Contingency in International Law

Contingency in International Law

On the Possibility of Different Legal Histories

Edited by

INGO VENZKE AND KEVIN JON HELLER

OXFORD
UNIVERSITY PRESS

OXFORD
UNIVERSITY PRESS

Great Clarendon Street, Oxford, OX2 6DP,
United Kingdom

Oxford University Press is a department of the University of Oxford.
It furthers the University's objective of excellence in research, scholarship,
and education by publishing worldwide. Oxford is a registered trade mark of
Oxford University Press in the UK and in certain other countries

First Edition published in 2021

Impression: 1

Published in the United States of America by Oxford University Press
198 Madison Avenue, New York, NY 10016, United States of America

British Library Cataloguing in Publication Data

Data available

Library of Congress Control Number: 2020952230

ISBN 978–0–19–289803–6

DOI: 10.1093/oso/9780192898036.001.0001

Printed and bound in the UK by
TJ Books Limited

For NCV and ST
GD and BD

Acknowledgements

The present volume builds on the conference 'Contingency in the Course of International Law: How International Law Could Have Been', which we held in Amsterdam in the summer of 2018 under the auspices of the Amsterdam Center for International Law (ACIL). It was a sparkling event exceeding our expectations in substance and form; in the depth of the exchange; in open curiosity and intellectual rigour; and in sheer interest and numbers.

We invited a few colleagues to the conference but wanted to seek out unfamiliar voices. About 140 scholars replied to our Call for Papers, and 60 presenters filled the conference. Fleur Johns opened the proceedings and Sam Moyn closed them. Both gave memorable keynote lectures that now, in revised versions, frame the present volume. We are truly grateful to all of the presenters and conference-participants for their engaged contributions and spirited exchanges, and to the contributors to the volume for their continued commitment, ongoing debate, and regular input.

Neither this volume nor the conference would have been possible without the financial and logistical support we received from ACIL and the Amsterdam Law School. Several colleagues were of particular assistance in bringing the conference to fruition, including ACIL's administrative assistants Yvonne ter Horst and Kaan Özdurak, as well as the helping hands of Teresa Cabrita, Corina Heri, Jackson Oldfield, and Wim Zimmermann. Kathryn Skinner was a superb student assistant during that time.

The volume would not have obtained its present shape had it not been for Bianca Dillon's outstanding support in finalising it. She closely read and edited every chapter with exceptional diligence and dedication. We are further grateful to Brittany Feldman, who took over from Kathryn as a student assistant to work on the volume.

We wish to thank Merel Alstein from OUP, who attended the conference in 2018, for her kind support for the project from its beginning. And we are grateful to Jack McNichol for steering the volume towards production.

With deep gratitude to our interlocutors and all who have helped.

Ingo Venzke and Kevin Jon Heller
Amsterdam and Copenhagen, October 2020

Table of Contents

III. LOCATING & RESISTING CONTINGENCY

A. MIGRANTS & REFUGEES

B. SEA & RESOURCES

C. HUMAN RIGHTS

D. ARMED CONFLICT

List of Contributors

Mohsen al Attar, Dean of the Faculty of Law, University of the West Indies; Associate Professor, University of Warwick

Amanda Alexander, Lecturer, Australian Catholic University

Jochen von Bernstorff, Professor, University of Tübingen

Kevin Crow, Assistant Professor of International Law and Ethics, Asia School of Business; International Faculty Fellow, MIT

Ana Delic, PhD Researcher, Tilburg University

Justin Desautels-Stein, Associate Professor, University of Colorado

Filipe dos Reis, Assistant Professor, University of Groningen

Saïda El Boudouhi, Professor of Law, Université Polytechnique Hauts-de-France (Valenciennes)

Matthias Goldmann, Junior Professor, Goethe University Frankfurt; Senior Research Fellow, Max Planck Institute for Comparative Public Law and International Law

Geoff Gordon, Senior Researcher, T.M.C. Asser Instituut

Kathryn Greenman, Lecturer, University of Technology Sydney

Kevin Jon Heller, Professor of International Law and Security, Centre for Military Studies, University of Copenhagen; Professor of Law, Australian National University

Mats Ingulstad, Researcher, Norwegian University of Science and Technology

Fleur Johns, Professor, University of New South Wales

Michelle Staggs Kelsall, Lecturer, SOAS University of London

Edward Kolla, Associate Professor, Georgetown University

Lucas Lixinski, Associate Professor, University of New South Wales

Emma Stone Mackinnon, Lecturer, University of Cambridge

Bianca Maganza, PhD Candidate, Graduate Institute of International Development Studies (Geneva)

Kathryn McNeilly, Senior Lecturer, Queen's University Belfast

Frédéric Mégret, Professor, McGill University

Samuel Moyn, Professor, Yale University

Nicholas Mulder, Assistant Professor of Modern European History, Cornell University

Janne E Nijman, Professor, University of Amsterdam and the Graduate Institute of International Development Studies (Geneva); Academic Director, T.M.C. Asser Instituut

Josef Ostřanský, Visiting Fellow, Australian National University; Associate Researcher, Geneva Center for International Dispute Settlement

Alex Oude Elferink, Netherlands Institute for the Law of the Sea (NILOS); Utrecht Centre for Oceans, Water and Sustainability Law, Utrecht University

Umut Özsu, Associate Professor, Carleton University

Genevieve Renard Painter, Assistant Professor, Concordia University

Surabhi Ranganathan, University Senior Lecturer, King's College, University of Cambridge

Silvia Steininger, Research Fellow, Max Planck Institute for Comparative Public Law and International Law

Christopher Szabla, Global Academic Fellow, University of Hong Kong

Michele Tedeschini, Research Fellow, Centre for Global Cooperation Research, Universität Duisburg-Essen

Boyd van Dijk, McKenzie Fellow, University of Melbourne

Ingo Venzke, Professor, University of Amsterdam; Director, Amsterdam Center for International Law (ACIL)

List of Abbreviations

AIIL	American Institute of International Law
API	Additional Protocol I
APIII	Additional Protocol to the Geneva Conventions
ARSIWA	2001 Draft Articles on the Responsibility of States for Internationally Wrongful Acts
ASEAN	Association of Southeast Asian Nations
BBNJ	Biodiversity Beyond National Jurisdiction
BIPM	*Bureau International des Poids et Mesures*
BIT	Bilateral Investment Treaty
CA3	Common Article 3
CBD	Convention on Biological Diversity
CILT	Critical International Legal Theory
CIPEC	Intergovernmental Council of Copper Exporting Countries
CLCS	Commission on the Limits of the Continental Shelf
CLH	Critical Legal History
CLS	Critical Legal Studies
CSOP	Commission to Study the Organisation of Peace
DSU	Dispute Settlement Understanding
ECHR	European Convention on Human Rights
ECOSOC	United Nations Economic and Social Council
ECT	Energy Charter Treaty
ECtHR	European Court of Human Rights
ESC rights	Economic, Social and Cultural rights
EU	European Union
FAO	Food and Agriculture Organization of the United Nations
FET	Fair and Equitable Treatment
FLN	Front de Libération Nationale
GA	United Nations General Assembly
GATT	General Agreement on Tariffs and Trade
GCs	Geneva Conventions of 1949
HCCH	Hague Conference for Private International Law
IACtHR	Inter-American Court of Human Rights
IBA	International Bauxite Association
ICA	International Commodity Agreement
ICCPR	International Covenant on Civil and Political Rights
ICEM	Intergovernmental Committee for European Migration
ICESCR	International Covenant on Economic, Social and Cultural Rights
ICJ	International Court of Justice
ICL	International Criminal Law
ICRC	International Committee of the Red Cross
ICSID	International Centre for Settlement of Investment Disputes
ICTY	International Criminal Tribunal for the Former Yugoslavia
IDI	*Institut de Droit International*
IFI	International Financial Institution

IHL	International Humanitarian Law
IIL	International Investment Law
ILC	International Law Commission
ILO	International Labour Organization
IMA	International Migration Administration
IMF	International Monetary Fund
IMO	International Maritime Organization
IOM	International Organization for Migration
IOPC Funds	International Oil Pollution Compensation Funds
IRO	International Refugee Organization
ISA	International Seabed Authority
ISDS	Investor-State Dispute Settlement
ITLOS	International Tribunal for the Law of the Sea
ITO	International Trade Organization
ITU-R	International Telecommunications Union—Radiocommunications
LE	Legitimate Expectations
LoN	League of Nations
LOSC	Law of the Sea Convention
MAI	Multilateral Agreement on Investment
NAFTA	North American Free Trade Agreement
NGO	Non-Governmental Organisation
NIAC	Non-International Armed Conflict
NIEO	New International Economic Order
OAS	Organization of American States
OECD	Organisation for Economic Co-Operation and Development
OPEC	Organization of the Petroleum Exporting Countries
PSNR	Permanent Sovereignty over Natural Resources
R2P	Responsibility to Protect
RSR	Reciprocating States Regime
SG	Secretary General
SPLOS	Meeting of States Parties to the Convention
TDM	Transnational Dispute Settlement
TFEU	Treaty on the Functioning of the European Union
TNC	Transnational Corporation
TWAIL	Third World Approaches to International Law
UDHR	Universal Declaration of Human Rights
UN	United Nations
UNCITRAL	United Nations Commission on International Trade Law
UNCLOS	UN Convention of the Law of the Sea
UNCLOS III	Third United Nations Conference on the Law of the Sea
UNCTAD	United Nations Conference on Trade and Development
UNGA	UN General Assembly
UNHCR	United Nations High Commission for Refugees
UNICEF	United Nations International Children's Fund
UNRRA	United Nations Relief and Rehabilitation Agency
US	United States
UTC	Universal Coordinated Time
VCLT	Vienna Convention on the Law of Treaties
WPLC	World Peace through Law Conference
WTO	World Trade Organization

I

INTRODUCTION

1
Situating Contingency in the Path of International Law

*Ingo Venzke**

I. Introduction

The present volume asks a question that is deceptive in its simplicity: Could international law have been otherwise? In other words, what are past possibilities, if any, for a different law? The path of law was long understood as expressing a natural plan, given fate or divine fiat. The mark of enlightened modernity was then to no longer see the world, and the law in it, as so predetermined that contingency was just puzzling.[1] The ramifications of this move were tremendous across theory and practice. The individual became the focal point of legitimate order and the master of a now disenchanted, freer world. Ridden with contradictions, enlightened modernity evoked anxieties about how to bear the weight of one's choices, if not of the whole world. The newfound freedom triggered a longing for guidance and explanation within this world of possibility, for foundations that were now evasive.[2] Still, today there is hardly a serious account left that would consider the path of international law to be necessary and that would refute the possibility of a different law altogether.

If that is so, then thinking through how international law could have been otherwise should not be too hard, neither in theory nor in practice. In our original conference pitch, Kevin Jon Heller and I claimed that 'international law's past... is ripe with possibilities that have been forgotten'. We wanted to reveal and remember them. We did not, however, want to engage in stories of miracle counterfactuals, hypothetical changes that are withdrawn from worldly constraints. We set out in search of plausible possibilities that arose within given circumstances. Many chapters in the volume now meet precisely that ambition, retrieving contingency from the margins of collective memory.

For none of the contributions has this been an easy task, nor should it have been. Behind every possibility of the past stands a reason why the law developed as it did after all.[3] The search for contingency appeals to opposing critical sensibilities of wanting to show possibilities of the past and wanting to reveal the determining forces that compel the law down

* Email: i.venzke@uva.nl. I am truly grateful to all the participants of the conference 'Contingency in the Course of International Law: How International Law Could Have Been', University of Amsterdam, 14–16 June 2018 for the spirited discussions and all their input.

[1] Niklas Luhmann, *Kontingenz und Recht* (Suhrkamp 2013) 36; Nicholas Onuf, '"Tainted by Contingency" Retelling the Story of International Law' in Nicholas Onuf (ed), *International Legal Theory: Essays and Engagements 1966–2006* (Routledge 2002) 359, 374.

[2] See Theodor W Adorno and Max Horkheimer, *Dialectic of Enlightenment* (John Cumming tr, Verso 1997).

[3] Compare Tedeschini, in the present volume, noting that '[t]he more we look for it, the more contingency slips away'.

Ingo Venzke, *Situating Contingency in the Path of International Law* In: *Contingency in International Law.* Edited by: Ingo Venzke and Kevin Jon Heller, Oxford University Press. © The Several Contributors 2021. DOI: 10.1093/oso/9780192898036.003.0001

one path rather than another.[4] Many chapters encounter tensions when they want to recover past possibilities without downplaying patterns of determination and domination. While those warring critical sensibilities may point in different directions, both are crucial to keeping inquiries on the terrain of contingency, situated precisely between necessity on one side and chance on the other. Only with a keen sense of why things turned out the way they did is it possible to argue about how they could plausibly have turned out differently.

The present search for contingency in international law, as I see it, is motivated in the first instance by a refusal to resign to the present state of affairs, to accept 'all ... senseless wretchedness [as] an unchangeable force of nature, a fate beyond man's control', as Max Horkheimer put.[5] In the second instance, it is motivated by the hope that recovering possibilities of the past facilitates change in the present for a different future.[6] Situating contingency in the course of international law counters dynamics that depict law's course as next to necessary. Those dynamics rationalise in hindsight and preach with foresight. They understand the past not out of its own possibilities but as a prequel to the present, and the present in light of the future to come. When they flatten law's history and iron out contingencies, the law appears to be next to necessary and progressive change is deemed undesirable and impossible anyway.

'If there is a sense of reality, there must also be a sense of possibility',[7] Musil claimed in an early chapter of *The Man Without Qualities*. He immediately continued to write of delicate fools who are so overwhelmed by such a sense of possibility that they daydream with their heads in the clouds—fools, he wrote, that are 'called idealist by those who wish to praise them'.[8] Those daydreamers 'cannot comprehend reality or ... in their melancholic condition, avoid it. These are people in whom the lack of a sense of reality is a real deficiency.'[9] But there are also those who keep their feet on the ground and embrace—still with Musil—a 'conscious utopianism that does not shrink from reality but sees it as a project'.[10] That may well be the core of most critical projects, including the present volume: upholding the possibility of a different law.[11] Recovering contingency in the course of international law wishes to cultivate pockets of freedom that exist within and against a world presently beyond reach.

In this introduction, I will situate contingency on the terrain between necessity and chance. I will also discuss what makes the search for contingency so politically charged and so valuable—its link with human freedom. Ultimately, historical inquiry cannot do without the presumption of contingency, as I will submit in agreement with others (II). Expanding on the agenda behind the present volume as I see it, I will then sketch dynamics that portray

[4] Yemima Ben-Menahem, 'Historical Necessity and Contingency' in Aviezer Tucker (ed), *A Companion to the Philosophy of History and Historiography* (Blackwell 2009) 120.

[5] Max Horkheimer, 'Traditional and Critical Theory' in Max Horkheimer, *Critical Theory: Selected Essays* (Continuum 2002) 188, 204. Searching for contingency of course has a history or, better, histor*ies* within different disciplines. See in detail Painter, in this volume. While debates about critical legal histories come close, international law is at a different moment, as I have argued on another occasion, see Ingo Venzke, 'Possibilities of the Past? The Histories of the NIEO and the Travails of Critique' (2018) 20 Journal of the History of International Law 263.

[6] See Nijman, in this volume.

[7] Robert Musil, *The Man Without Qualities* (Sophie Wilkins tr, Vintage 1995) 10.

[8] Musil (n 7) 22.

[9] ibid.

[10] ibid.

[11] Christoph Menke, 'Die Möglichkeit eines anderen Rechts' (2014) 62 Deutsche Zeitschrift für Philosophie 136. In her seminal article, Susan Marks, too, sees this as 'a cardinal principle of progressive thought', Susan Marks, 'False Contingency' (2009) 62 Current Legal Problems 1, 2. She further agrees that 'it is quite right to hammer the point that history is a social product, not given but made. For if it is made, it can be remade differently.'

the path of international law as next to necessary (III) to then specify what the practice of searching for contingency might do about those dynamics, and what other potential this practice may hold (IV). One benefit that puts thinking about contingency ahead of much normative theorising is that it also asks why something that may seem desirable has not materialised. That question must guide those on pathways of transformation in their sobering search for change (V). Closely aligned is the question of what would actually have made a difference in the path of international law, and what still can (VI). Often it seems that the law only reflects given conditions—an impression that is frequently unassailable. But there is a risk of undervaluing how the law escapes its determining context (VII). Inquiries into what happened and what else could have happened are two sides of the same coin.[12] It still remains difficult to actually convey a sense of contingency, not in the least due to strictures of narrative style (VIII). In conclusion, I see sites of contingency in the law's contextualisation, the reading of its context, and the rendering of its history (IX).

II. Contingency situated

Searching for contingency in the path of international law probes what else could plausibly have happened. Whatever actually happened, while possible, did not become necessary only because it happened.[13] What *is* might also *not be*. Likewise, something is not impossible only because it did not happen. Contingency delineates the field of what is possible, bounded by necessity, on one side, and chance on the other.

Occasionally, some authors elide contingency's distinction from chance. Such an elision is more common and easier in the English language than in others, a point to which I shall return.[14] The concept of contingency has also been the target of spats between those who defend spheres of freedom to act differently and others who decry the emphasis on seemingly free-floating actors.[15] I briefly revisit those well-known debates because they clarify what is at stake. The stand-off between Isaiah Berlin and EH Carr remains classic and demonstrative.[16] Their arguments about whether and how to locate contingency in the path of history extend to the reasons and responsibilities for pretty much everything that is right and wrong in the world. These debates also attest to the manner in which the conceptual contours of contingency are shaped and sometimes blurred under the impact of political leanings.

Berlin's *Historical Inevitability*—one of his *Four Essays on Liberty*— argues persuasively in favour of historians' focus on contingency. For him, historical judgement 'consists precisely in the placing of what occurred (or might occur) in the context of what could have happened (or could happen) and in the demarcation of this from what could not.'[17] But his text is also an unpersuasive polemic against Stalinism and a caricature of Marxism, castigating them both for their supposedly 'impersonal and unalterable' view of history.[18] Berlin

[12] See Aviezer Tucker, *Our Knowledge of the Past* (CUP 2004) 226.
[13] Luhmann (n 1) 32–33.
[14] See (n 91).
[15] One of the most notorious targets for that latter critique is Niall Ferguson, *Virtual History: Alternatives and Counterfactuals* (Basic Books 1999).
[16] It is also the point of entry for Marks (n 11) and Allan Megill, 'History's Unresolving Tensions: Reality and Implications' (2019) 23 Rethinking History 279.
[17] Isaiah Berlin, 'Historical Inevitability', in *Liberty* (OUP 2002) 94, 121.
[18] Berlin (n 17) 155.

warns loudly against the implications of such a view of history as it shifts responsibility from individuals and their action towards the forces that be, and that cannot be changed.[19] EH Carr's powerful retort—*What is History?*—contends that historical developments are ill understood as the product of individual choices that abstract from causal factors at work. 'To say that the Russian revolution was due to the stupidity of Nicholas II or to the genius of Lenin is altogether inadequate', Carr notes.[20] Placing emphasis on individual agency impoverishes historical understanding and misguides assessments of why something happened. Pushing back against Berlin, Carr folds contingency into chance and conflates arguments about what was possible—plausibly so—with counterfactual speculations about what would have happened if only Cleopatra's nose had been shorter.[21]

In my understanding as in that of others, contingency is not only opposed to necessity, but also to the *im*possible—that which was just not possible under given conditions.[22] It is opposed to chance, to the random and arbitrary occurrence of events that would have been impossible were it not for some kind of sudden change of circumstances.[23] Inquiring into the determining forces that bear on all action does not lead towards necessitarian views of history, nor does probing alternative possibilities slide into chance. As Susan Marks noted in her formative article, the verb 'to determine has its roots in the Latin word *terminare*, meaning "to set bounds" to something'.[24] Like Marks, I would see thinking of contingency to be in line with Marx's well-received affirmation that '[m]en make their own history, but they do not make it just as they please; they do not make it under circumstances chosen by themselves, but under circumstances directly encountered, given and transmitted from the past.'[25] In her chapter in this volume on Arvid Pardo's role in the development of the law of sea, Surabhi Ranganathan is careful to carve out conditions of possibility, placing particular attention to shifts in the discourse and the importance of timing. The same may be said of Ana Delic's narration of the history of international private law through the initiatives of Pasquale Stanislao Mancini, Estanislao Zeballos as well as Tobias Asser, and for Bianca Maganza's history of Common Article 3 to the 1949 Geneva Conventions.[26]

Historiography only makes sense on the presumption of contingency. Without this presumption, all that would otherwise be left to do would be to chronicle events as vindications of the laws of history (for which no plausible theory has survived) or to chronicle them while resigned to the apparent incapacity to learn anything about them.[27] Stronger still, if contingency was not presumed, Samuel Moyn argues in the present volume with the support of Roberto Unger, 'action risks paralysis through the belief that the forces of history are all controlling, a self-fulfilling prophecy that feeds much demobilisation and withdrawal past and present.'[28] And yet, debates similar to those of Berlin and Carr continue to pervade historical inquiries generally, and (international) legal history in particular.[29] Those

[19] ibid 121–22. Also see the reading by Marks (n 11) 4.
[20] EH Carr, *What is History?* (Penguin 1982) 120.
[21] ibid 98–100; also see at 105, where Carr speaks of 'devotees of chance and contingency in history'.
[22] Luhmann (n 1) 32–33.
[23] In agreement, Marks (n 11) 2 writing that 'things can be, and quite frequently are, contingent without being random, accidental, or arbitrary'.
[24] Marks (n 11) 7.
[25] Karl Marx, *The Eighteenth Brumaire of Louis Bonaparte* (Progress Publishers 1934) 10.
[26] Ranganathan, Delic, and Maganza, all in this volume.
[27] Megill (n 16) 284. For the chronicler's view of history, see Walter Benjamin, 'Über den Begriff der Geschichte' (1940) in Walter Benjamin, *Gesammelte Schriften* (Suhrkamp 1974) vol 1, 694.
[28] Moyn, in this volume.
[29] Painter, in this volume.

debates are also gendered, economically stratified, and they reflect complex colonial histories, adding further reason to tread carefully.[30]

A key question when putting the search for contingency into practice is deciding exactly when to stop looking for the next underlying reason: that is, late enough so as to not exaggerate possibilities that did not exist, and early enough to not reduce all actions to a necessary expression of their context.[31] This is nothing other than the domain of historiography. Historiography does not stop asking why something happened until it is adequately explained, nor does it deny the possibilities of something different happening. For Reinhart Koselleck inquiries into historical causation are thus anthropologically centred:

> The historical facts of the past, as well as those of the future, are possibilities that either have been or can be realized and which preclude compelling necessity. Facts remain contingent, however much they can be grounded; they arise in the space of human freedom.[32]

Such a conception of contingency is, as Umut Özsu writes in his chapter, well at home in a Marxist tradition where it takes that place between necessity and impossibility. Something that is contingent must first of all be possible.[33] It is not a requirement, however, that an outcome was willed by any actor, as Edward James Kolla makes clear in his history of national self-determination after the French Revolution.[34]

III. Rationalising with hindsight

Later in his book, Musil paraphrases a professor at a quotidian social gathering thus:

> He spoke of the path of history. When we look ahead, he said, we see an impenetrable wall. If we look left and right, we see an overwhelming mass of important events without recognizable direction. But looking back, everything, as if by a miracle, has become order and purpose.[35]

The professor's intervention reflects the experience of uncertainty with regard to most things that will happen in the future, however near, and the simultaneous certainty with

[30] Beliefs in the possibility of different action—and possibilities of a different law—are spread much more widely among male elites. See respectively for the emphasis on gender and strata Hilary Charlesworth, 'International Law: A Discipline of Crisis' (2002) 65 Modern Law Review 377; Marks (n 11) 14, noting that 'to those at the less comfortable end of social relations ... the patterning of privilege and deprivation will be quite plain.' cf Antony SR Manstead, 'The Psychology of Social Class: How Socioeconomic Status Impacts Thought, Feelings, and Behaviour' (2018) 57 British Journal of Social Psychology 267.

[31] cf Martti Koskenniemi, 'Histories of International Law: Significance and Problems for a Critical View' (2013) 27 Temple International and Comparative Law Journal 215.

[32] Reinhart Koselleck, *Futures Past: On the Semantics of Historical Time* (Columbia University Press 2004) 127. cf Carr (n 20) at 95, who makes the analogy between historical determination and causes of a crime: 'It would not, I feel sure, occur to any of those engaged in investigating the causes of crime to suppose that this committed them to a denial of the moral responsibility of the criminal.' It should be noted that different disciplines have good reasons to set up contingency differently. Also see HLA Hart and Tony Honoré, *Causation in the Law* (2nd edn, Clarendon 1985).

[33] Özsu, in this volume, making that argument with particular reference to Marx's account of the struggle over the hours of the working day—the outcome was contingent, within bounds.

[34] Kolla, in this volume.

[35] Musil (n 7) 182.

which the past tends to be explained.[36] There is a deeply human longing for reasons in a world that is contingent.[37] As Hannah Arendt noted, people find reasons 'in order to get rid of contingency and unexpectedness'.[38]

Granted, we really are smarter after the fact, but much less so than we think. The bias of hindsight and the rush to explain what has happened cloud ex post judgments and exaggerate assessments of likelihood. Baruch Fischhoff placed his pioneering work on hindsight bias squarely within discussions about historical methodology, subscribing to the view espoused by the historian Georges Florovsky:

> [t]he tendency toward determinism is somehow implied in the method of retrospection itself. In retrospect, we seem to perceive the logic of the events which unfold themselves in a regular or linear fashion according to a recognizable pattern with an alleged inner necessity. So that we get the impression that it really could not have happened otherwise.[39]

Fischhoff drew attention to psychological dynamics working towards what he called 'creeping determinism'.[40] In a similar fashion, Richard Evans more recently warned that, in the end, historians 'pile up causes until events are overdetermined, that is, they have so many causes that if one did not operate, the others would and the event in question would still have occurred'.[41]

In the specific domain of law, while certain dynamics sustain the appearance of necessity, other opportunities may arise to challenge that appearance.[42] Roberto Unger has famously blamed 'rationalizing legal analysis' as a mode of argument that creates 'false necessities'.[43] That mode of analysis continues to pervade many accounts of legal developments, especially those developments of the law that are carried along in the practice of adjudication. Similarly, many accounts are outright functionalist as though legal developments were a necessary response to societal changes—as if economic globalisation itself fatefully determined international investment law, for instance. Some functional explanations, especially those relating to an analysis of underlying political economies, can claim considerable plausibility, but they also efface alternative possibilities, including those alternatives that might have opened up through different understandings of the 'given' circumstances and the challenges they present. Facts do not speak for themselves.[44]

[36] Richard Ned Lebow, *Forbidden Fruit: Counterfactuals and International Relations* (Princeton University Press 2010).

[37] See already Adorno and Horkheimer (n 2).

[38] Hannah Arendt, interviewed by Roger Errera in October 1978, excerpts published in *The New York Review of Books* (New York, 26 October 1978) 18.

[39] Georges Florovsky, 'The Study of the Past' quoted in Baruch Fischhoff, 'Hindsight ≠ Foresight: The Effect of Outcome Knowledge on Judgment Under Uncertainty' (1975) 1 Journal of Experimental Psychology: Human Perception and Performance 288, 288.

[40] Fischhoff (n 39) 288.

[41] Richard J Evans, *Altered Pasts: Counterfactuals in History* (Little, Brown 2014) 82.

[42] See Ingo Venzke, 'Cracking the Frame? On the Prospects of Change in a World of Struggle' (2016) 27 European Journal of International Law 831.

[43] Roberto Mangabeira Unger, *What Should Legal Analysis Become?* (Verso 1996) 36; Roberto Mangabeira Unger, *False Necessity: Anti-Necessitarian Social Theory in the Service of Radical Democracy* (Verso 2001); cf Duncan Kennedy, *A Critique of Adjudication* (Harvard University Press 1997) 18.

[44] Section VII in this chapter.

Moreover, other views on the course of international law see it as bending towards a singular, just future.[45] In legal practice, finally, the past is used instrumentally and unabashedly to support claims in the present.[46] The operation of the law thrives on hindsight. In contradistinction, the search for contingency heads in the very opposite direction, trying to unsettle certainty about law's path and to make it more malleable. In the following two sections I will first deal with beliefs in the changeability of the law (IV) and then discuss how change might occur—and what the practice of situating contingency in the path of international law might engender in this regard (V).

IV. Reality as a project

I have suggested that upholding the belief in the possibility of a different law may well be the core of most critical projects, not to shrink from reality, but to take reality itself as a project, as Musil put it.[47] What might sustain such a belief, and why is it important? First and foremost, the hope that the law, and the world at large, might in principle be different is foundational to understandings of agency. Even those critiques of international law that portray it as a relentless tool of imperialism tend to be followed by cries for reform, as Mohsen al Attar points out in his chapter.[48] If nothing can change, why bother? There needs to be some *hope* in the changeability of conditions as a precondition for self-determined action, as Theodor W Adorno noted.[49] Such a hope does not need to be grounded in certainty, nor should it wane into wishful thinking.[50] In her history of human rights in the present volume, Kathryn McNeilly approaches hope that way, as a 'latent force with politically transformative potential in the context of restrictive power relations'.[51] Even those who keep their feet firmly on the ground must realise that whatever is (im)possible also depends on dreams and aspirations, as McNeilly also suggests. That is the conscious, grounded hope expressed in the slightly worn slogan of the 1960s: 'Be realistic and demand the impossible.' One need not be an idealistic fool to acknowledge that shifting hopes for whatever *should be* influences what *can be*, and vice versa. Necessity and (im)possibility are modalities unconnected to any object, formed instead through practices, experiences, and expectations.[52]

While introductory lessons of political philosophy teach that something *should not be* only because it *is*, first pages of social psychology teach that assessments of what is bound to be the case (necessary) and what is desirable (just) are in fact closely aligned—whenever one changes, the other follows suit swiftly.[53] Georg Jellinek wrote of the

[45] For a critical appraisal see Thomas Skouteris, *The Notion of Progress in International Law Discourse* (Asser 2010); cf Sundhya Pahuja, *Decolonising International Law: Development, Economic Growth and the Politics of Universality* (CUP 2011) 117.

[46] Anne Orford, 'On International Legal Method' (2013) 1 London Review of International Law 166; David Kennedy, 'Primitive Legal Scholarship' (1986) 27 Harvard International Law Journal 1.

[47] See above notes 10–11 and accompanying texts.

[48] Al Attar, in this volume.

[49] Theodor W Adorno, *Minima Moralia: Reflections from Damaged Life* (EFN Jephcott tr, Verso 1974) 97–98 (s 61). See in further detail, Tilo Wesche, *Adorno: Eine Einführung* (Reclam 2018) 187–95.

[50] Adorno (n 49).

[51] McNeilly, in this volume.

[52] Luhmann (n 1) 44; cf Hayden White, *Metahistory: The Historical Imagination in Nineteenth-Century Europe* (Johns Hopkins University Press 1973) 283.

[53] Vicky M Wilkins and Jeffrey B Wenger, 'Belief in a Just World and Attitudes Toward Affirmative Action' (2014) 42 Policy Studies Journal 325.

normative force of the factual in that vein, basing the origins of positive law and legal obligation on the human tendency to infer norms from recurring events.[54] More recent social psychological research confirms peoples' strong desire to live in a world that is in principle just, and that this is a world in which things appear to happen for a reason—hence the human inclination to explain, and in fact also justify, whatever has happened.[55] The longing for reasons—both causal and normative—even increases when certain conditions otherwise seem all too brutal. Rather than leading to increased contestation by the disadvantaged, glaring levels of inequality within societies have often evoked stronger justifications of the root conditions. Even those who drew (or rather: were dealt) the short straw may find it easier to blame themselves than the system whose structure and levers lie beyond reach.[56] Exposing contingencies in the law, and the ways in which the law partakes in shaping unjust outcomes, might challenge acceptance that the current situation is desirable and unchangeable.

This leads me to a still more principled argument on how to think about the pursuit of progressive change in a non-naïve fashion and the role that the search for contingency can play in this regard. In the wake of Marx, a theory of justice must aim at a *political* understanding of the economic conditions in order to oppose their appearance as natural and necessary—'a fate beyond man's control'.[57] Those conditions, for Marx, must first be made transparent, and most of his travails were dedicated to precisely that purpose. A critical theory of justice starts with a radical realism about the conditions of exploitation and injustice before attempting to strategise about their transformation.[58]

How that transformation might happen is of course the golden question. One common approach would be to postulate normative demands to which reality should simply adjust without further ado. That is clearly not the approach of critical theory, whose agenda would at the very least include the question of why such demands have not yet been met, a question which tends to be quite revealing. Nicholas Mulder and Boyd van Dijk, for instance, ask in their chapter why it took so long for starvation to become a war crime, exposing British and US resistance against such a norm.[59] Matthias Goldmann, in turn, shows how an overly narrow conception of human rights made them of little use in countering austerity policies imposed by the International Financial Institutions.[60]

[54] Georg Jellinek, *Allgemeine Staatslehre* (Wissenschaftliche Buchgesellschaft 1960) 337–40. See in further detail Nicoletta Bersier-Ladavac, Christoph Bezemek, and Frederick Schauer (eds), *The Normative Force of the Factual: Legal Philosophy Between Is and Ought* (Springer 2019).

[55] John T Jost, 'A Quarter Century of System Justification Theory: Questions, Answers, Criticisms, and Societal Applications' (2019) 58 British Journal of Social Psychology 263; Gary Blasi and John T Jost, 'System Justification Theory and Research: Implications for Law, Legal Advocacy, and Social Justice' (2012) 94 Ideology, Psychology, and Law 1119.

[56] John T Jost and others, 'Social Inequality and the Reduction of Ideological Dissonance on Behalf of the System: Evidence of Enhanced System Justification among the Disadvantaged' (2003) 33 European Journal of Social Psychology 13.

[57] Rainer Forst, 'Gerechtigkeit nach Marx' in Rainer Forst, *Normativität und Macht* (Suhrkamp 2015) 171–85.

[58] See Theodor W Adorno, *Negative Dialektik* (Suhrkamp 2003) 29, 354.

[59] Mulder and van Dijk, in this volume.

[60] Goldmann, in this volume.

V. Pathways of transformation

The agenda that I see behind the search for contingencies in the path of international law forms part of a critical tradition devoted to the high-flying aim of emancipatory politics. The search for contingencies involves taking the gamble that at least occasionally such contingencies will be revealed, and that their exposure is important to critical theory's aim, be it in a marginal and mediated fashion. How so? I see two main pathways of transformation. They are rooted in idealism and materialism, where idealism's gist is still best captured, albeit crudely, in Hegel's famous dictum that 'once the realm of imagination has been revolutionised, reality will not withstand',[61] and materialism is captured in Marx's equally crude and famous retort that 'philosophers have only interpreted the world, in various ways. The point, however, is to change it.'[62] While it has clearly been a central aim of critical legal thought to transcend this distinction, its success on this count is debatable.[63] In any event, both pathways continue to offer direction for transformation.

The first pathway connects to constraints that arise from how action in the present is held captive by dominant knowledge, consciousness, and imagination. This notably includes knowledge about the modalities of past developments, their (im)possibilities. The project of revealing contingency places itself at a distance from the present in order to denaturalise and critique it. It thus enlarges the present sense of possibility, hoping to open up a different future, as Janne Nijman elaborates in her chapter. The task has purpose because this just 'cannot be how the world was meant to be', as she puts it with reference to Philip Allott.[64] And it is an important task not the least because 'once [collectively] desired effects fail to happen and refuse to come into the world, the fact that they were originally counted on is likely to be not only forgotten but actively repressed'.[65]

The necessity and (im)possibility of certain developments depend on the observer and the history she writes out of an entangled present—histories that can open up and close down the realm of possibility.[66] As Emma Stone Mackinnon notes in her chapter on the legacy of the Algerian Revolution, 'contingency arises in the question of how the past will be remembered and made relevant for the future, and in which intellectual legacies will be carried forward and which will be left behind'.[67]

Kevin Crow likewise illustrates how perceptions of possibility are shaped through shifting discursive structures, in his case with regard to the 1955 Bandung Conference and

[61] GWF Hegel, *Briefe von und an Hegel, Band 1: 1785 bis 1812* (Johannes Hoffmeister ed, Meinert 1952) 253, 'ist das Reich der Vorstellung revolutioniert, so hält die Wirklichkeit nicht aus' (my translation).

[62] Karl Marx, 'Theses on Feuerbach' in Karl Marx, *Selected Writings* (Lawrence H Simon ed, Hackett 1994) 98, 101 (Thesis XI).

[63] See David Trubek, 'Where the Action is: Critical Legal Studies and Empiricism' (1984) 36 Stanford Law Review 575, 609. Trubek also pointed out that critical legal theory has remained vague in its account of how change should happen.

[64] Nijman, in this volume, with reference to 'Review Essay Symposium: Philip Allott's *Eunomia* and *The Health of Nations* Thinking Another World: "This Cannot Be How the World Was Meant to Be" (2005) 16 European Journal of International Law 255.

[65] Albert O Hirschman, *The Passions and the Interests: Political Arguments for Capitalism before its Triumph* (Princeton University Press 1977) 131; also quoted in Fuad Zarbiyev, 'A Genealogy of Textualism in Treaty Interpretation' in Andrea Bianchi, Daniel Peat, and Matthew Windsor (eds), *Interpretation in International Law* (OUP 2015) 251, 267.

[66] dos Reis, in this volume, on the contingency of the observer.

[67] Mackinnon, in this volume. cf Christopher Tomlins, 'How Autonomous is Law?' (2007) 3 Annual Review of Law and Social Science 45, carving out the implicit assumption of relating law's autonomy to societal context, and suggesting to instead relate it to both justice and, notably, memory.

its reception in major English-language newspapers like *The Times*. 'Much of Bandung's contingency', Crow writes in his chapter, 'does not rest on the event itself, but on how the event was used by future actors'.[68] A lot of recent historical work has been motivated precisely by that ambition, wanting to account for alternatives that are suppressed in the forgetful conceptions that operate in the past and present.[69] Many chapters take aim at such dominant, hegemonic visions that overshadow alternative possibilities, also targeting more general modes of thought. Justin Desautels-Stein draws attention to underlying structures that shape thinking about sovereignty— the analogy to property, for example.[70] And Frédéric Mégret focuses on the regime of border control, drawing out the 'epistemological limitations that concretely bound our legal imaginations' and recalling that 'freedom of movement was once the default assumption in international law'.[71]

But few authors—and none in the present volume—would argue that merely raising awareness is enough to do the job, let alone that writing history on its own could enact social change. Too many are the constraints working on any actor. It is also clear that actors may not be constrained by ignorance but instead may act against their better judgement.[72] Working on awareness, in short, may be beside the point. Stronger still, as Fleur Johns demonstrates in her contribution, upholding beliefs in the possibilities of making the world differently may facilitate the conservative and stabilising forces that work in the meantime. Such beliefs may end up obscuring the underlying dynamics guaranteeing that the haves come out ahead.[73] Geoff Gordon warns in a similar fashion in his chapter that 'the normative affirmation that it could have been otherwise upholds material commitment to the actually-existing distribution of goods that it supports'.[74] He suspects moreover that the agenda behind the search for contingency resuscitates an enlightenment conception of the subject who can simply act on the world. And Johns draws attention to all the 'stuff around the world', that prescribes quite physically what can and cannot be done.[75] One might add to this the toll of the enlightened subject's action on the natural world, that endangers the bare conditions of life.[76]

Those points are well taken. Whether the recovery of contingency is a valuable practice depends on the reasons that obstruct a better reality. For the idealist, it is enough that at least occasionally those reasons include the suppression of alternatives that render the present all too natural, necessary, and just. For the materialist, it is the monolithic reality that a

[68] Crow, in this volume.

[69] cf Stefan-Ludwig Hoffmann, 'Human Rights and History' (2016) 232 Past & Present 279, 307; Christopher Tomlins, '"Be Operational, or Disappear": Thoughts on a Present Discontent' (2016) 12 Annual Review in Law and Social Science 1, 2 arguing that '[l]egal history fulfills its responsibility by undertaking a dual task, of recovery and rejection—the recovery of memory and right, the rejection of regimes of interpellation'.

[70] Desautels-Stein, in this volume.

[71] Mégret, in this volume.

[72] Susan Marks, 'Human Rights and Root Causes' (2011) 74 Modern Law Review 57, 75, 'So the point is not to clear up delusions, but to bring out the effects of action, including action "against better knowledge"', with reference to Peter Sloterdijk, *Critique of Cynical Reason* (University of Minnesota Press 1988) 5.

[73] Johns, in this volume.

[74] Gordon, in this volume.

[75] Johns, in this volume.

[76] Anna Grear, 'Towards "Climate Justice"? A Critical Reflection on Legal Subjectivity and Climate Injustice: Warning Signals, Patterned Hierarchies, Directions for Future Law and Policy' (2014) 5 Journal of Human Rights and the Environment 103.

recovery of contingency may discard, instead showing cracks and contradictions that, too, may support a hope in the changeability of conditions.[77]

VI. *Plus ça change*

I now turn from the agenda underpinning the search for contingency, and from how such a search might possibly make a difference in the present for a different future, to questions that arise when conducting such a search in practice. The current section focuses on what might actually have bent the path of international law in a different direction. The analytic difficulties in particular concern time-frames and the distance one takes from the law. The following sections then pursue the question of where to locate contingency inside and outside the law (VII) and how to convey such contingency narratively (VIII).

Several authors in the volume note that the law may have looked differently for a moment, only for it to then regain its tracks: *plus ça change, plus c'est la même chose*. Josef Ostřanský argues in his chapter that it was like a decision pulled out of thin air to protect foreign investors' legitimate expectations as part of the guarantee of fair and equitable treatment.[78] The leading precedent making that claim was soon contradicted and, overall, there is nothing necessary about these legal developments, according to Ostřanský. He argues further, however, that if investors' interests had not been accommodated in this way—as part of the guarantee of fair and equitable treatment—they would nonetheless have been accommodated by other means.[79] Even if the law had been a bit different, its effects would have been the same. Silvia Steininger and Jochen von Bernstorff argue similarly in their chapter on the extension of human rights protections to corporations. '[T]he transformation of corporate interests into human rights was a contingent development', they show with emphasis on three critical junctions. But the pattern fits all too well with the increasing dominance of neo-liberalism since the 1980s.[80]

The effects of what appears like a plausible alternative fade in the *longue durée*. Kathryn Greenman highlights in her chapter how Latin American countries successfully resisted the codification of state responsibility for the treatment of aliens in the 1930s and that international law developed to affirm such responsibility regardless. As long as resistance fails to break through 'international law's structural biases and fails to work against fragmentation, it is unlikely to effect change', Greenman notes.[81] While the UN Convention of the Law of the Sea (UNCLOS) is often hailed as a lasting legacy of the New International Economic Order (NIEO), Alex Oude Elferink notes that much of that legacy was undone by the implementation agreement concerning the relevant Part XI of the Convention. He also carefully argues that little would have changed even without such an agreement.[82]

It may further be the case that plausible alternatives initially welcomed would have produced undesirable consequences down the line. In an earlier piece on counterfactual

[77] cf Ingo Venzke, 'The Practice of Interpretation in International Law: Strategies of Critique' in Jeffrey L Dunoff and Mark A Pollack (eds), *International Legal Theory: Foundations and Frontiers* (CUP forthcoming).
[78] Ostřanský, in this volume.
[79] ibid.
[80] Steininger and von Bernstorff, in this volume.
[81] Greenman, in this volume.
[82] Oude Elferink, in this volume.

histories—which can be broader, more varied than queries into contingency—I have asked what would have happened if the International Court of Justice (ICJ) had accepted its jurisdiction in *South West Africa*. According to John Dugard, this would have ended apartheid about ten to fifteen years earlier, not because a judgment would have worked miracles on South Africa, but because it would have swayed the United States and United Kingdom to no longer prevent the Security Council from taking meaningful action.[83] The judgment would arguably have tipped developments towards economic sanctions, at least earlier than 1986.[84] The assumption is that the Court's judgment on the merits would have condemned South Africa and vindicated the applicants. But that is far from certain. Judge Jessup, who voted in favour of the Court's jurisdiction and followed the applicants' argument to quite some extent, notably denied one of their most crucial substantive claims—that there is an international legal norm prohibiting differential treatment based on group membership (ie, race).[85] Whereas it was indeed unlikely for the Court to decline its jurisdiction in 1966, more would have had to change for a decision on the merits to favour the applicants. If the Court had accepted to exercise its jurisdiction, it is likely that this alternative would have led to an outcome even worse than the fiasco of 1966, namely letting South Africa off the hook on the substance of its claims, not on the technicality of jurisdictional competence.

In her contribution to the present volume, Saïda El Boudouhi works with the tension between thinking about big changes that would certainly have left their mark and the aim to learn something about the law as it is. She notes that it is more productive, but also 'more challenging to imagine "small tweaks or adaptations"' rather than big overhaul.[86] Her focus rests on the ICJ's close decision in *Barcelona Traction* to consider what impact it might have had on the development of international investment law. What if—quite possibly—Belgium's standing had been affirmed? A tweak with some likely repercussions indeed.

Whether a specific change in the law makes a difference for the course of international law is surely related to the pathways of transformation I discussed in the preceding section. It is difficult for any single decision to make more than a dent in the long run. Had the arbitral tribunal in *AAPL v Sri Lanka* not been the first to affirm the foreign investors' standing on the basis of the underlying investment treaty, the next tribunal around the corner would likely have done so.[87] What matters is a change in the structures of discourse that distribute the chances for any claim about the law to succeed—those structures are stabilised by that

83 Comment made at the symposium, 'A Court for the World? Trust in the ICJ 50 years after South West Africa' (The Hague, 30 November 2016). See in further detail Ingo Venzke, 'What If? Counterfactual (Hi)Stories of International Law' (2018) 8 Asian Journal of International Law 403.

84 This is when the Security Council actually took meaningful action, including economic sanctions—a whole forty years after the onset of apartheid and twenty years after the Court's *South West Africa* judgment. See 'The Question of South Africa', UN SC Res 591 (28 November 1986).

85 *South West Africa (Ethiopia v South Africa; Liberia v South Africa)* (Second Phase) (Judgment of 18 July 1966) Dissenting Opinion of Judge Jessup [1966] ICJ Rep 6, 325, [432]-[433]. cf Ingo Venzke, 'The International Court of Justice in the Battle for International Law: Colonial Imprints and Possibilities of Change (1955–75)' in Jochen von Bernstorff and Philipp Dann (eds), *The Battle For International Law* (CUP 2019) 235.

86 El Boudouhi, in this volume.

87 There is notably a wide range of determination between rational design and accidental evolution, pace: Joost Pauwelyn, 'Rational Design or Accidental Evolution? The Emergence of International Investment Law', in Zachary Douglas, Joost Pauwelyn, and Jorge E Viñuales (eds), *Foundations of International Investment Law: Bringing Theory into Practice* (OUP 2014) 11. Compare the critique by Ntina Tzouvala, 'The Ordo-Liberal Origins of Modern International Investment Law: Constructing Competition on a Global Scale' in John D Haskell and Akbar Rasulov (eds), *New Voices and New Perspectives in International Economic Law*, European Yearbook of International Economic Law Special Issue (Springer 2020) 37, 51. Also see Muthucumaraswamy Sornarajah, 'Power and Justice in Foreign Investment Arbitration' (1997) 14 *Journal of International Arbitration* 104.

mix of ideas and material constraints.[88] Quite a few chapters assume that change is unlikely to come from within the law and must instead be sought elsewhere.

VII. Contingency outside and inside legal practice

It should not be a surprising observation that the law and its development are largely shaped by conditions that the law does not itself control—neither in treaty-making, in the practice of adjudication, nor in other instances. In the search for contingent developments that might have shifted the course of international law, one may well be thrown back onto distributions of power in their material as well as ideational manifestations. It is only fitting that the pathways of transformation also account for developments in the past. So Ostřanský is in good company when he concludes that real change in the law is only possible if the underlying political economy were to change. Nor is Amanda Alexander alone with her chapter in the present volume that targets the narratives that tend to be told about international humanitarian law, highlighting those narratives as the constraints that circumscribe the realm of possibility.[89]

Arguments such as those of Ostřanský and Alexander, while highly plausible, may however underrate the degree to which the law itself matters in shaping the conditions of which it is part. There is even a risk that responsibility for transformative action dissipates between domains of life and related academic disciplines, between law and politics, for instance. It cannot always be the respective other who should do something to face the recalcitrant reality. It is most alarming—though not uncommon, alas—for legal scholarship to relegate questions of possibility to politics and to the almost mythical, if not deified, choices of sovereign 'States' (typically with that capital 'S'). It is paradoxical, too. Who, if not (international) lawyers, would be better placed to appreciate the degree to which the law structures those choices, through the constraints the law imposes and the possibilities it offers?

One might still say, as Hegel did in English translation, that international law is 'tainted by contingency' because it 'always depends on particular sovereign wills.'[90] But one would then learn little about the law's contingency unless the query extended into the vicissitudes of sovereign will. The translation is important here because the German original speaks not of contingency (*Kontingenz*), but of *Zufälligkeit,* whose literal translation is 'coincidence'—something quite different.[91]

There is a still deeper problem that troubles the practice of contextualising legal developments. Placing the law in relation to its context may put in motion a line of argument

[88] For such an understanding of legal interpretation, see Ingo Venzke, *How Interpretation Makes International Law: On Semantic Change and Normative Twists* (OUP 2012) 40–49.

[89] See Alexander, in this volume, for the argument centred on international humanitarian law, as well as Nijman, in this volume.

[90] GWF Hegel, *Grundlinien der Philosophie des Rechts* (Suhrkamp 1986) 500 [§333]. On this understanding of contingency in international law also see dos Reis and Delic, both in this volume.

[91] For the original see Hegel (n 90), 'Die *Kantische* Vorstellung eines *ewigen Friedens* durch einen Staatenbund ... setzt die *Einstimmigkeit* der Staaten voraus, welche auf moralischen, religiösen oder welchen Gründen und Rücksichten, überaupt immer auf besonderen souveränen Willen beruhe und dadurch mit Zufälligkeit behaftet bliebe' (italics in original). It is also particularly in English language literature that contingency sometimes slides into chance. In other languages that I read it is not possible to say, as is perfectly fine in English, that something is 'contingent on' something else, which only expresses a relationship of dependence but says nothing about possibilities.

that is bound to find law's fateful determination in that context.[92] It may be compelling and insightful, for example, to tie legal developments to the rise of neo-liberalism to thereby expose and critique neo-liberalism's trenchant operation. But the possibility of alternative legal arrangements tends to get lost, lest the context was to change.[93] Also under the spell of neo-liberalism the law continues to be riddled with tensions. The law remains to some degree pliable, not least because what neo-liberalism demands from the law is not so straightforward. Struggles on the inside of the law about what to do with those demands must be part of the story.[94] No context speaks for itself, nor are its boundaries given—questions of what counts as context and how to read it are crucial sites of contingency, of politics, and of intense academic debate.[95] Exactly the same could also be said about what counts as law, adding yet another layer to the indeterminacy of the context.[96] Historical anthropology has made that point beyond refute, also in the field of international law.[97]

It is for instance common to read the 1977 Additional Protocol I (API) to the Geneva Conventions, which ended up internationalising 'armed conflicts in which people fight against colonial domination or alien occupation and against racist regimes in the exercise of their right of self-determination',[98] against the background context of anti-colonial struggle. Emma Stone Mackinnon demonstrates in her chapter, however, that the outcome of API was contingent on lawyers' battles over how to read that background. Legal positions varied widely, also among those vested in anti-colonial struggles. Mackinnon thus notes more generally that '[l]aw is not simply determined by its context, but is itself a site for argumentation over the meaning of that context.'[99]

It may occasionally be that the law meets its fateful determination in its context, which is tantamount to saying that, in that moment, the law has no autonomy or normativity to speak of.[100] That is the case when decisions are legally groundless, as Michele Tedeschini argues in his contribution with the example of the *Tadic* case before the International Criminal Tribunal for the Former Yugoslavia (ICTY).[101] For Tedeschini, this was an unprecedented decision—it was the first that the ICTY rendered and the first to assess the legality of the UN Security Council Resolution establishing the ICTY. Unprecedented as the decision was, Tedeschini shows, it was next to necessary as judges fell back on how they saw their role in the history of international criminal law, which seemed to leave them with no choice.[102]

[92] See Painter, in this volume.

[93] For an insightful account where, however, contingency gets lost, see Quinn Slobodian, *Globalists: The End of Empire and the Birth of Neoliberalism* (Harvard University Press 2018).

[94] This resonates with Justin Desautels-Stein's argument to not reduce the law to its context but to look at the legal process instead (in this volume), as well as Filipe dos Reis' distinction between contingency in origin and as origin (in this volume).

[95] See Venzke (n 5).

[96] I thank Genevieve Painter for this point in particular, next to many other invaluable comments.

[97] See Madelaine Chiam and others, 'History, Anthropology and the Archive of International Law' (2017) 5 London Review of International Law 3. See especially Genevieve Painter, 'A Letter from the Haudenosaunee Confederacy to King George V: Writing and Reading Jurisdictions in International Legal History' (2017) 5 London Review of International Law 7.

[98] Art 1(4).

[99] Mackinnon, in this volume.

[100] cf Koskenniemi (n 31) 216, arguing that the law, as a normative phenomenon, cannot just be reduced to its context. See more generally, Christoph Möllers, *Die Möglichkeit der Normen—Über eine Praxis jenseits von Moralität und Kausalität* (Surhkamp 2016).

[101] Tedeschini, in this volume.

[102] ibid.

The pseudo-formalist position that legal arguments determine a legal decision is surely difficult to maintain, but reaching through the law for the real underlying reasons may dismiss the autonomy of the law all too quickly. The law tends to have its own reasons that are no less real, its own realm of possibility.[103]

VIII. Conveying contingency

I have suggested that inquiries into what happened and what else could have happened are indeed two sides of the same coin.[104] Following this analogy, however, it is impossible to simultaneously see both sides of the coin without further ado. We can keep turning it around, but whenever we look at one side, it is difficult to also have a sense of the other. And when we flip the coin, the side of contingency tends to land face down, like all the historical material once it is locked into and arrested in writing. As Moyn notes, contingency tends to be banished narratively.[105] No one knew that better than Musil, whose *dramatis personae* remained fully invested in organising Kaiser Franz Josef's approaching 70th anniversary in 1918, oblivious to the imminence of the First World War as well as the Kaiser's natural death in 1916. The novel remained unfinished. Musil had sketched several endings and remained unsatisfied with each: How could he close his opus without undercutting the power of all previous pages? How could he end without imposing a direction on everything he had written before?

I have been particularly interested in contingencies in the history of international economic law, including the history of the International Trade Organization (ITO).[106] The ITO's statute was backed by the United States and signed in 1948 by fifty-three states at the time (for comparison, the UN counted fifty-eight members). Will Clayton, chairman of the closing conference in Havana had crowed that '[t]his may well prove to be the greatest step in history toward order and justice in economic relations among the members of the world community and toward a great expansion in the production, distribution and consumption of goods in the world.'[107] It did not happen, the ITO never saw the light of day.

My point here is that existing histories repeatedly omit the possibility of the ITO's success. Douglas Irwin recently offered a most informed account, piling up reasons for the ITO's fate—it could not have been otherwise. What happened against the expectations of almost all actors at the time is a given for Irwin: The US Congress did not ratify the statute, other countries turned away, and the ITO's statute ended in the dustbin of history.[108] The actions of the ITO's most ardent supporters are tragic as they approach the organisation's preordained downfall. In contrast, as Irwin moves up to the 1990s, the establishment of the North Atlantic Free Trade Agreement (NAFTA) comes as a surprise.[109] But contingency is

[103] Venzke (n 77); cf Ino Augsberg, 'Some Realism about New Legal Realism: What's New, What's Legal, What's Real?' (2015) 28 Leiden Journal of International Law 457.

[104] Tucker (n 12).

[105] Moyn, in this volume.

[106] I offer a small account of its history as a plausible counterfactual in Venzke (n 83) 424–28.

[107] Statement by the Honourable William L Clayton at final plenary session, on 23 March 1948, quoted in Richard Toye, 'The International Trade Organization' in Martin Daunton and others (eds), *The Oxford Handbook on the World Trade Organization* (OUP 2012) 85, 95.

[108] Douglas A Irwin, *Clashing Over Commerce: A History of US Trade Policy* (University of Chicago Press 2017) 502–505.

[109] ibid 636–42.

lost again because early on Irwin foreshadows what we know—NAFTA was established. He thus conveys no sense that it was possible, perhaps even quite likely, that NAFTA would not be established. The certainty that is portrayed about NAFTA's establishment makes those who did not see it coming look a bit foolish and their anxieties overblown. If the first instance is rendered tragic, the second is comic.[110] Contingency is lost twice.

Moyn claims in his chapter that exposing contingency requires a markedly different style, a style of side-shadowing, which Musil mastered, as opposed to the much more common fore- and back-shadowing that is inherent in Irwin's account as in many others. The technique of side-shadowing recalls Musil's passage quoted above: '[i]f we look left and right, we see an overwhelming mass of important events without recognizable direction.'[111] One way of achieving a similar effect may be to dwell on particular events, rather than 'engulf[ing] events into international law's evolutionary narratives', as Genevieve Painter writes in her chapter.[112] But as Fleur Johns, Richard Joyce, and Sundhya Pahuja know from their efforts in 'eventing international law', that is easier said than done.[113] Musil despaired over how to end his novel, but he had the literary luxury of keeping it unfinished. Can we end an inquiry into the contingency of international law's past without taking a stance on what could (not) have happened—reviving past expectations, perhaps, and showing beliefs in possibility? We then indeed feel the strictures of our professional standards and expectations.[114] And other than in fiction, there are things we know to have happened in the world's non-fictitious history.

Fiction may, however, offer ways of breaking from narratives that are embedded in international law, as Alexander demonstrates in her chapter. She resorts to Cixin Liu's science fiction trilogy to show what a non-humanist narrative about international humanitarian law might look like, thus replacing the two-sided coin with a different currency altogether.

IX. Conclusion: Three locations of contingency

'How not to run from a history that we cannot make?' Isabel Feichtner recently asked echoing the historian Heinz Dieter Kittsteiner.[115] The question draws together the seemingly defeatist recognition that history is beyond reach with the wavering hope that there may still be something left to do. It is not a suggestion to run (where to?) but an invitation to stand, stay, and strategise. The present volume, as I see it, translates this invitation into the search for pockets of possibilities, tucked away by rationalising (legal) histories that

[110] For these modes of emplotment and their narrative effects, White (n 52); also see Painter, in this volume.

[111] Musil (n 7) 182.

[112] Painter, in this volume, referring to Walter Rech, 'International Law, Empire, and the Relative Indeterminacy of Narrative' in Martti Koskenniemi, Walter Rech, and Manuel Jiménez Fonseca (eds), *International Law and Empire: Historical Explorations* (OUP 2017) 74; cf William H Sewell Jr, *Logics of History: Social Theory and Social Transformation* (University of Chicago Press 2005) 100–103, offering a theoretically rich conception of events as 'the conceptual vehicle by means of which historians construct or analyse the contingency ... of social life'.

[113] Fleur Johns, Richard Joyce, and Sundhya Pahuja, 'Introduction' in Fleur Johns, Richard Joyce, and Sundhya Pahuja (eds), *Events: The Force of International Law* (Routledge 2011) 1.

[114] Painter, in this volume. cf Rose Parfitt, *The Process of International Legal Reproduction: Inequality, Historiography, Resistance* (CUP 2019); Jean d'Aspremont, *The Critical Attitude and the History of International Law* (Brill 2018).

[115] See Isabel Feichtner, 'Critical Scholarship and Responsible Practice of International Law. How Can the Two be Reconciled?' (2016) 29 Leiden Journal of International Law 979, 979; Heinz Dieter Kittsteiner, *Naturabsicht und unsichtbare Hand. Zur Kritik des geschichtsphilosophischen Denkens* (Ullstein 1980).

tend to be so closely intertwined with the operation of power at any given moment.[116] 'The struggle of man against power is the struggle of memory against forgetting', Milan Kundera averred.[117]

I see three such sites of struggle to recover contingency in the path of international law, each built on the other. First is the practice of contextualising the law, which works against its abstract rationalisation, its inherent logic that lifts the law above and beyond politics. The operation of the law hardly has a place for its own uncertainty. While legal histories could take greater distance from that theatre of the law, often they do not, instead offering linear histories that arrive at the present without much difficulty, laden with secondary sources that support each other in a self-referential fashion. Contextualising the law deprives it of its seemingly unsituated rationality, making it messy and malleable. Second, however, law's contextualisation must resist treating the context as fatefully determining the law. It should neither consider that context as a given, nor law's relation to it as somehow evident. A key site of contingency that tends to be glossed over all to quickly is the struggle over what counts as context, what to make of it; and what counts as law to begin with. The context is determinative in the sense that it sets bounds to what was (im)possible. Not everything could be done within and against that context, made of that context. But within those bounds, possibilities have often varied quite significantly. The third site of struggle lies within historiography itself and the way in which it contributes to the creation of (im)possibility. It includes the other two: what was possible in international law within and against its context?

Situating contingency in the path of international law struggles against forgetting what was the case and what may still be.[118] All of that in the '[h]ope that fate and power will not have the last word.'[119]

[116] It would indeed be a serious lack of self-reflexivity if inquiries into the contingency of international law did not consider their own relationship with power, as Johns warns in the present volume.

[117] Milan Kundera, *The Book of Laughter and Forgetting* (Michael Henry Heim tr, Knopf 1981) 2.

[118] Compare Michelle Staggs Kelsall, in this volume, arguing that the refusal to compromise on the UN Code of Conduct on Transnational Corporations has kept alive an alternative that would otherwise have been lost.

[119] Theodor W Adorno, 'Spengler After the Decline' in Theodor W Adorno, *Prisms* (Samuel and Shierry Weber tr, first published 1967, MIT Press 1983) 51, 72.

II

THEORISING & NARRATING CONTINGENCY

A.

ENACTED STRUCTURES & STRUCTURED ACTORS

2

On Dead Circuits and Non-events

Fleur Johns

I. Introduction

> Uncut devotion to the critique of . . . illusion makes us delusional. In the trick of politics we are insufficient, scarce, waiting in pockets of resistance, in stairwells, in alleys, in vain. The false image and its critique threaten the common with democracy, which is only ever to come, so that one day, which is only never to come, we will be more than we are. But we already are. We're already here, moving. We've been around. We're more than politics, more than settled, more than democratic. We surround democracy's false image in order to unsettle it. Every time it tries to enclose us in a decision, we're undecided. Every time it tries to represent our will, we're unwilling.[1]

What if? Those two little words can, and have, carried international lawyers so far, so high. What if the actual world with which we feel compelled to grapple—in all its inequality, intolerability, and inertia—might quite plausibly have been, and might yet be, otherwise? It is valuable and productive to forbid 'the verification of a possible world by the actual one'.[2] It is important to pursue, in one way or another, the 'radical counterfactual'.[3] Many have shown this. It is possible, too, to understand much that surrounds us in terms of the appeal of this line of thought. Trump, Duterte, Bolsonaro: their rise signifies, to some degree, collective fascination with the road not taken.[4]

In this chapter, however, I wish to steel myself against the appeal of the 'what if?'. The revelation of contingency has become something of a trope in international law and it

[1] Stefano Harvey and Fred Moten, *The Undercommons: Fugitive Planning and Black Study* (Minor Compositions 2013) 19. In quoting this work epigraphically, I think it behooves me to acknowledge that it is clearly not a book written for me, or for much of the audience of this chapter, and that I am uncomfortably positioned in relation to the text, as Bernard Harcourt and Allegra McLeod have acknowledged also being (albeit differently so): see Allegra McLeod, 'Toward Abolition' (*Critique & Praxis 13/13*, 27 February 2019) <http://blogs.law.columbia.edu/praxis1313/allegra-mcleod-toward-abolition/> accessed 8 October 2019; Bernard Harcourt, 'Introduction to the Undercommons: Beyond Critical Praxis' (*Critique & Praxis 13/13*, 25 February 2019) <http://blogs.law.columbia.edu/praxis1313/bernard-e-harcourt-beyond-critical-praxis/> accessed 8 October 2019).

[2] Gayatri Chakravorty Spivak, *Outside in the Teaching Machine* (Routledge 1993) 79.

[3] ibid.

[4] Ernesto Londoño and Manuela Andreoni, 'Brazil Election: How Jair Bolsonaro Turned Crisis Into Opportunity' *New York Times* (New York, 29 October 2018) <https://www.nytimes.com/2018/10/29/world/americas/jair-bolsonaro-brazil-profile.html> accessed 8 October 2019 ('Many see in [Bolsonaro] the kind of disruptive, status quo-breaking potential that propelled President Trump's victory in 2016.'); John Reed, 'Rodrigo Duterte and the Populist Playbook' *Financial Times* (London, 26 July 2018) <https://www.ft.com/content/98589db0-8132-11e8-bc55-50daf11b720d> accessed 8 October 2019 ('Although heir to one of the country's oldest political families, Duterte painted himself as an outsider . . . and capitalised on popular discontent with "Imperial Manila", the disdainful term Filipinos use for their dynastic political and business elites.').

Fleur Johns, *On Dead Circuits and Non-events* In: *Contingency in International Law*. Edited by: Ingo Venzke and Kevin Jon Heller, Oxford University Press. © The Several Contributors 2021. DOI: 10.1093/oso/9780192898036.003.0002

carries some attendant risks. I want to dwell on those perils for a short time and try to sketch some possible routes around or against them. I will do so in three steps.

First, in Part II, this chapter will lay out something of what the routinised revelation of contingency in international law tends to make of people, and of social, legal, and political relations. A pattern tends to surround the unearthing of contingency in international legal work: a circuit linking capacity to insight, agency to awareness. I will start by simply drawing attention to this recurrent formation, with some illustrations. For all its orientation towards possibility, this pattern rules certain things in and out. Patterns tend to do that, of course; some elements will not fit the pattern and must be set aside.

The next two sections of this chapter will consider what gets foregrounded, and what gets foreclosed, by our continued propagation of the Enlightenment credo that knowledge and visibility—especially consciousness of contingency—are likely to enlarge transformative possibility. As explained further below, to fixate on revealing contingency for emancipatory ends is to presuppose that power, in the international legal field, rests upon the denial of contingency. On the contrary, however, there are many modes of power and hierarchy prevailing on the global plane that insist and thrive upon contingency. Holding fast to the idea that contingency begets negotiability makes it difficult to engage these latter modes of power. A focus on revealing contingency also makes it hard to grapple with global conditions and infrastructure that don't typically operate 'eventally': the terrain of what we might call non-events. An orientation towards unearthing contingency in international law thus leaves undisturbed and uninvestigated a very large range of distributive and normative operations on the global plane. I will offer some examples below, as I flesh this out.

After having sketched something of what the revelation of contingency tends to leave untouched, the fifth and sixth sections of this chapter, and the final concluding part, will attempt a little speculative rummaging around at these margins. If the conditions required to sustain the idea that contingency—together with knowledge of contingency—are predicates of action in the international legal field seem unacceptable for one reason or another (because they either require too much, or too little, of those meant to give effect to them), then what other conditions might we try to leverage critically? What is a 'what if?' that one could direct against the standard versions of the 'what if?' in international legal writing? How contingent are the knowledge-freedom associations in which analyses of contingency tend to trade? How might one engage with configurations of power in which contingency is imbricated, or in relation to which contingency seems beside the point? In short, what might be done about the following worry: that international lawyers might now be spending a little too much time identifying particular crossroads and turning points in international legal history and imagining those moments as relivable, while leaving more or less untouched vast swathes of the densely patterned terrain transected by these imaginary paths.

II. The cogency of contingency

I want to acknowledge, first, something that the other contributors to this volume already make plain: that many brilliant people are today fruitfully engaged in telling compelling stories about international law's contingency. They are, in earlier words of the editors of this volume, seeking to 'question the present state of international law by challenging its pretense to necessity' and 'draw out ... what could [or could not] ... have been' along its 'course'.[5]

To foreground contingency in this context is to highlight the extent to which worldly things and conditions that seem unavoidably what and how they are, became so, at least in part, through a combination of action and accident. Above all, it is to engender a sense of possibility and, often, to inspire action towards realisation of some of the possibilities so recognised. In the study of law and legal institutions, the aim is to 'sinter' the bars of the 'iron cage' of Max Weber's account, or to counter other influential accounts read as narratives of entrapment or inevitability.[6]

With important variations, this contingency-quarrying pattern in international legal work tends to go something like this: institution, rule, or thing C is often said to have evolved, in a reasonably coherent way, from predecessors A and B towards which it is said to have been reactive or corrective. There was, however, a moment or moments in C's history when it was expected to take, could have taken, or did take a very different form. Proceeding from the unearthing of this historical moment, one learns that C's current configuration cannot be explained by preference to progress, logic, or the rational alignment of interests. Rather C's current condition could equally be understood as an outcome of quite incidental factors, marginal interests, or momentary conflagrations of power and desire. In other words, C's current form could be attributed to contributors and catalysts of which relatively little notice has been taken. Alternatively, the factors to which C's emergence has been attributed may be seen sitting alongside other contributors and catalysts which had the potential to exert causal force in relation to C, but did not do so, or did not do so decisively at the time. All that is said to proceed naturally, logically, and non-negotiably from the sequence A to B to C might, accordingly, be open to question. C could—even yet—be made otherwise.

Now I take it that the motif to which I allude is familiar enough for me to spare you the recitation of specific examples of it. I had thought, at some point, to present a collage of quotes from articles voicing the kind of ambition to which I am referring, but that would entail a cheapening of the work in question. Contingency-unearthing work invariably does much more, and varies much more, than such a short-shrift, formulaic account would suggest. So, let me take it as read that, as Susan Marks observed so trenchantly in 2009, '[t]here is a great deal of talk about how things that are contingent are made to seem as if they were necessary, in virtue of being natural, universal, rational, eternal'.[7]

In that 2009 article, Susan Marks' primary target was the falsity of the contingency about which there has been so much talk. By that she meant 'what it leaves unsaid, in its unarticulated assumptions, implications and effects'.[8] In particular, Marks focused our attention on

[5] Kevin Jon Heller and Ingo Venzke, 'Call for Papers: Contingency in the Course of International Law' (*Opinio Juris*, 24 August 2017) <http://opiniojuris.org/2017/08/24/workshop-cfp-contingency-in-the-course-of-international-law/> accessed 8 October 2019.

[6] Stewart Clegg and Michael Lounsbury, 'Weber: Sintering the Iron Cage. Translation, Domination, and Rationality' in Paul Adler (ed), *The Oxford Handbook of Sociology and Organization Studies: Classical Foundations* (OUP 2009) 118. As Terry Maley highlights, however, Max Weber's work did not in fact put forward an account of history as 'determined or closed'; rather, Weber cast '[l]ife, with its irrationality and its store of possible meanings, [as] inexhaustible': Terry Maley, 'Max Weber and the Iron Cage of Technology' (2004) 24 Bulletin of Science, Technology & Society 69, 75 (quoting from Max Weber, 'Objectivity in Social Science and Social Policy' (original work published 1904)).

[7] Susan Marks, 'False Contingency' (2009) 62 Current Legal Problems 1, 14.

[8] ibid 17.

the way in which an emphasis on the contingency of historical events often served to de-link the study of those events from analysis of 'wider processes, tendencies and dynamics at work in the world' by which those events were conditioned.[9]

Aiming to build, here, upon Marks' work, I want to initially focus not so much on what gets cut away when we dwell on contingency so much as what tends to get smuggled in to the analysis of contingency in international law. Marks acknowledged these smuggled goods when she alluded to the 'voluntarist mystifications' in which analyses of contingency tend to trade.[10] Among these voluntarist mystifications, I contend, is a particular account of the relationship between consciousness and action, vision and capacity, awareness and agency. This presumed connection—and the idea of power on which it rests—is that with which I first take issue in this chapter.

What tends to get reproduced in the pattern that I just sketched is an idea that knowing, recognising, and seeing contingency in international legal affairs adds to the freedom and potential of those who are instilled with this knowledge, recognition, or insight. This is, as I earlier noted, a version of an idea strongly associated with the Enlightenment, albeit with a far older and longer provenance: namely, that knowledge and visibility enlarge transformative, emancipatory possibility in people and in human-made institutions.[11] I do not think it is an overstatement to say that there remains a tremendous investment in this idea at all scales, in all fields, and in many modes of law and politics, including in international law.

Now, it would be a bit absurd for me to try to disprove this credo wholesale. A claim that recognising the role of contingency in world-making, and otherwise learning more about its processes, never, in fact, occasions fruitful effort towards change: that clearly does not sound right. It would be similarly silly for me to argue that greater knowledge—knowledge of contingency in particular—promotes unfreedom across the board. Instead, this chapter will take a side-swipe at this idea, or rather a series of side-swipes. This chapter will record, in a number of different ways, what may be problematic about this association of consciousness of contingency with unbridling, or resistant capacity.

III. Consciousness-capacity confusion and the neglect of vectorial power

To cast the revelation of contingency as an emancipatory intervention anticipates a particular way of understanding power on the global plane. It suggests that insofar as the world is unequal, violent, and noxious, it has been made so in large part through the negation of contingency. That is, well-meaning people with power refuse to acknowledge that they are exercising power amid uncertainty, and so permit themselves and others to continue on one or other ruinous, exploitative path. That path is experienced as either predetermined, or as the best rational choice among only a very limited range of options. Alternatively, not-so-well-meaning people with power knowingly exercise that power in damaging ways.

[9] ibid 17.

[10] ibid 14.

[11] Immanuel Kant, 'An Answer to the Question: "What is Enlightenment?"' in Immanuel Kant, *An Answer to the Question: 'What is Enlightenment?'* (first published 1784, HB Nisbet tr, Penguin 2013). Admittedly, the relationship between knowledge and freedom put forward in this text is more complex than I am portraying, a little cartoonishly, here, in the interests of avoiding digression.

Meanwhile, others acquiesce in, or submit to, that harmful exercise of power because of a failure to recognise the contingency that surrounds these not-so-well-meaning people being invested with greater power in the first place.

Both of the foregoing accounts—which sometimes manifest in combination—evoke versions of relatively untrammelled and often un- or under-examined power: power that seems to trade on many people taking it for granted and paying little or no attention to its frailties, its paradoxical effects, or its potential alternatives. This kind of power is predicated on limiting people's sense of prevailing possibilities or denying those possibilities' existence. When Ambassador Nikki Haley, then US Permanent Representative to the United Nations, addressing a UN Security Council meeting on the situation in Libya in January 2018, remarked that '[t]here is no alternative to the UN process' and that the 'one key issue' to which attention should be paid was 'respect for human rights and fundamental freedoms', this is the kind of power she voiced.[12] There is certainly much of this kind of power in evidence amid global affairs today, and it definitely merits ongoing critical analysis.

Equally in evidence, however, are modes of power for which contingency is generative, indeed vital. An understanding of global institutions and operations as contingent is necessary to authorise and sustain those modes of power that lay claim to being self-sustaining, diffuse, and endlessly adaptable, rather than modes of power understood to emanate from particular sources or sites of authoritative decision.

It is in this mode that mechanisms of financialisation operate, from which so much financial capital has accumulated in so few hands of late.[13] John Maynard Keynes and Hyman Minsky are among those whose work explored the centrality of contingency to the 'normal' operations of modern financial markets. Keynes observed that 'the market will be subject to waves of optimistic and pessimistic sentiment ... where no solid basis exists for a reasonable calculation' and noted that the risk of 'the predominance of speculation' (which he defined as the 'activity of forecasting the psychology of the market' and anticipating and trying to profit from associated shifts in market valuation) increases '[a]s the organisation of investment markets improves', such that 'the capital development of a country [risks] becom[ing] a by-product of the activities of a casino'.[14] Minsky suggested, further, that over prolonged periods of prosperity, capitalist economies tend to become more and more dominated by forms of finance that are 'deviation amplifying'.[15]

It is in this mode, also, that uneven flows of digital data, and the machine learning increasingly involved in its collection, analysis, representation, and dissemination, work to create and allocate value on the global plane. Reflecting on 'the human experiences,

[12] 'Ambassador Haley Delivers Remarks at a UN Security Council Briefing on Libya' (*US Mission to the UN Office of Press and Public Diplomacy*, 18 January 2018) <https://ly.usembassy.gov/ambassador-haley-delivers-remarks-un-security-council-briefing-libya/> accessed 8 October 2019.

[13] Piketty and Saez's work has showed that, in the United States and other English-speaking countries, 'top executives (the "working rich") replaced top capital owners (the "rentiers") at the top of the income hierarchy during the twentieth century': Thomas Piketty and Emmanuel Saez 'The Evolution of Top Incomes: A Historical and International Perspective' (2006) 96 American Economic Review 200, 204. A number of researchers have attributed this and associated rises in income inequality to financialisation: see, eg, Ken-Hou Lin and Donald Tomaskovic-Devey, 'Financialization and U.S. Income Inequality, 1970–2008' (2013) 118 American Journal of Sociology 1284.

[14] John Maynard Keynes, *The Collected Writings of John Maynard Keynes, Vol. VII: The General Theory of Employment Interest and Money* (3rd edn, MacMillan 1973) 154, 158–59.

[15] Hyman P Minsky, 'The Financial Instability Hypothesis' (1992) Levy Economics Institute Working Paper No. 74, 7 <http://www.levyinstitute.org/pubs/wp74.pdf> accessed 8 October 2019. See further Susan Strange, *Casino Capitalism* (Blackwell 1983); Susan Strange, *Mad Money* (University of Michigan Press 1998).

routines, improvisations and accomplishments which implicate digital data in the flow of the everyday'—at least in the Global North—Sarah Pink, Shanti Sumartojo, Deborah Lupton, and Christine Heyes La Bond highlight some of the many ways in which experiences of 'digital living' foster a preoccupation with trying to 'deal with contingency, improvise in the face of uncertainty, adapt and move forward through the world'.[16] Shoshana Zuboff has described how the 'behavioral surplus' generated by these efforts has afforded a small number of technology firms immense power and wealth, while enmeshing those from whose behaviours it is extracted in what she describes as a 'dispossession cycle'.[17]

It is in this mode, furthermore, that 'development' is cast as an endlessly moving target, towards which 'developing' states, and most of the peoples and individuals inhabiting such states, are expected to continually innovate. Clive Gabay and Suzan Ilcan have shown how the Sustainable Development Goals may be read to extend the 'vitalising force' of a 'post-Second World War development orthodoxy' with a view to 'animating the capacities of Third World objects and turning them into active subjects'—specifically, creating 'entrepreneurial citizens' who might 'fare well in a world full of risk' amid contingency.[18] Ananya Roy has explored some of the ways in which the confluence of such ideals of 'creative capitalism' with those of 'millennial development' has fuelled the creation and extension of debt relations: a process she characterises as the 'financiali[s]ation of development'.[19] Paula Chakravartty and Denise Ferreira da Silva are among those who have explored how the '"new territories" of consumption and investment' that the global development project has sought to cultivate 'have been mapped onto previous racial and colonial (imperial) discourses and practices'.[20]

Some or all of the scholarly accounts I have just mentioned could, of course, be wrong. All of these efforts and operations could, perhaps, be said to be moving 'us' (whoever 'us' may be in this context) in a positive direction, although it does not seem so to many. This is not the place to rule on the existence or gradient of global trajectories. Nonetheless, insofar as the complex global phenomena to which these three terms—financialisation, datafication, and development—rather obtusely allude, and the distributions of power and resources that they tend to favour, might be making the world more unequal, violent, and noxious, they are doing so in large part through the amplification of contingency, not solely or even primarily through its negation. Legal techniques, artefacts, and professional sensibilities imbricated in these phenomena tend, on the whole, to work to cultivate and curate

16 Sarah Pink and others, 'Mundane Data: The Routines, Contingencies and Accomplishments of Digital Living' (2017) 4 Big Data & Society <https://doi.org/10.1177/2053951717700924> accessed 8 October 2019.

17 Shoshana Zuboff, *The Age of Surveillance Capitalism* (Profile Books 2019) 102, 138 and elsewhere. Admittedly, Zuboff's account is, as Eugeny Morozov observes, rather 'tunnel vision[ed]' including in relation to contingency. As Morozov writes: 'Are Zuboff's surveillance capitalists interested in turning us into a uniform gray mass, as she posits? Maybe, but they seem as interested in keeping us diverse and eccentric. How else would they get fresh viral content to monetize?': Eugeny Morozov, 'Capitalism's New Clothes' (*The Baffler*, 4 February 2019) <https://thebaffler.com/latest/capitalisms-new-clothes-morozov> accessed 8 October 2019.

18 Clive Gabay and Suzan Ilcan, 'The Affective Politics of the Sustainable Development Goals: Partnership, Capacity-Building, and Big Data' (2017) 14 Globalizations 468, 475–76, 482. On legal structures and accounts of 'best practice' designed to foster this developmental entrepreneurship on a larger scale, see Fleur Johns, 'On Failing Forward: Neoliberal Legality in the Mekong River Basin' (2015) 48 Cornell International Law Journal 347; Fleur Johns, 'From Planning to Prototypes: New Ways of Seeing Like a State' (2019) 82 Modern Law Review 833.

19 Ananya Roy, *Poverty Capital: Microfinance and the Making of Development* (Routledge 2010) 5, 7, 31 and elsewhere.

20 Paula Chakravartty and Denise Ferreira da Silva, 'Accumulation, Dispossession, and Debt: The Racial Logic of Global Capitalism—An Introduction' (2012) 64 American Quarterly 361, 368.

contingency, not to cover it up. That they do so is not epiphenomenal. Rather, these phenomena are predicated on the pervasiveness of, and pervasive attunement to, contingency; that is how they work. They certainly interact and intersect with technologies of power that work otherwise, but this does not negate the role of contingency in their operation.

Alain Pottage draws this out beautifully in his article on power as an 'art of contingency', interpolating the work of Michel Foucault, among others.[21] Pottage observes that Foucault's investigations of power and its modern transformation 'describe two attitudes to contingency, one which avoids or absorbs contingency … and another which presupposes, and thrives on, contingency'.[22] The latter entails social and historical operations 'hav[ing] to take responsibility for themselves' through mechanisms to which Foucault gave the name bio-power.[23] The point is not that humans are no longer agents of history. Rather, people are enrolled in history in a mode in which uncertainty about the effects of their actions and decisions is presupposed, indeed demanded. History becomes a series of contingent outcomes of practices that take those outcomes—whatever they might be—as a basis for the iterative extension and reproduction of the practices in question. As Pottage puts it: 'however events actually turn out, the expectation, rather than the event which "fixes" it, serves as the reference point for the next operation'; 'contingent events [serve] only as an occasion or stimulus to move from one operation to the next'.[24]

What those modes of global power that are dependent on the ubiquity and expectation of contingency capture is the geometric sense of the word contingency. That is, the idea of contingence as a matter of touching or contact at a particular angle—part of its etymology.[25] More precisely, they recall something of an angle of contingence: that is, the angle through which a plane curve bends between its extremities. Far from suggesting historical trajectories flying off in all directions as a matter of chance, contingency of the kind implicated in the operations of bio-power follows a curved trajectory between the extremities of life and death.[26] Its motions tend to be circular rather than scattered; directional rather than riveting. In this context, the directionality of power, and the sense of regulative force, rhythm, or momentum generated thereby, depend precisely on insistence on the unpredictability of power's effects.

Friedrich Hayek's understanding of the force of 'genuine' law is illustrative. Hayek argued that 'genuine laws … must … be intended to operate in circumstances which cannot be foreseen in detail' such that 'their effect on particular ends or particular people cannot be known beforehand'.[27] In Hayek's influential account, it was this predictably unpredictable quality of law (that is, the non-contingent contingency of laws' circumstances and effects) that would ensure that the law-making state would operate as a 'piece of utilitarian machinery' in the service of individuals' advancement, rather than as 'an institution that imposes on its members its views'.[28] It was only along this angle of contingence that Hayek could envisage law

[21] Alain Pottage, 'Power as an Art of Contingency: Luhmann, Deleuze, Foucault' (1998) 27 Economy and Society 1.

[22] ibid 9.

[23] ibid 9.

[24] ibid 14.

[25] 'Contingency, n.' (OED Online September 2019) <https://www.oed.com/view/Entry/40247?redirectedFrom=contingency> accessed 8 October 2019.

[26] Foucault explained bio-power as 'the set of mechanisms through which the basic biological features of the human species became the object of a political strategy, of a general strategy of power': Michel Foucault, *Security, Territory, Population. Lectures at the Collège de France 1977–1978* (Graham Burchell tr, Picador 2007) 1.

[27] Friedrich Hayek, *The Road to Serfdom* (first published 1944, Routledge 2001) 79–80.

[28] ibid 80.

being reconcilable with freedom, with the latter understood as requiring 'renunciation of direct control' over individuals as well as 'the absence of coercion of a people as a whole'.[29] The course and outcome of individuals' efforts to advance themselves and their interests, respectively, would remain unknowable in this account (and could thereby be said to be uncoerced), but only people who continued to move along the vector of 'development' towards ever-greater 'full[ness]' and interest-fulfilment might be understood to be acting in pursuit of freedom. It is by this kind of route that the expectation of people's contingent pursuit of 'the fullest development of their individual personality' has come to serve, in many settings, as both a vehicle and rationale for power in settings in which freedom-as-noncoercion is a vociferously defended value.[30]

Let us consider another example of this kind of power, expressed in material rather than textual or ideal form. Take the process of commodification.[31] That is, the making of a thing—a bale of wool, or a billable hour of a lawyer's time—that gives summative, objective expression to the social relations occasioning its production. This is an example of a process that has to be understood as contingent in order to operate. The global circulation of commodities—their purchase and sale—depends on their being capable of valuation more or less without regard to the conditions of their production. The process of releasing a commodity's value from the value that might have been contributed or attributed to it during the course of its production requires that this value be treated as somewhat unknowable in the abstract or in advance—that it be subject, in other words, to the contingencies of the market.[32] Of course, commodification depends also upon a sense of non-contingency too—that is, a sense that certain conditions are natural or necessary. Belief in the sufficiency of the pricing signal, for example, entails necessitarian thinking. Nonetheless, it is primarily through insistence upon contingency, and the ubiquity of choice under circumstances of contingency, that the thinking required for commodities' circulation gets reproduced. The operation of the global market in commodities (including the market in commodified labour) depends on the continued evocation, generalisation, and curation of contingency.

Brief recapitulation may be useful at this point. Recall that this chapter seeks to explain what might be problematic about the idea—implied in much international law work—that increasing consciousness of contingency is likely to enlarge transformative, emancipatory possibilities on the global plane. What I have suggested, in this section, is that greater consciousness of contingency is likely to be beside the point for many operations of global power, namely those that depend in large part on a sense of human and non-human actions and interactions taking place under circumstances of contingency and having contingent effects. To this extent, orienting critical effort towards the revelation of contingency might be misguided in so far as the possibilities that this promises seem to hinge on the ubiquity of more or less one style of power: determined and determinative power. Setting aside whether countervailing consciousness and knowledge are likely to defuse that style of

[29] Friedrich Hayek, *The Constitution of Liberty* (first published 1960, Routledge 2014) 28, 14.

[30] Hayek (n 27) 80.

[31] This account of commodification draws upon Karl Marx, 'The Fetishism of Commodities and the Secret Thereof' in Karl Marx, *Capital Volume I* (Samuel Moore and Edward Aveling trs, first published in German in 1867, Progress Publishers 1887) 76–78, 80–81.

[32] Keynes wrote of valuation as a practice premised on 'knowledge' of 'extreme precariousness', often premised on an assumption (frequently not sustainable for long) 'that the existing state of affairs will continue indefinitely': John Maynard Keynes, *The Collected Writings of John Maynard Keynes Vol. VII: The General Theory of Employment Interest and Money* (3rd edn, MacMillan 1973) 149, 152.

power—which is a question worth pursuing in its own right—it is far from clear that recognising contingency afresh could ever defuse, counteract, or re-route the vectorial modes of power to which I have just alluded. What is more, those vectorial, contingency-dependent, contingency-curating modes of power are especially prevalent in the global markets on which so much of the world's living and dying now depends.

IV. Discontinuous systematics and non-events

A second reason why an orientation towards unearthing contingency in international legal histories is problematic lies closer to the sorts of concerns to which Susan Marks has already drawn attention. It is, moreover, related to the problem that I just raised. Marks wrote: 'current arrangements are not simply arbitrary or accidental, but belong with the logics of a system which must also be brought within the analytical frame'.[33] A number of 'analytical frame[s]' might be brought to bear upon the 'systematicity' to which Marks drew attention, among them Foucault's 'theory of discontinuous systematicities'.[34] In Foucault's works, this was never just a matter of logic, or language, but also of stuff. The 'systematics' of Foucault's writings were, in part, material.[35] They were also discernible only as conditions under which certain phenomena emerged, rather than being knowable, with any certainty, in advance. Yet they were, nonetheless, regular and recurrent. As Foucault wrote: 'though it is true that these discontinuous discursive series each have, within certain limits, their regularity, it is undoubtedly no longer possible to establish links of mechanical causality, or of ideal necessity between the elements which constitute them'.[36] It is, Foucault explained, 'in ... practice that the events of discourse find the principle of their regularity'.[37] This regularity or seriality emerges, Foucault continued, not from some 'hidden nucleus' of 'thought or signification' of a kind that contingency-unearthing might ramify, but instead by 'go[ing] towards its external conditions of possibility, towards what gives rise to the aleatory series of [the world's] events, and fixes its limits'.[38]

Among the 'external conditions of possibility' by which this 'aleatory series' may be 'limit[ed]' (as well as enabled) is the physical, representational, and communicative infrastructure in operation (or latent) all around the global plane, including on the terrain of international law. There is simply so much legacy infrastructure with which international law and lawyers work that exhibits serial persistence and is, as a consequence, hard to activate as amenable to contingent recasting.[39] Much of this infrastructure is at stake in the kinds of operations to which I alluded earlier: the transmission and storage of data and

[33] Marks (n 7) 10.

[34] Marks (n 7) 14; Michel Foucault, 'The Order of Discourse' (Ian McLeod tr) in Robert Young (ed), *Untying the Text* (Routledge 1981) 48, 69.

[35] Mark Olssen (2014) 'Discourse, Complexity, Normativity: Tracing the Elaboration of Foucault's Materialist Concept of Discourse (2014) 1 Open Review of Educational Research 28.

[36] Foucault (n 34) 69.

[37] ibid 67.

[38] ibid.

[39] Fleur Johns, Richard Joyce, and Sundhya Pahuja, 'Introduction' in Fleur Johns, Richard Joyce, and Sundhya Pahuja, *Events: The Force of International Law* (Routledge 2011) 1, 4 ('In the reduction of the past and the future to a narrative of unfolding progress, it often seems that nothing could happen ... which [international law] has not either anticipated or claimed the ability to capture: nothing surprising, nothing confronting, nothing, perhaps, capable of constituting an "event" in "the strong sense"').

stuff around the world; the allocation and accumulation of value; the formats and fixtures of development programming and funding. The operations channelled through this infrastructure depend on an expectation of contingency. Yet the infrastructure itself is hard to experience in these terms.

For instance, if one is looking at the transmission of data around the Asia Pacific region for diplomatic, governance, development, and humanitarian purposes among others, as I have been doing in my own research of late, one needs to take account of the SEA-ME-WE3 optical submarine telecommunications cable and its various upgrades and successors.[40] One might focus on the arrangements surrounding its development in the mid-1990s, and its commissioning in 2000, under a consortium led by France Telecom and China Telecom. One might revisit the decision to contract out its administration to Singtel, a telecommunications operator owned by the Government of Singapore. One might focus on the contingent events of its failure and repair—some such incidents having been quite highly publicised—and the unconfirmed event of it having been tapped for surveillance purposes.[41] Yet no such event-oriented investigation would touch the matter and effects of this undersea cable still being there, transmitting multiple terabits per second of data, most of the time.[42]

Recuperation of the contingencies of human decision seems likely to have little if any bearing on the 'elaborate' structures of insulation and interconnection in which this and other undersea cables are encased: comprising 'fixed structures that shelter [their] power from natural and social threats, and … make[] it preferable to link systems with existing networks rather than branch out to new sites'.[43] It would be difficult, also, for investigations of contingency to engage the many automated and mechanical dimensions of undersea cables' operation, and yet these infrastructures remain utterly vital to the direction, resourcing, sequencing, and interruption of international legal work.

There remains, of course, tremendous potential to generate supernumerary 'evental' moments and 'evental' sites out of what seems to have been done and dusted—or to 'subtract the sheer "what happens" from the general determinations of "what is"' (as Alain Badiou has written, with a very specific, mathematical valence).[44] Nonetheless, the degree to which one can render international legal histories in these terms, and the effects of so doing, are themselves contingent. It cannot be the case that this is the way to go for all critical international legal work, for all people, places, and times and all operations of power. Moreover, for certain modes of power, and certain infrastructural operations, it could well be not the way to go at all.

[40] Network Administrator, 'SEA-ME-WE3' <http://www.smw3.com/smw3/SignIn.aspx> accessed 2 October 2019; 'SEA-ME-WE3' <http://www.seamewe3.net/> accessed 2 October 2019; Nicole Starosielski, *The Undersea Network* (Duke University Press 2015) 45, 158, 242. See generally Adam Satariano, 'How the Internet Travels Across Oceans' *The New York Times* (New York, 10 March 2019) <https://www.nytimes.com/interactive/2019/03/10/technology/internet-cables-oceans.html> accessed 8 October 2019.

[41] James Griffiths, 'The Global Internet is Powered by Vast Undersea Cables. But they're Vulnerable' (*CNN*, 26 July 2019) <https://www.cnn.com/2019/07/25/asia/internet-undersea-cables-intl-hnk/index.html> accessed 2 October 2019; Olga Khazan, 'The Creepy, Long-Standing Practice of Undersea Cable Tapping' (*The Atlantic*, 16 July 2013) <https://www.theatlantic.com/international/archive/2013/07/the-creepy-long-standing-practice-of-undersea-cable-tapping/277855/> accessed 8 October 2019.

[42] Yin-can Ye and others, *Submarine Optical Cable Engineering* (Academic Press 2018) 66.

[43] Starosielski (n 40) 232.

[44] Alain Badiou, *Badiou: Theoretical Writings* (Ray Brassier and Alberto Toscano trs, Continuum 2004) 98.

Let us, at this point, register the surfacing of an apparent contradiction. I suggested earlier that many modes of power thrive on contingency. Now I raise a concern about those modes of power having patterns, regularities, and bearings and being conditioned by enduring, relatively immoveable forms of infrastructure. The latter words suggest not so much contingency as the laying down of predetermined paths. There is a difference, however, between submission to the necessarily constraining power of circumstances (that contingency-unearthing work tries to counter) and observation of the patterning of contingency (that contingency-unearthing work tend to miss). The contingency of the commodity's circulation and valuation in the market is a routed, paced, and serialised contingency. It depends on a sense of continual motion, as well as the sequencing of that motion, and support for and reproduction of these properties is a feature of the infrastructure through which commodity circulation works. Again, Alain Pottage is helpful here when he observes, writing of Foucault's account of power taking the form of 'action upon actions' that:

> It is emergent in the sense that it originates neither in its protagonists nor in an abstract social-structural function. So, although a power relation presupposes a particular historical configuration of forces and discourses, it does not actualize or stabilize latent possibles or probables. Rather, it is produced in the relation sculptured by its exercise ...[45]

Another mixed message could have been received from the preceding paragraphs; let me deal with that too. It might be possible to hear some of this as a story of power shifting locales—of global power moving, say, from the visible domain of the public to the invisible domain of the private, and the failure of international legal scholarship to follow. That is, however, not at all what I am trying to highlight. My concern is not with the location of power so much as the patterns characteristic of its operation. As indicated earlier, I am worried that international lawyers might now be spending too much time identifying particular crossroads and turning points in international legal history and imagining those moments as relivable, while leaving more or less untouched vast swathes of the densely patterned terrain transected by these imaginary paths. To recast my concern in the positive, we might—public international lawyers, that is—do well to recall the tactical advice offered by Foucault in *The History of Sexuality*—when he put forward some '[r]ules of continual variations':

> We must not look for who has the power ... and who is deprived of it ... nor for who has the right to know and who is forced to remain ignorant. We must seek rather the pattern of the modifications which the relationships of force imply by the very nature of their process.[46]

V. 9/11 and some patterns of modification

What could this entail, this seeking 'the pattern of the modifications which the relationships of force imply by the very nature of their process'? Power, in this account, is intransitive. It is not possessed by subjects and objects, or set against or cast over them, so much as expressed through them. It cannot be located definitively; it may be grasped only obliquely and in

[45] Pottage (n 21) 22.
[46] Michel Foucault, *The History of Sexuality: An Introduction Vol. 1* (Robert Hurley tr, Vintage 1990) 99.

relational terms: as a 'pattern of ... modifications' that is 'impl[ied]' by the 'process' through which 'relationships of force' become apparent.

Perhaps one could take a scrap, familiar from among international laws' most oft-told histories, and retell it in this intransitive mode by recourse to a brief and rather audacious counterfactual. What if one were to speculate that the terrorist attacks of 9/11 might not have happened, or might have happened differently? Let me be clear that this is no voicing of conspiracy theory. Consider it, rather, a little thought experiment. Its purpose is to try to see what might become discernible if one were to redact, from one of the most familiar scenes and dates of recent history, the contingent event by which it has come to be defined, and to turn attention away from some of that scene's most notorious protagonists.

Can you contemplate 9/11 never having happened? Imagine several of the key figures in those attacks being stopped at the airport, their plans foiled. And now let us cast our minds back to how global affairs were tracking in 2001 before that event and consider what might have been different if those trajectories had continued uninterrupted. To open a small window into that time, and because my own memories of that day (out the front of my apartment in Lower Manhattan, looking down Greenwich Street at the burning towers) are a little blurry, let us consider the front page of the *New York Times*' online edition for 11 September 2001, as it stood at 12.05am on that morning, New York time.[47]

Headlines from that morning edition remind us that the US economy was weakening and that the Bush administration was under pressure. (The so-called 'Dot Com Bubble' had been bursting since 11 March 2000 and the Nasdaq Composite—the home of most of the United States's publicly traded tech companies—was already well into a slide that would see it lose 78% of its value by 2002.) Another headline story reported the Middle East having 'explode[d]' in 'all-but-declared war', as Shimon Peres, then Israeli foreign minister, and Yasir Arafat, then-leader of the Palestinian Authority, struggled to revive peace talks amid 'widespread pessimism' and 'growing militancy'. A third front page story recounted New York City voters being deluged with digital robo-calls in the primary campaign for city mayor. In the face of these, the *New York Times* reported, many voters 'ha[d] still not paid attention, ha[d] become wary, or ha[d] just fallen into a defensive stupor'. And in more front page stories from the New York region, a teacher and youth-worker and father of two in Westchester County, Patrick Dolan Critton, was reportedly charged for having 'hijacked a jetliner from Ontario to Cuba' in 'a black-power revolutionary' act some thirty years earlier. The 54-year-old allegedly worked, in the early 1970s, in 'a covert explosives factory' making 'pipe bombs with other members of a black liberation group, the Republic of New Africa'. Further down the front page of the online edition, under 'international', there was also a report about the United States blacklisting paramilitary groups as 'terrorist organizations' in Colombia. And the lower front page featured, too, inconclusive and conflicting reports of the outcome of a suicide bombing in Kabul aimed at Ahmed Shah Massoud, the leader of the Russian- and Iranian-backed United Front, described as the last remaining opposition to the ruling Taliban in Afghanistan. There was even a story about growing US sensitivity to Russian threats, and new surveillance efforts designed to counter them; 'Though Mr. Bush and Mr. Putin have declared that the United States and Russia are no longer enemies,

[47] 'A Snapshot of the World, Hours Before It Changed Forever' *The New York Times* (New York, 10 September 2011) <https://cityroom.blogs.nytimes.com/2011/09/10/a-snapshot-of-the-world-hours-before-it-changed-forever/> accessed 8 October 2019.

military leaders in both countries have said they are taking steps that reflect a decline in trust' the *New York Times* reported.

It is remarkable just how much of what tends to be understood, to varying degrees, as a direct or indirect legacy of 9/11 is already there, on the *New York Times* front page, some eight hours before the first plane hit the World Trade Centre. Rising militancy in the Middle East. Terrorist hijacking and suicide bombing, both near the US 'homeland', and much further afield, cut through by experiences of racialised violence, alienated youth, and long-lasting histories of occupation, clientism, and colonialism. The expansion of a discourse of terrorism and a practice of undeclared war, together with associated techniques of blacklisting and surveillance. A global economy starting to pivot away from the United States, and vice versa, heightening a growing sense of US vulnerability. Digital technologies becoming ubiquitous and arousing both suspicion and apathy. So many dimensions of the shift in global logic that 9/11 is supposed to have introduced or intensified—unexpectedly, contingently—are there, in plain sight, before jet stream ever scored the Lower Manhattan sky.

One could say, perhaps, that this confirms the value of unearthing contingency. All that we are now inclined to read as a prequel to 9/11 might just as easily have become groundwork for some other history-defining event lurking latently amid the detail on this front page. The 'war on terror' might have been otherwise, or not at all. That the United States and its allies invaded Iraq and Afghanistan, with devastating repercussions, seems all the more questionable when one contemplates that the United States was already grappling, in roughly routine ways, with at least some of the threats that those invasions ostensibly sought to counter. That is, if the morning of 9/11 dawned with a conviction in place that conventional tools of diplomacy and criminal law would (more or less) suffice to deal with known threats of terrorism and violent religious extremism, it seems all the more contingent, and indefensible, that those tools were so readily dispensed with in favour of war.

What the front cover of the *New York Times* on the morning of the event might also suggest, however, is that the process of redirecting, repurposing, and renaming those conventional tools and threats was already well under way, and the techno-material conditions for that rerouting were already in operation, before 9/11 ever happened. The 'pattern of ... modifications' that seem to underpin all that 9/11 would later become may require some mode of explanation or engagement *other* than that afforded by stories centred on individual consciousness, such as those of Dick Cheney's 'imperial presidency', to recall the title of a 2005 *New York Times* editorial.[48] In a grotesque rendering of the kinds of emancipatory possibility that contingency-unearthing is meant to unleash, that 2005 editorial invested Cheney with a kind of über-consciousness of contingency and of the potential embedded within it, claiming that 9/11 'was a chance Mr. Cheney ... [had] been dreaming about for decades' and describing an array of 'secret meetings' in which he had engaged. In other words, it sought to pinpoint, in Foucault's words, 'who has the power ... and who is deprived of it ... who has the right to know and who is forced to remain ignorant'.[49]

That *New York Times* editorial also rehearsed a familiar expectation of public consciousness-raising potentially diminishing this backroom power. Much international law scholarship has done likewise, albeit in far more nuanced versions. Yet the interlocking

[48] 'Mr Cheney's Imperial Presidency' *The New York Times* (New York, 23 December 2005) <https://www.nytimes.com/2005/12/23/opinion/mr-cheneys-imperial-presidency.html> accessed 8 October 2019.

[49] Foucault (n 46).

trajectories set out on the front page of the early edition of the *New York Times* that September day suggest that the aftermath of 9/11 need not have hinged upon Cheney's masterful intervention, nor on whether we knew about it (or not). Those pre-existing trajectories, apparent on the front page of the *New York Times*' early edition for 11 September 2001, make it harder to contend, also, that but for the iniquity and secrecy of Cheney and colleagues, heightened public consciousness might have afforded relatively untrammelled access to new horizons of possibility.

What exactly are some of the techno-material conditions or patterns to which this account gives short shrift, beyond the broad trends to which I've alluded? And how might we hope to engage those conditions and patterns, if not through knowledge-making and awareness-raising? I have suggested that many contemporary operations of power on the global plane work vectorially. That is, they take effect directionally, by orienting how and where resources, material aspirations, expectations and attention flow and the velocity and rhythms at which they do. If that is the case, then it is vital to investigate these operations directionally, in transit. They must be understood and investigated in action, as that is how they manifest.[50] Patterns and bearings of power—including those of power's transmission, leakage, incremental accumulation, drainage and so on—are as important to study as the sites where strategies may or may not contingently originate or ultimately 'land'. Yet studies of contingency that work on the assumption that contingency has been covered up, and must be recovered or re-announced, do not tend to be concerned with bearings. They are attuned to the origination and sedimentation or docking of power, not to its vectorial operations.

I recalled earlier that Foucault wrote that 'relationships of force' imply a 'pattern of the modifications' and that this pattern is discernible by 'the very nature of their process'.[51] Patterns indicative of shifts in power relations are, in this account, only ever implied in their processes of operation. That is, they are enfolded or entangled in those processes; they do not precede or succeed them. Let us explore this further by reference to one example of a force-laden process also on display on the front page of the *New York Times* on 11 September 2001: the formulation of tax policy—specifically, the lead story about tax cuts.[52] Here, once again, we encounter contingency in a mode configured to align with the accumulation of power and resources, rather than countervailing that accumulation or calling it into question.

Responding to a 'darkening economic outlook', and rising unemployment, both Republican and Democratic leaders were, in September 2001, talking tax cuts. Both parties contemplated spending an ever-greater proportion of social security receipts in order to fund these. And the Republican minority leader in the Senate, Trent Lott of Mississippi, insisted that any such package should include a cut in capital gains tax. What was clear,

[50] For other versions of this claim, see Gunther Teubner (ed), *Global Law Without a State* (Ashgate 1997) 286 referencing the theory 'Materia est in actu set nullius et actus' as one 'created' by Late Scholasticism and 'held by followers of Duns Scot in Paris during the second half of the fourteenth century'; Michel Foucault, 'The Subject and Power' (1982) 8 Critical Inquiry 777, 788: 'Power exists only when it is put into action'; Karl Marx, *Capital Volume II* (David Fernbach tr, Penguin 1978) 185: 'Those who consider the autonomization ... of value as mere abstraction forget that the movement of industrial capital is this abstraction in action.'

[51] Foucault (n 46).

[52] Alison Mitchell and Richard W Stevenson, 'Key Leaders Talk of Possible Deals to Revive Economy' *The New York Times* (New York, 11 September 2001) https://www.nytimes.com/2001/09/11/us/key-leaders-talk-of-possible-deals-to-revive-economy.html> accessed 8 October 2019.

then, at the time, is the extent to which economic policy-making was poll- and mood-driven and framed at a national scale. What was prompting policy 'move[ment]' was the experience of being '[c]onfronted with polls showing that support for Republicans was eroding'.[53] Also noteworthy is the limited range of options that were then under consideration. Looming especially large was the reflex assumption that the combination of more allowance for capital accumulation plus innovation would yield broad-ranging economic benefits. The story mentions Bush's national energy plan being 'geared toward economic growth'.[54] A few months earlier, announcing that plan, Bush made clear what he saw as the engine of that growth, remarking that '[o]ne thing we're not in short supply of is an entrepreneurial spirit'.[55]

The pattern discernible, looking back, is one of growing investment—both material and psychic—in entrepreneurship. Also evident in retrospect is an appetite, within US politics, for trying to unhinge national economic policy-making somewhat from the domain of the global, alongside conviction that the global circulation of an 'entrepreneurial spirit' might nonetheless redeem and empower a nation trying to stand apart. Positive enablement of capital on the part of the national government (through policy-making, including tax cuts, supposed to favour entrepreneurship and investment in entrepreneurship, and thereby to drive wealth- and job-creation) was being actively championed as a way of unshackling the seemingly spontaneous force of 'entrepreneurial spirit' to traverse the globe.[56] The regulatory embrace of contingency—through governmental championing of the risk-taking entrepreneur—was cast as a way of rejuvenating the national economy. And this legislative embrace of contingency seems to have been well in train by the early morning of 11 September 2001. Any decision to enact tax cuts may be treated after the fact as contingent, but the broader orientation towards contingency as a means of accumulating resources and shoring up power seems harder to trace to singular choice-events. In this context, the idea that contingency-unearthing tends to amount to counter-conduct seems worthy of question.[57]

VI. What may have been missed

If patterned contingency and its embrace have indeed become more or less a matter of rule, then this poses very real challenges for international law's standard recuperative response to injustice: a response that seeks to recover and rebuild foundations. Studies of contingency in international law tend to be oriented around the design and construction of global order, and how its formative architectures might have been, and might yet be, made otherwise, in some improved or simply another way. However, attention tends not to be drawn to places like the nondescript former eyeglass factory in Secaucus, New Jersey, where the 'colocation provider'

[53] ibid.
[54] ibid.
[55] 'Bush Energy Plan Looks to Future. Critics Say Help is Needed Now' (*CNN Inside Politics*, 17 May 2001) <http://edition.cnn.com/2001/ALLPOLITICS/05/17/bush.energy.plan/> accessed 8 October 2019.
[56] See, eg, William M Gentry and R Glenn Hubbard, 'Tax Policy and Entrepreneurial Entry' (2000) 90 American Economic Review 283; Robert Carroll and others, 'Income Taxes and Entrepreneurs' Use of Labor' (2000) 18 Journal of Labor Economics 324.
[57] On the notion of immanent 'counter conduct' in Foucault's writing, see Arnold I Davidson, 'Introduction' in Foucault (n 25) xviii, xx–xxi.

Equinix houses its NY4 data centre—one of a string of Equinix data centres encircling New York, including several at Secaucus.[58] It is through these centres that a very significant amount of US stock trading activity gets executed in the mode of 'high-frequency trading'.[59]

This chapter is not the place to try to examine precisely what kinds of change that high-frequency securities trading might, and might not, have brought about in global economic and social relations, nor its relationship to broader processes of financialisation.[60] The point of this sudden relocation from a singular location in Manhattan to 'colocation' in Seacaucus is this: international lawyers' habitual concern with the making of governance architectures at their headquarters—and the consciousness or blindness of their most prominent architects—led most international legal scholars to more or less miss the matter of the global financial markets' profound reshaping during the years just before and after 9/11. While one can point out a series of regulatory changes made in the late 1990s and early 2000s that helped new automated trading outfits and private exchanges get off the ground, the making of these automated markets may perhaps be better understood through attention to distribution than through the study of design and construction. And the infrastructures and practices on which their growth has depended are not likely to have been captured by attention to that which announces itself as globally significant. Perhaps if international lawyers had been tracking transmission, as much as they (or we) have been captivated by tragedy, they (we) would have been more engaged with the kinds of shifts of which high-frequency trading is illustrative.

A second, and related point is that expanded consciousness and improved visibility offer little bite on the kinds of contingent operations at work in high-frequency trading since around the time of 9/11. Learning about the phenomenon's existence, and its growing economic significance (over the past decade especially), opens no route at all to figuring out how to engage with these operations in the present. Recognising that these operations are highly contingent and internally contestable—being prone to contribute to 'flash crashes', in which broad stock market indices collapse and rebound with incredible velocity—adds nothing to their negotiability. Even the contingencies of policy reaction or non-reaction to high-frequency trading—such as the fate of various measures or proposals for taxation and 'throttling' around the world—seem, at times, to be fairly incidental to the broad changes that these activities signal are underway.[61] Declining volumes, regulatory changes, and increased costs may have slowed high-frequency trading markets of late, but there is likely

[58] 'Inside the Equinix NY4 Financial Trading Hub' (*Data Center Knowledge*, 14 October 2013) <http://www.datacenterknowledge.com/inside-the-equinix-ny4-financial-trading-hub/> accessed 8 October 2019; Paolo Gorgo, 'Equinix Opens New NY5 Facility—Expect Accelerated Revenue Growth' (*Seeking Alpha*, 6 August 2013) <https://seekingalpha.com/article/784831-equinix-opens-new-ny5-facility-expect-accelerated-revenue-growth> accessed 8 October 2019.

[59] Graham Bowley, 'The New Speed of Money, Reshaping Markets' *The New York Times* (New York, 2 January 2011) <https://www.nytimes.com/2011/01/02/business/02speed.html> accessed 8 October 2019.

[60] Maureen O'Hara 'High Frequency Market Microstructure' (2015) 116 Journal of Financial Economics 257 ('set[ting] out some important aspects of this high frequency transformation' and surveying some of the regulatory and policy changes that 'ushered in the high frequency era'). On financialisation, see Strange, *Mad Money* (n 15); Randy Martin, *Financialization of Daily Life* (Temple University Press 2002); Gerald Epstein, 'Introduction' in Gerald Epstein (ed), *Financialization and the World Economy* (Edward Elgar 2005).

[61] For discussion of various regulatory techniques used in different jurisdictions to try to temper the volatility associated with high frequency trading, see Imtiaz Mohammad Sifat and Azhar Mohamad 'Circuit Breakers as Market Stability Levers: A Survey of Research, Praxis, and Challenges' (2019) 24 International Journal of Finance & Economics 1130; Kjell Jorgensen, Johannes Skjeltorp, and Bernt Arne Ødegaard, 'Throttling Hyperactive Robots—Order to Trade Ratios at the Oslo Stock Exchange' (2018) 37 Journal of Financial Markets 1.

much more to come.[62] As Matt Haraburda, president of Chicago-based XR Trading, was reported to have said in January 2018: 'Maybe we are coming to the end of automating the things that were easy to automate . . . Now the real fun starts'.[63]

What has made it hard for international lawyers to take account of these shifts in tempo, technique, technology, and terrain? Fixations on necessity could perhaps have something to do with it—say, the tendency to accept the necessity of growth and the imperative of technological progress—but fixations on contingency also seem to have played a role. Regardless of the reason for international lawyers' past inattention to significant economic and financial changes (of which high-frequency trading is emblematic), continuing to challenge the pretence to necessity in these contexts seems, even now, to yield little by way of possibility. A more fundamental rerouting of the international legal endeavour seems called for.

Could it be that international lawyers' orientation towards salvation is a good place to start? So much critical scholarly effort has been put into bemoaning what international law has helped to destroy. So much work has been done trying to recover international law's costs, and to save its victims. So much labour is being directed towards recovering lost and little-known histories and showcasing international law's many strange, sometimes malformed constructions. Almost no time is being spent questioning the routine international legal impulse to minimise destruction. Yet on a global scale, salvation is not working. So much on the global plane is being discarded and degraded. Extinction rates are around 1,000 times pre-human rates.[64] Freshwater vertebrates lost 83% of their global population between 1970 and 2014.[65] Life expectancy in the US—higher than any other country's in 1960—is on the decline.[66] One 2018 study in the *British Medical Journal* blames substance abuse, despair, and the effects of long-term structural disadvantage.[67]

Could it be that international lawyers need to reflect less on salvation, and more on what to abandon, or set aside, including within their own critical repertoire, and how to do so? Another version of this suggestion might be the following: international legal scholarship would do well to assume a starting point of complicity, rather than cleanliness—to try to probe inside some operations of power in action, rather than try to arrest or arraign those operations from afar. This has long been the approach taken by some international humanitarian lawyers—those travelling on aircraft carriers, say—but sits less comfortably in other areas of doctrine and practice.[68] Assuming such a posture of complicity, it becomes important to ask: what ideas prevalent in international legal scholarship might warrant

[62] Gregory Meyer, Nicole Bullock, and Joe Rennison, 'How High-Frequency Trading Hit a Speed Bump', *Financial Times* (New York, 1 January 2018) <https://www.ft.com/content/d81f96ea-d43c-11e7-a303-9060cb1e5f44> accessed 8 October 2019. See further Alexander Osipovich, 'More Exchanges Add "Speed Bumps," Defying High-Frequency Traders' *The Wall Street Journal* (New York, 29 July 2019) <https://www.wsj.com/articles/more-exchanges-add-speed-bumps-defying-high-frequency-traders-11564401611> accessed 8 October 2019.

[63] Meyer et al (n 62).

[64] Jurriaan M De Vos and others, 'Estimating the Normal Background Rate of Species Extinction' (2015) 29 Conservation Biology 452.

[65] Monique Grooten and Rosamunde EA Almond (eds), *World Wildlife Fund. Living Planet Report—2018: Aiming Higher* (WWF 2018) 7, 95.

[66] Grace Donnelly, 'Here's Why Life Expectancy in the U.S. Dropped Again This Year' (*Fortune*, 10 February 2018) <https://fortune.com/2018/02/09/us-life-expectancy-dropped-again/?> accessed 8 October 2019.

[67] Steven H Woolf and Laudan Aron, 'Failing Health of the United States' (2018) 360 British Medical Journal 496.

[68] David Kennedy, *The Dark Sides of Virtue. Reassessing International Humanitarianism* (Princeton University Press 2011) 329 ('There is apparently something scandalous about an aircraft carrier sailing off to war as the *realization* of international humanitarianism . . . We prefer to think of humanitarians as gentle civilizers, lawyers whispering in the admiral's ear . . . ').

targeting? What could be dislodged and jettisoned in the patterns I've been describing? Could it be, for instance, that the idea that consciousness of contingency begets freedom is an idea worth setting adrift?

VII. Conclusion: Setting critical consciousness-raising aside?

The question above might sound glib. It is far from clear, of course, how one would go about destroying such an idea, or dispensing with it in practice. Reasoning against it seems unlikely to do the trick. Nonetheless, there *is* a vibrant tradition of internal critique in international law oriented towards unravelling or, broadly speaking, setting things aside, and it's a lineage worth recalling.[69] This is the tradition in which some international lawyers have dwelt upon grammar, sign, and erasure. This is the tradition in which some have cast legal order as an emanation of the unconscious. This is the tradition in which international lawyers have provincialised and fragmented legal consciousness. This is the tradition in which some have taken death rather than life, killing rather than birthing, waste rather than salvage, as the starting point for international legal work.[70] Writing on the ubiquity of contingency and its relationship to power in the key of this tradition is likely to yield accounts far more discomforting than accounts of contingency oriented towards recovery and redemption—an international law less ripe with possibilities than littered with remarkably resilient dead ends.

It would, however, be rather ungracious of me to conclude this chapter on such a note. The dead end is no place to take fellow travellers at the end of a short chapter such as this. Let me re-route and re-state with a more upbeat modulation, out of deference to the social norms of the international legal scholarly genre. Those radical counterfactuals that reside within the international legal tradition remain exhilarating to unearth. Following through on some of these, whether speculatively or programmatically, seems worthwhile doing in many instances. Yet, there are perils. Many mechanisms of power that prevail on the global plane thrive on contingency, rather than negate it. It is not clear that drawing out unacknowledged contingencies in international law's past can speak any kind of truth to this power. There is also the problem of engaging certain material dimensions of 'systematicity', or what I have called legacy infrastructure, and making these seem actionable, renegotiable. Pinpointing contingent events often seems rather incidental to the ongoing operations of one or other infrastructure channel. Not all dimensions of the actual are pliable to the critical touch. Much gets missed when international law scholars focus only on making

[69] It may be especially so in the face of the apparent forgetting of the richness of this tradition. I was rather taken aback when a talented and well-read researcher in the later stages of a doctorate at a world-leading university in the UK remarked to me, in early 2016, that she thought that writing international legal histories was simply how critical international law was done. David Kennedy's note of lamentation and surprise is worth recalling in this context: 'I continue to be struck . . . by the relative scarcity of work picking up, reworking, extending, or contesting the broad argument of *From Apology to Utopia*—or, for that matter, of my own *International Legal Structures*. Although often cited, Martti's book is rarely challenged or deeply engaged.' : David Kennedy, 'The Last Treatise. Project and Person (Reflections on Martti Koskenniemi's *From Apology to Utopia*)' in Russel A Miller and Peer C Zumbansen (eds), *Comparative Law as Transnational Law: A Decade of the German Law Journal* (OUP 2011) 75, 82.

[70] See generally Fleur E Johns, 'Critical International Legal Theory' in Jeffrey L Dunoff and Mark A Pollack (eds), *International Legal Theory: Foundations and Frontiers* (CUP forthcoming) UNSW Law Research Paper No 18-44 <http://dx.doi.org/10.2139/ssrn.3224013> accessed 8 October 2019.

that which seems fixed and unavoidable somewhat less so. Perhaps, in the face of one or other unequal or otherwise misshapen system of power, international law would do better to focus on patterns of transmission and superfluity, rather than trying to revisit or restage moments of origination. Perhaps international lawyers need to think about infiltrating and overloading some systems going forward, rather than trying so insistently to dial them back towards some earlier point of supposedly neglected opportunity. Fortuitously, there is much still left to do in this field, and many people around with whom to do it.

3

Contingency in International Legal History

Why Now?

*Genevieve Renard Painter**

I. Introduction

In the field of international legal history, contingency kindles heated controversy. For some, the idea that international law could have been otherwise affronts the natural law account of its evolution. For others, analysis of contingency weakens the claim that international law's telos has been relentlessly imperial. The battle is often joined on the terrain of 'context', where some scholars are charged with dealing in anachronism while others are decried as peddlers of international law's self-legitimating stories.

For a conference and edited collection on how international law could have been otherwise, I planned to write a story about contingencies and near misses. It would have been a story about an Indigenous leader in the early 1920s who appealed to the League of Nations for assistance in a dispute his nation had with Canada and the British Empire.[1] The leader was Chief Deskaheh from the Six Nations of Grand River, a polity in what is now called Ontario, Canada. The Six Nations are one of several nations in the Haudenosaunee Confederacy. In one of many assaults on Six Nations' sovereignty, Canada invaded their territories in 1922 and installed a police garrison.[2] This invasion was among the grievances that Deskaheh brought to the attention of the League of Nations. His campaign of political and legal advocacy put the Six Nations into alliance with several states, some bureaucrats, a few civil society organisations, and a remarkable number of Scottish women who advocated on his behalf.[3] Deskaheh's story has already been told by scholars, mostly rendered as a tragedy, a mission doomed to fail due to the might of empire and the meekness of the League of Nations.[4] I intended for my

* Sincere thanks to Liam McHugh-Russell, Ingrid Renard, Christopher Tomlins, Itamar Mann, Rose Sydney Parfitt, Tobias Smith, Alessandra La Posta, and the conveners and participants of the conference, 'Contingency in the Course of International Law: How International Law Could Have Been', University of Amsterdam, 14–16 June 2018. All errors are my own.

[1] Joëlle Rostowski, 'The Redman's Appeal for Justice: Deskaheh and the League of Nations' in Christian F Feest (ed), *Indians and Europe: An Interdisciplinary Collection of Essays* (Rader Verlag 1987).

[2] Amar Bhatia, 'South of the North: Building on Critical Approaches to International Law with Lessons from the Fourth World' (2012) 14 Oregon Review of International Law 131, 165.

[3] Letter, Deskaheh to Sir James Eric Drummond, Secretary General, League of Nations, 23 August 1923, League of Nations (LoN) Archives, File 11 30454 28075; Letter, Rica Flemyng Gyll to Deputy Superintendent General of Indian Affairs, 12 April 1924, Library and Archives of Canada (LAC), RG10, Vol 2287, File 57, 169-1X; Bureau International pour la Défense des Indigènes, Resolution, 25 September 1923, LoN Archives, File 11 31197 28075.

[4] Grace Li Xiu Woo, 'Canada's Forgotten Founders: The Modern Significance of the Haudenosaunee (Iroquois) Application for Membership in the League of Nations' [2003] Law, Social Justice & Global Development Journal 1; Bhatia (n 2); Arnulf Becker Lorca, *Mestizo International Law a Global Intellectual History 1842–1933* (CUP 2014) 281–86.

Genevieve Renard Painter, *Contingency in International Legal History* In: *Contingency in International Law*. Edited by: Ingo Venzke and Kevin Jon Heller, Oxford University Press. © The Several Contributors 2021. DOI: 10.1093/oso/9780192898036.003.0003

chapter to retell the story as a success, because Deskaheh very nearly gained a hearing of his petition by the Assembly of the League of Nations. Telling a success story would involve dwelling on why the diplomat from the Netherlands did not immediately discard his petition;[5] why Persia, Panama, Ireland, and Estonia campaigned on his behalf;[6] why Sweden, holding the Presidency of the Assembly, invoked his procedural rights of fairness;[7] to say nothing of why the diplomat from Latvia leaned on the diplomat from Estonia to sign a joint letter supporting the Six Nations, only to demur at the last minute from signing the letter himself.[8] If a claim by an Indigenous nation protesting colonial occupation had been heard by the Assembly in 1924, it would not have been insignificant: Rose Parfitt's work on the Abyssinian crisis points to the high stakes of questions of state recognition at this moment in international law's past.[9]

That story—a revisionist history of Chief Deskaheh's quest for justice at the League of Nations—did not get written because I stopped to wonder, 'why is the field of international legal history thinking about contingency and necessity now?' Structural approaches, more inclined to emphasise necessity, have long dominated the field. But no longer. Contingency's stock has risen so fast that Susan Marks warns of the siren call of 'false contingency', and Anne Orford worries that the emphasis on contingency has taken international legal history in a conservative direction.[10] The conference that generated this edited collection received nearly 140 submissions to its call for papers, far exceeding organiser expectations.[11] The present excitement for contingency in international legal history is notable, if only because in other academic quarters there has been a move *away* from contingency and context towards structure and necessity. Is this just another case of international legal scholarship catching up to trends in other disciplines? Or is there something peculiar about the history of international law that explains why studying it has generated so much current interest in the tension between contingency and necessity?

This chapter explores these issues, taking Deskaheh's mission to the League of Nations as a departure point. I show that the necessity-contingency debate holds together an assortment of intellectual preoccupations among a heterogenous community of scholars. The debate about contingency and necessity has become a cipher for anxieties and hopes about international law's differentiation from other fields, its futures, and the political stakes of writing its history. The chapter begins with a capsule history of the contingency-necessity debate. It then considers the question, 'Contingency, why now?' from three vantage points: context, narrators, and politics in the writing of international legal history.

[5] Letter, Rt Hon Sir Auckland Geddes, HM Ambassador at Washington, to Lord Byng of Vimy, Governor General, 15 December 1922, LAC, RG10, Vol 1330, File 1362 Part 1.

[6] Letter, Delegations of Persia, Panama, Estonia, Ireland to President, League of Nations, 27 September 1923, LoN Archives, File 11 31340 28075.

[7] Letter, Erik Boheman, Minister of External Affairs, Sweden to Captain FP Walters, League of Nations Secretariat, 21 January 1924, LoN Archives, File 11 33556 28075.

[8] Letter, H Montgomery Grove, British Consulate, Reval to JCT Vaughan, British Legation, Riga, 10 April 1924, LAC, RG10, Vol 1330, File 1362 Part 1.

[9] Rose Parfitt, *The Process of International Legal Reproduction: Inequality, Historiography, Resistance* (CUP 2018).

[10] Susan Marks, 'False Contingency' (2009) 62 Current Legal Problems 1; Anne Orford, 'International Law and the Limits of History' in Wouter Werner, Marieke De Hoon, and Alexis Galan (eds), *The Law of International Lawyers* (CUP 2017).

[11] Email to author, 20 December 2017.

II. A history of contingency and necessity

To situate the present interest in contingency in international legal history, I begin by sketching the modern history of the tension between contingency and necessity in several related intellectual fields. Due to varying definitions of the terms 'contingency' and 'necessity', I consider the contingency-necessity debate as a discursive space, rather than as a debate occurring with well-defined and commonly agreed terms.

1. In history

In twentieth-century discussions about methods and history, the relationship between contingency and necessity mapped onto nineteenth-century dichotomies between free will and determinism and between agency and structure. Many theories of history from Hegel, Marx, and their progeny had posited a determinist theory of history. Agency played a role but circumscribed by a master narrative. Against this theory of history came the Nietzschean retort that everything was less pre-determined and more contingent than once believed.[12] In the twentieth century, the debate's political stakes had the Marxists lining up on the side of structure and necessity and the liberals lining up on the side of free will, agency, and contingency.[13]

The idea that the past, whether shaped by contingency or necessity, was out there in the world, amenable to representation, was upended by the linguistic turn. After the turn, the world's history was no longer real but produced discursively, emploted in narratives that could be categorised into tropes, like the tragic or the epic.[14] Those influenced by Foucault's genealogical method sought to reveal the many alternative pasts to our present in order to examine why the present manifests as it does.[15] As the world of possible narratives from events multiplied, necessity was pushed to the wings and contingency took the spotlight. Because contingency (as a corollary of post-structuralism) was seen to divert attention from necessity and determinism, it was often decried as a conservative, or at least anti-Marxist, method.

Among intellectual historians, it was the rejection of grand narratives of philosophical history that gave rise to concern for contingency. Quentin Skinner and other adherents of the Cambridge School denounced projects where ideas like 'the state' or 'citizen' were imagined as moving, undisturbed, across time. Instead, they said, ideas had to be considered 'in context', meaning that ideas were best comprehended as contingent on their place and time.[16] In the fight against grand narratives, the emphasis on context yielded multiple interpretations that relied on the differentiation between the present moment and

[12] Yemima Ben-Menahem, 'Historical Necessity and Contingency' in Aviezer Tucker (ed), *A Companion to the Philosophy of History and Historiography* (Wiley-Blackwell 2009) 120, 129.

[13] Marks (n 10) 5–11.

[14] The narrativist school was shaped by disputes among these authors and others: Michel de Certeau, *The Writing of History* (Columbia University Press 1988); Hayden V White, *Metahistory: The Historical Imagination in Nineteenth-Century Europe* (Johns Hopkins University Press 1973); Paul Ricoeur, 'The Model of the Text: Meaningful Action Considered as a Text' (1973) 5 New Literary History 91; Roland Barthes, 'The Discourse of History [1967]' in Elinor Shaffer (ed), *Comparative Criticism: A Yearbook. Volume III* (Cambridge University Press 1982).

[15] Michel Foucault, *The Order of Things: An Archaeology of the Human Sciences* (Pantheon Books 1971).

[16] Quentin Skinner, 'Meaning and Understanding in the History of Ideas' (1969) 8 History and Theory 3.

other contexts. Much debate ensued about how to choose the 'proper context', what such a choice entailed, whether contextualism presumed a representational account of language, and so on.[17] Contextualism, at that time, was associated with contingency, not structure or necessity.

The Cold War context implied that historians had to declare their allegiances through methodology: being for or against necessity proxied for being with or against the Marxists. Today, historians are more willing to allow that, simply as a matter of logic, our methods must make room for both contingency and necessity. If humans had a good theory to explain everything that had ever happened, we would not need historiography to order and give meaning to the past. We would just point to the theory. If, on the other hand, it was known that all human events arise out of pure chance, it would be futile to impose order or meaning on past events.[18] '[H]istoriography, as an activity that produces knowledge about the past, can be justified' by the fact that we believe that human life is both determined and contingent.[19]

Now, in the early twenty-first century, some observers have diagnosed a retreat from methods foregrounding plurality and contingency and a return to an empiricist enterprise that tells chronological narratives shaped by structural and determinist explanations.[20] In the field of history, post-structuralism did not unseat the reign of a modernist epistemology.

2. In legal history

In legal history, contingency also achieved dominance by the end of the twentieth century, but through a path distinct from the field of history. American legal realism shook beliefs about law's roots in abstract principle, as it showed how law was susceptible to political, economic, and social forces. Subsequently, critical legal studies (CLS) generated a swarm of scholarly investigations into the law's myriad contexts and its attendant histories.[21] As these contexts multiplied, so did contingency.[22] The CLS-inflected historicist mode of writing legal history remains dominant, but it has been criticised for lacking meta-level explanations of change.[23] Contemporary monographs in law and history show an awful lot of the haves coming out ahead, the power of the carceral state expanding, and the reach of the global corporation spreading, but the dominant mode of doing legal history seems barely to notice, much less explain why.[24] The prevalence of contingency as the mantra of legal

[17] For introductions to the debate, see James Tully, *Meaning and Context: Quentin Skinner and His Critics* (Princeton University Press 1988); Martin Jay, 'Historical Explanation and the Event: Reflections on the Limits of Contextualization' (2011) 42 New Literary History 557.

[18] Allan Megill, 'History's Unresolving Tensions: Reality and Implications' [2019] Rethinking History 1, 7.

[19] ibid 5.

[20] Gary Wilder, 'From Optic to Topic: The Foreclosure Effect of Historiographic Turns' (2012) 117 The American Historical Review 723; Joan Wallach Scott, 'History-Writing as Critique' in Keith Jenkins, Sue Morgan, and Alun Munslow (eds), *Manifestos for History* (Routledge 2007); Ethan Kleinberg, Joan Wallach Scott, and Gary Wilder, 'Theses on Theory and History' (May 2018) <http://theoryrevolt.com> accessed 29 May 2018.

[21] For an overview, see Catherine L Fisk, '&: Law _ Society in Historical Legal Research' in Markus Dirk Dubber and Christopher L Tomlins (eds), *The Oxford Handbook of Legal History* (OUP 2018).

[22] Robert W Gordon, 'Critical Legal Histories' (1984) 36 Stanford Law Review 57.

[23] ibid; Christopher Tomlins, 'After Critical Legal History: Scope, Scale, Structure' (2012) 8 Annual Review of Law and Social Science 31.

[24] Tomlins, 'After Critical Legal History' (n 23) 33–37.

history has prompted calls for a return to, variously, black letter law, necessity, structure, and the meta-theoretical.[25]

To recap: In the broader field of history, historiography moved away from methods that focused on timeless truths, necessity, and structural explanations towards methods which evoked discourse, multiplicity, and contingency. But contingency has since lost ground with the revival of empiricist, objective, and event-narrating methods. In legal scholarship, a structuralism associated with legal formalism was unseated by CLS and the drive to study law in multiple contexts. For legal historians, this manifested in a near-obsession with contingency, at the expense of consideration of the structures and necessity in law's evolutions.

III. Temporal and spatial contexts for international law

Let me turn to my central question: Why is the field of international legal history presently interested in the contingency/necessity debate? In exploring this question, I consider trends in scholarly literature as composite effects of texts. I am concerned with understanding how the field of international legal history, as a multi-disciplinary intellectual space, contains patterns and tensions that are distinct from and independent of authorial intention.

I first consider an explanation rooted in changes in the methods of international legal history. The current enthusiasm for history has been prompted in part by post-colonial critique of international law. The traditional account traced international law's origins to the ideas of a few European progenitors. Anghie and Koskennniemi's work exposed this origin story as the scholarly manifestation of a partisan political project, the civilising mission.[26] Revisions of the discipline's origin story have brought about a flourishing of debates about historical methods.

The methodological debate about the relationship between international law and history pits contextualists (inspired by interpretations of the Cambridge School method) against other historians.[27] Thanks to new historiographies shaped by this debate, the scholarship is no longer only about the past, nor only about Europe.[28] Critics of these developments charge that the enthusiasm for revisionism has caused the field to harbour anachronism, one of history's outlaws. On its face, the controversy is whether the ideas of international law should be interpreted within their time or in light of present-day norms. Beneath the controversy is a question about how to theorise international law's role in creating and remedying present-day injustices. Third World Approaches to International Law (TWAIL) displaced Europe as international law's lodestar and exposed the link between international law and global imperialism. The classical foundation of the discipline had long insisted on a line separating 'law' from 'colonial administration', 'politics', or 'anthropology', with legal

[25] ibid.

[26] Martti Koskenniemi, *The Gentle Civilizer of Nations: The Rise and Fall of International Law, 1870–1960* (CUP 2002); Antony Anghie, *Imperialism, Sovereignty, and the Making of International Law* (CUP 2005).

[27] Lauren Benton, 'Beyond Anachronism: Histories of International Law and Global Legal Politics' (2019) 21 Journal of the History of International Law 7; Andrew Fitzmaurice, 'Context in the History of International Law' (2018) 20 Journal of the History of International Law 5; Orford (n 10); Martti Koskenniemi, 'Vitoria and Us' (2014) 2014 Rechtsgeschichte—Legal History 119; Anne Orford, 'On International Legal Method' (2013) 1 London Review of International Law 166.

[28] Doreen Lustig, 'Governance Histories of International Law' in Markus Dirk Dubber and Christopher Tomlins (eds), *The Oxford Handbook of Legal History* (OUP 2018).

scholars concerned only with the former.[29] TWAIL histories reclassified these peripheries as within the core of international law and, in doing so, they exposed international law as a violent, imperial, and intrinsically political and bureaucratic project.[30]

But studies under the banners of 'not only the past' and 'not only Europe' form only one part of the blooming field of revisionist histories of international law. A growing corpus of work in history, political theory, anthropology, and geography shows that international law has a social, political, cultural, and environmental history, not just a jurisprudential history.[31] International law has a history held by the lowly bureaucrats, the revolutionaries, and the poor, not just by the elites. It has a history shaped by non governmental organisations (NGOs), missionaries, and international institutions, not just by states.[32] In hindsight, it is astonishing that the field lasted as long as it did without some ideas about Chinese theories of international law or without a clear understanding of how bureaucrats, magistrates, foreigners, and Indigenous people grappled with concepts like 'sovereignty' or 'jurisdiction' at the coalface of empire-building.[33] This wealth of scholarship has added enormous complexity to the history of international law. It has become harder to tell a univocal story about international law's conspiracy with Western liberalism and its imperial ambitions, just as it has become harder to claim that all evil in the last 500 years can be laid at the feet of international law. In having to account for other actors, other terrains of analysis, and other forces of influence, we now have histories brimming with uncertainty, complexity, and lack of generalisation across the globe—and, consequently, brimming with more contingency, and less necessity.

This trajectory, in which revisionist histories dismantled tidier stories through their emphasis on contingency, parallels developments in the Anglo-American history of domestic (as opposed to international) law. CLS expanded the scope of the history of law, by asking about actors and processes usually sidelined in law. The historical strand of CLS foregrounded the agency of actors rather than structure and the contingency of law's development rather than its necessity.[34] A few decades of scholarly industry later, we gaze upon an ungainly pile of stories about contingent pasts and presents with a sense of intellectual exhaustion and bewilderment.[35]

Where did all this contingency in domestic legal history come from? Tomlins tracks the infection to the trend for putting law 'in context'—juxtaposing law against society, politics, the economy, and so on. This aetiology suggests that finding contingency and agency in law's past is a symptom of the methodology of putting the law in context. Indeed, the surest

[29] Antony Anghie, 'Imperialism and International Legal Theory' in Anne Orford and Florian Hoffmann (eds), *The Oxford Handbook of the Theory of International Law* (OUP 2016).

[30] Becker Lorca (n 4); Anghie (n 26); Luis Eslava and Sundhya Pahuja, 'Beyond the (Post)Colonial: TWAIL and the Everyday Life of International Law' (2012) 45 Verfassung und Recht in Übersee / Law and Politics in Africa, Asia and Latin America 195; BS Chimni, 'Third World Approaches to International Law: A Manifesto' (2006) 8 International Community Law Review 3.

[31] For sample reviews of the field, see Benton (n 27); Valentina Vadi, 'International Law and Its Histories: Methodological Risks and Opportunities' [2017] Harvard International Law Journal 311.

[32] The citations to all these studies appear in Lustig (n 28).

[33] Phil CW Chan, 'China's Approaches to International Law since the Opium War' (2014) 27 Leiden Journal of International Law 859.

[34] For elaboration, see Gordon (n 22).

[35] Kunal M Parker, 'Law in and as History: The Common Law in the American Polity, 1790–1900' (2011) 1 UC Irvine Law Review 587, 593.

way back to structure and necessity might be withdrawing to the black letter law, mining it for its inner logic and ordering principles.

Putting law in context causes law to appear as co-constituted with everything else to which it is related. This co-constitution puts pressure on the definition of law and our confidence about its autonomy.[36] How are we to distinguish law from other fields of human thought and action? In the *Law As* project, Tomlins offers respite from the relentless relational juxtaposition through a method of overlaying law with other things, rather than situating it relationally.[37] Under its aegis, law has been read 'as' text, mistake, archive, language, history, and so on. That this has been possible lends credence to the idea that the law 'is', somehow, or at least that we can collectively believe it is so in such a way that we understand one another.

The ceaseless contextualising of domestic law has taken place in the shadow of a time-worn, august edifice: law in the books. Domestic law has the security of tenure to allow itself to be read as text, mistake, language, archive, and so on. Can international law withstand the scandal of being dressed up as something else? Anxiety about the status of international law as law has defined the field in the modern era.[38] The nineteenth-century iteration of international legal history was aimed precisely at narrating a history that would justify the legitimacy and binding force of international law.[39] Ongoing debate about sources doctrine, the recognition of international legal personality, the efficacy of international criminal law, and the politics of humanitarian intervention suggest that insecurities about international law's existence have diminished rather than disappeared. The question is no longer whether international law exists as a field of practice and research, but how to delimit its boundaries and explain its foundations.[40] During my research on Chief Deskaheh's efforts at the League of Nations, I have searched for micro-histories of the etiquette of inter-war diplomacy in order to understand the differences in tone meted out by the British diplomats to their counterparts in Persia and Panama, and then worried about whether the social history of the salutations in diplomatic memos was a worthy international law topic.[41] I have wondered whether I could make intricate power struggles between factions of Six Nations of Grand River and Canada's Department of Indian Affairs relevant to readers of an international law review.[42] In writing about early twentieth-century Anglo-Persian relations, to explain Persia's obstinate defence of Deskaheh's cause, I have watched my international law story mutate into one of international politics.[43] It is not clear how to delimit the 'case' or 'event' that is proper to international law. Indeed, as I have argued elsewhere, the line classifying a

[36] Christopher Tomlins, 'How Autonomous Is Law?' (2007) 3 Annual Review of Law and Social Science 45.

[37] Christopher Tomlins, 'Law As ... IV: Minor Jurisprudence in Historical Key. An Introduction' (2017) 21 Law Text Culture 1.

[38] Frédéric Mégret, 'International Law as Law' in James Crawford, Martti Koskenniemi, and Surabhi Ranganathan (eds), *The Cambridge Companion to International Law* (CUP 2012).

[39] Martti Koskenniemi, 'A History of International Law Histories' in Bardo Fassbender and Anne Peters (eds), *The Oxford Handbook of the History of International Law* (OUP 2012).

[40] Mégret (n 38).

[41] Contrast communications with Panama and Persia: Telegram to Mr Wallis (Panama), 4 March 1924, LAC, RG10, Vol 1330, File 1362 Part 1; Letter, JH Thomas to Lord Byng of Vimy, Governor General, 30 January 1924, LAC, RG10, Vol 2286, File 57,169-1C Part 4.

[42] Sally Weaver, 'The Iroquois: The Grand River Reserve in the Late Nineteenth Century and Early Twentieth Centuries, 1875–1945' in Edward S Rogers and Donald B Smith (eds), *Aboriginal Ontario Historical Perspectives on the First Nations* (Dundurn Press 1994).

[43] Letter, Secretary of State for the Colonies to Governor General, 5 March 1924, LAC, RG10, Vol 2286, File 57,169-1C Part 4.

matter as one of domestic or international law is itself the product of recognising some jurisdictions over others, a political question concealed by a methodological choice.[44]

One might summarise the entire field of law and society as the quest for choosing and defining law's relational others.[45] Domestic law has a fairly clear set of others against which it can be related—politics, economics, and society. But international law's outside is much less clear. Who is the international society that offers a context for international law? How do we define the international economy that is distinct from international law? On what basis can we separate international law from international politics?

This analysis leads me to conclude that the growth in histories of international law foregrounding contingency over necessity is an effect of the method of putting international law in relation to other things. The prevalence of this relational method may be a symptom of the continuing search for a basis for the differentiation of international law.

IV. The narrators of international law's pasts

An alternative explanation traces the increased attention to the contingency/necessity debate to the scholars themselves, rather than to the methods they choose. Hayden White and other narrativists contend that the scholar plays a determinative role in giving meaning to an essentially formless past, through narrative techniques of form, emplotment, order, and sequence.[46] For example, when history is narrated as tragedy, contingency loses out to necessity; when history is narrated as comedy, necessity is overshadowed by contingent forces.[47] According to the narrativist school, the balance between contingency and necessity arises from the scholars' choices of emplotment. But even the more realist historians admit their trade is telling compelling stories. Whereas in the previous section I argued that the necessity-contingency debate is evidence of a methodological debate about the proper context for the analysis of historical 'raw material', now I ask if the debate is a proxy for disagreement about how to narrate international law's pasts. I begin by mapping the dominant and dissident narrative structures in international legal history before advancing some possible explanations for these disagreements over narrative structure.

One might say that the historiography of international law has been home to two diametrically opposed necessity stories. In one, international law's history is a tale of progress and humanity's redemption; in the other, international law's history is a story of imperialism and oppression. Both stories are structuralist, though one might be dubbed Panglossian and the other paranoid. Both narratives are held together by a belief in a teleology for international law. Contingency appears in either narrative mode, as pure determinism makes for a short story. But in the Panglossian mode of historiography, if international law errs in its arc towards justice, it is a symptom of bumps along the way, rather than a symptom of systematic injustice. In the contrasting historiographies associated with TWAIL, there is some give (or contingency) in the system. That the dispossessed have used international law's discourses and arenas to challenge empire proves not the senseless contingency of international law's

[44] Genevieve Renard Painter, 'A Letter from the Haudenosaunee Confederacy to King George V: Writing and Reading Jurisdictions in International Legal History' (2017) 5 London Review of International Law 7.
[45] Tomlins, 'How Autonomous Is Law?' (n 36) 64.
[46] White (n 14).
[47] Ben-Menahem (n 12) 128.

history, but that in the hands of those in struggle, any tool can be used as a weapon if you hold it right. Those carrying a brief for international law[48] tell stories framed by the belief that international law will come out on the right side of history in the end—for example, the narratives that describe Chief Deskaheh as a human rights activist 'before his time' and a pioneer in the international recognition of Indigenous rights.[49] Those carrying a brief for TWAIL tell stories framed by the idea that international law's aspirations for total (Eurocentric) domination of the globe will always fail due to Third World resistance. They might say that Chief Deskaheh's experience at the League of Nations reveals the spaces for resistance within international law and the enduring existence of non-Eurocentric international normative orders.[50] In both these structuralist narratives, the tension in their form is drawn from contingency pulling against the much more powerful force of necessity.

These structuralist narratives have been challenged by another way of narrating the past, one that focuses on contingency and complexity. The historicist variant of this alternative was discussed in the previous section in the survey of the wealth of studies about the complexity and contingency of international law's pasts. A post-structural manifestation of contingency in narrative form appears through the evental analyses of international law.[51] Whereas conventional historiography engulfs events into international law's evolutionary narratives, where 'nothing happen[s] . . . which it has not either anticipated or claimed the ability to capture', this approach scans the history of international law for 'an opening, or having to come to pass anew', for context-breaking events, for innovation, accidents, agency, and hopeful possibilities.[52] 'Eventing' international law makes it possible to avoid teleology and use emplotment to draw out the contingencies in international law's past.

If international legal history is awash with stories that emphasise contingency rather than necessity and narrate the past as a site of plural possibilities, it may be due to a retreat from structuralism and the waning of tragedy as the field's hegemonic trope.[53] If I told a contingency story about Deskaheh's efforts at the League of Nations, I would dwell on the Dutch diplomat who did not immediately discard his petition, and I would try to explain his reasons (or his incompetency!). I would study the relations between Great Britain and Deskaheh's allies, Ireland, Persia, Estonia, and Panama, to investigate their motives. In a counterfactualist mode, I might wonder what would have happened if Deskaheh had been allowed a full hearing of his complaint at the Assembly of the League of Nations. Stitched together, the focus on these micro-moments would show the agency exerted by minor players and challenge the tale of structural necessities in the international legal order.

These alternative versions of Deskaheh's story suggest that a narrative perspective gives us a different angle on the question of why international legal historians are

[48] I borrow this phrase from Janet Halley, who takes it from Duncan Kennedy: Janet Halley, *Split Decisions: How and Why to Take a Break from Feminism* (Princeton University Press 2008) 189.

[49] Ronald Niezen, *The Origins of Indigenism: Human Rights and the Politics of Identity* (University of California Press 2003) 51–52.

[50] Becker Lorca (n 4).

[51] Walter Rech, 'International Law, Empire, and the Relative Indeterminacy of Narrative' in Martti Koskenniemi, Walter Rech, and Manuel Jiménez Fonseca (eds), *International Law and Empire: Historical Explorations* (OUP 2017) 74.

[52] Fleur Johns, Richard John Joyce, and Sundhya Pahuja, 'Introduction' in Fleur Johns, Richard John Joyce, and Sundhya Pahuja (eds), *Events: The Force of International Law* (Routledge 2011) 4, 1.

[53] Thomas Skouteris, 'Engaging History in International Law' in José María Beneyto and David Kennedy (eds), *New Approaches to International Law* (TMC Asser Press 2012).

currently preoccupied by the necessity-contingency debate. Whereas some scholars claim to be finding contingency (or necessity) in the relation between 'historical facts' and their context(s), the narrativist approach regards 'historical facts' as products of the *effet du réel* generated through emplotment.[54] This approach implies that contingency and necessity are effects of the narrative frame adopted by the legal historian; hence, the debate is rooted in us, the scholars, rather than in anything about international law and its pasts. The fact that some international legal historians are now drawn to contingency (rather than to necessity) is just the current answer to a question about 'what kinds of history appear to make themselves available in contemporary settings'.[55] It is not the object of research that has changed but the mentalities and contexts in which the historian is writing.[56] Methods shape international legal history because, as Craven notes, 'international law is not simply something that one can examine through the lens of history as if it were some historical artefact existing independently of the means chosen by which it is to be represented'.[57]

Explaining contingency's rise as an effect of narrative choices does not reduce scholarship to the idiosyncratic affinities of the scholar. Conventions particular to scholarly communities mean that some emplotments are taken as more valid than others. The conditions of validity of a historical narrative depend not on its 'correspondence to facts that are out there but because it rests on markers, periodisations, and causal sequencing that are socially accepted'.[58]

If the contingency-necessity debate is understood as a debate about the proper way to narrate history, what distinctions drive that debate? This question brings to the surface the heterogeneity of the community of writers of international law's histories. Legal scholars writing history and professional historians may be working with the same archival materials and on similar questions, but they will tell different stories and will be answerable to different professional standards.[59] I now examine whether differences between the professional historian and the legal historian help to explain the stakes of the contingency-necessity debate.

Legal scholars write as insiders to international law and as participants in an institution whose 'normativity resides, at least partly, in the historical past'.[60] The sources of international law draw some of their authority from their past-ness, as in international custom which crystallises through continued practices over time.[61] In fields like transitional justice and international criminal law, part of international law's power rests in its promise to close the door on the past.[62] Furthermore, as a type of legal reasoning, international legal

[54] White (n 14).

[55] Matthew Craven, 'Theorizing the Turn to History in International Law' in Anne Orford and Florian Hoffmann (eds), *The Oxford Handbook of the Theory of International Law* (OUP 2016) 35.

[56] Koskenniemi, 'Vitoria and Us' (n 27) 126.

[57] Craven (n 55) 34.

[58] Jean d'Aspremont, 'Critical Histories of International Law and the Repression of Disciplinary Imagination' (2019) 7 London Review of International Law 89, 97.

[59] Samuel Moyn, 'Legal History as a Source of International Law: The Politics of Knowledge' in Samantha Besson, Jean D'Aspremont, and Séverine Knuchel (eds), *The Oxford Handbook on the Sources of International Law* (OUP 2017) 288–91.

[60] Skouteris (n 53) 100.

[61] Robert Kolb, 'Legal History as a Source of International Law: From Classical to Modern International Law' in Samantha Besson, Jean D'Aspremont, and Séverine Knuchel (eds), *The Oxford Handbook on the Sources of International Law* (OUP 2017).

[62] Sofia Stolk, '"The Record on Which History Will Judge Us Tomorrow": Auto-History in the Opening Statements of International Criminal Trials' (2015) 28 Leiden Journal of International Law 993; Robert Meister, *After Evil: A Politics of Human Rights* (Columbia University Press 2011).

reasoning works by transposing meaning from one moment in time to another.[63] The past is not history, it is law.[64] In short, international law is an object of inquiry with its own theory of history. This theory of history may weigh more heavily on legal scholars than on professional historians.

The influence of international law's theory of history extends beyond jurisprudential reasons, however. The field acquired a historical topography in the nineteenth century, as 'its discourses and practice [came] to be organised in temporal terms, and its past "found" or "uncovered".'[65] The present became the measure of the past.[66] Past and present, figured in a linear temporal sequence, were mapped on to the world spatially: the colonised world was imagined to be stuck in a 'primitive' past, in need of the ministrations of empire (and later, development) to bring it into the European present.[67] The doctrinal history of international law views the past as a progression from ancient to modern events that culminated in the birth of the United Nations and the ongoing project to subordinate the world to a beneficent global law, a timeline that repeats Europe's idealised image of its own historical evolution.[68] International law is made to appear as an actor evolving 'in humanity's historical necessity for progress'.[69] Although progress has not been unbroken, 'unhappy moments in the history of law … are seen either as aberrations "never again" to be repeated or are ascribed to forces external … and hostile to the progressive core' of international law.[70] Thus, international law's normative force has partially relied on the narration—by legal scholars—of a specifically progressivist history.

Of course, this is not the only way that international lawyers narrate the discipline's history. The appearance of outsider and insurrectionary histories, like the Bandung project, speaks of a desire to escape the field's self-narratives.[71] Critical legal historians spurn the idea of linear and progressive history: 'Instead … they look for ruptures, discontinuities, and the uniqueness, rather than teleological nature, of legal phenomena.'[72] I hope to write the story of Deskaheh at the League of Nations because I want histories of international law that account for actors, events, and solidarities that evade the totalising teleology of human rights.

Some legal historians seek to displace the European narrative of progress as the constant referent. Notwithstanding these efforts, history written by jurists has 'maintained fealty to the idea that there is a specifiable history of international law whose "origins" may be traced back to the 19th century and beyond, and the central task is one of re-describing that history in a way that inserts the excluded "other" back into that story'.[73] The discipline cleaves to a prosaic understanding of progress, a forward-moving 'rationally comprehensible

[63] Orford (n 10) 174–75.
[64] Renisa Mawani, 'Law's Archive' (2012) 8 Annual Review of Law and Social Science 337.
[65] Craven (n 55) 22.
[66] ibid 29.
[67] Carol J Greenhouse, *A Moment's Notice: Time Politics Across Cultures* (Cornell University Press 1996); Anne McClintock, *Imperial Leather: Race, Gender, and Sexuality in the Colonial Contest* (Routledge 1995).
[68] Koskenniemi, 'A History of International Law Histories' (n 39).
[69] Skouteris (n 53) 110.
[70] ibid.
[71] Luis Eslava, Michael Fakhri, and Vasuki Nesiah (eds), *Bandung, Global History, and International Law: Critical Pasts and Pending Futures* (CUP 2017).
[72] Skouteris (n 53) 116.
[73] Craven (n 55) 34.

directionality in human history'.[74] This belief in progress, even if subliminal, may draw jurists to narrative structures with teleologies, thus tilting the scale towards necessity. By contrast, professional historians are less enmeshed in the practices that buttress international law's own self-understanding. Their distance from international law's meta-narratives may allow them the space to write stories full of contingency.

It may be that the influence of international law's own meta-narrative about history tips jurists towards structuralist narratives, whereas historians have more latitude about narrative form. But this is not a complete explanation, because some legal scholars write against this meta-narrative. Perhaps, the differences in the narrative affinities of legal historians and professional historians are rooted in divergent understandings of their ethos and office.[75] The legal scholar as historian remains a jurisprudent, bound by her office to care 'for the conduct of lawful relations or ways of belonging to law'.[76] The international legal historian as a jurist, too, bears duties of office that influence her approach to history. In McVeigh's framing, the legal scholar must 'judge the dead in relation to a law', and the failure to take responsibility for such judgements constitutes a legal historian's failure of office.[77] The law needs the legal scholar because the law strives for justice using knowledge furnished by the history of law.[78] In this sense, the legal scholar is not separate from or outside international law but embedded within international law, an actor bound by office 'to care for and be responsible for the practice, content, projects and damages of international law'.[79] And she is bound to a vision of the future in which international law matters. Koskenniemi asserts that one cannot write a history of international law without 'a teleological, forward-looking mode', because any such history must 'be about its imagined futures'.[80] Seen this way, it may be a failure of office for a legal historian to narrate stories which imply the radical openness of international law's past and, by inference, its future.

But what of the historian's duties and obligations of office? Historians write about a past that is fragile and easily lost. Its fragility entreats us to care for it.[81] Some care for the past by interpreting it in the proper context. Others care for the past by remaining alive to present-day constellations or, in another method, open-ended futures. But all write from the principle that willing agents can be held responsible for their words and deeds. Without this commitment to agency and responsibility, there would be no point to writing history, because providence and custom require little explanation. This is an element of modernity's understanding of the historian's role.[82] Fasolt explains that, in a prior early modern tradition, history was plainly political, written to undermine a contemporaneous form of political authority.[83] But, in modernity, the link between the office of the historian and political

[74] Vadi (n 31) 320; Thomas Skouteris, 'The Idea of Progress' in Anne Orford and Florian Hoffmann (eds), *The Oxford Handbook of the Theory of International Law* (OUP 2016) 947.

[75] For another perspective on the profession and disciplinary practices, see Orford (n 10) 306–10.

[76] Shaun McVeigh, 'Office and the Conduct of the Minor Jurisprudent' (2015) 5 UC Irvine Law Review 499, 499.

[77] ibid 506.

[78] Constantin Fasolt, 'History, Law, and Justice: Empirical Method and Conceptual Confusion in the History of Law' (2015) 5 UC Irvine Law Review 413, 418.

[79] Martin Clark, 'Ambivalence, Anxieties/Adaptations, Advances: Conceptual History and International Law' (2018) 31 Leiden Journal of International Law 747, 756.

[80] Koskenniemi, 'Vitoria and Us' (n 27) 129.

[81] Christopher Tomlins, 'The Strait Gate: The Past, History, and Legal Scholarship' (2009) 5 Law, Culture and the Humanities 11, 18.

[82] Constantin Fasolt, '*The Limits of History* in Brief' (2005) 6 Historically Speaking 5, 7.

[83] ibid 8.

authority has become obscured; now, it is hidden in plain sight, dressed as debates about historical method.

Both of the twentieth century's versions of modernity (bourgeois via liberal market capitalism and proletarian via Marxism) rested on a 'History' that was going somewhere, 'a way of looking at the past in terms that assigned to contingent events and situations an objective significance by identifying their place and function within a general schema of historical development'.[84] The disagreement between liberal and Marxist versions of modernity concerned the direction and the mechanisms for change in 'History'. As the twentieth century battled over which version of 'History' might prevail, a more discreet history developed in the shadow, 'history in the lower case ... plain, common-sense, humble "history" ... "academic" and "particularistic"', one that 'eschewed metanarrative claims that it was discovering in the past meaningful trajectories, purposes and teleologies'.[85] This lower-case history was just as ideological as 'History', as it expressed a history palatable to those who did not need a massive rupture or cessation of liberal capitalism's momentum.[86] Studying the past 'for its own sake' became dominant in universities fattened by Cold War-era financing of higher education, just as liberal and Marxist versions of 'History' fell from grace. This history 'for its own sake' is, in other words, not so different from 'History', whether in a liberal or Marxist mode. But its political nature is concealed under disciplinary essentialism and empiricist methodology.[87]

Thus, under modernity's epistemologies, ontologies, and forms of political authority, much of the professional practice of history has been confined to generating knowledge about 'the whole past, and nothing but the past'.[88] Appearances notwithstanding, historians are neither outside the political order that makes the writing of history possible and meaningful, nor are they inconsequential in holding up that political order.

Even though their intellectual practice is bound to a specific political order in which the world is an object of knowledge and individuals are responsible for their actions, modern-day historians rarely see themselves as office holders. Their office is concealed by the equivalence between objectivity and value neutrality in the modernist political order.[89] The post-structuralist turn exposed the inevitable political character of any act of narration of the past. Scholars always write from some position that is at once political, social, and material. Post-structuralism forces us to recognise that when contingency is favoured in narrations of the past and when doing so is explained through a commitment to value neutrality, the resulting narrative frame is a product of a modernist, liberal political order. While jurists may be bound by office to international law's theory of history and narrative tropes, historians are bound by modernity's. Neither bond is apolitical.

[84] Keith Jenkins, *On 'What Is History?': From Carr and Elton to Rorty and White* (Routledge 1995) 8.
[85] ibid.
[86] ibid 9.
[87] Kleinberg, Scott, and Wilder (n 20).
[88] Fasolt (n 82) 8.
[89] Scott (n 20) 22.

V. The politics of writing history

If both historians and legal scholars are beholden to modernity's theory of history and confronted by the post-structuralist rebuttal, differences in the duties of office may not do as much work as needed to explain the differences between historians and jurists. More pedestrian reasons might have more bite. Perhaps the debate about favouring contingency or necessity is the projection of a debate about intellectual authority within a heterogenous field of scholars.[90] Who gets to define the nature of our shared object of inquiry? Who can speak in the name of international law's past, present, and future? On what basis can one claim authority to speak? These questions fall on terrain shaped by the political economy of knowledge.

Institutional and material constraints shape the history that is written.[91] The fact that, until recently, international legal history written by legal scholars emphasised necessity/structure over contingency/agency may be attributable to the material exigencies of life as a legal scholar. The new wave of international legal history differs from its antecedents in that it relies on primary sources, often drawn from newly declassified repositories located in numerous archives scattered around the world.[92] Such archival research is time-consuming and expensive. It has been the exception, not the norm, in legal scholarship.[93] Deep dives into the archives are not possible if a doctorate is to be completed in four years, nor are they compatible with the publish-or-perish volume requirements of the Anglo-American legal academy. By contrast, early career historians (those who land one of the handful of research jobs available every year) have about half a decade worth of archival research from which to write narratives exposing agency and complexity, and their productivity is evaluated on corresponding metrics. International legal historians may feel academically insecure relative to card-carrying historians based on their hours billed in the archives, but, in the context of the gutting of the humanities, historians feel materially insecure, plain and simple. As these two professions feast on the body of international law, they do so to seek security in the academy, but without mentioning the political and material conditions that produce their insecurities. Disputes about the validity of different narrative forms—contingent or determinist—may be a polite way of avoiding discussion of the painstaking nature of archival research and the political economy of academic labour.

Faced with the evident methodological differences between legal scholars and historians, some suggest we should instead seek common ground. Benton, for one, argues that both legal scholars and historians can strive for evidence-based scholarship and analytical coherence.[94] But this search for common ground often flounders. Common ground is elusive, I posit, because when legal scholars and historians disagree about methodology, the dispute is a projection for disagreement about the question, 'What good will this scholarship do for the present and future state of international law?' If this is true, what separates the historian from the legal scholar, and what fuels the contingency-necessity debate, is the political

[90] Moyn (n 59) 308–9.
[91] Mary Fulbrook, *Historical Theory* (Routledge 2002) 174–75.
[92] Vadi (n 31) 318.
[93] Jacob Katz Cogan, 'Review. The Oxford Handbook of the History of International Law. Edited by Bardo Fassbender and Anne Peters' (2014) 108 The American Journal of International Law 371, 376; Randall Lesaffer, 'International Law and Its History: The Story of an Unrequited Love' in Matt Craven, Malgosia Fitzmaurice, and Maria Vogiatzi (eds), *Time, History and International Law* (Nijhoff 2007) 32–33.
[94] Benton (n 27).

stakes of writing history. The controversies about how to write about international law's pasts are controversies about imagining its futures. The fracas over contextualism is fuelled by the belief that colonialism is 'not a matter of past history but of present obligation'.[95] When Parfitt, invoking Tomlins and Benjamin, calls for a 're-enchanted' methodology, it is a dream of a 'more ethical history of international law', which for our waking moments would mean a more ethical present and future.[96]

The methodological debate between contingency and necessity is patently political. Telling a 'necessity' story meets with acclaim because it gives international law's history a political trajectory.[97] In contrast, telling the contingency story is maligned as apolitical, because even though contingency was once the rallying cry of radicals writing against truth and meta-narrative, contingency gores all narratives, even those dear to the oppressed.[98] In its caricatured form, historians are criticised for hiding from today's difficult political questions with their innumerable versions of the past, whereas legal scholars are criticised for believing the future can be righted if only the past can be known and used correctly.[99] Pushing the diagnosis to its most extreme articulation to make the point: because it has been historians rather than doctrinal legal scholars who have written all these dense, complex, and highly contingent historiographies, the implication is that historians may fiddle while Rome burns, but legal scholars have obligations to tell stories with future-oriented normative commitments.

Let us presume that scholars take up this call to imagine the future through stories of international law's pasts. How should this be done? One approach urges us to drop the endless relativising and the fealty to international law's own meta-narrative and offer a meta-history of our own through a head-on engagement with philosophies of history.[100] Another view counters that 'historians of international law must accept that the validity of our histories lies not in their correspondence with "facts" or "coherence" with what we otherwise know about a "context", but how they contribute to emancipation today'.[101] The opposite approach advocates 'unearthing the foundational premises upon which our social and political verities rest, in order ... to clear space for the operations of a history whose direction cannot be determined and whose end will never come'.[102] The tension between these approaches is about methodology, professional turf wars, and the obligations of office, but it is also about the scholar's place in the world.

Like everyone else, scholars of international law are struggling for ways to live with and resist the modern conditions of accumulation and dispossession. Historians are no less interested than legal scholars in a diagnosis and remedy to the unjust effects of international law in the present moment.[103] We voice these concerns in the language of method and narrative. Historiographies rich in contingency but lacking grooves and teleology tantalise with the implication that the present and future could also be different. But they are damnably

[95] Rose Parfitt, 'The Spectre of Sources' (2014) 25 European Journal of International Law 297, 306.
[96] ibid.
[97] Marks (n 10).
[98] Tomlins, 'The Strait Gate' (n 81) 32.
[99] See, further, Moyn (n 59) 306–9.
[100] Christopher Tomlins, '"Be Operational, or Disappear": Thoughts on a Present Discontent' (2016) 12 Annual Review of Law and Social Science 1, 14; Clark (n 79) 757.
[101] Koskenniemi, 'Vitoria and Us' (n 27) 129.
[102] Scott (n 20) 26.
[103] Fitzmaurice (n 27) 5.

mute on what that future should be and what we should do in the present to meet it. Even if counterfactual histories were a bigger part of the turn to history in international law, it would reinforce the point about the absence of vision about the future.[104] Convincing counterfactual histories do not throw open the gates to any possibility but represent the dreams of reasonable dreamers, offering 'conditional, constraining models that help us manage both the world and ourselves'.[105] The current interest in the contingency-necessity debate in international legal history may simply show our distress that we do not know what to do about the present and the future.

VI. Conclusion

Stories of contingency in international law capture the raw possibility for a better world without committing us to a theory of how to achieve it. To some, that may be precisely their appeal. Contingency gives neither freedom nor a course to achieve it; it gives the hope for freedom within determined parameters—the blue sky visible through the prison window. For others, necessity stories might appeal because they offer a narrative arc that explains past, present, and future. Both versions are held together by international law's faith in the future: in its modest form, lower-case progress; in bolder terms, the promise of emancipation.

Making progress or emancipation a metric for assessing the validity of scholarship does not tell us what kind of narrative, and what balance between necessity and contingency, will get us there. Some may find it absurd to imagine the possibility of progress or emancipation within the structure of international law.[106] Others might observe that populism, nativism, and authoritarianism also promise emancipation, but they have a plan to get there and a theory of history to support it. Indeed, 'very few modern political movements ... do not claim to be concerned with the advancement of freedom'.[107] International law has already sowed misfortune with universal rights applicable to all humanity, so it seems foolhardy to have another crack at it by re-writing its histories under the banner of 'emancipation'. Let us not forget the places and the human and non-human lives that would rather be emancipated from international law than emancipated through it. When scholars debate about contingency and necessity in international law's histories, I hear them as engaging with the messy, here-and-now of ethical, material, and political struggle within intellectual communities—a mess that cannot be sorted by beating the disciplinary bounds.[108] Rather than exposing either contingency or necessity as 'false', a reflection on the debate's present manifestation suggests that writing international legal history 'is more than a form of knowledge. It is a form of political activity'.[109]

[104] Ingo Venzke, 'What If? Counterfactual (Hi)Stories of International Law' (2018) 8 Asian Journal of International Law 403.

[105] Marnie Hughes-Warrington, 'If: Counterfactual and Conditional Historiography' (2019) 58 History and Theory 268, 280; Adam Kożuchowski, 'More than True: The Rhetorical Function of Counterfactuals in Historiography' (2015) 19 Rethinking History 337.

[106] Anghie (n 26) 168–72.

[107] Fitzmaurice (n 27) 13.

[108] Rech (n 51) 77.

[109] Fasolt (n 82) 5.

4

The Necessity of Contingency

Method and Marxism in International Law

Umut Özsu

I. Introduction

Of all the standard criticisms of Marxism, the claim that it is wedded to a mechanical and deterministic account of history is among the most pervasive. It is also among the least defensible. To some degree, Marx himself is partly to blame for the confusion, as he occasionally uses language that suggests (or has been thought to suggest) such an account.[1] But it is often forgotten (or conveniently neglected) that his work is grounded not only in the view that history can and must be explained, and that a key task of the critique of political economy is to explain the history of capitalism, but also the view that any adequate explanation of this history must attend closely to the contradictions, class struggles, and complex social and technological developments that fuel capitalism. Marx highlights the twists and turns of political struggle under capitalism in all of his historico-sociological writings, most famously 'The Eighteenth Brumaire of Louis Bonaparte' and 'The Civil War in France'.[2] Oft-cited for its claim that agency is historically and materially conditioned—'[m]en make their own history, but they do not make it just as they please in circumstances they choose for themselves'—'Eighteenth Brumaire' probes relations between different classes and class fractions during and after the 1848 revolution, as well as the process whereby Louis Bonaparte subsequently rose to power and established the Second French Empire.[3] Similarly, Marx warns that his discussion of colonial capitalism in *Capital* is restricted to 'the *countries of Western Europe*', cautioning those who would transform his account of 'so-called primitive accumulation'—the institution of capitalist production through the forcible separation of direct producers from their land and means of subsistence—into a supposedly universal and supra-historical model for the transition to capitalism.[4] This account, he stresses, is not intended as an 'historico-philosophical theory of general development, imposed by fate on all peoples, whatever the historical circumstances in which they are placed', noting that

[1] Perhaps most famously in the preface to the first edition of *Capital*, where he explains that his focus is on the 'laws of capitalist production' and their attendant 'social antagonisms', 'winning their way through and working themselves out with iron necessity'. He adds: 'The country that is more developed industrially only shows, to the less developed, the image of its own future.' Karl Marx, *Capital: A Critique of Political Economy* (Ben Fowkes tr, Penguin 1990) vol 1, 91.

[2] Karl Marx, 'The Eighteenth Brumaire of Louis Bonaparte' [1852] and 'The Civil War in France' [1871] in Karl Marx, *Marx: Later Political Writings* (Terrell Carver ed, CUP 1996) 31, 163.

[3] Marx, 'Eighteenth Brumaire' (n 2) 32.

[4] Karl Marx to Vera Zasulich, 8 March 1881, in *Collected Works of Karl Marx and Frederick Engels* (International Publishers 1989) vol 24, 370 (original emphasis). On 'primitive accumulation', see Marx, *Capital* (n 1) pt 8.

Umut Özsu, *The Necessity of Contingency* In: *Contingency in International Law.* Edited by: Ingo Venzke and Kevin Jon Heller, Oxford University Press. © The Several Contributors 2021. DOI: 10.1093/oso/9780192898036.003.0004

'events strikingly analogous, but occurring in different historical milieux, [have often] led to quite disparate results', and that explanation in history 'will never be arrived at by employing the all-purpose formula of a general historico-philosophical theory whose supreme virtue consists in being supra-historical'.[5] It is for related reasons that Marx refrains from offering detailed blueprints for the revolutionary overcoming of capitalism—'recipes ... for the cook-shops of the future', as he himself puts it derisively.[6] He prefers instead to speak open-mindedly about proletarian dictatorship and the 'expropriation of the expropriators'—the elimination of capitalist private property and the inauguration of common possession of land and means of production—as a transitional phase en route to the achievement of full socialism, a condition that has never actually been achieved anywhere.[7]

This sensitivity to contingency is not limited to Marx, but is rather a distinctive feature of the Marxist tradition. Lenin's theory of revolutionary practice, rooted in the 'concrete analysis of the concrete situation', presumes unpredictability and the ability to respond to it quickly, effectively, and sometimes in contravention of existing commitments.[8] Trotsky's theory of uneven and combined development—a theory developed in no small degree to explain why it was Russia, not Germany or another advanced capitalist country, that played host to the world's first successful large-scale anti-capitalist revolution—is unintelligible without recognition of the contingent.[9] Similarly, most contributions to Marxist state theory—from Antonio Gramsci through EP Thompson and Nicos Poulantzas to contemporary scholars like Bob Jessop—are designed to capture the to-and-fro of political and institutional contestation, paying heed to the role of different classes, class fractions, political parties, historical blocs, social movements, and trade unions and rank-and-file worker associations in the class composition and ideological profile of the state.[10] Still, the accusation of technological determinism remains prevalent, with many unable to imagine a Marxism not infected by the stagist account of history that was first cobbled together through positivistic reconstructions of Marx during the Second International and then elevated to the status of a hyper-mechanical grand theory during the height of Stalinism's power in the 1930s and 1940s. Ignored here is the fact that the specificity of Marx's own project—the critique of political economy and its categories as an immanent account of the dynamics of capitalism, itself understood as a specific mode of production—is incomprehensible if he is misread as a conventional nineteenth-century positivist in the grand Kantian tradition.[11]

[5] Karl Marx to editors of *Otechestvenniye Zapiski*, November 1877, in *Collected Works of Karl Marx and Frederick Engels* (International Publishers 1989) vol 24, 200–1. On this see Kevin B Anderson, *Marx at the Margins: On Nationalism, Ethnicity, and Non-Western Societies* (University of Chicago Press 2010) 224–36.

[6] Marx, *Capital* (n 1) 99.

[7] ibid 929–30. But for one attempt to work out an account of this sort see Peter Hudis, *Marx's Concept of the Alternative to Capitalism* (Brill 2012).

[8] For the 'concrete analysis' formulation see especially VI Lenin, 'Kommunismus' [1920] in VI Lenin, *Collected Works* (Progress Publishers 1965) vol 31, 165.

[9] See especially Leon Trotsky, *History of the Russian Revolution* (first published 1932, Max Eastman tr, Haymarket 2008); Leon Trotsky, *The Permanent Revolution and Results and Prospects* (first published 1929/1906, 3rd edn, Pathfinder 1969). For Trotsky's reliance upon the earlier work of Alexander Helphand (Parvus), the Second International theoretician and arms dealer, see Michael Löwy, *The Politics of Combined and Uneven Development: The Theory of Permanent Revolution* (first published 1981, Haymarket 2010) 40–42.

[10] Antonio Gramsci, *Prison Notebooks* (3 vols, Joseph A Buttigieg and Antonio Callari eds and trs, Columbia University Press 1992–2007); EP Thompson, *Whigs and Hunters: The Origin of the Black Act* (Pantheon 1975); Nicos Poulantzas, *The Poulantzas Reader: Marxism, Law and the State* (James Martin ed, Verso 2008); Bob Jessop, *The State: Past, Present, Future* (Polity Press 2015).

[11] See eg Patrick Murray, *Marx's Theory of Scientific Knowledge* (Humanities Press 1988). Note further that this positivistic rendering of Marx—often branded 'orthodox' or 'traditional' by critics both Marxist and non-Marxist—bore strong family resemblances to the type of modernisation theory later espoused by Walt Rostow and

Similarly ignored is the fact that Marx and all significant figures in the Marxist tradition, including all of those just mentioned, have been engaged in political action, often at the highest levels, and therefore intimately familiar with all manner of contingencies, practical and conceptual.

Accusations such as these have often discouraged those who would otherwise be inclined to mine the Marxist tradition for useful explanatory tools. For those concerned with international law, particularly its history, the charge of determinism is akin to a death knell, signalling a methodological rigidity wildly out of step with the stress on particularity and ambivalence that remains central to most non-doctrinal forms of international legal scholarship today, from the oft-lauded 'turn to history'—now a full two decades old—to more recent engagements with Cambridge School contextualism.[12] The roots of this aversion to Marxism are complex and variegated, and causes of Marxism's lack of legitimacy among specialists in 'legal science' range widely, including the fact that Marx and Engels are often deemed to have been relatively indifferent to questions of law, rights, and the state. In the context of the legal-theoretical debates of the past half century, though, a particularly important source of opposition to Marxist social and political thought has come in the form of the critical legal studies movement, particularly its US variant. Deepening the early twentieth-century legal realists' critique of formalism, which they merged with successive waves of French structuralism and post-structuralism, the critical legal movement of the 1970s and 1980s mapped the codes that structure legal rhetoric and argumentation. It did much to destabilise the hold of facile legalism in the minds of students, scholars, and activists, but its tendency to dispense with class analysis and fetishise doctrinal and adjudicative indeterminacy often had the effect of displacing specifically Marxist modes of examining law and legal reasoning under capitalism. Critical legal studies may have 'died' long ago as a movement,[13] but its effects continue to be felt far and wide, not least in the growing field of international legal history and theory.

This chapter argues that Marxism affords an especially strong set of analytical tools for explaining the contingencies of international law. Far from being oblivious to historical dynamics, the Marxist tradition, at once politico-economic and ideological in critical orientation, is essential for elucidating the causes and consequences of such dynamics. Romanticising the concept of contingency as illuminative of aporia or ruptures—moments of radical uncertainty utterly at odds with the broader social contexts in which they register—risks relegating the events under scrutiny to the status of mutually unrelated accidents, to be lauded or lambasted in isolation or loose association. By contrast, a Marxist analysis of international law, one that is alive to the co-constitutive relations between class

other Cold War liberals. WW Rostow, *The Stages of Economic Growth: A Non-Communist Manifesto* (CUP 1960) ch 2. His explicitly anti-Marxist aims notwithstanding, Rostow was alive to the Soviet analogue, see ibid 148.

[12] See especially Anne Orford, 'On International Legal Method' (2013) 1 London Review of International Law 166; Martti Koskenniemi, 'Histories of International Law: Significance and Problems for a Critical View' (2013) 27 Temple International and Comparative Law Journal 215; Anne Orford, 'International Law and the Limits of History' in Wouter Werner, Marieke de Hoon, and Alexis Galán (eds), *The Law of International Lawyers: Reading Martti Koskenniemi* (CUP 2017) 297. See further Nijman, in this volume.

[13] On the movement's social dispersal see Duncan Kennedy, *A Critique of Adjudication (Fin de Siècle)* (Harvard University Press 1997) 9–10. For the corresponding 'death' of the 'New Approaches to International Law' project, which extended critical legal studies to international legal discourse, see Thomas Skouteris, 'Fin de NAIL: New Approaches to International Law and Its Impact on Contemporary International Legal Scholarship' (1997) 10 Leiden Journal of International Law 415.

power and juridical authority, provides an explanatory framework within which contingencies may be comprehended. Rather than encouraging enthralment with the unpredictability of a given event, Marxism lays the groundwork for a systemic account of its conditions and implications.

The corpus of rules, practices, and institutions to which we have become accustomed to ascribe the term 'international law'—a term with its own tangled history—cannot justifiably be regarded as either natural or necessary. The law governing relations between states and other 'subjects of international law' might have been assembled in any number of different ways, and with any number of different materials. A theory of international law is needed to understand how and why it came to be assembled in the way that it did (and how and why it may therefore yet be reassembled). This theory would neither reduce the legal form to the extra-legal outright, eliminating law as a socially and analytically meaningful category, nor succumb to an aestheticised celebration of contingency, exaggerating law's autonomy, malleability, and receptivity to 'play'. In this sense, it would break with conventional legal instrumentalism, which reduces law to a policy tool, as well as conventional legal formalism, which purports to confer upon law the status of a closed, normatively self-sustaining system.[14] Put differently, it would explain international legal structures as outgrowths of capitalism, a mode of production driven by the competitive exploitation of human labour-power for the creation, appropriation, and accumulation of surplus value. But it would do so while remaining attentive to the distinctly legal forms that encase these structures, particularly as the capital-relation may find expression in 'endless variations and gradations in its appearance'.[15] Such a theory would demonstrate that international law reflects the capital-relation, formalising the struggle between dominant and dominated states, peoples, and classes, but also demonstrate that reliance upon rights-based claims and organisational methods may prove to be important, sometimes crucially so, for anti-capitalist political struggles.

In a series of pathbreaking articles, Susan Marks has called for a renewed focus on the processes of dispossession, capital accumulation, and social reproduction sanctioned (and sometimes countered or at least limited) by law.[16] This chapter builds upon Marks' suggestion, arguing that contingency, rather than posing an intractable problem for Marxist thought, showcases its enduring explanatory power. The argument proceeds in two stages. I first revisit some of the ways in which Marx engaged directly with questions of law and rights. I then draw upon Poulantzas' theory of the state to propose a new Marxist approach to international law. My contention is that the question of law under capitalism is closely

[14] For an instructive Marxist critique of both approaches see Isaac D Balbus, 'Commodity Form and Legal Form: An Essay on the "Relative Autonomy" of the Law' (1977) 11 Law and Society Review 571, 571–73, 585–87. For the view that such approaches elide the fact that law is best understood as a social field, and that both instrumentalism and formalism fail to explain the elements and dynamics specific to this field, see Pierre Bourdieu, 'The Force of Law: Toward a Sociology of the Juridical Field' (1987) 38 Hastings Law Review 805.

[15] Karl Marx, *Capital: A Critique of Political Economy* (David Fernbach tr, Penguin 1993) vol 3, 927. For analysis of this passage in the context of a critical discussion of the 'base'/'superstructure' motif, see Ellen Meiksins Wood, *Democracy Against Capitalism: Renewing Historical Materialism* (CUP 1995) 57–59.

[16] Susan Marks, 'Exploitation as an International Legal Concept' in Susan Marks (ed), *International Law on the Left: Re-Examining Marxist Legacies* (CUP 2008) 281; Susan Marks, 'False Contingency' (2009) 62 Current Legal Problems 1; Susan Marks, 'Human Rights and Root Causes' (2011) 74 Modern Law Review 57. Marks characterises her position as a form of 'anti-anti-Marxism'; see 'False Contingency', 21. By contrast, I situate myself within the Marxist tradition (while drawing upon analytical tools from non-Marxist critical social theory, particularly the work of Bourdieu); see Umut Özsu, 'Legal Form' in Jean d'Aspremont and Sahib Singh (eds), *Concepts for International Law: Contributions to Disciplinary Thought* (Edward Elgar 2019) 624.

related to the question of contingency under capitalism, that the Marxist tradition's responses to both questions are considerably more nuanced than they have generally been made out to be, and that being a 'Marxist' requires commitment not to the view that all contingency is illusory but simply to the view that contingency (like agency) is socially conditioned.

II. Marx as legal theorist

That the Marxist tradition has long made a point of grappling with contingency, and that this is related closely to its engagement with the question of legal struggle, finds significant support in Marx's own writings. Arguably the strongest source of such support is chapter ten of the first volume of *Capital*, in which Marx analyses the struggle waged by the working class and trade union movement for stronger legal protections in nineteenth-century Britain. However, such support reaches at least as far back as the 1843 tract 'On the Jewish Question', in which Marx famously emphasises the limitations of strictly rights-oriented social and political movements. Against the Hegelian philosopher Bruno Bauer, who had argued that Germany's Jewish minority ought not to struggle for religious equality but against the religious state as such, Marx devotes most of 'On the Jewish Question' to questioning the very idea of 'political emancipation'. For Marx, it is not enough for a disenfranchised and persecuted group to secure legal rights of equality and citizenship. The achievement of formal equality and full citizenship through law is merely a smokescreen for the continuation, even fortification, of the exploitative social relations that characterised the substance of life for all Germans, Jews included. Marx concedes that '[p]olitical emancipation is certainly a big step forward', but he ultimately maintains that it is not 'the last form of general human emancipation'.[17] On his account, the attainment of citizenship, with corresponding civic and political rights and even the 'rights of man', is deeply individuating: it presupposes and further entrenches social atomisation, each person being reduced to a 'self-sufficient monad' distinguished by the bare capacity to bear abstract formal rights, particularly rights of private property and contractual freedom.[18] Since the task of socialism is to rid the world of such atomisation, mere 'political emancipation'—which effects a 'reduction of man on the one hand to the member of civil society, the *egoistic*, *independent* individual, and on the other to the *citizen*, the moral person'—is fundamentally insufficient.[19]

Although 'On the Jewish Question' is often presented as recommending an across-the-board repudiation of all law and legally framed modes of struggle, a more faithful and accurate reading of the text is that Marx advances his critique of formal legal equality in order to underscore the limits of exclusively rights-based tactics, not in order to do away with reliance upon law under all circumstances. More simply, Marx's point is not that rights-based tactics are always and necessarily useless, but that, in isolation, specifically legal efforts are not enough to overcome capitalism—or, as he eventually puts it in *Capital*, 'that revolutions are not made with laws'.[20] 'Political emancipation' in the form of formal equality and full

[17] Karl Marx, 'On the Jewish Question' [1843] in Karl Marx, *Early Writings* (Rodney Livingstone and Gregor Benton trs, Penguin 1992) 211.
[18] ibid 230.
[19] ibid 234 (original emphases).
[20] Marx, *Capital* (n 1) 915.

citizenship is the 'last form of human emancipation *within* the prevailing scheme of things', even if it is also a 'partial, *merely* political revolution' that 'leaves the pillars of the building standing'.[21] The year prior to the essay's publication, Marx had invoked the 'customary rights of the poor' when inveighing against the move to criminalise the gathering of wood in the *Rheinische Zeitung*, the newspaper of which he had recently come to be appointed editor, notably stressing that they were grounded in 'hybrid, indeterminate' forms of public/private property.[22] The trajectories of such struggle, never fully predictable, feed the formation of different regimes of right. Instead of attempting to impose a clunky analytical framework upon these concrete social contests, Marx recognises that they are seldom a sure bet—that the relation between capital and labour, while foundational to the prevailing mode of production, may take on a number of forms, with distinct crisis tendencies and contradictory characteristics. As would come to the fore powerfully in Marx's later writings on class struggles and state-reformation processes in France, the shifting balance of class forces is related closely to changing configurations of right, in the street as well as the courtroom.

'On the Jewish Question' is one of Marx's earliest essays, and readers are generally advised to take it with a grain of salt, situating it in the young and still somewhat moralistic Marx's tense relationship with Hegelianism and the various forms of anarchism and socialism that took hold among radicals in mid-nineteenth-century France and elsewhere. Yet what is often forgotten is that a rather similar view is articulated in the tenth chapter of the first volume of *Capital*, where Marx analyses the drive to enact new and stronger factory legislation in nineteenth-century Britain. Marx's principal aim in this chapter is to demonstrate that the length of the working day was an object of class struggle. This struggle was waged by workers through direct action, and also, in mediated form, by way of trade unions and other representative associations. And crucially, it manifested itself in disputes about law, rights, and state power.

For Marx, the working day embodies within itself a temporal and structural distinction that illuminates the core of the capital-relation—the struggle between those who absorb surplus labour in order to appropriate surplus value and those who produce surplus value after being forced to sell their labour-power. One part of the working day involves the expenditure of such labour-power as is necessary to produce the value of the worker's own labour-power, so as to ensure their continued subsistence. The remainder of the working day is devoted to the creation of surplus value through the expenditure of surplus labour—labour in excess of that required to produce the value of the worker's labour-power. This surplus value, produced through unpaid labour, is appropriated by the capitalist, and the accumulation of capital is driven by the reinvestment of at least a significant portion of that surplus value in the production process. The length of the working day is directly related to

[21] Marx, 'On the Jewish Question' (n 17) 221; Karl Marx, 'A Contribution to the Critique of Hegel's Philosophy of Right. Introduction' [1843–44] in Marx, *Early Writings* (n 17) 253 (original emphasis). On the implications for contemporary forms of 'resistance' see Stathis Kouvélakis, 'The Marxian Critique of Citizenship: For a Rereading of *On the Jewish Question*' (2005) 104 South Atlantic Quarterly 707, 718.

[22] Karl Marx, 'Proceedings of the Sixth Rhine Province Assembly: Third Article—Debates on the Law on Thefts of Wood' [1842] in Karl Marx and Frederick Engels, *Collected Works of Karl Marx and Frederick Engels* (International Publishers 1975) vol 1, 233. Marx would later explain that it was during the process of working on this and other political issues that he 'first encountered the embarrassment of having to discuss so-called material interests' after his earlier university studies in law, history, and philosophy. Karl Marx, 'A Contribution to the Critique of Political Economy', preface [1859] in *Marx: Later Political Writings* (n 2) 158–59. See further Peter Linebaugh, 'Karl Marx, the Theft of Wood, and Working Class Composition: A Contribution to the Current Debate' (1976) 6 Crime and Social Justice 5.

the rate at which labour-power is exploited and capital accumulates: the greater the quantity of labour-power expended during the course of a given day, the greater the number of hours the worker works beyond those needed for simple maintenance, 'creat[ing] surplus-value which, for the capitalist, has all the charms of something created out of nothing'.[23] Under capitalism workers must work in excess of the level necessary for their own subsistence. But the precise number of those additional hours is a function of concrete struggles, with no specific quantity fixed in advanced. As a result, the working day, while 'capable of being determined', is 'in and for itself indeterminate'; its duration is 'not a fixed but a fluid quantity', open to variation but 'only within certain limits'.[24] Marx points out that such contingency is ineradicable, and significantly compounded by varying socio-cultural customs and expectations with respect to the satisfaction of physiological and social needs.[25]

The struggle between worker and capitalist is 'necessary' in the sense that it presumes—and thereby helps to reinforce—commodity production and exchange, and the broader process of generating and appropriating surplus value, as its preconditions. It is 'contingent' in the sense that the configuration of power resulting from a particular contest, or set of contests, may yield a variety of different distributions of time and labour, some of which will be formalised in different legal rules. Capitalism's overcoming may be the long-term strategic objective of class struggle, but positional battles in the language of law, rights, and the state nearly always remain of paramount importance for short-term tactical purposes.[26] If '[c]apital is dead labour which, vampire-like, lives only by sucking living labour', this is because '[t]he time during which the worker works is the time during which the capitalist consumes the labour-power he has bought from him'.[27] On the one hand, the capitalist, panged by 'werewolf-like hunger for surplus labour', seeks to extend the duration of the working day as much as possible, so that greater 'absolute' surplus value may be produced and appropriated (to complement any 'relative' surplus value produced and appropriated through increases in labour intensity and productivity).[28] On the other hand, the worker, 'nothing more than personified labour-time', tries to bring the capitalist to heel by invoking the need for a 'normal working day'.[29] Since 'the nature of commodity exchange itself imposes no limit to the working day, no limit to surplus labour', requiring only that such labour be expended in order to motor capital accumulation, the two battle it out, capital armed with age-old rights and labour wielding increasingly significant rights of its own.[30] When he famously writes that '[b]etween equal rights, force decides', Marx means that the question of the length of the working day illuminates the 'struggle between collective capital, i.e. the

[23] Marx, *Capital* (n 1) 325.

[24] ibid 341.

[25] ibid.

[26] For reflections on this distinction in the context of international legal studies, see Robert Knox, 'Strategy and Tactics' (2010) 21 Finnish Yearbook of International Law 193.

[27] Marx, *Capital* (n 1) 342.

[28] ibid 353, 432–38. For Marx, the gradual legal limitation of the duration of the working day has the effect of pushing capital to devise new accumulation strategies indexed on greater productivity and intensity, partly through the introduction of new machinery and organisational structures that increased rates of exploitation. Chapter 10 of the first volume of *Capital* thereby plays a crucial role as a hinge between discussions of 'absolute' surplus value (in pt 3) to 'relative' surplus value (in pt 4). Chapter 15 discusses 'relative' surplus value in connection with the Factory Acts.

[29] ibid 343, 352–53.

[30] ibid 344.

class of capitalists, and collective labour, i.e. the working class'—a struggle waged on the skewed tactical terrain of law, though not solely on that terrain.[31]

Chapter ten is integral to *Capital*'s immanent critique of political economy. And like the chapters on 'primitive accumulation', the account it provides is concerned deeply with law.[32] Persuaded that '[n]othing characterizes the spirit of capital better than the history of English factory legislation from 1833 to 1864', and that '[t]he establishment of a normal working day is the result of centuries of struggle between the capitalist and the worker', Marx discusses the Factory Acts promulgated in response to the agitation of English factory workers, 'the champions, not only of the English working class, but of the modern working class in general'.[33] He also offers detailed descriptions of the lived experiences of different groups of workers, in a variety of British counties and also in the Caribbean and southern United States, devoting some of his most exacting prose to children as young as nine forced to work as many as three consecutive twelve-hour shifts.[34]

Marx's analysis of legal developments during this period of widespread social immiseration and rapid capital accumulation lays the foundations for a crucial intervention, at once political and conceptual: while the importance of rights-based modes of mobilisation should not be exaggerated, given that they are conditioned by the capitalist mode of production, simply repudiating all such struggle would do little to further the interests of the working class. Capital 'takes no account of the health and the length of life of the worker, unless society forces it to do so', making it imperative to secure in law (and not only law) whichever gains may be had in battles with capital, however undeniable it may be that protection afforded by law comes at the cost of further disciplinary repression.[35] If the Statutes of Labourers of the fourteenth through eighteenth centuries kickstarted and consolidated capital accumulation by deploying the state's legal and extra-legal powers on behalf of emergent capital, the Factory Acts about which Marx wrote extensively in *Capital* restricted the degree to which capitalists were able to lengthen the working day.[36] This change, which involved the 'formulation, official recognition and proclamation by the state' of new laws, resulted from a 'long class struggle' with countless setbacks.[37] That some capitalists now began to proclaim their everlasting dedication to 'science' while underscoring the wisdom of a 'legally regulated working day'—and their sage role in relenting to its introduction—did not justify scoffing at the push to secure improve working conditions through 'a protracted and more or less concealed civil war between the capitalist class and the working class'.[38]

31 ibid.

32 On the centrality of law to Marx's theory of 'primitive accumulation', in Britain and the extra-European colonial world, see Umut Özsu, 'Grabbing Land Legally—A Marxist Analysis' (2019) 32 Leiden Journal of International Law 215, 218–24.

33 Marx, *Capital* (n 1) 382, 390, 413.

34 ibid 369.

35 ibid 381.

36 ibid 382.

37 ibid 395.

38 ibid 409, 412–13. Marx polemically imputed such scoffing to Proudhon and his followers, among others; see eg Karl Marx, 'Political Indifferentism' [1873] in Karl Marx and Frederick Engels, *Collected Works of Karl Marx and Frederick Engels* (International Publishers 1988) vol 23, 392.

III. State power and international legal authority

The state has been understood in a number of different ways within the Marxist tradition. Indeed, in a sense, it could be said that the question of the state—its juridico-political form, class composition, and distinct claims to authority and legitimacy, as well as its role in social transformation and broader relations to other bases of social power—is *the* question of the Marxist tradition, at least in a specifically political register. Those accused of 'class reductionism' or 'economism' tend to stress passages in the classical canon supporting the view that the state, or at least its 'executive', is 'but a committee for managing the common affairs of the whole bourgeoisie', as Marx and Engels themselves put it, though only provisionally and with deliberately polemical zeal, in *The Communist Manifesto*.[39]

By contrast, Marxist state theorists like Poulantzas break explicitly with this orthodoxy, arguing that the state should be understood as a materialisation of the capital-relation. On this account, the state cannot be reduced to bourgeois power pure and simple. Instead, it must be understood as the regulatory and organisational expression of the logic of separation that informs the capitalist mode of production as a whole—the rift between those who do and those who do not control the means of production which cuts through the heart of all social relations anchored in the drive to accumulate capital. For Poulantzas, the state's juridico-political authority is derived from the fact that it codifies—and thereby channels and constrains—class struggle. The state is not a unitary and fully autonomous subject, a self-propelling agent of socio-historical change to which independent volition should be ascribed. Nor is it an inert 'thing' that may be captured from without, a passive, neutral, or pre-given instrument that may be manipulated by class forces constituted as such in advance. Rather than a monolith, a Leviathan of supreme authority that does not admit of any gaps or contradictions, nor of any changes over time and across space, the state (a concept in which Poulantzas includes a range of nominally private or 'non-state' sources of social power, such as schools, hospitals, and many religious institutions) is the crystallisation of class struggle. In this regard, the state is neither a normatively integrated system nor a simple tool of class rule, but the material realisation—the 'relatively autonomous' sediment, as has often been said—of the capital-relation, its ideological and institutional structures transcribing the class compromises and contradictions of capitalist society in general.[40] In addition to its central goal of ensuring capital accumulation, the state performs the crucial function of relaying market forces, integrating rival class interests, and containing crises of legitimacy and administration, most significantly those stemming from overproduction, over-accumulation, and long-term declines in the rate of profit. But since its apparatuses are provisional embodiments of an ongoing class struggle, there is, as Jessop has written, 'never a point when *the* state is finally built in a given territory and after which it operates, so to speak, on automatic pilot, according to its own, definite, fixed, and inevitable laws'.[41]

[39] Karl Marx and Frederick Engels, *The Communist Manifesto: A Modern Edition* (first published 1848, Verso 1998) 37.

[40] Nicos Poulantzas, *State, Power, Socialism* (Patrick Camiller tr, Verso 2000) 11–16, 35–46, 119, 127–36, 147–53, 173, 184–86; see also Nicos Poulantzas, 'The Capitalist State: A Reply to Miliband and Laclau' (1976) 95 New Left Review 63, 71–76. The idea of the state's 'relative autonomy', an expression of the separation of the economic and the political under capitalism, has often been criticised on the grounds that it is less an explanation than an unquestioned assumption (or a trope in need of substantive defence). For one discussion of the problem in Poulantzas' account of law and the state, see Sonja Buckel, 'The Juridical Condensation of Relations of Forces: Nicos Poulantzas and Law' in Alexander Gallas and others (eds), *Reading Poulantzas* (Merlin Press 2011) 154, 162–65.

[41] Jessop (n 10) 86 (original emphasis).

Poulantzas thought that the state's monopoly over coercive violence, coupled with its disciplinary and ideological techniques of ensuring 'consent', is continually reinforced through legal means. Law, for Poulantzas, is part and parcel of state power, and lends abstract generality to the project of managing and integrating divergent class interests. Yet it 'also organizes and sanctions certain *real rights* of the dominated classes (even though, of course, these rights are invested in the dominant ideology and are far from corresponding in practice to their juridical form); and it has inscribed within it the material concessions imposed on the dominant classes by popular struggle'.[42] '[S]truggles are always at the foundation of power', and state power—including, crucially, legal power—is a 'strategic field' on which are inscribed tactics flowing from 'the struggle of the working class against the bourgeoisie' in addition to 'the struggle of the bourgeoisie against the working class'.[43] The state's 'basic contradiction is located between tactics essentially polarized towards the interests of capital and its hegemonic monopoly fraction and tactics imposed by the struggle of the exploited classes', wrote Poulantzas, adding that it was this 'contradiction which, in varying degrees, traverses the networks and branches of the state economic apparatus *in their entirety*'.[44] This, among other things, is why Poulantzas rejected class instrumentalism no less than legal formalism, and why he remained unpersuaded by traditional claims that state power must always be confronted frontally (by way of a wholly exterior revolutionary force) rather than positionally (by, among other things, contesting elections, engaging in parliamentary politics, gaining control of state institutions, and working to socialise their power by transferring possession and ownership of the means of production from capital to labour).[45]

The question of the relation between class and state—or, in traditional European terms, between *dominium* and *imperium*—provides a useful perspective on the theme of law and contingency under capitalism. Marx never produced a book-length analysis of law, and he was never able to complete the volume on the state he intended for the long-term project that included *Capital* alongside other planned works, including books on international trade and the world market.[46] What he and Engels offer is therefore scattered throughout writings from different periods in their political and intellectual development. Yet the preceding discussion has demonstrated the untenability of slapdash claims to the effect that Marx and 'Marxism' are contaminated with a teleological determinism in which the state is nothing more than an unmediated expression or undifferentiated reflection of bourgeois power.

In this connection, it is notable that even Lenin, committed though he famously was to 'state-smashing', held that the state is the material embodiment of complex and changing social relations under capitalism. 'The State and Revolution', his unfinished 1917 essay in political theory and strategy, adopts as its premise what he calls a 'basic idea of Marxism'—that the state 'is a product and a manifestation of the *irreconcilability* of class antagonisms', and that it therefore 'arises where, when and insofar as class antagonisms objectively *cannot*

[42] Poulantzas, *State, Power, Socialism* (n 40) 84 (original emphasis).
[43] ibid 79, 119.
[44] ibid 173 (original emphasis).
[45] This second point is stressed in the retrospective analysis in Étienne Balibar, 'Communism and Citizenship: On Nicos Poulantzas' in Étienne Balibar, *Equaliberty: Political Essays* (James Ingram tr, Duke University Press 2014) 146–47.
[46] See eg Karl Marx to Ferdinand Lassalle, 22 February 1858, in Karl Marx and Frederick Engels, *Collected Works of Karl Marx and Frederick Engels* (International Publishers 1983) vol 40, 270.

be reconciled'.[47] While the bourgeois state is to be overthrown through violent revolution, a proletarian dictatorship is to carry out the 'expropriation of the expropriators' envisioned in *Capital* and deploy the coercive and distributive powers of a large workers' state in order to undertake the democratising measures necessary for its own eventual dismantling. Only with the completion of this final dismantling is capitalism finally to be overcome.[48] Unlike anarchists like Mikhail Bakunin and Pierre-Joseph Proudhon, Lenin is not fond of the idea of 'dispensing *at once* with all administration, with all subordination', insisting—like Marx[49]—that social relations would need to be transformed through such dictatorship before the final vestiges of the state and its system of bourgeois rights might disappear.[50] This requires a significant degree of analytical and political dexterity before and after the initial revolution, a willingness and ability to act 'in and against the state' in concrete struggles whose outcome is anything but predetermined.[51] It also entails reliance upon (and transformation of) rights and the state machinery, demonstrated with particular clarity in Lenin's case in his defence of nationalisations and the right to national self-determination.[52] Such tactical malleability is difficult to justify under a strict 'base'/'superstructure' model that accords little or no constitutive power to the state and its laws—the kind of model which Marx and Engels used sparingly and only metaphorically,[53] which Engels came to disown expressly,[54] and which Poulantzas, like many other Marxist theorists, repudiated as grounded in a mechanical distinction between the state and 'the economy'.[55]

[47] VI Lenin, 'The State and Revolution' [1917] in VI Lenin, *Selected Works* (Progress Publishers 1970) vol 2, 290 (original emphases). This view stems partly from Engels' historical-cum-conceptual argument that the state emerged when 'it became necessary to have a power seemingly standing above society which would alleviate the conflict and keep it within the bounds of 'order'. Frederick Engels, 'The Origin of the Family, Private Property and the State' [1884] in Karl Marx and Frederick Engels, *Collected Works of Karl Marx and Frederick Engels* (International Publishers 1990) vol 26, 269.

[48] The *locus classicus* of this view, premised upon the claim that the state 'withers away' (the most famous translation of *absterben*), is Frederick Engels, 'Anti-Dühring' [1877] in Karl Marx and Frederick Engels, *Collected Works of Karl Marx and Frederick Engels* (International Publishers 1987) vol 25, 268: 'State interference in social relations becomes, in one domain after another, superfluous, and then dies out of itself; the government of persons is replaced by the administration of things, and by the conduct of processes of production. The state is not "abolished". It *dies out*.' (Original emphasis.) Lenin quotes this passage, see Lenin, 'The State and Revolution' (n 47) 297–98.

[49] Karl Marx, 'Critique of the Gotha Programme' [1875] in Karl Marx and Frederick Engels, *Collected Works of Karl Marx and Frederick Engels* (International Publishers 1989) vol 24, 85–88, 95.

[50] Lenin, 'The State and Revolution' (n 47) 297–302, 311, 321–24, 330, 343, 346–47, 351–56, 359–62, 370–73 (quotation at 321, original emphasis). On 'smashing' the state, see ibid 306, 313–15, 321; cf Marx, 'Eighteenth Brumaire' (n 2) 116 ('All upheavals perfected this machine instead of destroying it').

[51] I borrow this expression from the London Edinburgh Weekend Return Group (A Working Group of the Conference of Socialist Economists), *In and Against the State* (rev edn, Pluto 1980).

[52] See eg VI Lenin, 'Speech on the Nationalisation of the Banks Delivered at a Meeting of the All-Russia Central Executive Committee, December 14 (27), 1917' and 'Declaration of Rights of the Working and Exploited People' [1918] in VI Lenin, *Selected Works* (n 47) vol 2, 511, 525; VI Lenin, 'The Right of Nations to Self-Determination' [1914] in VI Lenin, *Selected Works* (n 47) vol 1, 595.

[53] The best-known usage is Marx, 'A Contribution to the Critique of Political Economy', preface (n 22) 159–61; see also Marx, *Capital* (n 1) 175. Much ink has been spilled on the 'base'/'superstructure' metaphor. Here it is worth noting simply that the chapter on the working day in *Capital* complicates causal and deterministic interpretations of the metaphor, demonstrating that the struggle is contingent upon 'class alliances, conjunctural possibilities, discursive shifts in sentiments, and the outcome is never certain'. David Harvey, *A Companion to Marx's* Capital (Verso 2010) 199.

[54] See eg Frederick Engels to Joseph Bloch, 21[-22] September 1890, in Karl Marx and Frederick Engels, *Collected Works of Karl Marx and Frederick Engels* (International Publishers 2001) vol 49, 34; Frederick Engels to Conrad Schmidt, 27 October 1890, in Marx and Engels ibid 60–61.

[55] Poulantzas, *State, Power, Socialism* (n 40) 14–27, 50–51, 86–92; Nicos Poulantzas, 'Marxist Examination of the Contemporary State and Law and the Question of the "Alternative"' [1964] in Poulantzas (n 10) 28; Nicos Poulantzas, 'Preliminaries to the Study of Hegemony in the State' [1965] in ibid 77–78; Nicos Poulantzas, 'The Problem of the Capitalist State' (1969) 58 New Left Review 67, 68. For the argument that the state's segregation from 'the economy' receives full expression in marginalist economic theory, and that such theory lays the

Interestingly, a similar argument may be made in regard to international law. If law in general is a medium for formalising the capital-relation, encasing social relations under capitalism in distinct forms of authority and legitimacy, this is also the case for international law in particular. The World Trade Organization's Agreement on Trade-Related Aspects of Intellectual Property Rights (TRIPS) concentrates wealth in the hands of copyright, trademark, and patent holders, backing the global expansion of a preponderantly Euro-American regime of private property with a dispute-settlement mechanism.[56] No body of human rights law, not even the much-vaunted and half-mythological 'social, economic, and cultural rights', imposes strict legal obligations on states to cap wealth or counter income inequality as such.[57] At every turn, international law, like domestic law, extends formal legitimacy to the logic of separation between capital and labour. Yet to eschew engagement with international law pure and simple would be to elide the tasks of explanation and political intervention alike. The bourgeoisie's reliance upon state power to maintain its domination requires explanation, there being no immediately obvious reason why capitalist power should manifest itself in the specific form of the (nominally modern, national, and representative) state.[58] Similarly, the role of international law in facilitating capital accumulation and reproducing the social preconditions of such accumulation must be elucidated, there being no immediately obvious reason why a particular set of juridical constructs formalising relations between states and other 'international persons' should be expected to do heavy lifting in this respect. And this is by no means an 'academic' exercise. Understanding that international law is marked by a degree of ideological and institutional autonomy, and that its structures record earlier expressions of the capital-relation, is key to understanding how to wage effective struggles in its distinct force-field. At a minimum, it calls for considerable adaptability, a capacity to shift tactically depending upon context, and a significant degree of competence in international law's doctrinal analytics and argumentative practices—not for its own sake, or in the name of a nebulous humanitarian pragmatism,

foundations for much modern social theory through Weber, see Simon Clarke, *Marx, Marginalism, and Modern Sociology: From Adam Smith to Max Weber* (2nd edn, Macmillan 1991) 261 (contending that both marginalists and Weberians assume that 'although economic action depends on the existence of a legal and political order, it is legitimate to analyse economic action in abstraction from that order').

[56] Agreement on Trade-Related Aspects of Intellectual Property Rights (15 April 1994) Marrakesh Agreement Establishing the World Trade Organization, Annex 1C, 1869 UNTS 299. Ubiquitous in many circles, such criticisms of TRIPS have been identified as significant for the Third World Approaches to International Law (TWAIL) movement. See eg Makau Mutua, 'What Is TWAIL?' (2000) 94 American Society of International Law Proceedings 31, 37; BS Chimni, 'Third World Approaches to International Law: A Manifesto' (2006) 8 International Community Law Review 3, 8–9, 14, 17.

[57] The International Covenant on Civil and Political Rights (ICCPR) mandates that each state party 'undertakes to respect and to ensure to all individuals within its territory and subject to its jurisdiction the rights recognized in the present Covenant, without distinction of any kind, such as race, colour, sex, language, religion, political or other opinion, national or social origin, property, birth or other status'. ICCPR (16 December 1966) 999 UNTS 171 art 2. The International Covenant on Economic, Social, and Cultural Rights (ICESCR) merely requires that each state party 'take steps, individually and through international assistance and co-operation, especially economic and technical, to the maximum of its available resources, with a view to achieving progressively the full realization of the rights recognized in the present Covenant by all appropriate means, including particularly the adoption of legislative measures'. ICESCR (16 December 1966) 993 UNTS 3 art 2. On the limitations of human rights as a means of combatting socio-economic inequality, see Samuel Moyn, *Not Enough: Human Rights in an Unequal World* (Harvard University Press 2018).

[58] Poulantzas, *State, Power, Socialism* (n 40) 12, 52.

but in order to bolster the power of those who are (or 'just so happen to be', as some liberals might perhaps put it) on the losing side of the capital-relation.

For some theorists, the fact that international law is fuelled by capitalism means that decrying a given violation as a 'norm-breaching' act is either beside the point or simple bad faith. The relevant time, energy, and resources would be invested far more profitably in organisational and large-scale educational initiatives directed against the socio-economic forces that sustain a system marked by brutality and inequality at all levels. Adopting this approach, China Miéville in particular has analysed international law from the standpoint of Evgeny Pashukanis' theory of the legal form as a commodity form. According to Pashukanis, relations between the equal and autonomous rights-bearers presupposed by property and contract law are formally homologous to relations between qualitatively different commodities travelling through circuits of exchange.[59] Pashukanis extends this approach to international law, contending that '[b]ourgeois private law assumes that subjects are formally equal yet simultaneously permits real inequality in property, while bourgeois international law in principle recognises that states have equal rights yet in reality they are unequal in their significance and their power'.[60] Miéville amplifies this position, arguing that the trouble with international law is not that it lacks sufficiently robust enforcement mechanisms or that it has yet to develop domestic law's technical capacity and doctrinal sophistication, both classic and generally overdrawn liberal grievances. Rather, Miéville argues, international law is very much law, and it is often socially and politically effective, but it is rooted in precisely that system of production and exchange which has generated our massively unequal and exploitative world.[61] Since 1945 the General Assembly has adopted thousands of resolutions lauding sovereign equality, underscoring the importance of self-determination, stressing the need for international peace and security, and calling for political solidarity and economic cooperation. Neither these instruments nor the countless treaties and customs that criss-cross international law's social field challenge the fundamental coordinates of capitalist production and exchange. For Miéville the conclusion is clear: just as 'without violence there could be no legal form', so too 'without imperialism there could be no international law', which means that it is a mark of hypocrisy, self-deception, or plain inanity to seek to transform the world by upholding or reforming international law, an effort that 'can only ever tinker with the surface level of institutions'.[62]

For other theorists, the key point of emphasis is that international law is possessed of considerable constitutive power, directly feeding the contradictions and transformations of the capitalist mode of production, and cannot therefore be relegated to the 'superstructural' sphere and accorded no more than secondary or representational status.[63] Poulantzas is instructive once again, alive as he is not only to the distinct authority of the state and its laws but to 'the increasing *internationalization* of capital, to the massive dominance of American

[59] Evgeny Pashukanis, 'The General Theory of Law and Marxism' [1924] in Piers Beirne and Robert Sharlet (eds), *Pashukanis: Selected Writings on Marxism and Law* (Peter B Maggs tr, Academic Press 1980) 37.

[60] Evgeny Pashukanis, 'International Law' [1925] in ibid 178.

[61] China Miéville, *Between Equal Rights: A Marxist Theory of International Law* (Brill 2005) 25.

[62] ibid 293, 316. For a closely related argument that is similarly grounded in Pashukanis, see Grietje Baars, *The Corporation, Law and Capitalism: A Radical Perspective on the Role of Law in the Global Political Economy* (Brill 2019) chs 1, 6. For a more generous reading of Pashukanis than the one offered by Miéville, see Robert Knox, 'Marxism, International Law, and Political Strategy' (2009) 22 Leiden Journal of International Law 413.

[63] See especially BS Chimni, *International Law and World Order: A Critique of Contemporary Approaches* (2nd edn, CUP 2017) 449–62. For an authoritative Soviet-positivist articulation see Grigory I Tunkin, *Theory of International Law* (William E Butler tr, Harvard University Press 1974) 234 ff.

capital, to the political and economic decadence of the bourgeois class and to the increasing tendency towards an *asymmetrical* relation of *dependence* between the old centres of imperialism (notably in Europe) and the USA.'[64] This international economic order, which has undergone several rounds of systemic reshuffling in the hands of finance capital since the early 1970s, is enveloped and reinforced by law at every turn, from investment treaties and joint business venture agreements down to shop floors and office workplaces governed (in theory if not in practice) by safety regulations and basic employment legislation.[65] And it has unfolded alongside the re-composition of legal, political, and economic institutions in states forced to adapt to changes in the mode and scale of transnational capitalist power.[66] Yet the state and its laws (including its international laws) are not entirely reducible to the interests of a given class, and its 'relative autonomy' is derived not from the power of the capitalist class as such but from the confrontation of this class, in its various fractions, with the working class, in its various fractions.[67] What we now call 'international investment law' has, for instance, traditionally extended protection to corporations in the face of efforts by host states to expropriate and nationalise their assets. When such protection has proven insufficient, it has generally counselled some form of 'prompt, adequate and effective' compensation—a formula famously first proposed by US Secretary of State Cordell Hull in response to Mexico's move to nationalise American oil assets in the country.[68] Yet the 'international development law' of the 1960s through the 1980s, crafted in no small part by socialist and non-aligned lawyers, sought to bolster the power of capital-importing states to nationalise foreign-held assets, often with minimal compensation and for the purpose of using resulting windfalls to redistribute resources and undertake rapid industrialisation. It was not, of course, fully successful in this regard. But opposition to investment arbitration and investor-state dispute-settlement has been organised, international labour law and international Indigenous law have been expanded, and strong models of economic self-determination and permanent sovereignty over natural resources have been popularised, with the result that some Indigenous peoples, for instance, have enjoyed a limited measure of success with a range of territorial and resource-related claims and complaints, in inter-governmental fora like the UN Human Rights Council and also before the Inter-American Court of Human Rights and the African Court on Human and Peoples' Rights (though not before the European Court of Human Rights).[69]

[64] Nicos Poulantzas, 'On Social Classes' [1972] in Poulantzas (n 10) 201 (original emphasis).

[65] On the legal dimensions of neoliberal capitalism see especially Moyn (n 57); Quinn Slobodian, *Globalists: The End of Empire and the Birth of Neoliberalism* (Harvard University Press 2018); Honor Brabazon (ed), *Neoliberal Legality: Understanding the Role of Law in the Neoliberal Project* (Routledge 2017); (2014) 77 Law and Contemporary Problems (symposium entitled 'Law and Neoliberalism').

[66] See Nicos Poulantzas, 'Internationalization of Capitalist Relations and the Nation-State' (1974) 3 Economy and Society 145. For recent consideration of this approach in the context of debates about international trade and economic law, see Ntina Tzouvala, 'Neoliberalism as Legalism: International Economic Law and the Rise of the Judiciary' in Ben Golder and Daniel McLoughlin (eds), *The Politics of Legality in a Neoliberal Age* (Routledge 2018) 116.

[67] For different variants of this line of argument, see Chimni, *International Law and World Order* (n 63) ch 7; Bill Bowring, 'Positivism Versus Self-Determination: The Contradictions of Soviet International Law' in Marks, *International Law on the Left* (n 16) 133; Paul O'Connell, 'On the Human Rights Question' (2018) 40 Human Rights Quarterly 962; Umut Özsu, 'Humanitarian Intervention Today' (2019) 55 Socialist Register 271.

[68] US Secretary of State Cordell Hull to Mexico's Ambassador Francisco Castillo Nájera, 22 August 1938, reproduced in *Foreign Relations of the United States Diplomatic Papers, 1938* (Government Printing Office 1938) vol 5, 687. For its legal implications see especially Muthucumaraswamy Sornarajah, *The International Law on Foreign Investment* (3rd edn, CUP 2010) 414–43.

[69] From a growing literature on the international legal facets of decolonisation, see especially S James Anaya, *Indigenous Peoples in International Law* (2nd edn, OUP 2004); Antony Anghie, *Imperialism, Sovereignty, and the*

Short of a socialist utopia in which states and classes have gone by the wayside, it is difficult to imagine many social relations, in any context, that are not mediated at least to some degree by law. The legal and extra-legal, though conceptually distinct under capitalism, are bound together in complex relations of social co-constitution: 'the economy' and the political order with which it is coupled are configured to a significant degree through law, just as legal developments are responsive to and ultimately anchored in shifting distributions of politico-economic power. Marxist theorist Louis Althusser was certainly right about that much—we are 'always already' constituted as subjects of capitalism, and as such of its laws, rights, and states, outgrowths one and all of a competitive system of producing and amplifying surplus value.[70] The question for anyone who finds themselves on the hither side of the post-capitalist moment—which is to say all of us—is not, then, *whether* but rather *how* to engage law. A range of responses have been developed within the Marxist tradition to the question of international law's authority and usefulness in recent years. Some diverge sharply on issues of first-order significance. But most such responses have sought to capture the contingency of real struggles conducted partly in the name of law, rights, the state, or the international order.[71]

IV. Conclusion

Marxist dependency theorist Samir Amin may have bent the stick a touch too far when he suggested that 'what counts in history are the unexpected accidents'.[72] Few accidents, whether in the core or the periphery, are ever entirely accidents—purely spontaneous irruptions of sheer contingency in a plane of otherwise uninterrupted uniformity. Yet there is nonetheless an important kernel of truth in Amin's observation. Marxism is best understood not as a deductive, mechanical science, wedded to the proposition that the 'Real is the Rational' and clinging to the presumption that 'base' must necessarily precede 'superstructure'. Rather, Marxism is best understood as a method of explaining the deep-structural conditions that make seemingly unprecedented developments possible in the first place, limiting the range of pathways and outcomes possible in any given social context. The notion of the pure accident is the notion of the unintelligible rupture. The task of Marxism, as a

Making of International Law (CUP 2005); Nico J Schrijver, *Sovereignty Over Natural Resources: Balancing Rights and Duties* (CUP 1997); Matthew Craven, *The Decolonization of International Law: State Succession and the Law of Treaties* (CUP 2007); Sundhya Pahuja, *Decolonising International Law: Development, Economic Growth and the Politics of Universality* (CUP 2011); Jochen von Bernstorff and Philipp Dann (eds), *The Battle for International Law: South-North Perspectives on the Decolonization Era* (OUP 2019); Jorge E Viñuales (ed), *The Friendly Relations Declaration at 50: A Study of the Fundamental Principles of International Law After Half a Century* (CUP 2020); Umut Özsu, *Completing Humanity: The International Law of Decolonization, 1960–82* (CUP) (forthcoming).

[70] Louis Althusser, 'Ideology and Ideological State Apparatuses (Notes Towards an Investigation)' [1970] in Louis Althusser, *Lenin and Philosophy and Other Essays* (Ben Brewster tr, Monthly Review 1971) 170–83.

[71] In addition to those referenced in the notes above, see Akbar Rasulov, '"The Nameless Rapture of the Struggle": Towards a Marxist Class-Theoretic Approach to International Law' (2008) 19 Finnish Yearbook of International Law 243; Mark Neocleous, 'International Law as Primitive Accumulation; Or, the Secret of Systematic Colonization' (2012) 23 European Journal of International Law 941; Brabazon (n 65); Susan Dianne Brophy, 'An Uneven and Combined Development Theory of Law: Initiation' (2017) 28 Law and Critique 167. For a compendium that showcases the range of positions available within the Marxist tradition respecting questions of law, see Paul O'Connell and Umut Özsu (eds), *Research Handbook on Law and Marxism* (Elgar forthcoming).

[72] Samir Amin, 'Self-Reliance and the New International Economic Order' in Herb Addo (ed), *Transforming the World Economy? Nine Critical Essays on the New International Economic Order* (Hodder & Stoughton 1984) 213.

theory of history, is not to revel in such mysteries but precisely to explain them. If structure is baked into Marxism, so too is conjuncture.

Adopting the second of the two approaches sketched in this chapter yields a view of international law that is attuned to long-term tendencies but also responsive to short-term developments. On the one hand, by tethering international law to class struggles, to structurally constrained social contests between those who command and those who sell their labour-power, such an approach helps us understand why some (and not all) claims come to be recognised widely as 'legal norms', why some (and not all) arguments come to be accepted as valid and defensible, why some (and not all) actors come to be endowed with 'international legal personality', why some (and not all) states are gifted veto-bearing permanent seats on the Security Council, why some (and not all) UN organs are accorded the right to issue resolutions that are legally binding and not simply recommendatory. To take but one example, a Marxist approach of this kind would explain the development of international human rights law over the past seventy odd years neither as an incremental unfolding of some inexorable logic nor as a hierarchy of norms of the type exemplified by Karel Vasak's tripartite taxonomy,[73] but as an outgrowth of a series of wide-ranging but systemically constrained struggles over which social claims and relations were to receive greatest legal sanction. It is on account of these struggles, for instance, that property and inheritance rights came to be enshrined in widely ratified treaties like the Convention on the Elimination of All Forms of Racial Discrimination, while the idea of reparations for wrongs committed during colonial occupation was relegated to non-binding and generally forgotten instruments like the General Assembly resolutions that launched the New International Economic Order project in 1974.[74] It was by no means preordained that international human rights law would come to privilege civic and political rights over social and economic rights, nor that it would frame the former in preponderantly individualistic terms, as entitlements to be harnessed first and foremost against the state. These were, after all, developments which many socialist states often resisted, if generally unsuccessfully.

A focus on class and capital alone is insufficient to explain international law in its entirety. It would be a serious error to neglect the (explicitly or implicitly) racial dimensions of many international legal doctrines, old and new. So too would it be unjustifiable to ignore the fact that some areas of international law, such as international human rights law, are informed by distinctly gendered logics. Yet an explanation of the domestic and transnational class conflicts that sustain the production and reproduction of international law remains key. And importantly, it is precisely such attention to shifting class relations that enables the messiness of concrete legal decisions and developments to be understood. If law is the formal expression of the relation between dominant and subordinate classes (and peoples, states, and other social formations), it is also the formal expression of their ongoing and ceaseless struggle, a lopsided record of their respective victories and defeats. Legally

[73] Karel Vasak, 'A Thirty-Year Struggle: The Sustained Efforts to Give Force of Law to the Universal Declaration of Human Rights' (1977) 30 UNESCO Courier 29.

[74] International Convention on the Elimination of All Forms of Racial Discrimination (7 March 1966) 660 UNTS 195 art 5; Declaration on the Establishment of a New International Economic Order (1 May 1974) GA Res 3201 (S-VI), UN Doc A/Res/S-6/3201; Programme of Action on the Establishment of a New International Economic Order (1 May 1974) GA Res 3202 (S-VI), UN Doc A/Res/S-6/3202; Charter of Economic Rights and Duties of States (12 December 1974) GA Res 3281 (XXIX), UN Doc A/Res/24/3281. For consideration of the NIEO from the standpoint of this volume's overarching theme, see Ingo Venzke, 'Possibilities of the Past: Histories of the NIEO and the Travails of Critique' (2018) 20 Journal of the History of International Law 263.

formalised distributions of power are neither entirely settled nor strictly inevitable. The legal rules, practices, and institutions with which we operate are historically specific, deeply contested, and thereby revisable class compromises. If we are truly serious about understanding why international law is what it is today, we must be attuned to the social bases of the struggles whereby it has been formed and reshaped over time, indirectly if not directly. Far from ignoring the vicissitudes of history, a Marxist approach to the study of these struggles is especially well-placed to explain them.

5

The Realist and the Visionary

Property, Sovereignty, and the Problem of Social Change

Justin Desautels-Stein

I. Introduction

In the United States of a hundred years ago, lawyers and legal thinkers found common cause in their dissatisfaction with what became known in liberal legal thought as a 'right to exclude.'[1] In classic liberal legal theory, this was a right of individual owners to leverage the coercive force of the state against the world.[2] The owner could build walls (conforming to local regulations), determine who might enter the owner's territory and for how long they could stay, take another's land for his own, and generally shape the land to the will of the owner's political, social, and cultural life-story. Historically, the owner's right to exclude had served as the juridical enforcer for his general pursuit of self-determination.[3] Similarly in liberal legal theory, this traditional portrayal of individual ownership was also suggestive of what it meant to be a sovereign state. In what we can call the 'traditional' style of liberal legalism, sovereignty is rooted in a fundamental right of non-intervention: a raw reflection of the property owner's right of exclusion. Indeed, the private owner and the sovereign's rights to exclude, or rights of non-intervention, enjoy an identical argumentative structure. Both rights are justified through reference to an autonomous will, and the operationalising of that will in the context of territorial possession. Once an individual becomes an owner, and once some group of individuals become sovereign, a natural right to repel outsiders simply comes into being.[4] In this traditional vision of property and sovereignty, the legal structure begins and ends with a right to exclude the world.[5]

[1] On the right to exclude, see Anna di Robilant, 'Property: A Bundle of Sticks or a Tree?' (2013) 66 Vanderbilt Law Review 869.

[2] Morris Cohen, 'Property and Sovereignty' (1927) 13 Cornell Law Review 8; Francis Philbrick, 'Changing Conceptions of Property in Law' (1938) 86 University of Pennsylvania Law Review 691. On the use of 'liberalism' in this chapter, see Justin Desautels-Stein, *The Jurisprudence of Style: A Structuralist History of American Pragmatism and Liberal Legal Thought* (CUP 2018).

[3] A good nineteenth-century statement of the idea is available in John Dillon, 'Property—Its Rights and Duties in our Legal and Social Systems (1895) 29 American Law Review 161. A contemporary example is Thomas Merrill, 'Property and the Right to Exclude' (1998) 77 Nebraska Law Review 730.

[4] On the history of the sovereign's right to exclude in the context of migration, see E Tendayi Achiume, 'Migration as Decolonization' (2019) 71 Stanford Law Review 1509; Vincent Chetail, *International Migration Law* (OUP 2019).

[5] Eric Posner has canvassed various angles of the image in some of his most recent writings. See Eric Posner, 'Liberal Internationalism and the Populist Backlash' University of Chicago, Public Law Working Paper No 606 available at <https://papers.ssrn.com/sol3/papers.cfm?abstract_id=2898357> accessed 1 June 2020; Eric Posner and E Glen Weyl, 'Property is Only Another Name for Monopoly' (2017) 9 Journal of Legal Analysis 51 available at <https://papers.ssrn.com/sol3/papers.cfm?abstract_id=2818494> accessed 1 June 2020.

Justin Desautels-Stein, *The Realist and the Visionary* In: *Contingency in International Law*. Edited by: Ingo Venzke and Kevin Jon Heller, Oxford University Press. © The Several Contributors 2021. DOI: 10.1093/oso/9780192898036.003.0005

Until relatively recently, however, the right to exclude had been somewhat out of favour.[6] It had been out of favour, that is, among American judges, lawyers, and law professors as a way of explaining property law's social purpose. Intensely popular in the nineteenth century, the right to exclude came under heavy criticism in the early years of the twentieth as an unrealistic ivory tower affair and ugly artefact of the laissez-faire era. Indeed, for much of the twentieth century there was something like a consensus about what the course of such an explanation should look like, and the right to exclude played only a bit part.[7] As the story goes, everything from the American Law Institute's Restatement of Property Law (First) to state and federal judicial opinions to the law journals trumpeted the metaphor that property was a 'bundle of sticks.'[8] In this bundle, in which each stick represented a discrete property right, the right to exclude was only one stick among many.[9] This understanding of property law dominated the profession until the early years of the twenty-first century, and it remains powerful today. Despite its contemporary prevalence, however, the bundle of sticks metaphor has been steadily giving ground to a view that situates the right to exclude as much more than just a stick in the bundle; it is the whole 'kit-n-caboodle'.[10] In this currently popular 'retro' view, property is not a bundle of legal relationships best interpreted in the light of social needs and purposes. It is a *thing* over which an owner has a *right to exclude the world*.[11]

If we switch over from American property law to international legal thought, there has been a similar story at work with regard to sovereignty.[12] For just as the retro-view of property emphasises a return to *things* over which *individual owners* have a right to exclude the world, so too does the retro-view of sovereignty suggest a renewed orientation towards *territories* over which *governments* have a right to exclude the world. Furthermore, it is worth noting that just as the retro-view of the owner's right to exclude fell out of favour at the beginning of the twentieth century, so too did the retro-view of the sovereign's right.[13] Not

[6] For discussion, see, eg, Ezra Rosser, 'Destabilizing Property' (2015) 48 Connecticut Law Review 397; Gregory Alexander, 'The Complex Core of Property' (2009) 94 Cornell Law Review 1063; Hanoch Dagan, 'Remedies, Rights, and Properties' (2011) 4 Journal of Tort Law 1; Thomas Merrill and Henry Smith, 'What Happened to Property in Law and Economics?' (2001) 111 Yale Law Journal 357; Kenneth Vandevelde, 'The New Property of the Nineteenth Century: The Development of the Modern Concept of Property' (1980) 29 Buffalo Law Review 325.

[7] Stephen Munzer, 'Property and Disagreement' in James Penner and Henry Smith (eds), *Philosophical Foundations of Property Law* (OUP 2013) 289.

[8] JE Penner, 'The "Bundle of Rights" Picture of Property' (1996) 43 UCLA Law Review 711.

[9] The classic treatment is Wesley Hohfeld, 'Fundamental Legal Conceptions as Applied in Judicial Reasoning' (1917) 26 Yale Law Journal 710.

[10] James Penner, *The Idea of Property in Law* (OUP 1997); Lee Anne Fennell, 'Lumpy Property' (2012) 160 University of Pennsylvania Law Review 1955.

[11] There are multiple ways to defend this thesis, and it ought to be noted that the two premises of (1) seeing property as *thing*, and (2) seeing the *thing* as triggering a right of exclusion, need not necessitate the other. For various articulations, see Thomas Merrill, 'The Property Strategy' (2012) 160 University of Pennsylvania Law Review 2061, 2068; Larissa Katz, 'Exclusion and Exclusivity in Property Law' (2008) 58 University of Toronto Law Journal 275.

[12] For scholarly approaches in the retro-classical style, see Jack Goldsmith and Eric Posner, *The Limits of International Law* (OUP 2005); Eric Posner, *The Twilight of Human Rights Law* (OUP 2014). A precursor to the retro-classical resurgence is Wilhelm Roepke, 'Economic Order and International Law' (1954) 86 Recueil Des Cours 203. For general discussion, see Jack Goldsmith and Eric Posner, 'The New International Law Scholarship' (2006) 34 Georgia Journal of International and Comparative International Law 463; Jens David Ohlin, *The Assault on International Law* (OUP 2015).

[13] As I explain in a forthcoming work, this is a complex thesis. My claim is that while the sovereign's right to exclude was diminishing as a policing mechanism for the boundaries of international society, it was emerging as a plenary right in the development of migration law. Thus, while support for the right was weakening as a right to exclude *peoples* from international society, it was strengthening as a right to exclude *people* from territorial jurisdictions. See Justin Desautels-Stein, *The Right to Exclude: Racial Ideology, Borders, and the Global Legal Order* (OUP 2022).

only did the timing of reformist thinking keep pace in the dual contexts of international legal thought and property law. The kind of reforms were similar as well.

These symmetries in the twists and turns of sovereignty and property are no coincidence, and as I will suggest, among the features that unite American property law and so much of 'mainstream' European-American views of international legal thought is the deeper structure of liberal legal thought in which they both play a part.[14] Or to put that another way, the claim I am making in this chapter about the structural connections between property and sovereignty are meant less as discussions of the United States or Europe and more as an analysis of the liberal structure of legal thought in which so much of US and European law is rooted. As a consequence, when we ask questions like, 'How could the concept of sovereignty have become something other than what it once was or, to put it the other way, why has so much of the sovereignty concept remained the same?', we should realise that we are dipping into the deepest reservoirs of our legal order, spaces in which property and sovereignty share a common language.[15] At this grammatical depth, our liberal conceptions of property ownership and sovereign right blur. As one moves out from the grammatical level to the various doctrines, important and practical differences do of course begin to pop out. Nevertheless, the basic point I want to make here is that, if we are to take seriously our concerns with the sovereign right to exclude, we should simultaneously register these structural connections with the owner's right to exclude. To be sure, reforming the one without the other is certainly possible, and I do not want to be misunderstood as saying that we can only reform our foreign policy if we are at the same time reforming the law of property. That really isn't the point at all. However, it may very well be that, in the structure of legal thought, the obstacles we face in the one context are the same as what we face in the other. Reckoning with the possibilities of sovereign change and transformation, the challenge is less like altering a small dialect, and more like transforming the syntactical range of an entire language.

At the same time, it is important to notice both how and why, in this context of liberal legal thought, the right to exclude has already travelled the road to reform. The modern reforms of the early twentieth century swirled around a common intellectual centre: that the law become more 'realistic'. On a view that is now a century old, the property owner's right to exclude ought to be de-emphasised because, among other things, to elevate that right was a disservice to the reality of property law and its social needs.[16] In its turn, the sovereign's right of non-intervention ought to be de-emphasised because it was out of touch with the reality of the international order.[17] Thus, the traditional right to exclude was saddled with a 'modern' demand for an alignment between law and the real social world.

The consequence, however, was not likely what any of the early reformers might have predicted. Rather than supplant its older rival, the modern style ended up commandeered by the 'retro' view referenced above, producing a situation in which the contemporary debate is no longer about whether the right to exclude ought to be reformed and made more realistic;

[14] David Kennedy references this symmetry in his 'International Law and the Nineteenth Century, History of an Illusion' (1997) 17 Quinnipiac Law Review 99, 123.

[15] For discussion of this sense of 'language,' see Desautels-Stein (n 2) 35–61; Martti Koskenniemi, *From Apology to Utopia: The Structure of International Legal Argument* (CUP 2006); Duncan Kennedy, 'The Semiotics of Legal Argument' (1991) 42 Syracuse Law Review 75.

[16] Joseph Singer, 'Property as the Law of Democracy' (2014) 63 Duke Law Journal 1287.

[17] JL Brierly, 'The Shortcomings of International Law' (1924) 5 British Yearbook of International Law 4.

it is rather about who has the better realism. Indeed, the entire discourse about exclusion is drenched in a law-and-society paradigm belief in the necessity of a socially-realistic law. The important question, in this discourse, is therefore about which view has the better grasp on reality, that of the retro-thinkers, or that of the moderns. Counter-intuitively, my argument is that it is this very discourse that today acts as a block on our collective abilities to think beyond the right to exclude, and what the law of sovereigns might one day become.

That is, before discussing the possibilities of how the ultimate contingency of the right to exclude might be pressed into the service of a transformative mandate, we should push further on an idea that was at the very heart of that first shift between the traditional view and the view of the moderns: the idea of *realism.*[18] There is little doubt that the modern efforts, both in American property law and in international legal thought, to transform the socio-legal order of the twentieth century enjoyed great success. Indeed, the law of property and the law of nations are not today what they once were. Of course, there is much disagreement about whether these changes were beneficial, but what very few seem to disagree about is whether we want our legal system to be more 'realistic'. Indeed, everyone wants that. Nobody is about to get behind the slogan, 'We Want Laws Out of Touch with Social Needs, and We Want Them Now!' Nevertheless, we need to continue to push harder on the question of what it means to make a more realistic legal system. 'Realistic' for whom, according to what?

The problem that I am suggesting unfolds in something like the following: After the 'triumph' of legal realism, and the 'fall' of formalism and natural law theory, we find ourselves increasingly committed to the effort to match our legal concepts with the social order those concepts are meant to reflect. This triumph, however, is magisterial in its ambiguity. In

[18] There is at present a wonderful amount of constructive debate on the contemporary significance of legal realism. In that debate there are currents concerning the 'real essence of American Legal Realism', the relation between this essential realism and critical legal studies, and the true realist account of doctrine. Brian Leiter, 'Legal Realism and Legal Doctrine' (2015) 163 University of Pennsylvania Law Review 1975, 1976. See also, Brian Tamanaha, *Beyond the Formalist Realist Divide: The Role of Politics in Judging* (Princeton University Press 2009). What often happens in this debate is a tendency I'd like to avoid, and that tendency is to identify 'realism' with some particular person, an identity that might be called 'realist'. That is, as Brian Leiter suggests, we could associate realism with the names of 'core' people, like Herman Oliphant or Leon Green, and then ask what it was that these people believed. The result: the essence of realism. For a more comprehensive example of Leiter's thorough analysis, *see* Brian Leiter, *Naturalizing Jurisprudence: Essays on American Legal Realism and Naturalism in Legal Philosophy* (OUP 2007). Without commenting on the overall usefulness of intellectual history in this way, I do want to suggest that one consequence is a tendency to collapse non-complementary styles of argument under the single banner of 'realism.' This happens, for example, in Dagan's recent discussion of realism where he begins with the challenges associated with what he calls the 'starting point of the realist account of law', and then moves to what he calls a realist answer to such challenges: Hanoch Dagan, 'Doctrinal Categories, Legal Realism, and the Rule of Law' (2015) 163 University of Pennsylvania Law Review 1889, 1891. Unlike Leiter, I want to shift the discussion away from realist 'movements' and 'personalities' and towards what we can call a realist style of argument. In doing so, I will call 'realist' that first part identified by Dagan, the challenging part, the part that views legal doctrines 'as patchworks of contradictory premises' necessarily interpreted by canons of interpretation. The second part, the part that both Leiter and Dagan construct as prescriptive and as about 'going institutions', normativity and the like, I want to call a 'legal process' style of argument: Neil Duxbury, *Patterns of American Jurisprudence* (OUP 1997). As a result of shifting away from the search for the 'real essence of American Legal Realism', it is possible to clarify an important cleavage in so many accounts of realism, and it is this cleavage between the critical assault on doctrine and the reconstructive effort to rehabilitate that doctrine. In the context of American Legal Thought, I agree with Duncan Kennedy that it is helpful to make this analytical separation between the critical slant of legal realism and the reconstructive programme of legal process, as the two styles are so at odds with respect to their contrasting normative commitments: Duncan Kennedy, 'The Disenchantment of Logically Formal Legal Rationality, or, Max Weber's Sociology in the Genealogy of the Contemporary Mode of Western Legal Thought' (2004) 55 Hastings Law Journal 1031. This distinction is more often drawn between legal realism on the one hand and sociological jurisprudence on the other. I suggest here that legal process, and more broadly, legal functionalism, are more appropriately seen as the heirs of sociological jurisprudence rather than legal realism.

the views of the retro-thinkers, for example, the social order is *really* about the primacy of owners and sovereigns, and the elevation of clear and simple rules servicing their protection and empowerment. That is, it is some version of the *traditional* style of property and sovereignty argument that is the most 'realistic'. In the view of those thinkers still carrying the modern banner, however, the social order is about the complex interactions between individual entities and social institutions, the relative rights of sovereigns and individual human beings, and the elevation of legal regimes sophisticated enough to capture and regulate those dynamics. It is, on this view, the *modern* style of property and sovereignty argument that remains the most 'realistic'. The winner in the clash between these post-realist camps is the one with the most 'realistic' social science. In today's world, who can possibly adjudicate such a dispute?

While this problem seems particularly messy, I want to suggest a way around it. In these various debates there is a persistent misunderstanding about realism and what I have been calling the modern style. This misunderstanding ought to be addressed not merely for reasons of intellectual history; it ought to be addressed because it is a misunderstanding that continuously affects the intellectual conditions for imagining reform. There is much work to be done here, and in the space that I have left the chapter tackles just one aspect of that nebulous transition in the middle of the twentieth century. It is the difference between a legal realism that helped hammer the traditional view and then vanished, and a legal realism that was understood to give the moderns a plan of action, later called the legal process school. To see what the right to exclude might become, we must reseed and harvest that first crop of realist thinking. And to do *that*, we must cease the practice of seeing legal process as the totality of what realism ever was.

In doing so, the discussion below suggests a different characterisation of the debate, which leads to a different kind of problem. First, it is helpful to break realist arguments into two kinds. The first kind of realist argument provides a particular way of understanding what the modern style was all about: the view of property and sovereignty as deeply complicated regimes of institutions, rules, processes, and more. To give this first kind of realist argument a name, this is the 'legal process' way of thinking. The second kind of realist argument is analytically separate from the question of intermixture between legal rules and social processes. It is instead a way of understanding concepts like sovereignty and ownership as structures of legal thought, operating in an utterly contingent sea of phenomena. We can call this kind of argument temporal naturalism, or more colloquially, experimentalism. The use in making a distinction between these two kinds of realist argument is to highlight what is distinctive about our contemporary situation, how one kind of post-realism serves as a block on our abilities to reimagine the right to exclude, and how another might open the door.

II. The legal process view

To get a sense for these two kinds of post-realism, consider Felix Cohen's 'realist' article from 1935, *Transcendental Nonsense and the Functional Approach*.[19] This much-discussed

[19] Felix Cohen, 'Transcendental Nonsense and the Functional Approach' (1935) 35 Columbia Law Review 809.

article remains a wonderful illustration of the general problem that modern efforts at social change in the United States were facing in the early decades of the twentieth century.[20] Whether he knew it or not, Cohen captured that general problem right in the article's title. There is the explosive and critical energy associated with the demolition of 'transcendental nonsense', and there is the professional work of getting down to business, the 'functional approach' that would give the moderns a blueprint for legal expertise. These two parts reflect the two kinds of realist orientation I have already alluded to: (1) should we think of legal concepts like property and sovereignty as clusters of transcendental nonsense from an *experimentalist* vantage point, or (2) should we think of our legal concepts as having specific social functions, purposes, and so forth? If we take the first orientation, we really don't have anything like an empirically-determined plan of action.[21] If the latter, the plan is to figure out the complex social reality in which our legal concepts are embedded, all the various interests in play, their functions, their social contexts, and so on.[22]

In turning to the 'functional' approach, Cohen helped lay the groundwork for what would become known as the legal process school. This was an approach that depended, in part, on the particular status and competence of the jurist, in which legal controversies might turn on 'questions of value or of positive fact'.[23] Sometimes, legal process people recognised that in hard cases judges find themselves in genuinely moral situations, where a judge's ethics necessarily played a decisive role in the outcome.[24] But more broadly, it was the question of 'positive fact' that predominated. As Cohen explained, 'we must regard functionalism in law as in anthropology, economics, and other fields, as a call for the study of problems which have been neglected by other scientific methods of observation.'[25] Here was the modern turn to the social sciences, to sociological jurisprudence,[26] to the legal process that was also an inextricably social one.[27] In a word, it was a turn to empirical legal studies, and the belief that in immersing ourselves in the social sciences we might come to see law as another type of social knowledge. As Charles Barzun has explained in the context of the Hart and Sacks materials:

> Hart and Sacks were thus groping, however awkwardly at times, to define law as an academic discipline with methods that could properly be understood as *scientific*, comparable to those employed by economists, psychologists, or sociologists. In short, Hart and Sacks sought to justify their characterization of law as a 'craft' on the grounds that all knowledge, including that derived from the social and even natural sciences, was, in a sense, *craft* knowledge—that is, knowledge of how to *do something*.[28]

[20] For discussion, see David Kennedy and William Fisher III (eds), *The Canon of American Legal Thought* (Princeton University Press 2006) 163.

[21] Instead, we seem to be dealing with what Chris Tomlins has described in the context of Walter Benjamin's writings. See Christopher Tomlins, 'Of Origin: Toward a History of Contemporary Legal Thought' in Justin Desautels-Stein and Christopher Tomlins (eds), *Searching for Contemporary Legal Thought* (CUP 2017) 23.

[22] A terrific discussion is John Henry Schlegel, *American Legal Realism and Empirical Social Science* (University of North Carolina Press 1995).

[23] Cohen (n 19) 820.

[24] ibid 841.

[25] ibid 829.

[26] Roscoe Pound, 'The Scope and Purpose of Sociological Jurisprudence' (1911) 25 Harvard Law Review 140; Roscoe Pound, 'The End of Law as Developed in Legal Rules and Doctrines' (1914) 27 Harvard Law Review 195.

[27] Cohen (n 19) 844.

[28] Charles Barzun, 'The Forgotten Foundations of Hart and Sacks' (2013) 99 Virginia Law Review 1, 7.

Consistent with Cohen's functional approach, legal process people believed in an analogy between the work of legal theorists and the work of social scientists—work that had the same aim, namely, to better describe and understand the world in which we live. Thus, as earlier thinkers like Roscoe Pound had suggested, it was the task of lawyers and judges to learn from the disciplines of economics, political science, and sociology in order to both better predict legal outcomes and chart the 'best' course for those outcomes.[29] As a consequence, the empiricism of legal process recommended special attention to the contexts in which the bundles of sticks were configured. Thus, the interest of legal process people in interdisciplinary work, where the real explanations often take place beyond law per se, and in the offices of power and privilege that are always elsewhere. The post-realist legal process vision therefore emphasised an empirical encounter with law in society, and demands that the lawyer do his utmost to uncover the law's social life.

The characteristic approach to this view of the legal process school, however, is to simply collapse it with realism altogether, rather than see it as just one possible way of doing juridical work after realism. Hanoch Dagan, a scholar of legal realism, explicitly aligns his process approach with that of the realists, favourably citing Karl Llewellyn's suggestion that we understand legal analysis as 'craft'.[30] Dagan's approach is 'guided by the realist conception of law'[31] and 'calls for an ongoing (albeit properly cautious) process of identifying human values underlying the existing property forms',[32] forms which might be thought of as 'institutions structuring and channelling people's relationships'.[33] He continues:

> More specifically, our existing repertoire of property forms offers a tentative suggestion to parse the social world into distinct categories of human interaction. People interact in a myriad of ways depending on their relationships with one another. The spectrum of relationships between strangers (or market transactors); through relationships between landlords and tenants, members of the same local community, neighbours, and coowners; to intimate relationships between family members.[34]

On the other hand, retro-thinkers like Henry Smith similarly conflate realism with the legal process approach. When Smith and others castigate the realists for their efforts at describing society in its every last detail, and complain that '[t]he bundle-of-rights picture of property draws on social science and accordingly aspires to be a scientific theory of property',[35] they are talking about Cohen's functionalism and its progeny: the legal process interpretation of the realist heritage. Rather than succumb to the endless complexity of constructing legal concepts as bundles of relative rights and relationships, the retro-classical style paints property and sovereignty in simpler, more basic, *more realistic* terms. For whereas the modern legal process approach gives us a picture of a social world filled with a never-ending series of entanglements, the retro-classical style constructs a physically possessed *thing*, unified,

[29] Holmes has suggested as much in an earlier piece, again pointing to how typical it was for thinkers to blend realist and process arguments in a single article: Oliver Wendell Holmes Jr, 'Privilege, Malice, Intent' (1894) 8 Harvard Law Review 1.

[30] Hanoch Dagan and Roy Kreitner, 'The Character of Legal Theory' (2011) 96 Cornell Law Review 671, 678.

[31] Hanoch Dagan, 'The Craft of Property' (2003) 91 California Law Review 1517, 1558.

[32] ibid 1561.

[33] ibid 1558.

[34] ibid 1559.

[35] Henry Smith, 'Property as the Law of Things' (2012) 125 Harvard Law Review 1691, 1695.

structured, and exclusive in its basic character. The question is therefore about which is the better style for rendering a realistic law, that of Henry Smith's cohort, or that of Hanoch Dagan's.

This debate between Dagan and Smith, in which they disagree about whether the legal process approach is truly realistic or not, and in which they implicitly agree that the legal process approach is what legal realism bequeathed in American Legal Thought, is replicated in international legal thought. As strands of sociological theory began weaving their way into European approaches to international law, by the early decades of the twentieth century the shift to more realistic, more functional demands on sovereignty became increasing popular.[36] With explicit roots in Lasswell and McDougal's work, Harold Koh's contemporary 'transnational legal process' approach to the relation between sovereignty and international institutions looks a whole lot like Hanoch Dagan's realist-process approach to property law.[37] Koh has argued for a critique of the old distinction between something called 'national' and another called 'international', a critique of the old idea that states are the sole or primary subjects of international law, an acceptance of the functional view that international law must shift and transform in accordance with the needs of international society, and an acceptance of the functional view that international law must be capable of providing normative compulsion.[38] Similarly, Joel Trachtman's recent recipe for global government is premised entirely on a functionalist approach to socio-legal institutions and processes.[39] Drawing on thinkers like David Mitrany, Trachtman sees international politics as an adjunct to international society, transforming in tandem with those transformations in the cultural and economic world. That is, Trachtman's predictions are essentially about changes in international society, and the trick is to get the very best analysis of society's problems that we can.

On the other side, retro-thinkers in the United States like Eric Posner and Jack Goldsmith mirror a version of Henry Smith's position in the property debates. Just as Smith has claimed that legal realism has led property law away from its truest foundations in things and rights of exclusive possession, so too have Posner and Goldsmith complained of the lure of international institutions. The turn to institutions, they argue, has resulted in a weak international law, governed by a useless 'legalism' totally out of sync with the drivers of international life, namely, the incidents of real state power and sovereignty itself. What is real, what is really useful in the international order, is anything but a focus on the relative rights of sovereigns and non-state actors. What is realistic is an international order that comes back to the sovereign's ultimate right to exclude, to remain free from interference, to put its own interests *first*. Posner and Goldsmith argue that international law is only obeyed when it is in the interest of a sovereign to obey it.[40] They argue that 'international law emerges from states' pursuit of self-interested policies on the international stage. International law is, in this sense, *endogenous* to self-interest.'[41] The implication is that international law is

[36] Léon Duguit, 'Objective Law' (1920) 20 Columbia Law Review 817; Georges Scelle, *Precis de Droit des Gens* (Editions du Centre National de la Recherche Scientifique 1932); Julius Stone, *The Province and Function of Law* (Harvard University Press 1946); Georg Schwarzenberger, 'Jus Pacis Ac Belli? Prolegomena to a Sociology of International Law' (1943) 37 American Journal of International Law 460.

[37] Harold Koh, 'Transnational Legal Process' (1996) 75 Nebraska Law Review 181, 183.

[38] ibid 184. For an early view, see Alejandro Alvarez, 'New Conception and New Bases of Legal Philosophy' (1919) 13 Illinois Law Review 167.

[39] Joel Trachtman, *The Future of International Law: Global Government* (CUP 2013) 289.

[40] Goldsmith and Posner, *Limits* (n 12) 3.

[41] ibid 13.

devoid of normative content; that despite what the global legalists keep saying, the rules of international law are incapable of telling states what they *ought* to do. When they are working, which is not always the case, the rules of international law tell states what they are doing already.[42]

What I am suggesting here is yet another dimension in the string of symmetries between property and sovereignty in the history of liberal legalism. As I discussed above, where the traditional view understood property and sovereignty as highly formal architectures, the modern view recommended a functionalist perspective and the metaphor that property and sovereignty ought to be conceived as bundles of legal relationships. In the account I am drawing here, I am suggesting that the modern effort at 'realistic reform' has hit something of an impasse. Today, a retro faction is working to adapt the traditional style to the realism associated with modern reform, yielding a situation in which a legal process school-infused view of realism sets the agenda, the problems to be worked out, and the range of potential reforms. Scholars like Dagan, Koh, and Trachtman all favour a view of embedding basic legal concepts in the working life of legal institutions, while scholars like Smith, Posner, and Goldsmith argue for the uselessness of thinking about law in the registers of bundles and institutions and the like. In an increasing number of these conversations, early twentieth-century legal realism is considered at the heart of the matter, as either the bad seed or the good idea that needs updating. As I suggested when we looked at Felix Cohen's article, however, it is a mistake to conflate realism with legal process. To be sure, the intensely empirical work of the legal process school was suggested by a number of 'realist' scholars. The creative potential of the realist legacy, however, needn't be so restricted. It can, and needs to mean, more.

III. The ideological block

Chief among the needs for a revitalised realism that can go beyond the stale realism at the heart of the debate between the retro and modern thinkers is the need sketched out in the first half of Cohen's article. After all, the critique of 'transcendental nonsense', the argument that there is nothing neutral or necessary about any given construction of a legal concept, is an argument about the inability of a legal concept to work itself 'naturally' outside of time.[43] The critique of a timeless state of nature was also right there in Hohfeld's analysis of legal relations, which we have already seen in the context of the formation of the 'bundle' metaphor. In Hohfeld, as in Cohen, it is a mistake to conflate 'legal rights' with rights that might be discovered in nature. Similarly, in the work of Oliver Wendell Holmes Jr, so-called natural rights were of little value to the real-world work of understanding a legal system.[44] It is only legal rights that were thought to count, and when we look closely at legal rights, what we find is a dizzyingly complicated picture. For one thing, legal rights lack any meaningful existence outside of the positive exercise of legal authority. If an agent with legal authority has yet to decide that you, in some particular controversy, enjoy a right that imposes a legal

[42] ibid 38–39.
[43] Cohen (n 19) 810–11.
[44] Oliver Wendell Holmes Jr, 'The Path of the Law' (1897) 10 Harvard Law Review 61.

obligation somewhere else, then you have yet to enjoy that right. Legal rights never exist in the abstract. Nothing does, as Cohen colourfully suggested.

No doubt, as we can see in the 'complexity' of Hohfeld's system, in Holmes' 'Bad Man', and in Cohen's title, all of this seems to be leading towards the legal process school and the 'functional approach' of the moderns. And in the lives of these thinkers, it may very well have seemed *logical* that the critique of nature's rights *led* to the functional approach. What we need to remember, however, is that there was nothing logical (or illogical) about this utterly contingent sequence of events. To believe otherwise, that property and sovereignty *had* to become modern because of the 'realistic' demand to align law with a given view of society, is to fall prey to exactly the kind of ideological obfuscation legal realism was trying to resolve in the first place.

This issue of obfuscation, or the 'ideological block,' is sometimes related to a process of 'reification.'[45] Then, as well as now, reification is an amazingly pedestrian activity for lawyers. It is a common process in which a jurist translates a legal *concept*, like '*right*,' into a physical *thing*, like a piece of pie. That is, to reify a concept is to 'thing-ify' that concept.[46] For example, a lawyer might say that one's rights have been 'lost' or 'trampled upon,' just as you might lose your shirt only to find that your children used it as a tarp in their pillow fort. But, from this point of view, once we reflect upon the 'nature' of our rights, we realise that a right is not something you can lose in the same way that you can lose a shirt. Rather, a right is a figure that can be 'spoken' in the name of power, such as when a court marshals the forces of the state, or a figure that can be 'silenced,' such as when a court does not.[47] In Cohen's article, this is what the critique of transcendental nonsense is meant to suggest: to view owners and sovereigns in relation to *things* is ... nonsense.

This may be what the critique of transcendental nonsense was all about. It is not, however, what functionalism was all about, and in important ways the functionalism that came into the hands of the legal process people was just as vulnerable to ideology-critique as anything that had preceded it.[48] In the simplest terms, we can say that this 'no-nonsense' realism was against the reification of property and sovereignty. The legal process *interpretation* of realism, in contrast, was not. The reification at work in the legal process interpretation is about what happens to 'society' as jurists look to it in the posture of Cohen's scientific method. As we have come to understand, empirical accounts of law can have powerfully naturalising effects, recommending a view of society that has come to be as it is.[49] Society,

[45] For discussion, see Justin Desautels-Stein and Duncan Kennedy, 'Theorizing Contemporary Legal Thought' (2015) 78 Law and Contemporary Problems i. The seminal twentieth-century work on reification is Georg Lukacs, *History and Class Consciousness: Studies in Marxist Dialectics* (Merlin Press 1975). There have been many analyses of the problem of reification in law. See, eg Duncan Kennedy, *A Critique of Adjudication* (Harvard University Press 1998); Peter Gabel, 'Reification in Legal Reasoning' (1980) 3 Research in Law and Society 25; James Boyle, 'The Politics of Reason: Critical Legal Theory and Local Social Thought' (1985) 133 University of Pennsylvania Law Review 685.

[46] Cohen (n 19) 811 ('Nobody has ever seen a corporation. What right have we to believe in corporations if we don't believe in angels. To be sure some of us have seen corporate funds, corporate transactions (just as some of us have seen angelic deeds, angelic countenances, etc.) But this does not give us the right to hypostatize, to 'thingify' the corporation, and to assume that it travels about from State to State as mortal men travel.')

[47] Marianne Constable, *Just Silences: The Limits and Possibilities of Modern Law* (Princeton University Press 2007).

[48] For an example of the critique, see Gary Peller, 'The Metaphysics of American Law' (1985) 73 California Law Review 1151.

[49] This literature is enormous. See, eg Bruno Latour, *We Have Never Been Modern* (Harvard University Press 1993); Richard Rorty, *Philosophy and the Mirror of Nature* (Princeton University Press 1981).

on this view, is a real thing that can be studied, dissected, and properly diagnosed, as if it was a dead frog in a classroom. And with this proper diagnosis in hand, so the thinking goes, we will produce an objective albeit extremely complicated understanding of law's social life. As Cohen explained, again in the register of legal process rather than realism: '*Just as every physical object* may be analyzed as a complex of positive and negative electrons, *so every legal institution*, every legal rule or concept may be analyzed as a complex of plaintiff decisions and defendant decisions.'[50]

This focus on social complexity is as much of a reification as is the retro-classical obsession with basic architectures. For while the retro style mystifies the legal concepts of sovereignty and ownership directly, the legal process approach mystifies the social world in which property ownership and sovereign rule are meant to happen.[51] In each case, the reifications pass off legal concepts as 'physical objects' for the purpose of creating what is ultimately an intellectual shortcut.[52] With this kind of shortcut in place, in which the style purposefully reduces the legal imagination, it assists in producing the idea of 'settled law'.[53] If the law is settled, then we might expect an awareness of the relevant rules and the given facts to be the end of the matter, in terms of a jurist's professional practice. In an area susceptible to shortcuts and the mirage of settled law, the law (and here comes the reifying move) becomes a machine: insert your facts (wherever they come from, whether they are empirically drenched or architecturally formalised), and the jurist ought to be able to produce a legal conclusion necessitated by a combination of facts and rules, a particular fact-rule matrix.

Reifications produce the experience of settled law, and so when we *counter* the effects of reification, we begin to have the unsettling experience that the law was hardly settled at all. That is, if by 'settled law' we mean an area in which competing lines of reasoning have been closed down, these competing lines re-open once we jeopardise the reification. When we dial back the reification effect of the so-called shortcut, what we find is a legal terrain that looks neither like bundles nor things. What we find instead is a language, with all its grammars, tropes, and codas.[54] There is very little settled at all, and instead what we face in property and sovereignty is a political world in which lawyers make decisions about how to distribute society's wealth and resources. But when we use shortcuts and reify these concepts, either in the post-realist styles of legal process or retro-classical people, we sideline these open-ended political choices and decisions. That is, it isn't that political choices and decisions are not being made—it is rather that reifications produce the experience of not having to face these decisions, that the decisions have already been made, by someone else, before we arrived.

As a result, the legal process school and the modern style of post-realist legal thought all too often perpetuate the very problem realism was initially intended to uncover: a reified

[50] Cohen (n 19) 842.

[51] Robert Gordon, 'Paradoxical Property' in John Brewer and Susan Staves (eds) *Early Modern Conceptions of Property* (Routledge 1995) 95.

[52] Henry E Smith, 'Emergent Property' in James Penner and Henry Smith (eds) *Philosophical Foundations of Property Law* (OUP 2014) 324 ('Actual property delineation in terms of things and exclusion is a huge short-cut over the fully articulated stick-by-stick method of elimination and many less economic intermediate versions as well.').

[53] See Stanley Fish, *Doing What Comes Naturally: Change, Rhetoric, and the Practice of Theory in Literary and Legal Studies* (Duke University Press 1990); Duncan Kennedy, 'The Hermeneutic of Suspicion in Contemporary American Legal Thought' (2014) 25 Law and Critique 91.

[54] Desautels-Stein (n 2) 262–99.

right to exclude. For this reason alone, it matters that legal process and its association with empiricism, functionalism, pluralism, institutions, social context, and the rest ought to be resituated at the heart of the debate about how to reform the right to exclude. It matters because, for proponents of the legal process view, the task really is to do something like that which Smith, Goldsmith, and Posner complain about: to understand the vast complexity of the relative rights and relationships that render the right to exclude merely one piece of a much bigger picture.[55] But as I have just suggested, because the process-oriented debates between retro-classical and modern thinkers never get away from the reifications and shortcuts, they seem destined to entrench the structures of exclusion, rather than push beyond them.

Fortunately, the legal process view of reform does not exhaust realism's imaginative potential. A taste for this potential is offered in the recent work of thinkers like Roberto Unger, Lee Smolin, and Chris Tomlins.[56] It is a view of realism that incorporates what Unger and Smolin call temporal naturalism,[57] and what Tomlins calls the 'Law as . . . ' approach.[58] Taken together, we might call it an 'experimental' interpretation of the realist legacy, in contrast with the 'legal process' interpretation already discussed.[59] The basic thrust of such an experimental realism is simple: time is for real. And if time is for real, then *everything* changes, even time itself. Nothing anywhere exists outside of time, not physics, not mathematics, not legal concepts. In this view, legal concepts never reflect sets of institutional arrangements that might exist outside of time, ways in which society just *is* or just *has to be*. Concepts always exist in a temporal naturalism, rendering them contingent, always changing. Of course, the pace of change depends on a lot, and sometimes structural transformation is very slow. How can we speed it up? How can structural transformation accelerate? A beginning is to look for and understand the grammars and styles of legal thought, what they have been, and what they might become. For if we cannot see what the structure of practice might come to be, if these imaginative possibilities remain mystified, structural transformation remains ever more difficult, and our present circumstances ever more frozen. From the perspective of an experimental realism, if something is *natural*, all we know for certain is that it will *change*.

When legal realism's experimentalist interpretation is favoured over the legal process interpretation, the metaphor of sovereignty and property as bundles of rights comes to nothing other than contingency and change. In this interpretation of the realist metaphor,

[55] Cohen (n 19) 829.

[56] Roberto Mangabeira Unger and Lee Smolin, *The Singular Universe and the Reality of Time* (CUP 2015); Christopher Tomlins, 'Historicism and Materiality in Legal Theory' in Maks del Mar and Michael Lobban (eds) *Law in Theory and History: New Essays on a Neglected Dialogue* (Hart 2016) 57.

[57] Unger and Smolin (n 56) 357 ('We would like to have a naturalism that does not reduce human experience and aspirations to illusions . . . The root of the crisis in naturalism is its being wedded to the picture of the universe as a machine. This in turn is a consequence of the idea that nature is governed by laws which are timeless, immutable, and mathematical. The path out of the crisis is to embrace a new form of naturalism based on the reality of time . . . ')

[58] Christopher Tomlins, 'Law "And", Law "In", Law "As": The Definition, Rejection, and Recuperation of the Socio-Legal Enterprise' (2013) 29 Law in Context 137. See also, Justin Desautels-Stein and Christopher Tomlins, 'Contemporary Legal Thought As' in Desautels-Stein and Tomlins (eds) (n 21) 533.

[59] I am hesitant to gather these approaches together under the banner of 'experimentalism', most importantly out of concern for conflating these views with those of Charles Sabel, William Simon, and the more sophisticated works associated with New Governance. See Charles Sabel and William Simon, 'Democratic Experimentalism' in Desautels-Stein and Tomlins (eds) (n 21) 477. Ideally, I would offer the figure of the chiasm as a more appropriate sigil. In the space available, however, experimentalism will have to do. On chiastic jurisprudence, see Desautels-Stein (n 2) 290–99.

the lawyer's job has very little to do with trying to describe the world in its deepest complexity, in its every last detail. Instead, experimental realism recommends a particular antimetaphysics—a belief that there is nothing natural or necessary at all about the structures of exclusion. Indeed, we might come to envision property and sovereignty in any number of ways, opening the door to structures of inclusion we have yet to discover.[60] This cannot happen out of whole cloth. Rather, on this experimental view, the routes towards doctrinal and institutional imagination emerge in a space of becoming: in order to see what sovereignty and property might *become*, we must first understand where they have been and what they currently are. In a word, to imagine what they might become, we must first inhabit their structure. This is what Unger meant in the cryptic, final paragraph of his *What Should Legal Analysis Become?*

Our interests and ideals remain nailed to the cross of our arrangements. We cannot realise our interests and ideals more fully, nor redefine them more deeply, until we have learned to remake and to reimagine our arrangements more freely. History will not give us this freedom. We must win it in the here and now of legal detail, economic constraint, and deadening preconception. We shall not win it if we continue to profess a science of society reducing the possible to the actual and a discourse about law anointing power with piety. *It is true that we cannot be visionaries until we become realists. It is also true that to become realists we must make ourselves into visionaries.*[61]

IV. Conclusion

We continue to live in a world in which xenophobia runs riot. The extent to which a retro approach to the right to exclude justifies and fortifies such a world warrants our attention, and ultimately our resistance. At the same time, all remains quiet on the western front when it comes to the practices of property law. The routines of property are belied, however, by the debate among property scholars about how its most basic elements should be conceived. This is a fight over the soul of property law, and whether a community-based or an individualist conception of ownership ought to drive our contemporary political economy. Less flammable as a headline-grabber, it is nevertheless a debate with far-reaching consequences. The reason for bringing these discourses about the right to exclude, sovereignty, and property into conversation is to provide a fuller perspective about liberal legal thought, and what we are up against as we fathom the structure of exclusion, and that structure's reform.[62] The fuller perspective that I have tried to provide is two-fold.

On the one side, prospects for socio-legal change depend on understanding the deeper structure of legal thought in which concepts like sovereignty and property take their form. In the traditional and retro-traditional style, the argumentative practices of sovereignty and property build out in very similar architectures. Rooted in a conceptual core of individualism and territorial possession, these concepts manifest in a system of background

[60] Roberto Mangabeira Unger, *Democracy Realized: The Progressive Alternative* (Verso 2000).

[61] Roberto Mangabeira Unger, *What Should Legal Analysis Become?* (Verso 1996) 189–90.

[62] For earlier examples of a similar critique in the context of international relations theory, see John Ruggie, 'Continuity and Transformation in the World Polity: Toward a Neorealist Synthesis' (1983) 35 World Politics 261; Friedrich Kratochwil, 'Of Systems, Boundaries, and Territoriality: An Inquiry into the Formation of the State System' (1986) 39 World Politics 27.

and foreground rules. The background rules have a singular mission: protect and enforce the right to exclude. When functioning properly, the background rules hardly seem like rules at all. Instead, they simply emanate as the natural outcome of our socio-economic arrangements. Foreground rules, in contrast, are artificial. They are, notoriously, man-made. In this retro-classical style, foreground rules regulate the excess of the right to exclude, providing forms of governance that the background rules are unable to provide on their own. Foreground rules, however, are inherently suspect. The fewer of them the better.

The modern style of sovereignty and property argument is a different animal. Birthed in the critique of classic liberalism, the modern style touts itself as a far more realistic configuration of the relation between law and society. It is empirical, scientific, and concerned with society as the primary unit of analysis. Nevertheless, it is a mistake to understand the modern style as a wholesale repudiation of the traditional view. It is better to see it as an update. Individual (and sovereign) rights remain crucial, and the right to exclude retains an important place at the table. The moderns were, in a word, out to save liberalism from itself, not destroy it. As a result of this reformist impulse, the modern style shifts away from the explicit use of background and foreground rules and moves towards two orienting directions. The first is legal functionalism, a style of legal reasoning in which jurists determine the answers to legal disputes in the light of social needs and the purposes of the laws meant to serve those needs. The second direction for the modern thinker is the emphasis on the relativity of rights and legal relationships. Articulated in the bundle of rights metaphor, sovereignty and property are 'unbundled' as various rights and duties. The right to exclude is certainly a big stick in the bundle, but it is only one stick among many. Crucially, pieces of the bundle never pre-exist an actual legal controversy—rather they only come into view in the crucible of positive governance and particular contexts. Indeed, *context* is a watchword in this empiricist characterisation of the 'bundle'. The modern thinker, as a result, needs to figure out how the right to exclude properly relates, all in the light of an empirically nuanced account of the social context in which the rights and duties make their home.

As the traditional view has returned in a 'retro' style, property and sovereignty mirror one another in the dance between modern and retro approaches. One takeaway is that the structures of exclusion in which both sovereignty and property perform is much broader and deeper than a parochial analysis might suggest. Another takeaway is that the same moment of reform served as the bridge between the traditional and modern views of the right to exclude. The name for that moment was 'legal realism'. As discussed, a splintering in the realist legacy has served to obscure the odd role that realism now plays in our conversations about whether and how we might further reform the right to exclude, in either of its property or sovereignty dimensions. That splintering was this. After the realist critique of the traditional people, there emerged the legal process interpretation of that critique. It was an interpretation that would inform a great deal of the modern style, with its substantial emphasis on institutions, competencies, complexity, context, and social science. Further, it is the legal process interpretation of the realist legacy which now sits the heart of our debates over the structure of exclusion—a debate between retro-thinkers like Henry Smith, Jack Goldsmith, and Eric Posner, and modern thinkers like Hanoch Dagan, Harold Koh, and Joel Trachtman.

In addition to the legal process interpretation of the realist critique is what I have called an experimental interpretation. Resting on the recent work of Roberto Unger, Lee Smolin, and Christopher Tomlins, this is a view that emphasises the importance of ideology-critique and de-reification. The idea here is that, if the old classic liberal style of argumentative practice was criticised for reifying property and sovereignty, and thereby removing these concepts from our constellations of institutional imagination, the new modern style perpetuated a reification all the same. To be sure, it was a different reification. Whereas the classic jurists reified the legal materials themselves, modern jurists reified the endless complexity of a social world in which law was forever destined a lady-in-waiting. And it is precisely here that we see the importance in not only analysing the structure of exclusion itself, but also the manner in which that structure has so powerfully adapted to the legal process interpretation of realist reform. The question of whether the right to exclude ought to be 'realistic' is not up for debate. Everyone agrees that realism is the guide. The problem is that as a guide, it isn't up for the job, for legal process 'realism' is anaemic in its imaginative powers. Relying on precisely the kind of mental shortcuts an experimental realism ought to upend, the retro-classical/modern debate is going nowhere fast.

6

An Enlarged Sense of Possibility for International Law

Seeking Change by Doing History

*Janne E Nijman**

I. Introduction

This Cannot Be How the World Was Meant to Be.[1]

This is a quote from Philip Allott, one of the most important international legal theorists of our time.[2] He chose it as the motto for a symposium organised on the occasion of his retirement from Cambridge University in 2004. Philip had penned it down when he was sixteen years old.

Many students and scholars today must have had a similar thought around that age. I know I have. Overwhelmed by the disorder and injustices of the world around us, one asks oneself several questions: Could humanity live differently? Could international law play a role in that change? If so, how?

This experience of dissatisfaction with the present state of the world and the role that international law plays gives rise to questions such as the central one pursued by this volume: *could* international law have been different? I am grateful to the editors for the invitation to contribute a chapter that engages with contingency in international law first and foremost through an argument that international law *can* be different and that doing history can help us realise the possibilities in this regard. An alternative past may help us in the present to see what international law *can* be in the future.

By way of illustration, I will recover a specific past possibility when discussing the conceptions of sovereignty and international legal personality that are available as an alternative to what became the dominant conceptions of international law. This is, however, not a chapter on what international law might have looked like had these alternative conceptions prevailed.[3] Rather, my overall aim here is to show how doing history creates space for the

* This chapter builds on the author's inaugural lecture at the University of Amsterdam.

[1] 'Review Essay Symposium: Philip Allott's "Eunomia and The Health of Nations Thinking Another World: This Cannot Be How the World Was Meant to Be"' (2005) 16 European Journal of International Law 255.

[2] See eg Philip Allott, *Eunomia: New Order for a New World* (OUP 1990); Philip Allott, *The Health of Nations: Society and Law Beyond the State* (CUP 2002).

[3] Historical counterfactualism has been on the rise for some time now in academic history and with this research project, it arrives in international legal scholarship. The methodological value of counterfactuality for international law relates to an attempt to uncover contingency and bring back human agency within historical processes after decades of (post-)structuralism in international legal thought. In the words of Simon Kaye: 'Counterfactualism is the handmaiden of agency and its crucial role in human life.' My intervention in this

Janne E Nijman, *An Enlarged Sense of Possibility for International Law* In: *Contingency in International Law*. Edited by: Ingo Venzke and Kevin Jon Heller, Oxford University Press. © The Several Contributors 2021. DOI: 10.1093/oso/9780192898036.003.0006

experience of contingency and for 'a lesson in self-knowledge' and how this is important for new versions of international law. First and foremost this is motivated by the thought that the future is not an inevitable, natural, necessary continuation of the past. Doing history confirms this thought as it reveals the past as—what our editors call—'a realm of possibility'[4] and it critically questions the beliefs, concepts, and theories with which we come to our choices for the future. Change does not merely depend on a present that could have been different; it also depends on the consciousness of that possibility, which questions what constitutes or defines one's choices. While revealing contingency or possibility in the past provokes methodological questions such as the way in which history should be narrated to reveal this, my main claim in this chapter is the broader proposition that doing history may contribute to change.

An argument underpinning this proposition is that historical awareness nurtures human consciousness and enables the uncovery of false necessity (and false contingency for that matter) in the present international law. Doing history and thus confronting past—perhaps alien—international legal thought evokes critical reflection on what we could easily take for granted as 'necessary', that is, our own conceptions, beliefs, and theories of international law and international society. Could they have been different? Can they be different and thus contribute to a different international law in the future?

In my view, the above-quoted words of Philip Allott hold a range of experiences: bewilderment of the present and the past that brought us here, rejection of the necessity of the present, and a sense of possibility for a different future. In short, it captures a desire for change. More than suggesting another necessary reality, I take 'meant to be' as referring to the possibility of justice and of human agency. This, however, cannot be appreciated without recognising the importance of deep—natural and social—structures, circumstances, and honouring the insights of materialism. Most international legal scholarship draws heavily on these necessitarian assumptions, which consequently makes freedom such a contested belief.[5]

In my view, the increased focus on history in international legal scholarship of the last two decades[6] is as much about the future as it is about the past. This growing interest has now been captured as the 'turn to history': an increase of historical inquiry into international law and—most notably—international legal thought. Whence emerged what may be called 'history and theory of international law'. As a relatively new subfield of international law,[7] it

chapter is equally methodological yet more than interested in alternative pasts, I am interested in alternative futures. The methods of counterfactualism and contextualism bring out histories and facilitate thinking about possible, even plausible alternative courses of history. My argument for historical contextualisations in the history of international legal thought shares with historical counterfactualism the objective to uncover and underscore contingency and human agency. Simon T Kaye, 'Challenging Certainty: The Utility and History of Counterfactualism' (2010) 49 History and Theory 38, 57.

[4] Ingo Venzke, 'Situating Contingency in the Path of International Law', in this volume.

[5] Samuel Moyn, 'From Situated Freedom to Plausible Worlds', in this volume.

[6] In 1990 the European Journal of International Law (EJIL) directly started publishing studies of the life and work of early twentieth-century international lawyers. The Journal of the History of International Law was launched in 1999. This first issue includes a bibliography: Peter Macalister-Smith and Joachim Schwietzke, 'Literature and Documentary Sources Relating to the History of Public International Law: An Annotated Bibliographical Survey' (1999) 1 Journal of the History of International Law 136; see also Bardo Fassbender and Anne Peters (eds), *The Oxford Handbook of the History of International Law* (OUP 2012)

[7] George Rodrigo Bandeira Galindo, 'Force Field: On History and Theory of International Law' (2012) 20 Rechtsgeschichte 86

is not well-defined—and that is a good thing. It brings together history *and theory*, which is not without its tensions and challenges, methodological and otherwise. The responses to a subtitle such as 'Seeking change by doing history' are wonderfully illustrative. Intellectual and legal historians are, in polite terms, *intrigued* by the 'seeking change' part of the title. Critical international lawyers praise the 'seeking change' part, but show some doubt with regards to the 'doing history' element of the title.

In this chapter, I aim to discuss the field of 'History & Theory' somewhat further. First, I will situate the 'turn to history'. Subsequently, I will discuss the relationship between history and theory and how, in my view, this can be a productive one. Here I will discuss the importance of historical contextualisation of law and legal thought while arguing that the law's normative potential is exactly why international lawyers use its concepts to *do* things. In short, I am interested in alternative futures more than in alternative pasts. Finally, as is only fair, I address a self-reflexive question: 'if doing history is a form of seeking change, then what is the change I am seeking?'[8]

II. Situating the 'turn to history'

International legal scholarship turned to history in the late 1990s to early 2000s. To understand this 'turn to history' in international law,[9] we should situate it in the political context of globalisation and the end of the Cold War, as well as in the intellectual context of postmodern or critical thinking.

The end of the Cold War impacted international politics, reinforced globalisation, and triggered high-level discussions on a New World Order. Some liberal internationalists turned to history out of optimism,[10] hoping that the cosmopolitan project of international law might be possible after all.[11] However, disappointment with the state of international law sank in soon after: the envisaged New World Order failed to materialise and instead the War on Terror developed into the new normal.[12] Accelerating economic globalisation and integration put pressure on the culturally diverse world. As a result, international legal scholarship was confronted with questions about the relevance and foundations of international law and institutions. The separation between national and international law, the

[8] This may come close to what Kaye, following Jon Elster, calls an '*ontological* or world-building counterfactual narrative as an exercise in imagination' challenging historical preconceptions of international law. Kaye (n 3) 43ff. Strictly speaking we move here from doing history to doing theory (or philosophy) but the latter emerges from the former. See section III.3 in this chapter.

[9] George Rodrigo Bandeira Galindo, 'Martti Koskenniemi and the Historiographical Turn in International Law' (2005) 16 The European Journal of International Law 539; Thomas Skouteris, 'Engaging History in International Law' in José María Beneyto and David Kennedy (eds), *New Approaches to International Law: The European and the American Experiences* (Asser Press 2012) 99; Martti Koskenniemi, 'Histories of International Law: Significance and Problems for a Critical View' (2013) 27 Temple International and Comparative Law Journal 215, 216; Anne Orford, 'On International Legal Method' (2013) 1 London Review of International Law 166, 171; Anne Orford, 'International Law and the Limits of History' in Wouter Werner, Marieke de Hoon, and Alexis Galán (eds), *The Law of International Lawyers: Reading Martti Koskenniemi* (CUP 2017) 297.

[10] For 1990s optimism, see, eg Harold Hongju Koh, 'The 1998 Frankel Lecture: Bringing International Law Home' (1998) 35 Houston Law Review 623.

[11] Martti Koskenniemi, 'Why History of International Law Today?' (2004) 4 Rechtsgeschichte 61.

[12] Randall Lesaffer, 'International Law and Its History: The Story of an Unrequited Love' in Maria Vogiatzi, Matthew Craven, and Malgosia Fitzmaurice (eds), *Time, History and International Law* (Brill 2007) 27, 29; see also Koskenniemi (n 11) and Koskenniemi (n 9) 215, 216: Koskenniemi points to what he captures, I think well, as a sense of failure and disappointment.

primacy of states and invisibility of non-state actors, state sovereignty and territorial jurisdiction, and universality of human rights are all illustrative of the traditional doctrines that were scrutinised. Dissatisfied with the conditions of international society, scholars started to ask about the history of the international legal system as well as about their own role in the development of international law. The unreflexive pragmatism that had dominated mainstream international legal scholarship during the Cold War decades and that had left little space for history or theory now became untenable for many international legal scholars.[13] This was all the more so because of the developing intellectual context. For years we have been aware that doing history of thought is a profoundly *hermeneutic* exercise: it is about the *interpretation* of historic texts and the construction of historical narratives, which necessarily has a subjective element.

In the course of the twentieth century, the grand narratives of Western thought came under scrutiny. 'Postmodernist' or 'critical' theories challenged the assumptions of mainstream international legal scholarship too.[14] Post-structuralist theory, post-colonial theory, linguistic studies, and other postmodern theories—which, in short, may be referred to as the 'linguistic turn' in the philosophy of history—have profoundly impacted the historical narratives of international law.[15] Post-structuralist philosopher Michel Foucault and post-colonial critic Edward Said revolutionised our thinking about doing history of thought as focus shifted to discontinuity and contestation. With his 'history of the present', Foucault stimulated the writing of genealogies of fundamental concepts that define a field, such as 'sovereignty' in international law.[16] Edward Said was one of the scholars who sensitised our discipline to the ongoing reproduction of orientalist and imperialist knowledge, to the link between the Western Enlightenment and colonialism, and to the possible value of doing history of thought as a *critique* of imperialism.[17] It is impossible to discuss all these '-isms' and 'post-somethings' here. I will come back briefly to their impact on international legal thought later but postmodern thinking shattered existing certainties and paradigms, such as the separation of object and subject. The discontent with international law and legal theory converged with a discontent with the orthodox teleological, Eurocentric, and hagiographic *histories* of international law.[18] When critical thinking arrived in international law scholarship, it hit hard, which for some resulted in having a cynical outlook on international law's possibilities.

[13] David Kennedy, 'International Law and the Nineteenth Century: History of an Illusion' (1996) 65 Nordic Journal of International Law 385; Fleur Johns, 'International Legal Theory: Snapshots from a Decade of International Legal Life' (2009) 10 Melbourne Journal of International Law 1; Janne Nijman, *The Concept of International Legal Personality: An Inquiry into the History and Theory of International Law* (Asser Press 2004); Martti Koskenniemi, '"The Lady Doth Protest Too Much" Kosovo, and the Turn to Ethics in International Law' (2002) 65 Modern Law Review 159, 175.

[14] Joan Wallach Scott, 'History-Writing as Critique' in Keith Jenkins, Sue Morgan, and Alun Munslow (eds), *Manifestos for History* (Routledge 2007) 19.

[15] Daniel Woolf, *A Global History of History* (CUP 2011) 493–99.

[16] Jens Bartelson, *A Genealogy of Sovereignty* (CUP 1995).

[17] Edward Said, *Orientalism: Western Conceptions of the Orient* (Penguin 1995).

[18] That is, histories that portray international law merely as a force for progress of humanity and international lawyers as prophets of peace. The EJIL series mentioned earlier in n 6 broke with that hagiographical writing of history. See also, eg, Thomas Skouteris' work on progress, also in history writing on international law: Thomas Skouteris, *The Notion of Progress in International Law Discourse* (Asser Press 2010). On the Eurocentric nature of international legal history, see, eg Arnulf Becker Lorca, 'Eurocentrism in the History of International Law' in Bardo Fassbender and Anne Peters (eds), *The Oxford Handbook of the History of International Law* (OUP 2012) 1034.

The recent 'turn to history' and historiography by international law scholars and the new orientation towards international affairs by intellectual historians[19] has been mutually reinforcing. The recent 'turn' also spurred a vibrant new scholarship that is different from the orthodox forms of international legal history because of the extent to which it is intertwined with international legal theory. As such, the field of 'History and Theory of International Law' may be characterised by historical work that is open to theory, and international legal theorisation that is grounded in the history of international legal thought.[20]

III. *Why* and *how* 'History and Theory of International Law'?

Let me first explore what the study of the history of international legal thought is *for*. Closely related to this is the question of *how* to study it. Twenty years on, 'History and Theory of International Law' is marked by what I would call a *Methodenstreit*—a debate about the methods of the field. For reasons of clarity, I stage three positions that mark the field. On the one hand, there are scholars who do international legal history for the sake of *history*. On the other hand, there are international lawyers who do history exclusively as critique or *theory*. Moving beyond these two positions, there is a third that I call 'history and theory'. I would argue that the significance of this field lies in the opportunity to organise a fruitful dialogue between history of international legal thought and philosophy or theory of international law.

Why do international lawyers study the past? Clearly, international lawyers turn to the past all the time. It is where lawyers go to find whether legal obligations have been forged through treaties or customary law. They also turn to the past to determine 'original title' of sovereignty. For example, in the 2008 *Malaysia/Singapore* case at the International Court of Justice, judges read Grotius' work to find evidence of the territorial sovereignty of the Sultanate of Johor.[21] In the context of 'history and theory of international law', by 'turning to history' and with 'doing history' we mean research and teaching focused on international legal thought, ideas, concepts, *mentalités*, historiographical narratives, principles, and so on and so forth. We also focus on the jurists who developed and worked with these, often in response to a contemporary event such as a peace treaty.

Let me turn to the three positions I mentioned before (with some necessary simplification) on why and how we study past international legal thought.

1. History for history's sake: history *without* theory

First, doing history for history's sake. There are those who argue that we do—and should do—history *out of sheer curiosity* about the past. These historians aim to 'approach the past

[19] David Armitage, 'The Fifty Years' Rift: Intellectual History and International Relations' (2004) 1 Modern Intellectual History 97; also David Armitage, 'The International Turn in Intellectual History' in Darrin McMahon and Samuel Moyn (eds), *Rethinking Modern European Intellectual History* (OUP 2014) 232–52.

[20] I use history or intellectual history of international law and history of international legal thought somewhat interchangeably.

[21] *Sovereignty over Pedra Branca/Pulau Batu Puteh, Middle Rocks and South Ledge (Malaysia/Singapore)* (Judgment) [2008] ICJ Reports 12.

"in its own right, for its own sake, and on its own terms";[22] as Quentin Skinner put it. Doing history of thought then is a technique to *conserve* political or legal ideas. It is empiricist and antiquarian in nature and it insists on *objectivist* representation as a standard for dealing with past thought.[23] Any social utility approach to history is rejected; the past should be respected as the past and not be taxed with today's concerns.[24]

Some international legal historians accordingly defend the position that historical inquiry into international law should come from a genuine, non-instrumentalist interest in past events and ideas. Randall Lesaffer has repeatedly condemned the tendency of doing international legal history out of a 'functional interest' and for needs and concerns of the present.[25]

The tone of the *Methodenstreit* gets quite harsh at times. Ian Hunter speaks of '*debilitating* anachronism' and 'self-congratulating' post-colonial moralism.[26] While I agree that avoiding anachronisms is valuable when doing history of international legal thought, I find these statements questionable. I would argue that respect for the context and intentions of a historical author when seeking to understand his ideas does not preclude an evaluation of how past texts and concepts produced *present* repression and injustices.

It is too easy to set aside evaluation as anachronistic, provided that historic contextualisation plays a role. It is, moreover, not true that moral concerns with the Vereenigde Oostindische Compagnie (VOC)'s violent conduct overseas are altogether anachronistic, as is often suggested. The VOC's violence in the protection of its trade interests around the globe was, for example, subject to serious criticism by its Anabaptist and Mennonite shareholders.

My main concern with this approach's sharp criticism of bringing the present to the study of past thought is its overly *objectivist* claim about the production of historical knowledge and the recovery of meaning. It fails to recognise the inseparability of subject and object, and it fails to recognise fully that any historian seeking to *understand* Francisco de Vitoria or Hugo Grotius, for example, comes with questions, assumptions, and categories that draw on a theorisation formed in the present. It also fails to see that reconstruction of the intended meaning of a text by de Vitoria or Grotius cannot be fully identified with the text's meaning. 'History for history's sake' resists *theorisation* and a *proper dialogue* with present-day international legal theory.

On a related side note, there is always more than one history in any event: thus the sixteenth-century Spanish scholar de Vitoria, who lectured and advised on Spanish rule in the Americas, expressed moral criticism of Spanish violent conduct against the Native Americans. At the same time, we should mention that by positing *equal* standing and natural *rights* to *both* Spaniards and Native Americans, he effectively constructed a legal framework for Spanish *domination* in the Americas. This *inclusion* of the non-European into the

[22] Quentin Skinner, 'Sir Geoffrey Elton and the Practice of History' (1997) 7 Transactions of the Royal Historical Society 301, 304. Doing history for a historian like Geoffrey Elton then is 'a search for the truth' by reconstructing the 'true facts' of the past.

[23] Wallach Scott (n 14).

[24] Geoffrey Elton's anti-theoretical empiricism set him in opposition to someone like Michel Foucault or Hayden White, whose *Metahistory* (Johns Hopkins University Press 1973) played a significant role in the 'linguistic turn' in history too.

[25] Lesaffer (n 12) 29.

[26] Ian Hunter, 'The Figure of Man and the Territorialisation of Justice in "Enlightenment" Natural Law: Pufendorf and Vattel' (2013) 23 Intellectual History Review 289.

legal system to then *disempower* the non-European is shown to be reproduced by the structure of international law, even today.[27]

2. History for the sake of critique: history *as* theory

At the opposite side of the spectrum we find 'doing history as *critique*'. This approach *deconstructs* disciplinary truths and underlying assumptions.[28] I mentioned Michel Foucault and Edward Said already. Critical international lawyers took on board the understanding that the production of knowledge, including historical knowledge, is never neutral and always political.[29] Historiography is always contextual and contingent upon power structures.[30] Therefore, the grand narratives that have presented international law as a naturally progressive project for humanity,[31] bringing civilisation and replacing power politics with the rule of law, were challenged.[32]

Harvard professor David Kennedy built on Foucauldian insights for his history as *critique* of human rights. While he values the emancipatory, humanitarian cause, he points to what he calls 'the dark sides of virtue': the humanitarian and human rights activist exercises power too; she too is 'a ruler'.[33] International legal scholars like Antony Anghie and Martti Koskenniemi have brought to light the violence of the 'civilizing mission' of international law in the colonial and post-colonial age; the language of rights comes with the risk of domination.[34] Anne Orford explains how history as *critique* involves a heads-on confrontation with—in her words—the 'willed forgetting of international law's imperial past'.[35] She explains how the colonial conception of sovereignty continues 'to shape international law in the post-colonial era'.[36] This perspective helps us discern that many of today's problems in the Global South are 'the *effects* of a historically constructed global political and economic system'. This sensitivity is crucial in order to prevent that the institutionalisation of domination continue today, for example in a United Nations or International Monetary Fund (IMF) and World Bank context where global policies are developed and international law is shaped.[37]

[27] Antony Anghie, *Imperialism, Sovereignty and the Making of International Law* (CUP 2004).

[28] Wallach Scott (n 14).

[29] Doing history is doing politics. See, eg Arnulf Becker Lorca, *Mestizo International Law: A Global Intellectual History 1842–1933* (CUP 2015) 16, 22–24. Anne Orford argues that 'historical work is itself a politics': Orford, 'International Law and the Limits of History' (n 9) 311.

[30] Paul Veyne, 'Foucault Revolutionizes History' in Arnold Davidson (ed), *Foucault and His Interlocutors* (University of Chicago Press 1997) 146.

[31] Becker Lorca (n 29) 15; See also Skouteris (n 18).

[32] Martti Koskenniemi, 'The Politics of International Law' 1 European Journal of International Law (1990) 4.

[33] David Kennedy, *The Dark Sides of Virtue: Reassessing International Humanitarianism* (Princeton University Press 2004) 329.

[34] Antony Anghie (n 27); see also Martti Koskenniemi, 'International Law and the Emergence of Mercantile Capitalism: Grotius to Smith' in Pierre-Marie Dupuy and Vincent Chetail (eds), *The Roots of International Law* (Martinus Nijhoff 2013) 3–37.

[35] Anne Orford, 'The Past as Law or History? The Relevance of Imperialism for Modern International Law' (2012) Institute for International Law and Justice Working Paper 2012/2 <https://ssrn.com/abstract=2090434> accessed 12 August 2019.

[36] ibid 2. A Third World Approach scholar like BS Chimni has also pointed to the negative consequences of treating the past as history. It would create blindspots for how colonialism-imperialism shaped contemporary international law. While I share his desire to prevent these blindspots and to reveal this impact, I would argue that doing history and theory enables us to do this with credibility.

[37] ibid.

The unravelling of these long-time 'givens' has contributed to the much needed 'unsettling' of the orthodox, self-congratulatory histories of international law.[38] That said, most of the new histories of international law take up another 'given': international law as a necessarily imperialist force or project. While I take no issue with uncovering international law's role in domination and (economic) imperialism, I do challenge the necessity motivating these new histories. That would mean we would forego the possible added value of doing history and risk replacing one 'History' with another, closing off possible alternative pasts and futures.[39] Paraphrasing Wendt to comment on our current state of global capitalism: inequality is what we made of it.[40]

In the *Methodenstreit* regarding doing history of international law, Anne Orford calls upon lawyers to adopt deliberately and wholeheartedly anachronistic devices,[41] or—in Kemmerer's words—to employ 'radical anachronisms'.[42] In increasingly sharp language, Orford distinguishes the 'historical method' from what she calls the 'international legal method', where the latter is 'necessarily anachronistic'. In my view, this distinction is exaggerated. While I fully concur with Orford's critical agenda, I disagree with the caricature she makes of the Cambridge School's contextualist approach as necessarily 'conservative'[43] and thus without any critical potential.[44] In a more general sense, to make the past fully subservient to the present amounts to effacing the *historicity* of international legal thought; *history dissolves into theory* altogether. As such, *history as critique* fails in creating a *true dialogue between* past and present international legal thought. The past dissolves into a politics of the present and thus loses its dialogic force.

3. History for self-knowledge and an enlarged sense of possibility: History *and* theory

From my perspective, beyond 'history for history's sake' and 'history *as* mere theory' lies a third possible approach: 'history *and* theory of international law'. This represents a conversation between past and present international legal thought that questions the strict distinction between what is 'merely historical' and what is 'genuinely philosophical'.[45] For it to be a fertile conversation, it should start with doing good history, which in turn enables us to

[38] Orford, 'International Law and the Limits of History' (n 9) 310.

[39] It seems to replace one foundation with another while the Cambridge School has made a persuasive argument for doing anti-foundationalist history.

[40] Alexander Wendt, 'Anarchy is What States Make of it: The Social Construction of Power Politics' (1992) 46 International Organization 391.

[41] Orford (n 35); Orford, 'On International Legal Method' (n 9); Orford, 'International Law and the Limits of History' (n 9).

[42] Alexandra Kemmerer, '"We Do Not Need to Always Look to Westphalia ... " A Conversation with Martti Koskenniemi and Anne Orford' (2015) 17 Journal of the History of International Law 1, 2.

[43] Orford, 'International Law and the Limits of History' (n 9) 301: 'The conservative effects of history as method.'

[44] Kemmerer (n 42) 2: Jacob Katz Cogan has pointed out that many international law scholars 'focus only on the precursors to contemporary law, its institutions and actors, and seek merely to provide the law as it stands with an affirmative historical foundation.' Skinner is not affirmative history, on the contrary.

[45] Quentin Skinner, 'Interpretation and the Understanding of Speech Acts' in Quentin Skinner, *Visions of Politics Volume 1: Regarding Methods* (CUP 2002) 125.

question present international law and legal thinking and produce alternative theories. In my view, the Cambridge School approach may well facilitate such a conversation.[46]

The famous historian and philosopher RG Collingwood said that 'history is "*for*" human self-knowledge'.[47] Cambridge School historian Quentin Skinner builds on this insight. He says:

> [T]he very reason for regarding [. . .] histories [of ideas] as indispensably 'relevant', [is] not because crude 'lessons' can be picked out of them, but because the history itself provides a lesson in self-knowledge. To demand from the history of thought a solution to our own immediate problems is thus to commit not merely a methodological fallacy, but something like a moral error. But to learn from the past—and we cannot otherwise learn at all—the distinction between what is necessary and what is the product merely of our own contingent arrangements, is to learn the key to self-awareness itself.[48]

The point is firstly that, from doing history, we may learn how present international legal concepts result from past political choices. This means that doing history of thought is an opportunity to realise that the concepts we use are in fact not 'timeless'; they change over time. They are not inevitable and necessary, but contingent on a different (past) society—a specific historical and linguistic context within which they were used with a scholar's 'complex intention'[49] to address a timely problem or question. Doing history of ideas assists us in seeing how our beliefs and arrangements are 'the merest contingencies of our peculiar history and social structure'.[50] Doing history helps us realise that we live in a political but also legal world, that we have constructed through thinking—and thus doing—and to understand where possibilities lie for deconstruction and reconstruction. For history of international legal thought to be such a learning experience and to assist us in questioning our own assumptions, conceptualisations, and theories, the material initially needs to be distinctively historical. As such, the study of history offers the experience of an 'overwhelming element of contingency' and alienation (not in a teleological or pejorative sense). It is precisely the 'alien character' of past international thought, beliefs, and concepts as products of their time that makes them so 'relevan[t]' to our thinking about international law, and the questioning of it.[51] Doing history of thought crucially is about 'preventing' our current moral, political, and legal theories from, as Skinner puts it, 'degenerating into uncritically accepted ideologies'.[52]

Doing history of international legal thought creates a necessary *distance* from our own understandings, beliefs, assumptions, and theories about international law. Thus, it also offers a means to question these in a more self-critical manner and allows us to test them against 'alternative possibilities'.[53] With this self-critical perspective comes what Skinner

[46] 'History wishes to be objective but it cannot. . . . It wishes to make past events contemporary, but it must at the same time restore the distance and depth of historical remoteness': Paul Ricoeur, *History and Truth* (Charles Kelbley tr, Northwestern University Press 1965) 76.

[47] RG Collingwood, *The Idea of History* (Jan van der Dussen ed, rev edn, OUP 1993) 10; He gave the epistemological debate on doing history a definite hermeneutical turn.

[48] Quentin Skinner, 'Meaning and Understanding in the History of Ideas' in James Tully (ed), *Meaning and Context: Quentin Skinner and His Critics* (Princeton University Press 1988) 29, 67.

[49] ibid 63.

[50] ibid.

[51] Quentin Skinner, 'A Reply to My Critics' in James Tully (ed) (n 48) 231, 287.

[52] ibid 287.

[53] ibid 286.

calls an 'enlarged sense of possibility' of *changed* assumptions, conceptualisations, and theories.[54]

I return to this sense of possibility below. First, I would like to concentrate a bit more on the Cambridge contextualist approach to history by providing an example, while making three methodological points in passing.[55]

For history of international legal thought to have the alienating—and thus critical—force just mentioned, the method of interpretation must recognise that a classic text, for example Leibniz's 1693 *Praefatio* to his *Codex Iuris Gentium*,[56] was written in response to a specific political 'issue at stake' at the time. Therefore, reading such a historical text is not about learning timeless answers to 'perennial problems'.[57] To understand the text, its intellectual and political ideological contexts should be reconstructed. Additionally, the prevailing discursive conventions should be identified, in order to understand what Leibniz was *doing* by writing the text and developing his ideas. Leibniz lived during the disintegration of the Holy Roman Empire into what would become the modern Europe of sovereign states, which is characterised as a time of disorder, diplomatic confusion, and warfare. The traditional 'universal' legal order headed by Emperor and Pope was in disarray. Leibniz worked as a legal advisor to both the weakening Emperor and the emerging new actors on the international stage such as the Elector of Hannover, who wanted to be recognised as an international player. For Leibniz, the prime concern was the restoration of order and justice in Europe. In that context, Leibniz in the *Codex* argued for *relative* sovereignty for all those who were powerful enough to influence international affairs—that is, those who had a degree of military or treaty-making capacity. He also introduced *international* legal personality (a key doctrinal concept and tool of international law). As legal persons, *all of these new actors* counted as lawful and thus legitimate players at the international stage. At the same time, they were all conferred with the moral *and* legal *obligation* to comply with the demands of universal law and justice. A brilliant conceptual move.[58]

This brings me to my first methodological remark. A contextualist approach prevents oversimplified interpretation induced by meta-narratives.[59] In the late 1990s/early 2000s, the predominant narrative was (still) that the 1648 Westphalian Peace Treaties established a European order of *absolute* sovereign states and therewith the inter-state legal order. In light of this idea, an interpretation of Leibniz's 1693 text would have never allowed for the findings just mentioned. Contextualist studies of this text have contributed to a critique of the Westphalian Myth because it revealed the unfamiliar understanding of *relative* sovereignty and the *innovative* character of Leibniz's introduction of international legal personality. (What if this conception had taken hold all along?)

That leads to the second methodological remark. The Cambridge School approach avoids anachronisms, yet it allows us to recognise that a scholarly reconstruction of the context of a text and the identification of the author's intentions involves assumptions, understandings, beliefs, and theories that a scholar brings to the reading of the historical text. In other words,

[54] ibid 287.

[55] This example holds an implicit counterfactual—as history often does—but my concerns are elsewhere.

[56] Gottfried W Leibniz, 'Praefatio to the Codex Iuris Gentium' in Gottfried W Leibniz, *Leibniz: Political Writings* (Patrick Riley ed, CUP 1988) 165–76.

[57] Skinner (n 45) 3.

[58] Nijman (n 13).

[59] Skinner's contextualist approach was itself a methodological response to—and a break away from—the grand narratives of British imperialism and colonialism.

a subjective element exists when determining the 'relevant' or 'appropriate context' for an historical text's interpretation. As Skinner observes, '[t]here is no implication that the relevant context need be an immediate one'.[60] Denying that the present-day context marks the questions with which we turn to the past is scientifically obsolete. I turned to Leibniz' *Codex Iuris Gentium* wondering why he needed the concept of international legal personality because I was triggered by the vibrant debate on new actors and the subjects of international law in the late 1990s. Similarly, it is no coincidence that at a time of economic globalisation and violent capitalism, there is a marked revival of interest in the Dutch East and West India Company (VOC and WIC) and Hugo Grotius as a corporate lawyer of the VOC. Research on the legal history of the trade companies is an antidote to the forgetfulness regarding the dark history of Dutch trade wars and slave trade and their justifications. It is not uncommon for such research to be motivated by questions about the possibilities to hold multinational corporations accountable under international law for corporate injustices today. This so-called 'motivational presentism'[61] of course *impacts* our reconstructions. Perhaps more than Skinner, I would argue that contextual readings additionally generate new, different histories through time.

The third methodological remark goes to the critical potential of the contextualist approach by focusing on so-called 'evaluative-descriptive terms'.[62] These are terms that perform both a descriptive and evaluative function. As such, they are crucial disciplinary terms where thought and action meet and agency happens. They are used to legitimise 'untoward' action as moral and/or legal. An agent does something by using such a term; she manipulates an existing normative vocabulary to seek, for example, support for conduct that previously was not considered moral/legal. Analysing the use of such a term enables us to get a hold of conceptual innovation. Approaching the history of ideas, in a Wittgensteinian sense, as the history of the *use* of ideas or concepts enables us to wonder what is done in using these concepts in context.

This is particularly relevant when it comes to intellectual history of international legal thought where the legal practice or argumentation is all about using existing concepts to legitimise conduct and if needed to change their meaning and therewith change what is legitimate practice. International law concepts may thus be used to perform a particular (linguistic) task within a timely context to address a timely problem. History of international legal thought then is about what international law scholars were *doing in* using these core concepts in their intellectual context. As such, interpretation highlights choice and agency, strategy and tactics.[63]

With the introduction of 'international legal personality', Leibniz coined such a term for international law. As fundamental *and* ambiguous concepts of political or legal thinking, these terms are the *locus* of change: their meanings are contested, 'manipulated' and

[60] Skinner (n 45) 116. He explains in 1988 in 'A Reply to my Critics' and in 2002 even more concisely that '[t]he *appropriate* context for understanding the point of such writers' utterances will always be *whatever context enables us to appreciate the nature of the intervention* constituted by their utterances. To recover that context in any particular case, we need to engage in extremely wide-ranging as well as detailed historical research.'

[61] David Armitage, 'Modern International Thought: Problems and Prospects' (2015) 41 *History of European Ideas* 116, 119.

[62] Quentin Skinner, 'Some Problems in the Analysis of Political Thought and Action' in James Tully (ed) (n 48) 97, 112; Nijman (n 13) 23.

[63] Here we also find an implicit possibility for counterfactualism.

'moving', and create change in a thought system as a whole.[64] 'International legal personality' has been such a place of political struggle over the international legal system and the moral identity of international society.[65] This is visible in the work of Leibniz, whose political agenda and theory of universal justice as, in his words, 'wise charity' were the drivers for his introduction of the concept of international legal personality. It meant to ground a new *universal* system of law and justice that applied to European, Chinese, Indian, and Russian rulers alike and obliged them to rule justly—that is, wisely and charitably.

In the nineteenth century, another struggle over who did and did not 'count' in international law defined the use of international legal personality as a legal concept. By denying full international legal personality to so-called 'uncivilised' nations, international law was reinforced as a system of domination and subordination, while the injustices of colonisation and exploitation were facilitated. In the twentieth century, Hersch Lauterpacht among others focused on international legal personality (or in his time: the subjects of international law) in order to argue for radical change of the international legal system. Lauterpacht held that the human individual, not the 'State', was the true international legal person with rights and duties in international law. These intellectual histories challenge us to question the politics and morality of today's conception of international legal personality. Thus, a historical inquiry into a fundamental concept turns into an inquiry into the politics and justice concerns behind the conceptual innovations or commitments of today.

As such, *doing history* opens up a critical space for dialogue between past and present international legal thought, which enables us to question our present-day conceptions underlying politics and notions of justice. Subsequently, this allows us to theorise change of present-day international law and international legal thought.[66] This is the philosophical value of *doing history* of international legal thought.

Skinner describes this as 'a kind of exorcism' that historical inquiry offers to prevent our thinking from 'fall[ing] under the spell of our own intellectual heritage' and be paralysed by it. He calls upon us to 'do our own thinking [for the future] for ourselves'.[67] Residing at the interface of history and theory/philosophy provides an opportunity to liberate our capacity for imagination from the constraints—now recognised—that past thought and beliefs place upon our thinking (and doing):

> An understanding of the past can help us to appreciate how far the values embodied in our present way of life, and our present ways of thinking about these values, reflect a series of choices made at different times between possible worlds. This awareness can help to liberate us from the grip of any one hegemonial account of those values and how they should be interpreted and understood. Equipped with *a broader sense of possibility*, we can stand

[64] The study of these fundamental concepts as places of political struggle gives us insight into how conceptual change happens, how concepts change while moving through time, and where and how 'ideological innovation' is sought.

[65] Skinner (n 62) 112: 'It is essentially by manipulating this set of terms that any society succeeds in establishing and altering its moral identity.'

[66] The subjectivist dimension of contextual readings recognises the generation of new, different meanings through time. It suffices to add here that theorising change may be fostered by including what Paul Ricoeur called the acquired 'public meanings' of a historic text. Paul Ricoeur has taught us that any text always has more meaning than the one intended by the author. See Ricoeur (n 46).

[67] Skinner (n 48) 66.

> back from the intellectual commitments we have inherited and ask ourselves in a new spirit of enquiry what we think of them.[68]

Here, intellectual history moves into the domain of political philosophy and possibly of politics. It creates a conception of historical or political change that allows for both structures and agent—*what the past gives us, is not such a 'given' after all.*[69]

I think this is really where Quentin Skinner and Robertò Mangabiera Unger meet. Doing history of political or international legal thought—and therewith the experience of contingency—provides us with an awareness that comes very close to the empowerment Unger is after: realising that our present social arrangements are not necessary or natural but socially constructed. Therefore, these social arrangements can be deconstructed and/or reconstructed provided that such 'social reconstruction [does not] fail to respect our nature',[70] which in this sense refers to 'who we are, and how we can and should remake ourselves. The living person lies at the center of these ideas as the agent and the result, the subject and the object of history.'[71]

Unger's image of 'frozen politics' for domestic society and institutions applies equally to international society and institutions.[72] Doing international legal history—and thus taking a lesson in self-knowledge—provides us with a critical stance towards our theories and assumptions and towards our social arrangements and institutions; it empowers us to reconstruct them. As Unger says: 'We are our fundamental practices. But we are also the permanent possibility of revising them.'[73] In Skinner's words, '[w]e may be freer than we sometimes suppose.'[74] Doing history then produces awareness of the contingency of received beliefs, values, and institutions, and as such produces a sense of possibility—and arguably—responsibility. It suggests/recognises a capacity to reimagine and act. It is transformative and empowers to establish (institutional) change and get our (global) act together.[75] This is an empowerment we desperately need.

IV. Seeking change by doing history

If I claim that 'history and theory' projects are also about the present and about theorising change, it is only fair to say something about my own normative interests or the change I would be seeking.

[68] Skinner (n 45) 6.

[69] Roberto Mangabeira Unger, *False Necessity: Anti-Necessitarian Social Theory in the Service of Radical Democracy* (new edn, Verso 2001) xxviii: 'What seems to be given and presupposed is merely what we have temporarily refrained from challenging and remaking.'

[70] Unger explains his ambition very clearly: 'We must explain society and history in a way that takes the fate institutions impose on society and on us as decisive but not definitive: for real, but not for keeps. Then we shall already be doing transformative politics in the mind even before we have begun to do it in society.' ibid xxvii.

[71] ibid.

[72] ibid xxviii.

[73] ibid 351.

[74] Quentin Skinner, 'Introduction: Seeing Things Their Way' in Quentin Skinner, *Visions of Politics Volume 1: Regarding Method* (CUP 2002) 7.

[75] cf Moyn, in this volume. Doing history and theory in the way I argue here adds another productive use of contingency to this list.

I would like to engage with this question while drawing on recent research on Hugo Grotius' understanding of the human subject, society, and law. Reading Grotius and Hobbes together provided a means to ensure that I did not uncritically accept the so-called 'Westphalian model' of the international legal system, which is grounded on a Hobbesian anthropology. Rather, it allowed an experience of 'an enlarged sense of possibility' and to theorise an alternative conception of international law and justice that is based on the social or intersubjective nature of international life.

Hobbes transposed what he conceived of as the characteristics of humans living in a state of nature—solitary, fearful, distrustful, and pre-emptively aggressive—to the state agent in international affairs. The fully autonomous, self-interested and shrewdly calculating state then has defined the liberal tradition: self-preserving and self-serving actions are by definition legitimate. International life is nothing more than a perpetual struggle for survival. The so-called Westphalian model of sovereignty and international order then has effectuated a strict separation between subjects of law and justice within the territorial state—mostly its citizens—and outside the state. Justice only exists *within* the state, not *among* states. International law and institutions then are merely pretextual.

I have two problems with this reading. Firstly, in my view, the emphasis on Hobbes is unwarranted and has set mainstream positivist thinking about international society and international law on the wrong track.[76] All the more so—and this brings me to my second contention—as the globalised and hyperconnected world of today demands an alternative for the traditional Westphalian, let us say Hobbesian, model.

For Grotius, humans are not solitary but social creatures by nature. They have the capacity to reason, will freely, care, make a promise, and keep their word.[77] As such, they are capable of being trustworthy and acting responsibly, individually and collectively. In Grotius' understanding, international society is also a natural society of subjects or agents seeking personal as well as impersonal—that is, institutionally mediated—relations. International legal thought that builds on Grotius' insights thus tends to explain international law and institutions as developing *naturally* from social life, enabling production of trust and solidarity. *Naturally* in this context does not refer to being 'necessary'; it is rather meant to describe the natural capacity of human judgement of what serves the social.[78] Notwithstanding the ambivalence of Grotius' thinking, the recovery of his anthropology of the capable subject is an important counterpoise to the prevailing Hobbesian anthropology of contemporary international law; it creates the earlier mentioned 'enlarged sense of possibility' about international society and international law. Bringing Grotius into a conversation with the philosophical anthropology or 'hermeneutics of the self' of the French philosopher Paul Ricoeur[79] helps us theorise and operationalise human potentiality in this respect.

[76] Again, there is an element of implicit counterfactualism here.

[77] Grotius' theorisation of the capable subject was in a way an early modern version of what we deal with today as the necessity/contingency debate: in his days, the predestination and salvation debate—and the possible role of human will on (determination of) salvation—was central. See Janne Nijman, 'Grotius' *Imago Dei* Anthropology: Grounding *Ius Naturae et Gentium*' in Martti Koskenniemi and others (eds), *International Law and Religion: Historical and Contemporary Perspectives* (OUP 2017) 87–110.

[78] Anthony Carty and Janne Nijman (eds) *Morality and Responsibility of Rulers: European and Chinese Origins of a Rule of Law as Justice for World Order* (OUP 2018) In this book, Carty and I reconceive natural law thinking as found in Grotius in terms of the natural judgement of humans.

[79] Paul Ricoeur, *Oneself as Another* (Kathleen Blamey tr, University of Chicago Press 1992); Paul Ricoeur, *The Course of Recognition* (David Pellauer tr, Harvard University Press 2005)

Drawing on Ricoeur, I argue for a reconceptualisation of 'international legal personality' as a stage in the phenomenology of the human subject, as the ethico-legal identity of humans.[80] I concur with Ricoeur on the point that human desire for the good life includes the desire 'to live well with and for others in *just* institutions'.[81] International legal personality then is reconceived as a dimension of the capable human subject, who seeks just institutions to constitute selfhood reflexively through relations with others.[82] In my view, Ricoeur's philosophy helps us conceive of international law and institutions as ways to mediate mutual recognition and respect globally and to effectuate international or transnational social life. There are obvious reasons—both for normative and explanatory power—to move from the understanding of international life as a struggle for survival to its understanding as a struggle for mutual recognition.[83]

As a second and related point, in today's hyperconnected and globalised world, I would argue that the human desire for life together in just institutions moves rapidly beyond so-called Westphalian, modern territorial state-based thinking and traditional notions of citizenship to a scale that includes international or global institutions. I see this paradoxically confirmed in the current backlash against these institutions. For example, disappointment with the EU and with neo-liberal global trade regimes that fail to safeguard social justice. The traditional notions and beliefs that define our thinking today rely on past, highly contingent political, moral, and legal thought. *Doing history* such as the history of the international economic order undermines the current neo-liberal beliefs and arrangements as necessary. They are a form of 'frozen politics' and therefore challengeable on the basis of our 'exorcised' or scrutinised politics and justice concerns. For me, this is where Ricoeur and Unger come together and where the reimagination of *just* institutions—and thus an alternative future—becomes available to us.[84] It is where doing history offers a space for the human subject capable of reimagination. Drawing on Erasmus, Grotius, Ricoeur, Skinner, and Unger we find a space for responsible human agency between necessity and hyper-contingency.

Being self-critical in relation to past thought challenges us to do 'our thinking for ourselves'. This is a necessary, albeit not a sufficient, condition for change. The first step to an alternative future for international law is an enlarged sense of possibility. Subsequently, a philosophical discussion is needed about our moral, political, and legal values for the future. We can then do our thinking with new, enlarged horizons of expectation.[85]

[80] Janne Nijman, 'Paul Ricoeur and International Law: Beyond "The End of the Subject"—Towards a Reconceptualization of International Legal Personality' (2007) 20 Leiden Journal of International Law 25.

[81] Ricoeur, *Oneself as Another* (n 79) 239; Paul Ricoeur, *The Just* (David Pellauer tr, Chicago University Press 2000) 1–10.

[82] Nijman (n 80) 25–64.

[83] Understanding international life as a struggle for recognition rather than for survival helps us better understand international relations and the possibility of international law. It remedies, moreover, the traditional obfuscation of international theorisation. International theory in the sense of speculation about relations between states becomes *possible*. Martin Wight, 'Why is There No International Theory?' in Herbert Butterfield and Martin Wight (eds), *Diplomatic Investigations: Essays in the Theory of International Politics* (Allen and Urwin 1966) 33.

[84] Both Ricoeur and Unger aim to bring our thinking beyond structuralism, naturalism, and positivism and allow for human freedom, human agency, and institutional reimagination and reconstruction. If human existence is a gift that unfolds in a constructed social world, looking back provides us with the realisation that what limits our freedom today can be cast off.

[85] Ricoeur draws on Koselleck in *Time and Narrative Volume 3* (University of Chicago Press 1990).

V. Conclusion: Between cynicism and commitment

'This Cannot Be How the World Was Meant to Be.' Philip Allott's words bespeak a disappointment with the world as he found it. Here the citation points to a general dissatisfaction with international law and international legal historiography that actuated the field of 'History and Theory of International Law'.

I have argued that doing history is not merely about understanding past and present-day international legal thought; it is also about seeking change. It is about stepping outside old assumptions, conceptualisations, and theories, and about creating a critical space to question them and then theorise alternatives in order to *change* international law and society.

Allott's complaint may reflect one part of what Martti Koskenniemi has described as an inherent condition of the international law profession: the life-time oscillation 'between commitment and cynicism'.[86] On one side, there is commitment to international law and institutions because of their potential for emancipation and justice. On the flip side, there is looming cynicism, or at least profound doubt, because of the dark sides of international law. I agree with Koskenniemi that we cannot escape these two positions, but that is not the same as being trapped. For the international lawyer doing history, this oscillation is no longer unreflective. Freely and consciously navigating the critical space that has opened up between present and past international legal thought, the international lawyer is able to situate herself historically and orient herself morally and politically to new horizons when reimagining international law and institutions.

[86] Martti Koskenniemi, 'Between Commitment and Cynicism: Outline for a Theory of International Law as Practice' in Martti Koskenniemi, *The Politics of International Law* (Hart Publishing 2011) 271–93.

B.

SITUATED PERSPECTIVES & POSSIBILITIES

7

Contingencies in International Legal Histories

Origins and Observers

Filipe dos Reis

I. Introduction

The so-called 'turn' to history and historiography in international legal scholarship[1] puts in place, on the one hand, a *return* of history into the discipline as it can be found in traditional accounts already.[2] On the other hand, however, it is also a *turning away* from the specific 'use' of history in traditional, earlier histories. Such traditional accounts of the history of international law are portrayed, exceptions notwithstanding, as lacking engagement with and reflections upon their mode of history production. However, the emerging body of new international legal histories does not only provide fresh accounts of international law's past(s) but, as we are told, opens up, if done rightly, new avenues of critique and emancipatory futures. The more recent interest in international legal histories has motivated *some* scholars to tackle broader conceptual and theoretical themes as well.[3]

This is where discussions about contingency and the history of international law might emerge. As Nicholas Onuf observed some time ago, international legal histories, old and new, are linked (often implicitly) to discussions of contingency: the history of international law can be reconstructed as a 'long history of confronting contingency'.[4] For Onuf, international law's history is linked to contingency for two reasons. Firstly, international law exists under conditions of contingency. Onuf draws here on Hegel's discussion (in the *Philosophy of Right*) of international law (*äußeres Staatenrecht*) and, in particular, Hegel's critique of Kant's idea of a federation of states. For Hegel, such a federation will hardly work as it 'presupposes an *agreement* between states. But this agreement ... would always be dependent on particular sovereign wills, and would therefore continue to be tainted by contingency [*Zufälligkeit*]'.[5] Within international theory, this theme has been explored

[1] Matthew Craven, 'Theorising the Turn to History in International Law' in Anne Orford and Florian Hoffmann (eds), *The Oxford Handbook of the Theory of International Law* (OUP 2016); George Rodrigo Bandeira Galindo, 'Martti Koskenniemi and the Historiographical Turn in International Law' (2005) 16 European Journal of International Law 539; Alexandra Kemmerer, 'The Turning Aside. On International Law and its History' in Russell A Miller and Rebecca M Bratspies (eds), *Progress in International Law* (Brill 2008) 71.

[2] Jean d'Aspremont, 'Critical Histories of International Law and the Repression of Disciplinary Imagination' (2019) 7 London Review of International Law 89, 90; David Kennedy, 'The Disciplines of International Law and Policy' (1999) 12 Leiden Journal of International Law 9, 88.

[3] This becomes visible, for example, in the publication of topic-related textbooks: cf Bardo Fassbender and Anne Peters (eds), *The Oxford Handbook of the History of International Law* (OUP 2012); Anne Orford and Florian Hoffmann (eds), *The Oxford Handbook of the Theory of International Law* (OUP 2016).

[4] Nicholas Onuf, '"Tainted by Contingency": Retelling the Story of International Law' in Richard Falk, Lester Edwin J Ruiz, and RBJ Walker (eds), *Reframing the International: Law, Culture, Politics* (Routledge 2002) 378.

[5] Cited in ibid 359; GWF Hegel, *Elements of the Philosophy of Right* (HB Nisbet tr, CUP 1991) para 333R.

Filipe dos Reis, *Contingencies in International Legal Histories* In: *Contingency in International Law*. Edited by: Ingo Venzke and Kevin Jon Heller, Oxford University Press. © The Several Contributors 2021. DOI: 10.1093/oso/9780192898036.003.0007

prominently (and been iterated) by various generations of political realists in their conceptualisation of the international as characterised by anarchy and the endless repetition of power politics, violence, and war.[6] Yet, such a conclusion does not necessarily follow from Hegel's original formulation, as for Hegel contingency outside of the sphere of the state is, as it would be framed in social theory from Parsons onwards, one of double contingency: the interaction and reasoning process between *ego* and *alter* (here, in the form of states). Such an understanding would make it possible to describe the international as a social situation—the core claim of Onuf's version of constructivism in international relations theory.[7] Secondly, contingency is for Onuf inscribed in the international legal field itself, both in the way it reconstructs its history and in its underlying logic of history. In this aspect, international law is no exception to other fields. As Onuf notes, 'every field of scholarship has a story about the field's origins and the large contours of its development'. He continues:

> Stories about fields emerge from within fields; they take on weight but not density. Without them scholars would be less certain of their field's distinctive character and its place in the world of learning. This is the reason we hear simple stories, easy to learn and marked by a relatively high degree of consensus. We might even expect such stories to take mythical propositions.[8]

In the case of international law, the story is usually linked to the story of modernity, particularly its Weberian version, where 'universal reason gave way to instrumental rationality, and natural law to positive law'—as an attempt to come to terms with the contingencies of modernity.[9]

There are, however, exceptions to the conventional Weberian narrative. Onuf presents David Kennedy's reflections on the link between history and authority in international legal scholarship as one of these exceptions. Kennedy explores the link between history and authority by reconstructing the varying relationship of authorship and (legal) authority in the history of international law: while early (or 'primitive', as Kennedy puts it) international legal scholarship invokes authority through direct reference to authors, modern texts derive their authority through the absence—the writing-out—of the author.[10] Moreover, Kennedy problematises how 'mainstream international lawyers use history' and identifies here two modes of argumentation, which he calls 'history-as-provenance' and 'history-as-progress': while the task of the former is to present, *inter alia*, a stable origin of the international legal enterprise, the latter argument unfolds in order to create the impression of its steady and linear progress.[11] Put differently, both modes of argumentation,

[6] RBJ Walker, *Inside/Outside: International Relations as Political Theory* (CUP 1993).

[7] For a reconstruction of the link between contingency and constructivism, see Oliver Kessler, 'The Contingency of Constructivism: On Norms, the Social, and the Third' (2016) 45 Millennium 43. For a discussion of the role of international legal theory within different strands of constructivism, see Filipe dos Reis and Oliver Kessler, 'Constructivism and the Politics of International Law' in Anne Orford and Florian Hoffmann (eds), *The Oxford Handbook of the Theory of International Law* (OUP 2016) 344.

[8] Onuf (n 4) 361.

[9] ibid 363–364. The observation that modernity is characterised by contingency led Weber to develop his theory of action. For a reconstruction of Weber's take on contingency, see Kari Palonen, *Das 'Webersche Moment': Zur Kontingenz des Politischen* (Springer 1998).

[10] David Kennedy, 'Primitive Legal Scholarship' (1986) 27 Harvard International Law Journal 1, 5–7.

[11] Kennedy (n 2) 88–94.

'history-as-provenance' and 'history-as-progress', are recurring *topoi* in the 'long history of confronting contingency' in international law.

In this chapter, I take this observation as my vantage point and explore the relationship between contingency and international legal histories on two levels. In the next section (II), I recast how arguments of contingency and origin work in international legal histories. Bearing in mind of telling too easy a story, I argue that we can identify two different, yet complementary, ways of conceptualising origin and contingency: contingency *of* origin and contingency *as* origin.[12] To develop an analytical vocabulary and to get some conceptual grip, I turn to some basic ideas developed in the writings of Hans Blumenberg and, to a lesser extent, Niklas Luhmann. Both Blumenberg and Luhmann examine the relationship between contingency and origin. Yet they do so differently: while Blumenberg's work is concerned with the ontotheological foundations of modern Western philosophical thought and the contingency of its origin, Luhmann's theory of social systems conceptualises contingency as the origin of social order through the interaction of *ego* and *alter*, ie, under conditions of double contingency. In other words, where Blumenberg emphasises the lack of determination of origins of our social world (as these origins could have been different), Luhmann reconstructs how the stabilisation of contingency is tied to communication processes—communication processes which are in particular mobilising (legal) norms. While most international legal histories are engaged in 'finding' the origin of international law (and here contingency is tied to the observation that this origin could have been different), some international legal histories take, in addition, the contingent encounter of *ego* and *alter* (in the form of, for example, peoples, states, and empires) as the origin—here contingency becomes a productive force in order to create the origin of an international (legal) order.

Section III explores then more briefly, and again with the danger of oversimplification, arguments of progress in international legal histories—arguments in the context of 'history-as-progress'—by focusing on the interplay of what is observed and the position of the observer, and how this relate to contingency. In other words, I inquire into the observance of contingency—and the contingency of the observer—when it comes to writing international legal histories. Inquiring into the contingency of the observer means to problematise the role and position of the scholar when writing history. Inquiring into the observance of contingency means to problematise the contingency of history itself. To be sure, and this is what I seek to emphasise, both hang together. Here again, Blumenberg and Luhmann are helpful as both connect their discussions of contingency (the observance of contingency) with a problematisation of the position of the observer (the contingency of the observer).

I argue that in the work of more traditional international legal scholars (including both the more positivist and naturalist inclined ones), the use of history is usually intertwined with the history of international law as, for example, knowing the history of international law helps to identify custom or to improve treatises. Moreover, for these accounts, being part of the project of international law results in telling the history of international law as a linear and (quasi)teleological history of success and progress. In the end, contingency can be excluded by making international law 'better'. More recent historical studies in international law take this as their starting point and seek to destabilise this narrative of

[12] I take this distinction from Rüdiger Campe, 'Contingencies in Blumenberg and Luhmann' (2012) 158 Telos 81.

steady progress by, for example, reflecting upon the Eurocentric nature of their field or by foregrounding events instead of linearity and historical structures. In other words, these accounts use history in order to show the contingency of international law. What remains nevertheless often unconsidered—even in 'critical' international legal histories—is the contingency of the observer of these histories, ie, the contingent position of who writes these histories.

Section IV concludes the chapter with a brief discussion of what it could mean to open international legal histories for different conceptualisations of origin, and to give up the idea of progressive history and the firm standpoint of the observer at the same time, namely to conceptualise origin, observer and observed as contingent.

II. Contingency of origin, contingency as origin in international legal histories

The question of international law's historical origin(s) has attracted much attention during the history of international law itself. International legal histories, new and old, have devoted much energy 'finding' the right answer. The identification of origins helps not only to legitimate (or criticise) the project of international law as it creates narratives of adequate (or questionable) provenance, but is also intertwined with such fundamental questions as when is international law 'law' and when is law 'international'.[13] Put differently, histories of and debates about the origins of international law are concerned with the ontological status of both the 'international' and 'law' in 'international law'. Their function is to provide a stable ground(ing) for subsequent, more systematic inquiries into the field. This makes them very much debates and histories of the present, of today's politics of international law.[14]

It is the question of origins, and how origin relates to contingency, that concerned much of the work of the German philosopher Hans Blumenberg. Blumenberg's approach is historical, with a core interest in the epochal change of worldview that came along with the emergence of the modern age (*Neuzeit*). For Blumenberg, contingency 'is one of the few concepts of specifically Christian decent in the history of metaphysics'.[15] Whereas the medieval cosmology was characterised by necessity and the idea that a Christian God guarantees the homogeneity of reality, this has shifted fundamentally with the emergence of the modern world. The omnipotence of a late-medieval God is not available anymore. This shift is a 'stepping-out of the "universe of taken-for-grantedness"'; it is a 'turning of all characteristics of taken-for-grantedness of reality into contingency'.[16] Thus, as Blumenberg writes, the 'post-Christian age' is characterised by a 'culture of contingency': the 'basic idea' is now

[13] cf Craven (n 1). Moreover, the 'search for origins' is part boundary drawing exercises between different strands of international law. For a discussion of what this means in the context of international criminal law, see Immi Tallgren, 'Searching for the Historical Origins of International Criminal Law' in Morten Bergsmo, Yi Ping, and Cheah Wui Ling (eds), *Historical Origins of International Criminal Law*, vol 1 (Torkel Opsahl Academic EPublisher 2014) xi.

[14] cf Anne Orford, 'The Past as Law or History? The Relevance of Imperialism for Modern International Law' [2012] International Law and Justice Working Papers 2012/2 1; and Onuma Yasuaki, 'When Was the Law of International Society Born?–An Inquiry of the History of International Law from an Intercivilizational Perspective' (2000) 2 Journal of the History of International Law 1, 2–7.

[15] Hans Blumenberg, 'Kontingenz' in Kurt Galling (ed), *Die Religion in Geschichte und Gegenwart*, vol 3 (3rd edn, Mohr 1959) 1793.

[16] Hans Blumenberg, *Wirklichkeiten in denen wir leben* (Reclam 1986) 46.

'that it has not to be, what is'.[17] Or, as Blumenberg defines contingency elsewhere, it is the 'judgment of reality from the standpoint of necessity and possibility'.[18] Contingency makes it possible *and* necessary for humans to construct their own reality (eg, through technology); a reality that could have been constructed differently. Blumenberg explains:

> The awareness of the contingency of reality is, however, the foundation of a technical attitude towards the given: if the given world is only an accidental instantiation from the infinite range of the possible, if the sphere of natural facts no longer produces higher justification and sanction, then the factuality of the world becomes the primary impulse not only to judge and criticize the real from the possible, but it becomes possible, by realizing what is possible and by using the range of what is possible to invent and construct, to justify the cultural world as consistent and necessary.[19]

It is the construction of reality where, as Campe recently summarised, the contingency of origin becomes central in Blumenberg, as 'the world may be structured this way or another; there can be this world or a different one; the world might even emerge or not'.[20] In the end, reality has multiplied; the modern age is composed of 'realities we live in'.[21]

Stories of and debates about the origin of international law have multiplied. In this section, I reconstruct several exemplary attempts of 'finding' international law's origin and how these debates are tied to different understandings of international law's history. Moreover, these stories are often encapsulated in larger controversies over the nature of the field. In particular, I identify and discuss in this section the following international legal histories and how they study the origin of international law: the traditional international legal histories of Arthur Nussbaum and James Brown Scott and the question of international law's founding figures; the early controversy between Wilhelm Grewe and CH Alexandrowicz on international law's Eurocentric origin; David Bederman's and Onuma Yasuaki's diverging attempts to decentre the origins of international law by pointing to multiple origins in time and space; and finally more recent inquiries of international law's Eurocentric origin as formulated by Antony Anghie and Arnulf Becker Lorca.

1. Origins in traditional international legal histories: finding founding figures

A first type of controversy can be found in more traditional accounts of international legal history. For decades, *A Concise History of the Law of Nations* by Arthur Nussbaum was probably the most-read history of international law. Formerly an expert in private international law and commercial arbitration, Nussbaum was forced to emigrate from Germany to the United States in the 1930s. The first edition of the *Concise History* was published in 1947, with a second edition coming in 1954. The book forms part of the international legal positivist tradition. It can be seen as an example of what Kratochwil described as at least on the

17 Hans Blumenberg, *Die Sorge geht über den Fluß* (Suhrkamp 1987) 57.
18 Blumenberg (n 16) 47.
19 ibid.
20 Campe (n 12) 89.
21 Blumenberg (n 16).

first view 'strange symbiosis'[22] between legal positivism and political realism in the aftermath of the Second World War, where international legal positivists like Nussbaum follow the rather 'grim' picture of international politics of realist scholars like Hans Morgenthau and thereby accept a limited role to international law. As a result, for Nussbaum, 'it is unwarranted to assume ... something in mankind like an innate idea of international law'.[23] International law is, instead, positive law, it is fabricated by states and 'govern[s] relations among independent states as such'.[24] Studying the history of international law can help to determine the scope and potential of international law as it would 'indicate the presumable line of evolution and eliminate extreme assumptions'.[25] Nussbaum focuses here mainly on treaties between states as well as diplomatic and doctrinal developments. Historical progress is presented as a long detachment of international law from morality and, importantly, religion. It is for this reason that Nussbaum attributes the origin of international law to Hugo Grotius, as Grotius 'made an important step toward the emancipation of international law from theology [as] his system was designed as one of secular and juristic international law. And international law can only be secular.'[26]

To conceptualise the origin of international law in terms of secularisation was further developed in the second edition of the *Concise History*, in which Nussbaum included an appendix discussing whether international law originated with Grotius or the Spanish scholastics.[27] Nussbaum's primary opponent in this regard was James Brown Scott, one of the central figures of international law in the United States during the first half of the twentieth century. Scott argued in a series of publications during the 1920s and 1930s that international law is of Spanish (and Catholic) origin, with the Dominican theologian Francisco de Vitoria as the 'founder of the modern law of nations'.[28] As Scott writes, 'Vitoria was a liberal. [...] He was an internationalist by inheritance. And because he was both, his international law is a liberal law of nations.'[29] For Scott, Vitoria is a liberal thinker as he included

[22] Friedrich Kratochwil, 'How Do Norms Matter?' in Michael Byers (ed), *The Role of Law in International Politics: Essays in International Relations and International Law* (OUP 2000) 254. This observation is, of course, only strange on the first view as legal positivism and political realism have much in common. This observation also mirrors what Judith Shklar had suggested earlier in her seminal study of 'legalism'. As Shklar notes, the 'realistic picture of politics is [...] that of legalism gone sour'. For Shklar, this is the case as a closer look reveals that realist scholars are using the same method as international legal positivists, their 'professed opponents', as they 'have simply applied the same type of arguments that legal theorists have used in separating law from morality to the task of preserving politics from both law and morality'. One consequence of this development consists for Shklar in an impoverished picture of both the concept of politics as well as the concept of law as 'politics' gets reduced to a permanent war-like struggle for power while 'law' is boiled down to an image of extreme formalistic legalism, Judith N Shklar, *Legalism: Law, Morals, and Political Trials* (Harvard University Press 1986) 126, 122–123. See also Tanja Aalberts and Ingo Venzke, 'Moving Beyond Interdisciplinary Turf Wars: Towards an Understanding of International Law as Practice' in Jean d'Aspremont, Tarcisio Gazzini, André Nollkaemper, and Wouter Werner (eds), *International Law as a Profession* (CUP 2017) 287.

[23] Arthur Nussbaum, *A Concise History of the Law of Nations* (The Macmillan Company 1947) 7.

[24] ibid 19.

[25] ibid 1.

[26] ibid 105. For further discussion on Grotius and secularism see John D Haskell, 'Hugo Grotius in the Contemporary Memory of International Law: Secularism, Liberalism, and the Politics of Restatement and Denial' (2011) 25 Emory International Law Review 269.

[27] Arthur Nussbaum, *A Concise History of the Law of Nations* (2nd edn, The Macmillan Company 1954) 296–306.

[28] See, in particular, James Brown Scott, *The Spanish Origins of International Law: Francisco de Vitoria and His Law of Nations* (Clarendon Press 1934); and James Brown Scott, *The Catholic Conception of International Law: Francisco de Vitoria, Founder of the Modern Law of Nations; Francisco Suárez, Founder of the Modern Philosophy of Law in General and in Particular of the Law of Nations—A Critical Examination and a Justified Appreciation* (Georgetown University Press 1934).

[29] Scott, *The Spanish Origins of International Law* (n 28) 280.

the 'American principalities—as equals of Christian States' in the 'international community'.[30] It is this international community, and not states, which is central in Vitoria's (and Scott's) conception of international law. 'The international community' of Vitoria is, as Scott explains, 'not a superimposed State; it is coextensive with humanity—no longer merely with Christianity'.[31] In the international community, 'law and morality should be one and inseparable'.[32] To re-coin international law in terms of natural law brings Scott to the conclusion that Hugo Grotius should be 'considered as a member of the Victorian or, as it is usually termed, the Spanish school', but not as the founder of international law.[33] Moreover, it helped Scott, as one commentator pointed out, to envision Vitoria 'as the perfect ideologue for the US's emergence on the international stage ... by arguing that the communality of an international legal order was inextricably tied to its claim to offer "a single moral standard" applicable to all humanity, contrasting it against the colonial division in the global order established by the European empires'.[34] Thus, tracing the origins of international law back to Vitoria or Grotius has substantial implications as it not only renegotiates the relationship between (international) law, morality, and religion but also situates the foundation of international law either in the religious wars in Europe or the 'discovery' of America.

2. Origins and Eurocentrism: early debates

A second change, which Nussbaum introduced with the second edition of his *Concise History*, was the divisions of chapters into epochs instead of centuries, as it was still the case in the first edition. Nussbaum adopted this mode of periodisation from Wilhelm Grewe. Grewe, a German international lawyer and diplomat, published several articles in the first part of the 1940s, culminating in an extensive monograph on *The Epochs of International Law* in 1944. The book remained unpublished until 1984.[35] However, after its publication, it would become 'the standard book on the history of international law', a book of 'exceptional importance and influence'.[36] Grewe's history of international law is inspired by Carl Schmitt's *Großraumlehre* and adopts from Schmitt, among other things, the idea that international law is embedded in concrete orders (*konkretes Ordnungsdenken*).[37] 'An international legal order', Grewe argues, 'is a plurality of relatively independent (although not necessarily equal-ranking) bodies politic which are linked to each other ... and which are not subject to a superimposed authority having comprehensive law-making jurisdiction and executive competence.'[38] As such, the concept of international legal order is not

[30] ibid 282.
[31] ibid 283.
[32] ibid 11a.
[33] ibid 9a–10a. It was this idea, which Nussbaum should refute when he wrote in response to Scott 'that there is not the least proof for the assertion that the Spaniards of the "Golden Age" were the founders of international law', Nussbaum (n 27) 306.
[34] Kojo Koram, 'The Vitorian Recovery and the (Re)Turn towards a Sacrificial International Law' (2018) 6 London Review of International Law 443, 447; see also Orford (n 14).
[35] The English translation was published in 2000: Wilhelm G Grewe, *The Epochs of International Law* (Michael Byers tr, de Gruyter 2000).
[36] Bardo Fassbender, 'Stories of War and Peace: On Writing the History of International Law in the "Third Reich" and After' (2002) 13 European Journal of International Law 479, 479, 480.
[37] For a discussion of the influence of Carl Schmitt and the intellectual heritage of the 'Third Reich' on Grewe's work, see Martti Koskenniemi, 'Review: The Epochs of International Law. By Wilhelm Grewe' (2002) 35 Kritische Justiz 277; and Fassbender (n 36).
[38] Grewe (n 35) 7.

restricted to modernity and the 'inter-State law of a society of sovereign and equal States is only one possible configuration of an international legal order'.[39]

According to Grewe, we can find various international legal orders in antiquity and outside of Europe. Yet Grewe does not further explore these orders as they did not have a direct line of continuation to modern international law. This is different in relation to medieval law—in particular, late-medieval law—and it is important, as Grewe claims, to understand the 'medieval foundations and origins of modern international law'.[40] According to Grewe, the Middle Ages were not, as is often assumed in the literature, dominated by the universal powers of Pope and Emperor—their authority being for Grewe rather symbolic than effective—but by a plurality of independent political communities and a non-hierarchical notion of law. Nevertheless, Grewe observes a clear break between medieval and modern international law. Modern international law emerged simultaneously with the modern state system and its two major innovations of diplomacy and balance of power thinking. Grewe understands the history of the modern state system, in turn, as a sequence of empires, which can be grouped into 'three political systems, which are referred to herein an abbreviated fashion as the Spanish, the French, and the British system, produc[ing] its own unique, self-contained international legal order'.[41] It was only during the British epoch in the nineteenth century that the originally European international law became a legal order of worldwide and, thereby, universal scale. The twentieth century, Grewe's own century, was at initially characterised by an American epoch and later by the confrontation between the two blocs of the Cold War. Read differently, international legal orders are for Grewe the direct outcome of political struggles and different international legal orders stand, in the end, not only for different (historical) epochs but also for different traditions of hegemony, expansion, and empire. Importantly, these different traditions are all Western traditions, expanding from (medieval) Christian-Europe to the 'rest' of the world, where this 'rest' is conceptualised as a passive recipient of universalised European ideas.

Grewe contrasts his view of modern international law originating in Europe and expanding and diffusing into a universal international legal order with the approach of CH Alexandrowicz, who presents, as Grewe puts it, a 'striking oppositional thesis'.[42] Alexandrowicz, a Polish international lawyer who spent a considerable time of his career in India and Australia and who would influence the first generation of 'Third-World Approaches to International Law' (TWAIL) scholars, developed a distinctively non-Eurocentric conception of international law. Alexandrowicz did so by turning to the history of international law and argued that international law was, until the rise of international legal positivism in the nineteenth-century, universal law. Thereby, Alexandrowicz inverts Grewe's argument that international law was initially particular and became universal in the nineteenth century only. To prove his point, Alexandrowicz reconstructs non-European origins and notions of such a universal international legal such as, for example, in the Kautilyan tradition in East Asia;[43] and focuses on the encounters of Christian-European

[39] ibid 8.

[40] ibid 39. See also ibid 37–136.

[41] Grewe (n 35) 23.

[42] Wilhelm G Grewe, 'Vom europäischen zum universellen Völkerrecht. Zur Frage der Revision des europazentrischen Bildes der Völkerrechtsgeschichte' (1982) 42 Zeitschrift für ausländisches öffentliches Recht und Völkerrecht 449, 469.

[43] CH Alexandrowicz, *An Introduction to the Law of Nations in the East Indies (16th, 17th and 18th Centuries)* (Clarendon Press 1967) 61; CH Alexandrowicz, 'Kautilyan Principles and the Law of Nations' (1965) 41 British Yearbook of International Law 301.

rulers with their periphery—for example, the controversy between the Teutonic Order and the Kingdom of Poland at the Council of Constance (1414–18) over Poland's relations to pagan communities in Lithuania as well as the 'confrontation' between European sovereigns and their counterparts in Africa and, in particular, East Asia from the sixteenth century onwards.[44]

Alexandrowicz studies mainly treaty-making and diplomatic relations and reconstructs that, for instance, East Asian and European empires formed a universal and non-discriminatory international law. East Asian sovereigns had considerable agency in the making of treaties and the conduct of diplomatic relations, and they could become full members of the family of nations. As Alexandrowicz argues '[n]either is it possible to subscribe (from the legal point of view) to the idea of "colonialism" as explanatory of European-Asian relations prior to the nineteenth century.'[45] Alexandrowicz draws a similar picture of the relations between European and African rulers as treaties 'had to be negotiated and concluded on the basis of legal notions which prevailed at the time of their negotiation and conclusion.'[46] It is only the rise of international legal positivism in the nineteenth century, particularly after the Congress of Vienna, that brought this regime of equal treaty-making to an end as positivism 'discarded some of the fundamental qualities of the classic law of nations, particularly the principle of universality of the Family of Nations irrespective of creed, race, colour and continent (non-discrimination)' and it is with positivism that international law 'shrank into an Euro-centric system'—becoming a *Jus Publicum Europaeum* and running in 'parallel lines with colonialism as a political trend'.[47] Alexandrowicz conceives this notion of a Eurocentric international law as an anomaly—an episode in the long course of international law—which, as he hopes, can be overcome by including the new states of the decolonial era. This would then recover a universal notion of international law. Alexandrowicz differs here not only from Grewe, but also, as we will see below, from other critical inquiries into international law's Eurocentrism.

3. Multiple origins: decentring in time and space

Some of the more recent international legal histories seek to radicalise or even move beyond previous ideas. For instance, one stream of scholarship attempts to locate the origin of international law radically outside of Western modernity by narrating the history of international law in terms of multiple centres and, subsequently, multiple origins. In this regard, David Bederman has extended the history of international law into antiquity, challenging thereby the assumption that 'international law is a unique product of the modern, rational mind'.[48] Bederman is able to date the origin of international law back into antiquity

[44] As a result, Alexandrowicz directs our attention away from the European 'discovery' of the Americas (and related discussions of Vitoria) in two ways. He shows, first, that discussions on the relationship between Christian and non-Christian communities did not originate with the 'discovery' of the Americas but can be found prior *inter alia* in Eastern Europe and he emphasises, second, the importance of Africa and, in particular, East Asia for international legal controversies during the first wave of the European expansion. See CH Alexandrowicz, 'Paulus Vladimiri and the Development of the Doctrine of the Coexistence of Christian and Non-Christian Countries' (1963) 39 British Yearbook of International Law 441; Alexandrowicz (n 43); CH Alexandrowicz, *The European-African Confrontation: A Study in Treaty Making* (AW Sijthoff 1973).

[45] Alexandrowicz, *An Introduction to the Law of Nations in the East Indies* (n 43) v.

[46] Alexandrowicz, *The European-African Confrontation* (n 44) 6.

[47] ibid.

[48] David J Bederman, *International Law in Antiquity* (CUP 2004) 1.

by anachronistically employing and broadening concepts, ideas, and practices such as sovereignty, state, state system, balance of power, customary law—and international law. For Bederman, international law presupposes what the English school tradition in international relations theory, particularly Hedley Bull, understood as a system of states (or international society).[49] By reviewing the three institutions of diplomacy, treaty-making, and warfare, Bederman identifies three such systems, namely in the Near East (2800–700 BCE), the Greek city-states (500–380 BCE), and the Roman empire (358–168 BCE)—each of them based on a different kind of rule of law.

Bederman opposes, thereby, two sets of arguments. Firstly, instead of being governed by one 'single, cohesive body of rules for a law of nations, recognized by all States in antiquity', antiquity was composed of a plurality of different bodies of international law.[50] This plurality was facilitated by the widespread idea that relations between these states need to be based on a rule of law. It means that a certain *problematique* (inter-state relations in a system of states) created its own solution (rule of law). Secondly, the different variations of international law of antiquity are not only spatially disconnected but also temporally. Thus Bederman avoids telling a story of continuity between antiquity and modernity. Instead, one has 'to accept the ancient law of nations in its own terms'.[51] Bederman's story is, however, not the only one of multiple origins and multiple centres.

Another important intervention is the 'intercivilizational perspective' developed by the Japanese jurist Onuma Yasuaki.[52] Compared to Bederman, Onuma's work is considerably more reflective in terms of the transhistorical and transregional transferability of core concepts of international law and politics. The 'intercivilizational perspective' criticises Eurocentric accounts of the history of international law as it 'assumes the coexistence of plural civilisations, each of which had a normative system', each ordering its own 'world', and each based on its own 'egocentric universalism'.[53] Onuma identifies three self-contained regional civilisations, namely the Sinocentric tribute system in East Asia, the Islamocentric system of the Muslim world, and the Eurocentric system of Christianity. For many centuries, these regional civilisations coexisted mainly in isolation. From the eighteenth century onwards, however, the Eurocentric system extended and confronted the Sinocentric and the Islamocentric systems. As a result of the collision of worlds, the Islamocentric system collapsed in the eighteenth century, with the Sinocentric system following one century later.

Moreover, towards the end of the nineteenth century, international law became complicit with European colonialism, with the Berlin Conference as its most striking example. It is only in this period that the previously regional normative system of (European) international law became the one governing the world, something coinciding with the expansion of the (European) international society:[54] 'International society covering the entire globe with international law valid in such a global society did *not* exist until the nineteenth century.'[55] This Eurocentric idea of international law gained authority, inter alia, through

[49] Hedley Bull, *The Anarchical Society: A Study of Order in World Politics* (3rd edn, Columbia University Press 2002); Bederman (n 48) 16.

[50] Bederman (n 48) 267.

[51] ibid 15.

[52] See, in particular, Onuma (n 14).

[53] ibid 7, 6.

[54] Like Bederman, Onuma follows mainly Hedley Bull's notion of international society: Bull (n 49); see Onuma (n 14) 57.

[55] Onuma (n 14) 63 (emphasis in the original).

a presentist reading, starting in international legal histories from the nineteenth century. As Onuma explains: 'What appeared ... was a *projection* of the predominant [Eurocentric] view *onto the past* by *assuming* that such a reality had been existing during the period of Pope Alexander VI, or even much earlier. In this *projective interpretation of history*, what Europeans believed to be universal in those days ... were assumed to be actually universal.'[56] However, to be aware of the construction of such universals might help, as Onuma hopes, to come to terms with the situatedness of the European perspective and open up other, non-European perspectives, thereby creating an 'intercivilizational perspective'—a perspective that different civilisations come with different world views—as the basis of a truly global international law.

4. Origins and Eurocentrism: recent debates

Finally, an increasing number of studies seek to develop explicitly non-Eurocentric histories of international law by locating the origin of international law at the (semi)periphery of Europe and within the encounter between the European and non-European world. Antony Anghie has been the most prominent exponent of such a position. For Anghie, international law 'was created out of the unique issues generated by the encounter between the Spanish and the Indians' in the fifteenth century, with Francisco de Vitoria as the founding figure of international law.[57] However, in contrast to Scott, who identified (with) Vitoria as a liberal internationalist, Anghie considers the Dominican theologist a pivotal figure in the legitimisation of European colonial rule over non-European peoples. According to Anghie, Vitoria was confronted with the 'novel problem of the Indians'.[58]

While Vitoria argued that universal natural law applies to the Indians as he characterises them as human and in possession of reason, he conceptualised them at the same time as culturally different. This includes practices, shaped by their culture, which violate Vitoria's notion of universal international law. These violations, in turn, provide the Spaniards and other Europeans with a just cause for waging war against the Indians and, in the end, colonial conquest. However, Anghie claims that these 'colonial origins of international law' are often overlooked, sometimes even written out of the history of international law.[59] This silence is in particular problematic as, for Anghie, '*imperialism is a constant*' throughout the whole history of international law, whether it concerns sixteenth-century natural law, nineteenth-century positivism, or the pragmatism of the late twentieth century.[60] Thus, in contrast to Alexandrowicz, who saw colonialism as a nineteenth-century exception of an otherwise universal international law, Anghie insists that colonialism has been the normal condition in the course of international law and that the root dichotomy between coloniser and colonised, which was introduced by Vitoria, structures—in different articulations (civilised vs uncivilised, developed vs undeveloped, etc)—the international legal discourse

[56] ibid 54.

[57] Antony Anghie, 'Francisco de Vitoria and the Colonial Origins of International Law' (1996) 5 Social & Legal Studies 321, 322.

[58] ibid.

[59] Anghie (n 57).

[60] Antony Anghie, *Imperialism, Sovereignty and the Making of International Law* (CUP 2004) 315 (emphasis in the original).

until the present day: 'The colonial origins of the disciplines are re-enacted whenever the discipline attempts to renew itself, to reform itself.'[61] Attempts of renewal and reform are thereby 'Vitorian moment[s]', namely moments in which international law helps to re-establish an order of difference between core and periphery.[62]

It is here where Arnulf Becker Lorca's recent global intellectual history of international lawyers from the semi-periphery takes its vantage point.[63] In contrast to Anghie, who studies the direct domination of the core over the periphery, Becker Lorca zooms into the role of the semi-periphery and the making of the global (or universal) legal order. Such a legal order originated rather late. According to Becker Lorca, 'international law started to acquire a global geographical scope' only from the mid-nineteenth century onwards.[64] On the one hand, this has been facilitated by the first wave of economic, military, and political globalisation, which had occurred during the nineteenth century; on the other hand, however, it is only from this period onwards that 'non-European lawyers appropriated European international legal thought and established, along with Western international lawyers, a global profession that articulated a transnational legal discourse'.[65]

Becker Lorca emphasises in this context the agency of semi-peripheral jurists and how they were able to change international law through an immanent critique of Western rules: 'Semi-peripheral jurists internalized European legal thought in order to change rules. In changing rules, however, they also transformed international law. International law became universal ... only when non-Western jurists internalized European legal thought.'[66] Concerning the origins of international law, this has two significant consequences. First, Becker Lorca refrains from discussing 'international law's deemed founding fathers, be they Vitoria, Grotius or Vettel, in the sixteenth, seventeenth and eighteenth centuries' and focuses instead on the 'work and life of non-Western jurists'.[67] Second, it becomes possible to tell a 'history of an international law with hybrid origins and multiple sites of articulation'.[68] While Becker Lorca still assumes a privileged Western position in the international legal discourse, he is able to excavate the agency of semi-peripheral lawyers from such diverse places as Russia, Greece, Morocco, China, Japan, Ethiopia and, in particular, Latin America. Eventually, it is only this plurality that creates a single global legal order.

5. Conceptualising contingency and origins

By introducing the innovative work of the German philosopher Hans Blumenberg on the link between contingency and modernity, this section reconstructed how international legal histories identify the origin of international law in various ways. Different authors, with different projects within the discipline of international law, situate international law within a range of different origins. Sometimes authors with different projects even use a similar origin: as we have seen, for instance, both Scott and Anghie present Vitoria as international

[61] ibid 313.
[62] ibid 305.
[63] Arnulf Becker Lorca, *Mestizo International Law: A Global Intellectual History 1842–1933* (CUP 2015).
[64] ibid 10.
[65] ibid 138.
[66] ibid 45.
[67] ibid 10.
[68] ibid 22.

law's founding father—yet, their 'use' of Vitoria could hardly be more different as Vitoria is presented either as a liberal internationalist (Scott) or as a supporter of European colonialism (Anghie). Consequently, the origin of international law is not 'found' by referring to neutral facts 'out there', but is rather encapsulated in narratives linking past origins with present projects.

In addition, and this is the case particularly in the context of the various (and variegating) attempts of crafting non-Eurocentric international legal histories, a second notion of contingency operates in the background—a notion of contingency *as* origin of international law. To recapitulate, Alexandrowicz reconstructs the confrontation between European and non-European (Asian and African) sovereigns through the lens of treaty-making *as* the origin of universal international law; Onuma conceptualises the translation process between different civilisations *as* the origin of a truly global international law; Anghie points to the encounter between Europeans and non-Europeans *as* origin of (colonial) international law; and, finally, Becker Lorca retrieves struggles between peripheral and semi-peripheral jurists *as* origin of a simultaneously global and hybrid legal order. In other words, international law can only originate under *and* through confrontations, translations, encounters, and struggles of its various actors under conditions of contingency.

Thus, rather than taking the contingency of international law's origin as a problem—as something that needs to be tamed through a new, yet impossible, attempt of providing a more stable grounding—such a notion conceptualises it as the condition of possibility of a (hierarchical) international order. With this notion, we are now able to complement—when linking contingency and origin—the notion of the contingency *of* origin through an understanding of contingency *as* origin. While the former notion of contingency foregrounds the lack of determinacy (as contingency) of modern social order(s), the latter reconstructs how social order(s) emerge and stabilise when facing contingency.[69]

Within social theory, such a notion of contingency has been developed most comprehensively in Niklas Luhmann's theory of social systems. Luhmann defines the concept of contingency as simultaneously 'excluding necessity and impossibility. Something is contingent insofar as it is neither necessary nor impossible; it is just what it is (or was or will be), though it could also be otherwise.'[70] This is encapsulated in the idea of 'double contingency', ie, the encounter between *ego* and *alter* where (contrary to Mead) '*both* partners experience *double* contingency and that the indeterminability of such a situation for *both* partners in *any* activity that then takes place possesses significance for the formation of structures'.[71] Put differently, Luhmann is able to conceptualise contingency *as* origin because norms are the result of the evolutionary communication process between *ego* and *alter*; they do not (contrary to Parsons) exist prior to the interaction itself. Thereby, the emergence of norms (and a legal system) is one solution to the problem of double contingency, as 'norms restrict the contingency of the restriction of contingency, namely as they consolidate a proven consolidation of the arbitrary use of signs'.[72] Normative expectations 'bind' contingency in a certain way since norms remain valid even in the case of non-compliance. Hence, norms (and, in particular, the normative expectations of law) are part of an evolutionary process.

[69] Campe (n 12).
[70] Niklas Luhmann, *Social Systems* (Stanford University Press 1995) 106.
[71] ibid 108. I limit my analysis here to double contingency. For a discussion of 'triple contingency', namely that ego and alter are observed during their interaction by a 'third' in the form of social imaginaries, see Kessler (n 7) 57.
[72] Niklas Luhmann, *Das Recht der Gesellschaft* (Suhrkamp 1995) 128.

III. Observing progress, observing contingency in international legal histories

Within international legal discourse, the consolidation of norms is usually linked to a progressive history of international law. In this section, I recast arguments in the context of what David Kennedy has coined 'history-as-progress' by reconstructing the interplay of the observance of contingency and the contingency of the observer in international legal histories. Thus, I seek to problematise how and from where contingency is observed in international legal histories. I turn first to traditional international legal histories—and here Lassa Oppenheim's canonical account will serve as my example—and argue that this kind of scholarship separates and isolates the observer from what is observed: a 'neutral' observer analyses and finally tames the contingent course of international law. I then examine strategies of more recent international legal scholarship to destabilise narratives of international law's linear progress.

1. Progressive narratives of international law

As was the case with the question of international law's origins, Blumenberg and Luhmann provide us with conceptual tools when it comes to reconstructing how contingency is observed (and tamed) in progressive narratives of international law, as both theorise the role and figure of the observer by relating it to contingency. Blumenberg discusses the relationship between observance and contingency in particular in his essay *Shipwreck with Spectator*.[73] In this short, innovative piece, Blumenberg studies different actualisations of the seafaring metaphor throughout the history of Western philosophical thought. In this metaphor, the sea stands in principle for the space of contingency, as it represents, on the one hand, the 'naturally given boundary of the realm of human activities' and, on the other hand, 'the sphere of the unreckonable and lawless'.[74] Thus, for example, in antiquity seafaring stands for a transgression of boundaries where a fixed observer (or 'spectator') on land observes the struggle of sailors against the shipwreck on a contingent sea. In the modern age, in turn, the observer attempts to transform the sea into land by constructing a ship, which seems protected against shipwrecks and provides thereby a stable and neutral position for the observer. With Nietzsche, however, this position becomes destabilised, and the observer becomes stuck in permanent shipwrecks, where no stable position can be found and where the position of the observer itself renders contingent in the end.

What is important here is that Blumenberg draws our attention on the different ways the position of the observer is constructed vis-à-vis contingency. Similarly to Blumenberg, Luhmann conceptualises the relationship between what is observed and the observer as dynamic. Luhmann couples observation with contingency through the notions of first and second-order observation. For Luhmann, observation means to make a distinction and to indicate one side (and not the other side) of the distinction. Thereby, every observation includes and excludes—and creates a blind spot. While first-order observation presupposes

[73] Hans Blumenberg, *Shipwreck with Spectator: Paradigm of a Metaphor for Existence* (Steven Rendall tr, MIT Press 1997).

[74] ibid 8.

its distinction when describing, second-order observation (as the observation of observation) reflects these distinctions—but only from a social or temporal distance. This also signifies that first-order observation is not able to observe the contingency of making a distinction, while second-order observation is so (through distance).[75] Through second-order observation, as Luhmann puts it, 'everything becomes contingent, when what is observed depends on who is being observed'.[76]

A good example of the construction of a seemingly non-contingent observer, who attempts to tame the contingency of international law, is the canonical work of the British legal positivist Lassa Oppenheim. Oppenheim argued more than a century ago in his contribution on the 'task and method' of the 'science of international law' that the science of international law is not an 'end in itself', meaning that its purpose is not restricted to academia, but that its task is to identify legal rules.[77] In Oppenheim's view, this task is crucial as *international* law, compared to its domestic ('municipal') counterpart, presents a relatively low degree of codification: important international legal rules are not codified but 'merely' exist as rules of customary law. In this context, one of the main tasks of international legal scholars concerns, according to Oppenheim, engaging in historical research. Writing in 1908, Oppenheim notes that the 'history of international law is virgin land which awaits its cultivators' and, therefore, 'a master-historian of international law has still to come'.[78] Such a 'master-historian' would help to *identify*, on the one hand, customary rules as s/he would help to 'know of each rule of international law how it originated and developed, who first established it, and how it gradually become recognised in practice' and, on the other hand, serve as a 'master-builder' for the international law of the future.[79]

For Oppenheim, to write the history of international law would even be part of a larger project, as it would be part and parcel of the 'history of Western civilization'. This is possible as:

> All important events in the development of the state system of Europe from the last part of the Middle Ages downward to the French Revolution have had their bearing upon the development, the shaping, and the ultimate victory of international law over international anarchy, and so have all important events in the development of the state system of Europe and America since the French Revolution. And the master-historian, to whose appearance we look forward, will in especial have to bring to light the part certain states have played in the victorious development of certain rules and what were the economic, political, humanitarian, religious and other interests which have helped to establish the present rules of international law. Thereby the factors will be laid bare which have driven the different states into the community called 'family of nations' that will comprise in time the whole of humanity.[80]

[75] Niklas Luhmann, 'Kontingenz als Eigenwert der modernen Gesellschaft' in Niklas Luhmann (ed), *Beobachtungen der Moderne* (Westdeutscher Verlag 1992) 99–100.

[76] ibid 100.

[77] Lassa Oppenheim, 'The Science of International Law: Its Task and Method' (1908) 2 American Journal of International Law 313, 314; on Oppenheim more generally, see Mónica García-Salmones Rovira, *The Project of Positivism in International Law* (OUP 2013).

[78] Oppenheim (n 77) 316.

[79] ibid 316, 317.

[80] ibid 317.

More generally, Oppenheim's work is illustrative for the way traditional scholarship uses 'history-as-progress' arguments—arguments which are not restricted to the international legal positivist tradition but can also be found in various other projects of international law.[81] Here, a non-contingent observer seeks to construct a non-contingent international law within the contingencies of international politics and anarchy. These attempts of construction are then tied to a linear history (sometimes told with a number of drawbacks) of human progress (often told in Eurocentric terms).[82]

2. Critical voices and the question of progress

More recently, 'critical' international legal histories have started to question the linear and progressive history which dominated the field for so long. Here, in particular, two strategies stand out.[83] First, there is a growing scholarship problematising the Eurocentric nature of traditional international legal histories. In the words of Martti Koskenniemi, 'traditional histories [of international law] are terribly Eurocentric'.[84] As we have seen in the previous section, the critique of international law's Eurocentrism can take different forms. What scholars such as Alexandrowicz, Onuma, Anghie, and Becker Lorca have in common, however, is the idea that the history of international law has multiple perspectives and trajectories—and that traditional international legal histories privileged only one of these perspectives and trajectories, namely the Western one or, more precisely, the one of a Western observer. Thus, excavating perspectives and trajectories of non-Western observers renders the contingency of Eurocentric international legal histories intelligible.

Second, various authors started to criticise linear progressive narratives of international law by treating its history as constituted by a sequence of contingent disruptive 'events'.[85] As Derrida reminds us, 'an event implies surprise, exposure, the unanticipated' and, as such, 'it must never be something that is predicted or planned, or even really decided upon'.[86] Seen through events, history has no overarching structure or logic as 'myriad localized contingencies determine history's shape'.[87] However, for international law, events are not only disruptive, but international law carries at the same time 'an imperative to account for, respond to, contain, incorporate and overcome' events and, as a consequence, these events then 'become part of international law's evolutionary narratives'.[88] However, these

[81] For a discussion of progressive imaginaries within the natural law tradition, see Geoffrey Gordon, 'Natural Law in International Legal Theory: Linear and Dialectic Presentations' in Anne Orford and Florian Hoffmann (eds), *The Oxford Handbook of the Theory of International Law* (OUP 2016) 279. For international law in general, see Thomas Skouteris, *The Notion of Progress in International Law* (Asser 2010).

[82] Martti Koskenniemi, 'Histories of International Law: Significance and Problems for a Critical View' (2013) 27 Temple International and Comparative Law Journal 215, 217; Jennifer Pitts, 'The Critical History of International Law' (2015) 43 Political Theory 541.

[83] For a systematisation of similar strategies of critique within (Historical) International Relations scholarship, see Joseph MacKay and Christopher David LaRoche, 'The Conduct of History in International Relations: Rethinking Philosophy of History in IR Theory' (2017) 9 International Theory 203.

[84] Koskenniemi (n 82) 222.

[85] Fleur Johns, Richard Joyce, and Sundhya Pahuja (eds), *Events: The Force of International Law* (Routledge 2011).

[86] Jacques Derrida, 'A Certain Impossible Possibility of Saying the Event' (2007) 33 Critical Inquiry 441, 441.

[87] MacKay and LaRoche (n 83) 214.

[88] Fleur Johns, Richard Joyce, and Sundhya Pahuja, Introduction' in Fleur Johns, Richard Joyce, and Sundhya Pahuja (eds), *Events: The Force of International Law* (Routledge 2011) 3.

narratives remain unstable as they are exposed to the contingency and the disruptive force of (potentially) new events.

IV. Conclusion

This chapter explored how contingency is situated in international legal histories. In particular, it focused on how contingency relates to narratives of origin and progress. In both types of narrative, contingency is related to an idea of counterfactuality, namely, that the history of international law could also have been otherwise. Emphasising the contingency of international legal histories thereby redefines the borders of what can be thought and done; contingency becomes inextricably linked to politics.[89]

The chapter started with a reconstruction of how traditional and recent international legal histories locate the origin of international law. As it has attempted to show, different authors—pursuing different projects within the discipline—situate international law within a range of different origins. In the end, the origin of international law is contingent. Moreover, it is possible for some authors, particularly those problematising international law's Eurocentric origin, to conceptualise the link of contingency and origin not only as the contingency of origin but as well in the form of a contingency as origin, as contingency becomes inscribed in the communication processes (as confrontations, translations, encounters, and struggles) of various actors of international law. In a second step, I have turned to the question of how international legal histories deal with the observance of contingency when they advance arguments in the context of 'history-as-progress'. Here, more traditional international legal histories often rely on an understanding of a non-contingent observer, who seeks to create an international legal order that is able to tame the contingencies of international politics and anarchy. However, such narratives of international law's linear progress have come under scrutiny more recently, as several interventions by 'critical' international legal histories direct our attention to the multiple perspectives and the multilinear trajectories in the making of the current international legal order or invite us to conceptualise the history of international law as a history of contingent disruptive events.

Yet, even in more critical international legal histories the contingency of the observer, ie, the contingent position of who writes international legal histories, remains rather unconsidered; at least under-theorised. Here, it is worthwhile to come back to Blumenberg for the last time as he was well aware that attempts to fix the position of the observer—whether through science, norms, or language—might not bring durable solutions. In this context, however, the following observation from Blumenberg's essay *Shipwreck with Spectator* might be one possible starting point for such a reflection:

> Thus to think the beginning means […] to imagine the situation without the mother ship of natural language and, apart from its buoyancy, to 'reperform', in a thought experiment, 'the actions by means of which we—swimming in the middle of the sea of life—could build ourselves a raft or even a ship.' The demiurgical, Robinson Crusoe longing of the modern age is also present in the handiwork of the constructivist who leaves home and heritage

[89] See also Filipe dos Reis and Janis Grzybowski, 'The Matrix Reloaded: Reconstructing the Boundaries between (International) Law and Politics' (forthcoming) Leiden Journal of International Law.

behind in order to found his life on the naked nothingness of the leap overboard. His artificially produced distress at sea does not come about through the frailty of the ship, which is already an end result of a lengthy process of building and rebuilding. But the sea evidently contains material other than what has already been used. Where can it come from, in order to give courage to the ones who are beginning anew? Perhaps from earlier shipwrecks?[90]

[90] Blumenberg (n 73) 78–79.

8

Historical Base and Legal Superstructure

Reading Contingency and Necessity in the *Tadić* Challenge

*Michele Tedeschini**

It didn't enter my mind just then that anything could be different than it was.[1]

International criminal law (ICL) is living a difficult moment,[2] so much so that some authors cast doubt on the future of its main institutional actor, the International Criminal Court.[3] It is therefore possible to imagine a near future in which ICL has become a matter of mere historical interest. And with history often comes a certain itch for counterfactuals.[4] Could it have been different? Could the international criminal justice machinery as it exists today never have come into being, so that a significant amount of resources, time, and careers would have been invested somewhere else?[5] It is the latter query that this chapter considers. It does so by revisiting a particular point in time in which the entire ICL project was at risk of collapsing, at least at first glance. I am referring to the challenge to the jurisdiction of the International Criminal Tribunal for the former Yugoslavia (ICTY, or 'the Tribunal') filed by the Tribunal's first accused, Duško Tadić, in 1995 ('the *Tadić* challenge'). As the focus of this contribution is limited to the (key) legal practice of (international) adjudication, also limited is its explanatory potential in historical terms. The analysis simply aims to suggest that in instances of groundless adjudication, ie where international law is called to pronounce on the foundations of the very practices it is expected to support, structure determines outcomes much more than human agency does.

I develop my argument in six sections, followed by some concluding remarks. Section I briefly outlines a set of methodological considerations informing my approach to the topic, considerations which are mainly drawn from Susan Marks's scholarship. Section II summarises those issues raised by the *Tadić* challenge that the contribution revolves around, pointing at the legal contingency of both the Trial Chamber's and Appeals Chamber's

* I am grateful to Jason Beckett, Laura Fischer, Kevin Jon Heller, Foivi Sofia Mouzakiti, Scott Newton, Amanjit Kaur Sharanjit, Ingo Venzke, and Daniel West for their comments on earlier drafts of this contribution. All errors are my own.

[1] Knut Hamsun, *Hunger* (Sverre Lyngstad tr, Canongate Books 2016, first Norwegian edition 1890) 147.

[2] Joseph Powderly, 'International Criminal Justice in an Age of Perpetual Crisis' (2019) 32 Leiden Journal of International Law 1.

[3] Douglas Guilfoyle, 'The Future of International Law in an Authoritarian World' (*EJIL: Talk!*, 3 June 2019) <https://www.ejiltalk.org/the-future-of-international-law-in-an-authoritarian-world/> accessed 3 June 2019.

[4] Jeremy Black, *Other Pasts, Different Presents, Alternative Futures* (Indiana University Press 2015) 19.

[5] See Elies van Sliedregt, 'International Criminal Law: Over-Studied and Underachieving?' (2016) 29 Leiden Journal of International Law 1.

Michele Tedeschini, *Historical Base and Legal Superstructure* In: *Contingency in International Law.* Edited by: Ingo Venzke and Kevin Jon Heller, Oxford University Press. © The Several Contributors 2021. DOI: 10.1093/oso/9780192898036.003.0008

decisions on the matter. Section III exposes instead the determining pressure that the historical context exerted on the judges, adhering to Marks's invitation not to neglect structural factors in historical inquiry. Section IV attempts to explain the judges' attitude by employing Pierre Bourdieu's notion of *habitus*, history made conscience which orients agents towards certain choices and away from others. Section V maintains that using the *habitus* as an explanatory tool causes the analysis of counterfactuals to constantly refer back to structure, even when focusing on the behaviour of agents. Section VI offers some theoretical remarks suggested by previous sections. In particular, it issues a reminder that any historical explanation is no more than a politically driven construct for which the author must assume responsibility.

I. Marks: contingency and necessity in particular contexts

In her instant classic on the subject, Marks tells us that the analysis of contingency and the analysis of necessity must be pursued in tandem.[6] For it is precisely to the extent that one obscures the other, that contingency and necessity become false, thereby partially tainting the intellectual endeavour.[7] As critics,[8] instead, our job is to investigate the world as an organic whole, struggling to explain the relationship that exists between structure and agency.[9] And it is only by reference to particular contexts, that the investigation is likely to fulfil its epistemic purposes.[10] Taking this latter reflection as an invitation, in this contribution I intend to apply Marks's methodological framework to the field of ICL. In particular, the analysis will focus on a 'context-breaking moment'[11] in the history of the discipline. Such an approach is by no means innovative, of course. The idea (or diagnosis) that international law functions as 'a discipline of crisis'[12] which evolves along patterns of events,[13] incidents,[14] moments of rupture,[15] has been a recurring theme of the last three decades of scholarly debate. Further to this conceptualisation, revisiting the event emerges as a preferential practice for critically informed legal historians.[16] This is because events cannot be completely grounded in societal foundations,[17] but rather stand out as figures of contingency[18]—sites of political contestation pointing to possible alternatives to what actually occurred.

When considering a given event, therefore, contingency should be relatively easy to spot. We can expect the event to involve certain actors entrusted with the power to make

[6] Susan Marks, 'False Contingency' (2009) 62 Current Legal Problems 1, 10.

[7] ibid 17.

[8] Susan Marks, 'Human Rights and Root Causes' (2011) 74 Modern Law Review 57, 74.

[9] Marks (n 6) 9.

[10] ibid 20.

[11] Martti Koskenniemi, 'Histories of International Law: Significance and Problems for a Critical View' (2013) 27 Temple International & Comparative Law Journal 215, 239.

[12] Hilary Charlesworth, 'International Law: A Discipline of Crisis' (2002) 65 Modern Law Review 377.

[13] Fleur Johns, Richard Joyce, and Sundhya Pahuja (eds), *Events: The Force of International Law* (Taylor & Francis Group 2010).

[14] W Michael Reisman, 'International Incidents: Introduction to a New Genre in the Study of International Law' in W Michael Reisman and Andrew Willard (eds), *International Incidents: The Law that Counts in Worldpolitics* (Princeton University Press 1988).

[15] Charlotte Peevers, *The Politics of Justifying Force: The Suez Crisis, the Iraq War, and International Law* (Oxford University Press 2013) 244.

[16] Fleur Johns, Richard Joyce, and Sundhya Pahuja, 'Introduction' in Johns et al (n 13) 1.

[17] ibid 6.

[18] ibid.

significant decisions, by which the course of history is eventually shaped. Yet, the fact that a certain development cannot be *completely* grounded in some pre-existing circumstances, does not mean that it cannot be grounded in any circumstances *at all*. Here Marks's methodology comes to the fore, requiring that we expose the (partial) falseness of contingency by shedding light on the systematic constraints informing the context in which change occurred.[19] Accordingly, in the following pages I will aim to read both contingency and necessity in an event that is said to have been seminal to the development of ICL. I am referring to the *Tadić* case before the ICTY, and to the defendant's challenge to the Tribunal's jurisdiction specifically. On the surface, the *Tadić* challenge seems to mark a context-breaking moment not just for the ICTY's judicial activity, but for the much broader prospects of the ICL project at large. I shall explain why in the following section.

II. The *Tadić* challenge: contingency of a legal nature

The events warrant little more than a summary. In 1993, the UN Security Council established the ICTY as a judicial response to alleged violations of international humanitarian law committed in the context of the Balkans War.[20] For the first time since the Nuremberg and Tokyo trials, the project of international criminal justice was brought back to life. The Tribunal's beginnings were not easy, to put it mildly: no facilities, no prosecutor, not even robes for the judges to be decently sworn in.[21] But soon enough material sums of money were pumped into the brand-new judicial machine to get its work started.[22] There remained one problem, however. The Tribunal had no case to try, and the investment made by those states which had contributed to its funding had to be justified by a trial—any trial.[23] The awaited chance came with the arrest of Duško Tadić, a Bosnian-Serb cafe owner allegedly affiliated with Serb paramilitary organisations, who was accused of committing war crimes in Serb-run detention camps.[24] When the trial began, in 1995, the defendant immediately challenged the jurisdiction of the Tribunal. He did so by advancing several distinct claims, the first and arguably thorniest of which being that the Security Council did not have the power to establish a criminal tribunal, and accordingly that the ICTY had been illegitimately established.[25] In fact, before the Trial Chamber, which was invested of the matter in the first instance, the defence maintained that:

19 Marks (n 8) 74.

20 UNSC Res 827 (25 May 1993) UN Doc S/RES/827.

21 Antonio Cassese, 'The ICTY: A Living and Vital Reality' (2004) 2 Journal of International Criminal Justice 585, 585.

22 See UNGA 'Second Annual Report of the International Tribunal for the Prosecution of Persons Responsible for Serious Violations of International Humanitarian Law Committed in the Territory of the Former Yugoslavia since 1991', UN Doc A/50/365 (23 August 1995) <http://www.icty.org/x/file/About/Reports%20and%20Publications/AnnualReports/annual_report_1995_en.pdf> accessed 25 July 2019 (ICTY 1995 Annual Report).

23 Mark S Zaid, 'Trial of the Century? Assessing the Case of Dusko Tadic before the International Criminal Tribunal for the Former Yugoslavia' (1996) 3 ILSA Journal of International & Comparative Law 589, 593.

24 Raymond M Brown, 'A Fronte Praecipitium a Tergo Lupi: Towards an Assessment of the Trial of Dusko Tadic before the ICTY' (1996) 3 ILSA Journal of International & Comparative Law 597, 598.

25 George H Aldrich, 'Jurisdiction of the International Tribunal for the Former Yugoslavia' (1996) 90 American Journal of International Law 64, 64.

> to be duly established by law, the International Tribunal should have been created either by treaty, the consensual act of nations, or by amendment of the Charter of the United Nations, not by resolution of the Security Council.[26]

A number of considerations were advanced in support of this stance. Most importantly, the defence claimed 'that it was never intended by the Charter that the Security Council should, under Chapter VII, establish a judicial body, let alone a criminal tribunal'.[27] That contention provided the Tribunal with at least three possibilities:

(i) denying its power of judicial review over actions of the Security Council, or, alternatively, addressing the merit of its own constitution, either
(ii) dismissing the defendant's argument, or
(iii) upholding it.

The Trial Chamber and the Appeals Chamber handled the matter in radically different ways (although they both ended up dismissing the jurisdictional challenge, an aspect to which I shall return later). The judges of first instance accepted the arguments of the Prosecutor,[28] thereby rejecting the defendant's motion as raising non-justiciable issues.[29] The Appeals Chamber, instead, asserted its authority of judicial review over the Security Council's actions,[30] finding that the ICTY had been lawfully created[31] and ultimately denying the defendant's motion for appeal.[32]

Such a discrepancy is not particularly surprising. As a matter of legal interpretation, in fact, none of the three options listed above appears more grounded than the other two. The exercise of judicial review over the Security Council could be taken as falling within the incidental powers of the Tribunal,[33] yet its permissibility is a question that even the International Court of Justice (ICJ) had previously avoided.[34] As for the merits of such a review, on the one hand there is a presumption of legality that attaches to acts of UN organs,[35] accompanied by uncertainties as to the legal validity of the unlawfulness of a judicial body being declared by the judges of that same body.[36] On the other hand, Jeffrey Davis offers strong arguments in support of his assertion that '[b]oth traditional judicial doctrines and the customary practices for tribunal establishment lead to the clear conclusion that the ICTY was created illegally.'[37]

[26] *Prosecutor v Tadić*, (Decision on the Defence Motion on Jurisdiction) [1995] ICTY-94-1-T para 2 (*Tadić* Decision).
[27] ibid.
[28] *Prosecutor v Tadić*, (Decision on the Defence Motion for Interlocutory Appeal on Jurisdiction) [1995] ICTY-94-1-AR72 para 13 (*Tadić* Appeal).
[29] *Tadić* Decision (n 26) paras 5 and 40.
[30] *Tadić* Appeal (n 28) paras 14–22.
[31] ibid paras 32–40.
[32] ibid para 137.
[33] *Tadić* Appeal (n 28) para 18.
[34] Mia Swart, 'Tadic Revisited: Some Critical Comments on the Legacy and the Legitimacy of the ICTY' (2011) 3 Goettingen Journal of International Law 985, 999.
[35] M Cherif Bassiouni and Peter Manikas, *The Law of the International Criminal Tribunal for the Former Yugoslavia* (Transnational Publishers 1996) 24.
[36] Mohamed Shahabuddeen, 'The Competence of a Tribunal to Deny Its Existence' in Wang Tieya and Sienho Yee (eds), *International Law in the Post-Cold War World: Essays in Memory of Li Haopei* (Routledge 2001) 476.
[37] Jeffrey W Davis, 'Two Wrongs Do Make a Right: The International Criminal Tribunal for the Former Yugoslavia Was Established Illegally—But It Was the Right Thing to Do... So Who Cares?' (2002) 28 North Carolina Journal of International Law and Commercial Regulation 395, 397.

The above only confirms what we already expected, namely that some sort of contingency is involved in the unprecedented challenge raised by Tadić. It is a contingency of a juridical nature, so to speak—for 'the ethereal purity of formal legal analysis'[38] did not mandate any specific answer, at the same time seemingly permitting all of them. Under these circumstances, the event emerges in all its legal groundlessness. Which explains why the Appeals Chamber's debatable reasoning is accompanied by a separate opinion bluntly defining the exercise of judicial review 'ultra vires and unlawful'.[39] The judges, of course, feature as the agents who find themselves in the position to make a momentous decision. Momentous because its consequences were bound to reach far beyond the *Tadić* case.[40] The challenge questioned the very existence of the ICTY, and it did so right at the outset of the new organ's judicial activity. What would have happened, had the judges proclaimed the illegality of the Tribunal? 'Would the lights have been turned out and the microphones switched off?'[41] And would the untimely end of the ICTY have determined the abandonment of ICL, a project that the Security Council had just resurrected as part of its busy post-Cold War agenda?[42]

III. The *Tadić* challenge: reckoning into necessity

In the effort to read both contingency and necessity in the ICTY's handling of the *Tadić* challenge, the former of the two is easy to spot. Contingency (or false necessity) manifests itself in the variety of legally tenable options available to the judges. But then there is, according to Marks's paradigm, 'a kind of necessity which must be reckoned into'.[43] In *Tadić*, that kind of necessity is also not particularly difficult to expose. The fact that the Trial Chamber and the Appeals Chamber followed radically opposite lines of reasoning only to both ultimately dismiss the defendant's challenge, points at certain necessitating factors (or 'effective determinations')[44] that shaped the contours of the event. I believe that the clearest explanation of what those factors are can be found in another separate opinion, the one which Judge Sidhwa appended to the Appeals Chamber's decision. In it, both the question of judicial review in respect of actions of the Security Council and that of the lawfulness of the ICTY's establishment are addressed. Judge Sidhwa frames the former matter in rather enigmatic terms, invoking 'a somewhat liberal but cautious approach in an environment where international law seeks new mutations to meet unusual challenges thrown up by new situations'.[45] The 'environment', 'unusual challenges', 'new situations': all these references

[38] Jason A Beckett, 'The Deceptive Dyad: Falseness and Fantasy in International Law' (unpublished manuscript on file with the author, 2018) 20.
[39] *Tadić* Appeal (n 28), Separate Opinion of Judge Li, para 3. On the paradoxical effects of fundamental dissent in additional opinions, see Hemi Mistry, 'The Paradox of Dissent: Judicial Dissent and the Projects of International Criminal Justice' (2015) 13 Journal of International Criminal Justice 449.
[40] William A Schabas, *The UN International Criminal Tribunals: The Former Yugoslavia, Rwanda and Sierra Leone* (CUP 2006) 53.
[41] Colin Warbrick and Peter Rowe, 'The International Criminal Tribunal for Yugoslavia: The Decision of the Appeals Chamber on the Interlocutory Appeal on Jurisdiction in the Tadic Case' (1996) 45 International and Comparative Law Quarterly 691, 695.
[42] Dapo Akande, 'The International Court of Justice and the Security Council: Is There Room for Judicial Control of Decisions of the Political Organs of the United Nations?' (1997) 46 International & Comparative Law Quarterly 309, 309.
[43] Marks (n 6) 2.
[44] Louis Althusser, *For Marx* (Verso 2005) 113.
[45] *Tadić* Appeal (n 28), Separate Opinion of Judge Sidhwa, para 36.

seem to indicate a changing context that has little to do with formal legal analysis, but which nonetheless bears great relevance for the purposes of the decision. Better: decisive relevance, for that context alone prompts Judge Sidhwa to hold that 'whatever be the position, [. . .] the International Tribunal can examine the matter'.[46]

Having thus assertively disposed of the issue of judicial review, the opinion moves on to the next item. And it is here, I argue, that it evokes a strong sense of necessity. Because at this point, following the structure of the decision, one would expect an assessment of the legality of the Tribunal. Before getting there, however, Judge Sidhwa takes us on a historical tour that starts from Tito's death in 1980 and ends with the Tribunal's establishment by Security Council Resolution 827 of 1993. The bottom line of that 21-paragraph-long interlude seems to be a reminder that '[t]he brutality of the conflict [in former Yugoslavia] and the new horrendous dimensions in which it travelled, aroused the conscience of all nations.'[47] We are also offered a thorough list of the many international agencies, state missions, and NGOs whose agents were sent out to report on the crimes being committed.[48] By way of that reconstruction, what Judge Sidhwa seems to be telling us reads approximately like: 'against these documented atrocities, could we, judges, tell the world—the victims?[49]—that this Tribunal is illegal, therefore refusing to judge Duško Tadić or any other individual?' In Judge Sidhwa's eyes, history had decided for the bench long before Tadić filed his motion on jurisdiction. I will account for this take in the following section.

Eventually, in any case, Judge Sidhwa does address the legality of the Tribunal's establishment. Sort of, for the opinion fails once again to discuss the point as a matter of legal interpretation. 'What stands out prominently is that the Security Council did not take any hasty action' in creating the ICTY,[50] is what we learn. Moreover, given that a criminal tribunal can contribute to restoring peace, its establishment fell within the competences of the Security Council in accordance with Article 41 of the UN Charter. For 'it is too well known that peace can only bring amnesty', asserts Judge Sidwha, 'and those that desire peace do not have to wait for [the] Tribunal to be disbanded.'[51] Fair enough; but the defendant argued that, whether or not the Tribunal would be an appropriate measure for restoring peace, the Security Council had no authority to create a *judicial* body, under the wording of Article 41 of the Charter or any other provision thereof.[52]

Striking in Judge Sidhwa's separate opinion is the total absence of decisive formal justifications in support of the decision, as far as the propriety of judicial review and its merits are involved. The same absence is also captured by academic commentaries, in which it accompanies the contingency operating on the level of pure legal analysis. Jose Alvarez, for instance, notes how the *Tadić* case provided no solution to 'fundamental jurisprudential issues' about the legitimacy of the ICTY.[53] He also stresses the circularity of the judges'

[46] ibid.

[47] ibid, para 46.

[48] ibid, paras 47–50.

[49] See Sara Kendall and Sarah Nouwen, 'Representational Practices at the International Criminal Court: The Gap between Juridified and Abstract Victimhood' (2013) 76 Law and Contemporary Problems 235, 255.

[50] *Tadić* Appeal (n 28), Separate Opinion of Judge Sidhwa, para 62.

[51] ibid, para 63. As James O'Brien argues, historical 'factors have undeniable explanatory power but do not capture the legal basis for the Council's response to the situation': James C O'Brien, 'The International Tribunal for Violations of International Humanitarian Law in the Former Yugoslavia' (1993) 87 American Journal of International Law 639, 640.

[52] Nigel White, *The Law of International Organisations* (2nd edn, Manchester University Press 2005) 83.

[53] Jose Alvarez, 'The Likely Legacies of Tadic' (1996) 3 ISLA Journal of International & Comparative Law 613, 620.

arguments, based on the 'all-purpose answer that the legality of the tribunal *needs* to be affirmed'.[54] Alvarez, however, also points out that the defendant's challenge put the Tribunal 'between a rock and a hard place.'[55] One might expect such two alternatives to be either asserting the ICTY's legality, or denying it. But no: before that question is even posed, the answer has already been given.[56] The two choices are the options available to the judges 'to justify the legality of their tribunal'.[57] The verdict was the starting point of the decision, not its outcome. And, Alvarez adds, the appellate judges considered that refusing to review the ICTY's creation 'would not be a credit to the tribunal.'[58] A position echoed by former ICJ president Gilbert Guillaume, who finds it difficult to imagine 'how the Tribunal could have given a negative reply to [the issue of the legality of its creation], thus signing its own death warrant'.[59] In a later article which appraises the outcome of the *Tadić* trial, Alvarez claims that external historical narratives clearly influenced the judgment.[60] If that is true, we can only imagine the extent to which they influenced the decisions on jurisdiction. Among other commentators, George Aldrich accepts that the Appeals Chamber's ruling was 'controversial'.[61] At the same, however, Aldrich endorses the strategy to allow the defendant 'to *force* the Tribunal to confirm the validity' of its creation.[62] Finally, Mark Zaid notes that the legacy of the ICTY was already at stake in the *Tadić* trial.[63] It is a circumstance that the judges seemed to have very clear in mind, along with the conviction that faced with the horrors of the Balkans War, the world 'was compelled—if not forced—to act'.[64] Therefore the ICTY, and the inevitable outcome of the *Tadić* challenge.

IV. Bourdieu's *habitus*: a bridge between structure and agency

We have seen that some sort of contingency (false necessity) and necessity (false contingency) can be discerned in the ICTY's response to the *Tadić* challenge. These two entities must now be placed in the context of a mutual relationship, one that explains their modular functioning with respect to the particular case at stake: more systemic constraints, less freedom for the agents involved, more necessity, less contingency—and vice versa. In other words, it is not enough to state that both contingency and necessity were at play in 1995.

[54] ibid (emphasis added).

[55] ibid 615.

[56] '[T]he question can be inscribed only in the form dictated by the answer which awaits it, that is, which did not wait for it': Jacques Derrida, 'Form and Meaning: A Note on the Phenomenology of Language' in *Speech and Phenomena and Other Essays on Husserl's Theory of Signs* (Northwestern University Press 1973) 126. I am grateful to Jason Beckett for directing me towards this passage.

[57] Alvarez (n 53) 615.

[58] As William Schabas notes, the subsequent jurisprudence of international tribunals on the matter has been 'unwavering': Schabas (n 40) 52–53.

[59] A preferable solution, Guillaume claims, would have been for the ICTY to ask the Security Council to seek an advisory opinion from the ICJ: see Speech by His Excellency Judge Gilbert Guillaume, President of the ICJ, to the Sixth Committee of the UN General Assembly, 'The proliferation of international judicial bodies: The outlook for the international legal order', 27 October 2000 <https://www.icj-cij.org/public/files/press-releases/1/3001.pdf> accessed 14 July 2019, 4.

[60] Jose E Alvarez, 'Rush to Closure: Lessons of the Tadic Judgment' (1998) 96 Michigan Law Review 2031, 2034.

[61] Aldrich (n 25) 64.

[62] ibid 65 (emphasis added).

[63] Zaid (n 23) 589, 596.

[64] ibid 590.

Some more substance has to be given to the analysis.[65] I have emphasised the role of the judges in choosing between equally viable legal alternatives, but I have also argued that the historical context of the ICTY's establishment seems to have exerted a determining pressure for the chambers' respective decisions. Is there a conceptual framework capable of explaining this process?

I believe that there is, and that it can be found in Pierre Bourdieu's sociological notion of *habitus*. In Bourdieu's words, the *habitus* 'is a system of open mechanisms that can be constantly subjected to experience, and by the same token transformed by those experiences.'[66] It captures the circumstance that:

> agents have a history and are the product of an individual history and an education associated with a milieu, and they are also the product of a collective history, and their categories of thinking, categories of understanding, patterns of perception, systems of values, and so on, are the product of the incorporation of social structures.[67]

If we think about the *Tadić* challenge, it becomes apparent how a certain *habitus* could have oriented the judges' preferences towards a given outcome—upholding the Tribunal's legitimacy—that did not depend on legal argumentation. Judge Li's caustic remark on the unlawfulness of the Tribunal's judicial review, yet concurrence in the Appeals Chamber's decision, as well as Judge Sidhwa's tentative justification of the latter, both reveal that declaring the Tribunal to have been illegally constituted never appeared on the judges' horizon of possibilities. As Bourdieu explains:

> according to the habitus that I have, I either see or don't see certain things in a given situation. And depending on whether I see these things or not, I shall be incited by my habitus to do or not do certain things.[68]

The judges were free to decide, yet they did not perceive their freedom as such. Their actions were guided by unconscious interpretation of the surrounding context. And as Eric Hosbawm says commenting on Bourdieu's theory, 'the unconscious is history', history 'hidden [...] in people's minds and in the folds of their bodies'.[69] Bourdieu himself frames this concept in a vertiginous formulation: '[t]he *habitus*, a product of history, produces individual and collective practices—more history—in accordance with the schemes generated by history.'[70] The *habitus* is history itself, 'internalized as a second nature and so forgotten as history'.[71] If we look at the *Tadić* challenge through the lens of this theory, we can assert that it was the judges' *habitus* that turned the contingency offered by law into a kind of historical necessity. It is in this way, that the *habitus* 'occupies the space between structures and human activity, between conscious action and historical determination'.[72]

[65] False contingency calls 'for the expansion of analysis: [t]he abstract "merits" of a claim must give way to the likelihood of its realisation': Beckett (n 38) 16.

[66] Pierre Bourdieu and Roger Chartier, *The Sociologist and the Historian* (Polity Press 2015) 57.

[67] ibid 52.

[68] ibid 58.

[69] Eric Hobsbawm, 'Pierre Bourdieu: Critical Sociology and Social History' (2016) 201 The New Left Review 37, 40.

[70] Pierre Bourdieu, *The Logic of Practice* (Richard Nice tr, Stanford University Press 1990) 54.

[71] ibid 56.

[72] Hobsbawm (n 69) 43.

In this particular case, moreover, the *habitus* seems to provide a credible explanation for the attitude that the judges adopted when faced with an unprecedented occurrence—an event characterised by its legal groundlessness, as I have labelled it. According to Bourdieu, in fact, *habitus* and institutions are both 'modes of objectification of past history', whose dialectic relationship with one another 'constantly create[s] a history that inevitably appears [...] as both original and inevitable.'[73] When talking about institutions, Bourdieu refers to 'the monarchy', 'capitalism', 'the Church'.[74] It seems to me that for present purposes 'internationalism', or 'the international',[75] fits the label just as well. Those terms stand for the commitment to a benevolent international community[76] that moves forward and never backward, pursuing global betterment through projects (say, ICL)[77] that once underway can no longer be abandoned. Or, to say it differently, it signals an understanding of history as a progressive force inexorably moving towards a cosmopolitan order governed by human rights and the rule of law.[78] That history moves institutions and it moves through them, but it does so via the mediation of agency. In this process, the *habitus*:

> which is constituted in the course of an individual history, imposing its particular logic on incorporation, and through which agents partake of the history objectified in institutions, is what makes it possible to inhabit institutions, to appropriate them practically [...]. Or rather, the habitus is what enables the institution to attain full realization: it is through the capacity for incorporation, [...] that the king, the banker or the priest are hereditary monarchy, financial capitalism or the Church made flesh.[79]

By the same token, it is the *habitus* that enables the international to attain full realisation,[80] making of a judicial body the response to the Balkans' nightmare, turning international criminal *law* into international criminal *justice*. We can thus read the ICTY judges' attitude towards the *Tadić* challenge as an instance of 'regulated improvisation'[81] objectifying the sense of a historical path leading to the creation of the Tribunal. It is expression of a 'conditioned and conditional freedom [which is] as remote from creation of unpredictable novelty as it is from simple mechanical reproduction of the original conditioning.'[82] The judges became history, history incorporated in their unconscious and percolating through their actions, thus allowing history to move them and move through them.

[73] Bourdieu, *Logic* (n 70) 57.
[74] ibid.
[75] Sundhya Pahuja, *Decolonising International Law: Development, Economic Growth and the Politics of Universality* (CUP 2011) 26.
[76] David Kennedy, *The Dark Sides of Virtue: Reassessing International Humanitarianism* (Princeton University Press 2004) 22.
[77] [T]he constitution of the field of international criminal justice [...] requires an investment into an entirely new type of legitimacy that [...] stands in for a certain concept of international justice or *ordre public*.' As a result, practitioners in the field 'engage in a broader range of self-sustaining practices than would typically be required [...] for more established fields': Frédéric Mégret, 'International Criminal Justice as a Juridical Field' (2016) 13 Champ Pénal/Penal Field 13.
[78] Martti Koskenniemi, 'Global Governance and Public International Law' (2004) 37 Kritische Justiz 241, 241.
[79] Bourdieu, *Logic* (n 70) 57.
[80] Mégret (n 77) 47.
[81] Bourdieu (n 70) 57.
[82] ibid 55.

V. Re-producing contingency: back to structure

As I understand it, the notion of *habitus* suggests an elementary but important consideration. The fact that judges decide groundless cases because of *habitus*—a predisposition causing them to embrace a pro-institutional posture—tells us that someone's agency can easily become someone else's structure. For structure crystallises into the *habitus* and guides agency, favouring the reproduction of structure itself. This, at least, is what my analysis of the *Tadić* challenge seems to reveal: it is a point to which I shall return further later. But it seems evident that in the case under examination the *habitus* points towards necessity, ie towards determining factors pre-existing the event and channelled into the event itself by way of human behaviour. As a result, the investigation appears deficient on the side of contingency, that is when it comes to evaluating the potential of what could have happened differently but did not. And if we want to stay faithful to Marks' framework, contingency has to be retrieved; it has to be (re)produced, to say it with Ingo Venzke, showing its existence in the particular instance at stake.[83]

If we take the *habitus* seriously, the question to be asked in the search for alternative possibilities is no longer, as one might have thought: how likely was it that *the same judges* reach a different verdict? Rather, the query becomes: how likely was it that the benches be composed *of judges showing a different habitus*, ie judges (a majority, at least) reasoning in a different way and capable of denying the legitimacy of the very institution they were called to serve? To elaborate an answer, one could start by considering the profiles of the judges involved in the *Tadić* challenge, noting the relatively diverse array of geographical provenances[84] as well as the manifest gender imbalance—Trial Chamber's president Judge McDonald being the only woman among the judges of first and second instance. Or is it perhaps more important that seven out of the eight members of the chambers attended university institutions located in the Western world? Is this one of those patterns that prompted Anthea Roberts to warn of the risk that international lawyers remain trapped in bubbles of like-minded people?[85]

These might all be relevant considerations, while other factors might also have come into play. I am afraid, however, that this is not the appropriate venue for exploring the matter further. Doing so would inevitably require a much longer contribution than this chapter, one which builds on a(nother) methodology capable of justifying its approach to the counterfactual questions at stake. In this venue, I can only sketch what my operating hypothesis would be, if I had to undertake such a complex research venture. As I see it, the chances that any of the two benches may have consisted of judges whose *habitus* would lead to upholding the challenge raised by Tadić were really, really thin—almost non-existent. Discussing the work of the UN International Residual Mechanism for Criminal Tribunals—the body charged with bringing the ICTY's judicial activity to completion—Dov Jacobs argues that the outcome of some cases was determined before trial:

[83] Ingo Venzke, 'Possibilities of the Past: Histories of the NIEO and the Travails of Critique' (2018) 20 Journal of the History of International Law 263, 272.

[84] It is perhaps interesting that in both chambers the majority was composed by nationals of the five major contributing countries of the Tribunal, ie Canada, Italy, Malaysia, Pakistan, and the United States (see ICTY 1995 Annual Report, n 22).

[85] Anthea Roberts, *Is International Law International?* (OUP 2017) 231.

> *beyond individual Judges*, for some defendants [. . .] their fate was sealed on an institutional level, before their trial even started, given the ample discussion of their role in numerous other Judgments.[86]

In other words, no bench would have decided differently on the cases that Jacobs has in mind, because no judges would have departed from the findings made by their colleagues in other trials. No judges of international criminal tribunals as we know them, which is to say judges *who are likely to sit on an international criminal tribunal*.[87] This, also, is a consideration based on the observance of a certain *habitus*. And I believe that the same applies to the *Tadić* challenge, *mutatis mutandis*: no other bench, regardless of its composition as far as realistic possibilities for election are concerned,[88] would have declared the Tribunal to have been illegally established by the Security Council.

Much more important than my educated guess, however, is noticing that at this stage the investigation refers back to the analysis of structure. As tentative examples of the contingency-producing factors in the *Tadić* challenge, I have mentioned the selection of Judges, gender imbalance, and the prominent role of a handful of Western institutions in the politics of the production of knowledge about international law.[89] All these interrelated factors fundamentally concern structure, rather than individual choices (or mere chance). We started by pointing at a legal contingency that opens possibilities for the actors involved. We then shifted to necessity, aiming to expose the existence of what Althusser calls 'effective determinations',[90] a web of contextual pressures imposing limits on the relevant actors' agency. Now, in the attempt to recover contingency by better specifying how things could have been different, the investigation redirects us towards structure once again. This suggests some considerations to which I now turn my attention.

VI. The politics of counterfactuals

This section develops some theoretical remarks that the preceding analysis seems to suggest. As they arise out of a single case study in the realm of international criminal justice, such considerations do not embody an incontrovertible attitude towards the discipline of international legal history and the investigation of its counterfactuals. Rather, they should be taken as research hypotheses to be tested by reference to other momentous cases, sketches

86 Dov Jacobs, '3 Judges Removed from Mladic Appeal at the MICT for Appearance of Bias' (*Spreading the Jam: International Law, International Criminal Law, Human Rights and Transitional Justice*, 5 September 2018) <https://dovjacobs.com/2018/09/05/3-judges-removed-from-mladic-appeal-at-the-mict-for-appearance-of-bias/> accessed 14 July 2019 (emphasis added).

87 Mikkel Jarle Christensen notes that the judiciary of international criminal law is characterised by high levels of diplomatic and political expertise: Mikkel Jarle Christensen, 'The Judiciary of International Criminal Law: Double Decline and Practical Turn' (2019) 17 Journal of International Criminal Justice 537, 541.

88 Out of the twenty-two candidates standing for the first election of ICTY judges in 1993, for instance, seventeen had attended Western universities: see UNGA 'Curricula vitae of candidates nominated by States Members of the United Nations and non-member States maintaining permanent observer missions at United Nations Headquarters', UN Doc A/47/1006 (1 September 1993) <https://digitallibrary.un.org/record/172942> accessed 14 July 2019.

89 I borrow this expression from Balakrishnan Rajagopal, *International Law from Below: Development, Social Movements and Third World Resistance* (CUP 2003) 172.

90 Althusser (n 44) 113.

of an approach to the subject which partially departs from the methodological framework I assumed at the outset of this contribution.

In the attempt to substantiate the claim to contingency in the *Tadić* challenge, I have said that the investigation refers back to structure. If that is true, it follows that the event (at least, this particular event) points towards effective determinations more than it does towards freedom of choice on the part of individuals. The more we look for it, the more contingency slips away, remanding towards a chronologically deeper level of analysis. The *Tadić* decisions on jurisdiction are not a fitting avenue for stressing the freedom of its protagonists, the judges. If we wonder where to find the moment in which things could have taken another tack for Duško Tadić, for the ICTY, for ICL, then we have to look somewhere else. At the event juncture it is context that determines outcomes. It is not law, because international law is radically indeterminate, and even more so in extreme instances of groundless adjudication. Here, contra Koskenniemi,[91] law *is* context, the two cannot be disentangled from one another. Contra Koskenniemi but not necessarily contra Venzke, who states that '[t]here is no such thing as *the* context, it does not have clear borders in space or time.'[92] For while it is true that it is impossible, in retrospect, to frame the contextual background to a given event in accurate terms; that still does not mean that context does not exist, that it cannot play a decisive role in determining an event's outcome. My claim is only that at the event juncture under consideration there is nothing that breaks and escapes the context, *a* context as incorporated by relevant agents.[93] And if I refer to '*the* historical context' as the determining factor behind the judges' decision, it is because 'we need, after all, some word to designate the thing.'[94]

So, contrary to what I assumed at the beginning: as far as one key dimension of international legal practice—adjudication—is concerned, the event might emerge as a figure not of contingency but of necessity. Which does not amount to claiming that contingency is not there at all, but rather that its exposure is deferred to a different moment.[95] If in the judicial event law becomes context, then we always have to look for what produced that context to explain the contingency of the event and account for the sense of alternative possibilities that legal technique does no more than evoking. It is, of course, entirely possible to find out that (international) law itself played a role in the making of that context. In international legal practice, therefore, contingency should perhaps be looked for in those 'minuscule moments where the new is being articulated for the first time', nurturing what Koskenniemi calls 'a live sense of the possibility that even as everything seems to be bogged down in routine, we might already be living an event that finally breaks it up.'[96]

[91] Koskenniemi (n 11) 216.

[92] Venzke (n 83) 265.

[93] ibid.

[94] Louis Althusser, 'The Underground Current of the Materialism of the Encounter' in François Matheron and Oliver Corpet (eds), *Philosophy of the Encounter: Later Writings, 1978–87* (GM Goshgarian tr, Verso 2006) 171.

[95] The same may hold true for non-legal occurrences conventionally interpreted as context-breaking events. Scott Newton, for instance, argues that when the collapse of state socialism materialised, between 1989 and 1991, the 'real event, the moment of opening and release of possibility', had already happened. Accordingly, contingency 'was probably never in prospect in 1989': Scott Newton, 'Post-War to New World Order and Post-Socialist Transition: 1989 as Pseudo-Event' in Johns et al (n 13) 113.

[96] Koskenniemi (n 11) 240. See also Luis Eslava and Sundhya Pahuja, 'Beyond the (Post)Colonial: TWAIL and the Everyday Life of International Law' (2012) 45 Journal of Law and Politics in Africa, Asia and Latin America 195, 221: '[t]iny revolutions are everywhere, every day.'

Given that I have resorted to Bourdieu's *habitus* to account for the attitude of judges towards the *Tadić* challenge, the conclusion that contingency cannot be found in the event of groundless adjudication should not be surprising. It is clear, in fact, that the *habitus* is geared towards explaining social reproduction, not change. As far as the case study of this chapter is concerned, we might consider it as a factor of *legal* reproduction, continuation of the international enterprise. What the *habitus* cannot explain, instead, is how dramatic moments in which the existing context is broken unfold. As Hobsbawm holds, Bourdieu's *habitus* does not offer a convincing answer to the problem of 'profound, long-term historical' revolutions.[97] My contention here is simply that neither does (international) law—not at the event juncture of groundless adjudication, in any case, for judges are seldom revolutionaries. Which only amounts to restating the not-very-original position that law is a highly conservative business.[98] To quote Bourdieu:

> the choices which those in the legal realm must constantly make between differing or antagonistic interests, values, and world-views are unlikely to disadvantage the dominant forces. For the ethos of legal practitioners, which is at the origin of these choices, and the immanent logic of the legal texts, which are called upon to justify as well as to determine them, are strongly in harmony with the interests, values, and world-views of these dominant forces.[99]

On the international level, however, it is the law's very indeterminacy that constitutes the immanent logic of the legal texts.[100] At the moment of groundless adjudication, that indeterminacy is so radical that law can no longer be invoked to support any decision. Interpretation can justify different legal choices,[101] but it cannot justify the legal phenomenon itself.[102] Accordingly, the legal practitioner's *habitus* alone is what determines the outcome of events like the *Tadić* challenge.

The fact that in international legal practice the event features as a figure of necessity, more than as one of contingency, calls into question a major point made by Althusser and embraced by Marks. History moves through a process of accumulation of effective determinations, Althusser claims, the economic base being the last instance of such a process, the ultimately deciding factor. But '[f]rom the first moment to the last, the lonely hour of the "last instance" never comes', Althusser observes, for 'History "asserts itself" through the multiform world of the superstructures, from local tradition to international circumstance.'[103] If what I have said so far makes sense, however, I would venture to argue that in international legal practice the ultimate moment of base *does* come. When a momentous decision cannot be justified as a matter of legal technique, the legal superstructure refers to its contextual base, and contingency fails to show up at the site of the event. I would even

[97] Hobsbawm (n 69) 44.
[98] Gerry Simpson, 'Humanity, Law, Force' in Jeremy Farrall and Hilary Charlesworth (eds), *Strengthening the Rule of Law through the UN Security Council* (Routledge 2016) 79–80.
[99] Pierre Bourdieu, 'The Force of Law: Toward a Sociology of the Juridical Field' (1987) 38 Hastings Law Journal 805, 842.
[100] Beckett (n 38) 5.
[101] Martti Koskenniemi, 'What Is Critical Research in International Law? Celebrating Structuralism' (2016) 29 Leiden Journal of International Law 727, 732.
[102] Bourdieu (n 99) 814.
[103] Althusser (n 44) 112–13.

suggest that historical investigations limited to international law turn Althusser's paradigm upside down: in international legal practice, it is the moment of ultimate contingency that never comes.

To be sure: the foregoing holds true only so long as we assume that the law has definite boundaries, that it can be distinguished from what is *not* law. If we hold that the context has no clear borders in space,[104] however, then we also accept that it cannot be separated from law itself. For law operates through human beings—in my case study, the judges—who internalise the context and make it part of the legal endeavour, the *habitus* serving as a medium for this internalisation. Indeed, I have claimed that at the level of groundless adjudication law *is* context. As Beckett puts it, false contingency 'disrupts the formalists' neat distinction between inside and out, situating law in the realm of politics'.[105] When international law becomes context, it may not make too much sense to argue—as I have done—that contingency has to be sought outside international legal practice. For if law with its contingent interpretations cannot be disentangled from context with its effective determinations; if the *habitus* links structure and agency, challenging the common antinomies of determinism and freedom, the individual and society;[106] and if looking for contingency keeps redirecting to structure; we should perhaps also wonder if (false) contingency and (false) necessity themselves can be disentangled at all, if it is a realistic prospect to expect the (legal) historian to do so. Mala Loth makes a similar point in her remarks on the conference out of which this collection was born, arguing that 'the question whether "necessity" is an analytically useful category at all when all historical explanations are constructs anyway would have been interesting to discuss'.[107] Pair that view with Corey Robin's contempt for the 'misplaced mania for contingency, the fetish for the telling detail, that sinks the work of so many historians',[108] and doubts cannot but inflate.

By way of this blurring of methodological lines, I do not mean to destroy the intellectual enterprise, suggesting that investigations into contingency and counterfactuals are worthless. What I mean to do, instead, is issue a reminder that not only historical explanations, but the tools we use to offer those explanations are constructs as well. Obscuring contingency or necessity, thus favouring false contingency or false necessity, is primarily a choice of the author, and a political choice at that. It is, moreover, a choice which is both contingent and necessary. Contingent because different moves would be possible, necessary because one has to make it. As Constantin Fasolt notes:

> [s]urprising is the self-confidence with which historians seem to believe that it is possible to take a stand on history without excluding anything at all from comprehension. [...] Precisely because it is real, our knowledge is fuzzy, incomplete, and changing. Nothing is wrong with that. Taking no stand at all is certainly not an option.[109]

[104] See *supra* note 98 and accompanying text.
[105] Beckett (n 38) 7.
[106] Bourdieu (n 70) 55.
[107] Mala Loth, 'It Could Have Been Worse' (*Völkerrechtsblog*, 17 July 2018) <http://voelkerrechtsblog.org/it-could-have-been-worse/> accessed 18 July 2018.
[108] Corey Robin, 'Eric Hobsbawm, the Communist Who Explained History' *The New Yorker* (New York, 9 May 2019).
[109] Constantin Fasolt, 'The Limits of History in Brief' (2005) Historically Speaking 5, 10.

In other words: it is inevitable that (legal) history contains some falsity. And so it should, if it is to attend to the politics of its method, as Anne Orford suggests.[110] After all, even the most celebrated revisionist histories in the field of international law can be attacked for their selectivity and methodological arbitrariness.[111] Actually, their force lies precisely in their being provocative and 'endlessly controversial'.[112] It is thus essential to emphasise the political responsibility of the scholar 'in organizing material and asking questions', a responsibility which the analysis of counterfactuals takes 'a stage further, and indeed frequently a considerable stage further'.[113]

The likelihood of any given moment to yield different results and shape a different history than the one we live in is difficult, if not impossible, to measure.[114] What matters is that we can draw from the realm of history to catch glimpses of alternative worlds, worlds imagined if not realised.[115] The scholar's political responsibility calls for insisting on the inherent value of those alternatives, given that providing a wholly accurate account of how certain events were prevented from happening—of the interaction between structure and agency—is ultimately impossible.[116] But also, and finally, it is perhaps important to stress that the political role of the scholar does not exhaust itself with the choice to insist on either necessity or contingency, structural factors or human behaviour. This is because contingency and necessity are not political per se.[117] Going back to the *Tadić* challenge, in my analysis I employed Bourdieu's *habitus* to express a preference for a contextual reading of the legal decision. It is not difficult to see that such a reading says nothing about justice, or injustice.[118] Was it just to prosecute the defendant, who was ultimately sentenced to spend over a decade in a German prison?[119] Was it just to uphold the Security Council's bid to deliver criminal justice on the international plane? Methodological choices cannot answer these questions on the author's behalf.

VII. Concluding remarks

Needless to say, counterfactual narratives about ICL can and should revolve around more than a single event, however crucial. Accordingly, revisiting the *Tadić* challenge—a

[110] Anne Orford, 'International Law and the Limits of History' in Wouter Werner, Marieke de Hoon, and Alexis Galan (eds), *The Law of International Lawyers* (CUP 2017) 310.

[111] Samuel Moyn, *The Last Utopia: Human Rights in History* (Harvard University Press 2010) provides a fitting example. Philip Alston criticises its America-centric perspective, disregard of the power of ideas and exaggerate concern with formal political power: Philip Alston, 'Book Review: Does the Past Matter? On the Origins of Human Rights' (2013) 126 Harvard Law Review 2043, 2073. Antony Anghie notes that by the time Moyn starts analysing the explosion of human-rights discourse in the late 1970s, the 'Third World, which earlier in the book had featured prominently in his discussion [. . .], has [. . .] receded from view': Antony Anghie, 'Whose Utopia? Human Rights, Development, and the Third World' (2013) 22 Qui Parle 63, 72.

[112] Patrick William Kelly, 'What Is Hope For?' [2018] *Los Angeles Review of Books* <https://lareviewofbooks.org/article/what-is-hope-for/> accessed 17 July 2019.

[113] Black (n 4) 16.

[114] Venzke (n 83) 295.

[115] John Whitlow, 'Coming of Age at the End of History' (*Law and Political Economy*, 23 April 2019) <https://lpeblog.org/2019/04/23/coming-of-age-at-the-end-of-history/> accessed 24 April 2019.

[116] Bardo Fassbender and Anne Peters, 'Introduction: Towards A Global History Of International Law' in Bardo Fassbender and Anne Peters (eds), *The Oxford Handbook of the History of International Law* (OUP 2012) 15.

[117] Black (n 4) 10–12.

[118] Contra see Marks (n 6) 20.

[119] 'Press Release: Dusko Tadic Transferred to Germany to Serve Prison Sentence' (31 October 2000) <http://www.icty.org/en/press/dusko-tadic-transferred-germany-serve-prison-sentence> accessed 17 July 2019.

single moment in one among the many trials of one of a variety of international criminal tribunals[120]—is only relatively illustrative of what could have been different. Yet, the analysis does yield some results. It allows to say, for example, that we cannot *always* contextualise legal developments without reducing law to its context only.[121] It also suggests that Marks' theory falls prey to its own critique, as is common for critical theory in general.[122] For if Marks' argument is made in support of any 'anti-anti-ism',[123] then it also stands for a political approach to legal history that privileges one side of the contingency-necessity dichotomy to the detriment of the other. Thirdly, revisiting the *Tadić* challenge tells us something about the institutional thrust that stands behind the ICL enterprise, or at least stood behind it in the mid-1990s. I have claimed that contingency did not show up in those days of 1995. Better: it did show up for a flickering moment, the time it took to unveil the necessitarian force of the historical context made conscience through the *habitus*. In that sense, we know that *by that time* ICL had to be, precisely because we know that after the event it could no longer have been.[124] Or, we know that it had become necessary precisely because we know that its survival was subject to contingent legal choices. Which does not dispel another fundamental question: does ICL have to be?[125] What the analysis ultimately suggests is that its demise, should it materialise despite so much institutional support, would attest to the project's ultimate hopelessness.

[120] More broadly, '[f]ocusing on the prized institutions of international criminal justice […] risks […] blinding us to the extent to which even the force of institutions is derivative on the force of the field, and not simply the other way round': Mégret (n 77) 52.

[121] Contra see Koskenniemi (n 11) 216.

[122] David Kennedy, 'Critical Theory, Structuralism and Contemporary Legal Scholarship' (1985) 21 New England Law Review 209, 215, 226.

[123] Marks (n 6) 21.

[124] The present 'always emerges out of what existed yesterday, including the possibilities contained therein': Bertell Ollman, *Dance of the Dialectic: Steps in Marx's Method* (University of Illinois Press 2003) 3.

[125] '[T]he very need for ICL […] is controversial': Kevin Jon Heller, 'International Crime' in Jean d'Aspremont and Sahib Singh (eds), *Concepts for International Law* (Edward Elgar 2019) 524.

9

Subverting Eurocentric Epistemology

The Value of Nonsense When Designing Counterfactuals

Mohsen al Attar

I. Navigating idealism, cynicism, and Eurocentrism in critical international legal theory

Oscar Wilde says somewhere that a cynic is someone who knows the cost of everything and the value of nothing. He forgot to add that the cynic begins as iconoclast and ends as tragicomic. This caricature also marks the character of Third World Approaches to International Law (TWAIL).

As a theory *about* international law, TWAIL provides an analytical lens through which to examine elements of the global legal framework. Of predominant interest to TWAIL is the imbalance, usually inequity in outcomes, precipitated by international law. Through the use of counter-narratives, TWAIL scholars in particular, and critical international legal theory (CILT) scholars in general, expose the role of European imperialism and colonialism, of plunder and prejudice, of bigotry and barbarity in shaping the *architecture* of international law.[1] They have also uncovered the legacies of Eurocentrism in the *operation* of international law, legacies that persist in privileging some states at the expense of others. CILT scholars conclude that the international legal edifice is hopelessly tainted by original sin and thus destined to reproduce the same prejudicial outcomes. While they acknowledge that much of the language and at least some of the sentiment of international law has evolved, this is more curse than blessing: the form of international legal relations is designed to reproduce imperial violence albeit violence now coddled within the legitimising verbiage of legalism and humanitarianism.[2] By supplanting gunboat diplomacy with Security Council resolutions, International Criminal Court warrants, and loan conditionalities, prejudicial outcomes that appear contingent are legitimised with the imprimatur of lawfulness, legitimacy, and, ultimately, truth. We are led to a familiar nihilistic cul-de-sac. If international law is hopelessly prejudicial, if its aetiology means that it will forever remain so, why even bother? Cynicism indeed.

To many critical international legal scholars, however, the only thing more damned than a world with international law is a world without it. And since scholarship that ends at the point of no return has nowhere to go, they exercise a double-movement, employing aspiration to rescue international law from itself.[3] Enter the tragicomic. *If only* international law

[1] Antony Anghie, 'LatCrit and Twail' (2012) 42 California Western International Law Journal 311, 318.
[2] Robert M Cover, 'Violence and the Word' (1986) 95 Yale Law Journal 1601, 1610.
[3] Lorenzo Gradoni, 'Carlo Focarelli. International Law as Social Construct: The Struggle for Global Justice' (2014) 25 European Journal of International Law 605, 609.

Mohsen al Attar, *Subverting Eurocentric Epistemology* In: *Contingency in International Law*. Edited by: Ingo Venzke and Kevin Jon Heller, Oxford University Press. DOI: 10.1093/oso/9780192898036.003.0009

were '[to] listen ... to reconsider their way of seeing us';[4] *if only* international law became 'an instrument for or a site of liberation';[5] *if only* international law were not as international law is. Hope returns with a vengeance, in lockstep with the tragedy and farce of idealism. Anghie's declaration is the boldest of all: he tells us that the ambition of TWAIL scholars is 'to create a truly universal international law that promotes a compelling vision of international justice'.[6] Alas, the vision is rarely bolstered by anything beyond forceful appeals for better use of the current framework, warts and all, leaving even sympathetic readers either frustrated or despondent, usually both.

In this chapter, I propose that the use of counterfactuals could help overcome the impasse precipitated by TWAIL's almost schizophrenic double-movement. TWAIL's use of the counter-narrative has achieved its aim: far fewer are the denials of international law's barbaric past or of the contingency of the world's current configuration. The device has also run its course. Counter-narratives and condemnations, the bread and butter of TWAIL scholarship, has proven insufficient, stoking vexation and rage but doing little to alter the course of international legal history. To advance the causes of equality and equity in the reform of international law championed by TWAIL, something different is needed.

The counterfactual is an attractive device for critical legal scholars. It facilitates methodical explorations of alternative legal imaginaries, creating the means to test and finesse proposals for the reform of international law.[7] Indeed, the experimental yet methodical nature of the device allows, first, for better navigation of the muscular constraints that militate against reform—such as the mainstreaming of resurgent ethno-nationalism—and, second, for better advocacy against heavily contingent features of the international legal regime—such as the absence of debate on distribution inside international financial institutions. If deployed well, counterfactuals can help surmount the cynicism critical legal scholars bemoan by exploring alternatives to established trajectories. The catch, however, is that TWAIL must eschew the model of counterfactuals on display in this text and the antecedent conference. Ingo Venzke's parameters are sensible in achieving the type of critical and insightful exploration he promotes, highlighting the contingency of the contours of international law.[8] For TWAIL, however, the international legal regime must be reimagined root and branch. This translates into defying Venzke's list of cautions: our counterfactuals need not be probable or realistic nor, for that matter, need they *make sense* either. Borrowing from Quijano, Mignolo, and Walsh, I argue that the task of TWAIL parallels the task of decoloniality: to upend Eurocentric epistemology and knowledge, to imagine existence beyond the ideas that sustain the status quo.[9] For example, the state is the institutional

[4] Karin Mickelson, 'Rhetoric and Rage: Third World Voices in International Legal Discourse' (1998) 16 Wisconsin International Law Journal 353, 419.

[5] James Thuo Gathii, 'The Agenda of Third World Approaches to International Law (TWAIL)' in Jeffrey L Dunoff and Mark A Pollack (eds), *International Legal Theory: Foundations and Frontiers* (CUP 2019) <https://ssrn.com/abstract=3304767> accessed 18 June 2020.

[6] Anghie, 'LatCrit and Twail' (n 1) 320.

[7] Ingo Venzke, 'What If? Counterfactual (Hi)Stories of International Law' (2018) 8 Asian Journal of International Law 403.

[8] ibid 418.

[9] Walter D Mignolo and Catherine E Walsh, *On Decoloniality: Concepts, Analytics, Praxis* (Duke University Press 2018).

embodiment of coloniality and plutocracy and thus can never be decolonised nor democratised. As the framework for the mediation of relations between states, international law is equally toxic. In other words, the problem with international law is the very sense that it claims to possess, compelling TWAIL scholars to embrace 'non-sense' if they are to achieve the aims of the movement.

I proceed in three parts. I begin by exploring the paradox between cynicism and idealism in CILT scholarship with emphasis on TWAIL, underscoring the rationality of the putatively contradictory positions. My argument is that while these positions appear oppositional on their face, upon further investigation, we must conclude that both are required if the critique of international law is to remain within international legal fora. Next, I argue that frustration with the double-movement is precipitated not by disappointment with the supposed paradox but by dissatisfaction with the superficiality of the proposals. Calling for justice, equality, fairness does next to nothing to advance these struggles when the forms of justice, equality, and fairness are drawn from the same Eurocentric epistemology and knowledge that precipitates the injustice, inequality, and unfairness TWAIL laments. Seen through a decoloniality lens, the habitual rescue of extant international law is a core flaw in much critical international legal theory. In the third part, I detail how TWAIL scholars can leverage counterfactuals to advance a more robust debate on the type of legal reform that could counter the prejudicial design and practice of current international law.

II. Between cynicism and idealism: escaping the paradox of TWAIL scholarship

Theories rise and fall. Across academic disciplines, theories or systems of ideas are developed to explain and predict social phenomena. The dynamism of human existence means that theories are mostly ephemeral, relevant only for a specific temporal period or within a specific geographical space. Democratic capitalism, for instance, lost its explanatory force with the denationalisation of production, the rise of neoliberalism, and the triumph of executive democracy, in no specific order. Law is no different with varied theories developed and deployed across millennia to explain the phenomenon of law.

Of relevance for my argument are theories *about* law such as CILT, legal feminism, and, importantly, TWAIL.[10] Why is law the way it is? Who does law privilege, at whose expense, and how? Could it be otherwise? While *theories about law* exhibit both reflective and normative qualities, unlike their ideological counterparts, they do not offer a foundational architecture but critique aspects of an extant legal framework from a preferred angle and, sometimes, positing aspirational or applied solutions to the identified grievances. CILT and TWAIL self-evidently fall into the theories *about* law category, proffering reflections on international law as it is, as it fails, and as it could/should be.

[10] Robert Knox, 'What Is to Be Done (With Critical Legal Theory)?' (2011) 22 Finnish Yearbook of International Law 32; James Thuo Gathii, 'Alternative and Critical: The Contribution of Research and Scholarship on Developing Countries to International Legal Theory' (2000) 41 Harvard International Law Journal 263; Makau Mutua, 'Critical Race Theory and International Law: The View of an Insider-Outsider' (2000) 45 Villanova Law Review 841.

1. CILT in transition

While eclectic, occasionally contradictory, CILT and TWAIL are characterised by trends and patterns. Two stand out above the others. First, they are enamoured with both prejudice and privilege. Their scholars explain how, first, the architecture of international law and, second, its operation are biased in favour of and against certain established constituencies.[11] Second, they are also attracted to international law's ambivalence towards itself: many of the critical scholarly interventions problematise not just bias within international law but also its self-perpetuating character.[12]

According to Fleur Johns, CILT is characterised by multiple phases though, for my forthcoming discussion of TWAIL and counterfactuals, only the initial two are relevant.[13] The first emerged following the collapse of the post-war compromise. Once democratic capitalism ceased being democratic, liberal legalism ceased being liberal precipitating the emergence of a new explanatory theory. Enter the first iteration of CILT. First and foremost, scholars challenged 'the broad architectures of thought and allegiance by which the twentieth century had, to that point, been marked'.[14] Anyone familiar with CILT will immediately spot the works of David Kennedy and Martti Koskenniemi. Structuralist and post-structuralist critiques intermingled to devastating effect, undermining the historical purchase of text and doctrine (or positivism *tout court*) and demonstrating that both scholarly tools were inadequate in explaining the operation—not to say the character—of international law.

Koskenniemi is elucidative here. His *Politics of International Law* represents both a high and low point of CILT, a characterisation he acknowledges in his unoriginally titled sequel *Politics of International Law—20 Years Later*.[15] The initial iteration of the critique focused on doctrinal problems: what does sovereignty entail? How are sources adumbrated? Do historical accounts of international law cohere with the history of international law? Legal hermeneutics were deployed to advance a sweeping assault on international law's indeterminacy. Koskenniemi convincingly demonstrated that international legal arguments operate as fair weather fans, supporting one position one day and a contrary one another. As a glaring example of Koskenniemi's indeterminacy thesis, consider the International Criminal Court's ruling on South Africa's failure to detain Omar Bashir. In this instance, Sudan's non-assent to the Rome Statute proved insufficient in precluding the jurisdiction of the court over Sudan's head of state.[16] Official justifications for legal positions prove themselves something worse than fallible: they are, the indeterminacy thesis proclaims, fickle.

CILT's second phase was no less controversial. Disappointed with the critics' reproduction of the very hierarchies they bemoaned, CILT scholars and their Critical Legal Studies (CLS) predecessors were taken to task by the new kids on the block including Critical Race

[11] Anne-Charlotte Martineau, 'Overcoming Eurocentrism? Global History and the Oxford Handbook of the History of International Law' (2014) 25 European Journal of International Law 329.

[12] Knox (n 10).

[13] Fleur Johns, 'Critical International Legal Theory' in Mark A Pollack and Jeffrey L Dunoff (eds), *International Legal Theory: Foundations and Frontiers* (CUP 2019) <https://ssrn.com/abstract=3224013> accessed 18 June 2020.

[14] ibid 12.

[15] Martti Koskenniemi, 'The Politics of International Law—20 Years Later' (2009) 20 European Journal of International Law 7.

[16] Dapo Akande, 'The Immunity of Heads of States of Nonparties in the Early Years of the ICC' (2018) 112 AJIL Unbound 172.

theory, Feminist Legal theory, Post-structuralism, and, again, TWAIL. As Duncan Kennedy remarked, CLS was 'pushed hard [for] the ultra-white-male ethos of the New Left' and by post-structuralists for 'the super-straightness of that same white male ethos'.[17] 'Parochialism and privilege' undergirded both CLS and CILT as much as they did naturalism and positivism.[18] The irony was not lost on certain critical scholars who observed that the grievances raised by many of the movement's interlocutors reinforced the same paradigm of oppression CILT bemoaned. A similar sentiment informed TWAIL with Antony Anghie and Bhupinder Chimni dryly observing that, despite the putative arbitrariness of international law, 'indeterminacy very rarely works in favor of Third World interests'.[19] Critical international legal scholars were falling out of love with both international law and their critiques of it, creating conditions for the rise of a putatively anti-colonial legal scholarly movement known primarily by its *nom de guerre*: TWAIL.

2. TWAIL: hope, anxiety, and question marks

TWAIL evolved as a semi-autonomous movement, drawing on CILT when necessary, mostly in the early days, and spurning it once they came to acknowledge the ultra-white-male ethos that bleached the theory. TWAIL's anti-colonial character is key and the movement goes to great effort to centre international law's predations, placing emphasis on the countless ways that international law is used to plunder, subordinate, and delegitimise the Third World.[20] The scholars vary considerably in substance, style, and aspiration but unite in their recognition of international law's development as an instrument of conquest, central to the colonisation of non-European lands and peoples.

Both TWAIL's unity and its thesis are conveyed principally through the counter-narrative. One of the editors of this collection, Ingo Venzke, describes counter-narratives as 'unravelling rereadings' of international law that compel us to see history through a lens far removed from the orthodox representations conveyed in celebrated—and often unquestioned—texts.[21] As a scholarly device, counter-narratives are capable of much: 'Narratives that run counter to received wisdom are similar to histories counter to the facts. In both cases, the world changes.'[22] In her ethnography of CILT, Johns celebrates the impact of TWAIL on critical international legal theory through the successful deployment of counter-narratives: among others, TWAIL has produced 'a cogent counter-narrative ... surrounding the status, character and constitution of

[17] Duncan Kennedy, *The Rise & Fall of Classical Legal Thought* (Beard Books 2006) xxxii.

[18] Johns (n 13) 7.

[19] Antony Anghie and Bhupinder S Chimni, 'Third World Approaches to International Law and Individual Responsibility in Internal Conflicts' (2003) 2 Chinese Journal of International Law 77, 101.

[20] Gathii (n 5); Mohsen al Attar, 'TWAIL: A Paradox Within a Paradox' (2019) forthcoming International Community Law Review; Luis Eslava and Sundhya Pahuja, 'Between Resistance and Reform: TWAIL and the Universality of International Law' (2011) 3 Trade, Law and Development 103; James Thuo Gathii, Henry J Richardson and Karen Knop, 'Introduction to Symposium on Theorizing Twail Activism' (2016) 110 AJIL Unbound 18; John D Haskell, 'TRAIL-Ing TWAIL: Arguments and Blind Spots in Third World Approaches to International Law' (2014) 27 The Canadian Journal of Law and Jurisprudence 383; Mohsen al Attar and Vernon Tava, 'TWAIL Pedagogy—Legal Education for Emancipation' (2009) 15 Palestine Yearbook of International Law 7.

[21] Venzke (n 7) 410.

[22] ibid.

sovereignty in international law'.[23] Anghie's *Imperialism, Sovereignty, and the Making of International Law* was pioneering in this genre of TWAIL scholarship and we have since been regaled by invaluable counter-narratives on the relationship between international law and plentiful sub-topics including war and commerce (James Gathii),[24] the New International Economic Order (Sundhya Pahuja),[25] Latin American anti-colonial resistance (Arnulf Lorca),[26] statehood (Obiora Okafor),[27] Bandung and the decolonisation movement (Luis Eslava, Michael Fakhri, and Vasuki Nesiah),[28] and human rights (Ratna Kapur), among others.

Re-readings of the past make for enlightening stories, compelling us to rethink that which we once took for granted. As Venzke astutely proclaims, with each counter-narrative, the world changes. And yet, it bears mentioning that the world also stays the same. Permanent members of the Security Council remain permanent; Third World countries are still threatened with annihilation; and the International Criminal Court's African fetish has yet to be satiated. For all the brouhaha, the counter-narrative often appears more feel good than do good, achieving few of TWAIL's ambitions. Bhupinder Chimni is even less charitable:

> Unfortunately, TWAIL has neither been able to effectively critique neo-liberal international law or project an alternative vision of international law. The ideological domination of Northern academic institutions, the handful of critical third world international law scholars, the problems of doing research in the poor world, and the fragmentation of international legal studies has, among other things, prevented it from either advancing a holistic critique of the regressive role of globalising international law or sketching maps of alternative futures.[29]

Despite the cynical tone, Chimni is hardly a cynic. Much of his oeuvre is dedicated to reflecting on the foundations of the very alternative futures TWAIL has failed to articulate. Yet Chimni is the exception that proves the rule. Much TWAIL scholarship, including my own, excels at critique demonstrating with both conviction and panache the predation that underpins international law. Yet, the *cri de guerre* that ignited the TWAIL movement—'The regime of international law is illegitimate'—was followed by a yelp for reform. What we require is more justice, greater equality, respect for sovereignty, moral equivalency, all of which we are told is to be achieved through more international law. How does TWAIL reconcile the contradiction? Two answers are proffered, neither of which prove satisfactory.

[23] Johns (n 13) 11.
[24] James Thuo Gathii, *War, Commerce, and International Law* (OUP 2010).
[25] Sundhya Pahuja, *Decolonising International Law: Development, Economic Growth and the Politics of Universality* (CUP 2011).
[26] Arnulf Becker Lorca, 'Universal International Law: Nineteenth-Century Histories of Imposition and Appropriation' (2010) 51 Harvard International Law Journal 475.
[27] Obiora C Okafor, 'International Human Rights Fact-Finding Praxis in Its Living Forms: A TWAIL Perspective' (2014) 1 The Transnational Human Rights Review 59.
[28] Luis Eslava, Michael Fakhri, and Vasuki Nesiah (eds), *Bandung, Global History, and International Law: Critical Pasts and Pending Futures* (CUP 2017).
[29] Bhupinder S Chimni, 'Third World Approaches to International Law: A Manifesto' (2006) 8 International Community Law Review 3, 3–4.

3. Why do TWAIL scholars rescue international law from TWAIL?

For the first, we turn to Anghie and Chimni, luminaries within the movement. They play two separate but complementary hands. They begin by telling us that 'TWAIL scholars are unwilling to depart the arena of international law, notwithstanding the injustices that international law has inflicted on the Third World' for they, like others, believe in the 'transformative potential of international law and in the ideal of law as a means of constraining power'.[30] On what do they rest this belief? On a further belief in the potential of 'good argument based on law' to prevail against power.[31] Their idealist opening is following by a realist salvo: TWAIL scholars should not 'conced[e] the entire arena of international law to other methodologies and actors' in the hopes of stumbling onto a more compelling discourse for justice.[32] International law possesses both symbolic and regulatory gravitas, 'fram[ing] problems, suggest[ing] responsibility, and propos[ing] solutions'.[33] Unfortunately, neither argument proves persuasive leading many other TWAIL scholars to the cynical cul-de-sac bemoaned.[34]

Faith can be powerful; it can even be compelling. However, we are compelled to ask *faith in what* are Anghie and Chimni advocating for? Does international law have transformative potential? Of course it does. The world has been repeatedly transformed by international legal machinations as both Anghie and Chimni detail in their respective works. The counter-narratives verify, however, that Third World peoples have mostly suffered at the hands of these transformations. Curiously, the scholars side-line Koskenniemi's indeterminacy thesis at the very moment it proves most valuable. In every instance where the Third World was hammered by international law, cogent arguments were made to justify the intervention. Moreover, the two scholars had the misfortune of championing the constraining power of international law in the very same year that the United States and the United Kingdom invaded Iraq, an act committed in flagrant violation of international law. Until today, Blair continues to forcefully 'argue' that the invasion was lawful and necessary to bring Hussein to heel. The issue is not whether international law frames problems, suggests responsibilities, and proposes solutions but the indeterminacy underpinning every step of the exercise: for example, tackling certain matters (eg non-tariff barriers) while simultaneously effacing others (eg hunger-related deaths). In this instance, Koskenniemi is on point: the politics of international law are the politics of definition as the partialities of some are adopted at the expense of many others.[35] Anghie and Chimni conflate *their* ideal of law with the reality of law and appear to fall into the 'false contingency' trap Susan Marks cautioned against, admittedly some years after the publication of their article.[36]

For the second attempt to reconcile TWAIL's seemingly contradictory strands, we turn to a contributor to this volume, Umut Özsu, for his nakedly Marxist rescue of critical international legal theory's reformative aspirations. In his remarks during the Contingency in International Law conference that helped guide this scholarly collection, Özsu proclaimed

[30] Anghie and Chimni (n 19) 101.
[31] ibid.
[32] ibid.
[33] Anghie and Chimni (n 19) 101.
[34] SG Sreejith, 'An Auto-Critique of TWAIL's Historical Fallacy: Sketching an Alternative Manifesto' (2017) 38 Third World Quarterly 1511.
[35] Koskenniemi (n 15).
[36] Susan Marks, 'False Contingency' (2009) 62 Current Legal Problems 1.

that 'Marxism affords the strongest set of analytical tools for explaining (rather than simply describing) the contingencies of international legal history'.[37] He proceeds to detail two argumentative approaches that capture the Marxist tradition within international legal scholarship, self-evidently favouring the second. The juxtaposition is well known and figures prominently in much critical international legal scholarship. China Miéville is represented on one end of the spectrum, making his now familiar argument about the ideal of international law being the chaos of international law.[38] Both Özsu and Miéville articulate the argument more eloquently: 'if, as [Miéville] insists, "the chaotic and bloody world around us *is the rule of law*", and it is therefore delusional or hypocritical to invest in international law as a "progressive" force, one is effectively left with no choice but to espouse a kind of legal nihilism, adopting a preponderantly quietist posture with respect to the legal ramifications of "norm-breaching" acts of violence like unilateral humanitarian intervention'.[39] A nihilistic alleyway is where many iconoclasts inevitably end up, stumbling through the morass of hopelessness with the stink of surrender emanating from their garb.

Özsu is no fatalist, however, and he draws on both Poulantzas and Knox to rescue international law from itself. The regime is indeed grounded in the violence of capitalist production, not unlike the state system itself, but still 'law commands a degree of normative and institutional autonomy, claiming that its material and institutional structures register the settlements of past struggles, some of which are capable of being deployed as part of anti-capitalist and anti-imperialist programmes'.[40] The position Özsu endorses and encourages others to adopt is one of 'principled opportunism' and 'cautious investment' in legal arguments that can be deployed on 'strategic terrain'.[41] While his regard for Miéville's position rings shallow, his sincerity reaches deafening levels when cautioning against the 'erroneous and self-defeating' strategy of 'cast[ing] law aside on account of a puritanically romantic attachment to non-legal forms of resistance'.[42]

4. From principled opportunism to false contingency

The space afforded in this chapter is insufficient to engage fully with Özsu's powerful albeit eminently contestable claims. I limit myself to a few remarks that situate his argument in relation to my own and facilitate a segue into the next section, a position that I argue is more persuasive in addressing the contradictions of TWAIL. It would be churlish to doubt Özsu's overriding premise: law is both a site and an expression of struggle; it is denoted by class clashes and class compromises. This quality, too, enhances rather than undermines international law's indeterminacy. As Rajagopal and Lorca observed some years before Özsu, Third World peoples may have been victimised by international law but they were hardly passive in the exercise engaging in multiple forms of resistance, both legal and extra-legal,

[37] Umut Özsu, 'The Necessity of Contingency' (Contingency in the Course of International Law, Amsterdam, June 2018) 2.
[38] China Mieville, 'The Commodity-Form Theory of International Law: An Introduction' (2004) 17 Leiden Journal of International Law 271.
[39] Özsu (n 37) 3.
[40] ibid.
[41] ibid 4.
[42] ibid 5.

all of which inform international law as it now exists.[43] To deny this is to ignore both the dynamism and contestation that are part and parcel of the formulation of international law.

Yet, as highlighted in the introduction to this chapter, international law may not be determinate but neither is it random. As Marks persuasively argues, beware false necessity:

> I believe it is quite right to hammer the point that history is a social product, not a given but made. For if it has been made, then it can be remade differently. This is surely a cardinal principle of all progressive thought, and the work of drawing out its multifarious implications is as urgent as it is endless. The worry I want to explore, here, however, is that we may be undertaking this work in a way which causes us to neglect the equally important progressive point that possibilities are framed by circumstances. While current arrangements can indeed be changed, change unfolds within a context that includes systematic constraints and pressures.[44]

She goes on to label her worry that of 'false contingency'.[45]

Like Marks, I do not ignore the malleability of the constraints we operate within or the tensions that colour the exercise of power. To suggest that power has it easy is, indeed, naïve, not to say counter-productive in the extreme. And yet, I cannot help but feel that Özsu, like Anghie and Chimni, is expressing the misguided optimism that frequently characterises TWAIL scholarship. What do we make of the superstructure of law if even the Marxists deny law's superstructural character? The traditions of past scholarship frame our thinking in convincing but ultimately contingent ways. Özsu appears to fall into a similar trap as Anghie and Chimni: neither argument nor norms are truly autonomous, imbued with the predilections of those who articulate them and thus curbing their transformative potential. Their critical, even revolutionary thinking begins to sound less radical and more conformist than their passionate prose implies.

Notice that Anghie and Chimni speak of international legal problems and solutions as though these are divorced from the contingent rationalities of the original authors. Equally representative of their cognitive bias is their dismissal of the search for alternative discourses of justice, as if international law enjoys a monopoly over justice or, as some more radical scholars would assert, enjoys a relationship to justice at all. The same is true of Özsu and his reliance on international law's 'normative and institutional autonomy' inferring that this is not in itself constructed, artificial, and, ultimately, contingent. He even implicitly castigates Miéville for pursuing an 'erroneous and self-defeating' strategy. The gist of Özsu's argument is that operating within the system that he himself laments is realistic while operating beyond it is romantic and, incidentally, irrational. Özsu is aware of the thin ice he is treading, turning to Knox and advocating 'principled opportunism', 'cautious investment', and the distinction between strategies and tactics. In short, all three scholars believe their arguments rational, realistic, and politically savvy, seeming mostly oblivious to the fact that they may have fallen victim to the Eurocentric epistemology they bemoan.

[43] Balakrishnan Rajagopal, 'Counter-Hegemonic International Law: Rethinking Human Rights and Development as a Third World Strategy' (2006) 27 Third World Quarterly 767; Lorca (n 26).
[44] Marks (n 36) 2.
[45] ibid.

To be clear, I do not doubt the validity of their conclusions. Based upon their commitments and preferred modes of reasoning, the conclusions they reach are understandable, salient even. Whether they are convincing is another matter that goes beyond the scope of this article. What I draw attention to is an overriding flaw in their respective analyses as they conclude that theirs is a rational course of action rather than a contingent one that some others are likely to protest. The rationality they rely upon is itself sourced in the system they condemn, precipitating the cynicism that many students of critical international law graduate with. TWAIL problematises the consistently prejudicial operation of international law to the disadvantage of the Third World. The realist turn, especially when informed by the same prejudiced regime, does little to allay the feeling that we are merely legitimating what TWAIL itself regards as an illegitimate system. Consider, for example, that the impressive compendium of counter-narratives—*the untold story of international law*—all of which verify that the framework is hardly as just as frequently represented, has had little bearing on either dynamic of prejudice or dynamic of difference, exacerbating widespread cynicism among publicists towards international law's capacity for change.

In the following section, I introduce the concept of decoloniality, arguing that TWAIL and critical international legal theory more broadly must eschew the realism and good sense that many of its scholars champion.

III. Fighting Eurocentrism with Eurocentrism

International law is a totalising conceptual frame that describes the global but is rooted in the local. It could not be otherwise as all conceptual frames are culturally delineated. This claim is the starting point of TWAIL and, albeit to a lesser extent, CILT as well. As Anghie forensically detailed in *Imperialism, Sovereignty, and the Making of International Law*, embedded within TWAIL viewpoints on international law is censure of Eurocentrism, whether Third World critiques of Eurocentrism or, to use Walter Mignolo and Catherine Walsh's pithy phrase, 'Eurocentric critiques of Eurocentrism'.[46] Drawing on the work of Aníbal Quijano, Mignolo and Walsh explain how the 'colonial matrix of power' is rooted not just in the institutions and ideologies of modernity but also in many scholarly critiques and resistance movements. For example, despite his importance to critical reflections on law including TWAIL, to Mignolo and Walsh, Karl Marx remains a European thinker critiquing a European epistemology. Universalising Marx, as many Marxists do, often amounts to a form of misrecognition, as if non-Europeans are incapable of original critique themselves. Their assessment is relevant for TWAIL and to my preceding discussion of Anghie, Chimni, and Özsu.

To Quijano, coloniality is better understood not as an event—colonisation—but as a process of transformation whereby human experience and human aspiration are dictated by the preferences of a singular civilisational trajectory. Stated otherwise, coloniality encapsulates the drive to present European subjectivity as human objectivity. The distinction between coloniality and colonisation is essential to understanding the difference between decoloniality and decolonisation and the relationship of all of these to international law.

[46] Antony Anghie, *Imperialism, Sovereignty and the Making of International Law* (CUP 2004); Mignolo and Walsh (n 9) 3.

Decolonisation informs much of the TWAIL corpus, whether the earlier or later iteration of the movement.[47] Colonisation was a political, economic, and cultural project of coercion whereby Europe, following varying degrees of brutality, claimed and imposed dominion over the lands and lives of others. It is understandable then that liberation manifested as a movement to repel the invaders, both politically and economically. State sovereignty was the basis of political freedom and, to a lesser extent, the New International Economic Order was the basis of economic liberation.[48] Left out, however, was cultural autonomy as the Third World embraced the nation-state model, a political structure central to the colonial matrix of power and to the exploitative relationships that shaped modernity. Coloniality is thus present not only in the naked violence of right-wing ethno-chauvinistic nationalism but also in the pseudo-progressive discourses of decolonised states. Indeed, just as confrontation and exploitation were central to the Euro-American era, the advance of the Sino-Asiatic era would be impossible without equally shrewd programmes of exploitation. I return to Anghie, Chimni, and Özsu.

Özsu calls for cautious investment in the value of international law as an instrument in the struggle for something other than what we have. Anghie and Chimni go further, ascribing intrinsic value to international legal arguments and to international law itself. Yet, when deploying a decoloniality critique, we understand that the aim is not simply to make use of the master's tools to either dismantle the master's house or to build a slave's house. Instead, what is needed are tools that transcend Eurocentric political, legal, and epistemic frames. To place it in an inquisitive tone, 'once it [becomes] evident that the state can be neither decolonized nor democratized', why do critical international legal scholars continue to insist about the decolonisation and democratisation of international law? It is naïve, duplicitous even to insist that authoritarian trees can yield democratic fruit. The flaw then is the denial by critical international legal scholars of the bounded and colonial character of their rationality.

Mignolo and Walsh make a similar point. They explain the conundrum through an ontological lens. Ontology is comprised of two elements: first, cosmology or a narrative about the creation of world and, second, epistemology or the principles that guide our knowing of the world.[49] What we regard as disciplines—economics, politics, and law—are nothing more than enactments of knowledge, constituted by and through our knowledge. There is nothing transcendent about state, sovereignty, legal, illegal, or non-legal. These concepts, so revered among publicists, are mere enactments of the same epistemological frame, one that Mignolo and Walsh tell us is shot through with a colonial construct of knowledge. Consider, for example, that dispossession, oppression, inequality, predation, and destitution are as much a part of the narrative of modernity as are the rule of law, the notion of equality, and supposed oneness of humanity.[50] Yet while the latter are celebrated as constitutive of

[47] Sundhya Pahuja, 'The Postcoloniality of International Law' (2005) 46 Harvard International Law Journal 459.

[48] Antony Anghie, 'Legal Aspects of the New International Economic Order' (2015) 6 Humanity 145; Margot E Salomon, 'From NIEO to Now and the Unfinishable Story of Economic Justice' (2013) 62 International and Comparative Law Quarterly 31; Eric Allen Engle, 'The Failure of the Nation State and the New International Economic Order: Multiple Converging Crises Present Opportunity to Elaborate a New Jus Gentium' (2003) 16 St. Thomas Law Review 187.

[49] Mignolo and Walsh (n 9) 141.

[50] Ironically, the most rabid ethno-chauvinists are far likelier to acknowledge the exploitative character of capitalism (which they justify with eugenicist arguments) than the progressive liberals who conceal its core character by dressing capitalism in silk robes: productive, compassionate, and recently philanthropic capitalism.

modernity, the former are regarded as indiscretions, errors, or even pathologies, disassociating equally constitutive elements from the narrative:

> It cannot be said explicitly that slavery is the exploitation of human beings for the benefit of other human beings. It cannot be said explicitly that the war in the Middle East or West Asia is for the control of territory and natural resources and not for the liberation or well being of people ... Once weapons were fabricated to implement wars; the neoliberal inversion of the rhetoric consists in fabricating wars to implement and sell weapons.[51]

Such is the nature of coloniality or the colonial matrix of power. Created in the Third World, the theoretical construct exists to reveal that which modernity conceals. An assertion from the current British Prime Minster, Boris Johnson, encapsulates official denial of the dark side of history: '[Africa] may be a blot, but it is not a blot upon [British] conscience. The problem is not that we were once in charge, but that we are not in charge any more.'[52] And how to rescue 'Africa'? 'The best fate for Africa would be if the old colonial powers, or their citizens, scrambled once again in her direction; on the understanding that this time they will not be asked to feel guilty.'[53] While Johnson is routinely pilloried for his xenophobic views, he holds neither authorship nor monopoly over the white man's burden. Central to the narrative of modernity is jingoism. Whether we draw upon theology or science, upon law or economics, supposedly universal truths are tactically deployed to sustain a colonial matrix of power. Decoloniality involves an epistemic challenge to the principles of knowledge, a task that involves changing the terms of the debate altogether.[54]

Critiques of decolonisation will aid us in distinguishing decolonisation from the more reflective task of decoloniality. Few are the TWAIL scholars who do not regard decolonisation as a failure. Their grievances are many: the preference of political sovereignty over economic sovereignty, the use of repression to fudge national unity, a comprador class collaborating with former colonial powers, the embrace of capitalist, neoliberal, and even imperial logics, and, the internalisation and ratcheting up of racialised hierarchies.[55] Each disappointment is magnified by their lasting power. In a recent text, Bedjaoui asserts the purchase of political realism.[56] Even with Third World jurists and scholars' awareness of the dark side of sovereignty and statehood, the aim of the decolonising state was to force out imperial powers; only then can preferred modes of organisation and governance be deliberated and pursued.[57] Of course, the deliberation rarely happened, the pursuit even less and, in a form of autopoiesis, state logic sustained its self-expression, reinforcing new alliances and quarrels in quick succession. Yet, as Mignolo and Walsh accurately conclude: if the state

[51] Mignolo and Walsh (n 9) 141.

[52] Boris Johnson, 'The Boris Archive: Africa Is a Mess, but We Can't Blame Colonialism' *The Spectator* (London, 2 February 2002) <http://www.spectator.co.uk/article/the-boris-archive-africa-is-a-mess-but-we-can-t-blame-colonialism> accessed 18 June 2020.

[53] ibid.

[54] Mignolo and Walsh (n 9) 145.

[55] Pahuja (n 25); BS Chimni, 'An Outline of a Marxist Course on Public International Law' (2004) 17 Leiden Journal of International Law 1.

[56] Mohammed Bedjaoui, 'Les "TWAIL" et le Sort des Etudes Juridiques Postcoloniales' in Mark Toufayan, Emmanuelle Tourme-Jouannet, and Hélène Ruiz Fabri (eds), *Droit International et Nouvelles Approches sur le Tiers-Monde: Entre Répétition et Renouveau* (Société de Législation Comparée 2013).

[57] Rémi Bachand, 'Les Third World Approaches to International Law: Perspectives pour une Approche Subalterniste du Droit International' in Toufayan, Tourme-Jouannet, and Ruiz Fabri (n 56).

cannot be democratised, how do critical international legal scholars hope to achieve human emancipation?

By accepting the rule of law, Anghie, Chimni, and Özsu put forward what, on its face, appears as a familiar than a radical proposal: to leverage the rule of law and to springboard off international law's normative and institutional autonomy in pursuit of better outcomes for Third World peoples. TWAIL and Marxism begin to tread dangerously close to modelling a pretence to power proximate to that of the would-be rulers of the world. None of this is surprising as the questions we ask and the answers we proffer are 'a consequence of being embedded and living in a Western imaginary enveloped in the process of becoming itself'.[58] For law, like other components in the narrative of modernity, is coloured with the same flawed premise: that epistemology is the product of ontology. Decoloniality scholars invert the relationship, asserting that epistemology begets ontology. The same is true of law that begins not with a rule but a relation that we name and regulate: what constitutes a right, what constitutes a duty, and why is there a hierarchy between them? In this frame, liberation is achieved by pursuing new ways of thinking, knowing, and being.

What does liberation look like for critical international legal theory? As alluded to above, it means we '[transcend] rather than [dismantle] Western ideas [by] building our houses of thought', the theorising and praxis of decolonial liberation in law.[59] For this act, I propose the use of counterfactuals but I propose them in the vein of TWAIL.

IV. Exploring alternative epistemologies through Third World counterfactuals

Venzke provides an overview of counterfactuals in the introduction as do many other contributions to this volume. Rather than repeating the exercise, I accept their representations and speak directly to its value for critical international legal theory broadly and TWAIL specifically.

TWAIL scholars are ostensibly on the lookout for alternative normative and operative frameworks.[60] The desire for an alternative figures prominently in their scholarship even if their approach to alternatives is more *wait and see* than *develop and trial*, more critique than creation. For example, the New International Economic Order, perhaps the most systematic attempt by Third World states to conceptualise social organisation beyond an orthodox Eurocentric frame, is endlessly savaged by critical scholars, almost as a rite of passage.[61] The criticisms are many and layered though are consistently bookended with the Third World's surrender to capitalist logic.[62] Many Marxists are particularly virulent, skewering the Third World for failing to heed the most basic truths about capitalist economic relations. Drawing on counterfactuals, I argue that another approach would prove more supportive of TWAIL's ambition.

[58] Mignolo and Walsh (n 9) 147.
[59] ibid 7.
[60] Chimni (n 29).
[61] Salomon (n 48).
[62] John Linarelli, Margot E Salomon, and Muthucumaraswamy Sornarajah, *The Misery of International Law* (OUP 2018).

I draw inspiration from Venzke's 'garment workers as seals' paradigm.[63] To provide a bit of background, the European Union prohibits the import and trade of seal products. Due in part to a public campaign that sought to highlight the brutality of seal hunting, animal welfare concerns figure prominently in the EU's rationale for the prohibition, articulated most forcefully in the EU's defence under the public morals exception to a WTO challenge against the prohibition brought by Canada and Norway. Around the same period, 1,134 garment workers in the Rana Plaza in Bangladesh were crushed and suffocated to death when the plaza where they produced clothing for Primark and Matalan, among others, collapsed onto itself and onto them. While the brutal conditions and hazards in the factory were well known, the disposable fashion sector's business model—an endless supply of rapidly produced cheap garments—ensures that orders are filled even while a 'mass industrial homicide' is underway (neighbouring factories continued to operate the day after the massacre).[64] Utilising the EC-Seals case and the Rana Plaza catastrophe, Venzke explores the paradox between our regard for seals and our disregard for workers.

In his counterfactual, Venzke hypothesises a world where both constituencies are afforded equal regard, making an important contribution to the debate about First World exploitation of precarious Third World labour. His first observation is that, in contrast to the import prohibitions on seal products, similar restrictions on garments produced in reprehensible conditions, are opposed by a mix of stakeholders including clothing manufacturers and retailers, Third World states, and First World consumers. Consensus around the lovability of baby seals means that import prohibitions on seal products are controversial only to the seal industry. Next, he argues that opposition could be settled by denying market access to producers who fail to improve health and safety standards. While this would surely increase the costs of production and thus cut into the profit margins and affordability of disposable fashion, it would improve working conditions for Third World labour. While these points are unoriginal, they are essential in appreciating that 1,134 workers were crushed and suffocated as much by concrete as they were by European conceptions of public morals. Marx's writings on commodity fetishism have not lost their relevance, nor has Rodney's critique of First World predation on Third World bodies.[65] These points advance Venzke's core argument: that counterfactuals help us appreciate the peculiarity of the normativity that underpins the distinction in treatment afforded to seals and garment workers. According to Venzke, 'the main point remains the exposure of imbalances … [w]hy does the gruesome practice of clubbing seals trigger public action when the awful treatments of labourers in the garment industry is left to the choices of consumers, guided by voluntary and largely ineffective labelling schemes?'[66] The counterfactual provokes readers by drawing attention to the persistence of paradigms of racism and white supremacy in the operation of the global economy, albeit in abstract language, inferring that the lives of baby seals rank higher in the European cosmic vision than the lives of Bangladeshi garment workers.

[63] Venzke (n 7) 428.

[64] Michael Safi and Dominic Rushe, 'Rana Plaza, Five Years on: Safety of Workers Hangs in Balance in Bangladesh' *The Guardian* (London, 24 April 2018).

[65] Duncan Kennedy, 'The Role of Law in Economic Thought: Essays on The Fetishism of Commodities' (1984) 34 The American University Law Review 939; Walter Rodney, *How Europe Underdeveloped Africa* (Howard University Press 1981).

[66] Venzke (n 7) 430.

For TWAIL, more elucidative is what the counterfactual reveals about international law and its role in preserving Eurocentric visions of oppression and liberation. Quoting Lebow approvingly, Venzke declares that the counterfactual must 'arise from the context' and must be 'realistic'.[67] On its face, this seems sensible, much like the exhortations of Anghie, Chimni, and Özsu also do. Yet, for a Third World that is consistently bludgeoned by context and reality, these parameters provide little succour. To be clear, Venzke's counterfactual model works well for progressive critical international legal scholars who aspire to tweak aspects of international law while preserving the underlying framework and the overriding epistemology. While I do not doubt either Venzke's progressive credentials or sincerity, I also note that the counterfactual is itself laden with the West's corrosive institutions that constituted a tiered world in the first place. His counterfactual only works if we presume that nation-states, capitalism, endless production and consumption, disposable fashion, the WTO, global stratification, and the premise that legal strategies which limit the bludgeoning of seals, garment workers, or whatever entity that irks European sensibilities can lead to the amelioration of international law. Venzke's counterfactual successfully highlights the contingency of the dubious morals that underpin European practices in international trade law and explores a sensible response to inequality, depravity, and barbarity. Yet, it is a critique of Eurocentrism for Europeans and I wonder how it would transform if the Third World was invited to the conversation. Indeed, despite the publication of the counterfactual in the *Asian Journal of International Law*, it is difficult to imagine a lecture on the scenario gaining much traction at the Rana Plaza memorial site. Bangladeshi garment workers would be excused for wondering why they are being likened to seals.

From TWAIL and Third World garment workers' perspectives, this counterfactual is characteristic of the Eurocentrism that infects much progressive legal thinking.[68] The problem, however, goes beyond the specific counterfactual. By grounding counterfactuals in context and in reality, we are also embedding them in the European provincialism that informs international law. Yet critical international legal theory's rationalisation of the current system—whether the law of seas, the territorial integrity of states, or the United Nations—accepts the imperial ambition upon which the edifice is built. And while I appreciate the need to resist projecting present knowledge 'into the past and into the minds of historical actors', I am equally weary of re-readings of the past designed to exorcise the etiological role of European imperialism in shaping the current framework.[69] International law is shot through with predatory ambitions. And while it is true that international law has served to constrain some of Europe's worst instincts, it only succeeds when Europe consents to the constraints. Eurocentric international law remains a perfect paradox and thus an inadequate framework for Third World liberation.

Cue the baby and the bath water idiom. But if the baby represents international law, then it is a predatory, genocidal, and sociopathic infant bathing in the putrefaction of its own pathologies. We cannot kill it quick enough. To infer as Venzke does that we must remain close to reality legitimises a reality that, he himself points out, is contingent and mostly beneficial to its authors; just as indeterminacy consistently works against the Third World,

[67] ibid 419.
[68] Martineau (n 11); James Thuo Gathii, 'International Law and Eurocentricity' (1998) 9 European Journal of International Law 184.
[69] Venzke (n 7) 423.

so too do counterfactuals shackled by Venzke's parameters. We are compelled to accept that which is simply because Europe has authored it, denying in the process the contingency of the configuration and, more importantly, the contingency of the epistemology. Venzke, Anghie, Chimni, and Özsu accept the narrative of modernity despite modernity's reduction of 'the majority of the population to quasi-human'.[70] To raise some of these quasi-humans to the level of seals might be progressive in the current context but the same regressive epistemology continues to hold the Third World 'hostage [to] modernity's designs and desires'.[71]

Counterfactual thinking can prove valuable to TWAIL and to the Third World but the type of counterfactuals are those that operate outside the confines of good sense. The examples are plentiful: a democratic Security Council, an IMF whose president is selected by African states, the constitutionalisation of participatory economics, a global moratorium on intellectual property rights, and more. As outlandish as these counterfactuals may sound, each has the advantage of highlighting that what makes sense in today's international legal framework, the contingencies that now exist as legal truths, are little more than Eurocentric partialities designed to preserve Europe's ascendancy at the expense of non-Europeans. Neither the context nor the reality need be accepted; in fact, they should be jettisoned altogether as we seek to inject new epistemologies into international law and, for that matter, into human civilisation. A decoloniality approach to counterfactuals and to critical international legal theory would highlight the embedded nature of the Western imaginary and the importance of challenging those very elements that make the most sense. Only then will we come to appreciate that the dualism between optimism and cynicism, that the binary between realism and romanticism that colours much of the debate in critical international legal theory are borne of a Eurocentric ontology that sustains the brutality of the status quo.

V. Resisting international law's subordination of the Third World

Like history, international law is neither determinate nor random. Structural logic and historical contingency combine to corral the options available to us, facilitating the status quo and foreclosing radical alternatives. Yet, the boundaries are more malleable than the cynics and tragicomics would have us believe. Scholars make their own research, but they do not make it organically; they do not make it out of knowledge created by themselves, but out of such learning as they find close at hand. The tradition of past generations of scholars necessarily weighs on the thoughts of the current one, framing their thinking in convincing but ultimately contingent ways. And at the very moment that scholars appear to acknowledge the contingency of things that are and things that will be, at these moments of transformative potential and revolutionary thinking, they deploy the idealism of the familiar to freeze the contingency of the future: *if only* is the last bulwark of the vanquished.

A TWAIL-based counterfactual paradigm will open minds and possibilities. If deployed with creativity and verve, counterfactuals offer a way forward. But they must subvert reality, context, and sense to underscore that what we regard as real, contextual, and sensible are all contingent and, to those who suffer the predations and perversions of these categories, they are also nonsensical. Just as counter-narratives were needed to challenge inaccurate

[70] Mignolo and Walsh (n 9) 119.
[71] ibid.

accounts of international legal history that acted to prolong the violence of Eurocentrism, so too are radical counterfactuals needed to plot pathways towards alternative models of international legal relations that do not seek to legitimise the segmentation of humanity into First World agents and Third World subjects. Writing accounts of international law where Bangladeshi garment workers are not compelled to beg for non-lethal working conditions, where First World consumers express solidarity with humans alongside non-humans also, where International Covenants and treaties are not treated as voluntary codes of conduct, will throw into vivid relief the nonsense that we are committed to. And while some might regard the nonsensical accounts I propose as little more than nonsense, radical counterfactuals are capable of pushing both TWAIL and critical legal theory beyond the comfort of the status quo, igniting our creative imaginaries in the process.

And that is what I would hope to see from TWAIL: the embrace of what many of our antagonists regard as nonsense.

10

The Time of Contingency in International Law

Geoff Gordon

I. Contingency works

This chapter addresses ways in which contingency supports international law. It takes off from a supposition that contingency is a key element in the operation of international law as a mode of power. The underlying insight is simple and familiar: international law is indeterminate.[1] In an indeterminate field, contingency is part of the basic construction. Any given decision or disposition can always be otherwise. Determination is likewise relevant here: when a given rule or right is amenable to two or more divergent readings—when the rule or right is a contingent one—resolution will be driven by other powers and things; and when international legal controversies are resolved in consistent fashion over time, some other apparatuses contribute to stabilise the practice of international law.[2] But it is part of the argument of this chapter that these determining apparatuses operate in conjunction with contingency under international law, that their determining force does not contravene contingency and is not contravened by contingency.[3] In its relationship and interoperation with the things that determine its outcomes, the utility of international law resides precisely in its contingent possibilities. This puts international law in a co-productive relationship with these other apparatuses: by virtue of its contingent character, international law operates to sustain the apparatuses that work to structure the field of international law, as I will explain.[4] In this chapter, I look at temporal and economic structuring apparatuses with which international law has a co-productive relationship, and the ways in which contingency is mobilised among them.

To get at the relationship among these things, I first take a step back to sketch a larger context by which the contingency of international law can be made legible. The larger context that I gesture to here pertains to a Western humanist tradition stretching back at least to the Renaissance. Working with this context for what it makes legible, I will rehearse the following argument: international law relies on contingency to sustain the humanist fantasy of a temporal economic actor. This temporal economic actor presupposes an abstract but individualised subject understood to be sovereign over itself. The self-sovereign individual is defined by capacities for agency and rationality that are mobilised in social and political context to maximise (self-)interest in the name of utility. On these bases—individual

[1] Martti Koskenniemi, *From Apology to Utopia: The Structure of International Legal Argument* (CUP 2005); David Kennedy, *International Legal Structures* (Nomos 1987).

[2] China Miéville, *Between Equal Rights: A Marxist Theory of International Law* (Brill 2005).

[3] Susan Marks, 'International Judicial Activism and the Commodity-Form Theory of International Law' (2007) 18 European Journal of International Law 199.

[4] I rely on the analytic of co-production developed by Sheila Jasanoff, 'Ordering Knowledge, Ordering Society' in Sheila Jasanoff (ed), *States of Knowledge: The Co-Production of Science and Social Order* (Routledge 2004) 13.

Geoff Gordon, *The Time of Contingency in International Law* In: *Contingency in International Law.* Edited by: Ingo Venzke and Kevin Jon Heller, Oxford University Press. © The Several Contributors 2021. DOI: 10.1093/oso/9780192898036.003.0010

self-sovereignty, agency, rationality, interests and utility—the humanist fantasy includes an emancipatory pretension to political pre-eminence that is inscribed in its temporality, but at odds with its economic underpinnings. The pretension to pre-eminence corresponds historically with an ascendant normative regime that has succeeded as an economic programme but continuously failed in significant political respects. I will unpack the historical narrative in the next two parts of this chapter. The take-away will be this: the frustrated emancipatory political programme is a complementary counterpart to the successful economic one, and the pretension to emancipatory political pre-eminence persists not despite but on the basis of failure and contradiction. As a result, the frustrations of international law's progressive programme are construed as a function of its contingent character, establishing negatively the urgency of its redemptive promise. Contingency thereby becomes the principle by which the legitimacy of the normative programme is intelligible.

The alchemy of turning failure into promise is enabled by special attributes of humanist temporality. Humanist temporality (like any temporality) is a social construction; like other social constructions, it has concrete effects in the world. I will describe the construction and its effects in formal and material terms. The formal terms include internal logics rooted in Cartesian and Kantian theory, their legacies, and political imperatives that they represent. The material terms include situated institutional constraints and distributional concerns as well as actual technologies of time production. These things and conditions together have structured the temporal order of international law. In so doing, they have made contingency intelligible in support of a normative programme predicated on the temporal economic actor, one for whom linear time is an infrastructural technology supporting transactional conditions associated with competitive markets.[5]

As I will explain below, the material temporal order upheld by international law enables a linear narrative capable of supporting a self-affirming contradiction: in the face of historical failure, international law always already contains within itself the normative solution. This is part of its progress narrative.[6] Its past failures are always proof of future successes, a source of assurance and self-affirmation. In turn, international law supports the impossibly linear temporal order by which it is empowered. In doing so, international law sustains the humanist fantasy and with it, the economic actor and programme to which that fantasy is linked in two ways. One, by maintaining the actual technologies of time that undergird the linear order. Two, by guaranteeing the normative *rightness* of the overall historical programme, despite the failure of key emancipatory political aspirations. Equally, it redirects or transfers political energy otherwise directed towards social political objectives into subjective self-affirmation, leaving other forces at work for political purposes. This, in part, is the politics of contingency.

The economic success I am referring to can be described in terms of a transnational global economy organised according to what Philip Allott has called primitive capitalism. The correlated emancipatory failure might be described in terms of what Allott has called international unsociety, a place where political aspirations go to die with the ideals that cover them.[7] By this I mean also to refer to the sense of disempowerment among the classes of people who contribute every day to the growth of the transnational global economy. Among

[5] Geoff Gordon, 'Imperial Standard Time' (2018) 29 European Journal of International Law 1197.
[6] Thomas Skouteris, *The Notion of Progress in International Law Discourse* (TMC Asser Press 2010).
[7] Philip Allott, *Eunomia: A New Order for a New World* (OUP 1990).

them, those of us (I use the plural to include myself) who trade in expertise and managerialism are nonetheless alienated by their ubiquity. One response historically has been to double down on an individualised political ethic, celebrating its normative possibility despite its general futility. This, I argue, has long been the heroic register of international law. It can be observed today when the International Court of Justice (ICJ) courageously grants provisional relief to Iran from the United States' deadly sanctions regimes. The relief granted by the Court valiantly and futilely affirmed the ethical validity of the same system that enables the undeterred sanctions regime in the first place.[8] It can be observed also in critiques of international law, for instance in the present volume, which I mean respectfully to interrogate: the theme of this volume, how international law could have been otherwise, reaffirms—however critically—international law's ethical promise not merely in the face of its failures, but *on the basis of them*.[9] In both modes, heroic and critical, we can observe Kantian and Cartesian logics at work, as I will elaborate. These logics affirm a subject that retreats politically into solipsistic self-regard while carrying forward—and being carried forward by—material economic practices.

Universal Coordinated Time (UTC), or globally standardised time today, is the principle time technology in support of the temporality that I mean to describe. It comprises an infrastructure that reproduces a precise, linear time scale that is instrumentally useful and ideologically potent. Instrumentally useful for the work it does, apparent all around in the work done by the technologies that reproduce or rely on globally standardised time. Ideologically potent because it is a naturalised fiction, creating the temporal conditions for a conceptual truth that supersedes and comes to define the material world of lived experience. In terms of the humanist fantasy and international law, this combination of instrumental and ideological characteristics means a materially productive time scale that supports a normative programme that has always already been the ideal ethical and emancipatory regime, even if it never has been. As I will explain, when political ideals fail, these temporal logics enable an affirmation of the subject who maintains those ideals, for no other reason than persisting as the same idealistic subject in the same material system that produced the failure. In sum, here is what I mean to say overall about the contingency of international law: *the normative affirmation that it could have been otherwise upholds material commitment to the actually-existing distribution of goods that it supports*. On this basis, international law enables and sustains the reproduction of the modern economic actor despite its political discontents.

I will tell this story below in three more parts divided by two longish historical intervals. The first two focus on formal logics in historical context, the third on contemporary practices and socio-technical conditions. The first part establishes the humanist frame by reference to Descartes, and focuses on the material and political foundations of the Cartesian subject. The second jumps to Kant, for further contributions to the humanist programme, deontological and ethical, in light of a changed historical context. The third picks up in the present day, where I will look more closely at the work done by international law together with technologies of temporal order and contingency to support the economic actor of humanist fantasy.

[8] Geoff Gordon, 'Contradiction and the Court: Heterodox Analysis of Economic Coercion in International Law' (forthcoming) 34 Temple International and Comparative Law Journal.

[9] To be sure, the discussion that this volume represents is an important one; my contribution is part of that discussion, not a rejection of it.

II. Cartesian subjects

For this brief review,[10] I rely on Antonio Negri's close analysis of Descartes' politics.[11] Negri draws for his study on a wealth of historians and commentators to describe the historical context that produced the Cartesian subject.[12] I summarise it in extreme shorthand here. A rising merchant class, situated between the aristocracy and the multitude, had reached the cusp of political power at the time of the Renaissance. I will refer to this class at points as proto-bourgeois, on the basis that the class prefigures the development of a modern bourgeois category typically referred to as the middle class. The emergence of this merchant class as a viable social and political force was part and parcel of the humanist and scientific programme that would ultimately erode the orders of medieval hierarchies, religious and feudal. It arose out of a historically-specific material and political basis, fuelled by the relatively broad distribution of wealth at the height of the Renaissance. Following the height of the Renaissance, however, the political and economic community of merchants and similarly-situated figures suffered material setbacks resulting in political reversals and economic malaise.[13] Negri describes at that juncture a strategic choice or compromise to forego overt political power in order to consolidate economic gains. The productive energies of the proto-bourgeoisie were confined as a result to a private, civic realm, divided from recognised, institutional political authorities backed by tradition and force of arms. The compromise allowed merchants, artisans and other members of this group to sustain material gains at the expense of self-mastery. Moreover, this class was confronted politically from above and below: by feudal and monarchical figures above, and the popular multitude below. Likewise, the production of knowledges and sciences necessary to continued economic expansion proceeded, but without control of the elite institutions wielding political power and without a popular political base to challenge those institutions. The compromise—material gain without political capacity—conflicted starkly with the aspirations of Renaissance humanism and undermined the self-identity of this proto-bourgeois class that Renaissance humanism had enabled.[14]

Negri describes a peak moment of crisis at the time of Descartes.[15] The class was bound up with scientific-philosophical development within an overall programme that was exposed on two fronts, institutionally and metaphysically. Institutionally, by the failure of political authority, and metaphysically, by the failure of normative confirmation that political authority might confer.[16] By the time of Descartes, the foundering humanist project was

[10] The review here is genealogical rather than philosophical. It concerns the conditions of intelligibility for a political programme defined in part by an intellectual tradition. That tradition includes a constellation of influential humanist thinkers and publicists, prominently including Descartes and Kant. Accordingly, the focus here is on their place in and contribution to the historical constellation and programme, rather than philosophical coherence. With respect to Descartes, and in keeping with Negri's treatment, I am drawing in the background on the *Discourse on the Method*, *Meditations on First Philosophy*, *Principles of Philosophy*, *Rules for the Direction of our Native Intelligence*, and *The World*. The first four can be found in English translation in *Descartes: Selected Philosophical Writings* (CUP 1988); the last can be found in *The Philosophical Writings of Descartes: Volume 1* (CUP 1985).

[11] Antonio Negri, *Political Descartes: Reason, Ideology and the Bourgeois Project* (Verso 2007).

[12] A partial list representing a fraction of the historians and commentators canvassed in Negri's work includes: F Braudel, G Cohen, E Gilson, E Hobsbawm, J Huizinga, A Koyré, R Lenoble, RH Popkin, and R Romano.

[13] Negri (n 11) 114–15.

[14] ibid 115–21.

[15] ibid 125–26.

[16] ibid 148–49.

largely sustained alternately by the mechanists and the libertines. The former, often closely linked with monarchists, espoused a passive acceptance of a mechanically-determined universe;[17] the latter, associated with quietism, espoused a retreat into unbridgeable moral and intellectual isolation, conceding the social realm to other forces.[18] The mechanists turned order against the individual; the libertines turned the individual into an escape from order. Descartes' intervention aimed to redeem humanism differently from these defeatist movements. The significance of the relationship of Descartes to the mechanists and libertines is twofold: mechanism and libertinism constitute the points within the humanist project against which his own programme becomes legible, and in the process, these points become inscribed in his own programme. His intervention at once will surpass and preserve them. I will stay focused for the time being on the ways in which Descartes' programme overcomes mechanism and libertinism, but will return at points to the preservation of mechanist and libertine elements inscribed in the tradition that follows from Descartes' programme.

Descartes' intervention boiled down to this: redeeming the humanist project and its associated, proto-bourgeois class by doubling down on the individual, such that the autonomous individual would constitute the fundamental building block of a rational order.[19] 'I think therefore I am' made the (proto-bourgeois) individual an entirely self-sustaining phenomenon, and in such a way as to become the foundational and systematic point of entry into the perceived world. Independent of all material supports and constraints, independent of worldly limitations and frustrations, the individual in the humanist tradition now founds and so can appreciate the world it observes. In this way Descartes rejected the determinism of the mechanists, making the subject the starting point or engine rather than the passive extension of an ordered universe. Equally, by making the individual constitutive of a systematic order, rather than an escape from it, he rejected the retreat of the libertines. But still his humanist redemption entailed compromise. While the rational and logical place of the humanist or proto-bourgeois individual in the world was now assured, and at the foundations of that world, that place was still established outside and independent of contemporaneous sites of political authority.[20] Descartes validated the class through the individual but without reliance on the traditional structures of political power. He preserved the political possibility in the identity of the class but conceded existing political controls to conserve the historical humanist programme in its other interrelated dimensions: scientific-philosophical, cultural, and economic.[21]

To that point, the class of persons who aspired to Descartes' subject had shared a material situation distinct from aristocracy and multitude, with material interests to match, but lacked a coherent programme by which to sustain and advance them. Descartes established that programme and legitimated those interests in the identity of a systematic and self-affirming subject. Descartes' programme re-established the humanist fantasy as a viable ideological programme, redeeming the Renaissance affirmation of the human capacity to establish order and value in the world. He redeemed it in the face of political dispossession by antagonistic political forces, and in the face of fatalism and quietism by mechanists and libertines, otherwise adhering still to the humanist tradition.[22] The fantasy, and the key

[17] ibid 194–97.
[18] ibid 118–21.
[19] ibid 212–18.
[20] ibid 224–29.
[21] ibid 239–42.
[22] ibid 239–42 and 248–49.

to reconstructing its possibility for political pre-eminence, entailed comprehending material values within and through oneself, with emphasis on the special role played by reason and rationality.

In Descartes' solution, peculiar dimensions of the temporal economic actor today are already discernible: an abstraction rationally defined according to a capacity for rationality, an individual empowered as part of a class that prioritises acquisition and growth, but growth without end under constitutive economic imperatives. The same individual celebrates its own ends but within a determined historical project that admits no clear telos, and is constitutive of civil society independent of political authority. These dimensions are not exactly linear, but their non-linear characteristics are obscured by an affirmation of rationally driven, linear progress. 'I think therefore I am' is circular in its solipsism, but conjoined to linear temporal and economic systems. And at the end of the day, the individual's solipsistic metaphysical affirmation served to guarantee its material interests in the absence of any other assurance. This is the solution that I mean to suggest has become a template for the temporal programme I associate here with international law: a solipsistic self-assurance that underwrites historically-specific material distributions, within a deceptively linear time scale linked to notions of progress. In this context, as I will discuss later, contingency is part and parcel of the political project, not a break from it.

Moving on for now: Descartes' humanist subject and class would not remain forever locked out of political institutions, but nor would they ever attain to total political emancipation. That failure is consistent with the terms of their Cartesian guarantee, which abandoned terms of social and political possibility to achieve a different systemic possibility.[23] Here the inscribed remnants of mechanism and libertinism are visible: the law-like nature of the systemic condition, evident in its mathematical certainties, coupled to the individualistic retreat from public authority. What Descartes already establishes is a subject born out of economic conditions, and in the name of which the world is reordered *for the historical purpose of sustaining its capacity as an economic actor*, by virtue of which political aspiration remains suppressed even as the political possibility of the class is preserved.[24] The new ordering of the world on this basis anticipates the normative work that international law will do. I turn next to Kant to mark a turning point in the political condition and the addition of a deontological programme to the metaphysical one. That combination—a once more ascendant class founded in the individual subject, and the articulation (represented by Kant) of a rule-based community among them—will prefigure further aspects of what I mean to draw out of international law.

III. Kantian rules

By the time of Kant,[25] the programme founded by Descartes' subject is an ideologically successful one. It has sustained and defined the identity of an expanding proto-bourgeoisie.

[23] ibid 247–53.

[24] ibid 207–208.

[25] As indicated at footnote 10, the study here focuses on a genealogical situation of Kant's work, rather than philosophical exposition. I draw in the background especially on *Groundwork of the Metaphysic of Morals*, the *Critiques*, and *Toward Perpetual Peace*. All can be found in English translation in *The Cambridge Edition of the Works of Immanuel Kant*, in the following volumes: Mary J Gregor (ed), *Practical Philosophy (The Cambridge Edition of the Works of Immanuel Kant)* (CUP 1996); Paul Guyer and Allen W Wood (eds), *Critique of Pure Reason*

Despite this success, however, dilemmas in both the material and metaphysical constitution of the class nonetheless remain apparent. The self-sufficiency of its subjectivity and interests are problematised twice over: first, the material interests of the class are acquired at the expense of the multitude and still at the sufferance of traditionally powerful political institutions (thus the class is not in fact self-sufficient); and second, the ideological success has isolated the subject within the system that it enables (and by which it is sustained), the subject's power founded solipsistically in itself. The former reflects the material reality of the acquisitive economic dimension of the Cartesian subject. The latter reflects the Cartesian compromise to redeem humanism with private validation rather than public commitment. As a result, each subject individually is left unable to overcome the invariable separation between itself and every other person or thing on whom it systematically relies for its affirmation. This separation leaves the subject alone in a world of objects that may be possessed but not known, echoing again the libertine withdrawal. And here the mechanistic dimension of the Cartesian project also remains apparent: the isolation of the subject from object and system leaves the subject alienated from the world (material, social) that it would define and order. Despite these dilemmas, however, the ideological success underwrote the economic success and growth of this class of subjects, to create a historical situation of ascendant political possibility once more. That possibility had become a revolutionary one, but nonetheless remained conditioned by the terms of the Cartesian compromise that redeemed and re-established the subject and its class in the first place.[26]

Such was the historical juncture at the time of Kant's writing. His work aimed to address the dilemmas emergent along with the successes of the Cartesian subject and thereby to fortify the humanist programme at a moment of mounting political possibility on the European continent. This included an account of the rift left open by Descartes between subject and object, exposed in theory by Hume and others, thereby to 'promote a unity between individuals on the basis of their subjectivity'.[27] In short, if for Descartes the humanist fantasy entailed redeeming the Renaissance affirmation of the human capacity to establish order and value in the world, for Kant the stakes had changed. For Kant, at a time of increasing political possibility, the further realisation of the humanist programme called for development at last of an empowered community of Cartesian subjects. The project entailed a basic paradox: organising a group on the basis of individualism.[28] And just as with Descartes, and the mechanists and libertines before him, Kant in some ways surpassed the Cartesian compromise (a class redeemed by solipsistic empowerment of the individual subject), but in other ways the compromise remains inscribed in the Kantian solution.

That inscription is evident in the privilege accorded ethics and aesthetics in the Kantian project. Let me address them in reverse order, beginning with aesthetics. Kant bridged the individual and the community with the material world that would sustain them both and, in sustaining them, validate their ends. Beyond sustenance, the material world offers an object lesson in individual perception rightfully applied, for the possibility of communicating and confirming (across individuals) a rightful appreciation of order among things in the

(The Cambridge Edition of the Works of Immanuel Kant) (CUP 1998); Paul Guyer (ed), *Critique of the Power of Judgment (The Cambridge Edition of the Works of Immanuel Kant)* (CUP 2000).

26 Terry Eagleton, *The Ideology of the Aesthetic* (Blackwell Publishers 1990) 65–70.
27 Salim Kemal, *Kant and Fine Art* (OUP 1986) 76.
28 Eagleton (n 26) 71–74.

world, objects and subjects alike. Here is the appeal of the aesthetic.[29] The aesthetically-appreciated object enables a sense of identification with the object, but also with others who also appreciate that material object. In this way, it enables an objective ordering built up out of so many subjective perceptions made legible according to the assumption of a common code. I note again in passing the anticipation of international law: a pretension to an objective order in the world constituted out of so many subjective (sovereign) determinations understood according to the assumption of a common code.

Before proceeding to the privilege accorded ethics, let me go a bit more deliberately through what is at stake in Kant's aesthetic programme, applicable still today. I rely on Terry Eagleton for the purpose, who writes of the enduring relevance of the dilemma faced by Kant in terms that resonate with Negri's study:

> That the individual subject should come to occupy centre stage, reinterpreting the world with reference to itself, follows logically enough from bourgeois economic and political practice. But the more the world is thus subjectivized, the more this all-priviledged subject begins to undermine the very objective conditions of its own pre-eminence. The wider the subject extends its imperial sway over reality, the more it relativizes that terrain to its own needs and desires.... the more it thereby erodes any objective criteria by which to measure the significance or even reality of its own experience .... [This reflects] the double nature of humanism, which appears to know no middle ground between the mania of exerting its powers and the depressive knowledge that it does so in empty space .... The point will be to preserve that shaping energy without subverting the objective realm which guarantees its significance; and Kant will thus trace within the very texture of the subject's experience that which points beyond it to the reality of the material world.[30]

The increasingly (economically and politically) powerful subject is also an increasingly isolated one, still lacking any apparent basis beyond itself to confirm the world over which it exercises its ascendant (economic and political) power. Staying with Eagleton a moment longer, these stakes play out primarily in two interrelated fields: ideological and market-oriented. The ideological stakes are bound up with the value of freedom, 'the essence of subjecthood', understood also in terms of sovereignty.[31] The market-oriented stakes move in lockstep:

> If freedom is to flourish, if the subject is to extend its colonizing sway over things and stamp them with its indelible presence, then systematic knowledge of the world is essential, and this must include knowledge of other subjects. You cannot hope to operate as an efficient capitalist in blithe ignorance of the laws of human psychology; and this is one reason why the ruling order needs at its disposal a body of detailed knowledge of the subject, which goes by the name of the 'human sciences'.[32]

[29] ibid 82–84.
[30] ibid 70–72.
[31] ibid 72.
[32] ibid 73.

Today we might speak instead of data sciences. In light of the political economy of contemporary information markets, recently described by Zuboff in *Surveillance Capitalism*,[33] the present-day relevance of the combined ideological and economic dilemma seems clear, and Eagleton prescient when he writes '[w]ithout knowledge you cannot hope to be free; yet knowledge and freedom are also in a curious sense antithetical. If it is essential to my freedom that I should know others, then it follows that they can know me too, in which case my freedom may be curtailed.'[34]

These are some of the stakes facing Kant's programme, then and now, mixing the ideological aspiration to freedom with the material mandate founded in market practice. Like Descartes, Kant did not aim to collapse the categories of subject and object. Instead, like Descartes, he looked for new ways to overcome the discontents of their separation by doubling down once more on subjectivity. In keeping with changed historical circumstance, however, Kant's subject was less defensively reductive. Relative to Descartes, Kant's historical world was more available to the subject, at its service and perhaps even ready for its law. The changing political fortunes of the proto-bourgeoisie enabled these expanded possibilities. In referring here to law, I mean now to flag Kant's deontological emphasis: where Descartes had provided for the constitution of the world by the subject, Kant provided for a sort of legislation by the same. The expanded historical possibility for political power, however, did not change the historical reality and material condition of a class that had accrued power by denying its own political possibility. The expansive ambition resuscitated with Descartes was apparent in the universalistic nature of Kant's deontological programme, commonly known by its categorical imperative—do nothing to another that you would not have done to you—according to which each person is (negatively) known as an ends in itself.[35] The political compromise, however, continued to define (or equally, prevent the definition of) the political core of the humanist goal. The key rule to affirm and bind a community of equals would be a negative one. And here is the significance of the Kantian privilege accorded ethics. Kantian law or legislation is personal in nature. An ordered system of rules for community is founded, but still must pass through the individual subject. The expression of communal recognition occurs in the negative space of interactions that do not transgress a line articulated by reference to personal autonomy. Likewise, the material historical conditions that made community a Kantian priority presented an increasingly robust public space for the class of humanist subjects—but one in which value-determinative actions and interactions happened according to individual transactions, namely in the marketplace, more so than in any more classical political institution, which remained still just beyond the scope of bourgeois power. Thus economics (subsuming private activity) would (continue to) define the distribution of values in this ascendant political community, and Kant's law would take the character of a private code of ethics to check the behaviour of each participant in that value-determinative marketplace individually.

As I have been suggesting at points, the mix of aesthetic possibility and deontological imperative prefigured the ideological basis of modern international law. The ideology begins with the common starting point of the same solipsistic sovereign subject, capable of

[33] Shoshana Zuboff, *The Age of Surveillance Capitalism: The Fight for a Human Future at the New Frontier of Power* (Profile Books 2019).

[34] Eagleton (n 26) 73–74.

[35] Kant, *Groundwork of the Metaphysics of Morals* (n 25).

generating out of itself alone a rational order for the world. From this starting point, sovereign subjects interact according to rules established on the basis of common appreciation for material conditions, defined in the first place by territory. That common appreciation establishes ideologically the possibility to communicate as subjects but according to a shared code. The shared code in turn provides the terms for a set of fundamental rules predicated on equal and independent sovereignty, entailing the negative relationship (do nothing to another ...) of one subject to the next. Under this negative injunction, each sovereign individually represents the highest authority for its own purposes, and none represents a highest authority for public purposes. The communal commitment thus translates only into negative recognition of self-identical abstractions, rather than any more substantial interconnection. This is the communal consciousness engendered by Kantian law according to a Cartesian constitution.

The foregoing makes clear the compromise at the heart of the ascendant politics of the subject class as constituted by Descartes. Even as the ideological success of the Cartesian subject verged on revolutionary political power, it did not include recourse to a positive programme of public politics—much as Kant himself eschewed the same. At this point, let me describe again the mandate of international law as prefigured this time by Kant, working up from the deontology. Kant's ethical system was enabled by an aesthetic possibility that was both real and chimerical: chimerical insofar as it could not bridge the inevitable isolation inscribed in the solipsistic subject, but real to the extent that it enabled each subject to imagine a shared experience. The material object founded that imagination by making itself available to the value-coded perception of the subject. Recalling Eagleton's critique, however, the ideological value encoded in the Cartesian subject's experience is twofold and contradictory: simultaneously to overcome and sustain the sovereign subject's peculiar isolation from every other subject. This overall condition characterises both progressively and oppressively the paradox of international law and relations: all subjects simultaneously sustain and threaten each other in a world understood according to subjective enjoyment of material goods. Subjects constitute political community but leave an empty space at its communal core.

In keeping with the specific character of the Cartesian subject and its historical basis, a competitive economic logic fills this space, determining and distributing material values apparently according to so many individual acts. To validate the communal possibility founded on this contradictory basis, Kant articulates a progressive, ethical imperative always already operative at least negatively in the private capacity of each subject individually. The ethical imperative is always already at work to delimit and bring order to the system predicated on each subject *qua* subject: both the imperative and the order it founds remain immanent in the subject. The imperative and order are validated and made communicable by an aesthetic appreciation of the material world. But the material world is also the object of the economic programme that entails competition among the same subjects. Ultimately, in the wake of political authority, economic individualism prevails to define and determine material relations, while ethical individualism sustains the ideological pretension to a progressive political order. In other words: whatever discontents may result from the economic distribution, it is always possible still to imagine that the public consequences could have been and may yet be otherwise on the basis of the normative regime already constituted among its subjects.

IV. Contemporary times

International law today expands on the developments traced in sections II and III. Its temporal qualities remain crucial to its work. They reflect the progressive, solipsistic character described above and guarantee international order with the progressive promise of individualist ethics. That promise is communicated by international law on the basis of material categories: territory, resources, population. In this system, material values are distributed by economic means, creating an expansive normative programme of material consequence while limiting political authority for the same. Its temporal qualities and the contingencies that they make intelligible sustain its distributive functions.

To explain, let me begin here with an exceedingly brief overview of select time technologies and a dominant temporality they support today. The history of the mechanical clock in the West is roughly contemporaneous with Renaissance humanism. It promotes a linear conception of measured time. From the nineteenth century onwards, international law becomes mutually implicated with mechanical time, especially with respect to standardisation and global expansion. In other work, I have traced the co-production of international law with standardised time over the same time period around the world.[36] I have tried to stress in that other work the basic fact that standardised time as co-produced by and with international law is unreal but effective: the pretension to uniform and simultaneous measurements of time around the world is impossible but otherwise mostly adequate for purposes of identification and coordination. International law co-produces international law through the activity of the intergovernmental Bureau International des Poids et Mesures (BIPM), established pursuant to the Metre Convention of 1875, as well as the activity of the International Telecommunications Union—Radiocommunications Sector (ITU-R), a UN sub-agency. The BIPM administers the production UTC, while the ITU-R determines with the BIPM the technical standards by which UTC is produced. The BIPM administers the production of UTC by drawing on national time-keeping laboratories around the world to announce monthly the definitive time. Each national laboratory includes multiple nuclear clocks, their several time readings rendered into a single laboratory reading by algorithms that weight each clock differently with each reading. Likewise, the BIPM weights the various readings of each laboratory differently for each next monthly announcement. This assemblage of changing readings and weights is a recursive one and the definitive time is only ever announced after it has occurred, typically with a delay of several weeks. There is neither any one source of globally standardised time, nor is its production linear. Among other things, it is an utterly contingent construction, though it has all the authority and everyday acceptance as a natural fact supporting a linear conception of temporal progress.

To restate, the system of time production under international law is practical but not true. This is not a problem for global temporal order: the centre can go unfilled, so to speak, while the operating system of time management and measurement goes on with precision enough. Plenty of work is done on that basis, plenty of transactions are concluded, plenty of productivity is enabled, and plenty of discipline is meted out with a 'centreless' system of practically-effective standardised time. In that sense, it is not unlike the humanist programme itself, as it arguably continues to expand and entrench its normative reach over

[36] Gordon (n 5); Geoff Gordon, 'Railway Clocks' in Jessie Hohmann and Daniel Joyce (eds), *International Law's Objects* (CUP 2018) 387.

daily life without ever claiming a political centre, which is simultaneously reserved for and denied by the Cartesian subject. Likewise, international law, following Kant's deontological contribution, provides on this basis a centreless system of rules that privilege instead the private character of so many Cartesian subjects, vesting normative promise in an ethical imperative applicable to each individually. The Cartesian subject and Kantian ethic prefigure a career for international law that has carried forward globally the material, economic programme associated with bourgeois enterprise, while deferring political authority. The political institutions constituted under international law, such as the UN Security Council, defer political authority, while the juridical institutions, such as the ICJ, manifest an ethical mission to redeem a public project, the international community, that they never actually define or determine.[37] While the political centre goes unfilled, however, its economic counterpart continues ascendant. The situation is apparent also in the emergence of transnational law and administrative-regulatory law lacking any clear political core. Their ascendance tracks and is interrelated with the spread of transnational economic processes admitting little corresponding political restraint. The Cartesian compromise remains apparent: the bourgeois class of managers and experts who constitute these dominant fields of international activity (myself included) nonetheless exhibit an apparent lack of political agency and routinely deny their/our own political power. The jurisprudence of the ICJ provides a ready snapshot of the juridical character. The Court alternates between handwringing about its political limitations and futile pronouncements with progressive intent, for instance in *The Wall Advisory Opinion*, or the more recent decision to grant Iran provisional relief from US economic sanctions in the current *Treaty of Amity* case between the two states.[38] The futile pronouncements are not merely epiphenomenal, however, nor evidence of the irrelevance of international law. Rather, they define its real, productive contribution to the sustained expansion of the humanist programme: the solipsistic self-affirmation that guarantees a progressive promise while deferring political possibility. The promise sustains the ideology of its long-proliferating unpolitics (to add to Allott's vocabulary from the introduction) sustaining also the unsociety that the unpolitics have produced.

Alongside the ICJ, the UN Security Council is the prototype under international law of the political institution that defers a political centre. Its famous deadlock among permanent members needs no elaboration. But let me quickly sketch a recent example of the productive power of this deferral. The disputed state of Kosovo recently created an army out of what formerly was known as the Kosovo Security Force. Vladimir Putin called the army illegal under international law. He was right. Other states recognised the creation of the army as a legitimate act by the state of Kosovo under international law. They were also correct. International law has no rule barring the creation of an army per se. In that sense Putin would have been wrong. But Kosovo presents a special case, governed by the regime established by the Security Council under Resolution 1244 and related instruments. The 1244 regime provided for the reconstruction of Kosovo and established the terms for civil and security forces in the region. When Kosovo declared independence in 2008, it did so by commandeering civil and political institutions established under law by the 1244 regime. But

[37] Gordon (n 8).

[38] *Legal Consequences of the Construction of a Wall in the Occupied Palestinian Territory* (Advisory Opinion) 2004 ICJ Reports 136; *Alleged Violations of The 1955 Treaty Of Amity, Economic Relations, And Consular Rights (Islamic Republic Of Iran v United States of America)* (Request For The Indication Of Provisional Measures, Order of 3 October 2018) ICJ Reports 2018, as discussed in Gordon (n 8).

not all states recognised the unilateral declaration of independence, Russia among them. By Russia's non-recognition, valid as a matter of international law, the region of Kosovo remains subject to the terms of Resolution 1244, which would render the unilateral creation of a standing army illegal. Because the Security Council is deadlocked, there will be no statement from the body to affirm either or any set of arguments concerning Kosovo's independence and the 1244 regime. It bears recalling as well at this point that the 2010 ICJ opinion pronounced only that the Kosovo act of self-determination was not illegal, not that it legally established a new state, likewise deferring the positive political pronouncement.[39] Accordingly, with respect to the Kosovo army under 1244, neither set of arguments is wrong. Both are correct, and in this way the underlying deferral is productive. The army is both things, rather than neither, legal and illegal, enabling each set of parties to proceed according to its own calculus.

In this indeterminate space, what meaning does contingency have? That the question of legality could be or have been decided differently is not emancipatory in international law: it is definitive of it. International law facilitates the distributions and centres of material power established elsewhere, in multiple possible locations on the basis of interests established in coordinate fields of enterprise. It does this not as epiphenomenon, but actively, by producing a particular and particularly effective linear temporal order out of its recursive and indeterminate elements. The linear temporal order that it materially reproduces supports the particular economic programmes that define the interests at work in place of any political centre. On the same linear, historical basis it maintains its progressive normative character, for instance by the appraisal that it could have been otherwise.

In sum, while the political centre under international law is consistently denied or deferred, two things are happening. First, in its ethical capacity, international law continuously provides for the right answer that could have been, but only by reference to decisions made in a privileged private capacity, according to atomised, individual interests. Likewise, by its progressive character, international law will ultimately sanctify the terms by which any such decision today (such as the historical assertion of self-determination by Kosovo) will be rightly understood tomorrow. In the present, we the participants in international law refer back to past failures for the latent correction that they ultimately will have activated. Failure never undermines the system. To the contrary, failure always reinforces the importance of the system, and the importance of sustaining its ethical promise. This is a function of a temporality that is at once concretely linear and entirely unreal. The temporality of international law is the idealistic promise of a fantastic future on the basis of an artificial past and unforthcoming present. And this is the second thing happening: the economic interests that underwrite the temporal order of international law continue inexorably to grow. Facilitated by that temporal order, the material basis of the humanist project and its privileged classes continues to expand. So do corresponding capacities vested in regulatory and administrative authorities, managerial and expert in nature, assumed in lieu of any centred political regime. As a consequence, political agency is constantly deferred as material values are consistently reproduced and redistributed. Supported by the contingency of international law, the modern or temporal economic actor remains the primary world historical agent.

[39] *Accordance with International Law of the Unilateral Declaration of Independence in Respect of Kosovo* (Advisory Opinion) 2010 ICJ Reports 403.

III

LOCATING & RESISTING CONTINGENCY

A.

MIGRANTS & REFUGEES

11

The Contingency of International Migration Law

'Freedom of Movement', Race, and Imperial Legacies

Frédéric Mégret

I. Introduction

In the midst of a global migration crisis marked by ever more restrictive border practices, reforming but also perhaps entirely reimagining what a politics of human mobility might mean has never seemed more urgent. This has precipitated considerable thinking, on both the left and the right, about the possibility of 'open borders' scenarios by philosophers and political theorists notably,[1] occasionally from a human rights perspective.[2] The problem with many of these political theoretic accounts is that they are anchored in an analytical tradition that is under-historicised, and not particularly interested in the contribution of international law.

International lawyers, for their part, have often seemed wedded to the system as it is, seeking to humanise it at the margin (stressing, for example, states' duties to asylum seekers), but at the risk of condoning its very principle, namely the almost absolute prerogative of states to exclude aliens from their territory. States, it is often repeated, have the right to control their borders, no obligation to regularise illegal migrants, and must combat irregular migration.[3] International law scholars have not been in conversation with other disciplines—such as history, philosophy, or international relations—that have sought to renovate our understanding of the structures of global mobility.

As a result, international lawyers, one might say, have interpreted the crisis of migration as epiphenomenal, even contingent: a result of states not honouring their commitments under international refugee law or human rights approaches to migration, in a context of an upsurge of cross-border movement as a result of war and climate-change fuelled disaster.[4] That crisis, then, could be fixed if only states complied with their obligations, international law were more binding, or more remedies available. It is not seen, typically, as resulting from what the current system of global movement otherwise presupposes: a fundamental

[1] Joseph H Carens, 'Aliens and Citizens: The Case for Open Borders' (1987) 49 The Review of Politics 251.

[2] Jorge M Valadez, 'Is Immigration a Human Right?' in Roland Pierik and Wouter Werner (eds), *Cosmopolitanism in Context: Perspectives from International Law and Political Theory* (CUP 2010) 221.

[3] International Convention on the Protection of the Rights of All Migrant Workers (adopted 18 December 1990, United Nations General Assembly resolution 45/158), arts 79, 35, and 64.

[4] For a critique of this approach, see Chantal Thomas, 'Mapping Global Migration Law, or the Two Batavias' (2017) 111 AJIL Unbound 504.

Frédéric Mégret, *The Contingency of International Migration Law* In: *Contingency in International Law.* Edited by: Ingo Venzke and Kevin Jon Heller, Oxford University Press. © The Several Contributors 2021. DOI: 10.1093/oso/9780192898036.003.0011

asymmetry between the hyper-mobile and the almost unlimited enforced immobility for the rest, the majority of the world's population. The crisis is not seen, in short, as premised on an unchallenged core of *unfreedom* of movement.

In this chapter, I want to reflect on what Susan Marks has described as the problem of 'false contingency' of international law.[5] That there may be a certain 'false necessity'[6] to international migration law as it exists is obvious and chimes well with a sense among critics that some ways of seeing could be changed 'if only we put our minds to it'. It also fits well with a certain imaginary construction by international lawyers of themselves as the engineers of global social change. It is certainly important to see the limitations of the ideology of border control not just as ethical limitations calling for various humanitarian interventions, but as epistemological limitations that concretely bound our legal imaginations.

Nonetheless, I am interested in what may be missed in the process, notably the only 'relative contingency' of the international law of migration. Without subscribing, as Marks suggests, to a 'fatalistic determinism', it remains possible to think in terms of at least a determination of the law, one that does not let go of the idea that things (and particular legal formations) happen for a reason. Border control may only be a 'way of thinking' about migration, but we cannot treat it as 'simply arbitrary or accidental', as a pure form detached from its sedimented constitution when, in fact, it 'belong[s] with the logics of a system which must also be brought within the analytical frame'.[7] Unfreedom of movement is surely at least partly embedded in structural conditions and not merely the product of mental habits.

Rather than look to the future as is often the case in exercises of 'reimagining', I suggest that an understanding of how the past continues to structure the present is the unavoidable companion to any serious reflection about how change might come (or be brought) about. The suggestion will be that in order to imagine how one might change the law fundamentally, one must be simultaneously and perilously aware that: (1) it was not always what it is presented as being, so that it could conceivably quickly become something quite different from what it is; but (2) that it is also very much what it is for a reason, and that we ignore its underlying purposefulness at our peril. We condemn ourselves, in particular, to be forever surprised at manifestations of the system that were, in fact, always intended. In other words, I want to highlight both the contingency and the non-contingency of the system of border control as we know it.

On the contingency side, then, the starting point is the extent to which, for all the commitment to states' ability to control their borders, freedom of movement was once the default assumption in international law. This will probably come as a surprise to most international lawyers, even those specialising in migration, given the short memory span of a 'discipline of crisis'.[8] After all, do international lawyers not teach that the history of international law is all about erecting borders, consolidating the power of the state, and sanctuarising territory? And that, key to these functions, is the ability to effectively or at least selectively exclude foreigners? Surely, then, excavating this different past will point to the 'false necessity' of our current beliefs, the fact that *an* international law—classical nineteenth-century

[5] Susan Marks, 'False Contingency' (2009) 62 Current Legal Problems 1.

[6] Roberto Mangabeira Unger, *False Necessity: Anti-Necessitarian Social Theory in the Service of Radical Democracy* (Verso 2004).

[7] Marks (n 5) 10.

[8] Hilary Charlesworth, 'International Law: A Discipline of Crisis' (2002) 65 Modern Law Review 377.

international law, no less—clearly thought very differently about these issues. This strongly relativises claims that there is something inherent about international law's commitment to controlling borders.

But there may also be a story about 'false contingency' niched into what might be calls to resurrect this early liberal inspiration, or to suggestions that international law would be 'truer to itself' if it reconnected with them. What is striking as we will see, is how dramatically international lawyers went from having relatively uninhibited conversations about freedom of movement to having no conversation at all about it. What interest in the notion there was had basically evaporated by the middle of the twentieth century. Contemporary international lawyers, with only a few exceptions,[9] have had very little interest in resurrecting such earlier, perhaps excessively utopian visions of what an international law of human mobility could stand for. The question, then, is how one accounts for this rapid and imperceptible transition and how it might help us problematise both an a priori in favour of mobility and a bias in favour of immobility.

One of the key developments in uncovering the contingency of law is the emphasis on its indeterminacy. Of course, the international law on migration can be manipulated: every open-ended rule has an open-ended exception so that in the right circumstances and the mouth of the right decision maker, the law can mean one thing and its opposite. But as is well known, that indeterminacy still somehow ends up producing certain rather constant outcomes, that are no less real simply because they are not somehow mandated by the law.[10] Rather than indeterminacy as such, I want to suggest that the paradoxical experience of indeterminacy/predictability is a result of the fact that international law *is constantly about something else than what it seems*. In having conversations about the law as if they were only about the law or, more specifically, in having conversations about international migration law as if it were (only) about migration, we risk missing the 'underlying stake' of debates about mobility, stakes that have arguably always had to do with far more than mobility per se.

When it comes to what might be characterised loosely as the international law of migration, this can mean three things at once. First, the international law on migration is not really about *migration* at all; rather, it is and has always been a sophisticated conversation about political economy, nationalism, and sovereignty, including in their most exclusive aspects. Mobility did not 'come' to states; rather, it often made them, in the process of states trying to deal with it.[11] Second, the suggestion will be that international law conversations about immigration are not and have not ever really been only *international* law conversations. Rather, as will be shown, they have been conversations heavily mediated by alternative geographic rationalities, most notably that of imperial law. Third, the international law of migration is not even much of a conversation about *law*. Instead, race has been the variable hiding in plain sight when it comes to its constitution, the one that provides the key to the weird contingency and non-contingency of its evolution through the ages.

[9] James AR Nafziger, 'The General Admission of Aliens Under International Law' (1983) 77 American Journal of International Law 804, 816; Bas Schotel, *On the Right of Exclusion: Law, Ethics and Immigration Policy* (Routledge 2013).

[10] Martti Koskenniemi, *From Apology to Utopia: The Structure of International Legal Argument* (CUP 2005).

[11] Darshan Vigneswaran and Joel Quirk, *Mobility Makes States: Migration and Power in Africa* (University of Pennsylvania Press 2015).

In pretending that international migration law is, wholly and fully, about international migration law, then, international lawyers will appear either gullible or disingenuous, the only ones to, as it were, not be in on the joke that they are themselves propagating. Specifically, the chapter will juxtapose various histories of international migration law to show how debates about mobility that have occurred in seemingly relative isolation have in fact deeply mimicked, echoed, and mutually constituted each other. The chapter begins by showing how freedom of movement and, notably, a 'right to immigrate' emerged historically as a cardinal goal of a liberal international law (II). It then suggests that the declining trajectory of that right must be understood in the context of similar and parallel conversations that were happening within empires and that introduced practices of fundamentally asymmetrical mobility (III). Finally, it looks at the imperceptible but complete decline of the right to immigrate in international law in the second half of the twentieth century as a result of the fusion of these late-imperial proclivities and contemporary international legal discourse (IV). I conclude with a few thoughts on whether the right to immigrate can be rescued from its complex past as part of a historically sensitive reflection about the present moment.

II. The origins of freedom of movement

International law may paradoxically and within certain limits have allowed for much greater mobility than is typically understood as being possible today under even a human-rights oriented version of migration in international law. To begin with, it is worth situating the notion that states have broad discretion when it comes to access to their territory within a broader historical context. As has been periodically rediscovered,[12] such a power was not always seen as flowing logically from sovereignty; or, to be precise, that prerogative had to be weighed against the fact that 'humanity and justice require states to exercise that right whilst respecting, in ways that are compatible with their own security, the rights and liberties of aliens who seek to enter their territory, or who already find themselves there'.[13]

In fact, the absolute power to exclude foreigners, if it ever existed, would have appeared as a historical anomaly to international lawyers writing before the nineteenth century. As late as the second half of the nineteenth century and even into the first half of the twentieth, a number of international lawyers, notably operating through the *Institut de Droit International* (IDI), advocated vigorously for a presumptive right to immigrate. International legal statements at least up to the First World War reflected a subtle and multi-layered approach quite at odds with modern kneejerk apologies for absolute sovereign control. Although the right to forbid access to one's territory was ultimately seen as flowing from the state's sovereignty, that right could not be applied 'absolutely' and had to be reconciled with 'the idea of an international community which means that nations, as members of humanity, are bound to respect the links that unite them'.[14]

[12] See in particular the landmark James AR Nafziger (n 9).

[13] Institut de Droit International, 'Règles Internationales sur l'Admission et l'Expulsion des Étrangers' (1892) Session de Genève (Rapporteur: M Gustave Rolin-Jaequemyns) (my translation).

[14] 'Chronique des Faits Internationaux' (1894) 1 Revue Générale de Droit International Public 555 (my translation).

In an era when the West was of course a significant net exporter of persons (and in which various newly independent colonies such as the United States or Argentina were significant importers), it was willing, at least in theory, to back quite strong corresponding obligations to welcome aliens. The *Institut de Droit International* even accepted, at its 1897 session, a right to both emigrate and *immigrate*: 'Contracting states recognise the freedom to emigrate and immigrate to individuals in isolation or en masse, without distinction of nationality. This liberty shall only be restrained by a duly published decision by the governments and within the rigorous limits of the necessities of social order and politics.'[15] Later on, the question would at least attract controversy, for example between the United States' insistence that immigration was a purely domestic question that could not be the object of international negotiations, and states that framed their perceived obligation to welcome migrants within a framework of cosmopolitan duties.

But the key point is that even as the power of the state to exclude persons on its territory became increasingly dominant, there was at least a significant transitional period in which the a priori obligation to accept almost anyone gave way to an obligation to not deny access *arbitrarily*. As Alfred Verdross put it as late as 1931, the right for states to deny access to their territory was hardly unlimited: 'no State within the international community claims to have the right to arbitrarily close its frontiers to foreigners. All have, in fact, followed the rule that every denial of admission, to be legitimate from the point of view of the law of peoples, must be based on a reasonable title'.[16] The obligation to not arbitrarily deny access, then, clearly coexisted with the generally recognised sovereignty of states to control immigration, but it leaned towards a 'right of admission... freely accorded, subject to specific exceptions fully announced in advance and recognized as reasonable by international public opinion.'[17] A resolution of the *Institut de Droit International* adopted in that vein as early as 1892 stipulated that: 'The free entry of aliens on the territory of a civilised state can only be prohibited in a general and permanent way for reasons of public interest and extremely grave motivations.'[18]

Interestingly, even as the United States increasingly jealously guarded its borders, it protested discrimination by other states in denying entry to certain American citizens based on their race or religion (for example, in reaction to the Russian refusal to accept American Jews, admittedly pursuant to an 1832 treaty that granted nationals of both nations a right of sojourn, travel, and protection).[19] As Hall put it, providing the widely accepted rationale

[15] Justitia et Pace Institut de Droit International, 'Principes Recommandés par l'Institut, en vue d'un Projet de Convention en Matière d'Émigration' (1897) Session de Copenhague (Rapporteurs: MM Ludovico Olivi et CF Heimburger), art 1 (my translation).

[16] Alfred Verdross, 'Règles Internationales Concernant le Traitement des Étrangers' (1931) 37 Recueil Des Cours, Collected Courses 327, 343–44 (my emphasis and translation).

[17] Edwin Montefiore Borchard, *The Diplomatic Protection of Citizens Abroad; or, The Law of International Claims* (The Banks Law Publishing Company 1915) 46 available at <http://archive.org/details/thediplomaticpro00borc> accessed 14 October 2016.

[18] Institut de droit international (n 13) ('L'entrée libre des étrangers sur le territoire d'un État civilisé ne peut être prohibée d'une manière générale et permanente qu'à raison de l'intérêt public et de motifs extrêmement graves.' my translation).

[19] Interestingly for our purposes, the United States considered that Russia asking American citizens about their religion amounted to an 'assumption of a religious inquisitorial function within our own borders, by a foreign agency, in a manner . . . repugnant to the national sense'. As William Wharton, Acting Secretary of the Department of State put it in a letter dated 28 February 1893: 'It is not within the power of this Government, or of any of its authorities, to apply a religious test in qualification of the equal rights of all citizens of the United States.' *Papers Relating to the Foreign Relations of the United States* (US Government Printing Office 1894) 536.

for such protests, 'to exclude any (alien) without reasonable or at least plausible cause is regarded as so vexatious and oppressive, that a government is thought to have the right of interfering in favour of its subjects in cases where sufficient cause does not in its judgment exist'.[20]

It is true that absent a treaty specifically granting mobility rights, the protests were of a political rather than legal character, and sometimes distinctly underwhelming.[21] What is remarkable, nonetheless, is that the international law of aliens was widely understood not only as applying to actual aliens already on the territory of another state, but also to putative ones, those who aspired to move into another state and had not yet been either granted or denied entry. The normative foundation of this notion of freedom of movement bears paying attention to. In a landmark article written in 1924, Paul Fauchille, then head of the IDI, contrasted the 'theory of the interdependence and international community of interest of states' to that of 'absolute sovereignty of the state'.[22] I return to the latter later since in many ways it eventually became the dominant mode of thinking of international immigration law, but in this section I want to highlight what were thought to be the pillars of the 'interdependence thesis'. One particular emphasis was on the needs of trade, which was conceptualised as an almost inherent feature of international association, and militated for migration as an adjustment variable in the world economy. For Fauchille:

> The conduct of international trade, which implies continuous intercourse, does not admit the possibility of states isolating themselves by excluding foreigners from their territories, since the co-operation of states is, in the final analysis, solely made up of the co-operation of the individuals composing them. On this theory, therefore, unless the very idea of the international community is to be destroyed, individuals must be admitted to have a right of free movement from one country to another. … In view of the economic interdependence and community of interest of nations, no state can be at liberty to exclude at will not only the products but the nationals of other countries, who are the indispensable agents of trade.[23]

Behind the needs of trade, however, was a deeper and somewhat amorphous sense of what Bluntschli earlier had called 'la liberté des relations internationales'. As that Swiss author put it: 'States are members of humanity; they are bound to respect the links that connect nations to each other; their sovereignty is not absolute; it is limited by international law'.[24] This was, in other words, a sort of obligation to participate in the international community by opening oneself up to international interaction, including as it manifested itself in the opening of one's borders to aliens. In a similar vein, Hall had earlier insisted that the right to deny access to one's territory was 'necessarily tempered by the facts of modern civilisation'.[25]

Bluntschli went on to list a number of, in his mind most unfortunate, experiences in isolation, including Japan and Paraguay in his era. De La Pradelle insisted later that the

[20] William Edward Hall, *A Treatise on International Law* (Clarendon Press 1890) 211.
[21] Jan C Jansen and Jürgen Osterhammel, *Decolonization: A Short History* (Princeton University Press 2017) 173.
[22] Paul Fauchille, 'The Rights of Emigration and Immigration' (1924) 9 International Labour Review 317, 322.
[23] ibid 322–23.
[24] Johann Caspar Bluntschli, *Le Droit International Codifié* (Librairie de Guillaumin et Cie 1874) 381 (my translation).
[25] Hall (n 20) 211.

worst example of such 'antique' self-exclusion from the international system was China, which had behaved as a 'fossille' by withdrawing from the international community and subtracting from it resources that it had no intention to exploit.[26] The failure of these states to join the international community could no longer be tolerated since it would affect the freedom to trade and travel, understood here largely of course as the freedom of Westerners to exploit the Middle Empire's resources. Ernst Isay, in his Hague Course of 1924 also made clear that connection between freedom of movement and civilisation, emphasising that:

> It is contrary to the law of peoples that a State which is a member of the international community, build a great wall of China. China and Japan, as long as they remained systematically closed to foreigners, could not become parties to this community. A State would still act against the law of peoples by denying entry of its territory no longer to all foreigners, but to the nationals of this or that state. It would thus violate the fundamental rights of states to equality of treatment: a right which flows from the law of nations.[27]

In other words, allowing foreigners in was not only an obligation in international law, it was the very mark of civilised statehood. It is also interesting that, starting from these free trade premises, Fauchille equally came to the conclusion that freedom of movement made sense as a fundamental right. Indeed:

> [T]he liberty of the individual also calls for the adoption of this conclusion. It is no longer admitted in modern law that every man is indissolubly bound to his native land. He has the right to come and go as seems good to him, in order to seek, in a community which he considers more favourable, greater facilities for achieving his end, that is to say, material and moral perfection.[28]

In short, and in ways that as we will see were of course indebted to their particular world outlook, international lawyers were once adamant that freedom of movement for persons was one of the pillars of an international legal order. They formulated that freedom, within its implicit civilisational boundaries, in very general terms linking themes of trade, civilisation, and individual liberty into a compelling and today quite incongruous case for a 'right to immigrate'. Long before 'freedom of movement' would become fashionable among cosmopolitan political theorists, it was, for a while at least, an article of faith for that most antiquated discipline, international law.

III. Empires as laboratories for limited mobility

What is striking, however, is how that set of normalised assumptions about freedom of movement were discarded, almost imperceptibility. Indeed, by the second half of the twentieth century, ideas about freedom of movement were simply no longer discussed in polite

[26] Albert de La Pradelle, 'La Question Chinoise' [1901] Revue Générale de Droit International Public 336.

[27] Ernst Isay, 'De la Nationalité' (1924) 5 Recueil des Cours de l'Académie de Droit International 451 (my translation).

[28] Fauchille (n 22) 324.

international law circles. What is perhaps most noteworthy is that the move from a presumptive right to immigrate to an absolute prerogative of the state to deny immigration occurred almost without argument, as if through a series of imperceptible lapses that did not require justification. This suggests that the commitment to mobility was all along much more fragile than it seemed. How does one explain that puzzle? Was the commitment to freedom of movement perhaps contingent, and if so contingent on what?

I return in the next section to how one might retrace the abrupt decline of the right to immigrate in international law, but I want to suggest in this section that a key piece of the puzzle—in fact, *the* missing piece of the puzzle—is to be found in the history of intra-imperial mobility and its regulation. This section draws on historical work that has been more willing to see imperial law as one of the origins of international law, operating in its shadow but also with its blessing and sometimes as its *avant garde*.[29] This has created genuine indeterminacy in the discipline's core concepts, but also new found opportunities to understand its dynamics from the point of view of the vast reservoir of legal experimentation endogenous to empires.[30]

The argument here is that if international law could afford to be so supportive of human mobility it is because the mobility regulated by international law was really only a fraction of global mobility. Actual patterns of global mobility were shaped first and foremost by logics of empire (actual empires, not just the empire of international law), which themselves increasingly progressed towards and acted as real-size experiments for more controlling approaches to the movement of persons. The hypothesis is that it was those 'internal' practices that empires bequeathed to international law in the wake of decolonisation and that contained the seeds of one of the most dramatic (apparent) turnarounds in international law's history.

The literature on intra-imperial mobility is typically ignored by international lawyers, at some risk. Empires—notably the French and British, but also the Spanish, Dutch, and Portuguese—were vast spaces of *internal* mobility that affected huge numbers of people. They were also spaces of complex and sometimes contradictory experiences in regulating mobility that were constructed separately from the general realm of international law. Specifically, empires involved a triple movement of both mobility and immobility. First, the displacement of surplus metropolitan populations to the colonies, often to the 'protectionist' exclusion of non-imperial nationals.[31] In the first half of the twentieth century, the majority of British isle migrants moved to British dominions.[32] Their mobility was often financially supported, sometimes both on the metropolitan and peripheral ends, for example through subsidised tickets.

As has been pointed out by Tony Ballantyne '"settlers" were typically unsettled and mobility was their defining characteristic', even though the naturalisation of the nation-state has sometimes made it seem otherwise.[33] More generally, Ballantyne has suggested that:

[29] Lauren Benton and Lisa Ford, *Rage for Order* (Harvard University Press 2016).

[30] Lauren Benton, 'Made in Empire: Finding the History of International Law in Imperial Locations: Introduction' (2018) 31 Leiden Journal of International Law 473–78.

[31] For example, the Spanish and Portuguese empires long restricted immigration to their American colonies to Spaniards and Portuguese respectively.

[32] Judith Brown and WM Roger Louis, *The Oxford History of the British Empire: Volume IV: The Twentieth Century* (OUP 1999).

[33] Tony Ballantyne, 'Mobility, Empire, Colonisation' (2014) 11 History Australia 7, 27.

> At a fundamental level, the governance of the empire was dependent on mobility. It relied on the ability to move governors, clerks and imperial functionaries from metropole to colony, and from colony to colony. Its coercive instruments – army, navy, police – needed to be deployed and redeployed to extend imperial sovereignty, open up markets, enable 'settlement', suppress rebellion and symbolically display the realities of colonial power.[34]

Second and simultaneously, empires relied on a policing of some mobilities. In fact, the enforced immobility of indigenous and colonised peoples was just as central to the constitution of coloniality. Indigenous mobility—and occasionally the mobility of Western adventurers who had lost their Western ways—was perceived as a threat to orderly colonial society. To cite Ballantyne again:

> regulation of the mobility of indigenous and colonised communities was central to the operation of colonial power. Métis bands travelling out from Red River following bison and engaging in cross-border trade, 'travel-happy Samoans', nomadic tribal people and adivasis in India, and mobile Aboriginal communities were hard for colonial states to 'see', control and police.[35]

Whether in attempts to transform nomadic people into sedentary agriculturalists, or the effort to punish the 'thuggee' in India, the colonial project relied crucially on suppressing mobilities that were seen as subversive. In that respect, the regime in force in the British Empire, for example, was not that different from that applicable in Belgium Katanga and Congo or Italian Ethiopia which had put in place severe controls of domestic mobility.

Third, beneath arguments about freedom of movement, lied the harsh reality of coerced movement within the Empire, particularly of non-white and subaltern white manpower. This of course included the slave trade and the displacement of Africans to the US and other colonies in the Americas. It also included early projects of labour and manpower transfers. For example, millions of Chinese and Indian labourers were moved, often involuntarily or as part of indentured labour, to various locations in the Empire. Penal colonies were part of the same constrained movement effort, albeit focused on the white working class. Controlled migration, the more or less forceful transfer of populations from one area to another, was also part of political imaginaries of empires and colonial integration,[36] informed by a sort of authoritarian developmental streak in imperial policy.

Until relatively late in the life of the principal European empires and despite these contrary impulses, a certain belief in at least privileged intra-imperial mobility could nonetheless be sustained. For Great Britain, this was linked to an investment in the idea that free labour would inevitably go hand in hand with free trade; for France it was deeply implicated in ideas about French *mission civilisatrice*. In both cases, mobility came to be guaranteed at least theoretically within the imperial space. The British Nationality and Status of Aliens Act of 1914, for example, defined British subjects as those born 'within His Majesty's dominions and allegiances',[37] which implied their right to entry into Britain. In the same year,

[34] ibid 20.
[35] ibid 23–24.
[36] Peo Hansen and Stefan Jonsson, 'Demographic Colonialism: EU–African Migration Management and the Legacy of Eurafrica' (2011) 8 Globalizations 261.
[37] British Nationality and Status of Aliens Act 1914 art 1.

France guaranteed freedom of movement between the Algerian departments and the metropolis, after decades where it had required a special permit to leave Algeria, at a time when Algerian manpower was much in need.[38]

At the same time, empires eventually engaged in efforts to control mobility to the metropolis as soon as that mobility was deemed excessive or disruptive. In the case of the British Empire, the initial challenge to a politics of relative mobility came not from the metropolis but from the dominions themselves. The imperial ideal, in fact, slowly broke down under the pressure, its periphery increasingly claiming its autonomy in the first half of the twentieth century by asserting an unwillingness to give effect to the promise of imperial citizenship. Although this was also visible in the rise of tariffs as obstacles to intra-imperial free trade, there was little doubt that control over the flow of migrants—and in particular the ability to conduct white-only policies—was central to the dominions' claims for emancipation. The Colonial Office gradually sided with them. For example, the Marquess of Crewe at the Imperial Conference of 1911 insisted that it was not the case that 'every subject of the King, whoever he may be or where ever he may live, has a national right of travel, or still more to settle, in any part of the Empire'. Instead, 'it is the right of the self-governing Dominions to decide for themselves in each case who are to be admitted as citizens of the respective Dominions'.[39]

In France, the effort to slow down intra-imperial mobility came from Paris beginning in the 1920s and particularly in relation to Algeria. Gradually, the 'indigènes' were required to produce a certificate of hospitality ('certificat d'hébergement') in order to move to metropolitan France. This created an early problem of trafficking of migrants. By 1928, the law was made harsher and would-be migrants to the metropolis needed to be in possession of an identity card, a criminal record devoid of conviction, as well as possession of at least 150 francs and the deposit of a 'caution' in case they need to be repatriated. That regime was extended to French Western Africa and subsequently Indochina, and empowered local colonial authorities to deliver the necessary papers.[40] It reinforced the foundational distinction in the French empire between French 'nationals' and French 'citizens', only the latter of which could move freely.[41]

Similarly, the US limited mobility within its empire, notably from the Philippines. One of the main provisions of the Tydings–McDuffie Act, prior to Philippine independence, related to immigration. In reclassifying all Filipinos as aliens for the purposes of immigration and setting up a very strict quota, it made further Filipino emigration to the US challenging. But even before the Act, Filipinos in the US were excluded from naturalisation and risked never being allowed to return if they left as a result of the Filipino Repatriation Act of 1935, which extended to the Philippines the Asian-exclusion policy of the Immigration Act of 1924.

The subtext of these assertions however was not merely claims for sovereignty for sovereignty's sake. It was, rather, largely informed by concepts of race and the desire to police what Du Bois would famously describe as the global 'colour line'.[42] It was as non-whites

[38] Décret of the 18th June 1913, confirmed by the Law of 15th July 1914.

[39] Dominion Law Reports, 184 (1914).

[40] Olivier Le Cour Grandmaison, 'Colonisés-Immigrés et "Périls Migratoires": Origines et Permanence du Racisme et d'une Xénophobie d'Etat (1924–2007)' (2008) 69 Cultures & Conflits 19.

[41] Emmanuelle Saada, 'Citoyens et Sujets de l'Empire Français' (2003) 53 Genèses 4.

[42] WEB Du Bois, *The Souls of Black Folk* (originally published 1903, CosimoClassics 2007) xv.

started to migrate to the dominions and, later, to the old imperial metropolis, that walls began to be raised. New meanings were given to borders in the process that often paid lip service to ideals of imperial mobility, even as they increasingly sought to reinterpret it in limited and asymmetrical ways. The racial aspects of immigration discrimination could occasionally be masked, for example by excluding nationals of certain countries or regions rather than on the basis of race, but such efforts were transparent.[43] An entire register of arguments was developed to explain why would-be intra-imperial migrants were not welcome, sometimes claiming to deny them access for their own good, but more often drawing on a eugenic register to resist 'mongrelling' and the loss of national character.[44] Institutional and administrative practices were also developed to increasingly control and police imperial migrants both in the colonies and the metropolis,[45] based on racialist ideas.[46] Ideas that had been used to justify the privileged freedom of mobility of Western settlers, then, were deployed to construct the unprivileged immobility of Southern migrants.

As a consequence of the bluff of imperial citizenship increasingly being exposed, those who had been denied entry often returned home with an increased sense of the need for national independence.[47] Restraints on mobility thus served not only to shape the reimagining of the colonial metropolis as a nation state relatively cleansed of its imperial past (and, most notably, of any debt it may have owed, including in terms of continued mobility, to former colonial subjects); it also precipitated the movement by which former colonies became independent. That independence, in turn, could be invoked against them: you cannot both be independent and continue to claim the (as it turns out, already quite theoretical) privileges of intra-imperial mobility.

This does not mean that intra-imperial mobility could not survive for quite long, both as an idea and as a practice, depending first and foremost on underlying material conditions and the need for labour. One irony is that the phase of most intense decolonisation for both France and the UK coincided with decades of economic boom following the Second World War. Even as the moment was ripe politically, in the midst of independence struggles, for setting limits to transnational mobility, European economies had never been more in need of labour. In fact, post-imperial mobility was often intensified in the dying years of empires as a way, perhaps, of staving off the inevitable and no doubt as part of a nostalgia for what empire had once portended. British citizenship covered some 800 million subjects in the 1940s, which provided many of the migrants to Britain. In a context where the colonies of France and Portugal 'had never been so strongly integrated into the political structures of their metropoles as they were after 1945', this 'included a relatively broad freedom of mobility for citizens inside a shared imperial space'. Even in the case of Britain and the Netherlands, 'the period after the Second World War brought about a lowering of imperial barriers to geographic mobility'.[48]

[43] Sherally Munshi, 'Race, Geography, and Mobility' (2016) 30 Georgetown Immigration Law Review 245.

[44] See, for example, René Martial, *Traité de l'Immigration et de la Greffe Inter-Raciale* (Larose 1939).

[45] Gérard Noiriel, *Immigration, Antisémitisme et Racisme en France (XIXe-XXe Siècle): Discours Publics, Humiliations Privées* (Fayard 2007).

[46] Laurent Dornel, 'Les Usages du Racialisme: Le Cas de la Main d'Oeuvre Coloniale en France Pendant la Première Guerre Mondiale' (1995) 20 Genèses 48.

[47] Sherally Munshi, 'Immigration, Imperialism, and the Legacies of Indian Exclusion' (2016) 28 Yale Journal of Law and the Humanities 51.

[48] Jansen and Osterhammel (n 21) 173.

Nonetheless, and in stages, ideas about imperial mobility appeared—again—increasingly *passé*. This was most visible in the former British metropolis which, now experiencing qualitatively larger migration from its former colonies and no longer as fixated on the imperial 'ideal', went from having been the key architect of imperial mobility to being its prime dismantler. This was even as, ironically, the dominions themselves gradually did away with (overt) ethnic discrimination. The 1948 British Nationality Act is perhaps the last one that guaranteed entry of all Empire subjects into Britain. In 1962, the Commonwealth Immigrants Act for the first time subjected Commonwealth citizens to immigration control. By 1971, the regime of Commonwealth immigrants had been aligned with those of other immigrants 'thus repudiating the Imperial mobility and the integrity of the Empire upheld since the beginning of the century'.[49] Notoriously, most Chinese residents of Hong Kong would eventually be denied the right to emigrate to Britain.

On one level, it is quite clear that the experience of intra-imperial mobility bore only tangential relation to that of international law. When talking about freedom of movement, the distinguished international jurists of the nineteenth century could not have been and were not talking about imperial mobility. Conversely, within empires whatever opening or limiting of mobility there was could not be said to occur specifically as a result of international law. Nonetheless, the distinction between international law and imperial law was at times paper thin: international law, in its collective imagining of the 'other', was largely imperialistic; and empires, notably the British Empire, were so broad and disarticulated that their internal legal relations often took quasi-international forms. The questions of extra and intra-mobility were therefore bound to be interrelated. The experience of the rise and the breakdown of imperial mobility, then, sheds some light on and has some lessons to yield for the broader understanding of how the liberal commitment to global mobility eventually broke down.

IV. The breakdown of freedom of mobility under international law

Although it is difficult to find a 'smoking gun', the most plausible hypothesis is that international lawyers, many of whom had worked at the interface of international and imperial law anyhow, were from the start subtly attuned to the realities of limited imperial mobility and ready to import that baggage into international law writ large. The more utopian *Institut de Droit International* resolutions did not need to be repealed or critically re-evaluated; they could just as well be forgotten, consigned to an earlier, imprudent era of liberal optimism. As to emerging postcolonial states, they were so committed to their projects of national development and often so ambivalent about those of their new citizens who joined the former metropolis, that they often opted to not insist on having at least mobility to the former metropolis inscribed as a key component of the post-imperial compact.

Just as interesting is how knowing that story can help us reinterpret that earlier era of international legal mobility retrospectively as itself more fraught and ambiguous than is typically thought. The turn towards exclusionary migratory practices had also been long in the making in international law itself. If anything, imperial legacies bring attention to

[49] Brown and Louis (n 32) 28.

the degree to which the trajectory of ideas about international mobility as conceived by international lawyers both anticipated and followed those that emerged in the context of intra-imperial mobility. The idea of non-arbitrary immigration restrictions in international law, in particular, was a very flexible one. It is true that it was sometimes interpreted broadly and ambitiously, as when it involved an obligation on peripheral states to open their borders to European traders and settlers. The entitlement to human mobility was part and parcel of logics of imperialism, an obligation imposed on other countries to keep their borders open that had been evident as early as Vitoria's musings on Spaniards' right to travel Indian lands. As Eve Lester has underlined, the 'foreigner' was typically thought of as a 'European insider'.[50]

But it was not particularly anticipated that obligations to allow mobility might be reciprocated, perhaps simply because the question did not arise but also because it would have raised obvious discomfort. In fact, early on and in ways that were not always betrayed by the bland generality of proclamations about the duties of states to welcome all immigrants, mobility was significantly restricted when it came to non-Westerners. International law, in particular, 'did not seriously contemplate the non-European as a foreigner entitled to benefit from legal rights and protections on that account'.[51] Freedom from discrimination in immigration, such as it was imagined, was intimately linked to the 'network of commercial treaties by which the states, *of the white race at least*, are bound together'.[52] A significant concern when it came to inward mobility to the European world was the need to limit mixity and its attendant dangers. In fact, among the 'extremely grave motivations' suggested by the IDI in 1892 to justify restrictions to mobility were 'a fundamental difference of mores and civilisation or … a dangerous organisation or accumulation of aliens who would turn up *en masse*'.[53]

Fauchille, like most authors, recognised that 'although there is a legal obligation on a state to open its frontiers to foreigners, it may legitimately close them, justifying its action not by its rights of sovereignty but solely by its right of self-preservation'.[54] In particular, the state could 'exclude individuals only in order to effect a necessary selection among those useful and hostile to its national life'.[55] Although this may have sounded reasonably narrow, the list of what might contradict the goals of national life was so large as to make it questionable whether the initial principle was ever taken seriously. Even the quite liberal Fauchille noted that although it was dubious whether 'for its own preservation, a state might wish to prevent a fusion of races which might alter its ethnic character or obliterate its national culture', that would not be the case if 'this race belonged to an absolutely different civilisation and its members wished to enter the territory of the state in large numbers'.[56]

In practice, this meant that the obligation to allow aliens to immigrate had long been moderated by various exclusions. Among the seemingly random list of groups that one early twentieth-century American scholar cited for legitimate exclusion from the territory were 'alien races considered inferior or not capable of assimilation' such as 'Chinese and

50 Eve Lester, *Making Migration Law: The Foreigner, Sovereignty, and the Case of Australia* (CUP 2018) 77.
51 ibid 78.
52 Borchard (n 17) 46.
53 Institut de Droit International (n 13) ('une différence fondamentale de mœurs ou de civilisation ou à raison d'une organisation ou accumulation dangereuse d'étrangers qui se présenteraient en masse': my translation).
54 Fauchille (n 22) 325.
55 ibid 325.
56 ibid 325.

certain Japanese laborers in the United States and many of the British colonies, the gypsies in many European countries, and Turks in Panama'[57] to which one might add the case of the exclusion of Syrians from Haiti.[58] As can be seen, Western states were particularly keen on restricting movement from the semi-periphery (perhaps because this was where most of the movement came from), in ways that would in due course powerfully motivate Japan to militate for the racial-equality clause at the Versailles conference. The clause was successfully resisted by the US, Canada, Australia, and New Zealand which saw it, precisely, as threatening their immigration policies, notably as they applied to Asians.

Although there could be said to exist a general international law of aliens, therefore, in practice that law was mediated by a strong emphasis on 'friendship, commerce and navigation' treaties which arose within quite narrow civilisational confines. That this basic fact long remained hidden was largely a result of the fact that at the time of the great proclamations of liberal mobility, the dominant issue had been allowing Westerners to penetrate the Global South. Yet as soon as migration flows began to reverse, if not from the South to the North, at least from the less 'desirable' segments of the North (particularly Southern and Eastern Europe) to the North (the US) legal scholars quickly turned their attention to making the exception the norm. Earlier texts had certainly pointed to the powers of the state in that respect. For example, the Preamble to the International Rules on the Admission and Expulsion of Aliens highlighted that 'for each State, the right to admit or not admit aliens to its territory or to admit them only conditionally or to expel them is a logical and necessary consequence of its sovereignty and independence'.[59] But international lawyers, henceforth, conveniently omitted that such preambular clauses had been strongly moderated by a sense of obligation to would-be migrants.

By the mid-1920s, many authors began to recognise that control over immigration (and emigration) was a largely domestic question, part of the state's *domaine reservé*. The US, which had not only tolerated but actively encouraged immigration in the nineteenth century, was central in making the case that it should have control over its immigration policy, regardless of international legal niceties. Louis Varlez, contemplating the normalisation of assertions of sovereign power over entry onto territory in his Hague General Course in 1927 had no doubt that 'certain domestic issues are exclusively within the relevant governments' jurisdiction' and that these include most questions of emigration and immigration. Immigration states could, he argued, 'decide the number of foreigners from each country which could cross (their) borders and which should be considered undesirable: they determine in that respect the number, sex, age, nationality, moral and physical health, level of instruction, race, religion, origin, profession, which they judge necessary to their national development'.[60] It was for states, in short, to address questions of emigration and immigration as they saw fit.

The inter-war period paved the way for increasingly restricted mobility that largely tracked parallel intra-imperial developments. Mobility came to be associated specifically with labour mobility, with bilateral and multilateral treaties, often encouraged by the

[57] Borchard (n 17) 47.

[58] Brenda Gayle Plummer, 'Between Privilege and Opprobrium: The Arabs and Jews in Haiti' in Ignacio Klich and Jeffrey Lesser (eds) *Arab and Jewish Immigrants in Latin America: Images and Realities* (Frank Cass 1998) 80.

[59] Institut de Droit International (n 13) (my translation).

[60] L Varlez, 'L'évolution du Droit d'Émigrer' (1927) 20 Recueil des Cours de l'Académie de Droit International 329–30 (my translation).

International Labour Organization, to cater to the needs of certain immigration countries.[61] As Leila Kawar has pointed out, the International Labour Organization was one of the vehicles through which separate regimes of labour migration were launched, one for migrant worker recruiting and one for native labour recruiting, which inscribed within international law, perhaps for the first time, the idea of parallel yet deeply asymmetrical mobility rights regimes.[62]

Simultaneously, the League of Nations was laying the basis for the normalisation of passports. Passports had been introduced after the First World War to manage relatively large numbers of displaced persons. They had, however, always been meant to be a temporary measure. In the early 1920s, a spirit of optimism about international association made it seem as such temporary measures would soon no longer be necessary. Indeed, the League, backed by many states, although it recognised 'the legitimate concern of every Government for the safeguarding of its security and rights' and the fact that this 'prohibit(ed), for the time being, the total abolition of restrictions and (the) complete return to pre-war conditions', nonetheless hoped to phase out passports 'in the near future'.[63]

However, states quickly became accustomed to the technology and some suggested a strong inclination to make the temporary permanent. As Mark Salter has argued in his mastery study of 'the passport', states (notably the UK) made a range of claims about its utility, including the rather opportunistic argument that no state could be expected to abandon them until every other state did so.[64] Although passports were a technology which in and of itself did not necessarily collide with a right to immigrate, it certainly had the potential to be used to control and discipline would-be migrants (and emigrants, although this is not my focus), and has of course since become associated with exactly that.

After the Second World War, arguments about the need to exercise control over immigration generally connected to and fused with arguments about the need to restrict post-imperial immigration, as the two became essentially the same thing. The general right of states to prevent foreigners from immigrating into their territory drew on late imperial denials of mobility to inhabitants of the periphery. One of the conditions of independence was thus that newly independent states relinquish any claim that their nationals might have a right to emigrate to the old metropolis—although the need of former European colonial powers for labour meant that this reality would remain hidden for decades.

The idea of sovereign control over migration, including a control that was largely arbitrary and absolute, was increasingly taken for granted.[65] References to international law's earlier, much more ambivalent position almost entirely disappeared. It is difficult to point to a moment of inflexion; instead, it is as if the issue simply vanished from international law debates. The focus on refugees in itself attests to the changing nature of the problem: if refugees exist as a distinct category in international law and as a relatively privileged form of movement linked to the discourse of rights, it is because the migrant cannot, fundamentally, frame her own movement from a rights perspective.

[61] Varlez (n 60).

[62] Leila Kawar, 'Equivalence and Exclusion: Constructing Europe and Its Others in Interwar Migrant Labor Conventions' (Annual Conference of the Canadian Council on International Law, Ottawa, 24–25 October 2019).

[63] Cited in Sarah Dehm, 'The Passport' in Daniel Joyce and Jessie Hohmann (eds) *International Law's Objects* (OUP 2019) 342.

[64] Mark B Salter, *Rights of Passage: The Passport in International Relations* (Lynne Rienner 2003) 80.

[65] Carter Goodrich, 'Possibilities and Limits of International Control of Migration' (1947) 25 The Milbank Memorial Fund Quarterly 153.

One sees, in fact, a convergence of the post-imperial and international legal conversations; or, rather, a situation in which the post-imperial moment henceforth fundamentally framed the international legal conversation. As imperial oceans receded as it were, they revealed fully constituted sovereign islands for whom discretion over entry was quickly a *fait acquis*. All international law had to do was then draw the consequences of that reality, meekly forgetting that it had once stood, rather imprudently perhaps, for a much broader project but, in the end, was fully reconciled with and attuned to a reality which it had of course contributed to bringing about. The dominions in a sense merely had the courage to say loudly what international lawyers had been thinking all along and would soon ratify, with the blessing of the former imperial powers.

In many ways, human rights took over where the necessities of international life or imperial citizenship had once occupied the centre stage, but in ways that consolidated rather than disrupted the consensus. As with previous versions of liberal freedom of movement, the impact of human rights was ambiguous and certainly did not challenge the definitive entrenchment of state power. On the one hand, human rights did extend the right to entry in the narrow case of refugees (*non refoulement*) and in a more limited way in the context, for example, of family reunification. On the other hand, in almost every other respect human rights came nowhere close to recognising a right to immigrate, and in fact, very much ratified the state's prerogative over its borders. Article 13 of the Universal Declaration made it clear that the right to free movement was restricted to the borders of one's state.

The European Court of Human Rights has, on that matter as in so many other matters, deferred to 'well-established international law' according to which 'a State has the right to control the entry of non-nationals into its territory'.[66] Lest there be any ambiguity, human rights instruments went out of their way to clarify that they were not upsetting the dominant order of limited movement. For example, the Declaration on the Human Rights of Individuals Who are not Nationals of the Country in Which They Live, adopted by the General Assembly in 1985 insisted that:

> Nothing in this Declaration shall be interpreted as legitimizing any alien's illegal entry into and presence in a State, nor shall any provision be interpreted as restricting the right of any State to promulgate laws and regulations concerning the entry of aliens and the terms and conditions of their stay or to establish differences between nationals and aliens.[67]

V. Conclusion

International law gradually but effectively abandoned ideas of freedom of movement with which it had been deeply associated in the nineteenth century. If nothing else, this forgotten legacy could be testimony to the sort of legal system that might have given rise to a norm of freedom of movement, or which freedom of movement could give rise to. It shows arguments based on 'false necessity' in their best light, given the evidence that quite clearly international migration law could involve something else than surrender to the idea of strict

[66] *Abdulaziz, Cabales and Balkandali v The United Kingdom* (Application nos 9214/80; 9473/81; 9474/81, Judgment 28 May 1985) para 67.

[67] Res 40/144 (13 December 1985) art 2.

borders and harsh migration control. At the same time, it might be evidence of the way in which freedom of movement was always a relatively weak project, one that ultimately relied on an implicit exclusionary bias that makes it highly suspicious today. Or it might bring attention to the 'false contingency' of imagining alternatives to the current system 'on the cheap', if one is not disposed to challenge its deep structure.[68] The current regime of extreme unequal mobility did not spring from nowhere, and therefore nor do we have reason to believe that it will go away easily.

As I have tried to argue, this gradual abandonment was paralleled by the history of colonial empires' decay, and their increasing incapacity and unwillingness to enforce a regime of at least nominal freedom of movement within their midst. This led me to re-explore the extent to which freedom of movement had always been a coded enterprise, one that operated in very different way depending on whether the mobility at stake was that of Europeans or non-Europeans. Along the way, I have suggested some darker legacies of ideas about freedom of movement, including the idea that freedom of movement—its 'whiteness', as it were—served as a crucial signifier for racialisation. Freedom of movement was not only replaced by but often coexisted with a system of control of mobility and hyper-selectivity that was almost limitless in its discretion.[69]

International lawyers themselves were often deeply and uncritically involved in glossing over contradictions between their earlier commitments and the emerging reality and tended to act as uncritical handmaidens of the post-imperial liberal order. The point about the hypocrisy of the system, however, is trite. Rather, this chapter suggests that the discussion of migration in international law can help frame three lines of inquiry about the nature of contingency in international law and the elusive promise of freedom of movement.

First, apparent changes in international law may hide surprising continuities. The nineteenth-century commitment to freedom of movement is maybe, in the end, not that different from the late twentieth- and early twenty-first-century commitment to closure of borders. The former only existed against the background of actual discriminations; the latter is based on a seemingly unilateral assertion of the ability to close borders but the constant reality of their porosity and the crafting of significant exceptions for certain populations. In other words, one argument is that the global regime of migration was already in the late nineteenth century, for all its superficial embrace of mobility, in effect not that different from ours. It reflected a familiar combination of hyper-mobility within and from the industrialised North, with significantly reduced South-North mobility. Today, for example, the European Union is typically understood as both an area of hyper-mobility within, and a fortress for those without. In that respect, the perception of a commitment to global mobility from classical international lawyers may be based on a misunderstanding: it was a commitment framed in general terms only because a significant part of humanity was, evidently, excluded from it.

Closely linked to those continuities may be the constancy of the assertion of a sort of racial sovereignty. Indeed, it is not so much that an already constituted sovereignty was naturally asserted to oppose claims to immigrate, but that claims to sovereignty and what it meant were triggered and reinforced by the tendency of non-white groups to migrate.

[68] Marks (n 5).

[69] Eric Neumayer, Unequal Access to Foreign Spaces: How States Use Visa Restrictions to Regulate Mobility in a Globalized World' (2006) 31 Transactions of the British Institute of Geographers 72.

As Radhika Viyas Mongia put it, migration, rather than 'disrupt(ing) notions of the purity and (fictive) homogeneity of the national', in fact 'precipitated the emergence of nationality as a staunch territorial attachment': 'it is precisely "raced-migration" that generates a state monopoly over migration practices'.[70] Drawing on Anthony Anghie, one could argue that sovereignty did not *deal* with the problem of migration as much as it was *constituted* by it. Our current international legal framework, such as it emerged, was shaped by responses to migration (and implicitly the question of race), much more than the other way around. It focused on the idea of the 'rights of states', an evolving compact of ideas that increasingly included a notion of almost absolute control over one's borders and the entry of aliens on one's territory.[71]

Second, one question is whether the original commitment to a much more liberal regime of global human mobility can be rescued from its exclusionary undertones. The ambivalence here is that a relative freedom of movement was only secured, at least theoretically, in a context of imperialism, real asymmetry, and racism. Its racism was not accidental but inherent to the global regime of mobility. Yet these earlier pronouncements are also unmistakably part of the history of international law. There is something to the fact that, in a context of arbitrary religious bans with strong ethnic overtones, for example, international law once candidly affirmed a principle of non-arbitrariness in immigration, even as it was blind to its own underlying exclusions. In the generality of its utterances, the international law of aliens did set out the conditions for a global regime of mobility that was on its face surprisingly more liberal than anything that has been witnessed since (except, of course, within regional arrangements).

Perhaps what is recoverable from that earlier era or at least worthy of study are some of the deeper justifications for the mobility part of the equation. Interestingly, in emphasising the equal right of all to travel and settle abroad, international lawyers made clear that such a right resulted from the equality of *states* rather than human beings, the former having a right to their citizens being treated as well as those of other nations. This meant that the willingness of a sovereign to exercise its diplomatic protection over the rights of some of its citizens arbitrarily denied entry into another state might provide the backbone of a strong regime of transnational mobility. The idea, then, is that there is a deep public international, inter-state undercurrent to the possibility of migration. As contemporary scholars put it, 'that immigration policy necessarily implicates our relationships with other nations is self-evident'.[72]

Although perhaps less appealing to our cosmopolitan contemporary sensitivities than human rights, such a foundation for global mobility may also have been more effective. It suggested the continued relevance of one's state of citizenship as a source of protection for aliens, something particularly relevant in a context where one may not have rights as a landed immigrant yet, but where one's 'bare' rights as a human count for little in the no-mans' lands of the Mediterranean and the Rio Grande. The insistence by Gambia for example that the International Criminal Court investigate migrant disappearances in the

[70] Radhika Viyas Mongia, 'Race, Nationality, Mobility: A History of the Passport' (1999) 11 Public Culture 527, 528.

[71] Peter Schuck, *Citizens, Strangers, and In-betweens: Essays on Immigration and Citizenship* (Perseus 2000).

[72] Joan Fitzpatrick and William McKay Bennett, 'A Lion in the Path—The Influence of International Law on the Immigration Policy of the United States Immigration and Naturalization Policy'(1995) 17 Immigration and Nationality Law Review 223, 224.

Mediterranean suggests that states of origin at least have a role in denouncing the fate of their citizens that are persistently denied the ability to immigrate legally.[73]

It may therefore be tempting, by way of thought experiment, to take earlier international law at its word and seek ways in which that broad liberal commitment to freedom of movement could be updated through a contemporary commitment to anti-racism. One is reminded of the way in which decolonisation elites appropriated the European international law notion of a right to self-determination and turned it against their oppressors. Could something similar be done with this earlier notion of a right to immigrate? Maybe, but it would involve a considerable degree of Global South solidarity, and not simply the attempt by Southern states individually and divided to secure privileged regimes of labour mobility for their own nationals. There may be more leverage, if asymmetrical mobility is fully understood to be a by-product of colonial and imperial relations, in thinking of migration today, as Tendayi Achiume notably has, as itself a form of decolonisation.[74]

At any rate, international law should be haunted by the bad conscience of this earlier good conscience. A historical contextualisation of the global law of migration might at least help us question the absoluteness of the equation of sovereignty and the sort of capricious, arbitrary and racist attitude to the entry of foreigners that has come to define it, even as we should entertain no doubt that every regime of freedom of movement has always tended to be inherently discriminatory. The nineteenth-century regime may not have been that different from today's, but it at least inverted the presumption, putting the onus on states to justify their restrictions to freedom of movement rather than trying to at best carve out narrow exceptions to an otherwise reified commitment to borders.

Third, the study of the early international law of migration can help us more generally think about the relationship of international law to history, and its role in conceptualising the limits and potential(s) of international law and justice. One larger lesson for change in international law in this book, is that the discipline may often be only dimly aware of having not taken certain roads and perhaps, as a result, fail to quite understand on what road it actually is or perhaps could be. This can also foster a revisionist inclination in international legal historiography that includes a tendency to write the past in light of the present, and is oblivious to the contingency of the present. For example, whilst it has been claimed that '[s]ince the development of the modern state from the fifteenth century onward, governments have regarded control over their borders as the core of sovereignty',[75] that statement needs to be substantially unpacked and is in some ways a gross simplification. As has been seen, international lawyers' notion of the 'rights of states' when it comes to immigration is a much more complex story than this conventional narrative suggests.

The discipline, it seems, is often complicit in the writing of its own 'false necessity'. The ability of international lawyers involved in the debate over migration across the nineteenth

[73] I have explored the idea that 'sovereign protection' should be a more central plank of human rights elsewhere. See Frédéric Mégret, 'From a Human Right to Invoke Consular Assistance in the Host State to a Human Right to Claim Diplomatic Protection from One's State of Nationality?' in Andreas von Arnauld, Kerstin von der Decken, and Mart Susi (eds) *The Cambridge Handbook of New Human Rights: Recognition, Novelty, Rhetoric* (CUP 2020) 453; Frédéric Mégret, 'Mixed Claims Commissions and the Once Centrality of the Protection of Aliens' in Ignacio de la Rasilla del Moral and Jorge Viñuales (eds) *Experiments in International Adjudication: Historical Accounts* (CUP 2019) 127; Frédéric Mégret, 'Beyond UN Accountability for Human Rights Violations: Host State Inertia and the Neglected Potential of Sovereign Protection' (2019) 16 International Organizations Law Review 68.

[74] Tendayi Achiume, 'Migration as Decolonization' (2019) 71 Stanford Law Review 1509.

[75] Myron Weiner, 'The Global Migration Crisis' in Wang Gungwu (ed) *Global History and Migrations* (Routledge 2018).

and twentieth centuries to constantly and subtly rewrite its fundamental tenets in ways that suited the needs of the day is striking. It attests not only to the well-known plasticity of international legal argument, but also to the importance of framing the law and its underlying social reality through narrative practices. The world of migration is portrayed at times in the language of liberal freedom, at times in the language of political economy, at times in the language of race, and at times in the language of sovereignty. Discourses of demography, eugenics, or public order are deployed to encourage migration here, limit it there. International lawyers are more handmaiden than demiurge, but in believing and claiming authority for the particular tales they weave, not entirely innocent of the forms of power they ratify.

One motif that this chapter hopes to have put in focus is the relative *amnesia* of international law, a sense of a discipline constantly reinventing itself for the age, even at the cost of turning its back on its own history. The danger is that the discipline will fail to see its history for what it is, at the risk maybe of missing out on its own occasional emancipatory promise, but also on the extent to which it is less detached from its darker legacies than it thinks. Because it is so amnesic, the discipline is a bizarre mix of being both unduly resigned to the broader status quo yet excessively confident about its potential to tinker with it at the margin. By failing to recontextualise debates about the current migrant crisis within the larger construction of unfreedom of movement, it condemns itself to reproducing the conditions against which it seeks to present itself as a precarious and tragic bulwark.

12

Contingent Movements?

The Differential Decolonisations of International Refugee and Migration Law and Governance

Christopher Szabla

I. Introduction

Why does no dedicated international organisation exist to oversee and enforce a concrete set of rights of all global migrants? Why are those rights fragmented among, *inter alia*, human rights, labour law, and the law of the sea?[1] Why has most migrant movement been left largely to the direction of states rather than being mediated internationally? In other words, why does no clear international legal and institutional *regime* exist to protect all migrants akin to that which exists for those covered by the mandate of the United Nations High Commission for Refugees (UNHCR) and the Convention on the Status of Refugees?[2] Or why does no such regime exist to regulate migrant movement akin to the one for the movement of goods formed by the General Agreement on Tariffs and Trade (GATT) and World Trade Organization (WTO)?[3] While an International Organization for Migration (IOM) exists, scholars such as Jan Klabbers have demonstrated how it lacks the scope, power, and incentives to address migration in the way the aforementioned organisations do their focal

[1] See Vincent Chetail, 'The Architecture of International Migration Law: A Deconstructivist Design of Complexity and Contradiction' (2017) 111 AJIL Unbound 18–23.

[2] Political scientists define 'regimes' as 'sets of implicit or explicit principles, norms, rules and decision-making procedures around which actors' expectations converge in a given area of international relations'. Stephen D Krasner, 'Structural Causes and Regime Consequences: Regimes as Intervening Variables' (1982) 36 International Organization 185, 186. Regimes typically describe 'more specialized arrangements that pertain to well-defined activities, resources, or geographical areas and often involve only some subset of the members of international society': Oran R Young, *International Cooperation: Building Regimes for Natural Resources and the Environment* (Cornell University Press 1989) 13. International legal scholars have acknowledged that regime theory expands legal thinking about restraints on state action. See eg Anne-Marie Slaughter, Andrew S Tulumello, and Stepan Wood, 'International Law and International Relations Theory: A New Generation of Interdisciplinary Scholarship' (1998) 92 American Journal of International Law 367, 367–68. This chapter includes international law and norms and the structures framed by international organisations as part of 'regimes'. Other scholars have already applied 'regime' terminology to refugee law and institutions. See eg Claudena Skran, *Refugees in Inter-War Europe: The Emergence of a Regime* (OUP 1995). Scholars have also noted that a similar regime is lacking for migrants as a whole. See eg Rey Koslowski, 'Global Mobility and the Quest for an International Migration Regime' (2008) 21 Center for Migration Studies Special Issues 103.

[3] Scholars posing this question from the perspective of political economy include eg Leah Haus, 'Migration and International Economic Institutions' in Aristide Zolberg and Peter Benda (eds), *Global Migrants, Global Refugees: Problems and Solutions* (Berghahn 2001) 271. Others propose new migration treaties along the lines of the GATT. See eg Koslowski (n 2) 107. Some treaties already regulate migrant movement—including the General Agreement on Tariffs for Services (GATS) and some International Labour Organization (ILO) instruments. See Koslowski (n 2) 114–15; Khalid Koser, 'Introduction: International Migration and Global Governance' (2010) 16 Global Governance 301, 308. Yet the former represents only a small number of elite migrants, and each represents a part of international migration law's fragmentation problem.

Christopher Szabla, *Contingent Movements?* In: *Contingency in International Law.* Edited by: Ingo Venzke and Kevin Jon Heller, Oxford University Press. © The Several Contributors 2021. DOI: 10.1093/oso/9780192898036.003.0012

areas.[4] Alexander Betts observes, consequently, that '[t]here is no formal or coherent multilateral ... framework regulating ... international migration' as a whole.[5] Neither the recent adoption of a non-binding Global Compact for Safe, Orderly and Regular Migration nor the IOM's rebranding as the 'UN Migration Agency' have fully altered this fact—though they illustrate how global governance continues to struggle with the absence of a migration regime.[6] The purpose of this chapter is to re-evaluate how and why such a regime never truly emerged in the same way as others—and particularly as compared to the regime for refugees—distilling lessons that this holds for future reform.

The histories of the refugee and migration regimes have been closely tied to institutional initiative and oversight. The Institute of International Law put forth a model treaty on the rights of all emigrants in 1897—and in the aftermath of the First World War, the League of Nations and the International Labour Organization (ILO) separately addressed the widespread problems of stateless refugees and large-scale unemployment, which created renewed pressure to faciliate labour migration.[7] During the interwar period, both organisations actively sponsored the production of treaty and soft law applicable to their respective charges.[8] Just after the Second World War, 'displaced persons'—including refugees and other migrants—came under the remit of organisations that treated them together. Yet soon a separate refugee regime was rearticulated, while the future of the institutional framework for the remainder of migrants came into question.

In the course of accounting for the missing migration *regime*, therefore, scholars have focused on the lack of an effective migration *organisation*, tracing its absence to the United States' decision, in 1951, to withhold critical funding for an ILO-linked International Migration Administration (IMA) because it would have involved the participation of communist states. But Cold War-centric explanations have not adequately explained why the United States did not prevent the creation of an international *refugee* regime in which communist states participated. Scholars have also not considered the extent to which a migration organisation arose in the form of the Intergovernmental Committee for European

[4] Klabbers has characterised the IOM as providing 'tailor-made solutions' for member states rather than a 'regulatory mandate' over them: Jan Klabbers, 'Notes on the Ideology of International Organizations Law: The International Organization for Migration, State-Making, and the Market for Migration' (2019) 32 Leiden Journal of International Law 383, 384.

[5] Alexander Betts, 'Introduction: Global Migration Governance' in Alexander Betts (ed) *Global Migration Governance* (OUP 2011) 1.

[6] See Global Compact for Safe, Orderly and Regular Migration, United Nations General Assembly (UNGA) Res 73/195 (LXXIII) (19 December 2018) United Nations (UN) Doc A/RES/73195; Agreement Concerning the Relationship between the United Nations and the International Organization for Migration, UNGA Res 70/296 (LXX) (5 August 2016) UN Doc A/RES/70/296. Even champions of the Compact concede it only begins to address serious migration governance challenges. See eg Linda Bishai, 'It's a Start—Why the Global Compacts on Refugees and Migration Matter' (*Just Security*, 12 September 2018) <https://www.justsecurity.org/60649/its-start-global-compacts-refugees-migration-matter> accessed 11 June 2019. Some are concerned that its provisions are weaker or less specific than existing norms, undermining the latter. See Alessandro Bufalini, 'The Global Compact for Safe, Orderly and Regular Migration: What is its Contribution to International Migration Law?' (2019) 58 Questions of International Law 5, 11–18. The IOM's rebranding, meanwhile, seems unlikely to end its fractious relationship with other UN agencies claiming competency over migration. See Alexander Betts and Lena Kainz, 'The History of Global Migration Governance' (2017) Oxford Refugee Studies Centre Working Paper 122, 7 <https://www.rsc.ox.ac.uk/publications/the-history-of-global-migration-governance> accessed 11 June 2019.

[7] On the Institute of International Law proposal see eg'Emigration from the Point of View of International Law', in James Brown Scott (ed), *Resolutions of the Institute of International Law Dealing with the Law of Nations: With an Historical Introduction and Explanatory Notes* (OUP 1916) 137. On interwar refugee and migration developments see eg Susan Martin, *International Migration: Evolving Trends from the Early Twentieth Century to the Present* (CUP 2014) 26–57.

[8] Martin (n 7) 26–57.

Migration (ICEM)—the forerunner to the IOM. ICEM was initially similar to (and arguably more potent than) UNHCR in its aid function and largely limited, like the early refugee regime, to aiding Europeans. While its membership was exclusive, ICEM was not unlike regimes such as the GATT, in being originally a Western club. Still, both the refugee and trade regimes later 'globalised' more effectively than the one focused on migrants. Why did the emerging migration regime *diminish* instead?

This chapter argues that decisions about the regimes made within the Cold War's context were not entirely determined by it, and that another framework—decolonisation—helps make sense of (but also did not determine) how those decisions led the refugee regime to expand while the migration regime declined. Cold War-era political dynamics helped ensure that ICEM did not become linked to United Nations (UN) or ILO oversight and initiatives. Consequently it decoupled, unlike the UNHCR, from processes of creating and interpreting relevant law. Nonetheless, the regimes began similar in their focus and operation.

Yet resolve by newly decolonised states to seize upon their membership in the UN helped expand the remit of the refugee regime beyond Europeans. ICEM was not a component of the UN, did not automatically admit new members, and thus faced no similar pressure. Its membership resisted altering the organisation's constitutional stipulation that it be limited to assisting Europeans alone.[9] Its constitution *did* allow ICEM to 'be concerned' with non-European *refugees*—leading it to become, as European emigration declined, an adjutant of UNHCR.[10] As such, it also drifted further from organizations more concerned with international law applicable to all migrants—which did increasingly apply to non-Europeans.

ICEM formally 'globalised' its mission around the same time as the GATT/WTO (becoming IOM) but unlike the trade regime, its purpose had shifted—to 'emergency management'—by the time it did so. Without the pressure that had been placed on the refugee regime to become relevant to the wider world, ICEM's work—and thus the migration regime as a whole—diminished in relation to the world's migration concerns.

Section II of this chapter examines US participation in the reshaping of the refugee and migration regimes in the early 1950s, demonstrating how its relative influence on each regime was instrumental in the creation of a refugee system under UN auspices and ICEM outside it. This section will also demonstrate that US decisions were less consistent and more complicated than earlier depicted—and were thus not straightforwardly *determined* by the Cold War alone.

Section III focuses on how decisions made in the context of decolonisation differentially impacted the refugee and migration regimes. It chronicles how newly decolonised states used UN fora to highlight refugee issues outside Europe, pull UNHCR towards crises elsewhere, and remove international legal restrictions on non-European refugee protection—while their inability to pressure ICEM reduced that organisation's capacity in the context of emerging postcolonial migration issues. Section IV concludes by addressing the extent to which these developments were 'contingent'—and what this demonstrates about the possibilities of reforming migration governance today.

[9] Constitution of the Intergovernmental Committee for European Migration (adopted 19 October 1953, entered into force 30 November 1954) 207 UNTS 189 (ICEM Constitution) art 1.

[10] ICEM Constitution (n 9) 210, Annex, e(4).

II. Refugee and migration regime divergence in the early Cold War

The years 1950 to 1952—with their dissipation of problems left over from the Second World War, the rise of Cold War dilemmas, and increasing concerns about the costs of humanitarian initiatives relating to both—witnessed a concerted effort to renegotiate the international governance of displaced and mobile populations. From 1943, these had been handled by the United Nations Relief and Rehabilitation Agency (UNRRA) and International Refugee Organization (IRO), which were both responsible both for the aid within Europe and resettlement overseas of 'displaced persons'—a category that effectively mixed forms of 'refugees' and other migrants.[11] In the early 1950s, however, global governance architects rearticulated a division between 'refugee' and 'migration' regimes.

Both UNHCR and the Refugee Convention were put in place by 1951. UNHCR replaced some monitoring and aid functions of the IRO, while the Convention imposed legal requirements on states not to return and to protect refugees—defined as individuals outside their countries of origin unwilling to avail themselves of those countries' protection out of a well-founded fear of persecution on account of their race, religion, nationality, political opinion, or membership in a particular social group.[12] Scholars have viewed adoption of this definition as a product either of a Cold War compromise, since political but not economic refugees from the Soviet bloc would be included, permitting both an ideological triumph for the West and repatriation of many to the East—or a product of concerns about the repetition of wartime atrocities.[13] Critically, however—owing to the desire to cap the number of potential refugees and to the character of the states represented in negotiations—the Convention also only pertained to those whose refugee status arose as a result of events before 1951, and gave states the option of defining this as meaning events 'in Europe'.[14]

The United States—the power by far the most capable of funding international programmes in the early postwar period—initially resisted participation in the refugee regime. It refused to agree to UNHCR resettlement or relief responsibilities, refused to fund the organisation until 1955, and did not become a party to the Convention until 1968. It was concerned not only with the cost of refugee programmes, but that they might involve refugees 'in which it had no political interest', who might want to settle in the United States.[15] Nevertheless, the United States assented to the regime's creation as part of the UN system—and its lack of enthusiasm was hardly fatal. The regime had advantages; the Convention definition of a refugee—focused on individual persecution—made it a potentially useful tool for ideological combat with the Soviet Union. Reasons the regime triumphed also went beyond the Cold War and US attitudes. A refugee regime without US participation was not

[11] See generally Mark Wyman, *DPs: Europe's Displaced Persons, 1945–51* (Cornell University Press 1998).

[12] Convention Relating to the Status of Refugees (adopted 28 July 1951, entered into force 22 April 1954) 189 UNTS 150 (Refugee Convention) art 1(A)(2).

[13] Michael Marrus, *The Unwanted: European Refugees in the Twentieth Century* (OUP 1985) 356; Skran (n 2) 110. A version of the definition was used by the IRO, but its use by the new refugee regime was not a foregone conclusion.

[14] Refugee Convention (n 12) art 1(B)(1)(b).

[15] Gil Loescher and Joan Scanlan, *Calculated Kindness: Refugees and America's Half-Open Door, 1945 to the Present* (Free Press 1998) 41. On US ratification of the Convention see Joan Fitzpatrick, 'The International Dimension of U.S. Refugee Law' (1997) 15 Berkeley Journal of International Law 1.

unprecedented and could be restarted. Thanks to private philanthropy, moreover, US unwillingness to provide funding also did not halt the regime's realisation.[16]

An organisation governing, facilitating, and aiding large-scale non-refugee migration, meanwhile, would have gone beyond systems put into place during the interwar period, and required more financial support. By 1939, ILO treaties governed migrant worker rights, indigenous labour recruiting, and treatment of passengers at sea, but a more comprehensive migration regime—particularly aid and assistance functions—had eluded advocates.[17] Postwar planners sought at least to replace the overseas transportation function of the IRO, which was not included in the refugee regime.

With US, British, and later UN encouragement, the ILO—with its history of experience in migration governance—drew up plans in 1950 for an IMA under its aegis. This institution would 'encompass the total European migration situation and reduce ... to a short-term problem' the masses in 'overpopulated' countries through emigration aid, and 'assist overseas countries to obtain the manpower and technical know-how desired for current economic and social development'. The proposed IMA, 'while acting only upon governmental request, was to draw up migration plans, negotiate agreements between sending and receiving countries, select, train, inform, and transport migrants, raise and disburse funds for transportation, and give loans to migrants in order to enable them to establish themselves in the receiving country'.[18]

The proposal was discussed at a 1951 conference in Naples, Italy, attended by European states and major recipients—including the US, Australia, and Latin American republics—of European emigrants.[19] One historian believes the conference failed because of the notion that even limited international governance of migration implied an unacceptable compromise of sovereignty—along with 'countries of immigration' feeling no need to cooperate in a 'buyer's market' for migrants.[20] Yet states had readily compromised to accept the *refugee* regime's restraints on their freedoms.

Other scholars point to the immediate historical context. Ernst Haas, for example, writes that 'a sudden *volte face* by the United States', led 'the Conference ... to kill the [IMA]'.[21] What produced this *volte face*? Several scholars blame Cold War politics for the United States ultimately refusing to participate in a migration governance effort that would have fully included the Soviet bloc.[22] Yet this does not fully explain *initial* US enthusiasm for the Naples proposal, which was in part *predicated* on the Cold War rationale that sapping 'overpopulated' Western Europe through emigration would diminish the communist threat. It also fails to address the fact that the United States found the prospect of Soviet participation in either the refugee regime or, initially, in the migration regime, unthreatening.

[16] Ingo Venzke, *How Interpretation Makes International Law: On Semantic Change and Normative Twists* (OUP 2012) 94.

[17] Aspects of this history are so far best covered in Martin (n 7) 26–48.

[18] Ernst Haas, *Beyond the Nation State: Functionalism and International Organization* (Stanford University Press 1964) 172–73.

[19] ibid 173.

[20] See Aristide Zolberg, 'Labour Migration and International Economic Regimes: Bretton Woods and After' in Mary Kritz, Lin Lean Lim, and Hania Zlotnik (eds), *International Migration Systems: A Global Approach* (OUP 1992) 317.

[21] Haas (n 18) 173.

[22] Haus (n 3) 278; Rieko Karatani, 'How History Separated Refugee and Migrant Regimes: In Search of Their Institutional Origins' (2005) 17 International Journal of Refugee Law 517; Martin (n 7) 98.

One alternative answer centres on sudden shifts in US domestic politics. In the midst of the Naples process, Congress passed the Mutual Security Act, providing $10 million to extend IRO activities—but stipulating that 'none of the funds available ... should be allocated to any international organization which has in its membership any Communist, Communist-dominated or Communist controlled country, to any subsidiary thereof or to any agency created by or stemming from such organization'.[23] The act 'was clearly aimed at the ILO' migration initiative, assessed a Brookings Institution report not long after; '[i]t undoubtedly contributed to the failure of the Naples conference'.[24] While the Executive Branch continued to support an IMA after passage of the act, it was regarded as 'unsellable' in Congress.[25] The increasingly Republican legislature had grown impatient with the Truman administration's costly overseas projects in the service of Cold War aims, from the Korean War to foreign aid.[26] The IMA may have simply come too late in the president's term to avoid electoral backlash to him and Congressional Republicans' hostility to one more expensive programme.

Still, the United States had also failed to support the refugee regime in its early years. Why was lack of US support *fatal* for the Naples plan? Haas' theory was that 'the [migration] program involved calls for ... large funds'.[27] Even other states found the ILO proposal 'grandiose and impractical in many of its aspects'.[28] The Brookings report went so far as to claim that its failure illustrated that migration was too 'economically complex' for *any* international organisation to tackle sufficiently.[29] While refugees might also require expensive programmes, UNHCR's aid function was limited at its outset, and a more extensive system of training and distribution for all migrants would have required prohibitively larger expenditures.[30] In effect, additional funding from the United States would have been more vital for the migration regime, making the timing and impact of the country's refusal more significant for that regime's fate.

Despite the IMA's failure, non-communist states still managed to forge an inter*governmental* migration organisation under US leadership. At Brussels in 1952 'the same governments that had first encouraged the ILO venture into migration, almost immediately proceeded to establish' the Provisional Intergovernmental Committee for the Movement of Migrants from Europe (PICMME)—soon becoming 'the totally autonomous [ICEM], which, while never joining the United Nations system, acquired many of the powers and functions originally claimed for the ILO' over the preparation and distribution of migrants.[31] While still costly, ICEM served US interests better than an organisation that would have sponsored migrants worldwide. ICEM's constitution limited its focus to European migrants, and its membership limited it to problems preoccupying Western and

[23] George L Warren, 'Report on the Conference on Migration and on the First Session of the Provisional Intergovernmental Committee for the Movement of Migrants from Europe' in United States Department of State, *Foreign Relations of the United States, 1952–1954, General: Economic and Political Matters, Volume I, Part 2* (US Government Printing Office 1983) 1576, n 10.

[24] Robert E Asher, *The United Nations and Promotion of the General Welfare* (Brookings Institution 1957) 525.

[25] Haus (n 3) 281.

[26] See generally Chester J Pach Jr, 'Mutual Security Act (1951)' in John Whiteclay Chambers II (ed), *The Oxford Companion to American Military History* (OUP 1999).

[27] Haas (n 18) 173.

[28] Asher (n 24) 525.

[29] ibid 527.

[30] See eg ibid 521 (emphasising the expense of land settlement and industrial training).

[31] Haas (n 18) 173.

Latin American states.[32] The United States would be able to eliminate 'surplus population' in Western Europe and to develop Latin America—tackling social unrest and poverty that it believed made both regions ripe for communism—without having to benefit the Eastern Bloc or finance attempts to address population problems elsewhere.[33]

Two similar regimes, therefore, emerged: UNHCR and the UN Refugee Convention, on the one hand, and ICEM—along with earlier treaties pertaining to migrant rights—on the other. Both were principally concerned with Europeans—given the de facto commitments of UNHCR during a period in which it was still occupied with postwar displaced persons and Cold War asylees, the temporal and optional geographical restrictions of the Refugee Convention, the constitution, membership, and purpose of ICEM, and the focus and application of the migrant rights treaties. While organisations arose in the late 1940s and early 1950s to handle Palestinian and Korean refugees, these were exceptions whose independent status proved the rule—and in the latter case, proved temporary.[34]

The purposes of the organisations were more distinct, but grew closer over time. While UNHCR—founded to oversee legal protection—gradually became more of an aid organisation, ICEM—founded to provide aid for transportation and settlement—became more invested in the safety, conditions of travel, and training of migrants to integrate into new cultures and labour markets. In effect, both organisations came to be concerned with the mobility of and the degree to which their respective charges enjoyed relatively frictionless experiences in host states.

As such, the principal distinctions between these systems were the fact that the refugee regime was accountable to a wider and potentially expanding number of states—a consequence of laying within the UN system—and that refugees were governed by a signal treaty linked to that system while migrants were not. The divergence in these regimes' legal architecture was not at first deeply consequential given migrants, unlike refugees, enjoyed some legal protection from their home states—and that the largely European migrants contemplated could often naturalise with relatively few problems in their new homes. Still, without a link between ICEM and UN or ILO treaties, the latter organisations still maintained that they had responsibilities for the legal oversight of migrants, while only ICEM focused exclusively on them.[35] The difficulties resulting from these agencies' fragmentation became prominently expressed when concern for migrants beyond Europe expanded in the UN and ILO, but not in ICEM.

III. The differential impact of decolonisation on the refugee and migration regimes

Owing to their distinct architectures, shifts in the late 1950s and early 1960s—both political and demographic—impacted what were, until then, relatively similar refugee and migration regimes in different ways. While attachment to the UN system made the refugee regime vulnerable to the critiques of newly admitted postcolonial states that it was not addressing their

[32] Richard Perruchoud, 'From the Intergovernmental Committee for European Migration to the International Organization for Migration' (1989) 1 International Journal of Refugee Law 501, 512.
[33] Loescher and Scanlan (n 15) 42–45.
[34] See Martin (n 7) 72–79.
[35] Asher (n 24) 526.

refugee problems, states outside the Western bloc and Latin America had little recourse within ICEM. More accountable international bodies outside ICEM, meanwhile, lacked its focus on migration. While these two systems' underlying structures diverged largely as a result of early Cold War-era decisions, therefore, these divergences became more *expressed* in a later era of intensified decolonisation, as Europe's demographic impact on the world softened and new states arose with different agendas.

1. Decolonisation and the refugee regime

Although the Refugee Convention did not obligate states to protect refugees created by events other than those that took place in Europe before 1951—which largely limited its applicability to those affected by the Second World War—UNHCR's mandate was left open. Still, most UN refugee discussion in the early 1950s concerned Europeans, particularly those who had originally lived in states that were now part of the Eastern Bloc. This focus continued despite the existence of outstanding refugee issues stemming from such traumas as the Chinese Civil War and Indian partition.

Major breakthroughs for non-European refugee issues came only after the independence of a critical mass of formerly colonised states. A watershed was the Algerian war, which caused a refugee exodus into neighbouring Morocco and Tunisia (both of which had become independent states and UN members in 1956). France, which considered Algeria an integral part of its territory, did not dispute conferral of refugee status on Algerians on the basis that Algeria was not 'Europe;' still less could it dispute that Algerians fell within the less-restricted mandate of UNHCR (it did not appear to consider raising the Convention's 1951 date limit). Yet it did consider conferral of refugee status on Algerians tantamount to admitting that it was persecuting them. French diplomatic documents concerned with Algerians rendered the term 'refugees' in scare quotes, often referring to Algerians who fled the war as '*repliés*' or 'those turned away' instead.[36] France insisted, therefore, that European countries not accord Algerians juridical refugee status. Nor, it argued, should Algerian '*repliés*' be given aid by UNHCR. France also claimed, on policy grounds, that refugee status might benefit disguised members of the pro-independence militant group *Front de Libération Nationale* (FLN).[37]

Nevertheless, Morocco and Tunisia, which bore the brunt of the refugee problem, continually lobbied in the UN General Assembly and UNHCR Executive Council for resolutions which would call on UNHCR to provide aid to Algerian refugees on their territories. Other Arab states, including Iraq and the United Arab Republic (the brief union of Egypt and Syria), joined and encouraged them.[38] France condemned such efforts as attempts to divert aid to the FLN. Yet its diplomats reported that Arab efforts succeeded by drawing the support of other 'Afro-Asiatic' delegations and 'embarrassing' Western states

[36] 'Note for the Secretary of Conferences by the Direction of Administrative and Social Affairs' (28 October 1957) (Archives Diplomatiques de France, site de Nantes [hereafter AD/N] New-York, ONU, 10POI/1, Carton 40).
[37] See eg 'Note by the Liaison Mission with Algeria re: "Problems of Algerian Refugees in Morocco and Tunisia"' (29 April 1959) (AD/N, New-York, ONU, 10POI/1, Carton 40) 3.
[38] See eg 8 November 1958 letter from Guillaume Georges-Picot, French Ambassador to the United Nations, to Ministry of Foreign Affairs (AD/N, New-York, ONU, 10POI/1, Carton 40) 5.

into agreement.[39] While scholars have attributed UNHCR policy shifts during the conflict to High Commissioner Auguste Lindt, their accounts also show Lindt was reacting to Moroccan and Tunisian remonstrations.[40]

The influence of the Cold War was not entirely absent in these decisions; Western states did not appear willing to alienate potential allies by supporting the French position—but alienating France was also a Cold War risk. Arab lobbying also drove these fears rather than the other way around. And while it might be expected that Soviet social justice concerns drove one or both Cold War blocs to embrace non-European refugee issues, the Soviet bloc did not consistently press them. The bloc did, on one occasion, call for UNHCR to focus entirely on non-European refugees given what it felt was a decreasing need for concern with humanitarian problems in Europe.[41] Yet on another it called for an end to UNHCR's *entire* mandate on that basis.[42] It also failed to support UNHCR aid for politically inconvenient non-European refugees, such as those from communist China entering Hong Kong before the Sino-Soviet split.[43] In supporting aid to Chinese refugees, African and Latin American states, in fact, prevailed over *both* the Eastern and Western blocs.[44]

Increasing cooperation among and advocacy by postcolonial states ultimately drove changes to the governance of UNHCR. Initial oversight of UNHCR operations involved states that contributed the most to the organisation's budget and hosted the most refugees.[45] But as newly decolonised states not only hosted more refugee challenges but became more vocal within the UN system, UNHCR administrators yielded to perceptions that its Executive Council needed to become more representative.[46] Newly elected African and Asian states then served as a voice both for non-European refugee issues and for further enlargement of the council to include *more* non-European states—and their concerns—in the early 1960s.[47] UNHCR consequently took on even more non-European refugee projects.

[39] 4 November 1958 telegram from the French Representation to the United Nations, New York, to the French Ministry of Foreign Affairs (AD/N, New-York, ONU, 10POI/1, Carton 40); 8 November 1958 letter from Guillaume Georges-Picot (n 38) 7.

[40] See Michael Barnett and Martha Finnemore, *Rules for the World: International Organizations in Global Politics* (Cornell University Press 2004) 89; Gil Loescher, 'The UNHCR and World Politics: State Interests vs. Institutional Autonomy' (2001) 35 International Migration Review 33, 37.

[41] 30 November 1962 letter from Roger Seydoux, French Representative to the United Nations, to Ministry of Foreign Affairs re: 'UNHCR' (AD/N, New-York, RP ONU, 10POI/I, Carton 113) 2–3.

[42] 1 December 1961 letter from Armand Berard, French Ambassador to the United Nations, to Ministry of Foreign Affairs re: 'General Assembly, 3rd Commission, on Refugees' (AD/N, New-York, RP ONU, 10POI/I, Carton 113) 3.

[43] 15 November 1957 letter from Georges-Picot to the Ministry of Foreign Affairs, re: '12th Session of the General Assembly, 3rd Commission' (AD/N, New-York, RP ONU, 10POI/I, Carton 113).

[44] 21 November 1962 telegram from Seydoux to the Ministry of Foreign Affairs (AD/N, New-York, RP ONU, 10POI/I, Carton 113) (noting a resolution on Chinese refugees passed with the support of Cameroon, Gabon, Madagascar, and the Central African Republic plus Paraguay and Guatemala, while Britain and France 'tried vainly to discourage' it).

[45] United Nations, '25th Session of the Economic and Social Council—Point 9: Executive Committee of the Program of the High Commission' (3 May 1958) (AD/N, New-York, RP ONU, 10POI/I, Carton 113).

[46] 23 March 1958 letter for M Wolfram from M Paolini (AD/N, New-York, RP ONU, 10POI/I, Carton 113) 2 (noting 'Afro-Asiatic states' were disfavoured on the earlier instantiation of the council); see also 27 October 1962 telegram from Ministry of Foreign Affairs to French Representation to the UN (AD/N, New-York, RP ONU, 10POI/I, Carton 113) (noting the High Commissioner found expansion to non-European states 'inevitable' given increasing UNHCR work in their regions).

[47] See eg 29 March 1958 letter from Georges-Picot to Ministry of Foreign Affairs re: 'Creation of the UNHCR Executive Committee' (AD/N, New-York, RP ONU, 10POI/I, Carton 113) 2 (noting inclusion of China on the council could 'deposit before the committee the problem of refugees in Hong Kong in all their extent').

A growing General Assembly even innovated expansions of the definition of 'refugee' that it served.[48]

The expansion of UNHCR activity to non-European refugees cleared the way for the adoption of the 1967 Refugee Protocol, which eliminated future geographic or temporal restrictions on refugee protection.[49] A 1964 UNHCR session that discussed the modification of the Convention in this direction found it widely supported in light of the de facto extension of the concept of refugee to the Global South when it came to the organisation's operations—the expansion that had been pressed by postcolonial states.[50] While the election of Prince Sadruddin Aga Khan as the first UN High Commissioner for Refugees from the Global South has been credited with advancing UNHCR's interest in refugees beyond Europe and the adoption of the Protocol, it is important not to exaggerate his role relative to new states'.[51] Support for Prince Sadruddin by the already decisive 'Afro-Asiatic' bloc was itself likely key in supporting his election.[52] Fears among Western states opposing Prince Sadruddin's election focused not on the likelihood that he would shift UNHCR activities to the Global South for the first time, but that he would fail to maintain a balance between them and activities in Europe.[53]

2. Decolonisation and the migration regime

In contrast to UNHCR and the Refugee Convention, the migration regime lacked mechanisms by which newly independent states could meaningfully influence its activities. Even as European emigration—the chief task ICEM was designed to facilitate—dwindled, ICEM's members tended to oppose extension of its original mission to non-European migration. They conceded, instead, to devoting resources to non-European *refugee* crises—which received more publicity from postcolonial states channelling their complaints towards the refugee regime through the UN system. This shift ultimately consumed ICEM's activities and diminished its role for migrants. It also decoupled ICEM further from the broadening focus of other organizations on international legal rights that those organizations could nonetheless not apply as effectively to migrants.

A 1952 General Assembly resolution illustrates the lack of influence that states outside ICEM had over the migration regime. It also demonstrates the emerging difficulties with fragmentation between ICEM and other organisations claiming competency over migrants stemming from ICEM's unique focus on Europeans. The resolution recommended that UN

[48] Venzke (n 16) 100 (on the expansion of UNHCR activity to Chinese refugees through its 'good offices).

[49] Protocol relating to the Status of Refugees (opened for signature 31 January 1967, entered into force 4 October 1967) 606 UNTS 267 arts 1(2)-(3).

[50] 'Note on the Work of the XIII Session of the Executive Committee of UNHCR' (Rome, 22–30 October 1964) (AD/N, New-York, RP ONU, 10POI/I, Carton 113) 2 (noting 'many delegations' saw the need to modify the Convention on this basis, and noting no objections).

[51] See eg Doreen Elliott and Uma A Segal (eds) *Refugees Worldwide, Volume 2* (Praeger 2012) 47, for a literal textbook view of Prince Sadruddin's role.

[52] French diplomats noted Prince Sadruddin had the support of 'the entire Third World'. 19 November 1965 telegram from French Representation at United Nations, New York to the Ministry of Foreign Affairs (AD/N, New-York, RP ONU, 10POI/I, Carton 113).

[53] 9 November 1965 telegram from Ministry of Foreign Affairs to French Representation at United Nations, New York (AD/N, New-York, RP ONU, 10POI/I, Carton 113).

'Member...and non-Member States ... conclude bilateral or multilateral agreements with a view to the equipment, transfer and resettlement of groups of emigrants, *without racial or religious discrimination*'.[54] Because of a lack of implementation mechanisms within the UN system, however—and their location, instead, within ICEM—this was merely a suggestion compared to calls to action that could be directed at UNHCR. As one contemporary wrote, the resolution's 'emphasis on direct agreements between governments rather than on international machinery is significant' for recognising the difficulty of influencing ICEM or creating a parallel organisation.[55]

Just as the UN had no tools to implement ICEM functions for non-European migrants, ICEM had little ability to monitor or advocate for their rights under UN or ILO-sponsored law, or for their treatment more broadly, despite growing concerns about them.[56] The resolution establishing ICEM—reaffirmed in its constitution—tied it to 'generally accepted international standards of employment and living conditions, with full respect for human rights'.[57] ICEM, the UN, and the ILO also squabbled over boundaries between their competencies.[58] Yet without an expansion of ICEM's mandate to non-European migrants, it had no ability to claim legal oversight of them.

By the early 1960s, with European emigration subsiding and other migratory—and political—pressures increasing, ICEM did begin contemplating the possibility of extending the institution's activities to non-European migrants. Yet with no avenue for postcolonial states' influence, there was never any serious movement for nor majority in favour of the idea. West Germany proposed that ICEM discussions should discuss facilitating migration *to* rather than merely *from* Europe, but French observers dismissed this as political jockeying within the organisation and little came of the suggestion.[59] Non-members' pleas fell on deaf ears; Australia and France viewed a Japanese petition for mere observer status in the organisation as an effort to become a full-fledged member, which each viewed as impermissible.[60] 'Do we want, or is there need for, an International Body dealing with *worldwide* migration?' one British diplomat in Geneva pondered in a brief to Whitehall in 1964. 'The short answer to this question', he continued, 'must, I think, be "no."' Non-European migrant groups neither required ICEM assistance nor, he believed, it would be desirable for ICEM to provide it. 'The overseas Chinese do indeed migrate', he considered, 'but ... *there seems no reason for the international community to organise such movement as there is.*' Referring to 'Jamaican migration to the United Kingdom', he was even more explicit, opining that '*we should certainly not wish these movements to be organized [sic] and subsidised* ... by any ... International Agency.' He dismissed any concern that similar needs might be driving

[54] Migration and Economic Development, UNGA Res 624 (VII) (1952) UN Doc A/2361, 16 (emphasis added).
[55] Asher (n 24) 528.
[56] Kathleen Teltsch, 'U.N. Study Shows Migrants' Plight,' *New York Times* (1 December 1974) 13 (noting the ICEM director's concern with the growing plight of non-European migrants in Europe).
[57] ICEM Constitution (n 9) Annex, 210.
[58] See 'International Organizations: Intergovernmental Committee for European Migration – Intersecretariat Meetings, ICEM - ILO' (ILO Archive file IGO 022-1000-01).
[59] 28 April 1961 letter from the French Ambassador to Germany to Maurice Couve de Murville, French Ministry of Foreign Affairs re: 'German Conceptions of the Future of ICEM' (AD/N ONU Representation Permanante à Genève, 11POI/1, Carton 601) 3.
[60] 13 February 1961 letter from G Gattand, French Ambassador at UN Office Geneva, to the Ministry of Foreign Affairs re: 'ICEM: Request to Admit Japan as an Observer' (AD/N ONU Representation Permanante à Genève, 11POI/1, Carton 601).

non-European migration as those that had inspired ICEM's creation: 'I believe it to be generally accepted that emigration cannot provide an acceptable answer to the problem posed by the immense annual increase in population in Japan, India, Pakistan or China', he concluded, supplying no rationale as to why overpopulation could be addressed by ICEM in Europe but not Asia.[61]

The United States was also opposed to expanding ICEM's remit, and even individual American politicians' proposals to expand its operations met with alarm. France reported with concern, for example, the belief that Senator Ted Kennedy would call for the organisation to aid all migrants.[62] Kennedy's eventual, watered down proposal rejected such an expansion explicitly and merely called on ICEM to de-emphasise assistance for European emigrants, be more inclusive of non-Western states, and focus, instead, even more on non-European refugees. French observers nonetheless noted that Kennedy roomed with Prince Sadruddin when he put forward this plan; they sought and received assurances from US diplomats that his words did not represent official policy. Latin American states, too, condemned the proposal for focusing on other migrants and thereby cheating them of their need for skilled European workers.[63] Only Bolivia appeared open to accepting non-Europeans.[64]

Only in the 1980s did ICEM finally—as Kennedy had advocated in 1966—drop 'European' from its name and change its constitution to eliminate geographic restrictions on its activities, becoming IOM.[65] But by then the organisation had already shifted its scope away from regular migration as a consequence of waning European emigration.[66] In recent years, over half of IOM's budget has been focused on emergency refugee and humanitarian activity.[67]

Opposition to ICEM's expansion not only illustrated its distinction from the UN-oriented refugee regime, but its substantive distinction from the equally exclusive and independent GATT. While GATT members could see an opportunity in the expansion of trade, however, Western states were reluctant to expand migration. Illustrating the ongoing effects of its status as an independent organisation subject to the influence of its wealthiest members, ICEM now even facilitates members' exclusionary immigration policies *against* migrants.[68]

[61] 23 November 1964 letter written on behalf of CP Scott, United Kingdom Mission Geneva, to KRC Pridham, UN (E & S) Department, London (1821/100/64) (British National Archives file FO 371/178510) (emphasis added).

[62] 26 May 1966 letter from Bernard de Chalvron, French Representative at UN Office Geneva, to the Ministry of Foreign Affairs re: 'Role of ICEM' (AD/N ONU Representation Permanante à Genève, 11POI/1, Carton 601) 6.

[63] See 'Extracts of Declarations Made at the 65th Meeting of the ICEM Council' (November 1966) (AD/N ONU Representation Permanante à Genève, 11POI/1, Carton 601) 19–21; 16 November 1966 telegram from Chalvron to the Ministry of Foreign Affairs (AD/N ONU Representation Permanante à Genève, 11POI/1, Carton 601); 22 November 1966 telegram from French Embassy, Washington to the Ministry of Foreign Affairs (AD/N ONU Representation Permanante à Genève, 11POI/1, Carton 601).

[64] 'Extracts of Declarations Made at the 65th Meeting of the ICEM Council' (n 63) 8.

[65] Perruchoud (n 32) 512.

[66] Francesca Fauri, 'European Migrants after the Second World War' in Francesca Fauri (ed), *The History of Migration in Europe: Perspectives from Economics, Politics, and Sociology* (Routledge 2014) 120.

[67] Martin (n 7) 143 (funds as of 2011).

[68] Klabbers (n 4) 384, 387. See also Rutvica Andrijasevic and William Walters, 'The International Organization for Migration and the International Government of Borders' (2010) 28 Society and Space 977; Sandra Lavenex, 'Multilevelling EU External Governance: The Role of International Organizations in the Diffusion of EU Migration Policies' (2016) 42 Journal of Ethnic and Migration Studies 554.

IV. Conclusion: From decolonisation to the present migration regime

As early as 1957, a Brookings report observed, in a prescient comment that was nonetheless relegated to a footnote, the effect of the exclusivity of the migration regime:

> The emphasis of the international community on European migration is significant ... organized migration was viewed by the Western world primarily as a European problem and scant attention was paid to migratory movements in other parts of the world. This tradition left its imprint on the international organizations interested in migration and left them ill equipped to render effective assistance in meeting the problems of non-European migrants.[69]

While the turn away from its emphasis on European refugees in the late 1950s and 1960s allowed the refugee regime to avoid these shortcomings, they remained applicable to the migration regime.

It is possible to debate how much of the history leading to this point resulted from contingent processes rather than the structural frameworks of 'the Cold War' or 'decolonisation'. To what extent, for example, were US spending priorities in the early 1950s—which undermined the formation of a more representative, less fragmented migration regime—a product of the wavering vicissitudes of American electoral politics placing an increasing number of Republicans in congressional power as enthusiasm for Truman, specifically, waned, rather than a necessary consequence of increasing Cold War pressures?

It is equally possible to view many important details of 'decolonisation' as contingent, despite overarching influences. Historians have demonstrated that decolonisation was a haphazard process.[70] Not all colonial territory broke into a predetermined number of states, achieved independence, or achieved it by the time postcolonial states' votes in the UN were reshaping refugee governance.[71] To suggest that 'the Cold War' or 'decolonisation' were monolithic and not characterised by shifting meanings or degrees of realisation might be to submit to an over-deterministic understanding of history or to fail to admit how turning points may be contingent even if shaped by context.[72]

Yet even taking a stricter understanding of 'contingency' that would see, for example, decolonisation necessarily producing a critical mass of new states, these states' concerted *advocacy* for a more representative refugee regime still appears no *necessary* product of the framework. Newly independent states of course advocated in their self-interest, yet this could have simply resulted in ad hoc expansions of UNHCR activity rather than a solidaristic campaign for international legal and institutional reform. Even the broader currents of the non-aligned movement or a 'spirit of Bandung' would not necessarily present

[69] Asher (n 24) 525 n 46.

[70] See eg Ronald Hyam, *Britain's Declining Empire: The Road to Decolonisation, 1918–1968* (CUP 2007) 398–99.

[71] Scholars have recently emphasised the real but lost possibility of postcolonial federations, for example. See eg Frederick Cooper, 'Alternatives to Nationalism in French Africa, 1945–60' in Jost Dülffer and Marc Frey (eds), *Elites and Decolonization in the Twentieth Century* (Palgrave Macmillan 2011); Adom Getachew, *Worldmaking After Empire: The Rise and Fall of Self-Determination* (Princeton University Press 2019) ch 4.

[72] On these possibilities see Susan Marks, 'False Contingency' (2009) 62 Current Legal Problems 1, 1–3.

a deterministic framework, but a context of encouragement for further acts.[73] There is certainly no reason to believe that this campaign was the result of *pressure*. Decolonised state advocacy for refugee regime reform may have been less a structurally-imposed process than a 'possibility'.[74]

Given the questions it presents about the inevitability of today's migration regime, the above begs counterfactual questions: what if circumstances had permitted more integration of the migration regime with other international institutions, or permitted more representation in its governance? Beyond its focus on emergency aid, IOM has clearly been held back by the lack of a clear protective mandate, a legacy of its failure to maintain a link with the oversight and creation of treaty law relevant to migration that an IMA would have had as part of the ILO. Yet maintaining this link would have also required it to keep pace with the focus of other international institutions on non-European migrants. In other words, this drawback may not have been as significant if ICEM had been forced to respond to the concerns of postcolonial states.

An ICEM that had expanded its remit and remained, consequently, a relevant international organisation overseeing all migration may have not only more effectively coordinated with the UN or ILO on rights, but even grown, like UNHCR, into a role promoting and monitoring international migration law, and overcoming its fragmentation. It may have built on its constitutional requirement to conform its activities to good treatment and human rights to serve as a focal point for codifying international norms and for publicising and monitoring implementation of migrant rights—as UNHCR's statute empowers it to do for refugees.[75] It may have become a site for interpreting existing rights and protections in migrants' favour, as UNHCR currently does for refugees.[76] It may have helped promote ratification of, oversee implementation of, and expand agreements such as the UN's Convention on the Protection of the Rights of All Migrant Workers and Members of their Families—today the least ratified major human rights treaty—as well as ILO migrant worker treaties and the embattled Global Compact for Migration.[77]

Even if it could not have addressed fragmentation problems in law, however, an organisation that had functioned for all regular migrants worldwide as ICEM had for European migrants—devoting resources to training migrants for skilled tasks and integration into host societies—may have succeeded in reducing some of the contemporary hostility towards migrant intake. It may have helped match migrants and employment opportunities and reduced critiques that migrants 'steal jobs'. And in planning and overseeing increased and safer avenues from migration, it may have helped migrants avoid smuggling via unsafe, underground routes. In short, it may have been a cornerstone of a better-governed world for migrants that the international community has only begun struggling towards again. With international politics reshaped and contingent developments inevitable, the question may not only be whether a new regime is possible, but whether it allows a representative group of voices, and whether they seize opportunities to be heard.

[73] By contrast to a context for contingent acts, Marks recounts that 'necessity' in its broadest conception has been linked to 'constraint', including 'external forces that mould, structure, or check'. 'Determinism' has been considered, at its broadest, 'the setting of limits and the exertion of pressures': Marks (n 72) 5, 8.

[74] Marks (n 72) 10.

[75] UNHCR Statute, UNGA Res 428 (V) (1950) UN Doc A/1775 art 8(a).

[76] Venzke (n 16) 109–30.

[77] On ratification status see Martin Ruhs, 'Rethinking International Legal Standards for the Protection of Migrant Workers: The Case for a "Core Rights" Approach' (2017) 111 AJIL Unbound 172, 173.

B.

SEA & RESOURCES

13

What If the United Nations Convention on the Law of the Sea had Entered into Force Unamended

Business as Usual or Dystopia?

Alex Oude Elferink[*]

Wenn es Wirklichkeitssinn gibt muß es auch Möglichkeitssinn geben[1]

I. Introduction

The oceans, comprising the larger part of the surface of our planet, are currently governed by one basic legal framework, the United Nations Convention on the Law of the Sea.[2] The Convention was adopted in 1982 and entered into force in 1994 and is generally considered to be a success story, as it has received broad support from all interests represented in the Convention. The Convention continues to be hailed as the 'Constitution for the Oceans'.[3]

On 16 November 1993, Guyana became the sixtieth state depositing its instrument of ratification,[4] meaning that the Convention would enter into force on 16 November 1994. At the time, none of the major industrialised states had ratified the Convention. These states rejected its mining regime for the deep seabed beyond national jurisdiction (Area). That regime largely was inspired by the idea of the New International Economic Order (NIEO) that was propagated by developing states in the 1970s. To allow the participation of the industrialised states in the Convention, the Secretary General of the United Nations had been organising consultations concerning the adaptation of the regime for deep seabed mining since 1990. From the perspective of the developing states, that participation was required

[*] I would like to thank Robin Churchill, Liesbeth Lijnzaad, Erik Molenaar, Joanna Mossop, Rozemarijn Roland Holst, Don Rothwell, and the editors for their comments on a draft of this chapter.

[1] Robert Musil, *Der Mann ohne Eigenschaften* (Rowohlt 1987) vol I, 16.

[2] (adopted 10 December 1982, entered into force 16 November 1994) 1833 UNTS 3.

[3] At the same time, serious questions could be raised concerning the effectiveness of this regime in ensuring the sustainability of the oceans. See eg Group of Experts of the Regular Process, *The First Global Integrated Marine Assessment: World Ocean Assessment* (United Nations 2016). However, this has not led to broadly supported calls to overhaul the jurisdictional scheme contained in the Convention.

[4] The term 'ratification' refers to all modalities through which states may become a party to the Convention. The current chronological lists of ratifications of, accessions and successions to the Convention and the related Agreements are available at (*United Nations Oceans and Law of the Sea*) <www.un.org/Depts/los/> accessed 18 August 2020. It lists Guyana as the fifty-ninth state ratifying the Convention. However, that list excludes Yugoslavia, which ratified the Convention on 5 May 1986 (see (1989) 14 Law of the Sea Bulletin 5).

Alex Oude Elferink, *What If the United Nations Convention on the Law of the Sea had Entered into Force Unamended* In: *Contingency in International Law.* Edited by: Ingo Venzke and Kevin Jon Heller, Oxford University Press. © The Several Contributors 2021.
DOI: 10.1093/oso/9780192898036.003.0013

for a viable mining regime to work. Only the major industrialised states had the capacity to engage in mining and create the benefits that would accrue to developing states under the Convention. From the perspective of the developed states, a widely accepted Convention provided a guarantee against unilateralism that might erode the freedoms of communication essential to international trade and maritime security. The consultations resulted in the adoption of an implementation agreement on Part XI of the Convention (Part XI Agreement), in July 1994,[5] just months before the entry into force of the Convention in November of that year. Notwithstanding its name, the Part XI Agreement significantly amends the Convention's deep seabed mining regime, removing most NIEO aspects.[6] Still, most governments accepted this outcome, and the Convention currently has 168 States Parties, including most industrialised states.

After 1994, the development of the law of the sea did not come to a halt. For instance, it has been necessary to take into account developments in international environmental law and advances in science and technology. Intensified use of the oceans has required a more detailed regulation of such diverse issues as transboundary fisheries, the protection of underwater cultural heritage, and marine genetic resources. Notwithstanding the expanding regulatory framework and calls (and actions) to amend the law set out in the Convention by individual states, the basic jurisdictional framework contained in the Convention has proven to be stable, in particular if the period between 1982 and the present is compared to developments in the period between 1945 and 1982.[7]

This chapter's analysis starts from the counterfactual that the consultations organised by the Secretary General did not result in the adoption of the Part XI Agreement prior to the entry into force of the Convention. This counterfactual is further considered in section II. Next, the chapter explores two counterfactual scenarios: 'Business as usual' and 'Dystopia'. The former scenario posits that the law of the sea would have developed largely in similar fashion as in the real world (section III). The scenario 'Dystopia' submits that a breakdown of the consultations on Part XI would have limited the participation in the Convention largely to the Global South (section IV), leading to a rift between the law as defined in the Convention and customary international law, increased tensions, and a failure to successfully deal with issues requiring a further elaboration of the law of the sea. The two scenarios are intended to sketch the range of possible futures of the law of the sea. After this *tour d'horizon*, section V assesses the likelihood of specific events included in both scenarios. Section VI provides some concluding reflections.

A detailed discussion on methodology is beyond the scope of this chapter. In writing it, I have taken into account the discussion in the introduction to this volume and literature on counterfactual argumentation in law and international relations.[8] In particular, I have

[5] Agreement relating to the Implementation of Part XI of the United Nations Convention on the Law of the Sea of 10 December 1982 (adopted 28 July 1994, entered into force 28 July 1996) 1836 UNTS 42.

[6] The Part XI Agreement among others did away with the compulsory transfer of technology and production ceilings to protect land-based mining operations in developing states.

[7] This framework regulates the rights and obligations of coastal states and other states in maritime zones and defines the extent of these zones. For an excellent overview in this respect see Philip Allot, 'Power Sharing in the Law of the Sea' (1983) 77 American Journal of International Law 1.

[8] This concerns in particular Ingo Venzke, 'What If? Counterfactual (Hi)Stories of International Law' (2018) 8 Asian Journal of International Law 403; Olav Schram Stokke, *Disaggregating International Regimes: A New Approach to Evaluation and Comparison* (MIT Press 2012) 37–80; Richard Alan Barnes, 'Alternative Histories and Futures of International Fisheries Law' in Erik Molenaar and Richard Caddell (eds), *Strengthening International Fisheries Law in an Era of Changing Oceans* (Hart 2019) 25; Gregory Mitchell, 'Case Studies, Counterfactuals, and Causal Explanations' (2004) 152 University of Pennsylvania Law Review 1517.

sought to select a counterfactual that implies a minimal change of actual history and have populated the two scenarios with real-world fact patterns, while trying to determine how these patterns would play out under the scenarios.

II. The counterfactual: entry into force of the Convention prior to the adoption of the Part XI Agreement

The historical record suggests that the pace of ratification of the Convention played a significant role in brokering a deal on Part XI.[9] Only in 1990, when it became evident that the Convention might enter into force in the near future, did the consultations on fundamental issues that had prevented the universal acceptance of the Convention get started.[10] Although the G-77 had taken a conciliatory stance on adjusting certain less controversial aspects of the regime of deep seabed mining in the 1980s, the group at the same time had indicated that its willingness to discuss matters was 'not meant to slow down the ratification process which must proceed on course'.[11] In other words, the entry into force of the Convention would not be postponed indefinitely if a compromise on Part XI did not materialise.[12]

At the start of 1990, the year the consultations on Part XI were initiated, the Convention had attracted forty-two of the sixty ratifications required to bring it into force. In October 1991, this figure already stood at fifty-one.[13] In September 1992, the European Communities Council Presidency in a communication to the other member states of the European Communities expressed the concern 'that entry into force of the [C]onvention as it stands may well close the window of opportunity created by the SGs informal consultations; effectively ending efforts to amend [Part XI] in order to permit participation by industrialised countries'.[14] This concern was caused by the rumour that a number of states might be ratifying the Convention in connection with the tenth anniversary of the Convention's adoption on 10 December 1992.[15] Had these ratifications actually occurred—in reality there was just one ratification on 10 December 1992, by Uruguay—the Convention would have

[9] In constructing the counterfactual, I have taken into account contemporary documents from the archives of the Ministry of Foreign Affairs of the Netherlands (MinBuZa).

[10] For a good summary of developments in relation to Part XI after the adoption of the Convention in 1982 see Robin Churchill and Vaughan Lowe, *The Law of the Sea* (3rd edn, Manchester University Press 1999) 230–38.

[11] Statement of Zambia on behalf of the Group of 77 at the 1989 PrepCom (1990) 15 Law of the Sea Bulletin 54, 55.

[12] A message from the Netherlands Permanent Mission in New York to the Foreign Ministry from January 1993 reports the interest of the G-77 in an early entry into force of the Convention. Message nyvu019/520 of 25 January 1993 (MinBuZa, inventory number 00377, isn 397373 3).

[13] The remark in n 4 on the ratification by Guyana is equally applicable to these figures.

[14] CPE Message lonc1321/cpei7496 of 22 September 1992 (file number 49/05/41587, AIM-number dve/ara/01048); see also Message nyv13776 of 15 November 1993 (MinBuZa, inventory number 00377, isn 397373, 1); Message nyv1360 of 12 November 1993 (MinBuZa, inventory number 00377, isn 397373, 2). A similar concern was expressed in the United Nations General Assembly (UNGA). For instance, in 1992 an influential representative of a G-77th member state, observed:

> [T]he problems with the international seabed regime, if not addressed in due time, have in the long run the potential of becoming a destabilizing factor of the legally binding effect of the Convention when it comes into force. We should therefore take advantage of the remaining time before the entering into force of the Convention to work out a compromise.

UN Doc. A/47/PV.83, 18.

[15] CPE Message (n 14).

entered into force on 10 December 1993, before the consultations on Part XI would have been successfully concluded.[16] This might well have closed the window of opportunity the consultations had opened.[17] Not so much because states no longer would consider it worthwhile to pursue the goal of a universally adopted Convention, but rather because the feeling of urgency to do so would have been lost. In particular, due to the absence of imminent mining activities in the Area, a deal on Part XI could also be put together at a later point in time.[18] States might have adopted a waiting attitude to see if others would make a first move. At the same time, developments in relation to the Convention and the law of the sea generally beyond the regime of deep seabed mining would take their course. Enter our alternative histories of the law of the sea. To allow a meaningful comparison, both scenarios look into the same issues. These issues are considered to represent major developments relating to the law of the sea. In order to avoid duplication and in light of the word limit for this chapter, explanatory footnotes and references in general are only included at the relevant point in one of the scenarios.

III. Scenario 1: business as usual

The entry into force of the Convention in December of 1993 closed the window of opportunity to reach agreement on the adjustment of Part XI. However, notwithstanding the limited participation in the Convention, due to the developed world's rejection of Part XI, it proved to be possible to arrive at a workable solution for deep seabed mining. Mining companies from industrialised states started operating under the conventional regime using developing States Parties to the Convention as sponsoring states.[19] The reciprocating states' regimes, which developed states with an interest in seabed mining had developed in the 1980s as an alternative to Part XI, thus no longer posed a challenge to the Convention's mining regime.

One of the follow-ups to the Rio Earth Summit of 1992 was the United Nations Fish Stocks Conference, which was intended to elaborate the Convention's regime on straddling fish stocks and highly migratory fish stocks. In the years following the adoption of the Convention, these stocks had come under increased pressure due to the Convention's absence of specific regulation of fisheries on the high seas. Notwithstanding the fact that there was no prospect of the Convention being universally accepted, all states participating at the Fish Stocks Conference eventually agreed that a legally binding instrument on this

[16] At the same time, the pending entry into force of the Convention might have sped up the consultations on the Part XI Agreement. A major breakthrough in the consultations, which was essential to achieving an acceptable compromise, had already been reached in August 1993.

[17] Documents from the MinBuZa Archives also point to another threat to the timely conclusion of the negotiations. After the departure of Under-Secretary General of the United Nations Nandan in 1992, the UN Secretariat had been taking a wait and see attitude, posing the risk of the consultations being dragged out without any prospect for results. Message nyvi491/10864 of 28 May 1992 (inventory number 00325, isn 397372, 2). See also message nyvi167/4282 of 22 February 1992 (inventory number 00372, 1–3). Ambassador Nandan subsequently participated in the consultations in a different capacity, allowing him to play a crucial role in completing them successfully. This episode illustrates the significance of individuals in shaping events.

[18] See also Jonathan I Charney, 'The United States and the Revision of the 1982 Convention on the Law of the Sea' (1992) 23 Ocean Development and International Law 279, 290–91, who outlines various options to amend Part XI after the entry into force of the Convention.

[19] See also the text at (n 57).

matter was needed to avoid unilateral extension of coastal state jurisdiction, with its attendant conflicts between coastal states and states fishing on the high seas. The agreement was developed as an implementation agreement to the Convention, but states not party to the Convention were allowed to become a party to this Fish Stocks Agreement. The adoption of the Fish Stocks Agreement led to reinforcing cooperation in regional fisheries management bodies. Coastal states, as a consequence, refrained from further unilateral actions that might have threatened the balance of interest expressed in the Convention's provisions on fisheries in the exclusive economic zone and the high seas.

The limited participation in the Convention implied that the institutions set up under the Convention were underused. The Commission on the Limits of the Continental Shelf (CLCS), which is to issue recommendations to coastal states on the outer limits of the continental shelf beyond 200 nautical miles, had little business following a decision of the Meeting of States Parties to the Convention (SPLOS) that developing states would not have to meet the December 2003 deadline and could defer their submission for an indeterminate period of time.[20] The continued uncertainty about the outer limits of the continental shelf has not posed great challenges, as hydrocarbon activities beyond 200 nautical miles are only taking place in areas that undoubtedly are part of the continental shelf of coastal states. The International Tribunal for the Law of the Sea (ITLOS), with its seat in Rio de Janeiro, has had a very limited case load, as most disputes concerning the law of the sea that were submitted to compulsory settlement concerned at least one state that was not a party to the Convention. However, the International Court of Justice (ICJ) continued to play a role in interpreting the law of the sea in a manner that has unified the Convention and customary law. The Court had already started this development in the 1980s in its judgments dealing with the delimitation of maritime boundaries between neighbouring states.[21]

Another feature of the law of the sea that has been lauded by commentators is the array of institutional arrangements and the adoption of pragmatic approaches. The former had been envisaged by the drafters of the Convention, who had agreed on a light institutional framework under the Convention and otherwise included rules of reference allowing existing organisations to continue regulating (new) activities in the oceans, while working within the jurisdictional framework provided by the Convention and customary international law. This concerns both specialised agencies of the UN, including the Food and Agriculture Organization and the International Maritime Organization (IMO), and global treaties and regional seas conventions.[22] The UN General Assembly (UNGA), comprising both the parties and non-parties to the Convention, has continued to play its coordinating role on oceans and law of the sea, and in its annual resolutions on oceans and law of the sea and fisheries has provided guidance to states and international organisations on how to deal with, *inter alia,* the detrimental effects of deep sea fisheries on vulnerable marine ecosystems. The UNGA also played a crucial role in initiating the negotiations on a more detailed regime on biodiversity in areas beyond national jurisdiction (ABNJ). Negotiations on a Protocol to the Convention on Biological Diversity (CBD),[23] which started in 2012, are well underway.

[20] The SPLOS has adopted a similar approach in the real world. See 'Issues with Respect to Article 4 of Annex II to the Convention' (*United Nations Oceans & Law of the Sea*) <www.un.org/Depts/los/clcs_new/issues_ten_years.htm> accessed 28 August 2020.

[21] See also text at n 30.

[22] See also text at n 48 and following.

[23] Convention on Biological Diversity (adopted 5 June 1992, entered into force 29 December 1993) 1760 UNTS 79.

The involvement of the CBD should not come as a surprise, as it had previously dealt with the four issue areas concerned: marine genetic resources, area-based management tools including marine protected areas, environmental impact assessments, and transfer of technology and capacity building.[24]

In 2020, twenty-seven years after the entry into force of the Convention, it may be confidently concluded that the Convention, without achieving universality, has lived up to the promise of providing a viable framework for ocean governance.

IV. Scenario 2: dystopia

In 2020, twenty-seven years after the entry into force of the Convention in 1993, it may be concluded that the failure to achieve a compromise on Part XI has been detrimental to the regime governing the oceans. The limited participation in the Convention has led to a rift between the conventional regime as interpreted and applied by its mainly developing States Parties and customary international law, which provides the applicable law for about half of the international community of states. No doubt, this rift in large part is explained by the often-ambiguous formulations included in the Convention, which had been included to bridge the conflicting interests of different states. The States Parties to the Convention have interpreted these provisions in a way that favoured the interests of coastal states. Developed states have rejected the relevance of this exercise for customary international law. That development has been entrenched by a number of landmark judicial decisions. This can be illustrated by the decisions in *MV Darwin* and *MV Russel Wallace*.[25] In *MV Darwin* ITLOS confirmed the coastal state focus reflected in the practice of the States Parties to the Convention, and held *inter alia* that under the Convention the passage of warships through the territorial sea is subject to prior notification to the coastal state, a decision that was vehemently rejected by major maritime powers. The ICJ in *MV Russel Wallace* held that the navigation of foreign-flagged vessels in the exclusive economic zone under customary international law was not subject to the restrictions ITLOS had found to be applicable in interpreting the corresponding provisions of the Convention in *MV Darwin*.

The regime for deep seabed mining has continued to be one of the most divisive issues in the law of the sea. While developed states continue to rely on the reciprocating-states regime to justify mining operations as a high seas freedom, developing states have rejected that approach as being contrary to the principle of common heritage of mankind as recognised by the UNGA prior to the start of the Third United Nations Conference on the Law of the Sea (UNCLOS III) in 1973 and the *jus cogens* character of that principle.[26] In particular, the issuance of exploration licences by the International Seabed Authority (ISA) to companies for areas that overlapped with licence areas of the states participating in the reciprocating-states regime led to acrimonious accusations from both sides and dispelled any lingering hopes that a compromise on the regime for seabed mining might still be possible in the foreseeable future.

[24] This accords with the actual practice of the CBD.

[25] These counterfactual cases remain to be reported in our actual world.

[26] For an elaboration of these arguments see Churchill and Lowe (n 10) 232–35.

The international community was also unsuccessful in addressing unfinished business of UNCLOS III, at which the Convention was adopted. The Fish Stocks Conference, which was convened pursuant to a UNGA resolution in 1993 in the wake of the 1992 Rio Earth Summit, and included all UN member states, was unable to adopt a legally binding instrument.[27] States that were not parties to the Convention, including many distant-water fishing states, rejected this approach as they would have no control over the further development of the Convention, which would then provide the frame of reference for interpreting and applying an agreement on specific fish stocks. The bland compromise declaration that was adopted at the final session of the conference did little to strengthen the mandate of regional fisheries management organisations. Subsequent attempts by coastal states to extend their jurisdiction over fisheries on the high seas continue to this day and regularly result in incidents between coastal state law-enforcement officers and foreign-flagged vessels beyond the 200-nautical-mile limit.[28]

Perhaps the most critical development in the law of the sea since 1993 was China's 2010 ratification of the Convention. While China, like the industrialised West, had previously refrained from ratifying the Convention, the move to a more assertive foreign policy in the middle of the 2000s led China to reappraise its position. China is by far the most powerful party to the Convention and the major funder of the Convention's institutions. China's participation in the Convention led to a further divergence between the Convention and customary law. States Parties generally were supportive of China's interpretation of the Convention's provisions bearing on the navigational and overflight rights of foreign armed forces in coastal state maritime zones. In reaction, the United States stepped up its Freedom of Navigation Program in the South China Sea and other areas critical to its military. The fear has been expressed that in the absence of a universally recognised legal framework, these incidents have the potential to escalate into major hostilities.

Attempts in the framework of the CBD and the UNGA to initiate a process to arrive at a comprehensive regime for biological diversity in ABNJ, which started in the first decade of this century, have gone nowhere. The States Parties to the Convention made the start of an intergovernmental conference conditional upon accepting that both the living and mineral resources of the Area are subject to the common heritage of mankind, which proved unacceptable to the states participating in the reciprocating-states regime, as well as to the European Union.

The adoption of the Convention in 1982 and the conciliatory stance on both sides until 1992 seemed to hold the promise of a universally accepted regime for the oceans that could be further elaborated through the concerted action of the international community. Today, in 2020, that hope has foundered, and it is generally accepted that the law of the sea is in a worse condition than at the start of UNCLOS III.

[27] In our actual world the form the instrument should take was also controversial. According to Schram Stokke '[w]hat *tipped the balance* was the eventual preference among influential states that had mixed interests for achieving a binding treaty': Olav Schram Stokke, 'Introduction' in Olav Schram Stokke (ed), *Governing High Seas Fisheries: The Interplay of Global and Regional Regimes* (OUP 2001) 7 (emphasis added). Documents in the MinBuZa Archive suggest that certain states eventually were prepared to accept a binding instrument due to the prospect of a widely ratified Convention, following the adoption of the Part XI Agreement. See Message of PV/New York to DIO/JS of 18 August 1994 and Press Release of the Permanent Mission of Japan to the United Nations of 15 August 1994, both in file number 49/05/47180, AIM-number dve/ara/01662.

[28] The Netherlands delegation to the Fish Stocks Conference submitted that a failure to conclude the Agreement would have this result. Delegation Report No. 3 of 5 April 1994 (file number 49/05/47180, AIM-number dve/ara/01662, 2).

V. Assessing the scenarios

The two scenarios described in sections III and IV represent two extremes of an alternative history that branches off from our time-line as a result of the failure to reach agreement on Part XI of the Convention prior to its entry into force. The current section assesses the likelihood of the main events that are included in the two scenarios.

1. The Convention and customary international law

In the early 1990s, prior to our counterfactual entry into force of the Convention in December 1993, the Convention, apart from Part XI, largely reflected customary international law as regards the definition of maritime zones and their substantive regime, which provide the core of the Convention's constitutional framework.[29] Certain parts of the Convention, such as the substantive regime of the high seas and the continental shelf, were already included in 1958 Geneva Conventions, which at the time of their adoption reflected or subsequently became customary international law. In 1984, a Chamber of the ICJ had already declared that Part V of the Convention, containing the regime of the exclusive economic zone, which was one of the major innovations of the Convention, was 'regarded as consonant at present with general international law on the question'.[30] The definition of the continental shelf provided by the Convention, which is critical to preventing coastal state encroachment on the Area, was quite widely applied in state practice prior to the Convention's entry into force.[31] In addition, no viable alternative for claiming coastal state seabed jurisdiction had been espoused in that period.[32] Prior to our 1993 counterfactual, a clear recognition of the fundamental importance the international community attached to the Convention was provided by Chapter 17 of Agenda 21, adopted at the Rio Earth Summit in 1992.[33]

It has to be asked whether, in our counterfactual world, the uniformity of the Convention and customary law would have been maintained, as has been the case in our actual world. The fact that most states considered the Convention to represent an acceptable compromise, as is also witnessed by the attempts in the 1980s and early 1990s to address the pending issues in relation to Part XI, might suggest an interest in protecting that compromise from being eroded. However, a number of considerations suggest that this conclusion should not be taken for granted.

[29] That situation has not changed subsequently. Robin R Churchill, 'The Impact of State Practice on the Jurisdictional Framework Contained in the LOS Convention' in Alex G Oude Elferink (ed), *Stability and Change in the Law of the Sea: The Role of the LOS Convention* (Martinus Nijhoff 2005) 142.

[30] *Delimitation of the Maritime Boundary in the Gulf of Maine Area (Canada/USA)* (Judgment) [1984] ICJ Rep 246 para 94.

[31] See also Churchill (n 29) 136–39.

[32] ibid 139.

[33] United Nations Conference on Environment and Development (UNCED), *Agenda 21: Programme of Action for Sustainable Development*, section 17.1, 'International law, as reflected in the provisions of the United Nations Convention on the Law of the Sea … sets forth rights and obligations of states and provides the international basis upon which to pursue the protection and sustainable development of the marine and coastal environment and its resources' (footnotes omitted).

It has been suggested that the absence of widespread ratification of the Convention would have led to state practice diverging significantly from the Convention in order to serve their particular interests, leading to controversy and uncertainty about the law.[34] This possibility is reflected in the idea of 'creeping jurisdiction', which implies that where issues requiring further regulation present themselves, coastal states, in particular, will seek to extend their sovereign rights or jurisdiction.[35] The fact that creeping jurisdiction remains an issue in our actual world, with a widely ratified Convention,[36] suggests that this issue would have presented itself with even greater force in our two scenarios.[37] In addition, as states would have yielded to 'the temptation to adopt measures inconsistent with the Convention, their willingness and political ability to ratify it [would have] decline[d]'.[38]

Actual state practice indicates that states continue to have differing views on the interpretation of specific aspects of the Convention, such as the navigational regime of warships in coastal state maritime zones and the balance of rights between the coastal state and other states in the exclusive economic zone. To a large extent, the divide here is between developing and developed states. Had the developing states dominated the Convention, they likely would have pushed their agenda in interpreting and applying its provisions. Moreover, the States Parties to the Convention likely would have argued that customary international law did not accord maritime powers the same rights as the Convention. In that connection, States Parties could have referred to the package deal nature of Convention, implying that states cannot pick and choose specific elements from the Convention, while rejecting others.[39]

The above considerations clearly suggest that the absence of widespread ratification carried the risk of destabilising the compromise contained in the Convention. This, in turn, would have led to uncertainty about the law in the relations between parties and non-parties to the Convention. The likelihood of increased incidents at sea involving disputes over the content of the law, in turn, could have undermined future cooperation in developing the law.

[34] See eg John R Stevenson and Bernhard H Oxman, 'The Future of the United Nations Convention on the Law of the Sea' (1994) 88 American Journal of International Law 488, 492; Barbara Kwiatkowska 'Creeping Jurisdiction Beyond 200 Miles in the Light of the 1982 Law of the Sea Convention and State Practice' (1991) 22 Ocean Development & International Law 153, 175–76. As Kwiatkowska observes in discussing jurisdictional creep of coastal states beyond the 200 nautical mile limit of the exclusive economic zone:

> In view of the numerous actual and potential rights and interests of states beyond 200 miles, the entry of [the Convention] into force for the overwhelming majority of the international community would appear to provide the only sound guarantee of orderly development of interstate relations seaward of 200 miles.

ibid 176.

[35] See eg Kwiatkowska (n 34); Erik Franckx, 'The 200-Mile Limit: Between Creeping Jurisdiction and Creeping Common Heritage?' (2005) 48 German Yearbook of International Law 117.

[36] A recent example is provided by the negotiations at the UN on the regime for biodiversity in ABNJ. Coastal states have advanced the concept of 'adjacency' to further their interests, whereas this concept is not reflected in the Convention. See further, Alex G Oude Elferink, 'Coastal States and MPAs in ABNJ: Ensuring Consistency with the LOSC' (2018) 33 International Journal of Marine and Coastal Law 437.

[37] See also text after n 53.

[38] Stevenson and Oxman (n 34) 488.

[39] This idea was already expressed by Ambassador Koh, the President of UNCLOS III, at the closing session of the conference in December 1982. Tommy TB Koh, 'A Constitution for the Oceans' <www.un.org/depts/los/convention_agreements/texts/koh_english.pdf≥ accessed 22 August 2020.

2. Compulsory dispute settlement

The possibility of resorting to compulsory dispute settlement under Part XV of the Convention has been considered a critical aspect of its architecture. In the two scenarios presented above, courts and tribunals are seen as either safeguarding the uniformity of the Convention and customary law or contributing to their divergence. Different factors come into play in assessing the likelihood of these two options.

First, with a limited number of mainly developing States Parties to the Convention, the composition of ITLOS would have differed significantly from that of the ICJ, as the latter also has a significant representation of judges from developed states. If either of these fora would have been presented with issues that involved a divide between developed and developing states, different outcomes would indeed have been possible. ITLOS likely would have adopted a developing state perspective in interpreting the Convention, while the ICJ in applying customary international law could be expected to have taken into account the practice of developed states. It might be argued that such a divergence would have been unlikely, as ITLOS (and arbitral tribunals constituted under Annex VII of the Convention) would have had an even more limited caseload than is actually the case with a larger and more diverse participation in the Convention. Indeed, a number of high-profile cases might not have been settled under the Convention, such as *Chagos*,[40] *Arctic Sunrise*,[41] and *South China Sea*.[42]

However, the fact that ITLOS's Rules of Procedure provide for the possibility of issuing advisory opinions indicates that ITLOS could still have played an active part in shaping the law in the absence of contentious proceedings.[43] In our actual world, in an advisory opinion requested by the Sub-Regional Fisheries Commission, with a membership of Western African coastal states, ITLOS among others has elaborated on the duties of the flag state in relation to its vessels fishing in the exclusive economic zone of other states.[44] This example indicates that advisory opinions under our scenarios could have played an important role in interpreting the law. For instance, States Parties might have used this avenue to clarify the implications of the package deal nature of the Convention for the development of customary international law in order to reconfirm that non-parties would either have to accept the whole package, as interpreted by its States Parties, or have to refrain from seeking to profit only from those parts of the Convention that serve their interests.

[40] *Chagos Marine Protected Area Arbitration (Mauritius v UK)* Permanent Court of Arbitration (Award of 18 March 2015) (*Cour Permanente D'Arbitrage Permanent Court of Arbitration*) <https://pca-cpa.org/en/cases/11/> accessed 28 August 2020.

[41] *The Arctic Sunrise Arbitration (Netherlands v Russia)* Permanent Court of Arbitration (Award on the Merits of 14 August 2015) (*Cour Permanente D'Arbitrage Permanent Court of Arbitration*) <https://pca-cpa.org/en/cases/21/> accessed 28 August 2020.

[42] *The South China Sea Arbitration (The Republic of Philippines v The People's Republic of China)* Permanent Court of Arbitration (Award of 12 July 2016) (*Cour Permanente D'Arbitrage Permanent Court of Arbitration*) <https://pca-cpa.org/en/cases/7/> accessed 28 August 2020.

[43] The Convention itself does not explicitly refer to the advisory jurisdiction for the full tribunal, but the ITLOS has included such a provision in Rule 138. 'International Tribunal for the Laws of the Sea: Rules of the Tribunal' <www.itlos.org/fileadmin/itlos/documents/basic_texts/Itlos_8_E_17_03_09.pdf> accessed 28 August 2020.

[44] Request for Advisory Opinion submitted by the Sub-Regional Fisheries Commission (Advisory Opinion 2 April 2015) ITLOS Rep 2015, 4.

3. Participation in an unamended Convention

The scenario 'Business as usual' assumes that a number of developed states eventually would have become a party to the Convention. Indeed, particularly developed states without an interest in deep seabed mining might have gone down this road. These states would not have been directly affected by what the developed world considered to be the negative implications of an unamended Part XI. At the same time, being a party to the Convention would allow them to influence its future development more directly than being on the outside, including through participation in the Convention's institutions.[45]

Developing States Parties to the Convention would also have had an interest in including developed states in the ambit of the Convention and, in that light, might have continued to take a conciliatory stance on deep seabed mining.[46] Broad participation in the Convention would have limited the risk of a competing regime for deep seabed mining from developing under customary law. It would also have ensured that the implementation of other parts of the Convention would have garnered widespread support, limiting the risk of destabilising the law of the sea due to the diverging practice of parties and non-parties. The suggestion that China might have become a party to the Convention to use it as a vehicle for advancing its interests would have been in line with the development of a more assertive Chinese foreign policy.[47] The exact impact of China would obviously have depended on the extent to which Western states would have ratified the Convention, offering a counterweight to China's impact on the development of the conventional law.

4. The frameworks for developing the law of the sea

The Convention sets up a number of bodies for implementing its provisions: the International Seabed Authority (ISA) in relation to deep seabed mining, ITLOS for dispute settlement, SPLOS primarily for dealing with the administration of the Convention, and CLCS for assisting states in establishing the limits of national jurisdiction beyond 200 nautical miles. Equally important, the Convention recognises that many aspects of its implementation require the involvement of competent organisations and other frameworks beyond the Convention's own institutional mechanisms.[48]

For instance, shipping is considered in the framework of the IMO, while the protection and the preservation of the marine environment are considered in the framework of global conventions like the CBD, the Convention on Migratory Species,[49] and regional conventions such as the Convention for the Protection of the Marine Environment of the

[45] An internal memorandum of January 1994 to the Netherlands' Minister of Foreign Affairs submits that in case the consultations on Part XI were to fail, the Netherlands should consider ratifying the unamended Convention in consultation with its European partners, ie the other member states of the European Communities and the European Commission. Memorandum 043/94 of 17 January 1994, (file Mag.Loc. 70A-19-14 inventory nr 2360, 1-2); see also Letter of the Minister of Foreign Affairs of 1 February 1991 (file number 49/05/39969, AIM-nummer dve/ara/00797, 2).

[46] See also n 18.

[47] For the development of Chinese foreign policy in this period see eg Gideon Rachman, *Easternisation* (The Bodley Head 2016) 47–67; Henk Schulte Nordholt, *China & de Barbaren* (Querido 2015) 317–18.

[48] See, for instance, the reference in Parts IV, V, VII and XII of the Convention (n 2).

[49] Convention on the Conservation of Migratory Species of Wild Animals (adopted 23 June 1979, entered into force 1 November 1983) 1651 UNTS 355.

North-East Atlantic[50] or the Convention for the Protection and Development of the Marine Environment of the Wider Caribbean Region.[51] These other frameworks generally seek to elaborate on the generally-worded obligations contained in the Convention, without adjusting its jurisdictional framework. For instance, the CBD provides that its parties 'shall implement this Convention with respect to the marine environment consistently with the rights and obligations of states under the law of the sea'.[52] The significance of these institutions and instruments beyond the Convention's ambit is twofold. First, it indicates that to a large extent the further implementation of the Convention would have been guaranteed in the absence of universal participation in the Convention, even if the bodies set up under the Convention would not have been operating effectively. Specific issues are not taken up in these institutions and instruments because they have been charged to do so under the Convention, but because they fit under their mandate as defined by their membership.

Second, the fact that the mandate of those other institutions and instruments does not include the development of the jurisdictional framework of the law of the sea would have been an impediment to them directly challenging the balance of rights and interests contained in the Convention. Obviously, the latter consideration would have applied to a larger extent to global institutions and instruments, with a near-universal membership, representing the balance of interests that was also responsible for shaping the content of the Convention. Regional institutions and instruments, which more often than not will not reflect this balance of interests in their membership, might instead have been prone to expressing specific interpretations of the law diverging from the compromise contained in the Convention.[53]

The two scenarios refer to some specific instances of the further implementation of the Convention. In the real world, the Fish Stocks Agreement[54] of 1995 is seen as an important complement to the Convention, which deals with high seas fisheries in a rather cursory manner. The Agreement in particular reinforces the role of regional fisheries management bodies. Following the adoption of the Fish Stocks Agreement, existing management bodies have adjusted their polices to bring them in line with the modern fisheries law principles contained in the Agreement. New regional bodies, which fill in gaps in fisheries management at the regional level, have taken a similar approach. Could the failure to conclude the Fish Stocks Agreement, as is posited in the scenario 'Dystopia', have led to a different result? No doubt, the Fish Stocks Agreement, being an expression of a broadly supported elaboration of the Convention, exerted a normative pull on the developments in fisheries management in the latter half of the 1990s and beyond in our actual world. However, at the same time, the Fish Stocks Agreement was part of a broader development in environmental and fisheries law.[55] That development was not based on the widespread adherence

[50] Convention for the Protection of the Marine Environment of the North-East Atlantic (adopted 22 September 1992, entered into force 25 March 1998) (1993) 32 ILM 1072.

[51] Convention for the Protection and Development of the Marine Environment of the Wider Caribbean Region (adopted 24 March 1983, entered into force 11 October 1986) 1506 UNTS 157.

[52] CBD (n 23) art 22(2).

[53] An example in the real world is the Galapagos Agreement. Framework Agreement for the Conservation of the Living Marine Resources of the High Seas of the South Pacific (adopted 14 August 2000) (2001) 45 Law of the Sea Bulletin 70. This agreement, concluded by Chile, Colombia, Ecuador, and Peru, accords coastal states rights in the high seas going beyond the Convention.

[54] Agreement for the Implementation of the Provisions of the United Nations Convention on the Law of the Sea of 10 December 1982 Relating to the Conservation and Management of Straddling Fish Stocks and Highly Migratory Fish Stocks (adopted 4 August 1995, entered into force 11 December 2011) 2167 UNTS 3.

[55] See eg Francisco Orrego Vicuña, 'The International Law of High Seas Fisheries: From Freedom of Fishing to Sustainable Use' in Stokke (n 27) 32–35.

to the Convention and would also have taken place in its absence. On the other hand, the recognition expressed through the Fish Stocks Agreement that the jurisdictional balance between high seas fishing states and coastal states included in the Convention should not be tampered with, and which in our actual world has been broadly accepted, might have fared less well in an alternative world in which there was no such normative break on claims by coastal states to unilaterally manage transboundary stocks.[56]

The scenarios also consider how the regime for biodiversity in ABNJ might have developed. In actuality, this regime is presently under consideration by an intergovernmental conference, which has been charged by the UNGA to negotiate what likely will become an implementation agreement under the Convention. Of the four issues under consideration in these negotiations, for the purposes of the present discussion the regime for marine genetic resources is most critical. It is highly likely that this issue also would have come to the fore under our counterfactual scenarios. The scientific and technological advances that made the potential value of these resources apparent would have occurred in any case. Continued disagreement over the regime of Part XI likely would have prevented this issue becoming the subject of negotiations on an implementing agreement under the Convention, as is explained in the scenario 'Dystopia'. At the same time, as the other scenario submits, this issue provides another example for which a framework beyond the Convention, in this case the CBD, might have provided an alternative.

The scenario 'Business as usual' submits that the UNGA remained pivotal in developing ocean governance. In our actual world, developing states have tried to give SPLOS an active role in reviewing the implementation of the Convention, while most developed states have resisted such attempts, referring to the mandate of the UNGA. The current compromise consists of the meeting discussing the report of the UN Secretary General on oceans and law of the sea that is also presented by the UNGA, without the meeting taking any concrete actions. The UNGA as a follow-up to the report adopts a resolution on ocean and law of the sea containing concrete calls for action. The divide between developing and developed states suggests that a SPLOS dominated by developing states might well have taken upon itself a more active role in reviewing the law of the sea, with a potential for straining the relationship with the UNGA and complicating cooperation within the UNGA.

5. Mining in the Area

In the 1980s, developed states set up an alternative regime for seabed mining outside of the Convention through the reciprocating-states regime. In that sense, seabed mining perhaps offered the only example of an activity with an alternative regime to that of the Convention with the support of the most directly interested states at that time. Whether that alternative provided the seeds for an escalating conflict is another matter. Until this day commercial mining in the Area has not yet materialised. It seems unlikely that states would be willing to force the argument on the applicable legal regime without a practical need to do so. Moreover, mining companies likely would have been interested in avoiding conflict over the legality of their operations. In that light, they might have wanted to look for options that

[56] See also Stevenson and Oxman (n 34) 498.

would not bring them into open conflict with ISA.[57] At the same time, Part XI was a critical issue to many developing states during the negotiations of the Convention. This might have made any challenge to the unamended Part XI regime likely a sensitive issue to the developing States Parties to the Convention and an ISA dominated by those same states. A conflict over Part XI could have become a catalyst in fuelling the discontent of the States Parties to the Convention over the rejection of the overall compromise reflected in it by the developed world.

6. Has the Convention's institutional framework made a difference?

Another way of looking at the present counterfactual is to inquire into the impact of the institutional framework of the Convention on the development of the law of the sea in our actual world, asking whether the absence or limited participation in that framework would have made a difference. The ISA is a key element to a functioning regime in the Area. The near-universal adherence to the Convention in our actual world in this respect compares favourably to the possible impact of developments on the ISA under our two scenarios. ITLOS and ad hoc tribunals under the Convention have made a significant contribution to the law on specific aspects.[58] That role likely would have been less pronounced under our scenarios, due to the more limited number of cases that would have been submitted to compulsory dispute settlement. However, as was explained in section V.2, ITLOS could have been used to pronounce on the law through advisory opinions. The role of SPLOS in the real world has been limited. One might say that its biggest contribution to the functioning of the Convention is its deferral to the UNGA in addressing current issues in the law of the sea. Our discussion indicates that SPLOS possibly might have performed less well on this latter point in our counterfactual world. The existence of the procedure to determine the limits of the continental shelf beyond 200 nautical miles involving the CLCS likely has made a difference. In our actual world, all relevant coastal states have spent considerable resources to comply with the requirements of the Convention and coastal states generally have acted upon the guidance the CLCS has provided to them. Limited use of the CLCS under our scenarios likely would have resulted in more expansive claims by coastal states, either by a(n) (overly) broad interpretation of relevant provisions of the Convention or by the introduction of new criteria allowing seaward extension of coastal state jurisdiction.

VI. Concluding observations

The preceding analysis suggests that the law of the sea might have developed differently had states failed to reach an agreement on the adjustment of Part XI of the Convention prior

[57] Mining companies are required to have a so-called sponsoring state to engage in mining under Part XI of the Convention (n 2) art 153. Only States Parties are entitled to act as such under the Convention (ibid). To avoid conflict with the ISA, and with the States Parties to the Convention, a company from a state that is not a party to the Convention could opt to operate under the Convention with a State Party as a sponsoring state. see also Charney (n 18) 288.

[58] See eg Vladimir Golitsyn, 'The Role of the International Tribunal for the Law of the Sea in Global Ocean Governance' in Stephen Minas and Jordan Diamond (eds), *Stress Testing the Law of the Sea* (Brill Nijhoff 2018) 11.

to its entry into force. However, one should at this point face the question of whether the Convention actually was 'too big to fail'. The Convention was the culmination of a process that could be said to have started at least in the 1950s with the first attempt by the United Nations to establish a comprehensive legal regime for the oceans. That regime, as agreed upon in 1958, was overtaken by developments in the 1960s that resulted in the negotiation of the Convention. Preparatory work started in 1969 and UNCLOS III convened between 1973 and 1982. The outcome was the first comprehensive law of the sea treaty. Although there were, and to this day remain, many minor differences over the interpretation of specific provisions of the Convention, the only 'deal breaker' was the regime for deep seabed mining contained in Part XI. Would the international community have been prepared to jeopardise the future of the Convention for an issue that at the time hardly showed any promise of commercial potential in the near future?[59] Perhaps not by design. However, our discussion suggests that the consultations on Part XI might have been stalled and developments might have slowly eroded the basis for a compromise. Still, it is unlikely that this would have resulted in a radically different law of the sea regime. First, there would not have been a comprehensive alternative law of the sea regime that differed radically from the Convention. Challenges would have focused on specific issues and the shift away from the Convention, had it occurred, would have been gradual. Secondly, the law of the sea is embedded in institutional frameworks and substantive rules beyond the Convention. These frameworks and rules probably would have guaranteed continued cooperation without a direct challenge to the Convention's jurisdictional framework. Finally, the law of the sea is made up of a number of individual regimes that have relatively little impact on each other. In that light, a challenge to one part of the Convention would not necessarily impact on other parts of the overall package. States may indeed purposely challenge a specific rule in such a way that has the promise of the least spillover.[60]

Notwithstanding these cautionary notes, it seems likely that in our counterfactual world there would have been more conflicting claims involving coastal states and other states concerning such issues as navigation and fisheries resources, leading to less effective cooperation and higher transaction costs.

One may furthermore ask whether the developing states, by accepting the Part XI Agreement, lost their distinct voice. Were the ideals of development and distributive justice largely offered to ensure the participation of the developed world in the Convention? No doubt that has been the case, and in that sense the Convention has not delivered on the hopes the developing world entertained in the 1960s and 1970s. At the same time, it may be questioned whether these expectations were realistic to start with. The NIEO mostly found expression in one specific aspect of the Convention as adopted in 1982, mining in the Area, while most ocean resources remained beyond that regime.[61] Moreover, mining in the Area has yet to deliver on its promise of an economic bonanza, if it ever will.

[59] See also Laurent Lucchini, '1996: Où en est le Droit de la Mer' (1997) 1 Annuaire du Droit de La Mer 17, 22.

[60] This may be illustrated by the development of the regime of the continental shelf. Reliance on this concept for claiming sovereign rights over the resources of the seabed allowed to differentiate that regime from claims over the superjacent waters and air space that might have affected existing freedoms of communication.

[61] In that connection, it may also be noted that developed states have been the main beneficiaries of the newly developed exclusive economic zone, which gives individual states almost exclusive control over the living and non-living resources inside 200 nautical miles from their coast. Among the ten states with the largest exclusive economic zones are seven developed states. Churchill and Lowe (n 10) 178.

Considering alternatives to the actual history of the Convention allows gaining a better understanding of its contribution to the development of the law of the sea. This chapter demonstrates the complexity of developing such alternative scenarios. However, without a comparative yardstick against which to assess the Convention's contribution, pronouncements in that respect will remain speculative or at best be based on implicit assumptions.[62]

[62] See also Stokke (n 8) 41.

14

What If Arvid Pardo Had Not Made his Famous Speech?

(False) Contingency in the Making of the Law of the Sea

*Surabhi Ranganathan**

I. Contingency, *false* contingency, and a 'what if' moment

The headquarters of the United Nations (UN) in New York and those of the International Seabed Authority (ISA) in Kingston, Jamaica, are sites of significant ongoing legislative activity relating to the oceans. The UN is hosting an intergovernmental conference to negotiate an agreement on the conservation and sustainable use of marine biodiversity beyond national jurisdiction (BBNJ).[1] The ISA is drafting regulations for the exploitation of deep seabed minerals, to enable corporations to move beyond prospecting and exploration, and begin commercial recovery of those minerals.[2]

While these are distinct types of law-making activities in formal terms—the one a treaty, the other, rules issued by an international organisation—they share several parallels. Both are connected with, and presented as complementary to, the 1982 UN Convention on the Law of the Sea (LOSC)—colloquially known as the 'constitution of the oceans'.[3] The BBNJ treaty will be an implementing agreement to the LOSC, similar to the 1994 Agreement on Part XI (the international seabed area) and 1995 Agreement on Fish Stocks.[4] The

* University Senior Lecturer in Law, King's College, University of Cambridge. I would like to thank the volume editors, participants of the CRASSH, Cambridge works in progress seminar, and participants of the Contingency in the Course of International Law conference at the University of Amsterdam for their feedback on earlier drafts. As the footnotes will reflect, the papers draw on earlier work and I am correspondingly grateful to many more colleagues and friends than I can name here. I would also like to express thanks to the American Society of International Law for enabling my attendance of the BBNJ negotiations, the ISA Secretariat for permission to attend their annual meetings, and funding bodies of the University of Cambridge for sponsoring these research visits.

1 For the latest updates, see 'Intergovernmental Conference on Marine Biodiversity of Areas Beyond National Jurisdiction' (*United Nations*) <http://www.un.org/bbnj≥ accessed 1 June 2020.

2 For the latest drafts, see 'Draft Exploitation Regulations' (*International Seabed Authority*) <http://www.isa.org.jm/instruments-juridiques/ongoing-development-regulations-exploitation-mineral-resources-area≥ accessed 1 June 2020.

3 United Nations Convention on Law of the Sea (adopted 10 December 1982, entered into force 16 November 1994) 1833 UNTS 3.

4 Agreement Relating to the Implementation of Part XI of the LOSC (adopted 28 July 1994, entered into force 16 November 1994) 1836 UNTS 3 (1994 Agreement), and Agreement for the Implementation of the Provisions of the LOSC Relating to the Conservation and Management of Straddling Fish Stocks and Highly Migratory Fish Stocks (opened for signature 4 December 1995, entered into force 11 December 2001) 2167 UNTS 3. The LOSC together with these two agreements, is commonly viewed as 'provid[ing] the framework within which most uses of the seas are located': RR Churchill and AV Lowe, *The Law of the Sea* (3rd edn, Juris Publishing 1999) 24. This framework is supplemented by customary law and other treaties.

Surabhi Ranganathan, *What If Arvid Pardo Had Not Made his Famous Speech?* In: *Contingency in International Law*. Edited by: Ingo Venzke and Kevin Jon Heller, Oxford University Press. © The Several Contributors 2021. DOI: 10.1093/oso/9780192898036.003.0014

exploitation regulations will complete the mining code that the ISA has been developing pursuant to the instructions in the LOSC read with the 1994 Agreement. Moreover, both activities are proceeding concurrently, and on a similar timeframe: they gathered momentum in the past quinquennium, and 2020 was the designated year of completion for both. In both cases, it was likely that this deadline would be overrun, even without the disruptions of the Covid19 pandemic. Nevertheless, both hope to conclude in the short term.

Perhaps most importantly, both are efforts at simultaneously realising competing goals. On the one hand, they seek to foster new economic activities in the ocean: the recovery of marine genetic resources in the BBNJ's case, and seabed mining in the case of the ISA's exploitation regulations. On the other hand, they are expected to address the grave ecological threats facing the ocean, and to ensure some sharing of the benefits derived from marine resources among all states, to give meaning to the idea that the ocean is a global commons, even if only in the parts beyond national jurisdiction. These aims pull in different directions: increasing economic activities pose direct threat to marine ecosystems; while obligations to distribute benefits increase the costs to those undertaking the economic activities.

The challenges faced by both law-making activities are thus significant and there are valuable accounts to be written of the ways in which they engage in practice with their contentious goals. That practice, however, while providing the context for this chapter, is not at its focus. Rather, I simply note here that difficulties *have* arisen in both processes with respect to safeguarding ecological protection and distributive equity where these cut against economic exploitation. In both processes, it has become clear that while we might highly regard the LOSC for its statements of community obligations vis-à-vis uses of the oceans—not least in designating the deep seabed as the common heritage of mankind—that treaty effectively privileges exploitation over the other two goals.[5] Its scheme of rights and obligations is instrumentally invoked even by non-party states *against* suggestions to ban seabed mining, condition access to marine genetic resources, and introduce schemes for redistribution.[6]

In this chapter, I take such invocations of the LOSC, together with the injunctions upon these forums not to 'undermine' it, as my point of departure.[7] Considering what I note above, I do not think it is controversial to suggest that if ecology and distribution are to be taken seriously, the new law-making processes will have to rectify the LOSC's shortcomings. Some undermining of the LOSC *is* needed. But that is not to negate the productive potential of the idea of the constitution of the oceans. In fact, I argue here that in order to give appropriate weight to the LOSC's constitutional quality, we should place its history—so little articulated in the rooms in which the new negotiations take place—in the foreground.

The LOSC should be viewed not just as a text that continues to instruct current activities, but also as a reflection *both* of long-serving economic logic, expressed, *inter alia*, in

[5] See eg Isabel Feichtner, 'Contractor Liability for Environmental Damage Resulting from Deep Seabed Mining Activities in the Area' (2020) 114 Marine Policy.

[6] Here I draw on my observation of the BBNJ and ISA meetings. But these invocations might also be tracked in the accounts of the proceedings carried in the Earth Negotiations Bulletin (*IISD Reporting Services*) <https://enb.iisd.org/enb/> accessed 1 June 2020. An example of the ISA's own use of the LOSC argument is Michael W Lodge and Philomène A Verlaan, 'Deep-Sea Mining: International and Regulatory Challenges and Responses' (2018) 14 Elements 331, 336: 'it is useless and counterproductive to argue that an a priori condition for deep-sea mining is an existential debate about whether it should be permitted to go ahead or not. The international community passed that point already many years ago'.

[7] In this context, see also UNGA Res 71/312 'Our Ocean, Our Future: Call for Action' (14 July 2017) UN Doc A/Res/71/312.

the vested rights and interests that had to be accommodated in it[8] and the contingencies of the time in which it was negotiated. These contingencies included: changing geological, biological, and technological knowledge about the oceans, as well as changing political and economic configurations; acts of individual agency (such as the one that will be discussed in this chapter); and the coalescence of a broad-based political movement for a New International Economic Order, that also brought into focus questions about who and what international law was for, its forms, and the processes and practices by which it should be made. The LOSC is the outcome of the interactions between these factors, as is the ocean that it gave shape to in its turn.[9]

In short, I develop an account of the LOSC as reflecting continuity and change, a product of structure and agency, expressing material interests and transformative ideology. I hope this will allow us to recognise three things. First, that its details might have been different, for worse as well as for better. Secondly, that we must not lose sight of why the details are as they are, and why, particularly, more radical possibilities did not materialise. The LOSC in its shortcomings (and doubtless also its promise) illustrates what Susan Marks has described as 'false contingency', an orientation towards the pressures and limits that shape choices.[10] Thirdly, the route towards more radical re-readings remains open, perhaps requiring undermining certain aspects of the LOSC, but truer to its constitutional promise.

I will tease out these points by using a thought experiment, revolving around the LOSC's most striking conceptual innovation: the principle of the common heritage of mankind. To explore how this idea, and the cocktail of interests in exploitation, distribution, and environmental concerns that it represents, became part of the corpus of international law, I will start by interrogating the moment in which it emerged. Specifically, I will ask 'what if': what if the key intervention from which it emerged had not been made? How might the law of the sea have looked? I will then turn to how this thought experiment might assist us in present engagements with the law of the sea.

[8] In many respects the LOSC and its implementing agreements do instantiate a familiar logic of the law catering to the economic interests of a few. It is possible to draw a straight line between the Grotian argument on the freedom of the sea, and the present framework that transmutes the ocean into a concatenation of places, distinguished by zone, function, and medium, on the basis that while *then*, assertions of freedom most suited the interests of a few trading corporations and emerging colonial powers; *now* those same interests are served by carving up the sea into zones of freedom and enclosure. Thus, the LOSC brings continental shelves up to and in some cases even beyond 200 miles within national jurisdiction to serve the interests of oil companies, leaves the high seas free for fisheries, and ensures the freedom of navigation across all zones of water.

[9] See Surabhi Ranganathan 'Ocean Floor Grab: International Law and the Making of an Extractive Imaginary' (2019) 30 European Journal of International Law 573. The concept of 'co-production' is helpful for keeping in view that while the law of the sea both reflects and reframes how the ocean is understood and imagined, the ocean has also been a site of conceptual and procedural innovation in the law. On co-production, see Sheila Jasanoff (ed), *States of Knowledge: The Co-Production of Science and the Social Order* (Routledge 2004) 1–45; Sheila Jasanoff, 'Future Imperfect: Science, Technology, and the Imaginations of Modernity' in Sheila Jasanoff and Sang-Hyun Kim (eds), *Dreamscapes of Modernity: Sociotechnical Imaginaries and the Fabrication of Power* (University of Chicago Press 2015) 1–33.

[10] Susan Marks 'False Contingency' (2009) 62 Current Legal Problems 1. Marks's idea may be summarised by reference to the famous statement of Marx that she quotes: '[men] make their own history, but they do not make it just as they please in circumstances they choose for themselves; rather they make it in present circumstances, given and inherited': Karl Marx, 'The Eighteenth Brumaire of Louis Bonaparte' in Terrell Carver (ed), *Marx: Later Political Writings* (CUP 1996) 32. The first part of the statement directs us to agency, the second to constraints; together they remind us that choices offered and made are not simply a matter of chance.

II. Pardo's intervention

The intervention in question was that of the first Maltese Ambassador to the UN, Dr Arvid Pardo. In November 1967, in a speech before the UN General Assembly's (UNGA) First Committee, Pardo advocated designating the deep seabed as the common heritage of mankind to safeguard it from national appropriation.[11] This would mean, he explained, subjecting it to regulation by an international authority to ensure that its resources were exploited to the benefit of mankind as a whole, which could be achieved by redistributing the revenue obtained, especially amongst developing states. The international agency might also ensure attention to the marine environment. For this speech, and for his myriad follow-up activities for promoting these ideas, Pardo came to be described as the 'Father of the Law of the Sea Conference'; or—more expansively—'the father of the new law of the sea'.[12]

The Maltese initiative was founded upon information of the rapid development of seabed mining technologies and the apprehension that these would lead to the appropriation of the whole ocean floor by industrially advanced states.[13] As Pardo explained to the First Committee, he hoped that rather than permitting this outcome, the UN would facilitate the use of seabed resources as a source of development capital for poorer states. The speech, running to nearly three and a half hours, was part panegyric to the oceans, part tantalising description of the seabed's material possibilities, and part warning of its approaching enclosure.[14]

Pardo offered, first, an account of ocean riches and available technology—invoking figures such as 358 billion tonnes of manganese, enough for 400,000 years of human consumption, as compared to 100 years' worth available on land. He then set out a compelling combination of promise and threat: on the one hand, seabed minerals could feed accelerated economic growth, and a redistribution of their riches could replace development aid, thus benefitting developed and developing states, in a win-win solution for all. On the other hand, in a zero-sum game, unless regulated by law, technologically advanced states would rush to colonise the seabed to get exclusive benefit of these minerals. This, effectively 'reserving the plurality of the world's resources for the exclusive benefit of [a few] nations', would sharply increase world tensions. In fact, a scramble was already underway and would surpass 'in magnitude and implication [the] colonial scramble for territory in Asia and Africa'.[15] International law did not prevent this scramble; it even facilitated it.[16] It was thus up to the assembled delegates to initiate a change in the law to bring about the win-win situation and avert the zero-sum game.

The change he suggested was to designate the deep seabed as the common heritage of mankind. This was to be achieved via a treaty that would establish an international agency led by the same technologically advanced states that were currently threatening to grab it

[11] General Assembly, First Committee Debate (1 November 1967) UN Doc A/C.1/PV.1515–1516.

[12] UN Press Release 'Dr. Arvid Pardo, "Father of Law of Sea Conference", Dies at 85, in Houston, Texas' (16 July 1999) Press Release SEA/1619; Malta Department of Information Press Release 202 (19 February 2002).

[13] See UNGA 1582nd Plenary Meeting (6 October 1967) UN Doc A/PV.1582; Note verbale dated 17 August 1967 from the Permanent Mission of Malta to the United Nations addressed to the Secretary-General, UN Doc A/6695.

[14] Surabhi Ranganathan, 'Global Commons' (2016) 27 European Journal of International Law 693, 704.

[15] General Assembly (n 11) para 91.

[16] Pardo here relied on Shigeru Oda's reading of the 1958 Continental Shelf Convention as permitting the whole seabed, shallow and deep, to be regarded as the continental shelf, so long as states could claim it was exploitable.

(Pardo felt that only the offer of a leading role would bring them to the negotiating table). He proposed that the UNGA immediately establish a committee to begin work on such a treaty; and, in the meanwhile, freeze all claims to the area.

The speech, albeit received with a degree of caution by developed and developing states, had early impact: that very session saw the establishment of a UN Committee on the Seabed, with the UNGA paying little heed to the UN Secretary General's (SG) request that they allow the Secretariat to complete its ongoing study of the seabed first.[17] Moreover, as the Committee began its work, and as Pardo and his collaborator Elisabeth Mann continued their advocacy for the common heritage principle, developing states came to embrace it enthusiastically. That principle and its application to the seabed became part of their agenda for a New International Economic Order (NIEO).[18] Developing states also leveraged the issues arising in the Seabed Committee's deliberations, such as the extent of national jurisdiction over the continental shelf, into the claim that settling such questions required a re-evaluation of the law of the sea as a whole.[19] Thus, they pressed for treaty negotiations covering a wide range of ocean-related issues. Developed states, though initially resisting, ultimately agreed.[20] Thus, the Third UN Conference on the Law of the Sea (UNCLOS III) was inaugurated in 1973 with the mandate to negotiate a comprehensive treaty—the LOSC.

While Pardo only participated in the first two sessions of the conference, being dropped from his various official posts following a change of government in Malta,[21] the seabed remained a divisive issue until the very end of the conference, and even beyond. The seabed-mining regime was the reason why the United States and other Western states refused to join the LOSC, and tried to construct an alternative law of the sea, drawing upon customary international law for traditional uses, and a 'Reciprocating States Regime' (RSR) for seabed mining.[22] The United States remains a non-party even after the 1994 Agreement has substantially rewritten the seabed regime, bringing it into conformity with commercial principles and stripping back the redistributive elements (although it participated in those negotiations too), but attends the ISA and BBNJ meetings.

Pardo's speech (and follow-up activities) introduced a new legal concept, the common heritage principle; it contributed an issue that became important to the NIEO agenda; and it catalysed the demand for renegotiating the law of the sea as a whole. These must surely count as significant impacts. Perhaps, then, he did do enough to justify the sobriquets bestowed on him? What then, if he had not made his intervention? How might international law have looked?

[17] For the initial responses of various states, see UNGA First Committee Debate (16 November 1967) UN Doc A/C.1/PV.1524–1530, 8–16. For the position of the SG, see Note by the SG (31 October 1967) UN Doc A/C.1/952. The Committee was initially established on an ad-hoc basis: UNGA Res 2340 (XXII) (18 December 1967). It was placed on a regular footing the following year: UNGA Res 2467 (XXIII) (21 December 1968).

[18] See Charter of Economic Rights and Duties of States, UNGA Res 3281 (XXIX) (12 December 1974) art 29.

[19] See Shigeru Oda, *The Law of the Sea in Our Time—Part II: The United Nations Seabed Committee 1968–1973* (Springer 1977) 83–86; see also UNGA Res 2574A (XXIV) (15 December 1969).

[20] UNGA Res 2750C (XXV) (17 December 1970).

[21] See S-0844-0013-06, S-446-0771-0015, *Malta Papers*, United Nations Archives, New York.

[22] See Surabhi Ranganathan, *Strategically Created Treaty Conflicts and the Politics of International Law* (CUP 2014) 147–211.

III. What if?

1. Pardo in context

To evaluate the difference made by Pardo's intervention, it is worth thinking about, *firstly*, the ways in which it differed (or not) from the discourse of the time. We might then note that Pardo was not the first mover on the matter of the seabed. In fact, he came to the issue late and by accident—via learning of a US proposal for a UNGA resolution directing the SG to conduct a study of the mineral resources of the sea. Pardo writes, self-deprecatingly:

> I had never heard that the sea contained significant mineral resources, apart from salt, so I thought that this was yet another of the many less useful projects then engaging the attention of the UN. I was highly sceptical and I prepared to criticize the American proposal. At a cocktail party that evening, however, a member of the US delegation hinted that I should be careful to criticize something I knew little about, so I held my peace in the debate, but I was definitely intrigued.[23]

The US proposal, which culminated in GA Resolution 2172 of 6 December 1966, itself followed other another initiative at the UN: in March 1966, the UN Economic and Social Council (ECOSOC) had requested the SG to study the possibilities of harnessing mineral and non-fisheries food resources of the sea 'to raise the economic level of people throughout the world, and especially in the developing countries'.[24] The ECOSOC resolution was a response to a proposal by the United States, Ecuador, and Pakistan. Outside the UN, the International Law Association's Dutch Committee had initiated discussions on a treaty regime for seabed mining, administered by a UN special agency.[25] Moreover, US President Lyndon Johnson had made a public speech cautioning against colonial competition for the lands under the high seas, urging 'We must ensure that the deep seas and the ocean bottoms are, and remain, the legacy of all human beings'.[26] GA Resolution 2172, for its part, reiterated the ECOSOC's call for a study by the SG of the possibilities of harnessing marine resources for common benefit.

Further, Pardo was presumably developing his ideas in conversation with other initiatives, which made recommendations similar to those made by Malta to the UNGA. In July 1967, some weeks before the inauguration of the Maltese initiative, the World Peace through Law Conference (WPLC), held in Geneva with participation of 122 state delegations, adopted a resolution denoting the high seas (including the seabed) as the common heritage of mankind, and recommending that the UN extend its jurisdiction over its non-fishery resources.[27] In August 1967, three days after Malta announced its initiative, the Commission to Study the Organisation of Peace (CSOP), a think tank, submitted a draft UNGA resolution to the SG, declaring the high seas and seabed the common heritage of mankind, to be used for 'the benefit of all peoples of the world'.[28] It too called for the establishment of

[23] Arvid Pardo, 'The Origins of the 1967 Maltese Initiative' (1993) 9 International Insights: A Dalhousie Journal on International Affairs 65, 66.

[24] ECOSOC Res 1112 (XL) (7 March 1966).

[25] Shigeru Oda, *The Law of the Sea in Our Time—Part 1: New Developments 1966-1975* (Brill 1977) 9–10.

[26] Lyndon B Johnson, 'Remarks at the Commissioning of the Research Ship—Oceanographer' (*The American Presidency Project*, 13 July 1966) <http://www.presidency.ucsb.edu/documents/remarks-the-commissioning-the-research-ship-oceanographer> accessed 1 June 2020.

[27] WPLC, Resolution 15: Resources of the High Seas (13 July 1967) (UN Archives S-0442-0027-0003).

[28] CSOP, Draft Resolution and Working Paper (21 August 1967) (UN Archives S-0858-0005-03).

an international authority within the UN framework, with the power to regulate uses of high seas and the seabed. Pardo, introducing similar suggestions—albeit only in connection with the seabed, not also the high seas—thus drew upon ideas which were already in (some limited) public circulation.

Moreover, the language of common benefit had already been applied to other domains—the preamble of the Antarctic Treaty referred to the 'interest of all mankind' in the use of Antarctica exclusively for peaceful purposes;[29] while the Outer Space Treaty provided that the 'exploration and use of outer space, including ... celestial bodies, shall be carried out for the benefit and in the interests of all countries, irrespective of their degree of economic or scientific development, and shall be the province of all mankind'.[30] These utterances were not identical in form or substance with the suggestions made by Pardo or by WPLC or CSOP; in particular, they did not indicate any obligation to share the fruits of commercial exploitation of resources. However, the idea that designating a resource or domain as a commons required some regulation beyond protecting the freedoms of access and use was also present in them. In short, Pardo's suggestions for the seabed did not come entirely out of the blue.

Pardo also articulated those suggestions for reasons other than purely an interest in the law of the sea; although this no doubt became a field of (pre)occupation for the rest of his career. At the time, he had been principally concerned with accomplishing what he had been recruited to do: raise newly independent Malta's international profile. Malta's first Prime Minister, Giorgio Borg Olivier had headhunted him for this task, persuading him to resign from his career as a UN civil servant.[31] Up against resource constraints in the new role—a staff of just three—Pardo recognised that he needed a big-ticket issue through which Malta could project a distinctive presence at the UN, demonstrating 'consistency, impartiality, sensitivity to the concerns of other States, and an interest not only in our own concerns but also in those of the international community as a whole'.[32] He flirted with a few ideas, including UN reform, and arms trafficking, before the cocktail conversation led him to alight on the seabed. He recognised that speaking on maritime matters could enhance Malta's standing in Mediterranean disputes; and might even lead to Malta becoming the headquarters of some international body, which would bring economic, political, and technological benefits. These were possibly his key goals at the time: Pardo writes that when he first articulated it, he did not recognise 'the tremendous innovative potential of the common heritage concept'.[33]

It is also worth noting that, although I have spoken of Pardo's speech as contributing an issue to the NIEO agenda, and as catalysing the chain of events that produced demands for renegotiation of the law of the sea as a whole, he—and Malta—were not fully aligned with either cause. For example, in his UN speech, Pardo had favoured a regulatory mechanism

[29] The Antarctic Treaty (signed 1 December 1959, entered into force 23 June 1961) 402 UNTS 71.

[30] Treaty on Principles Governing the Activities of States in the Exploration and Use of Outer Space, including the Moon and Other Celestial Bodies (signed 27 January 1967, entered into force 10 October 1967) 610 UNTS 205 art 1.

[31] Prime Minister Borg Olivier wrote to the SG U Thant shortly after Malta's September 1964 referendum for independence, asking him to release Pardo on secondment to Malta. Secondment not being permitted to political posts, Pardo was permitted to resign and join the Maltese delegation in time for Malta's admission to the UN in December 1964: S-0844-0013-06, *Malta Papers*, UNA New York.

[32] Pardo (n 23) 65.

[33] ibid 68–69.

led by technologically advanced states; opposing as impractical one in which developing states would enjoy decision-making parity. He also opposed claims for extended zones of national jurisdiction over the seabed, which were favoured by many developing states. Moreover, Pardo, speaking for Malta in the UN, initially opposed and possibly voted against (until developed states had come round to it) developing states' demand for a comprehensive negotiation of the law of the sea.[34]

As we will see, it is probable that, even if Pardo had not made his speech it is likely that the seabed would have appeared at some point on the UN's law-making agenda given all the other initiatives that were concerned with it. However, the timing of his intervention, and the directions in which it catalysed UN activity mattered.

2. A heady moment

The seabed would have appeared on the UN's law-making agenda in some form even if Pardo had not made his speech. For, as discussed in the previous section, there had been other initiatives focusing upon it even before Pardo took it up. These included initiatives within the UN, and civil society initiatives that were actively seeking to engage the UN. The common heritage principle and its application to domains beyond national jurisdiction would have also appeared; this again was not Pardo's sole brainchild. Pardo was the carrier of these emerging tendencies to the UN; he was not their originator. It is more difficult to assess whether, without Pardo's intervention, the seabed would have become a prominent element of the NIEO agenda; or catalysed a comprehensive renegotiation of the law of the sea. To some extent, both might have been the case: developing states had been involved already in moving the above-mentioned ECOSOC and UNGA resolutions, which might have spurred them on to include the seabed in their NIEO agenda regardless of Pardo. Moreover, while the need for a seabed treaty provided leverage for comprehensive negotiations, there *were* other unsettled questions, such as the extent of territorial waters and fishing rights, which offered similar catalysing points.

Nevertheless, Pardo's intervention contributed towards distilling the broader discourse into concrete demands, including the redistribution of financial benefits derived from the exploitation of the seabed, and the regulation of that exploitation by an international body acting as trustee for all countries. It owed its impact perhaps most of all to fortuitous timing. The way in which Pardo framed the issues was particularly compelling in that moment; it accelerated political action and set in motion the dynamics that would guide the seabed debate for a long time. In the absence of his intervention, the Secretariat would have been able to complete its study. We cannot know what recommendations it might have made but its more gradual process—implying also a delay of a few years in beginning political discussions on the seabed regime and the common heritage principle—would have mattered, as I will discuss. And without Pardo's compelling framing—a heady cocktail of exaggerated excitement over seabed riches, and exaggerated fears of land grab by a few developed states—the negotiations might have proceeded in a less 'theological' register (to quote Pardo himself) than became the case at UNCLOS III.[35]

[34] UNGA Plenary Meeting (15 December 1969) UN Doc A/PV.1833 30-31. The votes to the relevant resolution, UNGA Res 2574A (n 19) were not recorded.

[35] Arvid Pardo, 'Before and After' (1983) 46 Law and Contemporary Problems 95, 102.

For Pardo presented the possibility and perils of the seabed in terms that became difficult to discount later. And, he was able to do so because the state of knowledge about the ocean was poised at a unique moment where scientific and technological knowledge was advancing at a dizzying pace; a moment of *revolution* in the earth sciences, according to historians of science.[36] For, the moment of Pardo's speech was the moment of startling new discoveries on the seafloor, which enabled major breakthroughs in understanding the formation and features of the earth's surface. Moreover, these developments came on top of other notable advances: telephone cables joined telegraph cables on the seafloor.[37] The first physiogeographic maps of the ocean floor appeared (the first 'artistic version' was painted in 1967; its scientific equivalent making its appearance some years before).[38] Deep sea drilling made rapid strides—the Joint Oceanographic Institutions' Deep Sea Drilling Project was inaugurated in 1966, construction began on its commissioned vessel, the *Glomar Challenger*, in October 1967, and it left for its first voyage in March 1968.[39] The recovery of hard minerals—diamonds, zirconium, tin, gold—from the continental shelf was a growing industry.[40]

More broadly, the 1960s were a period of heightened techno-utopianism in many fields, with the ocean, alongside outer space at the focus of grand visions and projects. And, as well as the sense of possibility, there was also a prevailing sense of need—especially in the US, but circulating outwards from its academies and public media—that the ocean (and outer space) would be increasingly turned to, as decolonisation, 'the population bomb',[41] and, of course the Cold War, generated resource shortages.

This heady moment made it easy to accept Pardo's overstatement of the wealth of the oceans and potential for technologically mastering this domain. And he did overstate the case rather significantly. Although relying upon calculations of the quantities of seabed minerals that had been published by John Mero, a scientist at the Scripps Institution of Oceanography who had rediscovered the mineral wealth of polymetallic nodules[42] (the nodules were first discovered by the nineteenth century *Challenger Expedition*), Pardo omitted Mero's caution that only a fraction of his estimated 1.66 trillion metric tonnes of nodules would prove economic to mine. Instead, he presented the figure of 'approximately 1.5 trillion tons' as a 'conservative' calculation.[43]

Pardo also overstated the danger of a colonial-style scramble, based on a legally marginal interpretation of the existing law of the sea. As the World Court would confirm just over a year later in the *North Sea Continental Shelf* cases, that law—the 1958 Continental Shelf Convention—did not include the deep seabed (where the nodules lie) within the definition

[36] See eg Naomi Oreskes, *The Rejection in Continental Drift: Theory and Method in American Earth Science* (OUP 1999) part III. Oreskes is the leading historian of science in the area; following her monograph, she also published an edited collection in which seventeen scientists recall the moment: Naomi Oreskes (ed), *Plate Tectonics: An Insider's History of the Modern Theory of the Earth* (Westview Press 2003).

[37] While the first trans-oceanic telegraph cables date back to the 1860s, the first telephone cables were laid in the 1950s. See Stewart Ash, 'The Development of Submarine Cables' in Douglas R Burnett, Robert Beckman, and Tara M Davenport (eds), *Submarine Cables: The Handbook of Law and Policy* (Martinus Nijhoff 2013) 19.

[38] See eg Cathy Barton, 'Marie Tharp, Oceanographic Cartographer, and her Contributions to the Revolution in the Earth Sciences' (2002) 192 Geological Society London, Special Publications 215, 218–21.

[39] Ken J Hsü, *Challenger at Sea: A Ship that Revolutionized Earth Science* (Princeton University Press 1992).

[40] William J Broad, *The Universe Below: Discovering the Secrets of the Deep Sea* (Touchstone 1997) 255.

[41] See eg Paul R Ehrlich, *The Population Bomb* (Sierra Club/Ballantine Books 1968).

[42] See John L Mero, 'Minerals on the Ocean Floor' (1960) 203 Scientific American 64; John L Mero, *The Mineral Resources of the Sea* (Elsevier 1965).

[43] General Assembly (n 11) para 26.

of the claimable continental shelf.[44] Nor were Western states scheming to extend their jurisdiction as far as Pardo feared: their own defence, fishing, and shipping interests were firmly opposed to a great carve up of the seabed. The CIA produced a scare map in 1971 precisely to warn of the threats to navigation were the ocean to become divided into great national lakes, a result that might follow from any complete division of the seabed.[45] Just before that, in 1970, US President Richard Nixon advanced a proposal to limit national jurisdiction over the seabed, allowing most of it to be designated as the common heritage, part governed by states as 'trustees', and part by an international body.[46] Yet Pardo's representation of the threat of division exercised great influence—no doubt his international standing as a prominent former civil servant at the UN Department of Trusteeship and Technical Assistance Programme (now UN Development Programme) and as a known and respected figure amongst developing states meant that his perception mattered. Developing states summarily rejected the Nixon Proposal, voicing suspicion about the language of trusteeship.[47] Notably, they expressed this rejection during the first Pacem in Maribus conference, which Pardo had organised in Malta, in 1970, to discuss the development of the law of the sea.

3. The importance of timing

The conditions which contributed to the impact of Pardo's speech no longer held some years later. The heady moment had given way to a steadier one; wild techno-utopian optimism about using the ocean as a 'last resource'[48] had given way to a more critical assessment of the possibilities.[49] Estimates as to the quantities and value of manganese nodules had come under scrutiny; with technology not ready, higher-than-expected costs, and new strikes on land, the case for seabed mining became weaker. In some circles this was known early on, even by the beginning of the 1970s.[50] Equally, the fear had dissipated: writings on the population bomb received due criticism for their alarmist tones and their sole focus on the numbers in the Third World, forgetting the much higher rates of consumption in the first.[51] And the ICJ judgment and evident opposition within developed states had—or should have—also mitigated fears of a colonial-style scramble. The seabed issue, if arising only a few years

[44] *North Sea Continental Shelf (Federal Republic of Germany v Denmark)* (Judgment) [1969] ICJ Rep 3, para 41. In support of this view, see also RY Jennings, 'The Limits of Continental Shelf Jurisdiction: Some Possible Implications of the North Sea Case Judgment' (1969) 18 International and Comparative Law Quarterly 819, 827.

[45] See Philip E Steinberg, The Social Construction of the Ocean (CUP 2001) 175.

[46] Draft UN Convention on the International Seabed Area (3 August 1970) UN Doc A/AC.138/25.

[47] See papers on the Pacem in Maribus conference in Malta (1970) (UK National Archives, London, FCO 76/161).

[48] Eg Tony Loftas, *The Last Resource* (Hamish Hamilton 1969).

[49] See GP Glasby, 'Lessons Learned from Deep-Sea Mining' (2000) 289 Science 551. Koskenniemi and Lehto also note that by 1974–75, '[t]he illusion of an "ocean bonanza" had been lost': Martti Koskenniemi and Marja Lehto, 'The Privilege of Universality: International Law, Economic Ideology and Seabed Resources' (1996) 65 Nordic Journal of International Law 533, 541.

[50] Per records in FCO 76/733, UK National Archives; see also Letter from the Chief Geologist, Ministry of Natural Resources, Kenya (10 September 1973) (Kenya National Archives KP/6/9).

[51] Ehrlich issued a revised edition of his book in 1971 in which he pointed to overconsumption by the rich in developed countries (which he now called 'overdeveloped' countries), especially the United States, as a key drain on the Earth's resources. These themes became more prominent in Ehrlich's later works: Paul R Ehrlich and Anne H Ehrlich, 'Too Many Rich Folks' (1989) 16 Populi 20; Paul R Ehrlich and Anne H Ehrlich, *One with Nineveh: Politics, Consumption, and the Human Future* (Island Press 2004); Paul R Ehrlich and Anne H Ehrlich, 'The Population Bomb Revisited' (2009) 1 Electronic Journal of Sustainable Development 63.

later, would not have been such an arresting one. It is unlikely, for instance, that associations of Quakers and Methodists would have been inspired to establish an NGO to lobby for the common heritage principle in the development of the law of the sea.[52]

Timing then, was everything, as far as the seabed's becoming a key topic in international relations was concerned. From 1967 onwards, until 1982 and even beyond, the seabed would become one of the main issues of the NIEO battle, as also in the Cold War tussle for power. More than 150 states spent enormous resources—money, time, people—on negotiating a regime for seabed mining, with significant involvement of civil society. Some might object to my suggestion that, had it come on to the UNGA's agenda some years later, the issue would not have achieved so much prominence. They might ask, reasonably, why then it did not lose significance once the economic and technological realities began to bite. But this objection has been addressed in the literature, which notes that given the initial prominence of the issue, positions around it had hardened rapidly. The seabed regime became partly a matter of prestige, and partly that of establishing precedent.[53] For, developing states, keen to be the rule makers—for once—on the use of an economic resource, thought that shaping the development of common heritage principle in relation to the seabed might facilitate shaping distributive rules in other areas as well. They thus insisted that the rules encompass not only a sharing of profits, but also: (i) financial and technological assistance from developed states to enable developing ones to undertake mining initiatives of their own; and (ii) administrative parity between developed and developing states in implementing the rules of the regime. Developed states, for their part, were keen to avoid conceding such visions of 'socialist' new international order.[54]

Moreover, in addition to reasons of prestige and precedent, there were others: the literature does not similarly highlight the extent to which developed states withheld or distorted information about the prospects of seabed mining, continuing to convey an inflated account of the possibilities of the activity to developed states.[55] Even after information about the diminished prospects of seabed mining began to circulate openly, the actions of developed states conveyed a more ambiguous message. Consortia sponsored by them reported successful testing of nodule mining technologies. These states also enacted unilateral legislation to enable early investments by mining companies and were as tenacious as developing states in the negotiations over the LOSC mining regime.[56] No doubt, they were as much in search of an ideological victory, but they did much to maintain developing states' belief in the material prospects of seabed mining. This is important to consider in view of the implications for the NIEO movement. For it is not clear that the seabed negotiations did much to advance NIEO claims, and it is possible that they may have also provided an expensive distraction from other elements of the NIEO agenda—a waste of developing state resources that could have been better applied elsewhere.

In any event, delusive facts—not just contesting ideologies—underlay the seabed negotiations. A UN Oceans Economics and Technology Branch Report of 1982 clearly recognised

[52] On the work of this NGO, the Neptune Group, see Ralph B Levering and Miriam L Levering, *Citizen Action for Global Change: The Neptune Group and the Law of the Sea* (Syracuse University Press 1999).

[53] See eg Koskenniemi and Lehto (n 49) 539ff.

[54] James L Malone, 'The United States and the Law of the Sea after UNCLOS III' (1983) 46 Law and Contemporary Problems 29, 31.

[55] For more on this point, see Ranganathan (n 9)</INT> 595.

[56] ibid.

this in its summing up of the seabed negotiations. It noted that the participants had been 'beset with a range of "facts" which are often contradictory, elusive and difficult to substantiate'.[57] It quoted the following sharp comment from an independent study conducted in 1976:

> [A] review of previous work on this subject and a study of how the resource estimates have been used have led us to conclude than an unfortunate coincidence of exaggerated resource estimates and misinterpretation of those estimates has resulted in a situation where national and international decisions have been and could be made on the basis of completely erroneous information.[58]

And the trend of exaggeration and misinterpretation began with Pardo.

Pardo himself became a critic of the negotiations, describing them—as mentioned earlier—as an 'almost theological debate' in which 'the viability of the future international regime for the seabed … and economic realities were largely forgotten by the contending parties'.[59] Other commentators express disappointment about the mutations produced in the common heritage principle, which became associated with a bureaucratic, centralised, and inefficient regime that imposed too many costs on developed states in the face of too much uncertainty about the benefits—the common heritage, in their words, became 'the common burden'.[60] Developed states rejected it, refusing to sign the LOSC. But disappointment was expressed also by prominent Third World voices, which considered the regime finally adopted in 1982 a corruption of the common heritage principle, because it did not secure sufficient redistribution.[61]

4. After 1982

Negotiated on the initial certainty of the rich economic prospects of seabed mining, the LOSC regime had a paradoxical benefit. In placing the seabed under a body (the ISA) at which developing states enjoyed effective representation, and in linking mining licences to obligations of financial and technological assistance to developing states, redistribution of part of the revenue and adherence to production quotas, it made seabed mining less attractive—causing companies to postpone planned investments into the activity. John Shaw, head of one of the most prominent mining consortiums, Ocean Management Inc, involving German, Japanese, American, and Canadian companies, writes as much in an article published in 1993. He describes completing the first ever successful pilot mining test in 1978, followed by the decision *not to invest* in developing a full-scale operation owing to the onerous character of the provisions then being written into the LOSC.[62] With such setbacks

[57] United Nations Oceans Economics and Technology Branch, 'Assessment of Manganese Nodule Resources: The Data and the Methodologies', Seabed Minerals Series Volume 1 (Graham and Trotman 1982) 1.

[58] Pasho and Mckintosh quoted ibid 2.

[59] Pardo (n 35) 102.

[60] Markus Schmidt, *Common Heritage or Common Burden? The United States Position on the Development of a Regime for Deep Sea-Bed Mining in the Law of the Sea Convention* (Clarendon 1989).

[61] BS Chimni, 'Law of the Sea: Winners are Losers' (1982) 17 Economic and Political Weekly 987.

[62] John L Shaw, 'Nodule Mining—Three Miles Deep!' (1993) 11 Marine Georesources and Geotechnology 181, 197.

to early mining ventures, the deep seabed remained protected from the deleterious effects of mining activity—mining, in fact, is yet to begin, though exploration activities have been taking place. This is fortuitous because in the 1970s the scale of damage that mining could cause was not well understood. The common view was that deep seabed mining was less harmful than mining on land (its remoteness being a key trope). Seabed mining, had it proceeded then, would have done so on the basis of relatively weak environmental provisions.

The law on the seabed continued to evolve after 1982. For a time, developed states floated their own alternative mining regime in the form of the RSR, reading the common heritage principle more or less in terms of the old principle of the freedom of the sea: minimal international administration and redistribution of benefits. Ultimately, following the major shifts in world order in 1989—the end of the Cold War, the spread of liberalisation, and the faltering of Third World solidarity—they were able to obtain changes in the LOSC regime itself by way of the 1994 Implementation Agreement.[63] The new regime shifted the balance in favour of exploitation, establishing seabed mining squarely on commercial principles, stripping back its distributive elements. It also altered the structure of the ISA, shifting greater control into the hands of its less representative organs—and thus, effectively, developed states. It reduced the common heritage of mankind concept mainly to a few provisions on revenue sharing. These changes, described as a 'mutilation' of the common heritage of mankind ideal by RP Anand,[64] were not however regarded as 'undermining' the LOSC by Western scholars: Louis Sohn, for instance, called it an 'excellent example of adapting international law to new circumstances'.[65] Developed states swiftly joined the altered treaty; enabling it to enter into force in November 1994 with nearly universal ratification. Even the United States, while still a non-party to the LOSC, provisionally signed the 1994 Agreement.

The ISA began its operations (in 1995) in a period when seabed mining had not been the focus of research and investment for a significant period. Its capacity to implement the (albeit changed) balance between exploitation and redistribution was thus not tested, and it was even able to adopt more ambitious environmental regulations, and tailor the rules for exploration to new types of mineral deposits—polymetallic sulphides and cobalt-rich crusts—which the LOSC had not accounted for, being solely concerned with polymetallic nodules. But the situation has now changed, with a reanimation of industry interest in seabed mining. The ISA recognises the challenge of ensuring that mining is both to the benefit of mankind (including future generations) and commercially viable and sustainable; but also believes—in the words of its current Secretary General, 'the international community has a unique opportunity to get it right'.[66] Yet, as noted in the opening section, ongoing work on the mining code has generated misgivings. The models developed for redistributing revenue suggest that little—if anything—will be available to share once contractors' risks, costs, and liabilities have been accounted for.[67] So far as ecological considerations

[63] 1836 UNTS 3 (1994). On the changes see Ranganathan (n 22) 174–76 and 376–79.

[64] RP Anand, 'Common Heritage of Mankind: Mutilation of an Ideal' in RP Anand, *Studies in International Law and History: An Asian Perspective* (Martinus Nijhoff 2004) 180, 196.

[65] Louis B Sohn, 'International Law Implications of the 1994 Agreement' (1994) 88 American Journal of International Law 696, 704–5.

[66] Lodge and Verlaan (n 6) 335.

[67] See eg African Group Submission on the ISA Payment Regime for Deep-Sea Mining in the Area, Submission to ISA Council, 25th Session (5 July 2019) <https://ran-s3.s3.amazonaws.com/isa.org.jm/s3fs-public/files/documents/agsmitmodelfinal.pdf> accessed 1 June 2020; see also Isabel Feichtner, Sharing the Riches of the Sea: The Redistributive and Fiscal Dimension of Deep Seabed Exploitation (2019) 30 European Journal of International Law 601.

are concerned, even the ISA's by no means trivial achievements are called into question by scientific studies that speak to the impossibility of reconciling mining with protection of marine environment and biodiversity.[68] The ISA does not yet acknowledge that 'getting it right' might now mean not getting started at all—that is, a moratorium on mining—or giving up the competitive model, envisaging multiple commercial mining ventures, in favour of other approaches. The paradoxically beneficial LOSC-induced postponement might thus yet come to naught.

IV. Contingency and critique

The LOSC as adopted in 1982 was shaped by multiple factors: scientific and technological change, political and economic upheavals, and a widely shared consciousness of the world being remade, albeit with many contrasting visions of what that might entail. Situating Pardo's intervention in this time, and by way of a thought experiment that asks 'what if' that intervention had not been made, this chapter tries to unpack the place of individual agency within a constitutional moment. It points out that Pardo's intervention may be regarded as a contingent action, without which the law of the sea might indeed have been different in some respects: the seabed regime might not have become a centrepoint of the NIEO movement; the common heritage principle might have remained at a more abstract level of elucidation; and UNCLOS III itself might have had an altogether different cast or at least a more limited scope. The chapter also teases out the element of contingency in Pardo's own uptake of the issue.

However, the chapter also seeks to show the element of false contingency, showing that 'what might have been' might resemble what did become in many respects. To this end, it highlights the factors that generated an interest in seabed mining, and underpinned Pardo's uptake of the matter, inspiring his exaggerated account; and permitting it to be received as credible. Those factors—new discoveries, techno-optimism, fears of resource scarcity—had catalysed discussions over seabed minerals at various venues, many of which might have also placed the seabed on the international law-making agenda. Moreover, and importantly, it also shows how the initial excitement sparked by Pardo's intervention was then co-opted and maintained by various groups of states to further their broader political agendas. It takes note of the gradual subordination of the redistributive element of the common heritage principle to commercial imperatives. Meanwhile, ecological issues, brought into view much later, also remain secondary to the goal of exploitation.

What might we take from all this? As noted at the beginning of the chapter, the ocean is poised at a delicate moment, and the ongoing law-making initiatives are critical to determining its ecological fate as well as its normative conception as a global commons. Yet, at the negotiations, a kind of LOSC-literalism is in use—even by non-parties to the treaty—to rebut efforts to shift the balance between exploitation on the one hand, and redistribution

[68] See eg Holly J Niner and others, 'Deep-Sea Mining With No Net Loss of Biodiversity—An Impossible Aim' (2018) 5 Frontiers in Marine Science 1; Cindy Van Dover and others, 'Biodiversity Loss from Deep Sea Mining' (2017) 10 Nature Geoscience 464; Daniel OB Jones and others, 'Biological Responses to Disturbance from Simulated Deep-Sea Polymetallic Nodule Mining' (2017) 12 PLoS ONE 1; Lisa A Levin and others, 'Defining "Serious Harm" to the Marine Environment in the Context of Deep-Seabed Mining' (2016) 74 Marine Policy 245.

and ecological protection on the other, towards the latter.[69] The LOSC's constitutional stature is also leveraged to this end, in reminders that the new rules and regulations should not undermine the old. Thus, calls for banning seabed mining are met with the response that that question was settled by the LOSC, and cannot be reopened now.[70] The history, when recalled, is equally instrumentalised: a valorised narrative in which mineral extraction is joined to the common heritage by the wisdom of the LOSC's progenitors; Pardo of course prominent among them. In these ways, the LOSC is imbued with a fixity that preempts challenges to its exploitation bias.

The chapter thus offers a more nuanced account of the LOSC's seabed regime, bringing into focus both the contingent nature of the decisions that underpin it, and the steady operations of the logic of exploitation to subordinate other aspects of the common heritage principle. To see the common heritage principle and seabed regime take shape in the fog of imperfect knowledge, via interventions of mixed motives, and without robust challenge to the extractive imaginary (in service to which they also underwent significant overhaul) is to recognise that we might step away from settled understandings to candidly assess what is desirable in our time. That is also to take seriously the idea of the LOSC as a constitution: both a guiding framework for engaging with the oceans, and the reason for embracing change in the direction of ecological and distributive justice.

[69] A point made, inter alia, by many observers to the BBNJ negotiations, and amply verifiable in the summaries produced by the Earth Negotiations Bulletin (n 6).

[70] Lodge and Verlaan (n 6) 336.

15

Contingent Economic Legal Ordering

Permanent Sovereignty over Natural Resources and International Commodity Agreements

*Lucas Lixinski and Mats Ingulstad**

I. Introduction

The principle of Permanent Sovereignty over Natural Resources (PSNR) is largely thought to be a counter-colonialism move to prevent great power exploitation of developing countries' natural resources after independence, one rooted in the demand to decide on the use of their own resources for their own benefit.[1] As such, it is a staple of historical approaches to international law, lending itself to normative and teleological histories of Third World empowerment, neatly supporting and affirming the aspirations underlying Third World Approaches to International Law (TWAIL).[2] PSNR is an important part of international law in the mid-twentieth century, serving as a monument to the unity of decolonising nations, and a significant moment in the legal history of decolonisation in the United Nations (UN) era. What if, however, PSNR had not been enshrined in international law? What would the international economic legal architecture look like in the absence of this principle? Those are the two key questions that animate this chapter.

Instead of making the PSNR Declaration's adoption our moment of break with history, we choose a pivotal, if under-appreciated, moment in the design of international economic institutions in the League of Nations period: the 1933 London Economic Conference, the aim of which was to tackle the Great Depression through international cooperation and revive international trade. This conference, critical in relation to PSNR, considered regulatory measures on the trade in commodities that in many respects spoke to the same tensions that led to the adoption of the PSNR Declaration in 1952.[3]

During the League of Nations era, but also in the early United Nations years, there were distinctive efforts to impose limits on the exercise of state sovereignty by the colonial powers, which had the effect of privileging decolonising forces in those territories. After

* The archival research for this project was generously funded by a grant from the Gerda Henkel Stiftung. The Fate of Nations project, funded by the Norwegian Research Council, supported further research and precious joint writing time. We are thankful to Bruno Pegorari for research assistance in the critical editing stages. All errors remain our own.

[1] For the most authoritative monograph-length treatment of the topic, see Nico Schrijver, *Sovereignty over Natural Resources: Balancing Rights and Duties* (CUP 1997).

[2] See generally Antony Anghie, *Imperialism, Sovereignty and the Making of International Law* (CUP 2007); and BS Chimni, *International Law and World Order: A Critique of Contemporary Approaches* (CUP 2017). See also Crow in this volume, exploring one of TWAIL's foundational moments (the 1955 Bandung Conference).

[3] Permanent Sovereignty over Natural Resources, UNGA Res 3171 (17 December 1973) UN Doc A/RES/3171.

Lucas Lixinski and Mats Ingulstad, *Contingent Economic Legal Ordering* In: *Contingency in International Law*. Edited by: Ingo Venzke and Kevin Jon Heller, Oxford University Press. © The Several Contributors 2021. DOI: 10.1093/oso/9780192898036.003.0015

the First World War, an expected post-war scarcity of raw materials gave rise to fears that the imperial powers might seek to increase production through resort to labour practices only vaguely different from outright slavery. It befitted the League of Nations to rein in excesses, uphold moral standards, and enable more rational practices. Despite the expectation that the colonial powers could be held accountable by outside pressure, these discursive shifts temporarily also served to reinforce their imperial legitimacies.[4] However, the League of Nations also became a vehicle for the attempt to wrest control over raw materials production and trade from private cartels that often acted with tacit or explicit state support. They were to be replaced by coordination through International Commodity Agreements (ICAs), institutionalised arrangements aimed at regulating international production and trade of specific raw materials. ICAs, supported by both the League of Nations and the UN, would have provided checks on the exercise of both imperial and corporate power over resources and resource rents in the Third World.

On the basis of this history, the counterfactual establishes the plausibility of an alternative historical trajectory. KR Khan has suggested that if PSNR had been fully implemented, there would have been little scope for post-war ICAs.[5] This does not point to a fundamental incompatibility between PSNR and ICAs, but rather their functional equivalency. Consequently, if the economic architecture projected by the League of Nations had been adopted, and then successfully replicated in the UN, there likely would have been no PSNR Declaration. As a consequence, in the eventuality that any subsequent demands for a New International Economic Order (NIEO) had been advanced,[6] they would have required a different legal basis.

By choosing the London Conference to break with history and pose our key counterfactual, we are pushing the chronological boundaries for the genesis of PSNR back into the interwar period. This timeline allows us to recover a forgotten historical trajectory, revealing a groundswell of support and the underlying strength of the Third World demand for control over resources, thereby exposing the forgotten possibilities of the past.[7] Our intervention weaves in the hitherto neglected Latin American regional push for what is now known as PSNR. In a revision of the established narrative of the emergence of PSNR, we show that it was only after an unsuccessful attempt to moot the principle in the Western hemisphere that Latin American policymakers targeted the UN. Doing so allows us to emphasise the stakes of international law-making, and the also often-neglected contribution of regionalism. The Latin American project interacted with and inspired the demands of the decolonising states. By bringing the fight to the UN, they could not only find allies, but also an arena where the hemispheric pressure of US hegemony was less stultifying. The Latin American states were seasoned diplomatic fighters, allowing an uneasy and tenuous South-South coalition to achieve critical mass.

[4] Susan Pedersen, *The Guardians: The League of Nations and the Crisis of Empire* (OUP 2015); Miguel B Jerónimo, 'A League of Empires: Imperial Political Imagination and Interwar Internationalisms', in Miguel B Jerónimo and José Pedro Monteiro (eds), *Internationalism, Imperialism and the Formation of the Contemporary World* (Palgrave 2018).

[5] Kabir-ur-Rahman Khan, *The Law and Organisation of International Commodity Agreements* (Martinus Nijhof 1982) 20.

[6] Declaration on the Establishment of a New International Economic Order, UNGA Res 3201 (S-VI) (1 May 1994) UN Doc A/RES/3201(S-VI).

[7] See the introductory chapter of this volume.

The history of Latin American involvement in the resources and PSNR arena is critical not only for the strength of the regional bloc, but also because international resource governance was a key part of the push for the creation of the Organization of American States (OAS), which, as discussed elsewhere, was pivotal for the positioning of regionalism in the making of the United Nations, much as it had been an important part of regionalism in the League of Nations.[8]

Thus, even though the legal regime might have been different than it is today, by uncovering both Latin American agency and the connection between ICAs and international economic law at this critical juncture, we see how important these elements were to make PSNR fall into place to afford at least some cover against transnational corporations. In other words, our counterfactual underscores the ripple effects of legal principles far beyond their ultimate target audience.

In order to support our entwined theses, we first look at the role of commodity agreements in international economic architecture, uncovering the story of a failed attempt at international rulemaking targeting commodities. Next, we introduce our counterfactual, and consider what might have happened if the London Conference of 1933 had been at least partially successful. Third, we move to ask 'so what?' of our counterfactual narrative, considering how the various constellations of law and regimes could have produced vastly different outcomes, either diverging or converging with the actual historical developments. Each of these three moves looks at both the universal and the Latin American perspectives, thus offering points and counterpoints that help us articulate our theses on the role of regionalism and subaltern narratives. After fleshing out the significance of counterfactual thinking for our double-helix account, we make some concluding remarks reconnecting this chapter to broader issues of methodology and the possibilities and limitations of counterfactuals for legal and historical analysis.

II. Commodity agreements and international economic architecture

1. PSNR and international economic law architecture

PSNR is a means to assert the right to the benefits accruing from the exploitation of natural resources, what economists often refer to as the resource rents.[9] From the outset of the movement to enshrine PSNR in international law, this legal concept was not merely conceived as a necessary concomitant of state sovereignty but was imbued with moral purpose and a teleological history of emergence, or in some cases, the re-emergence of economic sovereignty. But above all, PSNR was underpinned by a particular set of economic ideas. From the late 1940s and onwards, international lawyers, development theorists, UN officials, and Western classical economists understood the troubled relationship between the

[8] Mats Ingulstad and Lucas Lixinski, 'Pan-American Exceptionalism: Regional International Law as a Challenge to International Institutions' in Simon Jackson and Alanna O'Malley (eds), *The Institution of International Order: From the League of Nations to the United Nations* (Routledge 2018) 65.

[9] UN Economic and Social Commission for Asia and the Pacific, *Policies, Regulatory Regimes and Management Practices for Investment Promotion and Sustainable Development of the Mineral Resources Sector in Economies in Transition and Developing Countries of East and South-East Asia* (United Nations 2002) 39.

industrialised world and the underdeveloped peripheries as a function of specific power relationships that depressed raw materials prices to the advantage of the consumers.[10]

Furthermore, the future architects of the NIEO saw PSNR as a key part of their push to curb the power of the great multinational corporations, who at the time amassed substantial power in highly concentrated extractive industries. Anticolonial intellectuals argued that developing countries were subjected to a double bind: not only were the prices of commodities falling relative to the prices of manufactured goods; whatever remained of the resource rents were siphoned off by multinational corporations that controlled the extractive and intermediate stages in the value chain. As economic growth lagged, they demanded the right to undertake more invasive government regulation of corporate activities. Political independence had to be accompanied by economic independence.[11]

Since PSNR was intended to address the worsening terms of trade, the question is whether there existed alternative remedies. A system of ICAs sanctioned by a universal organisation provides a plausible alternative which could have made the push for PSNR redundant in the post-war era. The PSNR Declaration is pre-dated by blueprints for such alternative mechanisms. John Maynard Keynes had advanced proposals for direct government intervention to stabilise commodity prices in 1938.[12] Various international schemes to ensure adequate and equitable access to raw materials as a means to reduce political competition for resources were proposed and adopted in the run-up to the Second World War.[13] Particularly, the provisions for ICAs under the draft International Trade Organization (ITO) Charter directly addressed the grievances motivating the demand for PSNR. The Charter provided for the establishment of specific agencies, Commodity Councils, to monitor developments in a given sector, and would provide sovereign states with authority to use quantitative controls to affect the reduction of production or trade of a commodity, as well as regulation of prices, without resorting to outright nationalisation.[14]

We suggest that the ICAs envisioned under the ITO rules would have provided the Third World producers with access to internationalised machinery for monitoring raw materials exploitation and exports, as well as enforcement mechanisms. By ensuring that the raw materials consumers also had an interest in corporate compliance, the balance of power would shift decisively from the companies managing cross-border commodity flows. A comprehensive system of quotas and price regulation would reduce their possibility to utilise vertical integration to their advantage, as it would have removed the possibility to shift costs

[10] Christopher Dietrich, *Oil Revolution: Anticolonial Elites, Sovereign Rights and the Economic Culture of Decolonization* (CUP 2017), particularly 26-60; John Toye and Richard Toye, 'The Origins and Interpretation of the Prebisch-Singer Thesis' (2003) 35 History of Political Economy 437.

[11] Norman Girvan, *Corporate Imperialism: Conflict and Expropriation. Transnational Corporations and Economic Nationalism in the Third World* (Monthly Review Press 1976); Vernie Oliveiro, 'The United States, Multinational Enterprises, and the Politics of Globalization' in Niall Ferguson and others (eds), *The Shock of the Global: The 1970s in Perspective* (Belknap Press 2010) 147–48.

[12] John Maynard Keynes, 'The Policy of Government Storage of Food-Stuffs and Raw Materials' (1938) 48 The Economic Journal 449.

[13] Michael Fakhri, *Sugar and the Making of International Trade Law* (CUP 2014). Also, Mats Ingulstad, 'Regulating the Regulators: The League of Nations and the Problem of Raw Materials' in Andreas RD Sanders, Pål T Sandvik, and Espen Storli (eds), *The Political Economy of Resource Regulation: An International and Comparative History, 1850–2015* (University of British Columbia Press 2019).

[14] Havana Charter for an International Trade Organization (adopted 24 March 1948), art 61(a): 'The regulation of production or the quantitative control of exports or imports of a primary commodity and which has the purpose or might have the effect of reducing, or preventing an increase in, the production of, or trade in, that commodity; or (b) The regulation of prices.'

across political jurisdictions and between the extraction, processing, and manufacturing stages in the value chain. At the same time, the principle of representation from both consumers and producers could have ameliorated the frequently antagonistic relationship between the two groups. Consumers could also have benefited from reduced volatility of the price cycles since they are as likely to be as interested in stable prices as in low prices.[15]

The political economy of materials production and consumption patterns at this point in time formed an essential part of trade architecture. Therefore, the entire commodity control project was a much more ambitious take on economic architecture and political economy than what eventually was embodied in the General Agreement on Tariffs and Trade (GATT). The commodity control agenda, on the other hand, was vastly more ambitious, as it would require deeper intergovernmental cooperation, entailed stricter limits on their freedom to regulate, and finally its ambit also included the developing countries. It envisioned a potentially forceful system encompassing both production quotas and governance bodies and would require close business-government cooperation. GATT, on the other hand, was an interim measure to achieve tariff reductions on trade in manufactures between countries negotiating the ITO and was supposed to be absorbed by the latter. It was a far more modest attempt to effect changes in the international trade architechture, both in terms of its scale and scope, resting on a flimsy legal foundation with the support of a jerry-rigged secretariat salvaged from the detritus of the ITO.[16]

Meanwhile, the colonial powers continued to enjoy their sovereign prerogative to exploit raw materials in their colonies, even if it was increasingly dressed up as development of the colonised territory, both for its own sake, but also to the benefit of the entire world. The idea that non-Westerners could own, regulate, and reap the benefits from their own resources still seemed somehow unnatural. During a visit to oil-rich Venezuela in 1950, George Kennan was disgusted to see revenues flowing into the state coffers, denouncing them as a 'ransom to the theory of state sovereignty'.[17] The United States sought to stymie this growing assertiveness at great cost to both the Latin American societies and its own standing and long-term objectives.[18] Was there any workable basis for a more cooperative approach?

2. Commodity agreements and international security in the Americas

What we today know as PSNR started as an attempt to reclaim control over natural resources claimed by a regional power (the United States) to feed the war machine portrayed at home and abroad as fighting on behalf of 'good' to defeat 'evil'.[19] The Latin American

[15] There is a substantial economic literature devoted to whether consumers benefit from commodity price stabilisation. A notable early contribution was Frederick V Waugh, 'Does the Consumer Benefit from Price Instability?' (1944) 58 Quarterly Journal of Economics 602; see also Paul A Samuelson 'The Consumer Does Benefit from Feasible Price Stability' (1972) 86 Quarterly Journal of Economics 476.

[16] Robert E Hudec, 'The Role of the GATT Secretariat in the Evolution of the WTO Dispute Settlement Procedure' in Jagdish Bhagwati and Mathias Hirsch (eds), *The Uruguay Round and Beyond: Essays in Honour of Arthur Dunkel* (Springer-Verlag 1998) 101–20.

[17] Greg Grandin, 'What was Containment?: Short and Long Answers from the Americas' in Robert J McMahon (ed) *The Cold War in the Third World* (OUP 2013) 42.

[18] Glenn Dorn, *The Truman Administration and Bolivia. Making the World Safe for Liberal Constitutional Oligarchy* (Pennsylvania State University Press 2011).

[19] John M Blum, *V was for Victory: Politics and American Culture During World War II* (Harcourt Brace 1976).

pushback against US economic exploitation was not a wartime phenomenon, however, but a movement that had gathered strength over time. The interwar nationalisations of mineral industry properties by Mexico and Bolivia for instance, had been bitterly felt in the United States and also gave cause for concern outside the hemisphere.[20] During the Second World War, US rhetoric of war necessity became a vehicle for intensified exploitation of regional resources. For their part, Latin American states attempted to galvanise the momentum of the negotiations of what become the OAS to secure control over the exploitation and the benefits accruing from their resources. It was only when their regional efforts failed that they went to the UN, where PSNR took the shape it is known for. This is the revisionist angle of our narrative: it adds a pre-history to conventional accounts of PSNR that, alongside the alternative of the counterfactual, discussed below, allows us to underscore certain structural elements of international law that we take for granted.

This context feeds into a broader debate about Pan-Americanism, which for our purposes includes a legal turning point during the interwar period, and as the Second World War started. The insistence that Inter-American international law rested upon the principle of arbitration, ie the peaceful settlement of international disputes, allowed many countries in the region to remain neutral until the later stages of the war. But during this period, the United States signed bilateral agreements with all Latin American nations, which were subsequently legitimised in resolutions of the inter-American conferences. These arrangements had three main purposes: (1) to assure the supply of raw materials from Latin America; (2) to facilitate US use of Latin American air and naval bases; and (3) to root out Nazi subversion in the hemisphere. These agreements allowed a large degree of US control over internal political situations in vast areas of the Western hemisphere but also created the conditions for the formation of the OAS in 1948. They inextricably tied commodities to (at least regional) security, but only as a foundation: these agreements were framed in broader terms to allow ongoing preferential trade in commodities that favoured the United States and US corporations. These bilateral agreements were often disguised as general agreements of friendship and cooperation and were endorsed by the Pan-American Union.[21] In

[20] Anand Toprani, *Oil and the Great Powers: Britain and Germany, 1914 to 1945* (OUP 2019) 108–09.

[21] See, eg, Lend-Lease Agreement Between Bolivia and the United States (Bolivia-United States) (adopted 6 December 1941, entered into force 6 December 1942) 5 UNTS 749 art 4; Mobilization of Productive Resources Exchange of Notes between Brazil and the US at Washington (Brazil-United States) (adopted 3 March 1942, entered into force 3 March 1942) 5 UNTS 913; Agreement Between the Governments of the United States of America and the Republic of Chile on the Principles of Mutual Aid Applicable to the Common Defense of the American Continent (Chile-United States) (adopted 2 March 1943, entered into force 2 March 1943) 6 UNTS 598 art 2 on military defence, art 5 on trade; Procurement of Strategic Materials Exchange of Notes between Colombia and the United States of America at Bogotá (Colombia-United States) (adopted 29 March 1943, entered into force 29 March 1943) 6 UNTS 954 art 1; Lend-Lease Agreement between Costa Rica and the United States signed at Washington (Costa Rica-United States) (adopted 16 January 1942, entered into force 16 January 1942) 6 UNTS 1070 art 4; Lend-Lease Agreement between Cuba and the United States signed at Washington (Cuba-United States) (adopted 7 November 1941, entered into force 7 November 1941) 6 UNTS 1194 art 4; Lend-Lease Agreement between Haiti and the United States signed at Washington (Haiti-United States) (adopted 16 September 1941, entered into force 16 September 1941) 8 UNTS 748 art 6; Lend-Lease Agreement between Honduras and the United States signed at Washington (Honduras-United States) (adopted 28 February 1942, entered into force 28 February 1942) 8 UNTS 936 art 4; Purchase of Rubber Produced in Peru Exchange of Notes at Washington (Peru-United States) (adopted 23 April 1942, entered into force 23 April 1942, terminated 30 June 1947) 10 UNTS 1140 para 2; Purchase of Uruguayan Wool Exchange of Notes at Washington (United States-Uruguay) (adopted 23 November 1942, entered into force 23 November 1942, terminated 11 October 1943) 12 UNTS 1008; Lend-Lease Agreement between Venezuela and the United States Signed at Washington (United States-Venezuela) (adopted 18 March 1942, entered into force 18 March 1942) 12 UNTS 1156 arts 2 and 5.

many respects, these treaties lay the foundation for the hidden mechanics of geopolitical empire.

When the war did reach the hemisphere, the language of the Pan-American Union (the OAS predecessor, operating between 1890 and 1948) meetings shifted away from guaranteeing the neutrality of American states and became about rallying behind the United States as the defender of the hemisphere. This effort meant the United States enjoyed greatly facilitated access to strategic raw materials across the Americas, all in the name of the emergency of the war. The United States set about increasing the flow of Latin American strategic materials through an array of transportation, health, food, security, and technical assistance programmes that had the effect of reshaping sectors in the Latin American economies according to its needs. Agreements to secure access and at least ostensibly facilitate or regulate trade in commodities are thus largely at the core of the success of the creation of the OAS, in that they created a web of bilateral legal relations to which Latin American states attempted to respond, by ensuring access in terms more favourable to them.

Latin American countries' aspirations provided the first big push towards sovereignty over natural resources. That was reflected in the architecture of Pan-Americanism as a permanent set of institutions, which comprise a tripod: the OAS as its political leg;[22] an agreement on mutual security as the defence leg;[23] and an (ultimately failed) economic treaty as the leg that would correct the imbalance of resource exploitation, the Economic Agreement of Bogotá.[24] This latter treaty, signed three days after the OAS Charter, makes reference to the need to compensate developing countries for imbalances in the international prices of raw materials compared to industrial goods (article 3.1),[25] and determines that no coercive measures be allowed to influence the economic development (or affect the sovereignty) of American states (article 8).

The Bogotá treaty never came into force, receiving only three of the fourteen required ratifications (two-thirds of the twenty-one signatories, as per article 41, which is in line with the requirements of the OAS Charter—article 140—and Rio Treaty—article 22). According to Sundhya Pahuja, part of the reason the Economic Agreement did not receive enough support was a disagreement over the issue of compensation for expropriation of natural resources in the hands of foreign investors.[26] This not only underlines the influence of the US private or corporate interests in this area but also prefigures the clashes over nationalisation and compensation in the NIEO-debates of the 1970s.

OAS multilateralism, therefore, excludes any consideration of natural resources from its texts that entered into force and relegates them to the lesser spheres of bilateral or private economic relations, where inequalities in raw materials exploitation can continue, be reinforced, and perpetuated. The US military did advocate for funding for resource development programmes in Latin America prior to Bogotá, but deferred to the State Department's strategy of promoting foreign investment. In any case the Pentagon deemed the legal arrangements of the mutual security treaty to be sufficient, at least in the sense that it offered

[22] Charter of the Organization of American States (OAS Charter) (adopted 30 April 1948, entered into force 13 December 1951) 119 UNTS 3.

[23] Inter-American Treaty of Reciprocal Assistance (adopted 2 September 1947, entered into force 3 December 1948) 21 UNTS 77.

[24] Economic Agreement of Bogotá (adopted 5 February 1948, entered into force 5 February 1948) OASTS No 21.

[25] The United States made a reservation to this provision at the time of signature.

[26] Sundhya Pahuja, *Decolonising International Law* (CUP 2011) 107–08.

guaranteed access to Latin American strategic materials when planning for a future war.[27] Whatever little of the hemispheric rhetoric that could be used in this context, respect for sovereignty was counter-balanced by the commitment to solidarity, which played well in the hands of the United States. The military discourse of raw materials gained a glossy cover in the OAS in the form of its commitment to the economic development of the hemisphere, through 'improved conditions for trade in basic commodities' (article 39.b.i). The big question is: improved conditions for whom?

This Latin American history thus underscores the uses of militaristic and liberalist discourses to shift commodity regulation and make it a smaller part of international trade architecture (or, as the Economic Agreement example shows, to bypass it altogether). The bilateral agreements created a baseline that Latin American states could not re-set. What if, however, the bilateral agreements were not the baseline, but the deviation from it? What if there had been an earlier international instrument that created better conditions for the international trade in commodities? The next section introduces and explores this counterfactual.

III. What if?

1. A London Charter on Commodities (1933) as the basis for the ITO

The 1933 World Monetary and Economic Conference in London is widely regarded as a failure. This was the 'last, and lost, opportunity' to break the deadlock on international cooperation to deal with currency fluctuations, war debts, and as is less frequently noted, commodity prices.[28] US President Franklin Delano Roosevelt effectively sunk the conference with a 'bombshell' message offering stark criticism of its fixation on international monetary stabilisation, signaling that he would prioritise US domestic recovery.[29] But what if the delegates had been able to salvage something by reaching agreement on commodity stabilisation based on regulation of production, trade, or prices? Such an agreement is far from implausible. Over-production and falling commodity prices were then widely recognised as a problem of the first order. Even the League of Nations secretariat had abandoned its customary support for liberalisation and free trade to get behind the demands for restrictions on production and price controls. As Patricia Clavin relates, this was both practical politics and economics.[30] In the United States, President Hoover had come to support joint action to stabilise commodity markets, and his successor Roosevelt had publicly embraced it. Even after the London Conference was generally acknowledged to be over, Secretary of State Cordell Hull pushed for international agreement to check the growth of trade barriers, while allowing for measures to stabilise commodity prices.[31]

[27] 'JCS 626/3, February 3, 1948' in Thomas Etzold and John L Gaddis (eds) *Containment: Documents on American Policy and Strategy, 1945–1950* (Columbia University Press 1978) 311–15.

[28] Harold James, *International Monetary Cooperation Since Bretton Woods* (IMF 1996) 27.

[29] Rodney Morrison, 'The London Monetary and Economic Conference of 1933: A Public Goods Analysis' (1993) 52 American Journal of Economics and Sociology 307.

[30] Patricia Clavin, *Securing the World Economy: The Reinvention of the League of Nations, 1920–1946* (OUP 2015) 114–16.

[31] Gustave A Nuermberger and others (eds), *Foreign Relations of the United States, Diplomatic Papers, 1932* (United States Government Printing Office 1947) vol 1, doc 808; Rogers P Churchill, George V Blue, and Shirley F Landau (eds), *Foreign Relations of the United States, Diplomatic Papers, 1933* (United States Government Printing Office 1950) vol 1, docs 456, 492, 727–29; Morrison (n 29) 309.

While the conclusion and ratification of a London Charter on commodity stabilisation is entirely plausible, it is necessary to demonstrate that this agreement would have paved the way for a new economic regime with commodity agreements as a cornerstone. The groundwork at the London Conference was carried out by two separate commissions. Commodities fell within the purview of the Economic Commission, which set up a dedicated sub-committee to study coordination and marketing. It reasoned that since the purchasing power of the raw materials producers had to be restored, commodity prices needed to be shored up through concerted efforts. Controversially, the sub-committee concluded that only a general agreement to regulate trade and production would 'enable the evil to be attacked at the root'.[32] It suggested a set of principles to keep the commodity agreements from transmogrifying into predatory producer cartels. The commodity subjected to regulation had to be of great importance, and with an identifiable surplus. The agreement had to be comprehensive, command assent among exporting countries, and provide for cooperation with non-exporting countries. It should be flexible, durable and non-discriminatory, fair to producers and consumers alike, ensure stable prices, and support efficient production. It also specifically required that 'individual governments concerned must have the power and the will to enforce it in their respective territories'.[33]

Although some delegations were highly sceptical of making these provisions permanent, the committee concluded that the 'exceptional period' demanded 'exceptional remedies'.[34] Even if an agreement on these principles had been adopted merely on a temporary basis by the delegates, it is fair to assume that the lingering effects of the Great Depression, followed by rearmament, world war, and reconstruction, would have provided ample justification for prolongation.

While equitable access to raw materials featured heavily in the run-up to the Second World War, it is unlikely that this counterfactual London Charter could have appeased Germany, Japan, and Italy, the so-called have-not powers.[35] The 1937 League Inquiry into the raw materials problem offered little in the way of solution, and the political tug-of-war over raw materials steadily intensified until the outbreak of the Second World War. The onset of war forced the existing commodity schemes to suspend their operations. In their stead, the Great Powers turned to other means to ensure a stable and secure supply of raw materials,[36] like the bilateral treaties in the Americas discussed earlier. In short, the adoption of the London principles would not have decisively altered the developments that led to the eruption of the Second World War, nor would it have had a decisive influence on its course or outcome. The counterfactual consequences would only be felt as the planning for post-war order began in earnest.

As the planning for a post-war settlement began in the Western capitals, the problem of commodity stabilisation was high on the agenda. Despite the pause in their operations, the limited interwar experiences with commodity agreements provided important impetus for post-war planning. A 1943 International Labour Organization (ILO) report stressed

[32] 'Report of the Economic Commission' League of Nations Monetary and Economic Conference (27 July 1933), printed as Annex II in *Reports Approved by the Conference on July 27th, 1933, and The Resolutions Adopted by the Bureau and the Executive Committee* (League of Nations Publications 1933).

[33] ibid 47, particularly 3(e).

[34] ibid 18.

[35] Richard Overy, *The Origins of the Second World War* (Routledge 2017) 37.

[36] Edward P Cambio, *International Commodity Agreements: Selected Research Materials* (Library of Congress 1976).

the importance of commodity stabilisation for future welfare. It concluded that government involvement had become the norm, and that the necessity of commodity regulation commanded general recognition. As for the future, the inter-war experiences showed that commodity controls unsupported by production or export regulations had scant chance of success.[37] A revival of the counterfactual London Convention could likely have been agreed at Bretton Woods, where several delegates had hoped for decisive action to deal with problems relating to production and distribution of raw materials. Even if the political can had been kicked down the road on this occasion, the London principles were gaining acceptance. When the US State Department published proposals for a post-war trade organisation in late 1945, it did include somewhat hesitant provisions for commodity agreements. Such agreements would have to be publicised, non-discriminatory, and open to both producers and consumers.[38] These suggestions were then taken up by the Preparatory Committee for United Nations Conference on Trade and Employment under the auspices of the UN Economic and Social Council (ECOSOC). During negotiations on the draft ITO Charter in the preparatory committee, the United States found itself under heavy pressure from both the underdeveloped countries, but frequently also the Food and Agriculture Organization of the UN (FAO), Australia, and the United Kingdom, who saw a potential for commodity agreements to solve key problems in the post-war era. [39]

The post-war revival of ICAs brings us to the second decisive moment, the adoption of the ITO Charter. While it is generally acknowledged that the Charter was killed in the US Congress due to lack of political support, our counterfactual history would have made its passage all the more likely. Susan Aaronson points to the fact that the US State Department was late to present its proposals for an international trade organisation, thereby losing much of the momentum with Congress and other important constituencies.[40] The lack of support from the US military was another important factor. By the time the State Department changed tack and started arguing that the ITO Charter was a valuable safeguard that restricted the possibilities of the underdeveloped countries to impose unnecessary limitations on trade, it was too late. If the question of the ITO had been about re-activating the London Charter, the matter could have been put to Congress earlier, before the opposition had crystallised and the momentum had been lost. The ITO would have been brought into the UN system as a specialised agency.[41] An ITO-style treaty under UN oversight would then have guided the development of international commodity trade in the post-war world. As the outcome of an extensive drafting process at several international conferences, even if not ultimately ratified, the ITO Charter gives a close approximation of what was politically acceptable at the time. With the added benefit of precedence, a supportive, rather than permissive, attitude towards ICAs would have further animated the Charter.

The counterfactual adoption of an ITO-style treaty reaffirming the principles of the London Charter would in all likelihood have negated the need for the PSNR Declaration of 1952. After all, if the necessary control over corporate operations and the distribution

[37] International Labour Office, *Intergovernmental Commodity Control Agreements* (ILO 1943) 17.

[38] US State Department, *Proposals for Expansion of World Trade and Employment*, Commercial Policy Series 79 (Government Printing Office 1945).

[39] William Brown, *The United States and the Restoration of World Trade* (The Brookings Institution 1950).

[40] Susan Aaronson, *Trade and the American Dream: A Social History of Postwar Trade Policy* (University Press of Kentucky 1996) 60.

[41] Draft Agreement between the United Nations and the International Trade Organization (13 November 1947) UN Doc S-0472-0058-8.

of resource rents could be gained by other means, why risk nationalisation? That would bind up scarce capital for wages and operating costs, create domestic political liability for external market failures, all the while jeopardising access to foreign technology, management resources and antagonising Western customers. At a bare minimum, the concomitant success of Latin American negotiations on the basis of the London Convention would have shifted the political calculus for the elites in the hemisphere, thereby undermining the rapprochement between Latin American and Middle Eastern academics and politicians that provided the foundations for the PSNR Declaration.[42]

Without PSNR, would not the new nations emerging from the decolonisation process have been left at the mercy of international corporations without even the thin protective cloak offered by the principle? After all, the new entities depended on exports to provide the revenues necessary to expand their rudimentary state apparatus, and PSNR provided moral justification for their demand for an increased share of the revenues. Not necessarily. In our counterfactual, several of the new states would themselves have gained first-hand experience with participation in commodity regulation. Article 69 of the ITO Charter provided for the inclusion of dependent territories of members either jointly, or with separate representation if their interests diverged. Fortified by this experience, the new states would have been better placed to utilise their membership of the Commodity Councils once they became fully sovereign. That would have provided recourse to an international political mechanism that would have enabled them to exercise a much stronger degree of control over the foreign corporations. The commodity control agreements would yield better control of production and pricing. The multinational companies would no longer be in a position to reduce their tax burdens through transfer pricing, or wielding the threat of production cut-backs with consequent loss of local employment and tax revenues against their host government. Furthermore, the producing states could even have enlisted the assistance of the governments of the importing countries in the industrialised world, who would have shared an interest in maintaining stability of both supply and prices.

A world with economic architecture based on commodity agreements and stronger production controls, rather than laissez-faire economics, would, therefore, have congealed. This international regime would have put colonies and weaker states in an overall better position, in line with the vision that would have been echoed and reinforced in the Bogotá Economic Charter, ushering in alternative and more robust regionalisms.

2. The Bogotá Economic Charter and alternative regionalisms

While our counterfactual assumes that a logical consequence of the London Economic Conference is that its principles guiding commodity trade would have outlasted the League of Nations and the Second World War, there is a distinct possibility that the instrument would have succumbed to the international institutional iconoclasm of the war. But we pose that, even if the London Charter had not survived the Second World War, there would still be Latin America to promote these principles in the form of the Economic Agreement of Bogotá, but this time backed by the experience of the London instrument. These two

[42] Dietrich (n 10).

initiatives failed because they made too many compromises to rationalisation and a developmental project that did not suit developed nations. However, had the rationalisation doctrine of the Bogotá Economic Agreement prevailed in the Americas, supported by the London Charter, it would have also very likely prevailed in the global sphere, given that the United States was the big holdout, as Venzke explains.[43]

Anchoring the Economic Agreement of Bogotá in the London Charter, as opposed to the relative vacuum in which it was actually drafted, would have made a difference in at least two respects. First, more robust regionalism would have been enabled, generating increased revenues and unlocking developmental possibilities. Second, as a more abstract doctrinal point in international law, it would have been an instance of multilateralism being used to halt or correct strategic fragmentation, rather than multilateralism as the congealing of asymmetric bilateralisms. All of these points are of course interrelated, but deserve some individualisation for our analytical purposes, inasmuch as they point to different possibilities of counterfactual reasoning.

First, more robust regionalism would have ensued if the inter-American tripod would have been completed. That would necessarily lead to a better balance of powers between importing and producing nations, which would have helped mediate the core ambivalence of Pan-Americanism, stuck between the interests of the United States and those of Latin America. With a stronger inter-American system, and PSNR not a major issue, Latin American states would have been in a position to drive bigger projects in addressing their aspirations. In other words, had the Economic Agreement of Bogotá entered into force, the OAS would have turned out to be a far more muscular organisation, able to live up to the possibility of constraining US economic-imperial aspirations in the rest of the hemisphere. That would have set the tone for regionalism as a viable and possibly even desirable counterpoint to the UN, and different development economics would have been made operational.

The implication here is to underscore regionalism's excessive focus on specific approaches to enduring peace in the mid-twentieth century. The contingency, therefore, is how military cooperation rhetoric cloaked economic interests, and regional projects became hostages to these interests. The model, therefore, came to either have anaemic regional organisations like the OAS or to divorce security and development from structured economic policy, at least at first. For the American hemisphere specifically, a complete inter-American tripod would have created appropriate fora for the peaceful settlement of international disputes (an essential element of Inter-American international law dating back to the Pan-American Union's origins in the nineteenth century). The firmer anchoring on (regional) international legal principles and more robust institutions would have meant less of a need to go to the UN to vent and (re-)pursue grievances against the United States, which was a crucial motivation for PSNR.

Second, as indicated earlier, the Economic Agreement of Bogotá was a reaction to the interwar bilateral agreements between the US and Latin American nations. These agreements formed the basis for negotiations. Instead, had the London Economic Charter been adopted, the agreements would not have been the beginning of natural resources treaties in the Americas, but rather a typical example of strategic fragmentation.[44] Characterised as the

[43] Ingo Venzke, 'What If? Counterfactual (Hi)Stories of International Law' (2018) 8 Asian Journal of International Law 403, 424–28.

[44] Surabhi Ranganathan, *Strategically Created Treaty Conflicts and the Politics of International Law* (CUP 2014).

explicit exceptions, rather than the baseline, they would also have improved conditions for the adoption of the Bogotá Agreement. In other words, the US bilateral agreements with Latin America would have been made more visible as deviations at the time, and it would have been harder for them to be the invisible backbone conditioning resource trade in the Americas. With the rules of the Bogotá Agreement, too, PSNR would not have been needed, and commodities would have been regulated in a way that more aptly grappled with the power of transnational corporations, rather than being caught up in the state-centric rhetoric of PSNR.

Having fleshed out our key counterfactual, and the ensuing consequences, the question that remains is what, if anything, this counterfactual analysis helps elucidate about the nature of resource regulation in international law, economic architecture, or regionalism. More broadly, questions remain as well about method, the utility of counterfactuals in the turn to history in international law.

IV. So what?

1. Unravelling the tapestry of international economic law's history

Our alternative and revisionist history shows there are particular ways of thinking about PSNR and the connection between trade and natural resources. The Latin American layer of this revisionist story further shows how narratives of free trade obfuscate military interests, as well as the potential influence of organised blocs (as opposed to major economic players) in the design of international economic law and institutions. In particular, the contingency we introduced (our alternative history) shows that there is a potentially strong path dependency in the development of international economic architecture.

Had the London Conference been successful, and with it the Economic Agreement of Bogotá and connected Pan-American aspiration, it would have meant an important endorsement of a specific underlying rationale of global economic architecture. As Michael Fakhri has explained in contextualising specific commodities in the history of international trade law, there were three relevant doctrines underlying the international economic architecture at the time: rapprochement, rationalisation, and freer trade.[45] Rapprochement means that trade leads to peace among nations. As Cordell Hull poignantly summarised this outlook: 'unhampered trade dovetailed with peace; high tariffs, trade barriers, and unfair competition, with war.'[46] Rapprochement is thus a useful counterpoint to what became the smokescreen in OAS negotiations (where the defence of military interests overtook economic development, rather than seeing them as mutually reinforcing).

Rationalisation was the idea that at the macro-level, international economic architecture and law was supposed to stabilise and control the production, distribution, and consumption of certain products, conceived at the time as an alternative both to protectionism and free trade. With respect to strategic raw materials, this doctrine is immediately applicable, and at least on the surface, it is contained in the language of many of the bilateral instruments discussed earlier. This doctrine, in particular, blurred the line between public and private agents in the economy, by giving public agents a greater role in planning the economy.

[45] Fakhri (n 13) 83–91.

[46] Cordell Hull, *The Memoirs of Cordell Hull* (Macmillan 1948) vol 1, 81.

International institutions' role was precisely to mediate between public and private, eg through the establishment of a coordinating international authority supervising a series of internationally organised industries under control of dedicated boards or committees.[47]

Freer trade, lastly, was essentially about the reduction and eventual abolition of quantitative trade barriers and tariffs. This doctrine was tied with rapprochement (in the sense that tariffs could lead to conflict between nations that could escalate into warfare), but this tie was eventually abandoned in favour of further freedom for the private. The Report of the World Economic Conference in 1927 determined that 'the free circulation of raw material is one of the essential conditions for the healthy industrial and commercial development of the world', while recommending that export taxes and other barriers to the exchange of raw materials should be kept as low as possible, and never employed for political purposes.[48]

The same three doctrines echoed in the London principles and were re-formulated in the ITO Charter, particularly freer trade was promoted by the United States as the dominant force among the First World nations, and rationalisation from the perspective of the Third World with occasional support from other states.[49] Therefore, our counterfactual helps shed light on the divorcing of trade and development that happened institutionally, and the interests served by this bifurcation. It underscores also how dependent international lawyers generally are on a certain economic rationality to explain the international legal architecture and our teleological commitment to specific readings of history.

Our revisionist and alternative histories also call for more work to be done in uncovering the influence of non-state actors on the history of principles and ideas that are as state-centric as PSNR (or, for that matter, sovereignty). The specialised institutions and experts attached to universal organisations clearly have influence. But so do the private corporations, either as actors influencing domestic positions, as in the case of US corporations with regard to the ITO, but also as targets of international action as Michelle Staggs Kelsall relates in her chapter. Thus, counterfactual thinking in this context highlights that sovereignty is not just produced at the encounter of two states.[50] There is, in fact, a private history of international law that is not just that of private international law,[51] but what Koskenniemi has called for in his discussion of what the history of international law should become.[52] The issue here is not so much that international law has largely neglected these private aspects so far—it is more so that historians have engaged with these elements for a long time, and the turn to history in international law has somehow eluded this important methodological move.[53] In other words, contingency analysis also allows us to question larger

[47] Harold Greaves, *Raw Materials and International Control* (Methuen 1936), see particularly section II.

[48] 'Report of the World Economic Conference Adopted on May 23, 1927' (1927) 134 The Annals of the American Academy of Political and Social Science 174, 188.

[49] Fakhri (n 13) 156.

[50] cf Sundhya Pahuja, 'Laws of Encounter: A Jurisdictional Account of International Law' (2013) 1 London Review of International Law 63.

[51] Alex Mills, 'The Private History of International Law' (2006) 55 The International and Comparative Law Quarterly 1.

[52] Martti Koskenniemi, 'What Should International Legal History Become?' in Stefan Kadelbach, Thomas Kleinlein, and David Roth-Isigkeit (eds), *System, Order, and International Law: The Early History of International Legal Thought from Machiavelli to Hegel* (OUP 2017).

[53] But see Sundhya Pahuja 'The Changing Place of the Corporation in International Law' (Sir Hersch Lauterpacht Memorial Lectures of 2018, Cambridge 2018) <https://sms.cam.ac.uk/media/2696888> accessed 8 October 2019.

methodological points about the turn to history which speak even to very 'traditionally public' themes like sovereignty and can set free repressed disciplinary imaginations.[54]

Finally, our counterfactual helps underscore the stakes of PSNR. This principle is more than a decolonising move. It is also about, as Pahuja put it, a developmental project that followed from decolonisation.[55] But more than that, it is about international economic architecture and institution building. Had PSNR not come into being, as our counterfactual poses, the decolonisation narrative would not have eclipsed the principles' other potentials. In other words, counterfactual analysis also puts in stark contrast the problems of framing and imaginaries in the persecution of international legal causes and accompanying law-making, in that one principle's narrated aspirational values can hide away regulatory and world-making capacities. In other words, inasmuch as aspirational narratives and accompanying imaginaries help build momentum, they can also come at the expense of the very work they were meant to do.

2. Never say NIEO?

While an alternative regime for international economic governance could have developed on the basis of the adoption and subsequent strengthening of the London principles, it is uncertain whether the outcome ultimately would have been beneficial for Third World countries. The fear of control by foreign banks and multinational corporations was tangible both in long-established states in Latin America and the newly independent states in Asia and Africa. For them, as well as many UN diplomats, national control was a prerequisite for their strategies of import substitution and industrialisation on the basis of domestic resources.[56] Norman Girvan, one of the influential intellectuals in this movement, specifically pointed to the fact that as vertically integrated corporations, engaged in production of multiple products in several countries, transnational corporations (TNCs) had both incentives and opportunities to shift profits away from the point of extraction and to avoid taxation. Girvan concluded that given the demonstrable reticence of the minerals industry, nationalisation and domestic control over-extraction and refining was the most feasible course of action open to Third World governments.[57] The negotiations over a Code of Conduct for TNCs, as Kelsall shows in her contribution to this volume, embodied the NIEO demand for redistributive justice precisely through reining in the TNCs as agents of exploitation, particularly through shedding light on their inner workings.[58]

If the corporations had been deprived of opportunities to evade taxes through ICAs at an earlier stage, the grievances that gave rise to the sovereign rights movement and the establishment of producer cartels like the Organization of Petroleum Exporting Countries, the International Bauxite Association, and the Intergovernmental Council of Copper Exporting Countries could have been successfully addressed already during the 1950s and

[54] Jean d'Aspremont, 'Critical Histories of International Law and the Repression of Disciplinary Imagination' (2019) 7 London Review of International Law, 89 <www.ssrn.com/abstract=3382763> accessed 8 October 2019.

[55] See Pahuja (n 26).

[56] Mark Mazower, *Governing the World: The History of an Idea* (Penguin Books 2013) 280, 287, 301.

[57] Norman Girvan, 'Bauxite: The Need to Nationalize, Part I' (1971) 2 Review of Black Political Economy 72.

[58] Michelle Staggs Kelsall, '"Poisonous Flowers on the Dust-heap of a Dying Capitalism": The United Nations Code of Conduct on Transnational Corporations, Contingency and Failure in International Law' in this volume.

1960s. There would have been no need to spell out PSNR, or even more drastically, the right to establish commodity cartels in the Charter on Economic Rights and Duties of the State.[59] A less antagonistic relationship between consumers and producers might have ensued, based upon the London principles, taking the wind out of the sails of the NIEO. In this optimistic scenario, the TNCs would have faced less risk of nationalisation. Accordingly, at least for the evangelists of foreign direct investment, they might have been more willing to provide the capital and technology for further processing facilities, creating forward linkages that would have benefited the host society. Finally, by ameliorating the boom-and-bust cycles of commodity prices that can starve a government of the necessary financing to maintain essential services, before flushing them a few years later with cash that can be spent without oversight or accountability, the 'resource curse' would have been much less likely to afflict developing countries.[60]

Far less fortuitous outcomes can be imagined, even starting from the same initial premise. If the ICAs built along the lines of the London principles and the ITO had been successful, developing countries could have developed stronger appetites for regulation, demanding an ever-larger share of the resource rents. In this scenario, the ICAs would have provided an alternative means of asserting sovereignty against the TNCs, who would then have lost control as decisively as they did after the promulgation of PSNR and the subsequent wave of nationalisations in the Third World.[61] But it is still likely that the terms of trade would have continued to disfavour the producers, eg due to increased use of substitutes, or reductions of the input of raw materials, at least relative to the rising value of imported manufactures. Strong support for a new global economic order built on the very same principles that informed the NIEO is then likely to have emerged. Since the operating principles of commodity stabilisation had already been codified and embedded into the international economic architecture, a strong push along those lines could have stood a greater chance of success. But that would raise the question of whether conflicts over cost differentials, quota allocation, financing, free-riding, and other problems haunting any producer association could have been successfully navigated.[62] It is quite likely that an economic order built on ICAs might have been inherently unstable, particularly since the actual historical record of the ICAs inspire little optimism.[63] The spectacular collapse of the Tin Agreement, for instance, led to huge financial losses with drastic consequences for output, jobs, and welfare in the countries that were hardest hit.[64] A similar crisis in an entire system built on ICAs could have hit the Third World countries even harder than the debt crises and the restructuring programmes of the 1980s. The counterfactual London Charter could have produced worse development outcomes than the Washington consensus.

The two scenarios sketched out in this chapter underline both the value and the pitfalls of applying counterfactuals. A properly useful counterfactual forces us to consider the options that were available to policymakers, but it also lays bare the enduring strength of established

[59] Charter of Economic Rights and Duties of States, UNGA Res 3281 (XXIX) (12 December 1974) arts 2 and 5.

[60] Richard Auty, 'Economic Development and the Resource Curse Thesis' in Oliver Morrissey and Frances Stewart (eds), *Economic and Political Reform in Developing Countries* (Palgrave 1995).

[61] Geoffrey Jones, *Multinationals and Global Capitalism: From the Nineteenth to the Twenty First Century* (OUP 2004).

[62] Alfred Maizels, 'Commodities in Crisis: An Overview of the Main Issues' (1987) 15 World Development 537.

[63] Marcelo Raffaelli, *Rise and Demise of Commodity Agreements* (Woodhead 1995).

[64] Ian Mallory, 'Conduct Unbecoming: The Collapse of the International Tin Agreement' (1990) 5 American University International Law Review 835, particularly 868–71.

political and economic structures. The use of counterfactuals, although invaluable as a tool for historical enquiry, must be disciplined by attention to structural determinants.[65] The further we depart from the established factual record after a critical juncture, by constantly choosing paths that diverge, rather than converge with actual historical events, what we do know of subsequent developments becomes less useful as a guide to likely outcomes. Instead, we enter the realms of pure fiction, such as a stable world order without PSNR or NIEO, or one without PSNR but with NIEO and ultimately disastrous consequences for the commodity producers.

Counterfactual scenarios can also show us how some outcomes are very likely, such as Third World governments asserting control over their resources, even if different legal instruments would have been utilised for the purpose. Identifying critical junctures, and determining an alternative outcome may tempt us to fixate upon events that are spectacular and at least particular. Path dependencies might not hinge entirely on exactly which path is chosen at what time, as the range of available options depends on the lay of the land in a legal, economic, ideational, and political sense. It is the context that determines the consequences of the particular (non)-event, ie the passage of the ITO.[66] The potential equivalency of PSNR and ICAs, even if established, should remind us not to be too impressed by teleological narratives of legal developments, and to place less emphasis on the decisive significance of specific formulations or declarations contingent on specific historical events or constellations.

V. PSNR: Revisionist and alternative histories

Counterfactual thinking around PSNR forces a trip back in time: to engage with the stakes of PSNR is to engage with the cornerstones of international economic law's architecture. PSNR was the culmination of a range of ambiguous and often contradictory campaigns and impulses in international legal ordering, speaking to the nature of sovereignty, the role of political economy in choices about institutional architecture, and the ways in which the private is woven in and out of political slogans that have the effect of obfuscating economic stakes.

Our combination of counterfactual ('what if the London Economic Conference of 1933 had been successful?') and revisionist history (the Latin American pre-history of PSNR) sheds light on the baselines we take for granted in our accounts of international law's functioning today. For one, they evidence under-appreciated elements of international economic architecture, particularly resource regulation and the role of corporate actors. These histories also showcase that narratives of Third World or regional actors matter not only as counter-movements but also as pivotal seedlings of international legal ordering.

The light shed on these baselines necessarily transforms them, in at least two ways. First, by expanding and illuminating corners and foundations, characterising events and instruments as either the beginning of the making of a regime or the strategic fragmentation of pre-existing ordering. Second, by showing that the baseline was elsewhere all along, like the revisionist pre-history of regional efforts and their status. Both of these effects are significant

[65] Margaret MacMillan, *The Uses and Abuses of History* (Profile Books 2010).
[66] John L Gaddis, *The Landscape of History* (OUP 2002).

to international legal scholars engaged in the turn to history and can liberate disciplinary imaginations. Methodologically, too, this exercise stresses that scholars undertaking to recover legal histories should be more aware of the importance of political context and economic structures that have shaped the outcomes. After all, law constructed in a vacuum is the least plausible counterfactual of all.

C.

HUMAN RIGHTS

16

Rights for Daydreaming

International Human Rights Law Thought Otherwise

Kathryn McNeilly

I. Introduction

Within the international legal system, international human rights law has emerged as a particular focus for exploration of contingency and the counterfactual. An array of scholarship has revealed overtly or implicitly how this area of law could have been thought otherwise had various facts, actors, contexts, or power relations transpired contrarily.[1] This interest in international human rights law and contingency is unsurprising considering the emancipatory hope which this law has been thought to embody, and the various ways it has been assessed to have lived up to this hope.[2] Contingency is one way to understand how international human rights law might have evolved differently, or have been 'done better' as a hopeful and emancipatory discourse. In this respect, the impetus to think international human rights law otherwise is more than just an academic 'parlour game'.[3] Rather, it can be connected to deeper discussions about how such law might have fulfilled – and indeed may still fulfil – the hopeful expectations which were placed upon it.

In this chapter I remain with the theme of hope which pervades this subset of international law and undertake one counterfactual exploration of it which has not been considered to date. The specific question I pose is *what if international human rights law, in its mainstream form as a discourse shaped by the United Nations, had been developed as a discourse for daydreaming?* By this I mean a vehicle to help us dream individually but also collectively of a future of hope which is better than the present, and to do so in a politically-engaged way.[4] Asking this question is significant for international legal scholars interested in exploring the connections between international human rights law and hope in the past and, potentially, in the present. The question proceeds by reflecting on the near miss of a successful collision between the futural and the political in international human rights law during the mid-to-late twentieth century. In doing so, it allows the themes of hope and futurity to be engaged in a new way in this area.

[1] This includes the work of feminist, postcolonial, and Third World Approaches to International Law (TWAIL) scholars.

[2] See, for example, Wendy Brown, '"The Most We Can Hope For ...": Human Rights and the Politics of Fatalism' (2004) 103 The South Atlantic Quarterly 451; David Kennedy, 'The International Human Rights Movement: Part of the Problem?' (2002) 15 Harvard Human Rights Journal 101; Stephen Hopgood, *The Endtimes of Human Rights* (Cornell University Press 2013).

[3] EH Carr, *What is History?* (Penguin 1987) 97.

[4] In this respect, I approach hope as not just optimism, but a latent force withtransformative potential in the context of current power relations. For wider work on hope see, for example, Kathryn Sikkink, *Evidence for Hope: Making Human Rights Work in the 21st Century* (Princeton University Press 2017).

Kathryn McNeilly, *Rights for Daydreaming* In: *Contingency in International Law.* Edited by: Ingo Venzke and Kevin Jon Heller,
Oxford University Press. © The Several Contributors 2021. DOI: 10.1093/oso/9780192898036.003.0016

My discussion exploring the question above is divided into three sections. In the first I outline more of what daydreaming in the manner I am using it here means. In doing so, I draw from utopian thinking to contextualise more of what it might mean to dream about the future and enact it. In the second section, attention turns to explore how it is possible to understand the relationship between international human rights law, the futural, and the political throughout the twentieth century. I turn to historiographical scholarship for assistance, and find three readings of this relationship. The first two of these readings foreground periods where a commitment to either the futural or to the political defined international human rights. The third, however, draws attention to a period in the 1960s–1970s where these commitments did collide via the work of states from the Global South, albeit this work was not fully successful in shaping the mainstream development of human rights internationally. I argue that this latter collision, fleeting as it was, renders the idea of human rights as rights for daydreaming more than just a false contingency.[5] Rather, it may be viewed as a possibility that was marginalised by historic circumstances. In the chapter's final section, I investigate the difference that conceiving international human rights law as rights for daydreaming may have made. This includes consequences for this area of law's connection to grassroots social movements; development of its institutional processes and structures; and compatibility with neoliberalism in the twentieth century. In addition to a counterfactual exploration of the past, the difference that this alternative thinking would have made also includes consequences for the position and potential of international human rights law today in the twenty-first century.

II. On daydreaming

Before progressing further, it is important to pause and consider the daydream and what its activity might involve. Daydreaming as I am conceiving it here is consciously connected to hope, critical analysis of the present, imagination of alternative future possibilities, and to thinking about and actively approaching the future differently. This can occur individually, but daydreaming has a definitively collective element. Fundamentally, it serves to rouse us to bring an enhanced future into being in an expansive, social manner. It is, therefore, a futural and, at heart, an inherently political activity. Daydreaming together offers a way of thinking about the future that is grounded in hope and work to achieve better relations of living and being for all. The daydreaming that I am envisaging here can be contextualised against the work of utopian thinking.

Utopian thought has taken many forms, spanning literature and political theory from Plato's *The Republic* (370-380 BC) and More's *Utopia* (1516) onwards. Later work such as Francis Bacon's *The New Atlantis* (1627), Edward Bellamy's *Looking Backwards* (1888), and William Morris's *News from Nowhere* (1892) continued the tradition and were added to in the twentieth century by a range of critical utopian writing.[6] Across its various forms and manifestations, hope and the desire for a better way of being defines work in this vein as it serves to dream about the good place that is no place.[7] The future is imagined and thought

5 Susan Marks, 'False Contingency' (2009) 62 Current Legal Problems 1.
6 Tom Moylan, *Demand the Impossible: Science Fiction and the Utopian Imagination* (Peter Lang, 2014).
7 Ruth Levitas, The Concept of Utopia (Peter Lang, 1990).

through in more hopeful ways which serve to shine a critical light on the present.[8] In this respect, a future-focus is central to utopian work which is tied together by the concept of hopeful dreaming. In its focus on the future, and hope for better futures, much utopian thinking is also politically-engaged. As Ruth Levitas outlines, utopia is 'not just a dream to be enjoyed, but a vision to be pursued'.[9] The point is not just to dream about the future, but to enact such futures in everyday life to facilitate change.

Thinking on this latter point is evident in the work of many utopian writers. One of these is Ernst Bloch who identifies utopian imagining as falling into one of two categories: abstract fantastic and compensatory—or concrete—anticipatory and grounded in praxis.[10] It is only the latter which carries the future in a better form into the present by both anticipating and effecting such a future. In his consideration of utopia and the future-facing hope it embodies in its concrete form, a particular emphasis is placed on dreams.[11] Bloch distinguishes between night-dreams, which are concerned with the past, and dreams occurring during daytime, which are characterised by images of a better life and journeying forward and can push towards concrete utopia.[12] Other utopian writers who demonstrate the connection between dreaming and enacting change include feminist utopian authors. Imagining a range of gender equal futures, feminist utopian work such as Urusla Le Guin's *The Left Hand of Darkness* (1969), Marge Piercy's *Woman on the Edge of Time* (1976) and Sally Miller Gearhart's *The Wanderground* can be characterized as 'an exercise of wilful imaginiation' aimed towards achieving change.[13] In this respect, a connection between the 'not yet' and everyday action or political engagement must be understood as central to utopia as a concept underpinning human existence. As Levitas states, 'utopianism, in the sense of visualising, hoping for and *working for* a better world is an enduring and essential element of human aspiration and culture'.[14]

Utopian thinking, therefore, is united by a focus on future-facing dreaming as a means to venture beyond the present, in particular its limitations, and improve the world we live in through tangible action that stems from such dreaming. How might such a conception of dreaming relate to international human rights law? It is possible, I suggest, to read human rights as concepts which offer a means for future-focused daydreaming. Drawing from their central emphasis on creating a better world order, protecting basic human needs, and establishing an enhanced set of relations between citizen and state, international human rights from their outset offered a discourse of hope.[15] Their overarching objective reflects the fundamental dream of equality, freedom and the absence of oppression for all. Accordingly, human rights hold potential to be a vehicle through which daydreaming is stimulated and supported, providing tools to simultaneously anticipate and effect a better, hopeful future. International human rights law may, in other words, offer an additional, and productive, space in society for better relations of living and being to emerge via dreaming.

[8] Krishan Kumar, *Utopianism* (University of Minnesota Press, 1991) 20

[9] Levitas (n 8) 1.

[10] Ernst Bloch, *The Principle of Hope Volume 1* (Neville Plaice tr et al, MIT Press 1995). For discussion see Ruth Levitas, 'Educated Hope: Ernst Bloch on Abstract and Concrete Utopia' in Jamie Owen Daniel and Tom Moylan (eds), *Not Yet: Reconsidering Ernst Bloch* (Verso 1997) 65, 67.

[11] Bloch (n 11) 339-450.

[12] Bloch (n 11) 77–113.

[13] Frances Bartkowski, *Feminist Utopias* (University of Nebraska Press, 1989) 10.

[14] Levitas (n 8) xiii. Emphasis added

[15] See Eleanor Roosevelt, 'The Promise of Human Rights' (1948) 26 Foreign Affairs 470.

Overall, a relationship between international human rights law, the future, and the political which utopian thinking provides a context for is not easily recognisable in this area of law's mainstream history. Throughout the twentieth century, international human rights law was largely not understood as a vehicle for daydreaming about the future. The future—in the sense of hoping for a better world that is always 'not yet'—and the political—as a collective practice which challenges given relations of living and being—did not significantly align in the development of this international legal system. Yet, there does appear to be one period where a brief alignment of these elements did occur in a collection of activity at the international level. This provides the foundations for an important counterfactual investigation of human rights and daydreaming. To explore this assertion, and to further comprehend the relationship between international human rights law, the futural, and the political in the twentieth century, it is instructive to turn to historiographical scholarship.

III. The future and the political in the history of international human rights law

Human rights history has recently gained momentum as an area of scholarship, expanding how it is possible to understand the development of these rights, including their appearance and evolution in international law.[16] Much of this work has focused on providing competing understandings of the 'breakthrough' of human rights internationally.[17] This focus on the breakthrough debate has, however, inadvertently led to the neglect of wider themes that underpin human rights history in significant ways and thus warrant critical analysis. One such theme is how international human rights law has been understood to connect with ideas of futurity and the political. Surveying existing historiographical writing, three overarching accounts of this connection emerge.

The first of these provides a reading of this area of law in the twentieth century as a discourse which was future-focused, but apolitical in nature. This is evident in the work of orthodox, 'textbook' history focusing on the post-Second World War period.[18] This body of work understands the history of international human rights law as beginning with the Universal Declaration of Human Rights (UDHR) in 1948. The UDHR is presented as a document of hope facilitating a move from the horror of the Second World War into a new world order based on an alternative set of relations between the individual and the state. Bridging the past and future in such a way, the UDHR is decidedly apolitical: it is a document formed by consensus across diverse states and political persuasions which creates unity via a vision of a common humanity. While of course politics was not so absent from

[16] See Philip Alston, 'Does the Past Matter? On the Origins of Human Rights' (2013) 126 Harvard Law Review 2043.

[17] See Robert Brier, 'Beyond the Quest for a "Breakthrough": Reflections on the Recent Historiography on Human Rights' (2015) 16 European History Yearbook 155.

[18] Hersch Lauterpacht, *International Law and Human Rights* (Stevens & Sons 1950); Louis Henkin, *The Rights of Man Today* (Westview Press 1978); Mark Mazower, 'The Strange Triumph of Human Rights, 1933–1950' (2004) 47 The Historical Journal 379; Jack Donnelly, *Universal Human Rights in Theory and Practice* (2nd edn, Cornell University Press 2013). For discussion see Miia Halme-Tuomisaari and Pamela Slotte, 'Revisiting the Origins of Human Rights: Introduction' in Miia Halme-Tuomisaari and Pamela Slotte (eds), *Revisiting the Origins of Human Rights* (CUP 2015) 1.

drafting of the UDHR as this narrative might suggest,[19] the orthodox account remains that human rights emerged in the mid-twentieth century as a language of hope outside politics. A similar reading is also detectable in Samuel Moyn's revisionist history.[20] Rising as an apolitical utopian discourse in the 1970s after other emancipatory discourses—nationalism, socialism, etc—have failed,[21] in this reading human rights in international law offer a way of thinking about a better future above politics. They are again a uniting force transcending political division, this nature allowing them to gain traction globally at the height of the Cold War.[22] Accordingly, Moyn and orthodox 'textbook' authors observe human rights internationally as a vehicle for future-focused thinking in the twentieth century, but both see this future-focus as definitively apolitical. Furthermore, the apolitical is read as essential to why human rights gained traction in both the 1940s and 1970s. International human rights law emerges from these histories as compensatory, anchored in hope, but not necessarily defined by an anticipation which leads to action. Human rights in international law do not appear as a vehicle to facilitate political-engagement with utopia.

A second narrative, however, can be detected. This is located in the work of Stefan-Ludwig Hoffmann, who foregrounds the significance of the 1990s.[23] For Hoffmann, human rights increased in dominance in this period not because they offered an apolitical utopia, nor indeed any utopian impetus at all, but because they facilitated a focus *on the present*. He reads international human rights law as growing with force in the 1990s as a distinctively anti-utopian concept within a changing modern conception of time.[24] This leads human suffering to be engaged in the context of 'an emergency imaginary in the here and now, which suspends historical time',[25] contesting the utopian focus of previous political narratives. In place of utopianism, the present forms the predominant horizon of expectation.[26] In addition to eschewing a focus on the future, this account also contests international human rights as apolitical. Instead, Hoffmann observes human rights being invoked in the 1990s to legitimate humanitarian and military interventions, acting 'as a hegemonic technique of international politics that presented particular interests as universal'.[27] Human rights, therefore, are not a vehicle above politics, but very much a discourse of use for political ends in the present, albeit these were ends which reinforced rather than challenged existing power structures. This relationship to the present and the political is essential to the rise of human rights internationally in Hoffmann's view.

These historical accounts provide two contrasting perspectives. The first observes human rights internationally as future-focused but apolitical; the second understands this area of law as firmly political in nature but foregrounds the present. In neither do human rights

[19] Johannes Morsink, *The Universal Declaration of Human Rights: Origins, Drafting and Intent* (University of Pennsylvania Press 1999); Susan Waltz, 'Reclaiming and Rebuilding the History of the Universal Declaration of Human Rights' (2002) 23 Third World Quarterly 437.

[20] Samuel Moyn, *The Last Utopia: Human Rights in History* (Harvard University Press 2010).

[21] ibid 1–10.

[22] Albeit Moyn urges for a more political utopia for human rights today: Samuel Moyn, *Human Rights and the Uses of History* (Verso 2017).

[23] Stefan-Ludwig Hoffmann, 'Human Rights and History' (2016) 232 Past & Present 279, 282.

[24] Here Hoffmann is drawing from the work of Reinhart Koselleck: Reinhart Koselleck, *Critique and Crisis: Enlightenment and the Pathogenesis of Modern Society* (Harvard University Press 1988).

[25] Hoffmann (n 37) 303.

[26] ibid 304.

[27] Stefan-Ludwig Hoffmann, 'Introduction: Genealogies of Human Rights' in Stefan-Ludwig Hoffmann (ed), *Human Rights in the Twentieth Century* (CUP 2011) 1, 2.

come into view as vehicles for daydreaming which combine a future-focus with a political engagement. There is, however, a third reading that can be brought into view. This emerges from work focused on the 1960s–1970s which highlights the role of states from the Global South in mainstream human rights debate during this time. Steven Jensen, advancing yet another breakthrough narrative, re-prioritises the influence of these states in the 1960s.[28] Jensen reads Southern states as reviving the human rights project internationally, renewing emphasis on universality, and drawing attention to issues of race and religious intolerance. Here a different understanding of the futural and the political is clear. States from the Global South used human rights in the context of decolonisation to imagine and enact new everyday futures and constitutional orders. This movement fed back to the United Nations and stimulated developments such as the 1965 International Covenant on the Elimination of Racial Discrimination and the 1968 International Year for Human Rights, the agenda of which was innovatively pioneered by newly independent Jamaica.[29] However, this is where the political, future-focus appears to stop. While states such as Jamaica, the Philippines, Ghana, and Liberia were using human rights domestically and internationally as rights to daydream for a better future, it cannot be said that this impetus was completely successful in translating into the development of international human rights law foundationally. As Jensen documents, the pivotal role of these states soon declined[30] as Western states and their competing agendas quelled the futural vision which anticolonial perspectives had engendered for rights.

Beyond the decolonial politics of the 1960s, states from the Global South pursued an agenda for structural equality in mainstream international human rights fora in the 1970s. Exploring demands for structural equality, including demands for a New International Economic Order (NIEO),[31] in United Nations human rights spaces during this period, Julia Dehm highlights how visions of economic equality were engaged in attempts to redirect the possibilities, objectives, and conceptions of human rights.[32] These visions of alternative futures aimed for nothing less than a transformation of the international landscape, as well as a reimagining of the relationship between the individual, the state, and the international community. This was evident in debates on economic and social rights in the United Nations Commission on Human Rights 1968–1976; in General Assembly Resolution 32/130 of 1977;[33] and in discussion on the right to development throughout the late 1970s. As in the 1960s, however, this collision of the futural and a political focus in interventions from the Global South was not fully successful in shaping the long-term, mainstream development of human rights. With the changing political and economic climate of the early 1980s, this challenge soon became what Dehm terms a 'failed agenda'.[34] As the new decade

[28] Steven Jensen, *The Making of International Human Rights: The 1960s, Decolonization, and the Reconstruction of Global Values* (CUP 2016). Here Jensen is building on earlier work including Roland Burke, *Decolonization and the Evolution of International Human Rights* (University of Pennsylvania Press 2010).

[29] ibid 102–37, 69–101.

[30] ibid 277.

[31] See Nils Gilman, 'The New International Economic Order: A Reintroduction' (2015) 6 Humanity 1.

[32] Julia Dehm, 'Highlighting Inequalities in the Histories of Human Rights: Contestations Over Justice, Needs and Rights in the 1970s' (2018) 31 Leiden Journal of International Law 871. For additional discussion see Roland Burke, 'Competing for the Last Utopia? The NIEO, Human Rights, and the World Conference for the International Women's Year, Mexico City, June 1975' (2015) 6 Humanity 47.

[33] 'Alternative Approaches and Ways and Means within the United Nations System for Improving the Effective Enjoyment of Human Rights and Fundamental Freedoms' UNGA Res 32/120 (16 December 1977) UN Doc. A/RES/32/130.

[34] Dehm (n 46) 893.

continued, visions of human rights compatible with structural adjustment, as opposed to transformation, prevailed.[35]

The above activities in the 1960s and 1970s can be understood as examples of international human rights being engaged as rights to daydream, to imagine and facilitate a new, better future for humanity in a way that is grounded in collective hope. That they were not successful is due to a range of factors. These include the balance of power in the global political landscape, and the ability of Western states to reclaim the remit of human rights from what US Ambassador to the United Nations, Daniel P Moynihan described in 1975 as, 'something ominously close to looting' by Southern states.[36] Had the political environment both inside and outside the United Nations differed during this period to favour the direction of discourse initiated by the Global South, human rights internationally might have been shaped in an alternative way. While this may appear an unlikely outcome, the above analysis suggests that the traction Southern states achieved was at times not negligible. This might have extended further had dominant interests and prevailing modes of thinking during these decades not resisted this approach to human rights in favour of less radical models. This offers a useful launching pad to ask questions about the development of this area of law and its contingency. What would the consequences have been if international human rights law did develop from this period in a manner that was compatible with daydreaming? What if a future-focus anticipating the 'not yet' and an understanding of the political had successfully collided in international human rights law's mainstream development? Such would have shaped this law as one that was futural in its vision and attentive to the value of everyday, politically-engaged activity or dialogue to enact new futures. In the following section I investigate this counterfactual possibility.

IV. The future and the political thought otherwise in international human rights law

There are, of course, myriad consequences which might conceivably have followed international human rights being thought otherwise in the manner outlined above in the mid-to-late-century period. It is impossible to fully predict or capture all of these, but imperative to begin to explore them. Here I consider just three possibilities which signal towards the alternative trajectory international human rights law may have been set on, had the work of states from the Global South facilitated this different approach to human rights. These pertain to the use of this area of law by grassroots social movements; development of its institutional processes and structures; and its compatibility with neoliberalism. Collectively, these changes reveal the significance that thinking international human rights law as a discourse for daydreaming could have had.

[35] ibid 892–95.

[36] Daniel P Moynihan, 'The United States in Opposition' (1975) 59 Commentary 31. See also Dehm (n 46) 891–92 and Jensen (n 42) 275–82.

1. International human rights law and grassroots social movements

Beginning with the connection between this area of law and grassroots social movements, this relationship may have taken an alternative direction which would shape both international human rights law and grassroots practices worldwide. Twentieth-century human rights activity has been documented to take place in four waves.[37] Firstly, the 1940s period led by actors such as Eleanor Roosevelt shaping the early United Nations system. Secondly, the 1950s–1960s defined by the activity of anticolonialism. Thirdly, the 1970s driven by international non-governmental organisations (NGOs) interested in civil and political rights. Finally, the late 1980s–1990s which saw an explosion of wider NGOs and localised human rights activity. With the exception of anticolonial movements which, as above, have recently found an important place in international human rights history, the mid-to-late period of the twentieth century did not witness a strong connection between grassroots social movements and this area of law. A range of movements taking place at this time—including anti-apartheid activity, peace work, and women's liberation—are frequently not understood as 'human rights movements'.[38] One reason for this is entrenched views of what such movements looked like applied in retrospect after Western NGOs like Amnesty International had become closely associated with this term. An additional reason for grassroots social movements not being categorised as human rights movements during the mid-to-late-century point, however, is that often, and by their own definition, they in fact were not.

One example of this is the women's liberation movement of the 1960s–1970s in its Euro-American form.[39] While campaigning on issues protected by international human rights law since its inception—rights to non-discrimination; to be free from torture, cruel and degrading treatment; to health; to work, etc—grassroots women's liberation activity in Western states did not draw on rights language or provisions in a substantive way.[40] This work certainly did much to place discrimination on the basis of sex on the international human rights agenda in the 1970s—evidenced in creation of the Convention on the Elimination of All Forms of Discrimination Against Women in 1979—but it was not until the 1990s that local women's movements would use the language of international human rights with force.[41] As with the earlier civil rights movement,[42] grassroots activity on women's equality fed back into the shaping of international human rights law to a greater extent than it was shaped by such norms. Movements like Euro-American women's liberation were, undoubtedly, examples of concrete utopia, interested in translating dreams for a more egalitarian future into political action. It appears, however, that documents such as

[37] Kenneth Cmiel, 'The Recent History of Human Rights' (2004) 109 The American Historical Review 117, 126–35, with the addition of stage two following the work of scholars such as Burke (n 42).

[38] Joseph Slaughter, 'Hijacking Human Rights: Neoliberalism, the New Historiography, and the End of the Third World' (2018) 40 Human Rights Quarterly 735, 745–51.

[39] See Jan Bradshaw (ed), *The Women's Liberation Movement: Europe and North American* (Pergamon Press 1982). By virtue of connection to decolonisation and anti-imperialist activity, the women's liberation movement in the Global South had a different connection to human rights ideas: Elisabeth Armstrong, 'Before Banbung: The Anti-Imperialist Women's Movement in Asia and the Women's International Democratic Federation' (2016) 41 Signs 305.

[40] This is not to say, of course, that human rights had no part, but it was not the central stimulant or language of mobilisation. See Jo Freeman, 'The Origins of the Women's Liberation Movement' (1973) 78 American Journal of Sociology 792.

[41] Julie Peters and Andrea Wolper (eds), *Women's Rights, Human Rights: International Feminist Perspectives* (Routledge 1995).

[42] Jensen (n 42) 114–17.

the UDHR and the later International Covenants were not comprehended as immediately compatible with these dreams in the 1960s–1970s. At this point, human rights at the international level did not offer appealing or visible enough tools for such activity. Had this area of law developed differently to offer potential for collective daydreaming, this might not have been the case.

Embedding the future and the political at the heart of international human rights law in the 1960s–1970s period would have facilitated new ways for grassroots social movements to connect with the norms enshrined within it. Opening up the future-focus of this law—eschewing a dominant connection to Western, elite-defined utopias—would have allowed the better future which international human rights support to become democratised. This would have permitted more people and movements to dream via such rights, as the provisions of this area of law spoke to a wider range of hopes about the future. Similarly, foregrounding the political—and doing so beyond a focus on the agendas of Western states—would have allowed the dreams international human rights law connected with to better translate into political activity using the language of rights. With this change in relationship to the future and the political, a different awareness of this area of law and what it was about may have followed. Resultantly, an enhanced breadth of actors, such as the women's liberation movement, might have found purchase in international human rights law for daydreaming and have drawn upon it in their political engagements. Rights for daydreaming would be open to a wide range of dreams, to a variety of 'not yets' beyond the visions of the elite and those traditionally powerful within formal fora.

In addition to consequences for grassroots social movements, the change above would also have had consequences for how the politico-legal activity attached to this area of law was understood in this period and beyond. A very different interpretation of the term 'human rights movement' would have come into being with significant impacts for the global political landscape throughout the twentieth century. Amnesty International, Human Rights Watch, and other Western NGOs may not subsequently have taken centre stage as the flagships of human rights activity. Rather, a broader set of movements and actors might have been interpreted as also carrying out central international human rights work and come to define what it means to 'do' such work. As a result of this redefinition of the term 'human rights movement', international human rights could have developed a stronger connection to grassroots peace work, feminism, and similar emancipatory activities which did not find resources in such law until much later.

2. International human rights law structures and processes

The second consequence of rethinking international human rights law's connection to the futural and the political pertains to the institutional structures and processes of this legal system. The international human rights system developed in a distinctive manner throughout the twentieth century. Firstly, this was state-centric and elite-driven. Regardless of the connection between localised human rights activity and formal human rights institutions,[43] in its everyday operation, international human rights law became led by experts

[43] Sikkink (n 5) 232–35.

and focused on monitoring and implementing human rights in a state-centric way. Despite widespread efforts towards vernacularisation connecting the local and the global,[44] the international human rights system evolved quite detached from everyday people and the micro-activity of enacting the dreams of such people. Alongside this, secondly, focus in these structures and processes came to be placed on generation of consensus between actors in the system, and a desire to solve the problems of the past in the present through this consensus. This has led authors such as Jack Donnelly to characterise international human rights as representing an overlapping 'international political consensus'.[45] As a result, space for dissensus and the productive potential this can bring,[46] especially in thinking about and discussing the future, was limited.[47] These structural characteristics define many United Nations human rights fora, structures and bodies. They are not, at a foundational level, best designed to facilitate localised, everyday dreaming about future horizons.

If international human rights law had successfully been thought as compatible with daydreaming in the 1960s–1970s, its structures and processes may have evolved differently. These would be, responding to the first concern above, driven from the bottom-up as opposed to the top-down. This may have facilitated a revised conception of the role that states play in this system, a rethinking of the significance and use of experts, and a more accessible and dedicated set of channels for communication between the local and the global which meaningfully integrate everyday people. Addressing the second concern, it might have also involved designing structures and processes which better valued and encouraged political dissensus and which had the potential to embrace a variety of visions about the future, debating them from the ground up in an ongoing way.

One area likely to have been greatly altered by such a change is the treaty monitoring body system. Established in 1966 based on the importance of expert oversight, and regular reporting for states,[48] shortcomings soon appeared in this system. These included the ability of states to circumvent, manipulate, or evade scrutiny; the role of states in electing experts; lengthy delays and backlogs in the system; the deferential approach experts often take to states; and the lack of effective follow-up.[49] An additional limitation was the originally restricted role for NGOs in treaty body processes.[50] If thought as rights for daydreaming, NGOs, individuals and wider human rights movements would have driven these processes from the outset. This might have taken the form of additional voices in deliberation on state records, or expanding the idea of who is a human rights 'expert'. Changes could also have been made to ensure the work of treaty monitoring bodies was more accessible to the local level, including consideration of where monitoring processes take place geographically and better integration of local actors in follow-up activities. Focusing on the political to a greater

[44] Sally Engle Merry, 'Transnational Human Rights and Local Activism: Mapping the Middle' (2006) 108 American Anthropologist 38; Sally Engle Merry and Peggy Levitt, 'The Vernacularization of Women's Human Rights' in Stephen Hopgood, Jack Snyder, and Leslie Vinjamuri (eds), *Human Rights Futures* (CUP 2017) 213.

[45] Donnelly (n 32) 57–60.

[46] Jacques Rancière, *Dissensus: On Politics and Aesthetics* (Steven Corcoran tr, Continuum 2010).

[47] For wider discussion on this point, see Kathryn McNeilly, *Human Rights and Radical Social Transformation: Futurity, Alterity, Power* (Routledge 2017) 76–95.

[48] James Crawford, 'The UN Human Rights Treaty System: A System in Crisis?' in Philip Alston and James Crawford (eds), *The Future of UN Human Rights Treaty Monitoring* (CUP 2000) 1.

[49] Anne Bayefsky, 'Making the Human Rights Treaties Work' in Louis Henkin and John Lawrence Hargrove (eds), *Human Rights: An Agenda for the Next Century* (The American Society of International Law 1994) 229.

[50] The role of NGOs in these processes has subsequently been enhanced: Andrew Clapham, 'UN Human Rights Reporting Procedures: An NGO Perspective' in Alston and Crawford (eds) (n 63) 175.

extent in the development of the treaty body system would also have revised the differential approach taken in much state examination. Enhancing participation from a wider range of actors interested in making alternative futures via human rights would facilitate debate and dissensus which is unafraid of alienating states parties, one element which greatly impedes the system's effectiveness.[51] Through these changes, treaty body work might have been rendered more accessible, participatory, integrating a bottom-up approach and a meaningful commitment to agonistic dialogue.[52]

Such changes are not exclusive to the treaty monitoring body system. All areas from the creation of rights provisions to their implementation may have been affected, shaping processes to better focus on local people, contest, and agonism rather than documentation, consensus, and top-down legalistic problem solving. United Nations fora as a result would have been developed better as spaces for daydreaming together, in true diversity and collectivity, rather than sites for elite exchanges driven largely by states. Rights for daydreaming cannot be understood as underpinned by processes which operate in a top-down manner and which stress consensus. Beyond the treaty monitoring body system, alternative arrangements might also have been imagined for Charter bodies such as the later Human Rights Council and for mechanisms like the Special Rapporteur system and the Universal Periodic Review. In these processes states would not be understood as the primary directors of this area of law, but equal partners with local actors, everyday people and their visions of the future.

3. International human rights law and neoliberalism

The third consequence of successfully thinking this law otherwise relates to the relationship between human rights internationally and neoliberalism in the twentieth century, and into the twenty-first. This relationship is somewhat contentious. A number of views have been advanced on the form it has taken, focusing on the 1970s–1980s period. For Naomi Klein, international human rights as advanced by organisations such as Amnesty International during this time did not effectively investigate the link between oppression, terror, widespread inequality, and neoliberalism.[53] Accordingly, international human rights became complicit in the increasing dominance of Chicago School ideas. Challenging Klein's theory, however, Samuel Moyn observes a different relationship between human rights in international law and neoliberalism. For Moyn, 'the trouble was not so much that human rights obscured a necessary structural politics as that ... they stigmatized only the shame of material insufficiency while turning a blind eye to galloping material inequality'.[54] Whichever way we approach this relationship—one of abetting as per Klein, or one of inadequacy as per

[51] Scott Leckie, 'The Committee on Economic, Social and Cultural Rights: Catalyst for Change in a System Needing Reform' in Alston and Crawford (eds) (n 63) 131.

[52] For wider discussion of the value of agonism in human rights processes, see Kathryn McNeilly, 'After the Critique of Rights: For a Radical Democratic Theory and Practice of Human Rights' (2016) 27 Law and Critique 269.

[53] Naomi Klein, *The Shock Doctrine: The Rise of Disaster Capitalism* (Allen Lane 2007) 119–28. Klein's approach is further developed by Susan Marks, 'Four Human Rights Myths' in David Kinley, Wojciech Sadurski, and Kevin Walton (eds), *Human Rights: Old Problems, New Possibilities* (Edward Elgar 2013) 217.

[54] Samuel Moyn, *Not Enough: Human Rights in an Unequal World* (Harvard University Press 2018) 176. See also Antony Anghie, 'Legal Aspects of the New International Economic Order' (2015) 6 Humanity 145.

Moyn—dominant understandings of international human rights law in the 1970s–1980s placed a focus on an individualism which was compatible with neoliberalism.[55] Human rights violations were thought in terms of individuals, often in relation to physical integrity or status equality, with an accompanying privatisation of response.[56] The result was a developing international human rights discourse which prohibited focus on collective engagement and redistribution, both of power and of material resources. This individualism was assisted by a lack of focus on the futural and the political in rights which did not encourage daydreaming of a collective, better future beyond the present.

Yet, it was not inevitable that human rights internationally would develop in such a way and enter the twenty-first century with a question mark over their status as a language of resistant and emancipatory hope. This legal system could have embarked on a track which allowed it to be understood as a flexible and renewing tool to meaningfully challenge neoliberal trends. Had international human rights law developed in a manner which facilitated daydreaming in the 1960s–1970s, its relationship to neoliberalism may have taken a different direction. As a vehicle to imagine and enact a better future together—foregrounding the social nature of daydreaming—international human rights law would have been significantly less compatible with a focus on the individual and the possessive, bounded subject. Instead, these rights would have been tied to thinking meaningfully about collectivity and redistribution of resources, as per the agenda states from the Global South initiated. Their focus would firmly have been on a better future for all and challenge to existing relations of power which prohibit such. Responding to Klein's analysis, international human rights law would not have shied away from asking structural 'why' questions about rights violations, and would have been a resource to help pursue these deeper questions of power in the present and future for world-improvement. Similarly, responding to Moyn's approach, this area of law would not have contained its daydreaming to sufficiency alone, but would be compatible with dreams of material equality and redistribution. As a result of these changes, human rights and neoliberalism may have ceased to enjoy so much in common. The underpinning fabric of this international legal system would have contrasted more sharply with neoliberal impulses in the early 1980s.

This change, while influencing the impetus of human rights in international law in the late twentieth century, may also have had longer-term implications for the utility and relevance of its norms today. It is not an exaggeration to say that in the twenty-first-century human rights have been experiencing a period of crisis. A range of voices argue that the age of human rights is over, that there is little to gain from continuing engagement with human rights domestically or internationally.[57] One reason for this is the inability of these rights to speak back to continuing neoliberal relations of power and the global economic crises which have accompanied the opening decades of the new century. This was not inevitable. As tools to imagine a better future, to embrace our ontological status as 'not yet', and to stimulate dreams of hope which are characteristic of a vibrant human existence, international human rights law might have been better equipped to speak back to today's global context. It could have evolved with an inherent ability to imagine futures beyond

[55] Mary Nolan, 'Human Rights and Market Fundamentalism', Max Weber Lecture Series (European University Institute 2014) 2.

[56] Slaughter (n 52) 768.

[57] These authors include Hopgood (n 3), Kennedy (n 3), and Eric Posner, *The Twilight of Human Rights Law* (OUP 2014).

neoliberalism, an ability which could be returned to and engaged collectively in the new contexts of the twenty-first century.

The three consequences for international human rights law outlined above—a different connection to grassroots social movements; institutional processes and structures driven by alternative principles; and a less compatible relationship with neoliberalism—are of course speculative and suggestive. This reflects the nature of counterfactual exploration more generally.[58] They are, however, highly significant. The changes they gesture towards are wide-reaching, spanning across international human rights politics and law-making, popular as well as elite understandings and usages of rights. They envisage deep changes to the international human rights system and its everyday activity as we know it. Overall, an altered relationship to the futural and the political would have rendered this area of law more likely to be a channel for utopian dreaming, moving beyond the abstract, fantastic, and the compensatory to facilitate change in new ways. While such a counterfactual suggestion does require the deployment of imagination, its coming into being was not beyond the realms of possibility in the 1960s–1970s. The successful and widespread establishment of such a relationship in mainstream human rights discourse, stimulated by the activity of states from the Global South, remains one of the most significant 'what ifs' for international human rights law and its history.

V. Conclusion

Counterfactual exploration is a powerful tool that can be deployed to explore the development of international human rights law across its history. This chapter has sought to explore just one way in which this area of law might have been otherwise. The idea of daydreaming which it has employed can be engaged to stimulate a striking picture of human existence and society. This picture is one where hope is at the centre, taking a variety of forms which might range from the daydreams of an individual lost in thought to broader future visions of living and being together. Fundamentally, we can see hope as emerging through people's ability to dream, and to understand society as driven by such dreaming in multiple forms, individual and collective in nature. The impulse facilitated through the diverse forms of dreaming considered in this way is politically realistic, and capable of enacting the better futures which it is based upon. While daydreaming, on first glance, appears to have little in common with international human rights law, a closer analysis stimulates alternative insights and connections which can be considered, in particular regarding the history of this area of law. Human rights hold potential to be one location in society where daydreaming takes place, connecting to the hope which this area of law was founded on from its beginnings.

Rather than a purely speculative possibility, history does demonstrate a period in the twentieth century when mainstream international human rights law might have evolved as rights to daydream together. The diverse work of states from the Global South in the 1960s–1970s period reveals a unique moment where the future and the political did collide at the United Nations, albeit not for long. This collision might have taken hold had wider political contexts, relations of power, and the responses of Western states within the United Nations

[58] Ingo Venzke, 'What if? Counterfactual (Hi)Stories of International Law' (2018) 8(2) Asian Journal of International Law 403, 420.

differed. Thinking this lost opportunity today offers scholars and human rights actors food for thought. What daydreaming brings to reflection on this moment in international human rights law's history is a way to think otherwise about the hope that forms its central impetus. As an international discourse, human rights have always had the potential to foreground for us the unfinished nature of living and being, the 'not yet' of society, and the role of human actors and institutions in this. As norms laying the foundations for our relations with one another, with the state, and the goods we want to achieve in society, human rights can be understood as focused on dreaming from their beginning. Construction of an alternative future-facing foundation for international human rights law in the twentieth may have rendered this discourse another site in society where daydreaming for better futures could have been stimulated in alternative ways. While not exhaustive, the exploration above provides a sense of what international human rights law might have become as rights to daydream. This counterfactual investigation may hold a critical mirror up to this area of law today. Dreaming is central to our humanity, a capacity that must not be obscured or diminished. The question that remains is how international human rights law might re-emerge as one way to daydream together and affirm our humanity. In exploring this question, the counterfactutual can offer positive and productive possibilities for the present, how we think about and approach international human rights law today.

17

Who Turned Multinational Corporations into Bearers of Human Rights?

On the Creation of Corporate 'Human' Rights in International Law

*Silvia Steininger and Jochen von Bernstorff**

I. Introduction

Corporations are people, my friend! The infamous shouting match between Mitt Romney and a crowd of critics on the Iowa campaign trial quickly became a social media hit. Not surprisingly, his competitor Barack Obama was quick to rebut, 'Corporations aren't people. People are people!' While this particular debate took place in a specific historical context—the 2012 US presidential campaign and the aftermath of the *Citizens United* Supreme Court decision from 2010[1]—Romney's blunt statement still resonates in many public and academic circles: Should corporations enjoy 'human' rights similar to natural persons?

This contribution analyses the recognition and transformation of the idea of legal persons as rights holders from a rather isolated and restricted phenomenon in some domestic contexts, into a broader and fully-fledged recognition of corporations as human rights bearers in international law. The protection of corporations by international human rights law is rarely discussed among international lawyers.[2] It is heavily overshadowed by the parallel ongoing discourse on potential human rights obligations of corporations.[3] Hence, by analysing the historical junctures at which the arguably unlikely recognition of corporations as

* For helpful comments and remarks on earlier drafts, we are indebted to Kanad Bagchi, Isabel Feichtner, Matthias Goldmann, Kathryn Greenman, Kevin Jon Heller, Tom Sparks, Robert Stendel, Ingo Venzke, and the participants of the conference 'Contingency in the Course of International Law' at the University of Amsterdam (14–16 June 2018). Many thanks to Peter Pàzmàny for research assistance and to Bianca Dillon for editorial work.

[1] For an overview, see eg James G Wright III, 'A Step Too Far: Recent Trends in Corporate Personhood and the Overexpansion of Corporate Rights' (2016) 49 The John Marshall Law Review 889.

[2] For important critical accounts, see José E Alvarez, 'Are Corporations "Subjects" of International Law?' (2011) 9 Santa Clara Journal of International Law 1; Anna Grear, 'Challenging Corporate Humanity: Legal Disembodiment, Embodiment and Human Rights' (2007) 7 Human Rights Law Review 511; Turkuler Isiksel, 'The Rights of Man and the Rights of the Man-Made: Corporations and Human Rights' (2016) 38 Human Rights Quarterly 294; Julian G Ku, 'The Limits of Corporate Rights Under International Law' (2012) 12 Chicago Journal of International Law 729 See also generally, Grietje Baars, *The Corporation, Law and Capitalism. A Radical Perspective on the Role of Law in the Global Political Economy* (Brill 2019); David Ciepley, 'Beyond Public and Private: Toward a Political Theory of the Corporation' (2013) 107 American Political Science Review 139; Sundhya Pahuja, 'The Changing Place of Corporation in International Law' (2018) Hersch Lauterpacht Memorial Lecture <www.sms.cam.ac.uk/media/2696888≥ accessed 11 September 2019.

[3] See also Michelle Staggs Kelsall, '"Poisonous Flowers on the Dust-heap of a Dying Capitalism": The United Nations Code of Conduct on Transnational Corporations, Contingency and Failure in International Law' in this volume.

Silvia Steininger and Jochen von Bernstorff, *Who Turned Multinational Corporations into Bearers of Human Rights?* In: *Contingency in International Law.* Edited by: Ingo Venzke and Kevin Jon Heller, Oxford University Press. © The Several Contributors 2021.
DOI: 10.1093/oso/9780192898036.003.0017

rights bearers was advanced and cemented, we attempt to re-describe this highly problematic transformation of human rights into rights of multinational corporations.

Taking the question of historical contingency and counterfactual analysis seriously,[4] we intend to portray these historical developments in a non-determinist fashion, even if it seems to follow the general post 1970s neoliberal trend in international law to cement the rights of multinational corporations against international and domestic re-regulation.[5] We intend to analyse the interplay between events and discursive structures that led to the creation of corporate human rights in international law. International legal history inevitably must be a history of the interaction between legal and other societal structures, if it is not to be entirely submerged within a history of international relations.[6] Legal discourse as such is also a structural phenomenon. It constantly operates with specific semantic structures, which may be newly created or transformed by a specific historical event. At the same time, legal structures are also equipped by contemporaries with a claim to validity beyond that particular event. Such legal structures can also migrate to other fields of law or over time, often resurfacing in new contexts. 'Events' with an effect on legal discourse thus often reveal underlying societal (economic) structures, and may stabilise them or add to their transformation.[7] If events produce a significant impact on societal structures, they can be also called 'critical junctures'.[8] As to the issue of contingency, which is intricately connected with historical power relations, we thus have to look into the interplay between such historical events and societal structures. Contingency in that sense is an interstitial phenomenon. International law plays an ambivalent role here—it can help to stabilise power relations over time precisely through its own indeterminacy, allowing hegemonic forces to determine its meaning through the creation of new general norms or incrementally on a case by case basis.[9] But while international law can be used to sustain hegemony, the indeterminacy and revocability of its norms always also includes the possibility of contestation of entrenched structural conditions. Our research can perhaps demonstrate that by looking at the role of

[4] In this question, we follow Ingo Venzke, 'What if? Counterfactual (Hi)Stories of International Law' (2018) Asian Journal of International Law 403. According to Venzke, '[s]aying that international law is contingent does not mean that it could have taken any shape with equal probability. It rather means that the shape in which we find international law today was one possibility among others'. ibid 404. On the challenges for an analysis of historical contingency, see also Ingo Venzke, 'Possibilities of the Past: Histories of the NIEO and the Travails of Critique' (2018) 20 Journal of the History of International Law 263.

[5] See also Sundhya Pahuja and Anna Saunders, 'Rival Worlds and the Place of the Corporation in International Law' in Philipp Dann and Jochen von Bernstorff (eds), *The Battle for International Law: South-North Perspectives on the Decolonization Era* (OUP 2019).

[6] A point inspired by Koselleck's reading of the historical relevance of events and structures, see for its significance for international legal history Jochen von Bernstorff, 'International Legal History and its Methodologies: How (Not) to Tell the Story of the Many Lives and Deaths of the *ius ad bellum*' in Andreas von Arnauld (ed), *Völkerrechtsgeschichte(n). Historische Narrative und Konzepte im Wandel* (Duncker & Humblot 2017).

[7] For the significance of events in international law, see also Fleur Johns, Richard Joyce, and Sundhya Pahuja (eds), *Events: The Force of International Law* (Routledge 2011).

[8] The concept of critical junctures is being used in historical institutionalist theories in the field of comparative politics, see Seymour Martin Lipset and Stein Rokkan, 'Cleavage Structures, Party Systems, and Voter Alignments: An Introduction' in Seymour Martin Lipset and Stein Rokkan (eds), *Party Systems and Voter Alignments Cross-National Perspectives* (Free Press 1967); Ruth Berins Collier and David Collier, *Shaping the Political Agenda. Critical Junctures, the Labor Movement, and Regime Dynamics in Latin America* (Princeton University Press 1991). In short, 'a critical juncture is a relatively short period in time during which an event or set of events occurs that has a large and enduring subsequent impact', see James Mahoney, Khairunnisa Mohamedali, and Christoph Nguyen, 'Causality and Time in Historical Institutionalism' in Orfeo Fioretos, Tulia G Falleti, and Adam Sheingate (eds), *The Oxford Handbook of Historical Institutionalism* (OUP 2016) 71.

[9] Martti Koskenniemi, *From Apology to Utopia* (CUP 2005) Epilogue.

law in the interplay between historical events and underlying structures, the 'contingency' question can be productively posed.

So while the creation of corporate human rights seems to follow the general post-1970s neoliberal trend in international law to cement the rights of multinational corporations against international and domestic re-regulation, it can arguably be traced back to three critical historical junctures post 1945: the momentum of treaty-making in the late 1940s, the momentum of human rights adjudication in the 1980s, and the momentum of investment arbitration in the 2000s. In light of the overarching theme of this edited volume, we will also identify alternative visions to the three historical critical junctures, during which varying legal, political, economic, and social forces were at work.

II. Corporations as right holders

Throughout the last five decades, the highly contested and by no means obvious recognition of corporations as independent right holders has become a salient discursive element in two areas of international law; international human rights law and international investment law.

International investment law is long considered one of the most corporate-friendly fields of international law. Since investment law's early origin in the law of diplomatic protection in the middle of the nineteenth century, treaties of friendship, commerce and navigation have endowed individuals and private companies with procedural rights, such as the right to bring claims against sovereigns.[10] Naturally, the law of diplomatic protection required that it was a state party who needs to take action in the name of the corporation vis-à-vis another state party. This only changed over a century later when modern international investment law emerged, which empowered investors to directly access international arbitration.[11] The growing influence of international corporations coupled with the rise of investor-state arbitration transformed the legal nature of investors. They morphed from agents or beneficiaries of investment protection to independent right holders.[12] By reference to human (and consular) rights, they strategically portrayed themselves as holders of human rights and engaged in rights language in the defence of particular economic interests.[13] Some scholars argue that corporations even started to act as law-makers in international investment law.[14]

In international human rights instruments, the picture is more complex. Neither the Universal Declaration of Human Rights (UDHR) nor the two UN Covenants explicitly include corporate rights in their rights catalogues. However, the European Convention

10 See Ku (n 2) 739, citing in particular the Diplomacy Convention of 1853 Between Great Britain and the United States <http://avalon.law.yale.edu/19th_century/br1853.asp≥ accessed 11 September 2019. The law of diplomatic protection also played an important role for the establishment of human rights law, see Annemarieke Vermeer-Künzli, 'Diplomatic Protection as a Source of Human Rights Law' in Dinah Shelton (ed), *The Oxford Handbook of International Human Rights Law* (OUP 2013).

11 For the relationship between diplomatic protection and investment law, see Ben Juratowitch, 'The Relationship between Diplomatic Protection and Investment Treaties' (2008) 23 ICSID Review 10.

12 For the debate between direct versus derivate rights of foreign investors under international investment law, see also Zachary Douglas 'The Hybrid Foundations of Investment Treaty Arbitration' (2004) 74 British Yearbook of International Law 151.

13 Martins Paparinskis, 'Investment Treaty Arbitration and the (New) Law of State Responsibility' (2013) 24 EJIL 617.

14 See Julian Arato, 'Corporations as Lawmakers' (2015) 56 Harvard International Law Journal 229; Vaughan Lowe, 'Corporations as International Actors and International Law Makers' (2004) 14 Italian Yearbook of International Law 23.

on Human Rights (ECHR) has granted legal persons the right to property under the First Additional Protocol and also, in Article 34, opened up the right to petition to non-governmental organisations. There is only limited data on how frequently corporations claim these rights before the European Court of Human Rights (ECtHR). A 2006 empirical study identified that in the five-year period from 1998 to 2003 approximately 3.8% of the ECtHR's judgments were brought by companies or by people clearly pursuing corporate interests.[15] Most corporate actors claimed violations of due process guarantees and the right to property. However, in contrast to the European system, the Inter-American Court of Human Rights (IACtHR) has recently denied that corporations can hold rights under the American Convention on Human Rights. According to advisory opinion OC 22/16, only organisations of indigenous people and labour unions, when acting in the interest of citizens, can pursue judicial action; corporations cannot take recourse to the inter-American human rights system.[16] Yet, even when corporations are not explicitly mentioned in human rights treaties as right-bearers, in the last decades, scholarship and practice has started to recognise transnational corporations as holders of human rights, eg by broadly defining the term 'everybody' in these instruments.[17]

This trend in both human rights and investment law to endow corporations with human rights seems to mirror Marx's[18] reading of human rights in 'Zur Judenfrage'.[19] Specifically, Marx considers rights claims as rights of isolated individuals, who defend their property and subjective spheres of economic freedom against collective and redistributive projects. For Marx, rights are necessarily limited by 'the economic structure of society and its cultural development conditioned thereby'.[20] An entrenched notion of corporations as rights holders, which not only helps to balance the social rights of individuals affected by abusive corporate practices out of existence but also shields subjective spheres of economic activity against collective redistribution or communitarian projects, seems to confirm the Marxian claim, that this is what liberal human rights are all about—cementing existing power relations in a capitalist system.[21] Internationalised corporate 'human rights' can thus be seen to epitomise this assumed structural liaison between liberal capitalism and rights claims. Yet by showing that the creation of internationalised corporate 'human rights' was a contingent, recent, and in many ways unforeseeable development—as such dependent on various

[15] Marius Emberland, *The Human Rights of Companies. Exploring the Structure of ECHR Protection* (OUP 2006) 13f.

[16] Advisory Opinion OC-22/16 (IACtHR, 26 February 2016). For a more corporate/shareholder-friendly judgment of the IACtHR, see *Cantos v Argentina* (IACtHR, 28 November 2002).

[17] Lucien J Dhooge, 'Human Rights for Transnational Corporations' (2007) 16 Journal of Transnational Law and Policy 197.

[18] For a Marxist perspective on historical contingency, see also Umut Özsu, 'The Necessity of Contingency: Method and Marxism in International Law', in this volume.

[19] Karl Marx, 'On the Jewish Question (1843) in Robert C. Tucker (ed) *The Marx-Engels Reader* (2nd ed, W. W. Norton 1978) 40–46.

[20] Karl Marx, 'Critique of the Gotha Programme' (1875) ibid, 531.

[21] Upendra Baxi depicted this late twentieth- and early twenty-first-century trend as the rise of a new paradigm of 'trade-related, market-friendly human rights', a development which 'insists upon the promotion and protection of the collective human rights of global capital in ways that "justify" corporate well-being and dignity even when it entails gross and flagrant violation of human rights of actually existing human beings and communities', see Upendra Baxi, The Future of Human Rights (OUP 2002) 132; in recent years, scholars such as Susan Marks, Samuel Moyn, and Slavoj Žižek have engaged in a critical analysis of the relationship between neoliberalism and human rights, cf. Susan Marks, 'Human Rights and Root Causes' (2011) Modern Law Review 57; Samuel Moyn, *Not Enough: Human Rights in an Unequal World* (Harvard University Press 2018); Slavoj Žižek, 'Against Human Rights' (2005) 34 New Left Review 115.

critical historical junctures—we attempt to demonstrate that the 'corporate colonisation of human rights'[22] was and is by no means an inevitable legal development.

III. Historical juncture 1: treaty-making

This section attempts to trace the development of corporate human rights back to its origins in modern human rights law. Next to the UDHR, the most crucial advancements took place in the context of the drafting of the ECHR. As the first treaty to explicitly proclaim a right to property for legal persons, though not per se in the original Convention but in the First Additional Protocol, we will examine the drafting process to carve out the decisive motives and arguments.

For the drafters of the UDHR it went without saying that all rights of the Declaration pertain to natural persons only. The question of granting human rights to legal persons, let alone corporations, was not debated at all. Even during the controversial debate on the right to property, various factions, most importantly the Latin American states led by Chile, emphasised the social function of the right to property. For them including a right to property was supposed to be confined to a subsistence-core of an individual right to property.[23] Consequently, a right to property granted to commercial actors was never intended to be included in the first universal human rights catalogue.

However, the negotiations of the ECHR took place in a different environment. In contrast to the UDHR, the Consultative Assembly for the ECHR aimed at assembling a rights catalogue, which also established a shared ideological foundation for the European project. Hence, the representatives chose an inductive method and only listed rights, which were at present guaranteed on the territory of member states.[24] This inductive method resulted in a list of rights, which covered substantially less ground than the UDHR, but 'was to be a declaration of Western ideology; in a non-derogatory sense therefore its function was propagandist'.[25] During the negotiations, the question of legal persons as general right holders was not raised. However, the Convention did not only aim at defending the Western democratic ideal, but was also supposed to show 'the superiority of the economic and social aspects of a democratic society'[26] in order to successfully contain and exclude communism.[27] In this Cold War geopolitical climate, it is not surprising that corporations played a bigger role in the ECHR negotiations than in the UDHR, which was highlighted in the debate on the right to individual petition and the right to property.

Already in his inaugural speech as rapporteur, Pierre-Henri Teitgen had proposed ten liberties as the core of the rights regime, including the protection against arbitrary confiscation of property. He also requested the Legal Committee to clarify who may appeal to the

[22] Grear (n 2) 513.

[23] William Schabas (ed), *The Universal Declaration of Human Rights: The Travaux Préparatoires* (CUP 2013) vol I, 101.

[24] Council of Europe (ed), *Collected Edition of the 'Travaux Preparatoires' of the European Convention on Human Rights* (Brill 1975) vol I, 158.

[25] AW Brian Simpson, *Human Rights and the End of Empire. Britain and the Genesis of the European Convention* (OUP 2004) 605.

[26] Council of Europe (ed), *Collected Edition of the 'Travaux Preparatoires' of the European Convention on Human Rights* (Brill 1979) vol V, 218.

[27] ibid 298.

envisioned Court when a guaranteed right or liberty had been violated: 'Each one of the Member States? Corporate Bodies? Minorities? Individuals?'[28] The Committee was quick to accept that the right to petition could be exercised by both individuals and collective bodies, as long as they were victims of a violation of the Convention.[29] In order to exercise this procedural right, they therefore had to be bearers of at least one particular material Convention right.

The first historical juncture at which legal persons explicitly entered the stage of human rights instruments took place in the discussion on the right to property in the First Additional Protocol. As is well known, the Additional Protocol not only gave natural persons a right to property but eventually included 'legal persons' in the scope of the provision. The right to property in general was the object of a heated debate, it is no exaggeration to state that it was the most controversially discussed right of the Convention. Representatives differed on what the social function of property entailed.[30] Many representatives linked the social function of the right to property to the development of family life (eg arguing 'It is the function of private property to secure for the father of a family the true independence which he needs to discharge duties assigned to him by the Creator.'[31]). Most socialist and social democratic representatives argued, on the other hand, that in order for the right to property to serve social justice, it must be accompanied by economic, social, and cultural rights such as the right to work or the right to form trade unions. They argued that constituting an explicit right to property without including economic and social rights would mean that 'the whole of our declaration would be grossly distorted and misrepresented'.[32] This lack of balance would alienate ordinary men and women,[33] and thus endanger the future of the Council of Europe. However, those economic and social rights did not have a basis in the constitutional foundations of the state parties, hence, many in this camp favoured cutting the provision altogether.[34] Whether corporations should be included as holders of the right to property was not debated, the main narrative of property holders invoked by supporters of the provision were individuals and their immediate belongings. Yet, it is important to note that several state parties during that time had included a right to property for legal persons in their constitution.

Ultimately, a deadlock between several factions in the Consultative Assembly and the Committee of Ministers occurred. Belgian delegate, social democratic lawyer, and long-time supporter of the Convention project, Henri Rolin was tasked to table a proposal for the right to property to rescue the Convention. In the end, Rolin's proposal succeeded in accommodating those factions that insisted on a right to property as part of the Convention project and those delegates that opposed the inclusion of a right to property. The final draft was also presented as a compromise between the political left and right, as the supporters argued:

[28] Council of Europe (ed), *Collected Edition of the 'Travaux Preparatoires' of the European Convention on Human Rights* (Brill 1975) vol I, 160.
[29] ibid 224.
[30] Council of Europe (ed), *Collected Edition of the 'Travaux Preparatoires' of the European Convention on Human Rights* (Brill 1975) vol II, 104.
[31] Council of Europe (ed), *Collected Edition of the 'Travaux Preparatoires' of the European Convention on Human Rights* (Brill 1979) vol V, 312.
[32] Council of Europe (ed), *Collected Edition of the 'Travaux Preparatoires' of the European Convention on Human Rights* (Brill 1975) vol II, 56.
[33] ibid 80.
[34] ibid 92.

> that the new text went further to meet the socialist position than did that proposed at the first Session. For instance, Mr. Rolin, a leading Belgian socialist, was in fact the author of the Article under discussions. Equally, the text, which had been redrafted 7 times, and had been discussed for a whole year, represented the 'ne plus ultra' of compromise for conservative members of the Assembly. Were it not accepted, certain Members of the Committee said they would oppose the whole Convention as having been 'watered down' to such an extent that it had become useless.[35]

Shifting the provision to an Additional Protocol ensured that it did not officially belong to the core rights and freedoms and was subject to a separate ratification process. At the same time, in order to make this acceptable to the friends of the property provision, Rolin drafted the provision in a particularly encompassing fashion including a right to property for legal persons. In particular, France, Belgium, and Ireland had been adamant supporters of the inclusion of the right to property, while British and Swedish delegates had opposed this initiative.[36]

The British position is particularly interesting as the United Kingdom (UK) being in a weak economic position after the Second World War, was afraid of being sued by its own multinational companies for damages to property caused by operations of the British armed forces during and after the war. One example being the Burmah Oil Company, whose industrial plant in Burma was destroyed by advancing British forces in 1942.[37] Similar arguments were put forth in the context of the right to individual petition. British delegate Will Nally had been an outspoken opponent of a right to individual petition for legal persons, fearing that the British steel industry, which was then in the process of governmental restructuring, could appeal to the Commission and thereby block governmental legislation. It is therefore not surprising that the UK wanted to prevent a right of corporations to bring claims under the Convention until 1965. Almost prophetically, the British concerns regarding the empowerment of corporations anticipated the arguments brought forward fifty years later by critical voices pointing to the state's minimised regulatory power through international investment law.

Could this have turned out differently? Certainly so. The drafting history of both the UDHR and the ECHR reveals that the transfer of human rights guarantees to business actors in international law was disputed, met with considerable resistance, and was never intended to morph into a broad entitlement for corporations. An alternative positioning or framing of the property clause, such as the exclusion of business actors as legal persons seemed also possible. The final result in the case of the Additional Protocol to the ECHR can only be explained as the price that had to be paid by the opponents of the right to property for having rejected the insertion of the right in the main part of Convention. The wording of the initially excluded right in the Additional Protocol now had to accommodate the conservatives, who had threatened to scrap the treaty project altogether once it had become clear that the right to property as such would not make it into the main body of the Convention. Thinking counterfactually, the alternative to the insertion of the right to property for legal persons

[35] Council of Europe (ed), *Collected Edition of the 'Travaux Preparatoires' of the European Convention on Human Rights* (Brill 1985) vol VII, 136.
[36] ibid 134–35
[37] Simpson (n 25) 1092–97.

would have been a breakdown or collapse of the whole Convention project. However, if the right to property had been included in the core Convention, legal persons would probably not have been explicitly included in the rights catalogue. Ultimately, our analysis confirms the thesis of AW Brian Simpson that the 'European Convention and its First Protocol were the product of conflicts, compromise, and happenstance'.[38]

IV. Historical juncture 2: human rights adjudication

The second historical juncture took place in the time period between 1960 to 1980 in the emerging jurisprudence of the ECtHR. In this context, it is important to point out that this contribution does not deal with all legal persons taking recourse to the ECtHR, eg churches, labour unions, etc, but specifically focuses on for-profit corporate actors. Already in the 1960s, the first cases, in which individuals clearly pursuing corporate interests made use of their Convention rights, reached the Commission. The arguably first case, *X v the Netherlands*,[39] concerned a Dutch dairy farmer, who refused to join an association for cattle farmers and thus had to suffer financial losses. He invoked Articles 6, 7, 11, and in particular Article 9 of the Convention, but the case was declared inadmissible as the Commission found no violation of the incurred rights. Similarly, the case of *Fritz Neumeister v Austria*,[40] focused on the manager of a transport firm, who invoked Articles 6(1), 5(3), and 5(4) in connection with judicial proceedings against him and others in connection to allegations of tax fraud. This invocation of due process rights in connection with corporate activities is the beginning of a long line of cases leading to a situation, in which the most frequently invoked ECHR right of corporate actors is Article 6(1) concerning various due process guarantees.[41] This shows that even though the explicit inclusion of corporations is limited to very specific rights in the ECHR, corporate actors very soon discovered the potential of the human rights system and frequently relied on a whole range of other Convention rights. In the end, Mr Neumeister was successful in claiming those rights. A breakthrough for corporate human rights was the case of *A, B, C, and D v the United Kingdom*[42] brought by four shareholders of a steel company invoking for the first time Article 1 of Additional Protocol I. This case confirmed earlier concerns brought forward by the British delegation against the provision, as the shareholders alleged a human rights violation due to the 'Iron and Steel Act' 1967 which was part of the restructuring process of the steel industry by the British government. However, the Commission sided with the state party and held that the United Kingdom had not exceeded the margin of appreciation as to what measures were in the public interest.

Nonetheless, the elevation of corporations to a position of a human rights holder under the ECHR remained a dead letter until the 1980s. On the one hand, in 1986, the case of *Agosi v the United Kingdom*[43] was the first time a foreign company claimed a violation of Article 1 Additional Protocol I. Until this time, only nationals, respectively domestically incorporated companies, had appealed to the Court due to a violation by their state of origin.

[38] Simpson (n 25) vii.
[39] *X v Netherlands* App no 1068/61 (ECtHR, 14 December 1962).
[40] *Fritz Neumeister v Austria* App no 1936/63 (ECtHR, 27 May 1966).
[41] Emberland (n 15) 14.
[42] *A, B, C, and D v the United Kingdom* App no 3039/67 (ECtHR, 29 May 1967).
[43] *Agosi v the United Kingdom* App no 9118/80 (ECtHR, 24 October 1986).

Agosi, a German joint stock company, alleged that it was unaware that the gold coins it had bought from a private individual had been illegally smuggled out of the United Kingdom. The British customs authorities had seized the gold coins, but Agosi argued that it was still the rightful owner according to the contract of sale. On the other hand, cases such as *James and Others v the United Kingdom*[44] introduced distinctions on treatment, in particular the claims to compensation, between nationals and non-nationals when it held that:

> Especially as regards a taking of property effected in the context of a social reform, there may well be good grounds for drawing a distinction between nationals and non-nationals as far as compensation is concerned. To begin with, non-nationals are more vulnerable to domestic legislation: unlike nationals, they will generally have played no part in the election or designation of its authors nor have been consulted on its adoption. Secondly, although a taking of property must always be effected in the public interest, different considerations may apply to nationals and non-nationals and there may well be legitimate reason for requiring nationals to bear a greater burden in the public interest than non-nationals.[45]

While corporations are not explicitly discussed in this quote, nor the case itself, it is clear that the doctrine developed above was highly beneficial for multinational companies. This becomes even more apparent when we observe the discussion of *James* in the field of investment arbitration, where it is used as a crucial stepping stone and definition of the international minimum standard.

Consequently, during this second historical juncture, the ECtHR undertook through a line of cases a two-fold mission, promoting and expanding corporate rights against public institutions. Firstly, corporations successfully claimed the status of right holders not only under the right to property but also rights such as the right to a fair trial, thereby morphing from holders of a specific economic right to bearers of human rights in general. Secondly, the ECtHR in an activist fashion expanded the rights under the Additional Protocol by including far-reaching doctrines on the right to compensation in line with the Western position on the debate on the international minimum standard.[46] In cases such as *James*, the ECtHR put down a detailed list of entitlements of foreign corporations against public regulation of their property in the host state. This can be seen as a translation of the controversial Hull standard, promoted by the West as a principle of international law and opposed by the Third World, into the language of human rights. In a more strategic reading of the events, the European human rights discourse was instrumentalised in order to entrench the Western partisan position in the global debate on the New International Economic Order and became part of the 1980s backlash against Third World interests.

Most cases concerning corporate actors went largely unnoticed in the general public discourse on human rights and the Convention. Those early cases from the 1960s onwards, however, peaking in the crucial 1980s cases of *Agosi* and *James*, were highly influential in establishing the ECtHR as a corporate-friendly judicial forum. As the empirical work of Marius Emberland identified, the Court in these cases usually provided only a minimalist

[44] *James and Others v the United Kingdom* App no 8793/79 (ECtHR, 21 February 1986).

[45] ibid para 63.

[46] A similar example is the influential ECtHR jurisprudence on the principle of legitimate expectation in the context of Article 1 AP I ECHR, see also Josef Ostřanský, 'From a Fortuitous Transplant to a Fundamental Principle of Law?: The Doctrine of Legitimate Expectations and the Possibilities of a Different Law', in this volume.

reasoning. In many cases involving corporate actors, whether they result in business-friendly or a rather restrictive outcome, the Court remained silent on its motivations to expand or reject particular rights.[47] Thinking counterfactually, and given the vague legal basis in the Convention, each of these cases could have been decided differently. By denying human rights entitlements to corporations, judges would have put the ECtHR on a less-business-friendly trajectory. Up to this date, the jurisprudence of the ECtHR concerning the 'piercing of the veil' and the victim requirement of shareholders remains inconsistent. A strong, detailed decision on those issues could have brought the ECtHR closer to the stance taken by its inter-American counterpart, which distinguishes corporations from other legal persons that serve public interests of a particular social community and are thus eligible to hold independent human rights.

The ECtHR developed a different position, which becomes particularly explicit in the case of *Comingersoll SA v Portugal*.[48] This case exemplifies another pro-corporate development in the practice of remedies, as the Court decided to award non-pecuniary damages to a corporation for a violation of Article 6(1) of the ECHR by reason of the length of the judicial enforcement proceedings.[49] Just satisfaction for pecuniary damages of corporations under Article 41 of the ECHR had become established practice at the ECtHR since the 1980s, eg including compensation for loss of reputation[50] and decline in customers and business clientele[51] after violations of fair trial standards. Yet, the Grand Chamber in *Comingersoll* even extends this extensive remedial practice to non-pecuniary damage. In contrast to material loss, compensation for non-pecuniary harm in international human rights law requires the existence of mental anguish, pain, and suffering of the victim. The ECtHR typically awards non-pecuniary damages in situations of 'trauma, anxiety, anger, etc. coming with an attack on human dignity, the loss of trust in state institutions, the loss of beloved persons, the mental and physical pain lasting after torture, imprisonment, censorship, separation from family members, and so on'.[52] Awarding a corporation non-pecuniary damages thus assumes that the corporation itself—not the individuals standing behind it such as in the case of *Freedom and Democracy Party (ÖZDEP) v Turkey*[53]—has the capacity to feel mental anguish following a violation of its rights. In this context, the concurring opinion of Judge Rozakis joined by Judges Sir Nicolas Bratza, Caflisch, and Vajic is particularly revealing. In their view, corporations should actually even enjoy more autonomous protection than political parties or other 'looser' forms of organisations under the ECHR:

> I have voted in favour of finding a violation of Article 6 in this case and of awarding non-pecuniary damage to the applicant company because, in the circumstances of the case,

[47] Emberland (n 15) 200–1.

[48] *Comingersoll SA v Portugal* App no 35382/97 (ECtHR, 6 April 2000).

[49] See also Marius Emberland, 'Compensating Companies for Non-Pecuniary Damage: Comingersoll S.A. v Portugal and the Ambivalent Expansion of the ECHR Scope' (2003) 74 British Yearbook of International Law 409.

[50] See for instance in the case of *Tinnelly & Sons, Ltd and Others v the United Kingdom* App no 62/1997/846/1052–1053 (ECtHR, 10 July 1998).

[51] See for instance in the case of *Stratégies et Communications et Dumoulin v Belgium* App no 37370/97 (ECtHR, 15 July 2002).

[52] Szilvia Altwicker-Hámori, Tilmann Altwicker, and Anne Peters, 'Measuring Violations of Human Rights: An Empirical Analysis of Awards in Respect of Non-Pecuniary Damage under the European Convention on Human Rights' (2016) 76 Heidelberg Journal of International Law 1, 6. See also Dinah Shelton, *Remedies in International Human Rights Law* (OUP 2006).

[53] *Freedom and Democracy Party (ÖZDEP) v Turkey* App no 23885/94 (ECtHR, 8 December 1999).

> the company may validly claim that the length of the proceedings has adversely affected its reputation and has caused uncertainty in its decision-planning and a disruption in its smooth operation and management.... I think that the application by analogy of the test in the ÖZDEP case to the present one is not correct. In that case, the legal person was a political party (which, by its nature, is a looser organisation) and the protected right in question was the freedom of association of the members of that party who established and organised it. Here the situation is different: the company is an independent living organism, protected as such by the legal order of the State concerned, and whose rights also receive autonomous protection under the European Convention on Human Rights.[54]

Until the early 2000s, Convention-cases brought by foreign corporations, such as *Agosi*, were relatively rare. This changed at the start of the new millennium, when cases characterised by facts typical for investment arbitration, reached the Court.[55] At the same time, international investment law also entered into a new stage of corporate rights during the rise of investor-state arbitration.

V. Historical juncture 3: investment arbitration

While investment law naturally focuses on corporations by granting them a special status and explicit rights, their transformation to human rights holders in that context is a more recent phenomenon. We argue that this third historical juncture coincides with the rise of investor-state arbitration in the early 2000s. This moment of migration of corporate 'human' rights into the realm of investment arbitration indicated a shift in international investment law, elevating the status of corporations from beneficiaries to self-standing right holders. The general combination of human rights and investment law thus takes the form of a double-edged sword: On the one hand, merging human rights and investment law is often seen as an opportunity to strengthen public interests and to better protect the human rights of those affected by abusive corporate practices; on the other hand, by also transforming corporations into human rights holders, these positive effects may be neutralised or even outweighed by an even stronger position of the investor.

At its core, international investment law originated from the desire of the nineteenth-century Western great powers to protect the private property of their merchants and banks operating abroad. The predominant ratio of the law of diplomatic protection in the nineteenth and early twentieth centuries in particular aimed at preventing expropriation of alien property by establishing an international minimum standard for the treatment of foreigners.[56] This guiding motive led to the development of a broad range of investor rights today enshrined in more than 3,000 bi- and multi-lateral treaties. According to these treaty instruments foreign investors do not only have to be treated the same way as national

[54] *Comingersoll SA v Portugal* App no. 35382/97 (ECtHR, 6 April 2000) Concurring Opinion of Judge Rozakis joined by Judges Sir Nicolas Bratza, Caflisch, and Vajic 9.

[55] Ursula Kriebaum, 'Is the European Court of Human Rights an Alternative to Investor-State Arbitration' in Pierre-Marie Dupuy, Ernst-Ulrich Petersmann, and Francesco Francioni (eds), *Human Rights in International Investment Law and Arbitration* (OUP 2009).

[56] See eg Kate Miles, *The Origins of International Investment Law. Empire, Environment and the Safeguarding of Capital* (CUP 2013) 47–50.

companies; they are granted fair and equitable treatment and various other privileges. In particular, the 1980s turn to bilateral treaty-based investment protection has boosted the legal position of foreign investors at the expense of the regulatory authority of host states. While one can identify a general trend in investment arbitration to use comparative reasoning,[57] the increasing corporate reliance on human rights instruments in investor-state arbitration poses particularly grave normative challenges. References to human rights instruments in arbitral proceedings are not an isolated incident; they can be identified in approximately 10% of all investment arbitration cases.[58]

In contrast to the more recent perception that human rights are predominantly used by host states to circumvent their obligations under investment law,[59] foreign investors are heavily engaged in referencing human rights instruments to their benefit in arbitrations. Recent empirical research by Alvarez[60] and Steininger[61] identified that, in particular, references to European human rights law are as likely to be used by the investor as by the respondent state. In the words of Alvarez, '[references to European human rights law] are, in short, as likely to be used as a sword in favor of investor rights than as a shield to defend against them'.[62] Those human rights references serve a particular kind of 'human'—'namely foreigners armed with capital'.[63]

Reliance on human rights norms by investors and tribunals was not unexpected and perfectly in line with what is often described as the pro-investment bias of the regime and its institutional manifestations. A number of scholars believe that the commonalities between human rights and investment arbitration favour the inclusion of human rights,[64] arguing that both regimes share a common *telos*: protecting the individual against the power of the state.[65] Analysing this development from a perspective of historical contingency, however, makes us aware of the structural implications this entails for the nature of corporate rights.[66] Reliance on human rights reflects the active transformation of foreign investors from pure beneficiaries of bilateral investment treaties (BITs) to active 'human rights'-holders. It also signals a shift in the normative claim made by multinational corporations. By using analogies from human rights instruments, they engage in the 'rhetoric of rights' and claim a special form of legitimacy. While we do not question that investors can hold certain economic rights under bi- and multi-lateral treaties, this strategy of appropriating (and sometimes

[57] See among others, Stephan Schill and Katrine Tvede, 'Mainstreaming Investment Treaty Jurisprudence. The Contribution of Investment Treaty Tribunals to the Consolidation and Development of General International Law' (2015) 14 The Law and Practice of International Courts and Tribunals 94; Valentina Vadi, *Analogies in International Investment Law and Arbitration* (CUP 2015); Valentina Vadi, 'Critical Comparisons: The Role of Comparative Law in Investment Treaty Arbitration' (2010) 39 Denver Journal of International Law & Policy 67.

[58] See eg Silvia Steininger, 'What's Human Rights Got To Do With It? An Empirical Analysis of Human Rights References in Investment Arbitration' (2018) 31 Leiden Journal of International Law 33.

[59] An early analysis of this trend is Marc Jacob, 'International Investment Agreements and Human Rights' (2010) INEF Research Paper Series: Human Rights, Corporate Responsibility and Sustainable Development.

[60] José Alvarez, 'The Use (and Misuse) of European Human Rights Law in Investor-State Dispute Settlement' in Franco Ferrari (ed), *Impact of EU Law on International Commercial Arbitration* (Juris 2017).

[61] Steininger (n 58).

[62] Alvarez (n 60).

[63] ibid.

[64] *International Thunderbird Gaming Corporation v Mexico* (United Nations Commission on International Trade Law [UNCITRAL], 1 December 2005) Separate Opinion by Thomas Wälde.

[65] Bruno Simma, 'Foreign Investment Arbitration: A Place for Human Rights?' (2011) 60 International and Comparative Law Quarterly 573.

[66] On the choice of analogies in investment arbitration, see also Anthea Roberts, 'Clash of Paradigms: Actors and Analogies Shaping the Investment Treaty System' (2013) 107 American Journal of International Law 45.

misusing) 'human' rights concepts and standards in order to vindicate corporate interests has grave consequences for the nature, force, and moral authority of human rights. This corporate takeover of human rights can be understood under the prism of human rights mainstreaming[67] or the 'dehumanization of human rights'.[68] In the context of investment arbitration, this adoption of human rights language is used instrumentally to entrench an already fairly unbalanced pro-investor regime.

The European Convention human rights norms most frequently invoked by foreign investors concern the right to property, particularly questions of expropriation and compensation, as well as due process guarantees. In many cases, the jurisprudence of arbitral tribunals in the first two decades of the twenty-first century mirrors previous constellations and claims brought by corporations to the ECtHR. For instance concerning property claims, in the case of *ST-AD GmbH v Bulgaria*, the German company heavily relied on ECtHR jurisprudence to expand the protection of property and to grant compensation to corporate actors in the case of alleged infringements of that right.[69] It argued that the ECtHR case law is a source of 'fundamental information for concretising the act of expropriation as defined in the BITs... [and] is not contradicted even by the different wording, because the protection of human rights can, at the very least, be understood as a minimum standard below which the Investment Protection Treaty cannot in any case fall'.[70] In a similar vein, in the case of *Spyridon Roussalis v Romania*, the Greek shareholder argued that the Greece-Romania BIT extended to him the benefits of any additional obligation under international law between the two state parties.[71] He could thus claim the higher property protection under the ECHR before the arbitral tribunal.[72]

Foreign investors also use ECtHR jurisprudence to argue that a host state has violated the right to a fair trial under Article 6, such as the presumption of innocence in the case of *Hassan Awdi, Enterprise Business Consultants, Inc and Alfa El Corporation v Romania*, or the right to be heard in the case of *Tulip Real Estate and Development v Turkey*. In some instances, reliance on human rights is also used against governmental legislation. For instance, in the case of *Micula v Romania*, the Swedish individual and corporate claimants put forward an expert opinion which argued that the revocation of a law for the development of certain disfavoured regions in Romania would amount to a violation of ECtHR jurisprudence on legitimate expectations and legal foreseeability.[73] Moreover, European human rights law is not only invoked against signatories to the ECHR, but globally. For instance, in the case of *Toto v Lebanon*, an Italian construction company alleged violations of the right to a fair trial and due process guarantees from the ECHR and the International Covenant on Civil and Political Rights (ICCPR),[74] even though Lebanon is neither party to the ECHR nor has it ratified the Optional Protocol to the ICCPR, and thus cannot be summoned before the UN Human Rights Committee.[75]

[67] Martti Koskenniemi, 'The Politics of International Law—20 Year Later' (2009) 20 EJIL 11.

[68] Isiksel (n 2) 297.

[69] *ST-AD GmbH v Bulgaria* (United Nations Commission on International Trade Law [UNCITRAL], 18 July 2013) Award on Jurisdiction.

[70] ibid para 171.

[71] *Spyridon Roussalis v Romania*, ICSID Case no ARB/06/1 (7 December 2011).

[72] ibid para 158.

[73] *Ioan Micula, Viorel Micula, SC European Food SA, SC Starmill SRL and S. Multipack SRL v Romania*, ICSID Case no ARB/05/20 (11 December 2013) para 452.

[74] *Toto Costruzioni Generali SpA v The Republic of Lebanon*, ICSID Case no ARB/07/12 (11 September 2009) Decision on Jurisdiction, para 144.

[75] ibid para 158–60.

The responses of the tribunals when confronted with a human rights claim are complex. While some tribunals explicitly denied accepting arguments based on human rights,[76] others pro-actively engaged in human rights-based argumentation themselves. A particularly prominent example is *Tecmed v Mexico*. In this case the tribunal relied on two sources of external citations, the case of *Baruch Ivcher Bronstein v Peru* from the IACtHR and four cases from the ECtHR, including the aforementioned *James and Others v UK*, to decide on the proportionality of the expropriatory measure of the Mexican National Ecology Institute in the name of the public interest.[77] The growing inclusion of human rights arguments further emboldens unequal structures in investment arbitration by adding sacrosanct corporate 'human' rights to an already biased pro-investor regime.

Hence, the developments summarised in the first two historical junctures were absolutely essential for this structural change in investment arbitration. Thinking counterfactually, without this sanctification of corporate interests as human rights claims under the ECHR, the recognition of corporations as human rights holders in international economic law would not have come about, given that the landmark cases in investment arbitration on the issue of property/expropriation/compensation usually refer to the jurisprudence of the ECtHR. The lawyers and arbitrators involved in investor-state dispute settlement (ISDS) were mostly educated in elite universities in the Global North, hence it is not surprising that they are more accustomed to ECtHR jurisprudence and probably not familiar with the corporate-critical stance of the IACtHR.

Interestingly, the conceptualisation of corporations as right holders in ECtHR case law is increasingly accepted by both state parties and investors. Once a corporate human rights claim is on the table, the state will argue before the tribunal that its measures were a proportional restriction of that right. This shows that within this discursive field the elevation of corporations to human rights bearers is something like a done deal. In claiming or denying violations, both parties argue within the corporate human rights paradigm. From a historical perspective, however, the prevalent use of human rights by corporations seriously undermines the core idea of the 1940s–1970s human rights movement. The endless and somewhat fruitless 'business and human rights' or corporate social responsibility debates, which focus on potential human rights obligations of corporate actors have obscured to what extent corporations have over the last decade already achieved the transformation of their economic interests into human right claims. The corporate social responsibility discourse, from this perspective, deflects our attention from the fact that international law has further cemented economic structures by lending the authority of the human rights discourse to the rather mundane goal of maximising corporate profits. As European human rights law manifests and supports a structural pro-investor bias in investor-state arbitration, its appeal for cross-referencing in ISDS thus became almost inevitable.[78]

[76] For instance, in the case of *Pezold v Zimbabwe*, the Tribunal emphasised 'that due caution should be exercised in importing concepts from other legal regimes (in this case European human rights law) without a solid basis for doing so. Balancing competing (and non-absolute) human rights and the need to grant States a margin of appreciation when making those balancing decisions is well established in human rights law, but the Tribunal is not aware that the concept has found much support in international investment law.' (*Bernhard von Pezold and Others v Republic of Zimbabwe*, ICSID Case no ARB/10/15 (28 July 2015) para 465.

[77] *Técnicas Medioambientales Tecmed, SA v Mexico*, ICSID Case no ARB (AF)/00/2 (29 May 2003) paras 116, 122.

[78] Kathryn Greenman, 'The Law of State Responsibility and the Persistence of Investment Protection', in this volume.

Thinking counterfactually even under improbable conditions, if the first investment tribunal had denied the elevation of the investor under a bilateral investment treaty to the status of a human rights holder, and other tribunals had confirmed this reasoning as a precedent that should not be overruled, the legitimacy of corporate rights claims today would perhaps be much more precarious. Given the current backlash against investor-state arbitration, corporations could not be able to, for instance, argue that any attempt to redress the pro-investor bias of the regime constituted a violation of their 'human' rights. Corporate 'human' rights thus function as a particularly strong last line of defence for corporate interests against political reform. In that sense, human rights are not only 'not enough'[79] but become a concrete legal obstacle to more far-reaching collective projects aiming at a more just global society through redistribution and prohibitions.[80] Interestingly, the practice of the tribunals was by no means a uniform one; a number of tribunals for various reasons denied the transformation of business interests into human rights claims. Yet, the awards citing pro-corporate human rights have gained increased traction. Even when later tribunals do not explicitly cite ECtHR jurisprudence, they rely on prominent expropriation cases such as *Tecmed*. Of course, on a factual basis, corporations being faced with a bench that rejected their human right claims usually would still have been able to claim the far-reaching rights and privileges granted by the specific investment treaty regime.

VI. Conclusion

Our analysis has attempted to demonstrate that the transformation of corporate interests into human rights was a contingent development. At the first juncture, the inclusion of the rights of legal persons was a mere byproduct of a compromise to safeguard the Convention project. At the second juncture, the ECtHR for political reasons strengthened and expanded the notion of corporations as right holders in defence of a neoliberal economic project, joining the ranks of Western-dominated institutions like the World Bank, in order to create a sacrosanct and broad notion of corporate property protection. Unlike the IACtHR, the ECtHR did not limit the recognition of legal persons to non-profit institutions that are indispensable in order to effectively ensure Convention rights of natural persons, such as trade unions, newspapers, or churches. More than a decade later, this business-friendly jurisprudence then enabled investors to reformulate and expand their specific rights under bilateral investment treaties as 'human' rights.

Pointing to the contingencies in these developments, may reveal how the, at first sight unlikely, outcome of corporate human rights could have been prevented by vigilant diplomatic delegations or benches critically reflecting upon the ideological work they were engaged in. At the same time, our critical re-description of historical events might confirm a neo-Marxian reading of these events that emphasises the central role that human rights have for any modern capitalist economy. This of course is the issue of false contingency:[81] Do we, by constructing contingencies through historical re-description, necessarily underestimate or

[79] Moyn (n 21).

[80] For a philosophical critique of the notion of subjective rights along these lines, see Christoph Menke, *Kritik der Rechte* (Suhrkamp 2015).

[81] Susan Marks, 'False Contingency' (2009) 62 Current Legal Problems 1.

downplay deeply unequal structural conditions that would in fact have made another outcome highly unlikely or even impossible? To imagine another course of events during the 1980s and 1990s—a time of largely unrivalled US hegemony and the breakdown of Eastern European socialist economies—may be considered naïve and as such problematic.[82]

Corporate actors even without co-opting human rights during this time would perhaps have found other ways of promoting their interest in maximising their freedom to globally exploit human and natural resources without costly public interferences. And is the development of the bilateral investment regime itself not testament to the hegemonic economic constellation and belief-systems under which politicians, courts, and tribunals acted in this epoch?[83] While this is certainly the case, a critical re-description may nonetheless bring out the responsibility of all those involved in realising the three junctures that we have analysed in this contribution. 'Legal' persons could have gone unmentioned in the ECHR or courts, and tribunals could have adopted a restrictive stance towards extending human rights guarantees to business actors. Each diplomat, judge, arbitrator, or scholar could have acted differently and may have had the opportunity to convince colleagues to stall or at least delay the hegemonic course of events, which legally—we should not forget—aimed at an unlikely outcome: namely, at turning multinational corporations into bearers of 'human' rights.

[82] On false necessity or the contingency of existing institutions, see Roberto Mangabeira Unger, *False Necessity. Anti-Necessitarian Social Theory in the Service of Radical Democracy* (Verso 2004).

[83] On this era Jochen von Bernstorff, 'The Decay of the International Rule of Law Project (1990–2015)' in Georg Nolte and Heike Krieger (eds) *The International Rule of Law: Rise or Decline?* (OUP 2019).

18

Contesting Austerity in the 1970s and 1980s

When Human Rights Went Missing

*Matthias Goldmann**

I. Introduction

1. Debt, austerity, and human rights discourse

Since the emergence of sovereign statehood in early modernity, there have been sovereign debt crises.[1] Their resolution has regularly involved hardship for the population of the debtor state due to adjustments in fiscal and economic policy known as austerity. In the aftermath of the 2008 Great Financial Crisis, such hardship has often been addressed in terms of human rights.[2] As this chapter will explore, in historical perspective, this role of human rights represents the exception rather than the rule. Human rights discourse in the context of sovereign debt-induced austerity has varied enormously over time. Far from reflecting progress, its history reveals changing paradigms of human rights law. The understanding of human rights is contingent on the position and context of the participants in human rights discourse in a specific field at a particular moment and time. There is thus no single understanding, and accordingly no single historical trajectory of human rights. Rather, the closest one can come to a comprehensive history of human rights is by mapping the alternations of different discursive paradigms of human rights.

To track these paradigm shifts, this chapter situates human rights discourse in the context of austerity within the broader struggle between the 'economic' and the 'social' in society.[3] In the context of sovereign debt crises, the 'economic' stands for the interest of creditors to maximise their return. Conversely, the 'social' represents the interest of debtor states and their citizens to avoid austerity. Obviously, these two concepts represent ideal types. Concrete debt crises will always reflect a particular mix of the infinite varieties in

* This chapter is essentially an adjusted extract of my chapter 'Contesting Austerity: Genealogies of Human Rights Discourse' in Nehal Bhuta (ed), *Human Rights in Global Governance: Collected Courses of the Academy of European Law* (OUP 2021, forthcoming). For helpful critique I am indebted to Nehal Bhuta, Juan Pablo Bohoslavsky, Ingo Venzke, Anuscheh Farahat, Silvia Steininger, Margot Salomon, the students attending the human rights course of the Academy of European Law (AEL) in June 2017, and participants in the AEL Conference at the European University Institute in February 2018, and at the conference on 'Contingency in the Course of International Law' at the University of Amsterdam in June 2018. Thanks to Hannah Kull and Seoyoung Shin for research assistance.

[1] For defaults during early modernity, see Carmen M Reinhart and Kenneth S Rogoff, *This Time Is Different: Eight Centuries of Financial Folly* (Princeton University Press 2009) 86–87.

[2] For many: Aoife Nolan (ed) *Economic and Social Rights after the Global Financial Crisis* (CUP 2014).

[3] This distinction draws on Karl Polanyi, *The Great Transformation: The Political and Economic Origins of our Time* (Beacon Press 1944) ch 2.

Matthias Goldmann, *Contesting Austerity in the 1970s and 1980s* In: *Contingency in International Law*. Edited by: Ingo Venzke and Kevin Jon Heller, Oxford University Press. © The Several Contributors 2021. DOI: 10.1093/oso/9780192898036.003.0018

which we encounter each of these two ideal types in reality. Nevertheless, I believe that the simplification inherent in this dichotomy is justified as it offers helpful discursive orientation.

As the chapter will elaborate, the alignment of human rights with 'the social' has not been seamless. Rather, the role of human rights in the context of sovereign debt crises reveals certain contingencies of human rights discourse, which one might break down into two different, but intersecting, axes of discursive evolution. The first axis maps the dynamic relationship between human rights discourse and other concepts articulating concern for 'the social', including heterodox economic policies. The second axis tracks the complex relationship between human rights and different redistributive ideals. Human rights, like fundamental rights, their constitutional brethren, are not natural allies of an egalitarian vision of society or any particular idea of redistribution. Rather, as Samuel Moyn has masterfully shown, human rights oscillate between the idea of sufficiency, characterised by an emphasis on status equality, economic rights protecting against government interference, and only minimum guarantees of social protection, and a more egalitarian understanding based on a vision of relative material equality, which usually implies government intervention to realise welfare and prosperity for all.[4]

The history of human rights in the context of austerity deserves a more extensive treatment than this chapter allows.[5] This chapter restricts its focus to the 1970s and 1980s as a particularly interesting period, characterised by a crucial paradigm shift in the role played by human rights in the context of austerity. In the 1970s, when the International Financial Institutions (IFIs) began to lay the foundation of sovereign lending and conditionality as we know it today, human rights played a very different role compared to the 2008 crisis aftermath. Newly independent states invoked human rights mostly to assert their sovereignty, articulate their concern over the structure of the international economy, and avert international interference, rather than to promote specific social policies in the context of structural adjustment. I call this the structural paradigm in human rights discourse. Accordingly, the conditions imposed on debtor states during periods of financial distress did not trigger an explicit human rights critique. But the United Nations Conference on Trade and Development (UNCTAD) stressed the self-determination of debtor states, which was seen as a precondition for the realisation of human rights. Moreover, the notion of basic (human) needs articulated concerns about the social effects of austerity. While this concept was riddled with ambiguity, some understood it as devising the way towards a materially more equal society. To corroborate their position, they aligned the basic (human) needs approach with the duty of states to implement human rights.

The structural human rights paradigm abruptly disappeared from austerity debates in the 1980s, when the sovereign debt crisis hit the Global South. As demands increased to reconsider the social impact of structural adjustment programmes, the International Monetary Fund (IMF) shifted the terms of the debate decisively from human needs to human capital, thus entrenching a utilitarian perspective that considered structural adjustment policies purely from the perspective of how they would contribute to growth. Consequently,

[4] Samuel Moyn, *Not Enough: Human Rights in an Unequal World* (Harvard University Press 2018) 3–4. For a resounding defence of sufficientarianism: Liam Shields, *Just Enough: Sufficiency as a Demand of Justice* (Edinburgh University Press 2016).

[5] For a full account, see Goldmann, 'Contesting Austerity' (on file with author).

while human rights rose at the same time to the level of foundational global constitutional principles, to nothing less than the 'last utopia',[6] they had virtually no impact on the perception of austerity at the time. The erstwhile structural paradigm of human rights discourse gave way to a new, liberal paradigm of human rights discourse to be spread by international organisations to discipline governments, rather than to promote equality. This paradigm prevailed up until the end of the century. As I show elsewhere,[7] a critique of austerity based on a new, transformative paradigm of human rights law only emerged in civil society in the 1990s. It had little impact on the practice of austerity until the 'war against terrorism' leveraged the view that international organisations should be bound by human rights.

It therefore stands to reason that the evolution of human rights discourse did not neatly match the spread of neoliberal economic policies like austerity. The rise of the latter initially side-lined economic and social rights as a relevant perspective. Transformations in the economy and in international organizations may require shifts in human rights discourse, which cannot be taken for granted. In the case at hand, only coincidental developments in other fields restored economic and social rights discourse as a means to contest austerity, although with limited success.[8] Even so, this does not imply that one should not discard human rights discourse entirely. The (short) genealogy of human rights discourse set out in this chapter illustrates the high level of contingency inherent in human rights discourse.[9] Whether human rights discourse promotes social ends and equality is mostly a question of its particular context and time. This chapter ends by sketching out a political paradigm in human rights discourse that generates the potential for human rights discourse to contest austerity and entrench greater equality.

II. The 1970s: a human rights critique coming within reach

The crisis-struck decade of the 1970s marked a turning point in the politics of debt and austerity. The Global South compensated for the decline in official development aid from industrial countries by massively expanding their commercial borrowings, fuelled amongst others by the excess liquidity of internationally operating banks thanks to increased oil revenue in OPEC states ('petrodollars'). With progress in growth and development stalling and debt problems quivering on the horizon, the question emerged whether the IMF should expand its narrow focus on macro issues and tackle development issues more broadly. In 1971, it began advising on external debt, including debt ceilings, in the frame of its Article VIII and XIV consultations.[10] This resonated with the interests of lenders, who wanted to avoid any intermingling of the development aid they were providing with sovereign debt issues.[11] In

[6] Samuel Moyn, *The Last Utopia* (Harvard University Press 2010).

[7] Goldmann, 'Contesting Austerity' (n 5).

[8] In the latter respect, I concur with Samuel Moyn, 'A Powerless Companion: Human Rights in the Age of Neoliberalism' (2014) 77 Law and Contemporary Problems 147.

[9] On the different genealogies of human rights discourse: Stefan-Ludwig Hoffmann, 'Einführung: Zur Genealogie der Menschenrechte' in Stefan-Ludwig Hoffmann (ed), *Moralpolitik Geschichte der Menschenrechte im 20 Jahrhundert* (Wallstein 2010) 1, 26.

[10] Jérôme Sgard, 'How the IMF Did It—Sovereign Debt Restructuring Between 1970 and 1989' (2016) 11 Capital Markets Law Journal 103, 107.

[11] Minutes of the Executive Board meetings 71/33 and 71/34 of 21 and 23 April 1971, IMF Doc SM/71/80; cf Sundhya Pahuja, 'Technologies of Empire: IMF Conditionality and the Reinscription of the North/South Divide' (2000) 13 Leiden Journal of International Law 749, 766.

1974, the IMF established the Extended Fund Facility, a new lending functionality providing longer-term finance to overcome debt crises. Conditionalities included performance instruments, which went considerably beyond the erstwhile performance targets. The amendment of Article IV of the Articles of Agreement earlier that year provided the legal basis for these more stringent conditionalities.[12] The structural character of such conditionalities considerably increased their impact on domestic policies.

1. Background: interwar and post-war welfare statism

The post-war era up until the 1970s hardly saw criticism of conditionalities and the related austerity articulated in terms of human rights, even though their influence on the economic policies of debtor states was growing. Only at the end of the 1970s, the possibility of a human rights critique came within reach.

Several factors account for this development. For one, despite the inclusion of social rights in the 1948 Universal Declaration of Human Rights, discourse on economic, social, and cultural rights (ESC rights) hardly got off the ground in the industrialised economies during the *Trente Glorieuses*, the period of growth from the mid-forties to roughly the 1970s. The new historiography of human rights has explored the reasons for this silence in some detail.[13] In particular, the lack of ESC rights discourse had nothing to do with linear progress in human rights law, a common, self-gratulatory narrative according to which classical liberal rights devised the path on which the development of ESC rights could follow in a second step. Rather, it seems that ESC rights entered the legal and political vocabulary of the twentieth century on substance already during the interwar period. The decline of nineteenth-century bourgeois constitutionalism and the shift to mass democracy in many industrialised countries during the first half of the twentieth century indeed brought with it explicit constitutional recognition for social concerns. The classical, paradigmatic examples are the 1917 Mexican Constitution and the 1919 Weimar Constitution, to which one might add the 1931 Spanish Constitution, Roosevelt's 1941 Four Freedoms, or the 1948 Italian Constitution.[14] These fundamental charters articulated social concerns not only in terms of rights, but often in the form of programmatic provisions that would set in motion societal and political processes to build up the welfare state and balance the diverging interests of various segments of society.[15] Although constitutional rights adjudication (against the administration, not the legislature) in some cases goes back to this period,[16] the enforcement of ESC rights against the legislature was not part of this constitutional agenda

[12] UNCTAD, *Report of the Trade and Development Board on the First Part of its Fifteenth Session Held at the Palais des Nations, Geneva* (5–16 August 1975) A/10015/Rev.1 (1976) paras 161–63; Pahuja (n 11) 769; Axel Dreher and Roland Vaubel, 'The Causes and Consequences of IMF Conditionality' (2004) 40 Emerging Markets Finance and Trade 26, 32.

[13] For references see Joseph R Slaughter, 'Hijacking Human Rights: Neoliberalism, the New Historiography, and the End of the Third World' (2018) 40 Human Rights Quarterly 735, 741ff.

[14] Agustín J Menéndez and Matthias Goldmann, 'Weimar Moments: Transformations of the Democratic, Social, and Open State of Law' (2020) (on file with author).

[15] Michael Stolleis, 'Die Soziale Programmatik der Weimarer Reichsverfassung' in Horst Dreier and Christian Waldhoff (eds), *Das Wagnis der Demokratie Eine Anatomie der Weimarer Reichsverfassung* (CH Beck 2018) 195; Roberto Gargarella, *Latin American Constitutionalism, 1810–2010: The Engine Room of the Constitution* (OUP 2013) 101ff.

[16] Horst Dreier, 'Grundrechtsrepublik Weimar' in Dreier and Waldhoff (eds) (n 15) 175.

as this period, given the prevailing conservatism of the judiciary in many places, trusted in parliaments more than in courts.

After the Second World War, the framing of the social question remained essentially the same in Western democracies, although the urgency which the Cold War lent to this question required getting serious about implementing the welfare state.[17] The welfare state was part of a larger project of establishing an international economic order for the purpose of embedding capitalism to avoid a recurrence of the Great Depression and the war. Never again should the risks arising from uncoordinated, unchecked economic interests be allowed to materialise.[18] Domestically, this period coincided with the steep rise of the welfare state. Healthcare, the improvement of working conditions, and the expansion of secondary and tertiary education are visible signs of the profound entanglement between the economic and the social at the period. The Phillips curve dominated labour market policies, leading to macroeconomic policies that sought to achieve a balance between unemployment and inflation.[19] This context explains why ESC rights gained little significance as *rights* in industrialised countries even after the adoption of the Universal Declaration of Human Rights (UDHR).[20] Protecting social rights was a task for national welfare systems. Considering the context of its creation, and particularly the influence of Latin American constitutionalism,[21] one needs to understand the UDHR as setting out a programme for domestic welfare states, rather than as a compendium of judicially enforceable individual social rights.[22] ESC rights were more of a shibboleth for a new concept of the state, of a state that endorsed mass democracy and put the welfare of the people first.

The transnational dimension of welfare was formulated in an analogous language of development, breathing the air of modernisation theories, not of rights discourse.[23] Development became the means of choice to overcome global economic asymmetries, whereas ESC rights as entitlements would have raised more pressing questions of redistribution. Even states with autocratic leaders could participate in development, allowing developed democracies to cooperate with them under the premise of assisting them to 'mature' into fully-fledged democracy. Besides, ESC rights discourse would have exposed the failures of colonial powers.[24] That the asymmetry of the international economic order would undermine the plan of building up domestic welfare states was overlooked by many, with the exception of Gunnar Myrdal, who called for international welfare coordination.[25] But even Myrdal's highly egalitarian ideas rested much more on an idea of the state and of

[17] For Europe: Poul F Kjaer, 'The Transnational Constitution of Europe's Social Market Economies: A Question of Constitutional Imbalances?' (2019) 57 JCMS: Journal of Common Market Studies 143, 147ff.

[18] John Gerard Ruggie, 'International Regimes, Transactions, and Change: Embedded Liberalism in the Postwar Economic Order' (1982) 36 International Organization 379.

[19] cf Paul A Samuelson and Robert M Solow, 'Analytical Aspects of Anti-Inflation Policy' (1960) 50 The American Economic Review 177.

[20] Moyn (n 4) 57ff; Samuel Moyn, 'The Universal Declaration of Human Rights of 1948 in the History of Cosmopolitanism' (2014) 40 Critical Inquiry 365.

[21] Mary Ann Glendon, 'The Forgotten Crucible: The Latin American Influence on the Universal Human Rights Idea' (2003) 16 Harvard Human Rights Journal 27.

[22] Moyn (n 4) 55. As Moyn emphasises, a UNESCO publication of 1948 reveals great scepticism about the future of human rights, see Mark Goodale, *Letters to the Contrary* (Stanford University Press 2018).

[23] cf Reinhart Kößler, 'Development—Analytical Value and Ideological Baggage of an Elusive Term' in Uwe H Bittlingmayer and others (eds), *Education and Development in Afghanistan: Challenges and Prospects* (Transcript 2019) 48.

[24] Jessica Whyte, *The Morals of the Market: Human Rights and the Rise of Neoliberalism* (Verso Books 2019) 120.

[25] Calling for the international coordination of welfare planning: Gunnar Myrdal, *An International Economy: Problems and Prospects* (Harper & Brothers 1956) 51ff; cf Moyn (n 4) 104ff.

social morals than on rights as individual entitlements.[26] The welfare state should remedy the suffering caused by the Great Depression and the ensuring Great War.[27]

In fact, some saw rights as too individualistic to be relied upon for societal change. This position is reflected in Johan Galtung's 1969 definition of peace research. He advocates a broad notion of peace that includes social justice and considers starvation as a form of 'violence', whether structural or personal.[28] In a highly revealing footnote, Galtung concedes that the requisite standard of social justice may be found in international human rights agreements. However, he rejects using the notion of human rights because he believes them to enshrine at best personal entitlements, instead of addressing the structural causes leading to distributive unfairness. ESC rights would not challenge the power disparities responsible for unfair distribution.[29]

2. The twofold emergence of a structural human rights paradigm in the 1970s

The welfare state focus of post-war development cooperation began to fade in the 1970s with the realisation that the recipe of development through growth had reached an impasse. Despite economic growth, unemployment and inequality soared.[30] The rising debt crisis and related harsher austerity prompted two parallel, different but related discourses in international organisations that sought to challenge austerity and reframe the relationship between the economic and the social during debt crises: the UNCTAD debt debate and the basic (human) needs approach. While each of these discourses is fraught with ambivalence about the role of human rigths for economic policy, each of them reflects to some extent a new paradigm of human rights that notably differed from Galtung's view by emphasising their structural significance and using them to challenge austerity.

The first of these discourses emerged from the call for a New International Economic Order (NIEO). This initiative derived from heterodox, structuralist critiques of the post-war economic order prevalent particularly in Latin America. Sensing the risks implied in trade liberalisation for developing countries, Raúl Prebisch, the first Secretary-General of UNCTAD, advocated targeted measures of protectionism to allow for industrial development and diversification with a view to substituting imports and redistributing the benefits of development.[31] These efforts culminated in the NIEO proposal, an intellectually influential challenge to the economic hegemony of the industrialised countries.[32]

[26] Gunnar Myrdal, *Beyond the Welfare State: Economic Planning and its International Implications* (Yale University Press 1960) 95, 277–79. In fact, he mentions rights only once on page 277 near the end in a general, passing way, referring to the right to life, liberty, and the pursuit of happiness as part of the essence of the welfare culture.

[27] Moyn (n 4) 48.

[28] Johan Galtung, 'Violence, Peace, and Peace Research' (1969) 6 Journal of Peace Research 167, 171.

[29] ibid 181.

[30] Richard Jolly, 'The World Employment Conference: The Enthronement of Basic Needs' (1976) A9 Development Policy Review 31, 76; D John Shaw, *World Food Security: A History since 1945* (Springer 2007) 223.

[31] Nora Lustig, 'From Structuralism to Neostructuralism: The Search for a Heterodox Paradigm' in Patricio Meller (ed), *The Latin American Development Debate: Neostructuralism, Neomonetarism, and Adjustment Processes* (Westview Press 1991).

[32] Moyn (n 4) 113ff; Quinn Slobodian, *Globalists: The End of Empire and the Birth of Neoliberalism* (Harvard University Press 2018) 219ff.

This proposal ushered in a new view of austerity in the Global South. During the 1960s, a lot of attention had been absorbed by the question of whether the newly independent states would succeed to the debt of colonial powers incurred for the benefit of their territory, and under which circumstances the former could dismiss such debt as odious.[33] In the context of rising indebtedness and the NIEO initiative, the Global South shifted its focus in the 1970s towards improving international debt restructuring practice to reduce the need for austerity and the related abyss of despair by alleviating the debt burden in the first place. A sequence of resolutions sought to establish this desire on the international agenda. The second UNCTAD conference in 1968 emphasised the shortcomings of ad hoc frameworks for debt restructuring.[34] The Paris North-South Conference of 1974 on the NIEO gave rise to the UNCTAD Ad Hoc Group of Governmental Experts on External Debt Problems of Developing Countries. With this group, for the first time since the war, an international body came up with a series of recommendations for a broad-based, effective institutional framework for debt restructuring, which have lost little of their practical relevance.[35] A few years later, Tanzania made the proposal that the international debt commission should be competent to consider issues of social fairness when deciding about a debt restructuring.[36] This process culminated in Resolution 222 (XXI), which specifies in its annex the 'Detailed features for future operations relating to the debt problems of interested developing countries'.[37] The document constitutes a compromise. It dangles the prospect of debt relief in front of the debtor states, while falling short of institutionalising a formal debt restructuring mechanism.[38]

Even though the resolution does not mention human rights, the context of the NIEO and its relationship with human rights suggest that one might indeed understand these efforts within UNCTAD as a genuine human rights perspective by another name, as an approach that sought to safeguard human rights in a structuralist sense by rebalancing the relationship between the economic and the social at a global level. This follows from the role of human rights in the NIEO initiative, although this relationship was not free from ambiguity.

On the one hand, it did not go without saying for supporters of the NIEO that a language of rights as the implementation of this agenda, which was a variety of Keynes-inspired development economics, required in the first place a strong state, not individual entitlements.[39] Moreover, the NIEO debate mirrored certain general tensions between decolonisation and

[33] International Law Commission, 'First Report on Succession of States in Respect of Rights and Duties Resulting from Sources other than Treaties, by Mr Mohammed Bedjaoui, Special Rapporteur' UN Doc A/CN.4/204 (1968). For cases, see Jeff King, *The Doctrine of Odious Debt in International Law: A Restatement* (CUP 2016) 79–80; see also Marc Frey, 'A Revolutionary Process? Decolonization and International Law' in Norbert Frei and Annette Weinke (eds), *Toward a New Moral World Order? Menschenrechtspolitik und Völkerrecht seit 1945* (Wallstein 2013) 122.

[34] UNCTAD, *Beyond Conventional Wisdom in Development Policy. An Intellectual History of UNCTAD 1964–2004* (United Nations 2004) 33.

[35] UNCTAD, *Report of the Trade and Development Board (10 March—2 October 1975)* UN Doc A /10015/ Rev. 1, ANNEX A, 'Document Submitted by the Group of Seventy-Seven and Romania on Proposed Additional Policy Measures for Incorporation into the International Development Strategy for the Second United Nations Development Decade' para 22.

[36] Sgard (n 10) 108.

[37] UNCTAD Trade and Development Board, Resolution 222 (XXI) of 27 September 1980.

[38] Enrique Cosio-Pascal, 'The Emerging of a Multilateral Forum for Debt Restructuring: The Paris Club' (November 2008) UNCTAD Discussion Paper 192, 11.

[39] Upendra Baxi, 'The New International Economic Order, Basic Needs and Rights: Notes Towards Development of the Right to Development' (1983) 23 Indian Journal of International Law 225; Moyn (n 4) 117.

human rights.[40] Not all countries supporting the NIEO showed a high level of respect for democracy and human rights internally, which made their invokation a controversial issue. A case in point was the scepticism expressed towards civil and political rights at the Teheran Conference on Human Rights in 1968.[41] Some authors from the period also recognised the neo-imperialist potential inherent in human rights discourse, even though these concerns emerged in full only with the rise of Western human rights discourse in the subsequent decades.[42] It is probably for these reasons that the international documents setting out the NIEO hardly mention human rights. In fact, the NIEO Declaration contains only one reference to human dignity while placing emphasis on sovereignty and the construction of domestic welfare states.[43] The subsequent Charter of Economic Rights and Duties of States at least mentions the duty of states to comply with international human rights norms.[44]

On the other hand, the struggle for independence in the Global South, which provided the context for the idea of a NIEO, was closely aligned with a collective, structural understanding of human rights. Accordingly, sovereign equality and independence were considered as crucial prerequisites for realising human rights by way of economic development.[45] This framing of human rights is reflected in the first Article of each of the two International Covenants. Similarly, the 1968 Proclamation of Teheran emphasizes national liberation, anti-racism, and economic development as key challenges for human rights.[46] In the light of this, some go as far as to claim that the connection between human rights, self-determination, and development had become so strong that the Global South monopolised human rights discourse and made it unattractive for industrialised economies to engage in human rights discourse up until the rediscovery of human rights during the 1970s.[47]

The latter strand of thinking reveals a structural paradigm of human rights, one that supported the demand for a NIEO. It broke through in the debates surrounding the emergence of the right to development, a collective right expressing the desire for national economic self-determination and a fair international economic order rather than an individual entitlement.[48] The human rights practice of the United Nations during the 1970s, the incubation

[40] Jan Eckel, *Die Ambivalenz des Guten: Menschenrechte in der Internationalen Politik seit den 1940ern* (Vandenhoeck & Ruprecht 2014) 260ff.

[41] Roland Burke, *Decolonization and the Evolution of International Human Rights* (Univ. of Pennsylvania Press 2010) 99ff.

[42] Johan Galtung, 'The New International Economic Order and the Basic Needs Approach' (1979) 4 Alternatives 455, 462; Makau Wa Mutua, 'The Ideology of Human Rights' (1996) 36 Virginia Journal of International Law 589.

[43] Declaration on the Establishment of a New International Economic Order, UNGA Res 3201 (S-VI) (1 May 1974) UN Doc A/RES/S-6/3201.

[44] Charter of Economic Rights and Duties of States, UNGA Res 3281 (XXIX) (12 December 1974) UN Doc A/RES/29/3281 ch 1, lit k.

[45] RP Anand, 'Sovereign Equality of States in International Law—II' (1966) 8 International Studies 386, 406; Christian Reus-Smit, 'Human Rights and the Social Construction of Sovereignty' (2001) 27 Review of International Studies 519; Bradley R Simpson, 'Self-Determination, Human Rights, and the End of Empire in the 1970s' (2013) 4 Humanity 239; Moyn (n 4) 104, 111–12; Slaughter (n 13); Janne Mende, 'Are Human Rights Western—And Why Does it Matter? A Perspective from International Political Theory' (2019) Journal of International Political Theory (forthcoming); Burke (n 41) 37. This connection between sovereign equality and development recalls the Kantian idea of formal freedom and equality, which Kant believed to bring about social justice, see Frederick Rauscher, 'Kant's Social and Political Philosophy' in Edward N Zalta (ed), *The Stanford Encyclopedia of Philosophy Archive* (Spring 2017 edition) <https://plato.stanford.edu/archives/spr2017/entries/kant-social-political/> accessed 1 June 2020.

[46] United Nations, Final Act of the International Conference on Human Rights (22 April–13 May 1968) UN Doc A/CONF.32/41, chapter II 'Proclamation of Teheran'.

[47] Jan Eckel, 'Symbolische Macht. Antikolonialismus und Menschenrechte in den Vereinten Nationen' in Frei and Weinke (eds) (n 33) 134, 142–3. On the rebirth of human rights discourse in the West, see Moyn (n 6) 120ff.

[48] cf Declaration on the Right to Development, UNGA Res 41/128 (4 December 1986) UN Doc A/RES/41/128.

period of the right to development, reflects this understanding of human rights and its close alignment with the NIEO. Notably, General Assembly Resolution 32/130 of 1977 outlines a comprehensive set of 'alternative approaches and ways and means within the United Nations system for improving the effective enjoyment of human rights and fundamental freedoms'. The resolution stipulates that human rights questions require a global perspective, thereby shifting the focus from individual entitlements to collective plight characterised by structural Western dominance, including apartheid, colonialism, threats to national sovereignty and sovereignty over natural resources. It goes on declaring the realisation of the NIEO as essential for promoting human rights.[49] In this sense, UNCTAD Resolution 222 (XXI) on the debt problems of developing countries, a brainchild of NIEO, is a mosaic stone in the broader struggle for economic independence understood as a struggle for human rights.

The second discourse challenging austerity became known as the basic (human) needs approach. It began to thrive in virtually all international organisations charged with development issues since about 1970. The career of the concept received a decisive impulse from the International Labour Organization (ILO), which at the time grappled with the realisation that growth alone would not lead to equitable development, peace, and stability in the developing world. To bring redistribution on the table, it shifted its focus to basic (human) needs. The turns and twists of the debate about the basic (human) needs approach are too many to recount here in detail.[50] Suffice it to say that it was never fully resolved whether basic (human) needs implied a 'thick', egalitarian concept of welfare, or whether it amounted to ensuring sufficiency only.

On the one hand, the 1976 Tripartite World Conference on Employment, Income Distribution and Social Progress and the International Division of Labour suggested already by its title that it aimed for more ambitious levels of redistribution. Consequently, its Programme of Action explicitly extended the notion of basic needs beyond what was necessary for survival, and stipulated that full and fair employment should not only provide income, but also self-respect and dignity.[51] It advocated a participatory approach that drew on multiple influences, including heterodox economic policy approaches in China and Tanzania.[52] Accordingly, the concept of basic *human* needs was associated both with minimum floors and with income ceilings.[53]

Contrariwise, the World Bank's basic needs approach launched by President McNamara set itself less ambitious objectives by focusing on poverty, hence on those most in need.[54] This emphasis on efficiency and the alleged lack of respect for self-determination inherent in the basic needs approach drew criticism from representatives of the Third World,[55] but remained influential nevertheless through the institutional prowess of the World Bank.

[49] UNGA Res 32/130 (16 December 1977) para 1(d) and (f); see Baxi (n 39) 227; Julia Dehm, 'Highlighting Inequalities in the Histories of Human Rights: Contestations over Justice, Needs and Rights in the 1970s' (2018) 31 Leiden Journal of International Law 871, 882ff.

[50] See Reginald Herbold Green, 'Basic Human Needs: Concept or Slogan, Synthesis or Smokescreen?' (1978) 9 The IDS Bulletin 7; Assefa Bequele and David H Freedman, 'Employment and Basic Needs: An Overview' (1979) 118 International Labour Review 315; Dehm (n 49) 875.

[51] World Employment Conference, Declaration of Principles and Programme of Action (5 July 1976) UN Doc E/5857 paras 4–5.

[52] Green (n 50) 8; see also Jean Mouly, 'Employment: A Concept in Need of Renovation' (1977) 116 International Labour Review 1; Bequele and Freedman (n 48) 318.

[53] Green (n 50) 10.

[54] Moyn (n 4) 131, 190. Background on the World Bank discussions in Dehm (n 49) 879.

[55] Galtung (n 42) 461ff.

Given the ambiguity inherent in the basic (human) needs approach, some established a connection with human rights to tilt it towards a 'thick', egalitarian meaning. Such a shift was almost an obvious choice. The 1968 Teheran Proclamation had popularised the framing of development issues in human rights language.[56] The text of the Declaration of Principle of the 1976 World Employment Conference with its highly egalitarian aspirations took up the momentum, referring explicitly to the UDHR and specifically to the right to work. In fact, this Declaration prompted Philip Alston to highlight commonalities and differences between basic (human) needs and human rights, merging the two discursive strands with egalitarian objectives in mind.[57] Similarly, Upendra Baxi argued that the basic (human) needs approach reflected an egalitarian concept of ESC rights.[58] The association of basic (human) needs with human rights therefore represented a discursive strategy to vindicate the social against the economic in the ongoing rethinking of development economics. Once more, the understanding of human rights emerging in this context expresses a structural paradigm. Rather than guaranteeing individual entitlements or self-determination, human rights are meant to facilitate quality development, including fair and full employment, not mere sufficiency.

Hence, at the end of the 1970s, both the UNCTAD debt debate and the basic (human) needs approach (the two discourses relevant for framing austerity at the international level during this decade) were in various respects aligned with, and informed by, a structural paradigm of human rights that gave human rights a role to play in respect to the relationship between the economic and the social (axis 1). Each of these discourses showed a certain, though limited, affinity for more egalitarian forms of redistribution (axis 2). The NIEO debate followed an inchoate idea of human rights and only focused on the aggregate impact of the international order on the economic situation of states and groups. The basic (human) needs approach was caught up in disputes between equality and sufficiency. Nevertheless, despite these ambiguities, in retrospect, it seemed possible for a structuralist understanding of human rights in one form or another to become a highly relevant standard for the governance of sovereign debt crises and austerity.[59]

III. The 1980s: from human needs to human capital

The potential alignment between the governance of sovereign debt crises and human rights discourse did not materialise in the subsequent decade, even though this decade saw a massive wave of austerity befall the Global South. This wave followed on the heels of attempts to ensure greater respect for self-determination through a reform of conditionality in 1979 restricting the use of performance criteria.[60] The bulging debt crisis in the developing world, beginning with Mexico's default in 1982, quickly turned discourse on austerity in the reverse direction and led to a steady increase in performance criteria, imposing tougher austerity

[56] United Nations, Final Act of the International Conference on Human Rights (22 April–13 May 1968) UN Doc A/CONF.32/41, chapter II 'Proclamation of Teheran', paras 12 and 13.

[57] Philip Alston, 'Human Rights and Basic Needs: A Critical Assessment' (1979) 12 Human Rights Journal / Revue des Droits de l'Homme 19, 21.

[58] Baxi (n 39) 228–29.

[59] cf Baxi (n 39) 233.

[60] IMF Decision no 6056-(79/38) (2 March 1979) para 4; Erik Denters, *Law and Policy of IMF Conditionality* (Springer 1996) 96.

on debtor states. This revival of austerity was unwarranted and counterproductive. The debt crisis resulted chiefly from major global developments like rising interest rates in the United States and falling commodity prices as developed countries made the transition from industrial to service economies. However, the massive expansion of the IMF's lending activities created funding constraints on the part of the IMF that prompted it to impose tighter austerity to ensure timely repayment. In response to the crisis, the IMF opened two concessional lending windows, the Structural Adjustment Facility and the Enhanced Structural Adjustment Facility, in 1986 and 1987 respectively.[61] Another reason was ideological. The Baker Plan adopted in 1985 advocated the creed that debtor states should outgrow their debt crises in a grit-your-teeth-and-get-to-it mode. Harsh, shock-like adjustment and radical market orientation would ensure that growth would kick in soon and trickle down the echelons of the social hierarchy.[62] The Baker Plan was implemented thanks to a supportive coalition comprising the governments of developed countries, international banks, and senior staff at the IMF.[63] This rendered resistance from the Global South fruitless.[64] Legally speaking, the guidelines on conditionality left the IMF enough interpretative leeway for such a profound reversal of the 1979 reform, not least because the distinction between macroeconomic and microeconomic criteria is all but clear-cut since many measures cause both macro and micro effects.[65]

As a result, the management of debt crises became a much more tightly regulated, internationally coordinated endeavour involving significant levels of austerity, ie contractionary fiscal policies.[66] Not only did the number of conditionalities increase, but their quality changed, too. Of particular significance was the introduction of structural benchmarks.[67] They prescribe structural reforms with supposed long-term effects, such as an overhaul of public financial management. While entailing high sovereignty costs, the hope was that such benchmarks would send a powerful signal to creditors and restore the country's credit trustworthiness.[68] The price of this new brand of structural adjustment came in the form of a huge impact on ESC rights, effectuated mainly through cutting back subsidies and public services and their simultaneous liberalisation and privatisation.

Against the background of the debates during the 1970s, one might have expected some scope for the basic (human) rights critique to morph into a fully-fledged human rights discourse. In fact, one of the most powerful critiques, the one to which the IMF as the organisation in charge of approving adjustment programmes finally reacted, was advanced by other international organisations using the language of basic (human) needs. The activities of the World Bank and the United Nations International Children's Fund (UNICEF)

[61] Dreher and Vaubel (n 12) 37; James M Boughton, *Silent Revolution: The International Monetary Fund 1979–1989* (International Monetary Fund 2001) 644ff.
[62] Boughton (n 61) 417; Naomi Klein, *The Shock Doctrine: The Rise of Disaster Capitalism* (Macmillan 2007) 155ff.
[63] See the meticulous reconstruction in Alexander E Kentikelenis and Sarah Babb, 'The Making of Neoliberal Globalization: Norm Substitution and the Politics of Clandestine Institutional Change' (2019) 124 American Journal of Sociology 1720.
[64] Reinhart and Rogoff (n 1) 91–92; Pahuja (n 11) 782ff.
[65] Denters (n 60) 111.
[66] cf Mark Blyth, *Austerity: The History of a Dangerous Idea* (OUP 2013) 161ff.
[67] Dreher and Vaubel (n 12) 32; Boughton (n 61) 417.
[68] Wolfgang Streeck, 'The Rise of the European Consolidation State' (2015) Max-Planck-Institut für Gesellschaftsforschung Discussion Paper 15/1, 12.

were instrumental in this regard.[69] UNICEF is a particularly interesting case. It was probably among the first organisations to notice the effects of the new forms of austerity on rising malnutrition rates of children, difficulties afflicting the situation of women, and other vulnerable groups of society.[70] A 1983 report recommended a mix of different measures. Some of them aimed at better ensuring the most basic needs by proposing simple strategies for using scarce resources more efficiently, which would be compatible with the idea of sufficiency.[71] Others pursued more ambitious goals and connected the ordeal of children to greater global injustices, including problems of female education, income inequality, and the divide between the North and the South.[72] The seminal 1987 UNICEF report 'Adjustment with a Human Face' featured a similar mix of sufficiency and equality. Like other UNICEF reports, it avoided the term 'human rights', but on substance, it was all about them.[73] The report begins with Tanzanian President Nyerere asking his now-famous rhetorical question: 'Must we starve our children to pay our debts?'[74] The report then recommends expanding the focus of adjustment from radical short-termism to medium-term recovery, requiring larger financial volumes and debt relief. While it recognises the need to shield the vulnerable, it also considers measures that go beyond sufficiency, such as the idea of 'expansionary adjustment' to avoid deflation. One could therefore say that it combines a desire for more efficiency to ensure minimal standards with awareness of the need for greater overall redistribution.

The IMF response to these proposals was brisk at first.[75] In contrast to the World Bank, the IMF had not yet internalised the basic (human) needs approach at the time. It still understood itself as an organisation with a macroeconomic mandate, not one of development economics. From its point of view, the question was still open whether adjustment was the cause of troubles, or the cure. In fact, it had studied the distributive impact of adjustment since the 1970s, and its research had not established whether adjustment worsened the distributive effects of a debt crisis compared to a scenario without an adjustment programme.[76]

In the following, however, UNICEF and the Bretton Woods Institutions entered into a policy dialogue on the matter at the request of the latter.[77] This policy dialogue generated an astonishing result. IMF Managing Director Jacques de Larosière in a remarkable, frequently quoted speech did in fact recognise the urgency of ensuring basic human needs, but gave the notion a particular spin:

> Programmes of adjustment cannot be effective unless they command the support of governments and of public opinion. Yet this support will be progressively harder to maintain

[69] While reports by those involved on the side of UNICEF might overstate their role, the official IMF historian recognises such external influences, see Boughton (n 61) 694–95.

[70] Maggie Black, *Children First: The Story of UNICEF, Past and Present* (OUP 1996) 158.

[71] UNICEF, *The State of the World's Children 1984* (OUP 1983) 5ff.

[72] ibid 23, 57ff and 67.

[73] UNICEF, *Adjustment with a Human Face*, published as part II of UNICEF, *The State of the World's Children 1987* (OUP 1986). In 1977, UNICEF adopted a policy on basic services that sounds minimalistic, see Alston (n 57) 24. Nevertheless, by virtue of its different subject, this policy view did not address labour market issues and income distribution.

[74] UNICEF (n 73) 95.

[75] See the account in Richard Jolly, 'Adjustment with a Human Face: A UNICEF Record and Perspective on the 1980s' (1991) 19 World Development 1807.

[76] ibid 1811; Boughton (n 61) 696.

[77] Report of the Executive Director, UNICEF Executive Board (24 February 1987) E/ICEF/1987/2; Black (n 70) 158.

> the longer adjustment continues without some pay-off in terms of growth and while human conditions are deteriorating. Likewise, it is hard to visualize how a viable external position can be achieved if large segments of the work force lack the vocational skills – or even worse, the basic nutritional and health standards – to produce goods that are competitive in world markets. Human capital is after all the most important factor of production in developing and industrial countries alike.[78]

Within one paragraph, de Larosière switched from human conditions (which one might consider as equivalent to human needs) to human capital. On the way, the structural orientation and egalitarian component once associated with the basic (human) needs approach as introduced by UNICEF got lost and basic (human) needs became a lever to push through market liberalisation, as the speech further elaborates.[79] Hence, while income inequality goes unmentioned, the speech cultivates the image of the wasteful state. The recognition that cuts in investments can be detrimental provides little comfort as it leaves open whether it refers to private or public investments. In other words, this speech, rendered a few months after the launch of the Baker Plan and the Structural Adjustment Facility, aligns the basic (human) needs approach with what has later been called the Washington Consensus.[80] The shift was subtle, but clear. The concept of basic (human) needs, which might have become a placeholder for an egalitarian idea of human rights, was bent in the direction of sufficiency and bereft of its more egalitarian potential. The economic prevailed over the social.

This conceptual shift was paradigmatic for the austerity debates in the 1980s. It saw the near-complete abandonment of the structuralist paradigm of human rights familiar from the austerity debates in the 1970s. The void was not immediately filled by another human rights discourse or paradigm. To explain the absence of the voice of human rights in the choir criticising austerity, it is helpful to take into consideration the wider context within which these debates took place. For a number of reasons, it was not an obvious or even attractive choice for UNICEF or other actors to frame their scepticism of the new wave of austerity in the language of human rights.

To begin with, there is little evidence that the missing human rights-based critique of austerity resulted from the much-described rediscovery of human rights in the West towards the end of the 1970s in the context of the decline of the Soviet Union, the rise of neoliberalism, and terrorist threats, and the related rise of a new old liberal paradigm of human rights as primarily individual, negative entitlements.[81] While I do not have reason to doubt the accounts of the rise of that paradigm, it seems unlikely that it would have motivated UNICEF to refrain from a human rights critique of austerity in the mid-1980s. At this point in time, the shift towards a liberal paradigm of human rights was still ongoing, and alternative understandings of human rights actually found quite some resonance in international organisations. The United Nations was in the midst of the emergence of a third generation of human rights.[82] One important element of this process was the right to development,

[78] Remarks of de Larosière before the UN Economic and Social Council (4 July 1986) quoted in Jolly (n 75) 1816.
[79] See ibid.
[80] John Williamson, 'Democracy and the "Washington consensus"' (1993) 21 World Development 1329.
[81] Eckel (n 40) 343ff; Moyn (n 6) 120ff; Moyn (n 4) 70ff; on the neoliberal turn in human rights law, see Upendra Baxi, *The Future of Human Rights* (OUP 2007); BS Chimni, 'International Institutions Today: An Imperial Global State in the Making' (2004) 15 European Journal of International Law 1, 11.
[82] Philip Alston, 'A Third Generation of Solidarity Rights: Progressive Development or Obfuscation of International Human Rights Law?' (1982) 29 Netherlands International Law Review 307; Slaughter (n 13) 753.

endorsed in 1986.[83] UNICEF, for that matter, actively participated during these years in the drafting of the Convention on the Rights of the Child, an agreement bristling with second and third generation human rights reaching, at least prima facie, far beyond sufficiency.[84]

A different reason seems more plausible. There was simply no established practice of criticising the operations of international organisations for their human rights record. In fact, international human rights emerged in the post-war period as protection against nation states and their governments, not against international organisations. In the 1960s, liberation movements invoked human rights to claim sovereign equality from other states, not from international organisations. As I showed, the basic needs approach and the NIEO understood international organisations as instruments for the promotion and realisation of human rights. While it is one thing to debate how the IFIs should promote human rights, it is quite a different matter to claim that their operations threaten human rights. On the whole, the idea of international organisations as threats to human rights did not impose itself in the same way as it does today. This appears to result from the legacy of functionalism, the mid-twentieth-century theory which had depicted international organisations as agents of peace through rational bureaucracy.[85] Imagining IMF-imposed austerity as a human rights problem might therefore seem much more obvious for us than it appeared to UNICEF and its contemporaries at the time. It may have helped that the IMF's mandate, as the official doctrine claimed, did not extend to 'non-economic' considerations.[86] The limits of the mandate were the bone of contention regarding structural performance criteria,[87] and adding human rights to the equation would have potentially undermined the position of those desiring a more restrictive exercise of the mandate. In any case, the IMF could react much better to economic rather than non-economic arguments.[88]

It is presumably for these reasons that there are very few scholarly critiques of austerity from a human rights perspective up until the end of the 1980s.[89] Instead of invoking

[83] Declaration on the Right to Development (n 48).

[84] Documentation in Office of the United Nations High Commissioner for Human Rights, 'Legislative History on the Convention on the Rights of the Child' (2007) (*Save the Children's Resource Centre*) <https://resourcecentre.savethechildren.net/library/legislative-history-convention-rights-child-volume-1> accessed 1 June 2020.

[85] cf David Mitrany, 'The Functional Approach to World Organization' (1948) 24 International Affairs 350. On the emergence of the functionalist paradigm see Jan Klabbers, 'The Emergence of Functionalism in International Institutional Law: Colonial Inspirations' (2014) 25 European Journal of International Law 645. On the lasting effects see Jens Steffek, 'Max Weber, Modernity and the Project of International Organization' (2016) 29 Cambridge Review of International Affairs 1502. An intriguing example for the functionalist view of international organisations is Wolfgang G Friedmann, *The Changing Structure of International Law* (Stevens & Sons 1964).

[86] Joseph Gold, 'Conditionality' (1979) IMF Pamphlet Series No 31, 61. Hence, a Congressional Committee assumed in 1978 without further ado that membership rights could not be restricted by human rights, ibid 62; François Gianviti, *Economic, Social, and Cultural Human Rights and the International Monetary Fund* (2001). On the functionalist pedigree of this view: Mac Darrow, *Between Light and Shadow: The World Bank, the International Monetary Fund and International Human Rights Law* (Hart Publishing 2003) 205–06. For an early deconstruction of this doctrine: Richard Swedberg, 'The Doctrine of Economic Neutrality of the IMF and the World Bank' (1986) 23 Journal of Peace Research 377.

[87] Gold (n 86) 66 on the overlap between economics and politics and the ensuing desire of the Board to restrict performance criteria to macroeconomic indicators.

[88] Joseph Gold, 'Financial Assistance by the International Monetary Fund: Law and Practice' (1979) IMF Pamphlet Series No 27, 14–15; Laurence Boisson de Chazournes, 'The Bretton Woods Institutions and Human Rights' in Wolfgang Benedek, Koen de Feyter, and Fabrizio Marrella (eds), *Economic Globalisation and Human Rights* (CUP 2007) 210, 214.

[89] A rare example is Margaret Conklin and Daphne Davidson, 'The I. M. F. and Economic and Social Human Rights: A Case Study of Argentina, 1958–1985' (1986) 8 Human Rights Quarterly 227. See also James H Mittelman and Will Donald, 'The International Monetary Fund, State Autonomy and Human Rights' (1987) 34 Africa Today 49 (focusing, however, on violations of civil and political rights committed by governments of debtor states forcing adjustment programmes upon their people).

human rights, scholars and international organisations exchanged economic arguments, debating the most desirable and efficient path to growth and development.[90] Paradigmatic is a conference convened by the ILO in 1987 bringing together many relevant stakeholders. Participants agreed on the devastating effects of the recent debt crises on employment and human conditions, but no one formulated their critique of austerity in terms of human rights. Instead, UNCTAD and a number of developing states like Tanzania recalled the NIEO framework when demanding more resources and better distribution, both within and between countries,[91] whereas the IMF and Western countries insisted on structural adjustment through liberalisation as a path to growth. The conclusions of the conference combined a plea for basic needs with somewhat general concessions regarding procedures, stressing the need for a broad consensus on adjustment programmes in the debtor states.[92] A similar fate awaited regional initiatives that had voiced analogous critiques, refuting the encroachment of neoliberal adjustment policies and proposing more heterodox approaches. With the Consenso de Cartagena, heavily affected Latin American countries called for additional funding and debt relief,[93] to which the capital exporting countries responded with the Baker Plan. The UN Economic Commission for Africa's 1989 proposal for an African alternative adjustment framework made the case for a more holistic, long-term approach to adjustment that would allow the economies of the region to increase production and diversify, but was shrugged off by the IMF.[94]

In the end, there was practically no one with enough reason to invoke human rights against austerity during this period. The governments of crisis-ridden debtor states were frequently compromised as the implementation of austerity often enough involved flagrant human rights violations.[95] The case of Chile in the 1970s had illustrated the potential impact of human rights campaigns on global public opinion.[96] Conversely, the political opposition developed an interest in presenting themselves as the better debtors, both before and after ascending to power.[97] Calls for cancelling debt on the basis of its odious character only re-emerged with full force towards the end of the century.[98]

[90] ILO, 'High Level Meeting on Employment and Structural Adjustment' (23–25 November 1987) ILO Doc WEP 2-46-04-03.

[91] ibid para 18.

[92] ibid 28 (para 1), 30 (para 16); see Joel M Ngugi, 'Policing Neo-Liberal Reforms: The Rule of Law as an Enabling and Restrictive Discourse' (2005) 26 University of Pennsylvania Journal of International Economic Law 513, 570.

[93] Consenso de Cartagena (1985) 52 El Trimestre Económico 267; see also Arturo O'Connell, 'La Coordinacion de los Deudores Latinoamericanos: El Consenso de Cartagena y el Gruop de los Ochos' (1988) 21 Estudios Internacionales 373.

[94] United Nations Economic Commission for Africa, *African Alternative Framework to Structural Adjustment Programmes for Socio-Economic Recovery and Transformation* (1989); the ensuing common statement with the IMF reflects more disagreement than consensus, see Jolly (n 75) 1817.

[95] M Rodwan Abouharb and David L Cingranelli, 'IMF Programs and Human Rights, 1981–2003' (2008) 4 The Review of International Organizations 47.

[96] Eckel (n 40) 583ff; see also Horace A Bartilow, *The Debt Dilemma: IMF Negotiations in Jamaica, Grenada and Guyana* (Caribbean 1997); Jolly (n 75) 1816.

[97] cf Bartilow (n 96) 139.

[98] Klein (n 62) 156ff reports an odious debt debate in Latin American states overcoming autocracies. However, apart from a few occasional mentions, there is relatively little evidence for an odious debt debate in civil society and academia before the mid-1990s. Exceptions include Günter Frankenberg and Rolf Knieper, 'Legal Problems of the Overindebtedness of Developing Countries: The Current Relevance of the Doctrine of Odious Debts' (1984) 12 International Journal of the Sociology of Law 415; Luis Díaz Müller, 'El Derecho al Desarrollo y los Derechos Humanos' (1986) 4 Revista IIDH 5. Discussions related to odious debt in the 1980s and early 1990s predominantly refer to old cases, such as Chinese bonds from 1911, eg Tamar Lewin, 'Legal Claims against China', *The New York Times* (New York, 29 November 1983) Section D 2. Only the use of the concept in the South African Truth and Reconciliation Commission's 1998 report and the debt relief granted to Iraq after the 2003 war triggered a rich debate on the odious character of dictatorship debts. See South African Truth and Reconciliation Commission, 4

Thus, the conflict about austerity in the 1980s happened to be framed as a dispute over competing economic approaches, and the powerful actors favoured the neoliberal response. Not only their power of the purse deployed by the Baker Plan may have contributed to the ultimate success of their strategy, but also the fact that the structural approach advocated by post-war Latin American development economists had foundered precisely with this crisis.[99] The political left in Latin America and elsewhere found it difficult to formulate an alternative response to the growing neoliberal maelstrom.[100] Further difficulty arose from the fact that the debtor states did not agree on economic policies, with some of them even committing to austerity. It was certainly with the utmost delight that the Baker Plan quoted the Mexican president saying: 'The only way to overcome our economic crisis is to tackle at their root the structural problems of our economy to make it more efficient and productive'.[101] Such views added pressure on countries like Ghana, Zambia, or Tanzania desiring in word or deed a different economic policy.[102]

Unsurprisingly, one of the consequences of this debt crisis was the side-lining of UNCTAD as a relevant forum for debt issues, at least compared to its position during the 1970s. While it continued to monitor the debt situation, the momentum created by its earlier resolutions evaporated, and decisive impulses came from Western governments and the IFIs.

In conclusion, one might take from the development during the 1980s the insight that it is one thing to call for changes to the existing economic order in the name of human rights, but quite a different thing to operationalise human rights for a critique of adjustment programmes. Transiting from one paradigm to another requires a considerable shift in the function of human rights. The former view relies on state sovereignty; the latter view presupposes defining the role of human rights in global governance. Human rights virtually had to change sides, and this took some time. Human rights therefore did next to nothing to prevent the economic from prevailing over the social in austerity debates during the 1980s. Human rights discourse was simply unprepared for neoliberal globalisation.

Final Report (1998) para 151; Lee C Buchheit, G Mitu Galati, and Robert B Thompson, 'The Dilemma of Odious Debts' (2006) 56 Duke Law Journal 1201, 1220 (on past debates), 1230 (on Iraq). The debate critically revisited debt incurred by Argentina's military dictatorship, eg David Harvey, *The New Imperialism* (OUP 2003) 159–60; Eric Toussaint, *Your Money or Your Life!* (Pluto 2003) 200ff; Sabine Michalowski, 'Repayment of Sovereign Debts from a Legal Perspective: The Example of Argentina' in Janet Dine and Andrew Fagan (eds), *Human Rights and Capitalism A Multidisciplinary Perspective on Globalisation* (Elgar 2006) 303, 309. For a more cautious assessment, see Anna Gelpern, 'What Iraq and Argentina Might Learn from Each Other' (2005) 6 Chicago Journal of International Law 391. The debate continues. On Chile, see recently Juan Pablo Bohoslavsky, Karinna Fernández, and Sebastián Smart (eds), Complicidad Económica con la Dictadura Chilena. Un País Desigual a la Fuerza (LOM Ediciones 2019).

[99] Blyth (n 66) 161; Patrice Franko, *The Puzzle of Latin American Economic Development* (Rowman & Littlefield 2018) 70.

[100] Jolly (n 75) 1817; Barry Carr, 'The Mexican Left, the Popular Movements, and the Politics of Austerity 1982–1985' in Barry Carr and Ricardo Anzaldúa Montoya (eds), *The Mexican Left, the Popular Movements, and the Politics of Austerity* (University of California 1986) 1; Moyn (n 4) 128ff.

[101] The Baker Plan is reproduced in Detlev CHR Dicke (ed) *Foreign Debts in the Present and a New International Economic Order* (University Press Firbourg 1986) 290. Quote at 294.

[102] On heterodox persistence, see Jolly (n 75) 1817; on Ghana and Zambia see further John Baloro, 'African Responses to the Debt Crisis: the Relevance of Public International Law' (1991) 24 Verfassung und Recht in Übersee/Law and Politics in Africa, Asia and Latin America 28.

IV. Conclusion: contingencies of human rights discourse

The story does not end here.[103] The 1990s witnessed the birth of a transformative human rights paradigm in critiques of austerity that endorsed an egalitarian understanding of ESC rights. But even when austerity became virulent in the 1990s, human rights-based critiques remained marginal. The transformative paradigm was side-lined by a then-dominant liberal paradigm of human rights law as internationally guaranteed standards for domestic governments, attributing at the same time to socioeconomic rights at best the status of a backstop against abject poverty. Only the experience of September 11 and the ensuing human rights critique of international organisations, I argue, led to the breakthrough of human rights-based critiques of austerity in the aftermath of the Global Financial Crisis. Still, when human rights litigation against austerity abounded after 2010, it carried meagre success. The transformative paradigm kept struggling with the liberal paradigm, and courts often did not see it as their task to protect equality, including middle-class privileges.[104] In addition, the multilevel structure of structural adjustment programmes and their soft legal nature got in the way of judicial scrutiny.[105] Significant developments did, however, take place in the practice of international institutions. In the work of the UN human rights bodies, human rights discourse is now more firmly established than ever as a highly relevant standard for assessing structural adjustment.[106] The IMF reacted by reconsidering its policy on social spending, which emphasises the need for inclusive growth.[107]

What are the lessons of this account for human rights law? First, the history of human rights discourse is characterised by struggles between vastly different paradigms expressing highly diverging views about the role of human rights for the balance between the economic and the social (axis 1), and for material redistribution and equality (axis 2). These paradigms result from their specific historical situatedness. There is thus not one history of human rights, but many.

Second, human rights discourse adapts only very slowly. Whether a new paradigm gains traction or not depends on the interests of the actors involved, structural predispositions and path dependencies, and to some extent on sheer coincidence. The resulting paradigmatic clashes might render human rights-based critiques ineffective. One should therefore be careful to attribute the persistence of the IFIs in the face of scathing human rights critiques to the opposing economic interests of powerful member states alone. For there is also a conceptual side to such conflicts. The critique is always based on one particular paradigm of human rights, none of which has ever enjoyed universal acceptance. This might explain

[103] For a detailed account, see Goldmann (n 5).

[104] Claire Kilpatrick, 'Constitutions, Social Rights and Sovereign Debt States in Europe: A Challenging New Area of Constitutional Inquiry' in Bruno de Witte, Claire Kilpatrick, and Thomas Beukers (eds), *Constitutional Change Through Euro-Crisis Law* (CUP 2017) 313.

[105] Margot E Salomon, 'Of Austerity, Human Rights and International Institutions' (2015) 21 European Law Journal 521; Joe Wills and Ben TC Warwick, 'Contesting Austerity: The Potential and Pitfalls of Socioeconomic Rights Discourse' (2016) 23 Indiana Journal of Global Legal Studies 629.

[106] Eg Human Rights Council, *Guiding Principles on Human Rights Impact Assessments of Economic Reforms. Report of the Independent Expert on the Effects of Foreign Debt and other Related International Financial Obligations of States on the Full Enjoyment of Human Rights, Particularly Economic, Social and Cultural Rights* (19 December 2018) UN Doc A/HRC/40/57.

[107] IMF, 'A Strategy for IMF Engagement on Social Spending—Background Papers' IMF Policy Paper No 19/017 (14 June 2019).

why the IFIs often reacted to such critique at some point indirectly by adjusting their policies, yet without ever really adopting human rights language.

This leads to a third issue and a question. Is it worth employing human rights law as an effective remedy against austerity? Unsurprisingly, the answer is that it depends on the particular human rights paradigm employed. Under the current political paradigm, human rights allow consensus-building among a disparate field of austerity sceptics comprising intergovernmental organisations, transnational non-governmental organisations of vastly different ideological organisations, local actors, governments, and even international organisations. Given the deep cultural entrenchment of austerity,[108] such a function might not be the least of victories.

Related is the capacity of human rights discourse to increase complexity in decision-making. It may challenge economic discourse with non-economic arguments. This hits a weak point of the institutions potentially promoting austerity. As the field of economic expertise is the natural habitat of institutions promoting austerity like the IMF or the European 'troika', confronting them with (heterodox) economic approaches instead of human rights arguments allows them to carry on unabated. They can simply ignore it, claiming to know it better, and sweeping the underlying normative disagreement under the carpet. This was the fate of NIEO and of the related, interventionist brand of development economics proposed by Prebisch and hedged by UNCTAD. Even the towering authority of Joseph Stiglitz, who had decried the flaws of the orthodox creed for decades, eventually left his position as World Bank Chief Economist over disagreement about the World Bank's approach in tackling the Asian and Russian crises.[109] Unwelcome expertise can simply be dismissed.

Not so human rights. They shift the discussion from one about growth and efficiency to one in which the primacy of growth is no longer a natural given. Even if the Bretton Woods Institutions managed to reinterpret social challenges as questions of growth and effective programme implementation, particularly so with the shift to human capital, human rights defy their expertise to some extent. Ironically, the alleged neutrality of the Bretton Woods Institutions and particularly the IMF gives human rights their strength as it silences them on the issue. From this angle, much of the doctrinal debate on the human rights obligations of the IMF seems to be beside the point. As a discursive strategy for contesting austerity, its success is premised on the fallacy that there is only one right, universally shared understanding of human rights, which the critics of the IMF can control. Under the status quo, human rights discourse exposes institutions like the IMF to a yardstick of scrutiny whose terms they cannot control as much as they may control debates about the economic merits of austerity. It is therefore precisely the fact that the IMF considers itself unbound by human rights which makes it vulnerable to human rights discourse.

One more question remains. Is it possible to instil egalitarianism into austerity via human rights discourse and to effectively question sufficiency? In the literature, there seems to be disagreement about this point. Samuel Moyn argues that an egalitarian theory of socioeconomic distribution would be more demanding than human rights,[110] while

[108] Blyth (n 66).

[109] Richard W Stephenson, 'Outspoken Chief Economist Leaving World Bank' *The New York Times* (New York, 25 November 1999) <http://www.nytimes.com/1999/11/25/business/outspoken-chief-economist-leaving-world-bank.html> accessed 1 June 2020.

[110] Moyn (n 8) 168.

Paul O'Connell, among others, has called for invigorating human rights in the face of austerity.[111]

I believe it is not only possible but also worth trying to entrench more equality. For this to succeed, it is in a first step necessary to take the political paradigm seriously and to debunk the myth of the non-political character of human rights and of the allegedly political character of social rights.[112] This framing of human rights discourse bequeathed from the liberal paradigm only covers up the contingency implicit in the choice for sufficiency and conceals alternative, more egalitarian approaches which fully honour the promise of the progressive realisation of socioeconomic rights. Instead, one needs to reassert the transformative character of legal discourse as a potential receptacle for progressive ideas catalysing political processes of social development and integration, rather than a means of encoding capital, entrenching morality, or stifling overreliance on courts. As the transformative paradigm of human rights law comes with a heavy focus on courts,[113] the political paradigm proposal would require going back to the original idea of transformative constitutionalism built into constitutions from the interwar and post-war era that saw politics and social movements at the helm of social transformation,[114] and to advance such an idea of human rights in the context of contemporary institutional frameworks for human rights protection and expertise.

Those still sceptical of the political paradigm should consider one last aspect. Giving up on it would only give way for another looming paradigm. It would depoliticise human rights law again, only this time not in the service of capital but of the beneficiaries of authoritarian paternalism.[115]

[111] Paul O'Connell, 'On Reconciling Irreconcilables: Neo-Liberal Globalisation and Human Rights' (2007) 7 Human Rights Law Review 483.

[112] On this myth, see also Susan Marks, 'Four Human Rights Myths' in David Kinley, Wojciech Sadurski, and Kevin Walton (eds), *Human Rights: Old Problems, New Possibilities* (Edward Elgar Publishing 2013) 217, 229.

[113] Kilpatrick (n 104).

[114] Menéndez and Goldmann (n 14).

[115] For the legal manifesto of authoritarian paternalism, see Adrian Vermeule, 'Beyond Originalism' (*The Atlantic*, 31 March 2020) <www.theatlantic.com/ideas/archive/2020/03/common-good-constitutionalism/609037/> accessed 1 June 2020.

D.

ARMED CONFLICT

19

Contingencies of Context

Legacies of the Algerian Revolution in the 1977 Additional Protocols to the Geneva Conventions

Emma Stone Mackinnon

I. Introduction

The 1977 Additional Protocols to the Geneva Conventions contain one of the most explicit appearances of anticolonial political thought in and as international law. Additional Protocol I, Article 1, paragraph 4 extends to wars of national liberation the status of international armed conflicts, defining the scope of the application of the law of international armed conflict to include 'armed conflicts in which peoples are fighting against colonial domination and alien occupation and against racist regimes in the exercise of their right of self-determination'.[1] With paragraph 4, even as other provisions would work to contain its effects, the new text vindicated anticolonial claims to the legitimacy of independence struggles. In doing so, the document both commented on and helped reshape the relationship between state sovereignty and humanitarian concern, as well as between anticolonialism and international law as an historical project.

The 1977 clause is usually read as a reflection of the then-recent past and a projection of its lessons into the future. The Geneva Conventions, the first of which had been adopted in 1864, had last been expanded and updated in 1949. Initial drafts of what would become the Additional Protocols, having been drawn up by the International Committee of the Red Cross and Red Crescent (ICRC), were debated in a series of conferences and meetings in Switzerland between 1974 and 1977 under the title of the Diplomatic Conference on the Reaffirmation and Development of International Humanitarian Law Applicable in Armed Conflicts (CDDH). Where the 1949 Conventions were drafted in the shadow of two world wars, this time the delegates were working in the shadow of anticolonial conflicts, especially those in Algeria and Vietnam.[2]

[1] An overview and a link to the full text of Additional Protocol 1, along with a list of the 174 states parties and three signatories, is available on the ICRC's website at <https://ihl-databases.icrc.org/applic/ihl/ihl.nsf/INTRO/470> accessed 10 September 2019. The Additional Protocols, and all discussions that went into their drafting, are also available through the Library of Congress at <www.loc.gov/rr/frd/Military_Law/pdf/RC-Draft-additional-protocols.pdf> accessed 10 September 2019. Note the final text of Article 1, paragraph 4 continues from here: 'as enshrined in the Charter of the United Nations and the Declaration on Principles of International Law concerning Friendly Relations and Co-operation among States in accordance with the Charter of the United Nations'.

[2] The emphasis on the legacies of Vietnam and Algeria is a major theme of the ICRC's commentaries, discussed below. This theme is shared with much of the historiography; for an overview, see, Giovanni Mantilla, 'The Origins and Evolution of the 1949 Geneva Conventions and the 1977 Additional Protocols' in Matthew Evangelista and Nina Tannenwald (eds), *Do the Geneva Conventions Matter?* (OUP 2017) 35. On the legacy of the Algerian conflict in the 1970s, focused specifically on the 'principle of distinction', see Helen Kinsella, 'The Algerian Civil War and

Emma Stone Mackinnon, *Contingencies of Context* In: *Contingency in International Law.* Edited by: Ingo Venzke and Kevin Jon Heller, Oxford University Press. © The Several Contributors 2021. DOI: 10.1093/oso/9780192898036.003.0019

On some accounts—including, notably, that of the ICRC—the clause was the product of the desire to expand humanitarian provisions, and to adapt them to new circumstances. In this sense, it was part of the broader historical trajectory of the humanisation of war. As the ICRC's commentaries explain it, in the 1970s anticolonial conflicts were understood as an empirical fact; bringing them within the scope of international humanitarian law was something the ICRC and many of the delegates wanted to achieve.[3]

Others have argued that the clause was hardly the straightforward product of humanitarian sentiment alone, and emphasise instead changing political dynamics. When the Additional Protocols were debated, the group of delegates was very different from the earlier meetings: in 1949, sixty-three countries sent representatives or observers to the drafting meetings; during the four sessions concerning the 1977 Additional Protocols, as many as 124 countries took part, as well as eleven national liberation movements.[4] The shadow of anticolonial conflicts, in this sense, was manifest not only in the memory of violence, but in the empowerment of new state actors, who often worked as a bloc. As Giovanni Mantilla has shown, humanitarian concern, while part of the story, was not itself enough to get the United States, United Kingdom, or USSR to the table; mobilisation by Third World and socialist states, through what he describes as 'social pressure', provided crucial additional impetus.[5] In this way, paragraph 4 was possible because of the combination of newly independent nations and national liberation movements represented at the meeting, as well as the fact that multiple groups at the conference had an interest in adopting something along these lines, including several powerful delegations that argued for the pragmatic importance of extending international humanitarian law (IHL) to cover as much as possible and to adapt to the changing nature of armed conflict.[6]

The story I'll tell builds on these accounts, but focuses on a different kind of contingency in the making of the Protocols. In thinking about what it means to make law in the shadow of recent conflicts, it is easy to treat those conflicts as a kind of fixed background context. Instead, I want to suggest, the meaning and significance of that recent past was not fixed, but

the 1977 Protocols Additional' in Helen Kinsella, *The Image Before the Weapon: A Critical History of the Distinction Between Combatant and Civilian* (Cornell University Press 2011).

[3] See the ICRC's 'Commentary of 1987 on Protocol 1 Additional' <https://ihl-databases.icrc.org/applic/ihl/ihl.nsf/Comment.xsp?action=openDocument&documentId=78C0DA9A7B459ACEC12563CD0042F649> accessed 14 September 2019, as well as the ICRC's article 'The Geneva Conventions of 1949 and Their Additional Protocols' (1 January 2014) <www.icrc.org/en/document/geneva-conventions-1949-additional-protocols> accessed 14 September 2019. Also see former ICRC President Alexandre Hay, 'Statement made at the Plenary Meeting of the Independent Commission, New York, November 1983' reproduced in *Modern Wars: The Humanitarian Challenge, A Report for the Independent Commission on International Humanitarian Issues* (Zed Books 1986) 43–51.

[4] See ICRC, 'Commentary of 2016' on Convention 1 paragraph 73 <https://ihl-databases.icrc.org/applic/ihl/ihl.nsf/Comment.xsp?action=openDocument&documentId=5087F3472575591CC1257F150049C80B≥ accessed 15 September 2019. This change in representation in international fora with the growth in number of newly independent states was a more widespread phenomenon than this conference alone; the kind of optimism about remaking the world that it both embodied and encouraged is discussed, classically, in Mark Mazower's *No Enchanted Palace: The End of Empire and the Ideological Origins of the United Nations* (Princeton University Press 2009).

[5] The categories Third World and socialist are Mantilla's. See Giovanni Mantilla, 'Social Pressure and the Making of Wartime Civilian Protection Rules' (2019) 26 European Journal of International Relations 443.

[6] For a comprehensive account, see Giovanni Mantilla, *Lawmaking Under Pressure: International Humanitarian Law and Internal Armed Conflict* (Cornell University Press 2020). For an additional account of the inclusion of wars of national liberation, framed as a narrowing of the category of non-international armed conflict, see Anthony Cullen, *The Concept of Non-International Armed Conflict in International Humanitarian Law* (CUP 2010), especially chapter 3.

itself a matter of contestation. At stake in the very legal argumentation was not just a matter of how to better apply law to a new situation, but how to make sense of the previous few decades, and in particular how anticolonialism as an historical force should be understood in relation to international humanitarian law.

After all, if the goals of many delegates were alternately to bring more conflicts under the umbrella of humanitarian law, and to legitimise anticolonial struggle, there were multiple ways of achieving that; to assert that anticolonial conflicts are international armed conflicts was not the only option, and there was significant disagreement about whether and how that could be justified. These were not just abstract disagreements about law, nor the straightforward product of context. Rather than simply reflecting its context, we might think of law as adjudicating the significance of that context. Here, that meant adjudicating what kind of conflict an anticolonial conflict really was. The question facing the delegates was not simply how to best impose humanitarian limits on new types of violence, but of how to understand that violence, and its history, so as to render it legible in law.

That question was deeper than simply whether or not anticolonial conflicts were to be treated as international or not—and went far beyond a simple assertion that the coloniser and the colonised were two separate nations. Even in deciding to describe anticolonial conflicts as international armed conflicts, there were multiple legal arguments developed in the course of those conflicts themselves to which the delegates could appeal. There was no singular anticolonial legal position; anticolonial movements themselves presented differing legal views, which had evolved in varying relationships of competition and coordination with each other over the previous decades. In this sense, to the extent that the negotiations took place in the shadow of conflicts in Algeria and Vietnam, that shadow was present not only in cognizance of the violence of those conflicts, but in legal argumentation as well. The challenge was not only to address humanitarianism to new forms of conflict, but to encode certain intellectual legacies of the legal disputes that had flared alongside and as part of the conflicts. Those intellectual legacies presented distinct ways of understanding the significance of the conflicts for international law.

In what follows, I first return to the legal arguments of the Algerian resistance from around 1960 in order to bring forward the explanations that were offered to justify what made that conflict international such that the Geneva Conventions ought to apply. Here, I take issue with the standard summary of the Algerian case: that the conflict was international because Algeria and France were prima facie two different nations. Algerian activists, the story goes, saw Algerian nationhood as a basic historical fact; because it involved two nations, the conflict was international. In this way, the argument for the conflict's international status was not much more than an assertion of Algeria's nationhood, another way of demanding recognition of sovereignty as part of the revolutionaries' broader strategy. But while the Algerian argument was certainly itself a political claim, I'll argue that it also offered a more robust account of what made the conflict international, one that resisted the kind of straightforward nationalism usually attributed to it.

As I reconstruct below, the Algerian case involved three interrelated sets of arguments. The first concerned why the revolutionary government should be treated as legitimate, the second why France's effort to violently repress the rebellion should be understood as an act of aggression, and the third why the Algerian conflict specifically should be understood as an object of international concern. Algerian legal thinkers offered an account of sovereignty as constructed and performed in time, in part through the fulfilment of humanitarian provisions; a view of decolonisation as the progressive reshaping of international relationships in response to the aggression of imperialism; and a case for treating conflicts with international involvement as international. To bring these arguments forward, I make use of materials produced by the Provisional Government of the Republic of Algeria (GPRA), the writings of the GPRA-affiliated lawyer Mohammed Bedjaoui, and additional material from French archives and the archives of the ICRC.

After outlining the Algerian argument from during the revolution, in the second part of what follows, I turn to the 1970s and the debate over what became paragraph 4. Here, I trace a split within the Third World or anticolonial bloc. On one side were those who argued that both sides in an anticolonial conflict should be bound by the Conventions, for reasons that were compatible with that of the Algerian revolutionaries' first and second sets of arguments. On the other side were those who used an extreme version of a 'just war' argument to claim that only the aggressors should be bound by the Conventions, and in particular that captured soldiers fighting against anticolonial forces were not entitled to prisoner of war protections. Paragraph 4 does not clearly endorse one or the other of these positions, but simply designates anticolonial conflict as international. As others have shown, concern about the latter interpretation led to efforts to constrain paragraph 4's applicability elsewhere in the document. And notably, the more widely applicable of the Algerian arguments—that is, the third set, which did not concern colonialism specifically but emphasised involvement, loosely understood, by third parties—are absent from the final text.

Throughout, I argue against reading the ultimate text of the Additional Protocols as a straightforward product of its own recent history. Instead, it provides an account of the legal meaning of the recent past. Law is not simply determined by its context, but is itself a site for argumentation over the meaning of that context. This illustrates, I argue, how contingency arises not only from the uncertainty of diplomatic negotiations, nor only from law's unanticipated future usage, but from contests over law's relationship to the past. Certainly, humanitarian law engages with recent history as raw material, finding evidence of the kinds of armed conflict in need of greater regulation. But, because law itself stands in relationship to the recent past as a site of historical meaning-making, it also intervenes in contests over how to understand the significance and status of recent conflicts.

II. The internationalism of the legal arguments of the Algerian resistance

The Algerian War for Independence, among the most prominent and protracted anticolonial struggles of the mid-twentieth century, is more often remembered for its physical battles than for its legal ones. But the struggle was also distinctive for the Algerian resistance's extensive engagement with international law, in which the rebels, so often invoked as advocates of revolutionary violence, advanced arguments for humanitarian protection.[7] The

[7] On the role of the Geneva Conventions during the Algerian revolution, see Raphaëlle Branche, 'The French Army and the Geneva Conventions During the Algerian War of Independence and After' in Evangelista and Tannenwald (eds) (n 2) 161. For a broader account of the use and politics of torture as part of the war, Raphaëlle Branche, *La Torture et l'Armée Pendant la Guerre d'Algérie, 1954–1962* (first edition 2001, Gallimard 2016). On the memory of torture in the war for France, including continuities between the French wars in Vietnam and Algeria, see, classically, Benjamin Stora, *La Gangrène et l'Oubli: La Mémoire de la Guerre d'Algérie* (first edition

diplomatic and legal side was not just an afterthought, but a major site of conflict itself. As Matthew Connelly emphasises, the National Liberation Front (FLN) and the affiliated GPRA sought to discredit France and win legitimacy for the revolution through resolutions and lobbying at the United Nations. It also conducted extensive diplomatic communications both with other African and Asian independence movements and with national governments. The GPRA, headquartered in Cairo, appointed ambassadors and sent delegates to pan-Africanist conferences, and was deeply entwined in a transnational community of anticolonial movements.[8]

Among its more contentious legal claims, the Algerian resistance argued that the conflict was an international one, and therefore covered by the full force of the 1949 Geneva Conventions. At stake was not only the applicability of Common Article 3 protections for non-combatants in an armed conflict, but also, more contentiously, Article 4 of the Third Convention, covering combatants in international armed conflicts (including protections for prisoners of war). France disputed both, insisting that what was going on was a series of internal events that did not rise to the level of armed conflict; in keeping with this, Algerian resistance fighters were treated as criminals, subject to prosecution and, in many cases, execution. The French government eventually made concessions on protections for civilians and on the treatment of prisoners, but never agreed to the claims of the Algerian resistance that the conflict was international or that resistance fighters had the status of combatants, thereby also refusing to recognise captured fighters as having the status of prisoners of war.[9]

That violent fighters could also be humanitarian advocates is often explained by treating their advocacy as primarily a strategic gambit, combining public relations and legal action so as to embarrass France publicly and open another front in the battle. The GPRA appealed to the Geneva Conventions, the story goes, as a way of exposing the brutality of the French forces while also asserting Algerian sovereignty.[10] First and foremost, the GPRA was aiming to discredit and embarrass France internationally, making use of whatever tools it could find to generate bad publicity. Secondly, and more specifically, the GPRA was trying to establish that the conflict was international because Algeria itself was a nation; demands for humanitarian protections, in this sense, worked to underscore a nationalist argument. On this telling, the claim about the conflict's status as an 'international armed conflict' arose from a simple claim about the status of both France and Algeria as inherently separate nations.[11]

1991, Éditions La Découverte 1998). For an account of this in terms of both intellectual history and the history of social movements, see Eleanor Davey, *Idealism Beyond Borders* (CUP 2015).

[8] See, classically, Matthew Connelly, *A Diplomatic Revolution* (OUP 2003). Note his discussion does not explicitly cover the appeal to the Geneva Conventions.

[9] For more on the French position, see Kinsella (n 2) and Branche (n 7). A distinction is often made between treatment and status: while France would eventually agree to extend POW treatment to prisoners, it never conceded that those prisoners in fact had the status, and so legal rights, of POWs.

[10] See Fabian Klose, *Human Rights in the Shadow of Colonial Violence: The Wars of Independence in Kenya and Algeria* (Dona Geyer tr, University of Pennsylvania Press 2013).

[11] For a narrative of public shaming and internationalisation, see Connelly (n 8). For the latter story, see for example Jessica Whyte, 'The "Dangerous Concept of Just War": Decolonization, Wars of National Liberation, and the Additional Protocols to the Geneva Conventions' (2018) 9 Humanity 313. Note that, where Whyte takes all of the anticolonial arguments from the 1970s as offering a laudable and counterhegemonic version of just war theory, I read the arguments of the 1970s as between one group advocating a fairly banal version of just war theory, and another which rejected such language and offered a more promising notion of decolonisation as a process to reshape international law. (I expand on this in a response to Whyte published as part of a forum on the *Humanity* website, 'On the Language of Just War: A Reply to Whyte' (21 August 2019) available at <http://humanityjournal.org/blog/on-the-language-of-just-war-a-reply-to-whyte/> accessed 1 February 2021 .)

This story fits with a broader view of anticolonialism as emphasising the primacy of national sovereignty, a kind of nationalism potentially at odds with humanitarian concerns. Anticolonial thought is often described as involving a kind of sovereignty-first nationalism, in which sovereignty is prioritised before individual humanitarian concerns, and any appearance otherwise is understood as crudely instrumental. That charge may apply to certain versions of the argument about the applicability of Geneva Conventions protections in anticolonial conflict—but, despite the standard reading of their claims, it does not apply to the case made by the Algerian leaders.[12] Instead, by reconsidering the idea of sovereignty in the context of debates about humanitarian law and international status, I argue we can see how, even in arguments about Algerian nationhood, claims about sovereignty were connected with more robust guarantees of individual humanitarian protection and internationalist visions.

To begin, there was more to the GPRA's argument than simply an attempt to prove Algeria's own statehood. The GPRA's claims from the early 1960s about the Geneva Conventions combine a claim to international legal personality with a claim that decolonisation was, in itself, definitionally an object of international concern, and, in concert with those two claims, an assertion of humanitarian rights as well as responsibilities. The GPRA also described the conflict as an object of international concern, in which outside forces were interested and, in fact, already involved. Such claims were strategic, certainly—but most legal arguments are, and that itself does not mean such claims are incoherent or lacking in political vision.

The GPRA made a strong case not only for law to be applied to the conflict, but for the relevance of anticolonial conflict to international law. In the process, they staked claims about the meaning of the conflict and of the broader historical processes of which it was part. Looking back on the conflict in the 1970s, the meaning of its 'shadow' was not simply a memory of violence, but a question of how to interpret and encode the conflict and its historical significance. For that, there were multiple lines of argumentation available.

1. Approaching the Algerian argument

The strongest statement of the GPRA's argument appeared in a white paper, 'Livre Blanc sur l'Application des Conventions de Genève de 1949 au Conflit Franco-Algérien', ('Livre Blanc') published in New York and distributed to foreign governments at the UN and elsewhere.[13] The GPRA had previously announced its own adhesion to the Geneva Conventions in the (relatively brief) 1960 'Mémorandum sur l'Adhésion de la République

[12] In other contexts, the equation of anticolonialism with a nationalistic demand for sovereignty has been challenged by recent literature, in which critics have emphasised instead the federalist and internationalist orientation of anticolonial thinkers; here, I aim to contribute to that push, with respect more specifically to the relationship between individual humanitarian protection, sovereignty, and internationalism. See in particular Adom Getachew, *Worldmaking After Empire: The Rise and Fall of Self-Determination* (Princeton University Press 2019); Gary Wilder, *Freedom Time: Negritude, Decolonization, and the Future of the World* (Duke University Press 2015); and Christopher J Lee (ed), *Making a World After Empire: The Bandung Moment and its Political Afterlives* (Ohio University Press 2010), especially Lee's introduction.

[13] A copy of the 'Livre Blanc' is available in Alger Ambassade Box 72, folder Livre blanc, Centre des Archives Diplomatiques de Nantes (CADN); page numbers refer to this version. Note that pages are numbered independently by chapter; as such, citations here will include a chapter and a page number. Throughout, translations are my own.

Algérienne aux Conventions de Genève de 1949', which was included as an appendix to the 'Livre Blanc'. The second major statement took the form of a 1961 book by Mohammed Bedjaoui, *La Revolution Algérienne et le Droit* (also published in English as *Law and the Algerian Revolution*), offering an account of the relationship between the Algerian revolution and law with a large section devoted to the relevance of the Geneva Conventions; Bedjaoui also reproduced the 'Memorandum' as an appendix.[14] Additional FLN and GPRA materials augmented those arguments.

Alongside its official legal argumentation, the GPRA was also engaged directly with humanitarian actors.[15] The GPRA and its president, Ferhat Abbas, were in contact with the International Committee of the Red Cross. In Algeria, the French Red Cross was the officially recognised national society of the International Red Cross and Red Crescent Movement; the Algerian Red Crescent was founded in direct competition. The GPRA had close ties to the Algerian Red Crescent, the very existence of which served to challenge the legitimacy of French claims in Algeria. The Algerian Red Crescent served as an intermediary between the GPRA and the ICRC, negotiating prisoner releases both before and after Algerian independence.[16] That correspondence provides further archival material for understanding the GPRA's case.

The central texts combine an argument about Algeria's historical status with an argument about the GPRA's contemporary performance of sovereignty—arguments which complicate the reduction of the Algerian position to a straightforwardly nationalist one. The 'Livre Blanc' in particular argues that French governance was imposed from without, was never accepted by the people, and that the provisional Algerian government was acting more like a government than France was, through the protection of rights and the performance of sovereignty. Acting like a state—including by not using torture but also by providing medical care, organising services, and allowing everyday economic and social life to go on—was a crucial part of the story of what made the provisional government legitimate. It was because they were fighting on behalf of a state-like entity, and in a conflict that was the subject of international concern, the argument went, that Algerian prisoners should be considered prisoners of war, entitled to humanitarian protections and privileges. Notably, the GPRA's argument would imply that rebels in an anticolonial conflict were themselves also bound by humanitarian law—after all, their very claim to sovereignty rested in part on the fulfilment of humanitarian imperatives.

This first set of arguments, about the GPRA's performance of sovereignty, was embedded in an internationalist politics, evident in two other sets of arguments. Bedjaoui and the GPRA depicted French colonialism as a form of aggression, in conflict with humanitarian concern and in conflict with the imperative of national liberation. In addition, the GPRA pointed to existing involvement in the conflict by parties other than Algeria and France, as

[14] Mohammed Bedjaoui, *La Révolution Algérienne et le Droit* (Editions de l'Association Internationale des Juristes Démocrates 1961). For quotations, all translations are my own.

[15] Jennifer Johnson has documented the extent of the GPRA's humanitarian involvement, and, while other accounts, notably Raphaëlle Branche's, should serve to temper such claims, Johnson makes a strong case that the GPRA did engage in meaningful humanitarian actions. Jennifer Johnson, *The Battle for Algeria: Sovereignty, Health Care, and Humanitarianism* (University of Pennsylvania Press 2016).

[16] See correspondence in Archives de Comité International de la Croix Rouge (ACIRC), especially in B AG 202 008. Also see interview with Pierre Gaillard, 'The Algerian War: Memoirs of an ICRC Delegate' (*ICRC*, 19 May 2011), available at <www.icrc.org/en/doc/resources/documents/interview/2011/algeria-history-al-insani-2011-04-01.htm≥ (reproduced there from the magazine *Al-Insani*, October 2010) accessed 14 September 2019.

well as broader international concern and solidarity. These three pieces of the argument—concerning the performance of sovereignty, the status of anticolonialism in relationship to imperial aggression, and international involvement—offered a way of understanding law's relevance to the conflict, as well as meaning and historical significance of the conflict itself.

When the delegates met in the 1970s to debate the Additional Protocols, they would grapple with a similar question about the meaning of recent conflicts. Those conflicts did not present a fixed context for later debates; rather, the meaning of that context was itself contested. Aspects of the Algerian resistance's arguments, particularly the first and second sets, carried through to those debates, where they were part of a dispute not just over the applicability of law, but over how to make legal sense of the recent past. Other aspects, particularly those arguments about international involvement, largely dropped out.

2. Performing sovereignty

The GPRA put forward a set of claims about Algeria's status as a nation which highlight the historical and performative nature of national sovereignty itself, rather than appealing to nationhood as a fixed or essential quality. The 'Livre Blanc' made a careful case for why Algeria was a state on the basis of performing like one. This related to the claim, codified in the 1977 Additional Protocol, that the resistance was fighting colonial domination, but also goes beyond it. In the booklet's first chapter, the GPRA declares that 'the position of the G.P.R.A ... is that the country [*pays*] was conquered by France after a colonial war that lasted from 1830 to 1848'. Previously, it claims, Algeria was 'an independent state, maintaining diplomatic relations with a number of states'. The GPRA narrated a national history not just to establish the fact of past nationhood and conquest, but because possessing such a history was itself part of what it meant to be a nation.

Indeed, narrating and re-narrating the history of the nation was a persistent preoccupation of the FLN and GPRA's literature. French occupation was presented as an episode in a longer and continuous history, part of a recounting of a national past. As part of this, the 'Livre Blanc' suggests that France never enjoyed popular support in Algeria. While France incorporated Algeria into departments within France in 1948, treating it in this sense as part of the nation, Algerians, the GPRA claims, always contested French rule. In this sense, Algeria had never truly been conquered.[17]

The GPRA augmented those historical claims with performative ones. The GPRA argued that it was operating as a government, and so should be treated as one. It claimed it should be treated as a government because it looked like a government: it had separate wings; a president, vice president, and full set of governmental officers. It had appointed diplomatic officials and established foreign relations. To that end, it was recognised as a government by other nations; the 'Livre Blanc' lists seventeen.[18]

In addition to the GPRA's governing like a government, its army was, the white paper argued, fighting like an army: soldiers were trained and disciplined, they operated in regiments, they wore proper uniforms with clear insignia, and they carried sophisticated weapons. France would dispute this point, claiming that the resistance operated more as

[17] Quoted from first page of Chapter 1, 'Origine du Conflit Franco-Algerien', 'Livre Blanc' (n 13).
[18] 'Livre Blanc' (n 13) ch 1,7.

a loose terrorist network. France wasn't wrong that the FLN used such tactics, but parts of the Armée de Libération Nationale (ALN) were quite formalised.[19] As evidence, the 'Livre Blanc' offers quotations from French, British, and American newspapers on its army's conduct as an army, highlighting in particular the use of American-made grenades and German-made rifles.[20]

This tracks the requirements of the Geneva Conventions, and anticipates concerns raised during the drafting of the Additional Protocols, especially about maintaining the principle of distinction between military and civilian members in the context of anticolonial conflict. Notably, the claim to be observing the principle of distinction was used not only to prove that the ALN was capable of reciprocity were the French to also observe that distinction, so to prove the workability of the Conventions, but also as further evidence of the state-like quality of the state.

As further evidence that the Geneva Conventions should apply, the booklet points to the fact that the GPRA itself had ratified the Conventions. This provided proof of reciprocity, but was also a performance of sovereignty. The GPRA was already applying the Conventions, it claimed, to French prisoners of war in Algeria, and was cooperating with the Red Cross. What's more, the 'Livre Blanc' argues, France's insistence that the Conventions did not apply, and that it was instead domestic law that governed the conflict, was inconsistent with international law and even with French law, because France was a signatory to the Conventions; the Constitutions of both the Fourth and Fifth Republics stipulated that international Conventions ratified by Parliament took precedence over French laws and regulations.[21]

The longest chapter of the 'Livre Blanc' concerns 'Violation by France of Basic Humanitarian Principles', and catalogues France's alleged offences. Rather than an argument that the Conventions technically ought to apply, the chapter is presented as demonstrating the need for their application by documenting recent and ongoing humanitarian abuses. In doing so, it also underscores the argument that, while the GPRA had acceded to the Conventions, and was upholding humanitarian principles as a sovereign government should, the French government was doing nothing of the sort. The abuses are presented as breaking with not only the specific stipulations of Common Article 3, but the broader spirit of the Conventions, as well as of Article 5 of the Universal Declaration of Human Rights. In the chapter, the GPRA cites and quotes at length from a range of sources, including the leaked 1960 ICRC report from visits to detention facilities in Algeria, published (in excerpted form) in *Le Monde*, as well as public denunciations in the French press of the use of torture.[22]

The GPRA also underscored France's failure to act as a true sovereign in Algeria with the charge of genocide. The 'Livre Blanc' cites and quotes a report by Raphael Lemkin, perhaps the most prominent proponent for the regulation of genocide in international law. Lemkin submitted a report arguing that France was engaged in genocide in Algeria to the 1959 Monrovia conference of Independent African States. In the 'Livre Blanc', Lemkin's argument appears as part of a section documenting the destruction of entire villages in Algeria

[19] For more on this debate, see Kinsella (n 2).
[20] 'Livre Blanc' (n 13) ch 1, 2–3.
[21] 'Livre Blanc' (n 13) third page of chapter 3.
[22] See 'Livre Blanc' (n 13) chapter 6; for reference to UDHR, see first page.

and the use of military-run 'centres de regroupement'. In the portion quoted, Lemkin, like the GPRA, describes these as concentration camps. Both the Livre Blanc and the portions of Lemkin's report from which it quotes describe France as engaged in 'racial destruction' directed against Muslims, and so in violation of the UN Convention on the Prevention and Punishment of the Crime of Genocide (referenced as the 'convention on racial destruction').[23] In *La Révolution Algérienne et le Droit*, Bedjaoui explicitly uses the language of genocide in the opening of his argument about 'the colonial crimes', referencing 'genocide by the extermination of entire villages'.[24] Notably, in the GPRA's usage, genocide does not appear as a distinct and rival conceptual frame to that of human rights or of individual humanitarian protections, as we might now expect.[25] Instead, it was presented as one of multiple abuses that underscored both France's failure as a sovereign government in Algeria and the need for humanitarian protections.[26]

In responding to the 'Livre Blanc', rather than simply insist that Algeria was in fact part of France, the French government engaged seriously with the GPRA's arguments. This underscores that the legal dispute between Algeria and France represented more than empty posturing, but substantive argumentation over how to understand the legal status, and significance, of the conflict. Rebutting the GPRA's claims, the French government would argue that the GPRA represented a small minority of Algerians, and not the will of a nation. In claiming popular support for their own side, French officials claimed not that there was broad support for France or French rule, but support for peace, which implied continued French rule. Equating French rule with peace and stability, it depicted the GPRA as a minor faction without popular support.[27]

France's response reflected the notion that humanitarian concern and sovereign legitimacy were intertwined. The legitimacy of the rebel government was also disproven, French officials argued, by its use of violence. Indeed, French officials asserted that, in fact, the FLN was guilty of committing 'the extermination of populations' and of 'families'. It applied the label 'genocide' to the Melouza massacre.[28] Officials argued that France's willingness to let the Red Cross into Algeria, despite not being required to do so, was evidence France had nothing to hide.[29] In internal correspondence that was part of the development of those materials, French officials argued for highlighting what France was doing to promote economic and social progress in Algeria, and the general goals of decolonisation—tasks that, on their view, only France could carry out. Summarising the message the materials were meant to convey, one official put it this way: 'France intends to continue her work, not only

[23] See 'Livre Blanc'(n 13) page 9 of section 'Disparitions' of Chapter 6. Notably, the use of race as a framework here, and of Muslim as a racial category, is consistent with efforts not just to advocate for the rights of Algerians, but simultaneously to distinguish some Algerians from others.

[24] My translation; Bedjaoui's exact phrase is 'le genocide par l'extermination de villages entiers.' Bedjaoui (n 14) 209.

[25] For an account of the development of 'genocide' as a distinct category and Lemkin's role in it, see Philippe Sands, *East West Street: On the Origins of 'Genocide' and 'Crimes Against Humanity'* (Knopf 2016). Sands argues that genocide was defined in part through its opposition to the category of 'crimes against humanity' and that it focused on group as opposed to individual protections; the GPRA's use, however, subverts those distinctions.

[26] On the use of the charge of genocide within the French left, and its application to Algeria, see Christoph Kalter, *The Discovery of the Third World: Decolonization and the Rise of the New Left in France, c. 1950–1976* (CUP 2016).

[27] See 'Plan Possible d'une Response au Livre Blanc du FLN', Alger Ambassade Box 72, folder Livre blanc, CADN. All translations mine.

[28] See memorandum 'Plan Possible d'un Reponse au Livre Blanc du FLN' (n 26).

[29] 'Plan Possible d'une Response au Livre Blanc du FLN' (n 26).

because her honour is there engaged, but also because she alone can lead things forward in the interest of Algerians of the free world'.[30] While arguing that the Algerian rebels were the ones committing atrocities, French officials also, at least implicitly, posited respect for international law and humanitarian concern as criterions of legitimacy.

3. National liberation, decolonisation, and aggression as legitimising principles

As the discussion of the historical status of Algeria, as well as of the relevance of French abuses, already suggests, a central issue for debates about the applicability of the Conventions concerned the way in which French control of Algeria, and Algerian resistance to that control, should be understood. This question was an inherently historical one, and one which would remain important in the 1970s debates. That multiple interpretations were possible underscores the contingency of the latter moment: not merely how to respond to the violence of past conflicts, but how to understand the meaning of those conflicts and the historical trajectories of which they were part. As the GPRA's argument shows, there were multiple possible interpretations of the significance of anticolonial conflict for law.

In this earlier moment, several interrelated principles were put forward by the GPRA to frame the struggle against French rule: national liberation, a principle notably shared with recent French demands for liberation from Nazi rule; decolonisation, itself a world-historical force; and aggression, a way of understanding the wrongs of French occupation. Bedjaoui emphasised in particular the concept of national liberation, drawing comparisons with de Gaulle's Free French movement for national liberation against Nazi occupation during the Second World War. He also gestured towards ideas of decolonisation as a global, epoch-making event in international law; Bedjaoui expanded on that particular claim in later work, including his arguments for the New International Economic Order.[31] As part of both of those claims, French occupation was explained as a kind of 'aggression'—though not, as the argument would be used by others later, in order to justify a claim that resistance forces were not themselves bound by humanitarian law, especially as it concerned prisoners of war. In this earlier moment, the concepts of decolonisation and aggression were treated as interconnected, and tied to ideas of humanitarian concern.

The interconnection between ideas of national liberation, aggression, and decolonisation are outlined most clearly in Bedjaoui's *La Révolution Algérienne et le Droit*. Wider in scope than the 'Livre Blanc', the book explores Algeria's status in international law, and the specific issue of 'The Algerian War and the Geneva Conventions' as an issue within that. Before coming to the status of the provisional government, and to the Conventions

[30] Original: 'La France, entendant poursuivre son œuvre, non seulement parce qu'elle y a engagé son honneur, mais aussi parce qu'elle seule peut la mener à bien dans l'intérêt des Algériens du monde libre'. Comments under 'Critique General' on draft report, attributed to Oberdorff, page 5. Alger Ambassade, Box 72, folder Livre blanc, memo 'Brochure pour l'ONU' and 'Critiques Apportees a la Redaction de la Brochure Destinee a l'ONU'. These arguments are echoed in French correspondence with the ICRC as well; for that, see ACIRC, B AG 202 008 007, folder 2.

[31] My reading here is in keeping with and informed by Umut Özsu's account of Bedjaoui's approach to international law; see Umut Özsu, '"In the Interests of Mankind as a Whole": Mohammed Bedjaoui's New International Economic Order' (2015) 6 Humanity 129; and Umut Özsu, 'Determining New Selves: Mohammed Bedjaoui on Algeria, Western Sahara, and Post-Classical International Law', in Jochen von Bernstorff and Philipp Dann (eds) *The Battle for International Law: South-North Perspectives on the Decolonization Era* (OUP 2019).

specifically, Bedjaoui emphasises the legal personality of Algeria, focused on the past and present recognition of the state. His opening chapter tracks Algeria as 'subject of international law' prior to the French invasion; the second chapter then surveys the territories that had been 'liberated' since 1954.[32] Like the 'Livre Blanc', the book assesses the ALN, and the institutions of the GPRA, to establish the formal existence of the army and government.

Bedjaoui also argues specifically for the legitimacy of the GPRA as the government of Algeria, using the language of national liberation to compare the GPRA's status to that of de Gaulle's government in exile during the Second World War. He notes the similarities in their names—GPRA and GPRF, FLN and CFLN—as well as the names of their radio stations, and even of the neighbourhoods in which they were headquartered in exile—Garden City, Cairo, and Carlton Gardens, London.[33] More substantively, he cites the recognition of each movement by other governments. If the French liberation government was legitimate, surely the Algerian case, he claims, should be even clearer.

However, alongside arguments about the parallels to wartime France, Bedjaoui also highlights anticolonialism as a specific language and legal principle. He argues that anticolonialism has itself become a principle of international law, and the GPRA was engaged in an anticolonial struggle, making it legitimate 'both politically and legally'.[34] This broader view would be echoed in his 1976 *Towards a New International Economic Order*, written contemporaneously with the Additional Protocols themselves. Decolonisation, as he presents it, was a 'force', and a world-historical one, as epoch-making as colonialism itself. As he puts it in the opening to that book:

> The decolonization of the last twenty years, which is not yet a spent force and which is still causing surprise by the profoundly novel consequences to which it is leading in the international sphere, is just as important a phenomenon and just as decisive a turning-point in the 'rules of the international game' as the major geographical discoveries of the fifteenth and sixteenth centuries or the constitution of the great colonial empires following the industrial revolution.[35]

This perspective combines an argument about historical parallels with one about historical change. It offers an understanding of decolonisation as a creative movement, reshaping the world, both on the scale of and in the wake of colonialism itself. His 1976 book presents the 'shadow' of recent anticolonial conflicts not in terms of a memory of violence, but as part of decolonisation's direct reshaping of international rules.

Along these lines, Bedjaoui casts French abuses as 'colonial crimes', and the work of the resistance as both responsive to those crimes and also creative in its own right.[36] Among those colonial crimes, he includes torture, disappearances, and summary executions, as well as the blockading of villages and resulting famine, displacement of large parts of the population, and the use of incendiary napalm. In the face of this, Algerians were legitimately attempting to defend themselves. As evidence of that legitimacy, the GPRA was complying

[32] Bedjaoui (n 14) 18–39 and 40–47, respectively.
[33] Bedjaoui (n 14) 61–62.
[34] Bedjaoui (n 14) 69.
[35] Mohammed Bedjaoui, *Towards a New International Economic Order* (Holmes & Meier 1979) 11.
[36] Bedjaoui (n 14) 209, for example.

with the Red Cross, and had ratified the Geneva Conventions. Further, in keeping with the account in the 'Livre Blanc', he points out that the GPRA was providing medical services to the Algerian population and organising other social services.

Consistent with this, the GPRA and FLN described the French war in Algeria as a 'war of aggression', in line with the aggression of colonialism itself, and so part of a broader historical narrative. On the GPRA's account, Algeria had existed as a country before the French invasion, and the French presence had never been rightful. On this basis, the white paper claimed, the French were the aggressors, and the Algerian resistance was engaged in a kind of legitimate self-defence, one with a history that extended forward from France's 1830 invasion. But importantly, they did not argue that this rendered it exceptional, such that the rules of war should be suspended. Instead, the Algerian use of the term 'war of aggression' itself implied that this was an international conflict, in which the laws of war and international humanitarian law should apply.

In the context of the Algerian revolution, the categories of decolonisation, national liberation, and aggression went together as part of a narrative of the revolution's historical significance in relation to international law. The Algerian resistance claimed to be defending a coherent nation, one that existed prior to French invasion, from the aggression of colonial rule and the inhumanity of colonial crimes. In doing so, it was helping remake the rules of the international order, as part of an era of decolonisation. Claims about the applicability of international law arose from and as part of claims about the historical meaning of the conflict. In this sense, the decision to bring anticolonial conflict more clearly within the category of international armed conflict was not just a contest over whether to extend humanitarian concern to a particular category of conflict, but a contest over how those conflicts should be understood historically.

4. The conflict as international concern

A third line of argumentation in the GPRA's position concerned the status of the conflict as an object of international concern. Where the first two lines of argumentation were present, though contested, in the 1970s, this aspect of the GPRA's argument would largely drop out. The GPRA argued that the conflict had implications for international peace and security, as was reflected in interest in it evident at the UN. It also pointed to the growing number of refugees in Tunisia and Morocco, a situation the 'Livre Blanc' compared with those in Hungary and Palestine. It highlighted military involvement by other countries, on both sides, to underscore the conflict's international nature. While less specific to decolonisation as an historical moment, this set of arguments was premised on a view of decolonisation as a remaking of international relationships.

One aspect of the argument concerned support for the resistance beyond Algeria itself, including transnational networks of anticolonial solidarity. In presenting popular support as a source of legitimacy for the GPRA in his 1961 book, Bedjaoui underscored such support, and the two appendices to his chapter on the Geneva Conventions can be read as offering proof of that popular legitimacy. The second appendix, the more straightforward, contains quotations from press reports, testifying to the popular support for the GPRA. The first, more indirectly, provides a selection of press quotations, mostly from *Le Monde*, about the general strike organised by the GPRA in 1957, testifying to its extent and effectiveness, including its reach beyond Algerian borders.[37] His referent is a general strike called as the UN was preparing to hear a resolution on the 'Algerian question'. The strike was to take place, the organisers hoped, not only in Algeria, but also in metropolitan France, and in Tunisia and Morocco, which could be reached by FLN radio broadcasts; the GPRA's ambassadors were also meant to conduct wide publicity campaigns, and organise telegram campaigns to the UN.[38]

In addition to claims about public support beyond Algeria, the GPRA also argued that the war was an international one in the sense that other governments were involved militarily. The GPRA claimed France was receiving support from the United States and NATO, and that its military was using American-made equipment. France denied this, as the use of NATO resources was contrary to NATO rules. But US government materials offer corroboration of the Algerian claims. A US Foreign Service official, stationed in Algeria at the time, recounted later: 'The US was desperately trying to keep France in NATO', and so accepted much of the French strategy in Algeria, including looking the other way as France reassigned troops from NATO commitments to send them to fight in Algeria, and as it opted to 'use American equipment designated for NATO contrary to their commitments'.[39]

The deployment of NATO equipment was especially inflammatory in the broader context of NATO's relationship with Algeria. France had originally refused to join the treaty organisation unless French Algeria was included, insisting that Algeria was unlike other colonies or territories as it was part of France itself (other colonies and territories were excluded). The GPRA declared that Algeria was not a true part of NATO, as it was a continuously existing sovereign country and had never agreed to join. On these terms, Bedjaoui argued, France's use of NATO equipment in Algeria represented more than a domestic misallocation of resources, but was in fact a foreign action by NATO.[40]

The GPRA would also invoke the use of NATO arms prominently in its 1961 'Memorandum on the Recognition of Belligerence in the French-Algerian Conflict'. There, it declared that it 'considers after the 19th of September 1960 all participation of the Atlantic Organization, or any part of it, in the war of colonial reconquest and extermination conducted by France in Algeria, as an act of aggression against the Algerian people'. Recognition of belligerence in Algeria, they argued, went hand in hand with recognising the illegitimacy of NATO presence there.[41]

It was not only France making use of foreign military resources. The GPRA also had the recognition and assistance of other countries, especially Nkrumah's Ghana and Nasser's Egypt, leaders in the pan-African and Afro-Asian movements of the time. In addition to recognising the GPRA as a government and receiving its ambassadors, according to French

[37] Bedjaoui (n 14) 71–76.

[38] An intercepted three-page FLN memorandum regarding planning for the strike appears in French official files Alger Ambassade, Box 72, CADN.

[39] Virginia Crawford and Wendell W Woodbury, 'Interview with Wendell W. Woodbury' (The Association for Diplomatic Studies and Training Foreign Affairs Oral History Project, Library of Congress, June 4, 1993) 28–29 available at <www.loc.gov/item/mfdipbib001290> accessed 14 September 2019.

[40] See Chapter 9 of Bedjaoui (n 14) 'The Capacity of the GPRA to Conclude Treaties'. That chapter includes a reproduction of 'Memorandum Denouncing the Treaty of the North Atlantic by the GPRA' 202–9, which, the memorandum notes, goes beyond denouncing the idea of NATO membership to denounce the treaty itself.

[41] See 'Memorandum sur la Reconnaissance de Belligérance dans le Conflit Franco-Algérien' (Filed in ACIRC B AG 202 008 007, Folder 2, Appendix) 3–4.

surveillance Ghana was providing military support to the rebels, including arranging arms purchases and offering to send soldiers.[42]

Taken together, the GPRA's arguments about Algeria's own nationhood were closely tied to its claims about the international character of the conflict. The GPRA's and Bedjaoui's writings contain a robust understanding of what makes a state a state, and of what makes a conflict international. The argument was not simply that the war represented a conflict between two nations, France and Algeria, but that Algerians were engaged in legitimate self-defence against foreign aggression in a conflict with international implications and for which both sides received international support. The GPRA's position provided a view of the significance of the conflict in international law, including the relationship between the aggression of colonialism and the principle of national liberation. In this way, the conflict left legacies for the 1970s debates that went beyond either the memory of violence or an assertion of national sovereignty. What the debate involved was a set of arguments about the conflict's historical significance for international law. In the 1970s, the meaning of the past conflict was not fixed, but contested, and the matter of how to understand that conflict's significance itself became a source of contingency.

III. From 1962 to 1977

The legal arguments of the Algerian resistance would continue to be debated even after Algeria's independence in 1962. The question of whether the full humanitarian protections applicable in international conflicts should be understood to apply in anticolonial ones remained contentious, especially as other anticolonial movements made similar claims. Yet the nature of these claims was not always consistent, and the debates in the 1970s showcased multiple justifications for why national liberation struggles should be understood as international and brought under the purview of international humanitarian law. They involved, that is, different—and competing—ways of understanding the historical significance of the recent past for international law. The significance of the recent past was not a fixed fact, but a site of contestation and contingency.

By the 1970s, several rifts were evident. Some delegates made arguments which echoed the more recent histories told by the ICRC. They argued that anticolonial conflicts were a fact, and that the task was to ensure the widest possible practical purview for humanitarian protections. They described humanitarianism as a principle progressively encoded in law, and emphasised the need to extend international humanitarian law to as many circumstances as possible. But alongside that argument, representatives from newly independent states and their allies presented other, competing ways of interpreting the reason for including anticolonial conflicts, including alternative historical narratives to that of the gradual expansion of international humanitarian law. Some of these arguments echoed aspects of the Algerian arguments circa 1960, but others were very different. Among the anticolonial powers, there was a real split on whether anticolonial forces should themselves be bound by international humanitarian law.

[42] For information on GPRA requests for military assistance, see memorandum of JP Mauriat 'Position du GHANA à l'Égard du Problème Algérie' (9 December 1960) ('Ghana 1959–1986', 19910609-2, Archives Nationales).

This split may seem surprising: after all, during the Algerian conflict, other anticolonial movements and newly independent states had supported Algerian claims. Other countries—including, notably, North Vietnam—had affirmed to the UN and the ICRC that the provisional government was a real one, recognised by themselves and others, and that its stated accession to the Geneva Conventions was meaningful. In a December 1960 letter, Hoang Van Tién, the vice minister of foreign affairs for the Democratic Republic of Vietnam, wrote to the Swiss Federal Council: 'the Republic of Algeria, having all the attributes of a state or power and recognized by numerous countries, is plainly qualified to become party to these Conventions ... the GPRA has demonstrated the humanitarian spirit that animates the Geneva Conventions'.[43] This would seem to suggest agreement that the Geneva protections should apply to the conflict, and to those like it.

But during the debates about the Additional Protocols, several governments—including the North Vietnamese, as well as the Chinese and Albanian—would claim instead that the conflicts were just wars. They argued that the colonial forces were aggressors—meaning not, as the Algerian argument had run, that the conflicts were covered by the Geneva Conventions, but instead that such conflicts should be understood as battles between a legitimate force (the national liberation movement) and a criminal one (the colonial forces), and that the legitimate force therefore could not be restrained by the limitations arising from Geneva Convention protections for combatants from the criminal side. According to their reasoning, movements for national independence were justified in treating captured prisoners as criminals; such prisoners were guilty of waging a war of aggression, and so could be subject to interrogation, prosecution, and punishment.

The argument about just war offered a competing way to understand the historical meaning of anticolonial conflicts. The argument was not new in the 1970s, but continuous, conceptually and historically, with an earlier strand of argumentation. Geoffrey Best traces that strand forward from the USSR's position during negotiations in the late 1940s over the Third Geneva Convention, concerning the treatment of prisoners of war. According to the Soviet position at that time, prisoners of war (POWs) prosecuted for crimes prior to their capture would be subject to the same conditions as any other criminals in the country's justice system. Otherwise, adherents of this view maintained, POWs would have to be given preferential treatment, in terms of both living standards and sentencing, over a country's own nationals.

Initially, Best argues, this was the dominant view, not only for the Soviets but more generally. At first, only the ICRC had disagreed with the 'just war' stance, but the United States and United Kingdom eventually came around to their side, changing their position to endorse greater POW protections in the 1949 Conventions. This was, Best suggests, likely based in a concern that, in a conflict with Soviet-aligned states, captured American or British soldiers might be charged with crimes of aggression—a concern exacerbated by growing publicity about the conditions in prisons in the USSR and aligned states. That concern was realised during the US wars in Korea and Vietnam, leading the US position to become even more entrenched.[44]

[43] Letter filed in ACIRC B AG 041-083, Adhésion de l'Algérie (my translation).

[44] Geoffrey Best, *War and Law Since 1945* (OUP 1997) 135–38. Note Best groups the Chinese delegates with the Soviets.

When arguments about the justice of anticolonial conflict, echoing the arguments of the 1940s that Best describes, were made in the 1970s debates, they predictably drew the ire of the United States, United Kingdom, and other delegates. Those delegates painted with a broad brush, as if all arguments for including anticolonial conflicts relied on the same reasoning.[45] But, importantly, not all did: other proponents of including such conflicts argued that the international status of anticolonial conflict arose from the legal personality of the colonised group, and explicitly rejected language about the justice or injustice of the conflict. They described decolonisation as occurring in part through the remaking of international law, and as such, a legal principle on the march.

To support this, they emphasised the legitimacy-granting force of recent UN precedent supporting anticolonial struggles and affirming the right to self-determination. Such precedent was more meaningful, and should be applied to help revise, legal regimes that predated it. Its greater legitimacy arose precisely from the fact that it had been accepted by, rather than imposed upon, newly independent states.[46] In this way, the expansion of the definition of international armed conflict would reflect changing power dynamics in international law more widely. As one reflection of this, Egyptian delegate Georges Abi-Saab, refuting the idea that the language would mix *jus in bello* with *jus ad bellum* issues, argued that 'it was the existing system that gave preferential treatment to one of the parties', and that Article 1, rather than favour anticolonial forces, would serve an equalising function.[47]

The rejection of the language of just war by this latter camp was not a superficial disavowal, but an effort to draw a meaningful philosophical distinction. The legal personality of nations seeking independence, the argument went, arose not from a universal and timeless principle of just struggle, but had been conferred by agreements entered into in recent decades at the UN. Delegates emphasised the recognition of the right to self-determination in particular, though also argued that even agreements which described the appropriate treatment of territories or mandates served to implicitly recognise the legal personality of the nations placed under external governance.[48] In this sense, the legal status of national liberation movements was not a timeless principle of justice, but had been conferred through recognition by a system of international governance which was itself expanding.

Far from adjudicating these debates, the ultimate text glosses over the multiple positions that were articulated. But because the more hardline position had not been ruled out, powerful states, particularly the United States, remained concerned about it as a possible interpretation. As Mantilla has shown, those nations, anxious about the just war

[45] Full records of the CDDH are available in Federal Political Department, Records of the Diplomatic Conference on the Reaffirmation and Development of International Humanitarian Law Applicable in Armed Conflicts, Geneva, 1974–1977, Volumes 1–17 (Federal Political Department 1978) accessible at <http://www.loc.gov/rr/frd/Military_Law/RC-dipl-conference-records.html> accessed 10 September 2019. The discussions, along with draft text, relevant to the discussion here are helpfully compiled in Howard S. Levie (ed), *Protection of War Victims: Protocol 1 to the 1949 Geneva Conventions, Volume 1* (Oceana Publications 1979). For comments that embrace the framework of 'just war', see especially comments from China, 17, and Albania, 24, as well as, more implicitly, Romania, 74, and Somalia, 76. For attacks on the just war concept, see especially comments from the United Kingdom, United States, France, and Australia on pages at 7–8 and 43–47.

[46] For explicit disavowals of the language of the 'just war', see especially comments in Levie (n 45) from Egypt, 23–24; Norway, 44–45; India, 45; and Nigeria, 48.

[47] Levie (ed) (n 45) 24. Also see Georges Abi-Saab 'Wars of National Liberation in the Geneva Conventions and Protocols' (1979) 165 *Collected Courses of the Hague Academy of International Law* <https://referenceworks.brillonline.com/entries/the-hague-academy-collected-courses/*A9789024726271_03> accessed 10 September 2019.

[48] See especially comments from Syria, xxviii and 18; Romania, 4; Egypt, 23–24; Senegal, 32–33, in Levie (ed) (n 45).

implications of the first Article and concerned in particular that it introduced questions of political motivation into the applicability of the law, sought to undercut its significance elsewhere. They did so in part with Article 96, which stipulates stringent conditions which would have to be met by any 'national liberation movement' in order for it to receive the protections of the Additional Protocols. The addition of Article 96 greatly limits the applicability of Additional Protocol I.[49] Further limiting prospective applicability, the more expansive arguments made by the Algerian resistance in the period around 1960 dropped out by the 1970s—particularly the idea that external involvement in a struggle rendered it international. Had that been included, and still further if, by some chance, it had been ratified, it would have rendered Additional Protocol I more straightforwardly applicable in a greater number of conflicts.

As an historical exercise, the 1970s debates did not simply attempt to adjudicate the historical significance of the recent past as a reflection of the changing nature of armed conflict. The debate contained very different ways of understanding the ties between anticolonialism, humanitarianism, and international law. As this should suggest, the delegates in the 1970s were not simply responding to events around them and agreeing to bring them under the purview of international humanitarian law, but interpreting both the significance of recent history for armed conflict and the relevance of that history to the nature of international law as a project. The contingency of the outcome arose in part from contests over historical legal understanding.

Beyond the exact text of the Protocols, the 1970s debates have significance for how we understand anticolonial legal thought as a project. Both the Algerian arguments from the late 1950s and early 1960s, and the arguments made for the paragraph 4 text in the 1970s, are often presented as aligned with a form of anticolonial nationalism which emphasised sovereignty first, often in defiance of ideas of humanitarian obligation or human rights. The usual summary of the Algerian resistance's arguments about the international status of the conflict accords with a sovereignty-first story: France was a nation, Algeria was a nation, hence the conflict was international. While in this case anticolonial nationalism was part of a demand for greater humanitarian protection, the story goes, this was only because it served strategic purposes. Similar ideas would later be deployed not to extend humanitarian law, but to curtail it, insisting on the inviolability of sovereignty regardless of concern with humanitarianism or human rights.

Yet a reconsideration not only of the debates of the 1970s, but of the revolutionaries' claims from a decade and a half earlier, yields a far more robust conception of what might be seen to mark the conflict as international. Yes, the revolutionaries' argument was in part that Algeria and France were each nations—but to describe this as a kind of sovereigntist nationalism flattens a more nuanced view of what made Algeria sovereign. As the Algerian resistance presented it, sovereignty can be understood as connected both to an historical narrative of nationhood and to the performance of sovereignty, including the provision of humanitarian protections. And, in addition to an argument about Algeria's nationhood,

[49] For details of those restrictions, see Article 96, as well as ICRC, 'Commentary of 1987 on Protocol 1 Additional' (n 3). See Mantilla (n 6) especially chapter 5. On the Soviet role in helping to force the United States and United Kingdom to accept compromises, as well as the United States' own role specifically in negotiating a compromise on Article 44 on the treatment of prisoners of war, see Giovanni Mantilla, 'The Protagonism of the USSR and Socialist States in the Revision of International Humanitarian Law' (2019) 21 Journal of the History of International Law 181–211.

the resistance made arguments about the conflict as an object of international concern: a conflict with effects beyond Algeria's borders, and a conflict in which other countries were intervening. Bedjaoui's and the GPRA's arguments raised questions of whether internal armed conflict or civil war, involving outside intervention or generating flows of refugees, might properly be considered international. Those arguments allow us to see colonialism not simply as a violation of the right of national self-determination of the colonised nation—as the 1977 language suggests—but as a system maintained by international networks, and one that needed to be countered not with straightforward nationalism but with broader international organising and allegiances.

If the ICRC and others wanted the 1977 text to bring anticolonial conflict into the purview of international humanitarian law, there were multiple possibilities for how to do so. If the 1977 language was to encode the historical lessons of the previous few decades, those lessons were not fixed; rather, the frame through which to understand their salience and significance was actively contested. If law works to respond to the past and decide its significance for the future, contingency arises in the question of how the past will be remembered and made relevant for the future, and in which intellectual legacies will be carried forward and which will be left behind.

20

Unveiling Common Article 3 to the Geneva Conventions

Contingency, Necessity, and Possibility in International Humanitarian Law

Bianca Maganza

I. Introduction

With the inclusion of Common Article 3 (CA3) in the Geneva Conventions of 1949 (GCs),[1] situations of non-international armed conflict (NIAC) came to be regulated via treaty law for the first time.[2] The narrative surrounding the adoption of the provision and its interpretation is generally informed by ideas of linearity and progress: CA3 has been defined in various instances as the most basic and fundamental rule in international humanitarian law (IHL),[3] and its ground-breaking role for the development of the discipline has been highlighted on several occasions.[4]

While acknowledging the role of disciplinary pillar that CA3 plays in the field of IHL, this chapter addresses the provision from a different perspective, assessing the role contingency played in its negotiation, adoption, and interpretation—in particular as regards the choice of including CA3 in the GCs, the terminology that is used in the provision, and the way in which the latter has been (and is currently) interpreted. An analysis of the past contingencies that shaped the (hi)story of CA3, leading to the contingency of the contemporary

[1] Geneva Conventions I–IV (opened for signature 12 August 1949, entered into force 21 October 1950) 75 UNTS 31 (GCs).

[2] See Lindsay Moir, 'The Concept of Non-International Armed Conflict' in Andrew Clapham, Paola Gaeta, and Marco Sassòli (eds), *The 1949 Geneva Conventions: A Commentary* (OUP 2015) 391.

[3] See references to a 'minimum yardstick' reflecting 'elementary considerations of humanity' in International Court of Justice (ICJ), *Military and Paramilitary Activities In and Against Nicaragua (Nicaragua v USA)* (Merits) [1986] ICJ Rep 3 paras 218–19, to 'minimum mandatory rules' in the International Criminal Tribunal for the former Yugoslavia (ICTY), *The Prosecutor v Duško Tadić* (Decision on the Defence Motion for Interlocutory Appeal on Jurisdiction) ICTY-94-1-A (2 October 1995) para 102, and to 'minimal protection' in Supreme Court of the United States, *Hamdan v Rumsfeld, Secretary of Defense et al* 548 US 557 (2006) para 631. See also International Committee of the Red Cross (ICRC), 'Commentary to Art. 3' in *Commentary on Convention (I) for the Amelioration of the Condition of the Wounded and Sick in Armed Forces in the Field* (ICRC 2016).

[4] See, among others, Frédéric Siordet, 'Les Conventions de Genève et la Guerre Civile' (1950) 32 Revue Internationale de la Croix-Rouge 104; Georges Abi-Saab, 'Les Conflits Armés Non Internationaux' in Georges Abi-Saab (ed), *Les Dimensions Internationales du Droit Humanitaire* (Pedone 1986) 251; Antonio Cassese, 'La Guerre Civile et le Droit International' (1986) 90 Revue Générale de Droit International Public 553; Charles Zorgbibe, 'Pour une Réaffirmation du Droit Humanitaire des Conflits Armés Internes' (1970) 97 Journal du Droit International 658; Jean Simon Pictet (ed), *The Geneva Conventions of 12 August 1949: Commentary* (ICRC 1952); Sandesh Sivakumaran, *The Law of Non-International Armed Conflict* (OUP 2012); Moir (n 2); and ICRC (n 3).

Bianca Maganza, *Unveiling Common Article 3 to the Geneva Conventions* In: *Contingency in International Law.* Edited by: Ingo Venzke and Kevin Jon Heller, Oxford University Press. © The Several Contributors 2021. DOI: 10.1093/oso/9780192898036.003.0020

understanding of the provision, is important to realise that the concept of NIAC is far from being fixed and can, on the contrary, be contested.

To that aim, the contribution does not lay claim to proposing a single alternative reading of past events to the exclusion of all the others; rather, it sets out to encourage self-reflexivity and awareness of the existence of different interpretive possibilities.[5] Indeed, opening a certain concept to contestation does not necessarily mean condemning it. As Berman put it, 'normative biases may be defended with normative arguments':[6] acknowledging the contingent nature of some of our beliefs shall not prevent us from claiming that they still stand. As long as one is conscious that the questions posed will influence the answer, opening international law's past to discussion with the aim of questioning why and how we are where we are shall not only be an interesting exercise per se but also, hopefully, a means of seeking change by doing history.[7]

In order to track the contingencies that lie behind CA3, this chapter borrows from both contextual and critical approaches to history.[8] The analysis is premised on the assumption that, as much as any rigorous examination of the past entails taking into account the situation in which given historical facts have taken place,[9] awareness of the context should only be the first step, followed by a teleological account of the direction international law is taking.[10]

When it comes to the analysis of a treaty provision, this means balancing the context as it emerges from the *travaux préparatoires* with a textual interpretation of the Article in light of its object and purpose.[11] It is only in that way that it is possible to engage in an exercise of evolutionary interpretation, and advance a normative argument on the scope that a provision whose legal significance is largely perceived as a given could—or should—assume today.[12]

[5] On self-reflexivity in international law, see Andrea Bianchi, *International Law Theories—An Inquiry into Different Ways of Thinking* (OUP 2016). On history and international law, see Anne Orford, *On International Legal Method* (2013) 1 London Review of International Law 166 and Anne Orford, 'International Law and the Limits of History' in Wouter Werner, Marieke de Hoon, and Alexis Galán (eds), *The Law of International Lawyers: Reading Martti Koskenniemi* (CUP 2017) 297.

[6] Nathaniel Berman, 'Privileging Combat? Contemporary Conflict and the Legal Construction of War' (2004) 43 Columbia Journal of Transnational Law 1, 17.

[7] Janne Elisabeth Nijman, 'Seeking Change by Doing History' 591th Inaugural Lecture of the University of Amsterdam (24 November 2017).

[8] On the importance and the risks of historicising international law, see Paul Wrange, 'Historicizing International Humanitarian Law' in Mats Deland, Mark Klamberg and Pål Wrange (eds), *International Humanitarian Law and Justice: Historical and Sociological Perspectives* (Routledge 2019) 9 and Frédéric Mégret, 'International Criminal Justice History Writing as Anachronism' in Immi Tallgren and Thomas Skouteris (eds), *The New Histories of International Criminal Law: Retrials* (OUP 2019) 72.

[9] See Quentin Skinner, 'Meaning and Understanding in the History of Ideas', 'Some Problems in the Analysis of Political Thought and Action', and 'A Reply to My Critics' in James Tully (ed), *Meaning and Context: Quentin Skinner and His Critics* (Princeton University Press 1988) 29, 97, 231.

[10] See Martti Koskenniemi, 'Histories of International Law: Significance and Problems for a Critical View' (2013) 27 Temple International and Comparative Law Journal 215; Orford, 'On International Legal Method' (n 5) and Orford, 'International Law and the Limits of History' in Werner et al (n 5) as well as Thomas Skouteris, 'Engaging History in International Law' in José María Beneyto and David Kennedy (eds), *New Approaches to International Law: The European and the American Experiences* (TMC Asser Press 2012) 99.

[11] Vienna Convention on the Law of Treaties (opened for signature 23 May 1969, entered into force 27 January 1980) 1155 UNTS 331 arts 31–32. On interpretation in international law, see Ingo Venzke, *How Interpretation Makes International Law: On Semantic Change and Normative Twists* (OUP 2012) and Duncan B Hollis, 'Interpretation' in Jean d'Aspremont and Sahib Singh (eds), *Concepts for International Law: Contributions to Disciplinary Thought* (Edward Elgar 2018) 549.

[12] As Roberto Ago famously maintained, treaty interpretation is 'to some extent an art, rather than an exact science': see Report of the International Law Commission, 16th Session, UN Doc A/CN.4/173 (11 July 1964). On evolutionary interpretation in IHL, see Mark Klamberg, 'Evolution of Rules and Concepts in International Humanitarian Law: Navigating through Legal Gaps and Fault-lines' in Deland, Klamberg, and Wrange (eds) (n 8) 79.

As to the idea of contingency used in this chapter, the analysis is informed by the two sibling frameworks of false necessity and false contingency as developed by Unger[13] and Marks[14] respectively. The concept of false necessity warns us against a fatalistic determinism in the assessment of the history of international law. It is a powerful reminder that things do not have to be as they are, and confronts us with our mistaking the established order for something 'natural, necessary or authoritative'[15] when, on the contrary, it is a product of contingency—something that 'we have temporarily refrained from challenging and remaking'.[16] At the other end of the spectrum, we fall into false contingency when we consider history as something accidental, 'a matter of chance and will',[17] failing to take into account that there are necessary factors, limits, and pressures that orient change without predetermining it. Awareness of false contingency thus means acknowledging that history is made of certain conditions that make something possible but, crucially, may or may not be seized—in other words, 'that things can be, and frequently are, contingent without being random, accidental or arbitrary'.[18]

Throughout the chapter, the concepts of false necessity and false contingency are put in constant dialogue with each other, and tested against the background of each of the aspects analysed. As it emerges from the epistemological ambiguity of the term 'contingency' itself, referring to both uncertainty and dependence upon something else,[19] the two concepts can indeed be seen as two sides of the same coin, two faces of a *Janus Bifrons*.[20] It is only by taking into account both layers of analysis that we can escape seeing necessity where there is contingency but also avoid considering as purely accidental and arbitrary a system which is informed and shaped by *determined*—but not *pre-determined*—factors.[21]

And yet, for all the above, unveiling necessity and contingency is not meant to lead to pure relativism. As Craven put it, the past does answer our questions, but there is only a limited number of questions that we can ask.[22] This is why, while a critical approach to history is necessary to appreciate that possibilities are much wider than the reality we live in, keeping an eye on context means acknowledging that those possibilities are diverse and numerous but all the same finite.[23] Hence, as much as false necessity reminds us of the role of choices in history, false contingency balances the perspective by showing us the historical conditions that made choice possible in the first place. As Susan Marks, quoting Ellen Wood, tells us:

[13] Roberto Mangabeira Unger, *False Necessity: Anti-Necessitarian Social Theory in the Service of Radical Democracy* (Verso 2004).

[14] Susan Marks, 'False Contingency' (2009) 62 Current Legal Problems 1.

[15] Unger (n 13) xx.

[16] ibid xxviii.

[17] Marks (n 14) 10.

[18] ibid 2.

[19] 'Contingency' (*Merriam-Webster Online Dictionary*) <www.merriam-webster.com/dictionary/contingency> accessed 15 April 2019.

[20] See in the same direction Ingo Venzke, 'Possibilities of the Past: Histories of the NIEO and the Travails of Critique' (2018) 20 Journal of the History of International Law 263, 270.

[21] Marks (n 14).

[22] Matthew Craven, 'Theorizing the Turn to History in International Law' in Anne Orford and Florian Hoffmann (eds), *The Oxford Handbook of the Theory of International Law* (OUP 2016) 21.

[23] Venzke (n 20) 271.

> we are not obliged to accept a Manichaen choice between determinism and contingency – the real alternative to both is history: historical possibility, that is the existence of… social and material conditions which make something possible that was impossible before.[24]

The ultimate aim of the analysis is then not only to try and make sense of why things took a certain direction, but also to show that, with respect to the same object of analysis, the necessity stemming from a given historical moment can turn into contingency when tested today against the background of a different context.

II. The adoption of CA3: Much ado about nothing?

The first layer of contingency emerging from CA3 has to do with the very choice of regulating NIACs in the framework of a multilateral treaty, and with the claim of objectivity associated to this decision.

The magnitude of the novelty of adopting a provision covering situations of internal conflict is reflected in the extensive debate that led to its adoption in the context of the Diplomatic Conference of 1949.[25] As to the motives behind such decision, the official narrative points to the desire to create an objective standard for the application of the laws of war to situations of internal conflict, moving away from the subjectivity that was typical of the practice of recognition of belligerency.[26] In that respect, one of the main goals of the inclusion of CA3 in the draft convention was that of finding a way to provide for the immediate and automatic application of the most basic provisions of IHL in cases of NIAC by no longer leaving room for states to question the applicability of the laws of war to those situations.[27]

To be able to reach such goal, however, clear criteria to discern which situations would fall within the newly created category of NIAC would have been needed. On the contrary, the provision was born as a compromise adopted after long diplomatic negotiations:[28] as it was not possible to find an agreement on which situations should be covered by CA3,[29] the solution reached was that of simply avoiding a clear definition in order to prevent any dispute over specific requirements.[30] The result is that the text of the provision lacks any positive criteria to define what a conflict as per CA3 should look like. The category of NIAC is defined by what it is not, through a negative formulation, 'not of an international character'.[31]

[24] See Marks (n 14) 10.

[25] See Siordet (n 4) and ICRC, *Final Record of the Diplomatic Conference of Geneva of 1949*, in particular vol II B and vol III.

[26] On recognition of belligerency, see Hersch Lauterpacht, *Recognition in International Law* (CUP 1947), Antoine Rougier, *Les Guerres Civiles et Le Droit des Gens* (L Larose 1902) and Ernest Nys, *Le Droit International* (M Weissenbruch 1912).

[27] See in particular Robert Kolb, 'Le Droit International Public et le Concept de Guerre Civile Depuis 1945' (2001) 105 Relations Internationales 9, 16–17; and Lindsay Moir, *The Law of Internal Armed Conflict* (CUP 2002) 27; as well as Sivakumaran (n 4) and Gérard Aivo, *Le Statut de Combattant dans les Conflits Armés non Internationaux: Étude Critique de Droit International Humanitaire* (Bruylant 2013).

[28] See Giovanni Mantilla, 'The Origins and Evolution of the 1949 Geneva Conventions and the 1977 Additional Protocols' in Matthew Evangelista and Nina Tannenwald (eds), *Do the Geneva Conventions Matter?* (OUP 2017) 35.

[29] See extensively Aivo (n 27), Siordet (n 4), and ICRC (n 25).

[30] For a recent analysis of the compromising nature of the negotiations of CA3, see Giovanni Mantilla, 'Forum Isolation: Social Opprobrium and the Origins of the International Law of Internal Conflict' (2018) 72 International Organization 317.

[31] See, among others, Sandesh Sivakumaran, 'Re-envisaging the International Law of Internal Armed Conflict' (2011) 22 European Journal of International Law 219.

The provision does not contain any definition of the term 'party to the conflict', let alone any description of the conditions to be fulfilled in order to be considered as such.

Despite what may appear as an unsatisfying result from the point of view of the clarity of the law, such outcome was all but surprising in the eyes of many commentators. In particular, Rosemary Abi-Saab claimed that 'a legal text adopted after long and difficult negotiations within a diplomatic conference cannot but be a compromise text, where a vague formulation enables everyone to find an interpretation that does not excessively jeopardise their interests'.[32]

In light of the above, it is fair to say that CA3 was voluntarily left open to interpretation, leaving room for states to adjust any given situation to their preferences.[33] This decision clearly runs counter to the initial claim that the regulation of NIACs through treaty law would prevent subjective readings of given facts in light of the needs of the moment. To the contrary, it is quite easy to spot an inherent contradiction between the proclaimed goal of deciding *ex ante*, via treaty law, which situations could be considered NIACs and the absence of any explicit criteria for the applicability of the very provision adopted to that aim.

The scenario we are faced with ultimately amounts to a re-proposition of the situation that was to be eliminated in the first place. The fact that the applicability of CA3 often remains open to contestation because of—or thanks to—its own features challenges the very aim of its adoption: after all, we cannot claim that we have completely moved ahead of a subjective assessment of situations of NIAC.

Approaching the issue through the frames of necessity and contingency, it seems that the two forces have played different but complementary roles in the way CA3 was initially conceived and later brought to existence.

On the one hand, the adoption of CA3 must be read against the background of the historical context in which it took place. To begin with, the inclusion of NIACs in treaty law was part of the wave of codification of IHL that followed the Second World War;[34] moreover, right before the negotiation and adoption of the GCs, the Spanish Civil War had played a crucial role in providing the International Committee of the Red Cross (ICRC) with the occasion to discuss the possibility of regulating situations of civil war at the Diplomatic Conference.[35] On the other hand, it cannot be denied that the final formulation of the provision was strongly shaped by the need to find a compromise between irreconcilable positions.

[32] Rosemary Abi-Saab, *Droit Humanitaire et Conflits Internes: Origines et Évolution de La Réglementation Internationale* (Pedone 1986) 68–69 (translation by the author; original version: 'Un texte juridique adopté après de longues et difficiles négociations par une conférence diplomatique, ne peut être dans la plupart de cas qu'un texte de compromis, où chacun doit pouvoir trouver dans une formulation vague une interprétation qui ne porte pas atteinte de manière trop visible à ses intérêts').

[33] On indeterminacy in international law, see Cameron A Miles, 'Indeterminacy' in d'Aspremont and Singh (eds) (n 11) 447. For an interesting overview of the different forms of indeterminacy in IHL, see Adil Ahmad Haque, 'Indeterminacy in the Law of Armed Conflict' (2019) 95 International Law Studies 118. On complexity in international law, and in particular on the 'fundamental absence of any coherent original legislative design with respect to key regime applicability and threshold issues' in IHL, see Marko Milanovic, 'Accounting for the Complexity of the Law Applicable to Modern Armed Conflicts' in Christopher M Ford and Winston S Williams (eds), *Complex Battlespaces* (OUP 2019) 33, 36–38.

[34] On the formalisation of IHL, see Olivier Corten, 'Formalization and Deformalization as Narratives of the Law of War' in Beneyto and Kennedy (eds) (n 10) 251.

[35] See Aivo (n 27), Cassese (n 4) and Robert Heinsch, 'The International Committee of the Red Cross and the Geneva Conventions of 1949' in Robin Geiß, Andreas Zimmermann, and Stefanie Haumer (eds), *Humanizing the Laws of War: The Red Cross and the Development of International Humanitarian Law* (CUP 2017) 27.

The interchangeability and mutual reinforcement of the concepts of (false) necessity and (false) contingency emerges here quite clearly: depending on the perspective one adopts, it is possible to stress either aspect of the situation. In the face of the same historical moment, one can either choose to stress the need to find a compromise as an inevitable factor in the necessary choice of adopting CA3 with the features it has, or else consider the same result as highly contingent for its dependency upon a specific set of interests emerging at the Diplomatic Conference.

Be that as it may, it is important to ask ourselves if any alternatives were available and whether and how they would have changed the way in which international law deals with NIACs. This means considering the possibility that such a sensitive topic could have had a different story if managed differently, or even outside the boundaries of treaty law. Without engaging in an exercise of pure counterfactuals, the idea is to challenge the assumption that the choice of including CA3 in the GCs to provide for a more objective application of IHL to situations of internal conflict went without saying, as an unavoidable development of the laws of war.

To begin with, a different way of regulating the matter could have envisaged a different division of tasks among the actors that play the 'gatekeepers' of the field of IHL.[36] A different regulatory regime could have entailed, for instance, a prominent role assigned to the ICRC[37] or another specialised body.[38] To the contrary, as much as it was for states to have a say on the applicability of the laws of war under the practice of recognition of belligerency, the same actors are still exercising a sort of power of recognition by providing their own view on whether or not a given situation amounts to those covered by CA3.[39] Another way in which states could have maintained their central regulatory role without being free to interpret CA3 vis-à-vis each specific situation was proposed years later by Baxter: a procedure, analogous to that used to accept the compulsory jurisdiction of the International Court of Justice, through which states could specify via unilateral declaration under which circumstances they would apply the rules of NIACs.[40] Stretching our imagination a bit further, it seems even possible to imagine a situation in which conflicts that do not fall under the definition of international armed conflict (IAC) are only regulated by customary international law: according to Cassese, this is the direction IHL would have taken even in the absence of CA3, following a trend that started with the Spanish Civil War.[41]

The fact that in 1949, despite claims to objectivity, states chose to retain their power to decide on the applicability of IHL to situations of internal conflict shall not prevent us from asking whether any of the above-mentioned options could be viable today to confront new scenarios. Given the existing room for manoeuvre in the interpretation of the scope of CA3, and the fact that the concrete application of the provision in the aftermath of its adoption

[36] See Sivakumaran (n 4) 196–99.

[37] See Report of the Secretary General 'Respect for Human Rights in Armed Conflicts' (18 September 1970) UN doc A/8052 para 160 and ICRC, *Conference of Government Experts on the Reaffirmation and Development of International Humanitarian Law Applicable in Armed Conflicts* (ICRC 1971) part V, 39.

[38] See Report of the Secretary General (n 37) 145, 161; and ICRC (n 37) 40. Interestingly, the creation of an international authority with the role of determining, on application of either side, whether given requirements existed in relation to a specific case was already suggested by Lauterpacht in discussing potential future developments of the process of recognition of belligerency: see Lauterpacht (n 26) 254.

[39] On the similarities between CA3 and recognition of belligerency, see Zorgbibe (n 4) 676.

[40] See Richard Baxter, 'Ius in Bello Interno' in John N Moore (ed), *Law and Civil War in the Modern World* (Johns Hopkins University Press 1974) 533.

[41] See Cassese (n 4).

has been overall perceived as disappointing due to the denial of its relevance by either of the parties to the conflict,[42] we can ask ourselves whether the codification effort was, in the end, worth it. Provocative as these questions may sound, their purpose is to encourage us to think outside the box in the face of new scenarios—such as the use of artificial intelligence, new technologies, and new weapons in warfare. In light of the above, it is submitted that weighing the opportunity of adopting new treaties in the absence of a controlling body, and assessing the viability of other options (such as, for instance, the adoption of soft law instruments such as the Montreux Document regulating the use of private military and security companies),[43] are good ways to re-appropriate a sense of possibility towards the imagination of different solutions for situations that no longer fit the traditional boundaries of the discipline.

III. The armed forces of parties to the conflict—between contingent and necessary models

Another interesting example of how (false) necessity and (false) contingency intersect in the context of CA3 is the role played by historical context in shaping the provision around the paradigm of state armed forces.

Why does an Article that was inserted in the GCs precisely to cover conflicts involving non-state entities, and therefore deemed applicable to both sides,[44] provide as the only clue vis-à-vis the nature of the parties to the conflict a reference to members of their armed forces? At first sight, the reference to 'armed forces' is not easy to dismiss. The term is in fact consistently used throughout the GCs under an assumption of self-evidence according to which the reference builds on the criteria set forth by national legislation for the composition of the armed forces of the state.[45] On the other hand, to assume that the reference in CA3 was meant to be only addressed to the state's side would make very little sense, considering the ground-breaking role of the provision in regulating NIACs for the first time.[46]

Putting things in historical perspective helps address the conundrum posed by the apparently inconsistent use of the term.[47] In this respect, it is important to keep in mind that, notwithstanding the inclusion of the distinction between IACs and NIACs in treaty law, at the time of the adoption of the GCs, parties to the conflict still mirrored each other to a great extent in both situations. In particular, the negotiation and adoption of CA3 was based on the model of the Spanish Civil War—a context where the difference between the parties

[42] See ICRC (n 37) 38. For further details, see Sivakumaran (n 4) and David P Forsythe, 'Legal Management of Internal War: The 1977 Protocol on Non-International Armed Conflicts' (1978) 72 American Journal of International Law 277.

[43] See The Montreux Document on Pertinent International Legal Obligations and Good Practices for States Related to Operations of Private Military and Security Companies During Armed Conflict (17 September 2008).

[44] For an exhaustive account of the various theories explaining the binding nature of CA3 on non-state parties, see Sandesh Sivakumaran, 'The Addressees of Common Article 3' in Clapham, Gaeta and Sassòli (eds) (n 2) 415 and Andrew Clapham, 'Focusing on Armed Non-State Actors' in Andrew Clapham and Paola Gaeta (eds), *The Oxford Handbook of International Law in Armed Conflict* (OUP 2014) 766.

[45] See Pictet (n 4) and Aivo (n 27).

[46] See Nils Melzer, *Interpretive Guidance on the Notion of Direct Participation in Hostilities under International Humanitarian Law* (ICRC 2009) 28, and ICRC (n 3) para 530, building on the use of the wording 'armed forces' as opposed to '*the* armed forces'—in the French version, 'les membres *de* force armées' rather than 'les membres *des* forces armées'.

[47] On inconsistency as contradiction between different rules, see Haque (n 33) 138.

facing each other was one of legitimation rather than structure. At the time, civil wars often saw professional militaries on both sides. The average situation was characterised by the detachment of a dissident part of the army from the regular governmental forces: the opposing forces were thus very similar in size, discipline, means, and training, for they both possessed the features of a regular army.[48] If one takes into account that, at the time, it made perfect sense to think of a regular army and a dissident army facing each other, the use of the term 'armed forces' to refer to both sides becomes easier to explain. Seen against that background, the reference was not necessarily meant to leave much outside the picture:[49] since no real alternative existed, elevating the state's armed forces as a model was more the product of the contingent historical context than of political or ideological choice.

In principle, had they wanted, the drafters could have made clear that the reference to armed forces in CA3 had a different meaning from the way the term was used in the rest of the GCs. To be sure, the fact that this did not happen has to do with the compromise decision not to include any explicit criteria on the characteristics of the conflict and the entities involved therein. However, it is equally important to take into account that, at the time of the negotiation of the GCs, the structural features of the entities involved in internal conflicts were so similar that they would not have constituted a decisive criterion to draw a line between situations potentially falling within and outside CA3. In a context in which entities opposing each other in situations of NIAC shared many of their characteristics, avoiding the use of the term 'armed forces' wouldn't have had a big impact on the scope of application for CA3.

It is thus submitted that the real room for choice laid in the decision to adopt a provision covering NIACs, and not so much in a wilful choice to restrict its applicability to a selected kind of entity. To that extent, the reference to armed forces seems at the same time necessitated on the lack of alternative models but, in light of the historical context, also contingent inasmuch as it was not directly aimed at leaving particular kinds of conflicts outside the area of applicability of CA3. This seems confirmed by the language adopted in the following wave of codification of NIACs, with the Second Additional Protocol to the GCs (APII) making a clear distinction between state armed forces and 'dissident armed forces or other organized armed groups'.[50] Comparing the language of the two instruments, it is quite clear that the emergence of situations of conflict where opposing sides were not only different in legitimation but to a growing extent also in kind injected into the use of the term 'armed forces' an exclusionary potential that was not necessarily present at the time of the adoption of CA3.

What appears as a necessity related to the fact that the GCs were, to a great extent, the product of the legacy of the pre-Second World War world assumes another dimension if one expands the scope of the analysis to assess the historical context from a broader angle. While the term 'armed forces' was not directly meant to leave specific situations outside the area of applicability of CA3 within the Western world, the choice immediately stands out as

[48] See Aivo (n 27), as well as Pictet (n 4) 37, maintaining that NIACs as per CA3 are 'conflicts, in short, which are in many aspects similar to an international war, but take place within the confines of a single country'.

[49] See Zorgbibe (n 4).

[50] Second Additional Protocol to the Geneva Conventions of 12 August 1949 (opened for signature 8 June 1977, entered into force 7 December 1978) 1125 UNTS 609 art 1. A comparison of the use of the term 'armed forces' in CA3 and art 1 APII can be found in Nils Melzer, 'The Principle of Distinction between Civilians and Combatants' in Clapham and Gaeta (eds) (n 44) 296, 312–13.

the product of an exclusionary decision as soon as one starts zooming out of that part of the globe. The reference to armed forces relied indeed on the previous, deeply-rooted limitation of the conceptual scope of IHL to Western, structured, inter-state models of waging war and the consequent dismissal of any other practice as pertaining to 'others'.[51]

According to Mégret, the constitution of the 'other' has been central to the very emergence of the laws of war well before the negotiation and adoption of the GCs. In that sense, the GCs can paradoxically be seen as one of the first moments in which IHL started to slowly open up towards the inclusion of the Third World.[52] In that sense, it is possible to advance that the exclusion of the non-Western world from the horizon of the situations that would trigger the applicability of IHL was the product of a choice made centuries before, that was just beginning to loosen its grip.

At the time of the adoption of CA3, the contingency of a wilful exclusionary decision was in fact contaminated by the necessity of complying with an established paradigm that was taken for granted and, probably, not yet ready to be questioned: as Abi-Saab put it, referring to the GCs, 'it is ironically said ... that they are always one war behind'.[53] As ironic as history often is, the model that was used to build CA3 soon disappeared after the adoption of the GCs.[54] A cursory look at the use of the term 'armed forces' in the Additional Protocols suffices to understand that things took indeed a different direction in the First Additional Protocol to the GCs, where the choice of referring to organised armed forces without distinguishing between regular and irregular ones was made precisely to include wars of national liberation within its scope of application.[55]

IV. The interpretive space offered by CA3

Contingency and necessity can also be spotted in the way CA3 has been interpreted since its adoption. An analysis of how the provision's inherent contradictions have been handled by different actors offers interesting insights on the opening of historical possibilities in the aftermath of the adoption of a text characterised by structural ambiguity.[56]

In order to be able to shed some light on the different interpretations of CA3, we need to come back to the moment of its adoption. As discussed above, the compromise choice of leaving out of the text of the provision any reference to clear criteria to define NIACs and the actors involved therein was the product of the different views emerging during the negotiations at the Diplomatic Conference. On the one hand, several states meant CA3 to be

[51] See Frédéric Mégret, 'From "Savages" to "Unlawful Combatants": A Postcolonial Look at International Law's "Other"' in Anne Orford (ed), *International Law and its Others* (CUP 2006) 265 and Frédéric Mégret, 'L'Etatisme Spécifique du Droit International' (2011) 24 Revue Québécoise de Droit International 105.

[52] See Mégret (n 51).

[53] See Georges Abi-Saab, 'Wars of National Liberation in the Geneva Conventions and Protocols' (1979) 165 Collected Courses of The Hague Academy of International Law 435.

[54] See Abi-Saab (n 32).

[55] First Additional Protocol to the Geneva Conventions of 12 August 1949 (opened for signature 8 June 1977, entered into force 7 December 1978) 1125 UNTS 3 arts 1 and 43.

[56] On structural indeterminacy and textual interpretation, see Andrea Bianchi, 'Textual Interpretation and (International) Law Reading: The Myth of (in)Determinacy and the Genealogy of Meaning' in Pieter HF Bekker, Rudolf Dolzer, and Michael Waibel (eds), *Making Transnational Law Work in the Global Economy: Essays in Honour of Detlev Vagts* (CUP 2010) 34. On 'international law's relative stability in conditions of structural indeterminacy', see Frédéric Mégret, 'Thinking About What International Humanitarian Lawyers "Do": An Examination of the Laws of War as a Field of Professional Practice' in Werner, de Hoon, and Galán (eds) (n 5) 265.

applicable to civil wars characterised by control of territory and the existence of organised armed forces acting under responsible authority, following the model that would have traditionally triggered a recognition of belligerency.[57] This was not the case for the ICRC and a small number of other states that, on the contrary, thought that the whole point of CA3 was to cover internal conflicts less structured than civil wars.[58] As I have claimed, the aim of replacing a subjective recognition of belligerency with the objective applicability of CA3 was circumvented by the absence of any explicit criteria to define what a NIAC was. Once more, at the end of the day, the matter turned out to be one of interpretation, with the scope of application of CA3 acting as the bone of contention: the provision could at the same time embrace a wide range of situations or be interpreted restrictively.[59]

Soon after the adoption of CA3, the lack of a definition of NIAC started to emerge as problematic. In the face of its indeterminacy, different actors started to assume increasingly different positions as to whether certain situations were to be considered as triggering the applicability of CA3.[60] The ICRC kept trying to use the flexibility of the provision to advocate for a low threshold of applicability and to offer its services in situations that, on the contrary, many states saw as falling outside the scope of CA3. A growing gap in the interpretation of the provision started to arise between the ICRC and the majority of states, with the former deeming CA3 applicable to situations falling short of the characteristics of a fully-fledged civil war.[61]

No position clearly prevailed for quite a long time, until the International Criminal Tribunal for the former Yugoslavia (ICTY), in the famous Decision on Jurisdiction in the *Tadić* case,[62] provided a definition of NIAC and, from then on, began to elaborate related criteria of organisation of the parties and intensity of the hostilities.[63] Since then, a mainstream trend of interpretation[64] imposed itself in case law[65] and scholarly work,[66] was endorsed by the ICRC,[67] and later influenced the formulation adopted in the Rome Statute of the International Criminal

[57] See Zorgbibe (n 4) and Moir (n 27).

[58] See Abi-Saab (n 32) and Cassese (n 4).

[59] See Abi-Saab (n 32) and Abi-Saab (n 4).

[60] On the difference between semantic disagreement over the application of a concept to specific facts and substantive disagreement over the underlying standards see Haque (n 33) 126–29.

[61] See Abi-Saab (n 32) and Abi-Saab (n 4); as well as Mantilla (n 28). For an extensive survey of early state practice on the applicability of CA3, see Moir (n 27).

[62] See *Tadić* (n 3).

[63] See in particular *Prosecutor v Tadić* (Opinion and Judgment) ICTY-94-1-T (7 May 1997) para 562; *Prosecutor v Limaj* (Judgment) ICTY-03-66-T (30 November 2005); *Prosecutor v Haradinaj, Balaj and Brahimaj* (Judgment) ICTY-04-84-T (3 April 2008); *Prosecutor v Boškoski and Tarčulovski* (Judgment) ICTY-04-82-T (10 July 2008).

[64] See Alessandra Spadaro, 'International Humanitarian Law in the Jurisprudence of International Criminal Tribunals and Courts' in Dražan Djukić and Niccolò Pons (eds), *The Companion to International Humanitarian Law* (Brill 2018) 135, 139; Tamás Hoffmann, 'The Gentle Humanizer of Humanitarian Law: Antonio Cassese and the Creation of the Customary Law of Non-International Armed Conflict' in Carsten Stahn and Larissa van den Herik (eds), *Future Perspectives on International Criminal Justice* (TMC Asser Press 2010) 69 and Milanovic (n 33) 49.

[65] See International Criminal Tribunal for Rwanda, *Prosecutor v Akayesu* (Judgment) ICTR-96-4-T (2 September 1998) and *Prosecutor v Rutaganda* (Judgment and Sentence) ICTR-96-3-T (6 December 1999); International Criminal Court, *Prosecutor v Lubanga Dyilo* (Judgment pursuant to Article 74 of the Statute) ICC-01/04-01/06 (14 March 2012); Special Court for Sierra Leone, *Prosecutor v Sesay, Kallon and Gbao* (Judgment) SCSL-04-15-T (2 March 2009).

[66] See, among others, Moir (n 2), Sivakumaran (n 4), and Tilman Rodenhäuser, *Organizing Rebellion* (OUP 2018).

[67] See ICRC, 'How is the Term "Armed Conflict" Defined in International Humanitarian Law?' (Opinion Paper March 2008) and ICRC (n 3).

Court.[68]

In trying to read the interpretive direction introduced by the ICTY in terms of necessity and contingency, it is important to keep in mind both the authority of the actors involved in the interpretation of CA3 and the inherently ambiguous nature of the provision.

As for the first aspect, an overview of the different actors being called to express their opinion on the scope of applicability of CA3 reveals a panoply of different visions and projects. The ICRC, in light of its protection mandate, has always been interested in keeping the scope of the provision as broad as possible. At the other end of the spectrum, states generally advocate for a stricter application of CA3 as a way to protect their sovereignty. The ICTY, as a criminal court, had an interest in indicating criteria that would provide guidance clear enough to judge on individual criminal responsibility. Moreover, as it is well known, the gap created by the lack of internal adjudication mechanisms in IHL has more than once been filled by international criminal courts and tribunals.[69] In light of all the above, due to its authoritative role, the ICTY probably couldn't escape the expectation of providing some stability in an uncertain scenario—and, at the same time, it had enough relative power to decide how to do so. Against that background, it is possible to see the interpretive trend set by the jurisprudence of the ICTY as a context-breaking moment, in which the borders of the definition of a NIAC were shaped around the preferences and projects of actors who had a voice authoritative enough to set a direction for the future.[70]

When it comes to the role played by the structural ambiguity of CA3, it is fair to say that the lack of any explicit indication in the text of the provision created an interpretive space that needed to be seized through the development of some criteria.[71] At the same time, it is crucial to acknowledge that the decision as to the actual interpretive direction to be taken was contingent and not pre-determined. Contingency, however, does not mean arbitrariness: by and large, the interpretive choice of the ICTY can indeed be explained. First of all, the criteria spelled out in the ICTY's jurisprudence were not new: they had already been discussed at the Diplomatic Conference and purposefully left out of the final provision due to the lack of a common position on the matter.[72] The ICTY's choice of the interpretive criteria for NIACs also needs to be read against the background of the adoption of APII, as the tribunal had to square the circle between the scope of applicability of the two instruments and provide an interpretation that made the two ends meet halfway.[73] In that sense, if it was a choice, we could probably not expect anything different: our false necessity is at the same time a false contingency.

As to the actual content of the interpretive trend set by the ICTY, the standard is quite homogenously perceived as being broad and over-inclusive.[74] Far from denying

[68] Rome Statute of the International Criminal Court (opened for signature 17 July 1998, entered into force 1 July 2002) art 8(2)(f).

[69] See Spadaro (n 64) and Hoffmann (n 64), as well as Dino Kritsiotis, 'The Tremors of *Tadić*' (2010) 43 Israel Law Review 262; and Milanovic (n 33) 36–37.

[70] See Hoffmann (n 64). On normative power and semantic authority, see Ingo Venzke, 'Semantic Authority' and Anne van Mulligen, 'Normativity' in d'Aspremont and Singh (eds) (n 11) 662. On semantic authority as a 'piece of advice that cannot easily be disregarded', see Ingo Venzke, 'Between Power and Persuasion: On International Institutions' Authority in Making Law' (2013) 4 Transnational Legal Theory 354, 356.

[71] On the need for a 'mediating doctrine' to guide conduct when faced with vague concepts, see Haque (n 33) 127–28.

[72] For details on the discussion, see Anthony Cullen, *The Concept of Non-International Armed Conflict in International Humanitarian Law* (CUP 2010).

[73] See Kritsiotis (n 69).

[74] See among others Moir (n 2), Sivakumaran (n 4), and Rodenhäuser (n 66).

that claim, it seems at the same time important to realise that the ICTY's legacy, when confronted with contemporary situations of armed violence, provides a quite narrow reading of situations that are worthy of inclusion in the scope of application of the law of NIACs.[75] This is particularly true as, through a reference to NIACs in general, the ICTY's case law brought forward a paradigm that also includes criteria originally formulated around APII, partially conflating the interpretation of the two provisions.[76] In that sense, it seems that although the *strict* (in the sense of precise) requirements attached to CA3 were probably not aimed at being *restrictive* (in the sense of narrow) when they were developed in the jurisprudence of the ICTY, they nowadays lend themselves to being invoked against the applicability of IHL to contemporary realities of armed violence.[77] There are of course valid reasons to think that situations involving lightly organised armed groups or intermitting episodes of violence should not be covered by IHL (but, for instance, by human rights law). However, it is important not to invert the terms of the equation and mistake the cause for the effect: claiming that certain situations shall fall within other branches of the law is different from preventively denying the applicability of IHL because of the dogmatic application of criteria that have been developed in the past within a different context.[78]

A conjuncture of choices, happenstances, and determining factors created a situation in which the interpretive freedom left open by a structurally ambiguous provision is enjoyed in a way that seems rather narrow when confronted to new challenges: as a result, we are today witnessing an increasingly strict interpretation of CA3 in the face of increasingly broad scenarios. Criteria that were developed through case law are today largely perceived as being part of the provision since its inception, curtailing its flexibility and influencing its interpretation and application. The unkept promise of regulating the matter of NIACs once and for all through CA3, combined with subsequent authoritative readings of the provision, created an interpretive space burdened by sedimented interpreting practices that are taken as the law.[79] To the contrary, it is essential to remember that as much as the taking of a direction was probably inevitable, the way in which that happened was the product of a choice—certainly explainable, and partly necessitated, but a choice nonetheless. Awareness of the above seems key if we want to approach the law in a self-reflexive rather than dogmatic way.

[75] See Rodenhäuser (n 66) 71 n 61, highlighting how in its early case law the ICTY only analysed highly organised forces linked to state-like entities; and Laurie R Blank and Geoffrey S Corn, 'Losing the Forest for the Trees: Syria, Law, and the Pragmatics of Conflict Recognition' (2013) 46 Vanderbilt Journal of Transnational Law 693, 698 and 708.

[76] See in particular ICTY, *Prosecutor* v *Hadžihasanović, Alagić and Kubura* (Decision on Interlocutory Appeal Challenging Jurisdiction in Relation to Command Responsibility) ICTY-01-47-AR72 (16 July 2003). For details, see Cullen (n 72) 148 and Rodenhäuser (n 66) 86.

[77] One can think, for example, of situations involving forms of organised crime in the Latin American region or of transnational, horizontally-structured armed groups currently active in Yemen, Libya, and Syria.

[78] See Blank and Corn (n 75) 716. On the need to avoid taking a mere set of indicators as a definition of what constitutes a NIAC or a party thereto, see Tilman Rodenhäuser, 'Armed Groups, Rebel Coalitions, and Transnational Groups: The Degree of Organization Required from Non-State Armed Groups to Become Party to a Non-International Armed Conflict' (2016) 19 Yearbook of International Humanitarian Law Volume 3.

[79] As Venzke put it, the authority of discursive construction is incremental and rests on shared social beliefs: see Venzke (n 70) 366–70.

V. Conclusions

By challenging—in a sometimes purposefully provocative way—the mainstream narrative that surrounds CA3, I have argued that the way in which we understand the provision today is highly contingent, partly because of the context in which it was adopted and partly because of the way it has been subsequently interpreted: the finding is not necessarily new, but it is definitely something we are not always aware of.

I draw three main conclusions from the analysis. First of all, reflecting upon the outcome of the choice of regulating NIACs via treaty law shall encourage the imagination of alternative solutions for scenarios that do not fit the reality we are faced with. Regarding the features of the notion of party to the conflict emerging from CA3, we have to be mindful that criteria which today might appear restrictive were not necessarily meant to be so, and should not be seen as obstacles to evolutionary readings of the provision. Finally, and more importantly, the way we interpret the provision partly depends on us and on our goals and priorities, for the interpretive space we are left with is quite flexible and certainly not unidirectional.

Crucially, this means that other interpreting possibilities are available. That seems all the more true if one considers that, regardless of the two conflicting visions over which specific kinds of conflicts should fall within the scope of the provision, the aim of moving forward by adopting CA3 could be seen as the common intention of the parties which negotiated the GCs. In order not to engage in interpretations that would render the provision meaningless, the impact that CA3 was supposed to have when it was adopted needs to be taken into account in the exercise of evolutionary interpretation.[80] If we want to keep pace with an ever-changing reality and honour the forward-looking role the provision was expected to play in the context of the GCs, we might need to re-think the criteria that we have attached to it.

More broadly, my contribution aims at suggesting that awareness of the historical context, coupled with a sense of contingency, should have an emancipatory rather than freezing effect. The *pars destruens* must be always followed by a *pars construens*, for it is only when we get a sense of how and why things took a certain direction that we are able to make a step further and develop normative arguments, freeing ourselves from our own hurdles.[81] In the end, exploring past contingency is not only needed to take agency in the present but also to keep in mind that the future will be contingent as well.

According to Foucault, critique shall 'separate out, from the contingency that has made us what we are, the possibility of no longer being, doing, or thinking what we are, do, or think.'[82] By questioning the unquestioned, we can take back the intellectual possibility of conceiving things differently from what they are, and use the past as a guide rather than a dogma. Hopefully, as Marks and Lang put it, this is one of the ways in which we can prevent tradition from becoming conformism.[83]

[80] On the relevance of the 'temporal sense-intention' of the drafters in evolutionary interpretation, see Julian Wyatt, 'Using Intertemporal Linguistics to Resolve the Problem at the Origin and Core of the Evolutionary Interpretation Debate' in Georges Abi-Saab et al (eds), *Evolutionary Interpretation and International Law* (Hart 2019) 47, 54–55.

[81] See Rosalyn Higgins, *Problems and Process: International Law and How We Use It* (Clarendon Press 1995) 49.

[82] Michel Foucault, *What is Enlightenment?* in Paul Rabinow (ed), *The Foucault Reader* (Pantheon Books 1984) 32, 42.

[83] According to Lang and Marks, we only do history when we go back to tradition and reclaim it from the forces that would otherwise overpower it: see Andrew Lang and Susan Marks, 'Even the Dead Will Not Be Safe: International Law and the Struggle Over Tradition' in Werner, de Hoon and Galán (eds) (n 5) 321, referring to Walter Benjamin, 'Thesis V on the Philosophy of History' in Walter Benjamin (ed), *Illuminations* (Pimlico 1999).

21

Narrative Contingency and International Humanitarian Law

Crimes against Humanity in Cixin Liu's Post-Humanist Universe

Amanda Alexander

I. Introduction

International humanitarian law (IHL) is the term which names, and also conceptualises, the current regime of the laws of war. The name belongs to a particular narrative about the history and purposes of this regime. In the orthodox narrative that was built as this regime emerged in the 1990s, modern IHL was born when Dunant witnessed, with horror, the inhumanity of the Battle of Solferino. Dunant and the International Committee of the Red Cross went on to develop a humanitarian system of law, aimed at protecting the *hors de combat* and limiting the brutality of war.[1] One of the archetypal offences of this contemporary regime is crimes against humanity—that is assaults on civilian populations, whether they occur in international conflict or not. This offence makes the protection of civilians and the value of humanity a more powerful concern than the traditional respect for sovereignty in international law.[2]

The emergence of this humanitarian law of warfare and its shifting interpretation of crimes against humanity, from the Nuremberg Trials until the current day, has been dependent on the narratives that could be told about the law. These legal narratives are often informed by extra-legal discourses, such as strategic, moral, philosophical, or fictional narratives.[3] As the narrative possibilities change, so too does the ethical and aesthetic framework of IHL and, consequently, the interpretation and implementation of the provisions of law. This can lead to dramatic, yet often invisible, changes to the laws of armed conflict.

Critical international lawyers have, overtly or obliquely, acknowledged the importance of narrative as a source of meaning that shapes the interpretation and practice of international law. In their genealogies of the discourses of international law, these lawyers have argued that, although the prevailing narratives make universal claims, they are predominantly Western—arising from Western interests and facilitating Western hegemony.[4] Human

[1] See Amanda Alexander, 'A Short History of International Humanitarian Law' (2015) 26 European Journal of International Law 109.

[2] Ruti Teitel, *Humanity's Law* (OUP 2011) 50–60.

[3] Amanda Alexander, 'The "Good War": Preparations for a War against Civilians' (2019) 15 Law, Culture and the Humanities 227; Amanda Alexander, 'International Humanitarian Law, Postcolonialism and the 1977 Geneva Protocol I' (2016) 17 Melbourne Journal of International Law 15.

[4] See, eg, Prabhakar Singh, 'International Law's Intimate Animosity' in Abdulqawi Yusuf (ed), *African Yearbook of International Law Volume 18* (Brill 2010) 223, 224; Chris af Jochnick and Roger Normand, 'The Legitimation of

Amanda Alexander, *Narrative Contingency and International Humanitarian Law* In: *Contingency in International Law*. Edited by: Ingo Venzke and Kevin Jon Heller, Oxford University Press. © The Several Contributors 2021. DOI: 10.1093/oso/9780192898036.003.0021

rights and humanitarianism have not been exempted from this critique.[5] They are described as a language which has been shaped by Western concerns and imposed on others,[6] a language which legitimates some subjects of history and erases others,[7] while justifying imperialist and neo-imperial projects.[8] As a result, an important part of the critical approach to international law has involved challenging these dominant narratives with alternative accounts and interpretations of international law.[9] Some critical lawyers have sought a form of emancipation in such work—but many are less hopeful.[10] They have warned that attempts at counternarratives will always be undermined or co-opted by existing power arrangements.[11] Moreover, they have questioned whether it is even possible to shape new narratives within international law without adopting Western structures and liberal values.[12]

The difficulty of developing new forms of narratives is not just a problem for international law. It affects even the possibilities of the histories that underpin law and legal theory. In Hayden White's narrative theory of history, the possibilities of historical narratives are limited; only certain humanist approaches will count as 'History'.[13] Thus, IHL may be contingent on narrative possibilities, but it is hard to see these narratives, hard to change them, and even harder to imagine a different range of aesthetic and ethical possibilities.

Cixin Liu's science fiction epic, *Remembrance of Earth's Past*,[14] however, gives us an unusual opportunity to explore a vision of what such an alternative international law might look like if it were not based on Western narratives or humanist thinking. Science fiction provides an opportunity to create new worlds and, in Liu's case, to present new aesthetic forms.[15] Yet, even these new worlds are still a reflection of existing concerns and

Violence: A Critical History of the Laws of War' (1994) 35 Harvard International Law Journal 49, 50; Mohsen al Attar, 'Reframing the "Universality" of International Law in a Globalizing World' (2013) 59 McGill Law Journal 95, 111; Balakrishnan Rajagopal, 'International Law and its Discontents: Rethinking the Global South' (2012) 106 Proceedings of the Annual Meeting (American Society of International Law) 176, 176.

[5] Sébastien Jodoin and Katherine Lofts, 'What's Critical about Critical International Law? Reflections on the Emancipatory Potential of International Legal Scholarship' in Prabhakar Singh and Benoît Mayer (eds) *Critical International Law: Postrealism, Postcolonialism, and Transnationalism* (OUP 2014) 326, 330; Balakrishnan Rajagopal, 'Counter-Hegemonic International Law: Rethinking Human Rights and Development as a Third World Strategy' (2006) 27 Third World Quarterly 767, 768.

[6] Makau Mutua, *Human Rights Standards: Hegemony, Law, and Politics* (State University of New York Press 2016) 167.

[7] Joseph R Slaughter, *Human Rights, Inc: The World Novel, Narrative Form, and International Law* (Fordham University Press 2007) 5.

[8] David Kennedy, 'Reassessing International Humanitarianism: The Dark Sides' in Anne Orford (ed), *International Law and its Others* (CUP 2006) 133; Mutua (n 6) 165; Frédéric Mégret, 'From "Savages" to "Unlawful Combatants": A Postcolonial Look at International Humanitarian Law's "Other"' in Anne Orford (ed), *International Law and Its 'Others'* (CUP 2006) 265; Slaughter (n 7) 5.

[9] Jodoin and Lofts (n 5) 328.

[10] Ben Golder 'Beyond Redemption? Problematising the Critique of Human Rights in Contemporary International Legal Thought' (2014) 2 London Review of International Law 77; al Attar (n 4) 123; Rajagopal (n 5) 780.

[11] Ruth Buchanan, 'Writing Resistance Into International Law' (2008) 10 International Community Law Review 445, 446.

[12] Jodoin and Lofts (n 5) 334; John D Haskell, 'TRAIL-ing TWAIL: Arguments and Blind Spots in Third World Approaches to International Law' (2014) 27 Canadian Journal of Law & Jurisprudence 383, 403; Vasuki Nesiah, 'Resistance in the Age of Empire: Occupied Discourse Pending Investigation' (2006) 27 Third World Quarterly 903, 918.

[13] Hayden White, *The Content of the Form: Narrative Discourse and Historical Representation* (Johns Hopkins University Press 1987) 13. This is discussed further below.

[14] The trilogy consists of the books: *The Three-Body Problem* (Ken Liu tr, Head of Zeus 2015); *The Dark Forest* (Joel Martinsen tr, Head of Zeus 2015); and *Death's End* (Ken Liu tr, Head of Zeus 2016).

[15] Darko Suvin, 'Narrative Logic, Ideological Domination, and the Range of Science Fiction: A Hypothesis with a Historical Test' (1982) 9 Science Fiction Studies 1, 4.

concepts;[16] they can therefore be studied as a way of developing or playing with themes that are latent in reality.[17] This can be seen in *Remembrance of Earth's Past*, which presents law, crimes against humanity, and humanity itself in a way that feels very foreign—not just culturally, but aesthetically and theoretically. Liu rejects the individualistic, Kantian narratives of conventional Western thought, drawing instead from the post-humanist, non-anthropocentric theories that are beginning to emerge in various forms of ethical and environmental inquiry. These approaches may not be mainstream theories—but they are not completely marginal either. Their proponents hope that they will usher in a paradigm shift in law and ethics.[18] Such a shift may never come to pass, but in *Remembrance of Earth's Past* we can see what many feared impossible—a description of what a different law, dependent on alternative narratives, might look like.

II. Narratives and IHL

The importance of narratives for investing law with meaning has been demonstrated forcefully by scholars examining both domestic and international law. As Cover argued, no set of legal institutions or prescriptions exist apart from the narratives that give them meaning, the histories and teleologies that locate them.[19] These narratives, Cover states, entail a moral point.[20] Law, considered in this way, can be seen as not just a set of propositions or provisions, but, variously, a rhetorical system, a 'way of imagining the real',[21] of constituting possibilities, of 'apologising' for power,[22] justifying privilege,[23] and projecting an imagined future upon reality.[24]

The histories that are told about IHL give meaning to it as a system while shaping the interpretation of particular provisions. The orthodox history, which could be read in Hayden White's typology of historical narratives as a 'romance'[25] about the progress of IHL towards increasing protection for civilians and humanitarian values, means that the current legal regime is read as demanding a narrow interpretation of military necessity, a strict view of proportionality, and an overriding concern with the protection of civilian populations.[26] Orthodox international lawyers might not acknowledge the role of narrative, but they are practised in calling upon these histories and values of humanitarian law to interpret

[16] ibid 1; Fredric Jameson, *Archaeologies of the Future: The Desire Called Utopia and Other Science Fictions* (Verso 2005) 345.

[17] Mitchell Travis, 'Making Space: Law and Science Fiction' (2011) 23 Law and Literature 241, 252.

[18] Lorraine Code, *Ecological Thinking: The Politics of Epistemic Location* (OUP 2006) 61; J Baird Callicott, 'How Ecological Collectives are Morally Considerable' in Stephen M Gardiner and Allen Thompson (eds), *The Oxford Handbook of Environmental Ethics* (OUP 2017) 113-14.

[19] Robert M Cover, 'The Supreme Court, 1982 Term—Foreword: Nomos and Narrative' (1983) 97 Harvard Law Review 4, 4.

[20] ibid 6.

[21] James Boyd White, *When Words Lose Their Meaning: Constitutions and Reconstitutions of Language, Character, and Community* (University of Chicago Press 2012) 2–4; James Boyd White, 'Legal Knowledge' (2002) 115 Harvard Law Review 1396, 1398–99 quoting Geertz.

[22] Cover (n 19) 7.

[23] ibid 7.

[24] Robert M Cover, 'Violence and the Word' (1985–1986) 95 Yale Law Journal 1601, 1604.

[25] Hayden White, *Metahistory: The Historical Imagination in Nineteenth-Century Europe* (Johns Hopkins University Press 1973) 8–9.

[26] Alexander (n 1) 112–13.

provisions. Indeed, this is a normal technique in the development of customary international law.[27]

Critical international lawyers are well aware of the ability of such legal histories to shape and legitimise law.[28] Their accounts of international humanitarian law, however, present a law that has always been shaped by power, rather than humanitarianism.[29] It is a law that is, and has always been, contingent on the interests of Western states and on Western imaginaries of warfare.[30] Even the most fundamental crimes, such as crimes against humanity, have been shaped by these interests and stories.[31]

Although some critics have sought to unsettle these existing narratives by creating alternative histories of international law,[32] many have remained dubious about any real escape from the prevailing politics and narratives of international law.[33] International law might, according to this approach, be contingent, but its histories, narratives, and enactions tend to be shaped and reshaped in predictable and inescapable forms. The possibility of change, whether conceptual or practical, is, therefore, limited. These critical narratives could be associated with another of White's historical plots—the satire: 'a drama of diremption, a drama dominated by the apprehension that man is ultimately a captive of the world rather than its master'.[34]

However, there are some observers of the role of narrative in law who have suggested that there may be some scope for new narratives to change law—and new words to create new worlds.[35] Morgan and Slaughter have both pointed to the possibility of discourses from outside law leading to shifts in the interpretation of international law.[36] These writers suggest that novels and literary works may be especially important in creating new aesthetic and ethical frameworks for law.[37] Slaughter describes the relationship between novels and the law as:

> [M]utually enabling fictions: each projects an image of the human personality that ratifies the other's idealistic visions of the proper relations between the individual and society and the normative career of free and full human personality development.[38]

At one point Slaughter suggests that these possibilities are positive, the source of the emancipatory potential of international law.[39] Yet, even while he argues for the potential of

[27] See, eg, Janet Halley, 'Rape at Rome: Feminist Interventions in the Criminalization of Sex-Related Violence in Positive International Criminal Law' (2008–2009) 30 Michigan Journal of International Law 1, for an account of this sort of remaking of international law.

[28] See, eg, Walter Rech, 'International Law, Empire, and the Relative Indeterminacy of Narrative' in Martti Koskenniemi et al (eds), *International Law and Empire: Historical Explorations* (OUP 2017) 57.

[29] Chris af Jochnick and Roger Normand, 'The Legitimation of Violence: A Critical History of the Laws of War' (1994) 35 Harvard International Law Journal 49, 50.

[30] Mégret (n 8) 268.

[31] Claire Nielsen, 'From Nuremberg to the Hague: The Civilizing Mission of International Criminal Law' (2008) 14 Auckland University Law Review 81, 93.

[32] Jodoin and Lofts (n 5) 327.

[33] ibid 341, 342.

[34] White (n 25) 9.

[35] Boyd White, *When Words Lose Their Meaning* (n 21) 4.

[36] Ed Morgan, *The Aesthetics of International Law* (University of Toronto Press 2007); Slaughter (n 7).

[37] Morgan (n 36) 5. See also, Lisa Rodensky, *The Crime in Mind: Criminal Responsibility and the Victorian Novel* (OUP 2003) about the influence of literary fiction on the development of the domestic criminal justice system.

[38] Slaughter (n 7) 4.

[39] ibid 16.

narrative, Slaughter notes that literature has historically favoured and enabled some formulations of the law.[40] For Slaughter, like many critical lawyers, this literature and the law that it facilitates, can be understood as part of an imperialist vision that 'legitimates particular forms and subjects of history and subjugates or erases others'.[41] Thus, despite a moment of optimism, Slaughter returns to the critical stance that the possibilities of law, both in narrative and doctrine, are limited by existing power relationships and particular imaginaries.

The constraints of existing narratives, and particular approaches to history are not just a problem for lawyers, seeking an escape from an imperialist vision of law. Even Hayden White's accounts of narrative history articulate this problem. Although White may, at first, appear to give the historian choices in how to emplot and, therefore, give meaning to, the events of history, White attributes these choices of plot to precognitive ways of seeing the world—ways which are often shaped by the historian's own historical milieu.[42] This precognitive commitment will affect all the other narrative choices the historian makes.[43] Moreover, the whole process of creating narrative history is described by White as a subconscious desire to turn a meaningless reality into an imaginary order of coherence and integrity.[44]

The desire for this closure, this creation of an imaginary order, which constitutes historical narrativity for White, is linked with a concept of a legal system—which is itself an imaginary or symbolic order.[45] The main story of narrative history—indeed the necessary story—is humanity's relationship with the legal order. Narrative histories are, in White's account, ultimately stories about authority, power, and legitimacy acting on a certain understanding of the human.[46]

White felt that modern history, which was by its nature narrative history, could not escape this type of account of humanity and law. There had, he acknowledged, been those who had tried, like Braudel and other members of the *Annales* school.[47] These historians had attempted to bypass a history of individuals and 'events' and replace them with a history of structures, groups, and social categories.[48] Braudel had even produced a geo-history, focused on the Mediterranean.[49] These historians had tried to express a different form of temporality—a *longue durée*, a geographical time.[50] The history of individuals was, for the *Annales* school, a superficial history.[51] As Braudel wrote:

> The question is not to deny the individual on the grounds that he is the prey of contingency, but somehow to transcend him, to distinguish him from the forces separate from him, to react against a history arbitrarily reduced to the role of quintessential heroes. We do not believe in this cult of demigods, or to put it even more simply, we are against Treitschke's proud and unilateral declaration: 'Men make history'.[52]

[40] ibid 10–11.
[41] ibid 5.
[42] White (n 25) 38.
[43] ibid 29.
[44] White (n 13) 25.
[45] ibid 14.
[46] ibid 13.
[47] ibid 31–33.
[48] Paul Ricoeur, *Time and Narrative, Volume 1* (University of Chicago Press 1984) 102.
[49] ibid 103.
[50] ibid 103.
[51] ibid 103.
[52] Fernand Braudel, *On History* (Weidenfeld and Nicolson 1980) 10.

Yet, White, together with Ricoeur, considered that Braudel had not succeeded in avoiding a story of fragile human works and dramatic events.[53] Braudel was forced, they argue, to put entities and events on stage.[54] As such, he was not able to resist a narrative mode of discourse showing humans acting as agents.[55] Indeed, White suggested that a scientific history of structures, such as Braudel had hoped for, could never be more than 'quasi-history'.[56]

In this understanding of narrative history, it will always be forced to return to human agents and their encounter with a legal order. Critical and orthodox lawyers have worked within such limitations, telling histories of the law as a tool for human progress, or a constraint on human freedom. But must international law always be constrained by these aesthetic and theoretical commitments? What if there were other narrative forms? How might international law look if it were not Western, not humanist, not bound to a range of predetermined historical tropes, and a limited temporality?

III. *Remembrance of Earth's Past*

Cixin Liu has provided us with an example of what such a law could look like in his science fiction epic, *Remembrance of Earth's Past*. The advantage of science fiction in imagining difference is its ability to create new and strange worlds; a *novum*, in Darko Suvin's terms.[57] The science fiction writer can go where 'others will not, might not, dare not go,[58] playing with alternate social and legal systems and with different ways of being human.[59] Moreover, science fiction does all this in a format that resembles historical narrative,[60] turning our present into the past.[61] For Cixin Liu, the genre also allows the exploration way of producing a historical narrative. Indeed, I will go on to suggest that Liu has achieved something of the anti-humanist narrative that White and Ricoeur thought impossible.

Liu's trilogy consists of three books: *The Three-Body Problem*,[62] *The Dark Forest*,[63] and *Death's End*.[64] These books were published between 2006 and 2010 in China to increasing interest and acclaim. The last volume, *Death's End* was on the bestseller lists in China and the topic of nationwide discussions.[65] The trilogy has also achieved unprecedented success for a Chinese writer outside China.[66] *The Three-Body Problem* was been translated into twenty languages,[67] including English in 2014. In 2015 it became the first work by an Asian author to receive the prestigious Hugo Award for the best science fiction novel.[68] It has garnered

[53] White (n 13) 175.
[54] Ricoeur (n 48) 217.
[55] White (n 13) 174.
[56] ibid 174.
[57] Suvin (n 15) 4.
[58] Tom Moylan, *Scraps of the Untainted Sky: Science Fiction, Utopia, Dystopia* (Perseus Books Group 2000) 4.
[59] Travis (n 17) 242.
[60] Jeffrey C Kinkley, *Visions of Dystopia in China's New Historical Novels* (Columbia University Press 2015) 3; Istvan Csicsery-Ronay Jr, *The Seven Beauties of Science Fiction* (Wesleyan University Press 2008) 81–84.
[61] Jameson (n 16) 288; Moylan (n 58) 25–27.
[62] Liu, *The Three-Body Problem* (n 14).
[63] Liu, *The Dark Forest* (n 14).
[64] Liu, *Death's End* (n 14).
[65] Mingwei Song, 'After 1989: The New Wave of Chinese Science Fiction' (2015) 101 China Perspectives 7, 10.
[66] Stephen Dougherty, 'Liu Cixin, Arthur C. Clarke, and "Repositioning"' (2019) 46 Science Fiction Studies 39.
[67] Gwennaël Gaffric and Will Peyton, 'Liu Cixin's Three-Body Trilogy and the Status of Science Fiction in Contemporary China' (2019) 46 Science Fiction Studies 21.
[68] ibid.

acclaim from science fiction writers and generalist readers.[69] Reviewers have drawn connections between Liu's work and science fiction classics by Asimov and Arthur C Clarke.[70] Liu himself cites the influence of Arthur C Clarke.[71] Yet, even while the *Remembrance of Earth's Past* has been placed within this canon of science fiction, it has quite a different tone to both classic and contemporary Western works of science fiction.[72] Indeed, the narrative suggests a distinctive understanding of the universe, humanity, and law.

The Three-Body Problem begins with the story of a Chinese astrophysicist, Ye Wenjie, who is disillusioned with humanity after witnessing the Cultural Revolution and environmental destruction. When Ye Wenjie makes contact with an alien civilisation, she is warned not to reply, or her planet will be located and invaded by the Trisolarans.[73] The Trisolarans are unfortunate enough to inhabit a planet with an unstable, chaotic orbit, and are seeking a safer home. Ye Wenjie replies that humanity has lost the ability to deal with its problems and invites the invasion.[74]

Humanity soon learns that it is faced with an existential threat. In 400 years, the technologically advanced Trisolarans will arrive and they will almost certainly defeat and destroy humanity. One possible response, a response that would not be unusual in the science fiction genre, would be to ensure the survival of part of humanity by sending them out into the universe. Cixin Liu, however, suggests that humanity's laws will prohibit this possibility. In *The Dark Forest*, he has a special session of the United Nations General Assembly pass a resolution declaring 'Escapism' to be a violation of international law:

> In strong language, the resolution condemned the division and turmoil that Escapism has created within human society, and described Escapism as a crime against humanity in the eyes of international law.[75]

The Chinese delegate supports this resolution, pointing to the principle 'recognised by the international community, that all humanity has an equal right to survival'.[76] This seemingly odd definition of crimes against humanity is further explained by one of the characters:

> Put a little thought into it, and you'll realize that escape into the cosmos was never going to work. The critical question is who gets to leave, and who has to stay. This isn't ordinary inequality. It's a question of survival, and no matter who gets to leave – elites, the rich, or ordinary people – so long as some people get left behind, it means the collapse of humanity's fundamental value system and ethical bottom line. Human rights and equality have deep roots. Inequality of survival is the worst sort of inequality, and the people and countries left behind will never just sit and wait for death while others have a way out. There will be

[69] ibid.

[70] Peter Suderman, 'The Hidden Mind: A Best-selling Chinese Science Fiction Series on How to Survive Aliens and Authoritarians comes to America' (2017) 48 Reason 50, 50.

[71] Liu Cixin (Holger Nahm and Gabriel Ascher trs), 'Beyond Narcissism: What Science Fiction Can Offer Literature' (2013) 40 Science Fiction Studies 22, 23.

[72] Nick Richardson, 'Even What Doesn't Happen is Epic' (2018) 40 London Review of Books <www.lrb.co.uk/v40/n03/nick-richardson/even-what-doesnt-happen-is-epic> accessed 1 June 2020, 34; Suderman (n 70); Dougherty (n 66) 40.

[73] Liu, *The Three-Body Problem* (n 14) 296.

[74] ibid 300.

[75] Liu, *The Dark Forest* (n 14) 55.

[76] ibid 55.

> increasingly extreme confrontations between the two sides until there's world chaos, and then no one goes! The UN resolution is quite wise.[77]

Throughout the novels, every time a solution is suggested that will favour one part of humanity, it too is dismissed as a crime against humanity. Late in the trilogy, when humanity believes that their destruction will be brought about through an attack on the sun, Earth's population relocates to space stations past Jupiter. At this point in humanity's technological development, it might again be possible to give part of humanity a better option, by sending them out into the universe in lightspeed spaceships. All of humanity would still be saved, but some would be saved to live in better conditions. The construction of lightspeed ships would make humankind 'grand'[78] but it would also lead to manifest inequality and a threat to social stability.[79] The construction of lightspeed ships is, therefore, proscribed.

Yet, at the same time, many horrific acts of violence throughout the novels are not called crimes against humanity.[80] There is one incident when 'crimes against humanity' is invoked in what appears as a more appropriate setting. The crew of one spaceship is tried for crimes against humanity for killing (and consuming) all the members of another spaceship. Yet, the author clearly regards this as an unjust decision, and an inappropriate application of the law to a chaotic, survival situation.[81] Escapism may be a crime against humanity's values, but cannibalism is understandable when stranded in an amoral universe.

Thus, in Cixin Liu's universe, no individual can hope to make their own heroic escape, even while science cannot do much to prevent the eventual destruction of the species. Fortunately, a sociological breakthrough forestalls the arrival of the Trisolarans. Before her death, Ye Wenjie inspires Luo Ji to develop a field of cosmic sociology, suggesting the first two axioms:

> First, survival is the primary need of civilisation. Second, civilisation continuously grows and expands, but the total matter in the universe remains constant.[82]

She also suggests adding the concepts of chains of suspicion and technological explosion. That is, the difficulties of interstellar communication mean that no civilisation can predict whether another civilisation is a danger to it. Even if a civilisation seems benevolent it may consider you malicious. Moreover, any civilisation, even a weak civilisation, could have a sudden technological explosion and become a threat. As such, letting another civilisation exist, or letting it know you exist are both dangerous and violate the first axiom.[83]

Luo Ji uses these concepts to develop the theory of the universe as a dark forest: 'Every civilization is an armed hunter stalking through the trees like a ghost, gently pushing aside branches that block the path and trying to tread without sound.'[84] This discovery allows Luo

[77] ibid 55–56.
[78] Liu, *Death's End* (n 14) 491.
[79] ibid 473, 535.
[80] Some examples: the use of nanotechnology to slice a ship and its crew into strips; the Trisolaran relocation of the entire population of Earth to Australia, without food supplies, with the intention of reducing the human population through cannibalism; the reduction of our solar system to two dimensions.
[81] Song (n 65) 11.
[82] Liu, *The Dark Forest* (n 14) 6.
[83] ibid 517–20.
[84] ibid 521.

Ji to institute a system of mutually assured destruction: a threat to reveal the location of both Earth and Trisolaris to the universe if Trisolaris does not desist.

Luo Ji's reinvention of mutually assured destruction successfully deters the Trisolarans for a couple of centuries, but eventually it fails. Earth and Trisolaris are exposed. Trisolaris is destroyed first; one of its suns is blown up. The population of Earth retreats to space stations past Jupiter to avoid the same fate but the galaxy is reduced to two-dimensional space as, we discover, many others have been. Humanity becomes just another extinct species in the dark forest universe. Cixin Liu allows a few characters to survive to witness, over the course of 18 billion years, the death and rebirth of the universe.

In this way, Cixin Liu's epic narrative displays a vision of crimes against humanity, and humanity itself, that feels odd and even jarring. It is not unusual for the term 'crimes against humanity' to be invoked in situations that seem inappropriate to an international lawyer, but Liu's account seems more than the misuse of a legal or moral term. Why should escapism, which in many other narratives might seem like a good choice, an individual right or a heroic pursuit of autonomy seem so problematic? And why, at the same time, should Liu appear so cynical about the nature of civilisation, so accepting of a will to survive, and yet so dispassionate about the ultimate demise of humanity?

IV. Crimes against humanity in a harmonious society

The ability of science fiction to depict a different world is part of its distinctive appeal and importance. In this case, Cixin Liu's creation of such an original narrative is particularly interesting, given the limitations that seem to constrain the possibilities of law and narrative. Yet, for many commentators on science fiction, its true significance lies not in the invention of a *novum* but in the way in which the imagined world speaks to contemporary concerns, while shaping the way we understand the present and future.[85] Darko Suvin argued that the imaged world 'for all its displacements and disguises, always corresponds to the wish dreams and nightmares of a specific sociocultural class of implied addressees'.[86] Jameson suggested, in similar terms, that the true subject of science fiction is the historical present.[87] Even the most 'energetic imaginative leaps into radical alternatives', he states, are 'little more than the projections of our own social moment and historical or subjective situation'.[88] As such science fiction is often studied for insight into contemporary beliefs and anxieties, and occasionally as a source of socio-political critique.[89] For law and literature practitioners, this approach to science fiction tends to be directed towards its ability to imply a critique of law,[90] or think about how law might deal with new legal issues.[91]

Many reviewers and commentators have already sought these types of insights from Liu's work. They have pointed to the differences between Liu's writing and the Western canon of

[85] Suvin (n 15) 1.
[86] Moylan (n 58) 48.
[87] Jameson (n 16) 345.
[88] ibid 211.
[89] Hua Li, 'The Political Imagination in Liu Cixin's Critical Utopia: China 2185' (2015) 42 Science Fiction Studies 519, 519.
[90] Travis (n 17) 251.
[91] ibid 252; Orna Ben-Naftali and Zvi Triger, 'The Human Conditioning: International Law and Science-Fiction' (2018) 14 Law, Culture and the Humanities 6, 13.

science fiction and explained these differences by reference to Liu's socio-historical situation.[92] As such, they have tended to see in Liu's work a representation of current concerns in China,[93] such as ecological crisis,[94] rapid technological development,[95] and geopolitical tensions.[96] His work has also been situated against the background of recent Chinese history.[97] Mingwei Song observes the 'spectres' of communism, collectivism, and Maoism at play in his work.[98]

Thus, while *Remembrance of Earth's Past's* narrative and construction of an alternative law may hold some interest even when viewed as an unsituated fantasy, Liu's vision of law might be even more significant if it can be regarded as a translation of strands of thought that are already immanent in the world. Liu's concept of crimes against humanity may seem preposterous but I will suggest that, despite its originality, it does draw upon some existing ideas and narratives. These ideas clearly extend beyond any local narratives and concerns, as I will discuss in the next section on posthumanism. Nevertheless, in this section I, like other commentators, will consider whether Liu's work could be seen as reflecting Chinese narratives and concerns—although, for my purposes, I focus on rights discourse. I do not mean to suggest here that Liu is putting forward a Chinese position, official or otherwise. I am simply interested in the extent to which there may be elements of a particular, local understanding of rights within Liu's narrative.

Liu's assertions of crimes against humanity are extremely odd when considered within the prevailing legal and philosophical paradigm of crimes against humanity. Yet, despite the universal claims of concepts like crimes against humanity, the contemporary understanding is based on a specific narrative about rights and law. Within this narrative, individuals have rights because of their special human status. These rights are intended to uphold the autonomy and agency of the individual.[99] Rights, Ignatieff explains, are a language of individual empowerment—they allow individuals to define themselves, to decide what they will live and die for.[100] Rights will place limitations on the state, when necessary to protect the autonomy of the individual. This means that the values of liberty and autonomy will sometimes be more important than values of order.[101] Moreover, when a state allows crimes against humanity to violate this 'core humanity that we all share and that distinguishes us from other natural beings',[102] it is increasingly argued that the state may have surrendered the privileges of sovereignty.[103]

[92] Richardson (n 72); Suderman (n 70) 50; Dougherty (n 66) 40.

[93] Li (n 89) 522.

[94] Dougherty (n 66) 48.

[95] Jiayang Fan, 'Liu Cixin's War of the Worlds' (*The New Yorker*, 17 June 2019) <www.newyorker.com/magazine/2019/06/24/liu-cixins-war-of-the-worlds> accessed 1 June 2020.

[96] ibid.

[97] Song (n 65) 10; Li (n 89) 522; Dougherty (n 66) 53.

[98] Song (n 65) 10.

[99] Louis Henkin, 'The Universality of the Concept of Human Rights' (1989) 506 The Annals of the American Academy of Political and Social Science 10, 11.

[100] Michael Ignatieff, *Human Rights as Politics and Idolatry* (Princeton University Press 2003) 57.

[101] Henkin (n 99) 11.

[102] David Luban, 'A Theory of Crimes Against Humanity' (2004) 29 Yale Journal of International Law 85, 87.

[103] See, eg David J Scheffer, 'Toward a Modern Doctrine of Humanitarian Intervention' (1992) 23 University of Toledo Law Review 253; Francis M Deng, 'Frontiers of Sovereignty: A Framework of Protection, Assistance, and Development for the Internally Displaced' (1995) 8 Leiden Journal of International Law 249; Alex J Bellamy and Ruben Reike, 'The Responsibility to Protect and International Law' (2010) 2 Global Responsibility to Protect 267, 270.

This narrative has traditionally been associated with Western, liberal thought.[104] Both the universality of the narrative and the particular form it takes have been questioned—from a variety of Western and non-Western positions. As Chan puts it, 'human rights are not inherent in a person because of his or her being a human; they are recognised under particular national, historical, political, economic and socio-cultural circumstances at a given time and then, and only then, defined and protected by law.... evolve over time'.[105] The individualism of rights in the dominant narrative has been a perennial question,[106] while the growing priority of rights over sovereignty has become a more recent issue.[107] Even the tautological association of rights with humanity is starting to be questioned in some circles—an approach which will be discussed in the next section.

As China's international profile has grown, observers have become increasingly interested in the extent to which China might accept or seek to change the orthodox concepts of rights and principles of international law.[108] Although some have questioned the existence of 'Chinese values', or the possibility of expressing general views about their nature,[109] other scholars have held that China's vision of rights and the international order does diverge in some important ways from the dominant Western interpretations.[110] This divergence is variously attributed to recent Chinese history,[111] the experiences of imperialism,[112] and the values of Confucianism.[113] The result, according to Peerenboom, is an understanding of rights that could be seen by liberals as a 'dangerous threat to the legitimacy of human rights' or by supporters as a 'necessary corrective to the hegemony of liberalism and the neo-imperialistic tendencies of the Western-centric human rights movement'.[114]

In the international sphere, this difference can be seen in China's insistence on a traditional—or perhaps even more absolute[115]—view of sovereignty in the face of the increasing liberal emphasis on rights.[116] China has expressed discomfort with the idea of humanitarian intervention and the imposition of human rights standards as tools of imperialism and hegemony.[117] Human rights, from a Chinese perspective, are internal matters

[104] Slaughter (n 7) 5; Henkin (n 99) 12.

[105] Phil CW Chan, *China, State Sovereignty and International Legal Order* (Brill 2015) 168.

[106] Mutua (n 6) 169; Henkin (n 99) 11–12.

[107] BS Chimni, 'Sovereignty, Rights, and Armed Intervention: A Dialectical Perspective' in Hilary Charlesworth and Jean-Marc Coicaud (eds), *Fault Lines of International Legitimacy* (CUP 2010) 303; Sibylle Scheipers, *Negotiating Sovereignty and Human Rights: International Society and the International Criminal Court* (Manchester University Press 2009) 6-9; Roda Mushkat, 'China's Multi-Layered Attitude towards State Sovereignty: Theory, Practice and Broad Implications' (2017) 47 Hong Kong Law Journal 659, 671.

[108] Chan (n 105) 14–15; Mushkat (n 107). Anthea Roberts, *Is International Law International?* (OUP 2017) 15; Jonathan E Davis, 'From Ideology to Pragmatism: China's Position in Humanitarian Intervention in the Post-Cold War Era' (2011) 44 Vanderbilt Journal of Transnational Law 217.

[109] See, eg Marina Svensson, *Debating Human Rights in China: A Conceptual and Political History* (Rowman & Littlefield 2002) 7.

[110] Randall Peerenboom, *China Modernizes: Threat to the West or Model for the Rest?* (OUP 2008) 6; Chan (n 105) 132; Pinghua Sun, *Human Rights Protection System in China* (Springer 2014) 130.

[111] Davis (n 108) 278.

[112] Peerenboom (n 110) 164; Davis (n 108) 277.

[113] Chan (n 105) 110; James C Hsiung, *China into Its Second Rise: Myths, Puzzles, Paradoxes, and Challenge to Theory* (World Scientific Publishing 2012) 272–73.

[114] Peerenboom (n 110) 85.

[115] Andrew Coleman and Jackson Nyamuya Maogoto, '"Westphalian" Meets "Eastphalian" Sovereignty: China in a Globalized World' (2013) 3 Asian Journal of International Law 237, 254.

[116] Roda Mushkat, 'The Anatomy of China's Human Rights Regime: A Behaviourally Underpinned Analytical and Evaluative Account' (2014) 8 Vienna Journal on International Constitutional Law / ICL Journal 131, 136; Coleman and Maogoto (n 115) 244.

[117] Davis (n 108) 217–28; Peerenboom (n 110) 87.

for a state.[118] Moreover, it is suggested that, in the Chinese understanding, such rights are not something that are opposed to the state but something inseparable from the prosperity and dignity of the state.[119]

As such, China has stressed collective social and economic rights over what is perceived as a Western, liberal preoccupation with individual choices and liberties.[120] For example, the Chinese government's 1991 White Paper, in response to the Tiananmen Square massacre, puts forward a view of citizens' rights as deriving from the right of the nation to survive, develop, and increase wealth.[121] The nation, in this approach, creates and gives effect to the rights enjoyed by its citizens, and the development and survival of the nation is more important than individual paths.[122]

More recently, the introduction of the 'harmonious society' idea, by Hu Jintao in 2005, has further emphasised the importance of the stability of the whole society. The harmonious society policies were intended to ameliorate public anger in China about inequality, problems of basic livelihood, and environmental pollution.[123] In the quest for a harmonious society, instability and disorder are seen as serious dangers to society. Biddulph argues the prioritisation of harmony in China means that rights are balanced against the need to prevent disorder and protect social stability.[124]

The importance of harmony in the understanding of rights is also shown by other writers. Pinghua Sun asserts the idea of a fourth generation of rights, described as the 'right to harmony'.[125] This would cover a series of new rights, such as environmental rights and the rights of future generations.[126] When considering rights from the perspective of harmony, the rights of abstract individuals should not take precedence. Rather these are rights that function in the context of particular social relations and require coordination among various individuals, between various nations and cultures, between those who exist and those who are still to be born.[127] Harmony, Sun states, is the highest wisdom for the existence of the world:[128]

> Harmony, tolerance, benevolence, rites, virtue, morality, concern with others, and so on will play an important role in correcting ultra-individualism, egomania and antagonism contained in Western traditional human rights and in reconstructing the theory of international human rights discourse.[129]

Weiwei Zhang explains further that happiness, rights, freedom, and dignity are all considered individual values in the West but, in China:

[118] Chan (n 105) 121.
[119] ibid 111; Peerenboom (n 110).
[120] Ann Kent, *Between Freedom and Subsistence: China and Human Rights* (OUP 1993) 10; Weiwei Zhang, *The China Wave: Rise of a Civilizational State* (World Century Publishing Corporation 2012) 126; Peerenboom (n 110) 86; Chan (n 105) 113.
[121] Sarah Biddulph, *The Stability Imperative: Human Rights and Law in China* (UBC Press 2015) 22–23.
[122] ibid 22–23.
[123] ibid 4; Litao Zhao and Tin Seng Lim, *China's New Social Policy: Initiatives for a Harmonious Society* (World Scientific Publishing 2009) 1.
[124] Biddulph (n 121) 4.
[125] Sun (n 110) 15.
[126] ibid.
[127] ibid
[128] ibid.
[129] ibid.

> these values are both individual and collective, linked with the peace and stability of the nation, in part because China experienced too many chaos and wars in its long history, and people tend to view "peace under the heaven" as the top mandate of any competent central government.[130]

Remembrance of Earth's Past does not directly reflect these approaches, either philosophically or politically. Indeed, observers have found it hard to determine Liu's political position. Some consider that Liu Cixin's work reveals his distance from the state's ideology,[131] while others note his expression of illiberal views.[132] It is not my intention to assess his position, still less to reduce his *novum* to official or scholarly attitudes. Nevertheless, as fantastic as his work may be, it can be understood as indirectly playing with many of the ideas and concerns found in these broader discourses. The dangers of instability, the difference between a chaotic and a stable state is a constant theme running throughout *Remembrance of Earth's Past*. *The Three-Body Problem* is largely concerned with the problem of Trisolaris' unstable orbit, which means that it suddenly lurches into a chaotic state. Earth and humanity also descend, at various points in the books into terrifying chaotic eras, where there is no law. The importance of stability for both technological development and the happiness of humanity is repeatedly stressed.

If harmony, stability, and equality are prioritised over individual choices and self-determination, and entities like the environment, society, or future generations are granted some moral standing alongside individuals, then it becomes less odd to see escapism as an offence. Escapism, in the traditional rights perspective, looks like an individual right. Yet it showcases inequality; it causes social disorder, instability, and human unhappiness. A system committed to equality and harmony might consider escapism as a crime against both these values and its perception of humanity as a collective. Thus, by situating Liu's work within this wider discourse, his perception of crimes against humanity appears less nonsensical and fantastic. Rather, Liu's *novum* starts to suggest how an international law shaped by alternative, although already existing, discourses of rights and humanity might make sense within its own philosophical and aesthetic paradigm.

V. Crimes against post-humanity

Those writers who tried to posit a Chinese vision of rights suggested the possibility of attributing value to entities such as society or the environment. Liu, however, goes far beyond any such cautious, local, suggestions. His work engages with a much more radical criticism of traditional Kantian or Cartesian rights discourse, which can be found in post-humanist and biocentric ethical theories. Liu references environmental literature and he has spoken of his commitment to non-anthropocentric narratives.[133] In Mingwei Song's description, Cixin Liu is a 'cold blooded' critic of the rationalism and self-determination of humanism, and a surveyor of the post-human.[134] As such, *Remembrance of Earth's Past* offers an opportunity

[130] Zhang (n 120) 126.
[131] Gaffric and Peyton (n 67) 31; Li (n 89) 523.
[132] Fan (n 95).
[133] Liu (n 71) 22.
[134] Song (n 65) 12.

to not just consider how a different cultural view might inform the concept of crimes against humanity, but how an alternative theoretical and temporal paradigm might change the perception of humanity and the possibilities of international humanitarian law.

Cixin Liu has described his work as 'hard science fiction'.[135] He distinguishes this approach from mainstream literature, which, he says, focuses on humanity. Much like Hayden White, Liu argues that the traditional 'history of human society is the history of humanity's social development. From Spartacus brandishing his sword in the arena to the French revolutionaries shouting for rights, brotherhood, and equality, humanity's capabilities have helped to determine its goals'.[136] For Liu, such literature simply seems to indulge an 'intense anthropocentric narcissism'.[137]

This literary narcissism, Liu argues, is just a fleeting reflection of a short period in humanity's history. Liu claims that the narrative about humanity's internal experience only arose in the Renaissance. Before that, literature concerned the relationship between humans and the natural world or natural phenomena presented in the form of gods.[138] Now, Liu says, the anthropocentric narrative is even less plausible, since science has undermined humanity's status:

> Once we were formed by God as the wisest of all creatures and all other things in the universe were tools for our use; now no essential differences separate us from the other animals. Taking an even broader perspective, we become nothing more than irrelevant bacteria on a grain of sand in a remote corner of the universe.[139]

From this position, Liu attempts to replace the humanist narrative with a science fiction that attends to macro-detail, that 'allows authors to sweep across time and space, crossing billions of years and tens of billions of light-years with a simple stroke of the pen, leaving the world and the history described in mainstream literature to appear as nothing more than a tiny grain of dust, hardly worth mentioning'.[140]

Liu goes a long way towards achieving such a macro-narrative in *Remembrance of Earth's Past*. He cannot completely avoid using individual characters, but their characterisation is weak and they are increasingly used as ciphers to relate a larger narrative.[141] He uses various devices of the genre to extend his characters' life span so that he can transform them into observers of the passing of tens of billions of years, thereby reducing individual events and the story of humanity to insignificance.

This vision of a narrative that is not about humanity, a history that takes place over an extended time frame—a truly *longue durée*—recalls the *Annales* school attempts to write the history of structures. It also echoes the calls by some ecocentric environmentalists to rewrite a history of the Earth in geological time—a history in which humanity is just another species and a fairly new arrival at that.[142] The connection between this kind of environmental philosophy and Liu's posthumanism is made clear in *The Three-Body Problem*. In

135 Liu (n 71) 22.
136 ibid 27.
137 ibid 22.
138 ibid 27.
139 ibid 27.
140 ibid 25.
141 Suderman (n 70) 50.
142 Paul W Taylor, *Respect for Nature: A Theory of Environmental Ethics* (Princeton University Press 1986) 112.

its English translation, the first part of *The Three-Body Problem* is titled 'Silent Spring'—a clear reference to the foundational text by Rachel Carson that inspired the environmental movement. This section describes the depredations of the Cultural Revolution. These depredations are not, however, limited to humanity's violence towards humanity. Liu depicts humanity's assault on the environment in equally, if not more, censorious terms. Ye Wenjie, after witnessing the brutal murder of her father, joins the Production and Construction Corps. Here she experiences another expression of human evil:

> And so, under their chain saws, vast seas of forests turned into barren ridges and denuded hills. Under their tractors and combine harvesters, vast tracts of grasslands became grain fields, then deserts.[143]

Ye Wenjie grieves for the destruction of the trees. A reporter, Bai Mulin, recognises and shares her feelings. He calls attention to the smallness, the briefness of human experience compared to these ancient trees:

> More than three hundred years! A dozen generations. When this tree was but a shrub, it was still the Ming Dynasty. During all these years, can you imagine how many storms it had weathered, how many events it had witnessed? But in a few minutes you cut it down.[144]

Bai gives Wenjie a copy of *Silent Spring*.[145] It is this book, even more than the death of her father, which will later compel her decision to invite and assist the Trisolarans in their invasion of Earth.

> More than four decades later, in her last moments, Ye Wenjie would recall the influence Silent Spring had on her life. The book dealt only with a limited subject: the negative environmental effects of excessive pesticide use. But the perspective taken by the author shook Ye to the core. The use of pesticides had seemed to Ye just a normal, proper—or, at least, neutral—act, but Carson's book allowed Ye to see that, from Nature's perspective, their use was indistinguishable from the Cultural Revolution, and equally destructive to our world. If this was so, then how many other acts of humankind that had seemed normal or even righteous were, in reality, evil?[146]

Silent Spring, the book which prompted Ye Wenjie's complete disillusionment with humanity, had a critical influence on an environmental movement and an environmental ethics that, in its most radical forms, attempts to completely change the foundation of modern ethics, to reimagine the place of humanity in the world and to acknowledge alternative forms of temporality.[147] *Silent Spring* may just, as Ye Wenjie noted, have been a disturbing account of 'the direct killing of birds, mammals, fishes, and, indeed, practically

143 Liu, *The Three-Body Problem* (n 14) 20.
144 ibid 21.
145 Rachel Carson, *Silent Spring* (Penguin 1965).
146 Liu, *The Three-Body Problem* (n 14) 24.
147 Clare Palmer, 'An Overview of Environmental Ethics' in Andrew Light and Holmes Rolston III (eds), *Environmental Ethics: An Anthology* (Blackwell Publishing 2002) 15; Jason Kawall, 'A History of Environmental Ethics' in Stephen M Gardiner and Allen Thompson (eds), *The Oxford Handbook of Environmental Ethics* (OUP 2017).

every form of wildlife by chemical insecticides indiscriminately sprayed on the land',[148] but it introduced a shift in perception. It showed that human progress was not always beneficial and that humanity was not separate to its environment; there was no split between man and nature.[149] As such, it sparked an interest in ecologies[150] and pointed to the importance of the species over the individual, even amongst humans: 'For mankind as a whole, a possession infinitely more valuable than individual life is our genetic heritage, our link with past and future.'[151]

Within the environmental movement that emerged in the decades following the publication of *Silent Spring*, many advocates pointed to the importance of protecting the Earth for the benefit of humanity and future generations. Others, however, tried to move away from these anthropocentric arguments and create new ethical models that assigned value to other forms of life.[152] These environmental ethicists questioned the philosophical foundations for the belief in the superiority of humanity, such as the Judeo-Christian hierarchy of beings or Cartesian dualism.[153] They also dismissed the idea that rationality somehow made humans more valuable than other entities.[154] As Taylor argues, humans think that our aesthetic expression, our autonomy and self-determination are valuable in some way that makes us superior to other life forms.[155] But they are only valuable to us as humans because we have assigned value to them from a human point of view.[156]

In ecocentric or biocentric environmental ethics, there are other ways of assigning and understanding value or a valuable form of life. There are philosophical differences between how this value is justified, but biocentric thinkers tend to hold that all forms of life have some state of flourishing, a form of goal-directedness that has a value that can be protected.[157] This approach can apply to individual entities, but also to whole species or ecosystems. In *A Sand County Almanac*,[158] Aldo Leopold made biotic communities, species and ecosystems the subject of ethical consideration[159] by describing a 'land ethic' which 'enlarges the boundaries of the community to include soils, waters, plants and animals'.[160] His conclusion, much admired by environmental ethicists is that: 'A thing is right when it tends to preserve the integrity, stability, and beauty of the biotic community. It is wrong when it tends otherwise.'[161]

[148] Carson (n 145) 87.

[149] Margaret Atwood, 'Rachel Carson's Silent Spring, 50 Years On' *The Guardian* (London, 8 December 2012) <www.theguardian.com/books/2012/dec/07/why-rachel-carson-is-a-saint> accessed 1 June 2020.

[150] Joshua Schuster, *The Ecology of Modernism: American Environments and Avant-Garde Poetics* (University of Alabama Press 2015) 139.

[151] Carson (n 145) 185.

[152] See, eg, Taylor (n 142); Arne Naess, 'The Shallow and the Deep, Long-Range Ecology Movement. A Summary (1973) 16 Inquiry 95; Nicholas Agar, *Life's Intrinsic Value: Science, Ethics, and Nature* (Columbia University Press 2001).

[153] Agar (n 152) 14–15; Taylor (n 142) 145.

[154] Taylor (n 142) 145.

[155] ibid 129.

[156] Paul W Taylor, 'The Ethics of Respect for Nature' in Andrew Light and Holmes Rolston III (eds), *Environmental Ethics: An Anthology* (Blackwell Publishers 2002) 74, 79.

[157] Anna Wienhues, 'Sharing the Earth: A Biocentric Account of Ecological Justice' (2017) 30 Journal of Agricultural and Environmental Ethics 367, 377; Naess (n 152) 96; Taylor (n 142) 100.

[158] Aldo Leopold, *A Sand County Almanac: And Sketches Here and There* (OUP 1989); Palmer (n 147) 23.

[159] Callicott (n 18) 118–19.

[160] Palmer (n 147) 24.

[161] Leopold (n 158) 224–25; Callicott (n 18) 119.

Other environmental ethicists, such as J Baird Callicott and Holmes Rolston III, have continued to develop this holistic approach, arguing that the interests of the land community, species or ecosystem are not reducible to the interests of individuals and should take priority.[162] Rolston argued that the species is a bigger event than the individual[163]—it defends a particular form of life, resists extinction, and maintains a normative identity over time.[164] Indeed, Rolston says that an individualist view of environmental ethics will struggle, because of 'the fact that natural selection is rather careless with individuals; the test to which it puts them is whether they can pass on the historical lineage'.[165]

In the same way, these authors would sacrifice some species or members of species for other species. Rolston asks if we ought to save nature if this results in people going hungry or dying and he answers that, regrettably, sometimes, the answer is yes.[166] Callicott also argued that to sustain the health of the biological community of which human beings are a part, some individuals may have to be sacrificed for the whole. He suggests that it would be more important to save the most essential species, such as pollinating bees, over higher mammals that are less important in the biological community.[167]

Many of these ideas are echoed in *Remembrance of Earth's Past*, which displays a scepticism towards humanitarianism, a carelessness for individuals and, eventually, indifference towards humanity as a whole. When the impending destruction of Earth, together with disregard for the environment, leads to a civilisational breakdown—the 'Great Ravine'—the population is much reduced, but, Liu suggests, ultimately humanity is strengthened and improved.[168] Later, when five spaceships escape a devastating Trisolaran attack and find themselves alone in a dark universe, it soon becomes clear that one spaceship must destroy and plunder the others if any are to survive. Zhang Beihai, the acting captain of the ship *Natural Selection* and one of the wisest characters in the trilogy, is the first to realise this. He gives the rest of the crew time to come to the same realisation, affectionately watching over them as they busy themselves negotiating a political structure for their starship civilisation.[169] He only interjects occasionally to comment: 'Facing a disaster like the encounter with the Trisolaran menace, a society built upon principles of humanism is fragile, especially when our world needs the sacrifice of a part of it for the good of the whole.'[170]

Zhang Beihai knows that with this new civilisation will come a new morality and a new kind of human. Yet, despite his wisdom, Zhang Beihai waits a fraction too long to begin his attack on the other spaceships. As he is about to initiate his strike, *Natural Selection* is targeted by another ship—*Ultimate Law*. Zhang Beihei acknowledges his mistake, his humanist delay, somewhat ruefully, but he is not distressed. In fact, in the moment before destruction, he smiles at a colleague and says, 'It doesn't matter. It's all the same.'[171] Zhang has no more concern for his individual survival than Liu feels for his characters. In an extreme

[162] Gary E Varner, *In Nature's Interests? Interests, Animal Rights and Environmental Ethics* (OUP 2001) 11.
[163] Holmes Rolston III, 'Value in Nature and the Nature of Value' in Andrew Light and Holmes Rolston III (eds), *Environmental Ethics: An Anthology* (Blackwell Publishing 2002) 147.
[164] ibid 148.
[165] ibid.
[166] ibid 159.
[167] As discussed in Palmer (n 147) 24.
[168] Liu, *The Dark Forest* (n 14) 391–95.
[169] ibid 475.
[170] This quote is cited by Song (n 65) 10. My translation of the text states 'humanitarian' rather than humanist.
[171] Liu, *The Dark Forest* (n 14) 491.

situation, it is the survival of the biological species that is important—not its individuals, nor its morality, nor even its understanding of what it means to be human.

This incident reaffirms what Ye Wenjie learnt in the Cultural Revolution: humans have no special moral standing. The luxuries of humanism and self-determination can only be maintained in a stable era. In a crisis or extreme situation, it is the survival of the species that matters. Yet, even the biological survival of humanity is not that important to Liu. He is just as understanding of the use of violence by other species. The Trisolarans, who threaten Earth and occasionally carry out acts of extreme and devastating violence, are not presented unsympathetically. After all, humans are just 'bugs' to the Trisolarans, who have their own advanced civilisation and survival imperative. When another alien civilisation destroys both Trisolaris and Earth, this is described as a straightforward, understandable, bureaucratic decision. The need for each of these civilisations to survive is given equal weight—humans are not given any sort of special priority. Indeed, Liu shows appreciation for a bio-community without humans. When the Earth is left almost uninhabited at the end of the trilogy, he comments on its beauty and tranquillity.[172] The magnificence of the universe, long before and after human civilisation, is also noted. Although Liu uses three books to outline humanity's struggles to survive in the dark forest of the universe, its ultimate demise is not presented as an unusual tragedy, but just one of a series of extinctions.

In this way, Liu is able to use a post-humanist, biocentric approach, together with an extended view of temporality, to produce a narrative which dismisses the compressed human life of individual choices and self-determination. Instead he produces a vast narrative of species and structures in an amoral universe. By using these approaches, Liu has gone a long way in realising a very different narrative form—the sort of non-anthropocentric narrative that White and Ricoeur thought was an untenable form of history.

Moreover, it is through this unlikely form of narrative that Liu was able to introduce what seemed to be such a peculiar account of crimes against humanity. Yet, it may be that, within this ethical landscape and this narrative form, Liu's construction of crimes against humanity makes some sense. White thought that a traditional, humanist narrative history was an account of humanity's relationship with a 'Law' that constituted their individuality. But in Liu's macro-history, where humanity is just another species in a vast ecology of species, and the 'Law' that humanity confronts is a set of brutal Darwinian axioms, then the narrative becomes an account of a species' relationship with a 'Law' that constitutes its species' purpose. In this understanding of humanity and law, any desire to save individuals or allow them to follow their personal paths becomes less important. Indeed, if humanity is seen as a species, rather than a conglomeration of individuals endowed with personal rights and valuable autonomy, then the escapists' attempts to assert such autonomy, to separate from the species, could be seen not just as unimportant but as a crime against this concept of the human. In this way, Liu's post-humanist, macro-history facilitates a radically different account of humanity, law and, therefore, crimes against humanity.

[172] Liu, *Death's End* (n 14) 520–21.

VI. Conclusion

The ecocentric dispersion of value through a biotic community is not a mainstream view. Yet, at the same time, the move away from anthropocentric theories is not peculiar to environmental ethics; doubts about the value and nature of humanity have informed a variety of theories from the twentieth century to the present. As was shown above, some of the Chinese discourse suggested a similar approach, although in a much gentler form. More extreme, Western scholars have even explored the possibility of a non-anthropocentric jurisprudence—an Earth Jurisprudence that recognises the roles and rights of non-human entities and aims to strengthen the Earth community.[173] Scholars in these traditions have suggested that their views could introduce a paradigm shift[174] as significant as the Kantian paradigm shift that moved '"man" to the center of the philosophical conceptual universe'.[175] Philippe Sands is quoted as saying, in response to Earth Jurisprudence, that 'experience teaches us that what may seem as over-reaching at one time soon becomes conventional wisdom'.[176]

I do not mean to suggest that this will come to pass, nor am I advocating for such a change. Unlike Slaughter, I do not think that the existence of alternative possibilities in international law is always hopeful or emancipatory.[177] I have simply tried to show that there are other ethical and narrative schemas available, from alternative cultural and theoretical positions, and that once these are deployed it is possible to envisage law, humanity, and crimes against humanity quite differently. Liu's work should not be seen as a direct application of these schemas, nor as the only possible way to imagine their development. It does, however, show one way to play with these ideas, to draw out their possibilities in the extreme circumstances of his *novum*, and to use them to develop a new form of narrative. Thus, by exploring Liu's vision of law, it is easier to see how contingent the prevailing view of international humanitarian law is on the narratives that are told about it and within it, and to understand how it could potentially transform into something quite different.

[173] See, Cormac Cullinan, *Wild Law: A Manifesto for Earth Justice* (Green Books 2003).
[174] Callicott (n 18) 113–14.
[175] Lorraine Code, *Ecological Thinking: The Politics of Epistemic Location* (OUP 2006) 3.
[176] Ian Mason, 'One in All: Principles and Characteristics of Earth Jurisprudence' in Peter Burden (ed), *Exploring Wild Law* (Wakefield Press 2011) 44.
[177] See, Alexander, *The Good War*, (n 3) for an example of an ethical shift that facilitated aerial bombardment of civilians.

22

Why Did Starvation Not Become the Paradigmatic War Crime in International Law?

Nicholas Mulder and Boyd van Dijk

I. Introduction

At a meeting of Allied heads of state in December 1918, the British and French Prime Ministers David Lloyd George and Georges Clemenceau called for the prosecution of the exiled German emperor Wilhelm II by an international war crimes tribunal. The Kaiser's trial, they hoped, would show that 'there will be justice for all, and this will be a moral revolution in the world'.[1] In the wake of the First World War the Allies had an opportunity to reshape the principles of international law, but to do so in a way that could obtain wider legitimacy proved difficult. Although German conduct before and during the war had been illegal in various ways, the Allies themselves also broke international law; even after the Armistice, they maintained an economic blockade of Central Europe and the Middle East that had already caused hundreds of thousands of deaths.[2] To pressure the Dutch government to extradite the exiled Kaiser, British foreign secretary Arthur Balfour suggested imposing a blockade of the Netherlands; Lloyd George agreed with him, thereby accepting that the neutral country might have to be starved into submission.[3] It was a striking way to consider enforcing international criminal justice.

Balfour's proposal was not implemented, and the prosecution of the Kaiser was a dead end.[4] That economic coercion of such extreme nature was considered in the first place points to the absence of any recognition among Western elites in 1918 that depriving civilian populations of food supplies might itself be considered a war crime. As remarkable as it may seem, in the early twentieth century starvation was simply not legible as an act that might fit in the category of war crimes or crimes against humanity. Although abuses against civilians directly committed by regular soldiers such as murder and torture were widely

[1] 'Conférence à Londres' (2 December 1918) (Bibliothèque de Documentation Internationale Contemporaine [BDIC] Nanterre, France, F delta res 858/5/XIV) 10.

[2] Isabel Hull, *A Scrap of Paper: Breaking and Making International Law During the Great War* (Cornell University Press 2014); BJC McKercher, 'Economic Warfare' in Hew Strachan (ed), *The Oxford Illustrated History of the First World War* (OUP 2014) 125.

[3] William A Schabas, *The Trial of the Kaiser* (OUP 2018) 62, 76–79. Ultimately, no blockade was declared because Britain, France, and Italy could not obtain American support for their proposed tribunal.

[4] Kirsten Sellars, 'Trying the Kaiser: The Origins of International Criminal Law' in Morten Bergsmo, Cheah Wui Ling, and Yi Ping (eds), *Historical Origins of International Criminal Law: Volume 1* (Torkel Opsahl Academic EPublisher 2015) 195–211; Schabas (n 3).

Nicholas Mulder and Boyd van Dijk, *Why Did Starvation Not Become the Paradigmatic War Crime in International Law?* In: *Contingency in International Law.* Edited by: Ingo Venzke and Kevin Jon Heller, Oxford University Press.
DOI: 10.1093/oso/9780192898036.003.0022

recognised as crimes, the starvation of civilians only came to be identified as such in 1977 with the Additional Protocols to the 1949 Geneva Conventions. International criminal liability for the use of starvation is an even more recent phenomenon, passed as part of the 2010 Kampala Amendments to the ICC's Rome Charter.

What explains this extremely late emergence of starvation as a form of international injustice? Why was it not contested more successfully in previous days? Was this a matter of oversight, or had attempts to outlaw starvation strategies in wartime been deliberately undermined? This chapter argues that the late ban on wartime starvation can be best explained by the central role it plays in the use of blockade strategies in and around wartime. Purposely severing states and colonial territories from external resupply was a method that had been widely used by the same Western countries that played a key role in structuring modern international law, especially Britain and France. Blockade derived its attractiveness from being an essentially negative material intervention—prohibiting existing flows of resources, and diverting their course—with low public visibility and high pay-off as a war-fighting strategy. Moreover, liberal blockades distinguished themselves from earlier and more primitive blockades in that they worked *through* law and regulation, rather than extrajudicially. The legalised construction of blockade explains why international law has found it so incredibly difficult to contain the deadly effects of the starvation that this policy often causes.

Alex de Waal has recently assessed the history of man-made famines and the failure to effectively address starvation *as a crime*.[5] De Waal notes that we still lack 'a systematic study of famine perpetrators ... there's no comparative political scholarship on those who create famine and why'.[6] This chapter fills some of that gap by tracing how the Western states that shaped international public and humanitarian law to mitigate war during the twentieth century simultaneously used starvation as an instrument of war. Based on material from British, American, French, Dutch, German, Swiss, and Soviet archives, it highlights moments of contingency where a stronger legal regulation of hunger blockades was attempted. It also shows how Britain and the United States often successfully blocked restrictions on blockade or, alternatively, offered superficial safeguards against abuse that preserved the destructive core of the original practice.

The chapter proceeds in seven parts. It begins with a short survey of how starvation in war was justified in international law by invoking military necessity, and how it became progressively marginalised in inter-European conflict during the nineteenth century. It then focuses on the Allied legal revolution in economic warfare during the blockade of the Central Powers in the First World War. Thereafter it discusses attempts by humanitarian organisations such as the International Committee of the Red Cross (ICRC) to reduce the ability of blockades to lead to civilian starvation, first in the interwar period, then during the Second World War, and finally during the drafting of the Geneva Conventions in the late 1940s. Finally, the chapter charts some of the postcolonial after-effects of these processes of contestation by examining blockade and starvation during the Biafra War, before deriving some general conclusions from this story.

[5] Alex de Waal, *Mass Starvation: The History and Future of Famine* (Polity Press 2018).
[6] ibid 31–32.

II. Starvation and distinction in the age of imperialism, 1856–1914

In the early modern period, the law of nations placed some restrictions on the weapon of starvation through two kinds of distinctions: between civilians and noncombatants, and between contraband and free goods. The former involved the subjects governed by law, while the latter differentiated which goods would be allowed to enter blockaded areas in wartime. If civilians were recognised as such, and if food supplies were considered free goods, then legal protection against the use of starvation blockades could be made effective.

Nonetheless, it took time for these distinctions to take hold. According to Grotius, belligerent rights in war allowed the interception of items destined for war, which by their very nature were liable to be stopped as contraband. Grotius saw food as an item that would always be needed regardless of whether a country was at war or not.[7] It was therefore intrinsically worthy of legal protection. But he also allowed states to take any measures they thought necessary to bring the war to a quick end, especially if they had no other means of fighting at their disposal. In those cases depriving countries of food was licensed with a *jus necessitatis* argument.[8] Vattel was even more permissive, allowing food blockades 'in certain junctures, when we have hopes of reducing the enemy by famine', and his argument was used by Britain to seize food as contraband during the French Revolutionary Wars.[9]

The influence of the Enlightenment, the growth of civil society, and the proliferation of globalising economic connections, which made countries more dependent on foreign food supplies than under early modern agricultural regimes, exerted a strong influence on the laws of war. The explosion of inter-continental trade enabled by the transport revolution of the mid-nineteenth century made it possible for countries such as Britain to procure an increasing share of their food abroad. A major legal milestone was the 1856 Declaration of Paris, issued at the end of the Crimean War, which created a multilateral treaty governing the conduct of maritime warfare that any country could sign.[10] It enabled neutral vessels to carry any civilian supply (ie non-contraband), even if it was meant for an enemy recipient. Moreover, the Paris Declaration required that blockades were only legal if they were 'effective' (maintained by sufficient force close to the enemy coast). Thus countries could not issue mere 'paper blockades' but had to commit sufficient forces to uphold a real blockade. This limited their use to a small number of major powers. The effect of the Paris Declaration was not only to make much of the world as a space of exchange safe for trade, but also to pacify international economic relations between European empires. For almost half a century, starvation ceased to be the mark of major wars, even though there were plenty of wars, and semi-agrarian industrialising countries were uniquely vulnerable to disruptions in food supply.

Mass famine did occur during the nineteenth century, but less due to European inter-state war than as the result of civil wars and European imperialism overseas. The colonial appropriation of land, labour, and resources broke the existing structure of agrarian

[7] Hugo Grotius, *De Jure Belli ac Pacis* (originally published 1625) book III, ch 1, para 5.

[8] ibid, book II, ch 2, para 10.

[9] Emer de Vattel, *Droit des Gens* (Liberty Fund 2008) (originally published 1758), book III, para 112 530. Pierrick Pourchasse, 'Speculations and Embargoes on the Grain Trade at the Time of the Revolutionary Wars (1792–1795)' in Katherine B Aaslestad and Johan Joor (eds), *Revisiting Napoleon's Continental System: Local, Regional and European Experiences* (Palgrave Macmillan 2014) 69–80.

[10] Jan Martin Lemnitzer, *Power, Law and the End of Privateering* (Palgrave Macmillan 2014).

societies and reconfigured traditional networks of work and food provision that were very fragile and prone to breakdown. Precisely at the same time as Western food supplies became highly protected in international law from 1856 to 1914, imperialist expansion rendered the nutritional security of American, African, Asian, Australian, and Oceanic populations much more precarious.[11] The nineteenth-century age of empire should thus be regarded as the first epoch in which starvation was caused by changes in the international state system introduced by imperial powers. As a creation of this period and mindset, modern international law ensured the protection of Western property, but ignored the protection of food and medical provision for civilians outside the 'civilised' world. Nonetheless, imperialism was so destabilising that legal norms could not permanently contain the effects of unlimited colonial wars fought by European empires against non-Europeans in the periphery.

China was one of the places where famine struck repeatedly and harshly in the nineteenth century. The Qing Empire was undergoing slow disintegration at the hands of foreign imperial powers and suffered from periodic internal crises. One such episode was the Sino-French War, an undeclared conflict which began in the summer of 1884 as Chinese and French colonial troops clashed in Tonkin. France did not officially declare war even as it undertook a surprise attack on the Chinese fleet and blockaded Formosa. Prime minister Jules Ferry wanted to strike a quick and hard blow at the Qing government to intimidate Beijing into signing a new more advantageous treaty granting concessions to France. This undeclared *de facto* war meant that international legal protections did not obtain. When his initial attacks and maritime blockade did not work, Ferry allowed local French naval officers to increase the pressure. In early 1885, they began to intercept rice shipments travelling from southern China to the Qing capital region. The *blocus du riz* rested on the French argument that rice was used to feed the Chinese army and to pay tribute to the imperial capital, both of which were used to justify its classification as contraband.[12]

The Sino-French war lasted less than a year before China signed a new treaty and hostilities ended. Just as important as the treaty itself was the legal precedent that had been set: a European power could legitimately treat food as contraband and prevent another 'semi-civilised' state from feeding its population, even when they were not officially at war. Britain protested the French blockade and rejected its decision to treat rice as lawful prize. Bismarck was more opportunistic, arguing that 'the measure in question has for its object the shortening of the war by increasing the difficulties of enemy provisioning, and is a lawful measure of war if enforced equally against all neutral ships'.[13] That mass starvation was avoided in 1884 meant that France got away with committing a serious violation of the extant regime of international law.

Yet the rationale behind blocking food transport—to put as much pressure as possible on an enemy society in a short period—grew more attractive towards the end of the nineteenth

[11] de Waal (n 5) 67–73; Mike Davis, *Late Victorian Holocausts: El Nino Famines and the Making of the Third World* (Verso 2002).

[12] Bernard Brizay, *La France en Chine. Du XVIIe Siècle à nos Jours* (Éditions Perrin 2013) 283–301; Jean-Michel Gaillard, *Jules Ferry* (Fayard 1989) ch 6; Ernest Ragot, *Le blocus de l'île de Formose* (A Mellottée 1903); A Billot, *L'Affaire du Tonkin: Histoire Diplomatique de l'Établissement de Notre Protectorat sur l'Annam et de Notre Conflit avec la Chine, 1882–1885, par un Diplomate* (J Hetzel et Cie 1888) 272–73; Lewis M Chere, 'The Diplomacy of the Sino-French War (1883–1885): Finding a Way out of an Unwanted, Undeclared War' (PhD dissertation, Washington State University 1978); *La Campagne de l'Amiral Courbet en Chine. 1885: Les Pescadores, Le Blocus du Riz* (École Supérieure de Guerre Navale 1927).

[13] Letter by Bismarck to Kiel Chamber of Commerce quoted in *Norddeutsche Allgemeine Zeitung* (Berlin, 8 April 1885) 1.

century, as Western perceptions of the nature of war began to evolve. In the Russo-Japanese War, tsarist Russia followed the French precedent by treating food as contraband. Analysts of future war such as Ivan Bloch predicted that modern wars between food-importing industrialised powers would result in the rapid exhaustion of economic and logistical resources, leading to impoverishment, social revolution, and starvation.[14] It was in the hopes of fostering such societal collapse that the British government considered a far-reaching campaign of economic war against Germany in case of war. Great Britain and several other countries did not ratify the London Declaration of 1909, an attempt to create new regulations for war at sea and regulate its effects on civilian provisioning. This left the door open to a much more expansive use of economic pressure in future conflict.[15]

III. Starvation and international law in the First World War and interwar period, 1914–1939

In the First World War, the Allied powers of Great Britain and France mounted an economic, financial, and naval blockade of Germany, Austria-Hungary, the Ottoman Empire, and Bulgaria. Britain justified the blockade by issuing Orders in Council which changed the existing understanding of maritime law and the laws of war.[16] An important modification was the decision of 29 October 1914 to treat food shipments to the Central Powers as contraband. This decision was justified by reports that Germany had nationalised its food supply. Reasoning that state control of food obliterated the distinction between civilians and combatants as far as imports were concerned, the Royal Navy started to arrest food shipments bound for German ports. By February 1915 Foreign Secretary Edward Grey argued that under prevailing conditions 'the reason for drawing a distinction between foodstuffs intended for the civilian population and the armed forces itself disappears'.[17]

The blockade of Germany was continued beyond the end of hostilities and into the summer of 1919 to pressure the Reich into signing the Peace Treaty. By refusing the free entry of food into Germany, and admitting it only in small quantities, the Allies contributed to a major social, economic, and health crisis.[18] This is what led to the emergence of a group of moderate humanitarians such as Herbert Hoover, Jan Smuts, and Winston Churchill, who advocated immediate relief. The problem for most Allied decision-makers was not starvation as such, which had been pursued as one objective of the blockade—but rather its tendency to foment social and political revolution. Humanitarianism and *Realpolitik* came

[14] IS Bloch, *Is War Now Impossible? Being an Abridgment of 'The War of the Future in Its Technical, Economic and Political Relations'* (Grant Richards 1899) 294–318.

[15] Avner Offer has shown how the contradiction between British international law-making at conferences, which endorsed neutral rights and civilian protections, and the increasing ambition of all-encompassing naval war planning on the other can best be explained as a hedging of bets; if Britain would be neutral it would require protection for its imperial commerce on the world's oceans, but if it was a belligerent, it desired as unrestricted a hand to wage economic war against enemy societies as possible. Avner Offer, *The First World War: An Agrarian Interpretation* (Clarendon Press 1989) 277–80.

[16] Hull (n 2) 145–67.

[17] 'Wilhelmina Note in Full; England Intimates That All Food May Be Made Contraband' and 'Food Blockade Nears, Grey Hints' *New York Times* (New York, 20 February 1915) 1.

[18] NP Howard, 'The Social and Political Consequences of the Allied Food Blockade of Germany, 1918–1919' (1993) 11 German History 161.

together in starvation relief efforts conducted by private and public actors from the United States, Britain, and other Allied countries.

After the fact, the First World War was regarded by many Allied commentators as an existential shock that required a fundamental change in international law. Admiralty analyst and League of Nations advocate William Arnold-Forster claimed that 'in a war between organised modern States, the supposed distinctions are not only impossible to draw; they have actually ceased to exist as real distinctions'.[19] Arnold-Forster and other League of Nations supporters in the British political elite accepted that the use of blockade would cause starvation, but saw this indiscriminate approach as a price worth paying for an international order that could end war. 'The weapon of blockade is one and indivisible, it cannot be cut in half. It is no good trying to distinguish between civil and military supplies, between State property and private property, between food and other commodities … the weapon must be regarded as liable to be used in its entirety or not at all.'[20] Placing himself firmly within the just war tradition, Arnold-Forster was of the opinion that 'it is better to prevent war or economic pressure than to seek to humanise it … the world's best hope of mastering this fearful weapon of economic pressure is thus to begin by making it a servant of the public law'.[21] It would be the League of Nations that would henceforth be the only legitimate agency to inflict something as terrible as starvation on individual states.

Neutral countries opposed strong League economic sanctions because these measures affected their economic sovereignty and the livelihoods of their citizens. While the League outlined starvation as a last-resort peace preservation measure, the Swedish and Danish Red Cross Societies put forward proposals to mitigate the inhumane effects of blockade on civilian populations. In February 1921, they proposed a declaration that prevented states from stopping 'the imports into the blockaded or occupied country and the distribution in the form of gifts or advances, of foodstuffs, sanitary articles, medicine and clothing'.[22] To persuade belligerents to sign on, the Red Cross proposal allowed only 50% of the normal individual food ration to pass through a blockade, so as to avoid suspicions that the food might be passed on to enemy military forces. Despite its paternalistic attitude towards children, women, the sick, and the elderly, the ICRC still conceded the legitimacy of restricting food supplies in principle.

The League of Nations convened an International Blockade Committee (IBC) later that year to discuss when, by whom, and how economic sanctions against aggressor states would be implemented. Due to the efforts of the neutral countries (Norway, Switzerland, Spain, and Cuba) on this commission, the four permanent League Council members (Britain, France, Italy, and Japan) were forced to admit that member states retained quite far-reaching discretionary powers over when and how to impose sanctions. Economic pressure was meant to avoid war and restore peace, so it could be gradually built up. The IBC issued eighteen guidelines on the use of blockade, one of which (No. 14) specified that the interception of food supplies to the violator would only be used as a last-resort measure after all

[19] W Arnold-Forster, 'Maritime Law and Economic Pressure' (1925) 70 Journal of the Royal United Services Institution 442, 445.

[20] W Arnold-Forster, 'The Future of Blockade' (July 1920) II(1) *Foreign Affairs* 5.

[21] Arnold-Forster (n 19) 456.

[22] Prince Carl of Sweden and Harald Höffding, 'Projet Présenté par les Croix-Rouges Suédoise à la Xe Conférence Internationale de la Croix-Rouge Concernant l'Adoucissement des Conséquences du Blocus Économique pour les Malades et les Enfants des Pays Belligérants et des Territoires Occupés' (February 1921).

other means of conflict resolution had been exhausted.[23] Admitting such gradualism was an improvement over the automatic and comprehensive embargo envisioned by the Great Powers. But the IBC position still endorsed the idea that starvation was more humane and thus better than the horrors of war. This moral ordering explains why in the interwar period, starvation did not even register as a possible war crime; since the League would only use it as an alternative to war, it was by definition less bad than what it sought to avoid.

Within the organs of the League, the British-French argument that the material conditions of modern war necessitated the end of old legal restrictions on blockade was widely accepted. This worried interwar German elites, who were concerned that in a future economic sanctions regime the League would repeat its economic blockade against the Reich. The German Defence Ministry and Navy therefore supported Red Cross and neutral attempts to qualify and diminish the power of blockade.[24] German diplomats and military staffs took an interest not only in humanitarianism but also in developing international law to further this objective. They sensed that international law might help them regain protections and sovereignty which the Versailles Treaty had removed. In November 1929, US President Herbert Hoover drew on his credentials as a famine-relieving humanitarian to call for an international agreement to allow food ships unconditional access through blockade lines. But the main proponents of blockade, Britain and France, rejected what they saw as an attack on the deterrent function of the League's economic weapon.[25]

More battles over blockade brutality were waged in 1930, when both the International Law Association (ILA) and the International Committee of the Red Cross (ICRC) convened, the former in London in May and the latter in Brussels in October. At the ILA meeting, discussion concerned a new code of maritime law. The question at hand was whether seaborne commerce would be immune from seizure in war, as it had effectively been from 1856 to 1914. Article 15 of the draft destroyed any hope of protection by defining contraband as 'articles having an enemy destination and susceptible of belligerent use'—a definition wide enough to include any kind of good including civilian supplies.[26] As the German government well understood, this would 'make the English practice in the World War the foundation of the maritime laws of war'.[27] German jurist Georg Wunderlich took up the issue with his British counterpart, the Maltese maritime lawyer John Colombos. Attempts to amend the sweeping contraband Article by Wunderlich and his Norwegian colleague Boye ran into opposition from Colombos and two more British-trained jurists, Temple Grey and the Italian Giuseppe Palliccia.[28] The international legal milieu thus successfully defended the expansive redefinition of food blockade that had taken place in the wake of the First World War.

[23] 'Annex 18: The Economic Weapon of the League. Report of the Third Committee of the Second Assembly, Adopted on September 21st, 1921', League of Nations. The Records of the Second Assembly, Meetings of the Committees (Geneva, 1921) 380–94.

[24] Marineleitung, Reichswehrministerium to Auswärtiges Amt (25 May 1929) (Politisches Archiv des Auswärtiges Amt [PAAA] R 53167).

[25] 'Europe Sees Hoover Clash with League in Food Ship Plan; Holds the Economic Blockade, Geneva's Strongest Weapon, Would Be Nullified' *New York Times* (New York, 13 November 1929) 1.

[26] 'Draft Convention on the rights and duties of Belligerents with regard to neutral property'(1930) ILA Journal.

[27] Völkerrechtliche Vereinbarungen über die Milderung der Blockadewirkung, Gesandter Martius (Auswärtiges Amt) to Reichswehrministerium, Reichsverkehrsministerium, Reichsministeirum des Innern, Reichswirtschaftsministerium, Reichsministerium für Ernährung und Landwirtschaft, Reichsjustizministerium (15 April 1930) (PAAA R 53167).

[28] Wunderlich to Martius (Auswärtiges Amt) (14 May 1930) (PAAA R 53167).

Another route to regain lost protections was the humanitarian world of the ICRC. In the run-up to the Brussels Conference the German Red Cross delegate Paul Draudt wrote to ICRC Secretary Sidney Brown with a plea to consider reforming blockade practice along the lines of earlier Swedish and Danish ideas. Brown retorted that some protections for civilians would be possible, but that he saw little chance that major belligerents would ever agree to a serious restriction of their rights as blockaders. If soldiers could be starved but not civilians, then were workers in armaments factories to be considered soldiers or civilians?[29] Brown's broader argument was that as the dispenser of something close to global justice by multilateral agreement, the League had no other weapon than economic sanctions. To weaken this instrument with large numbers of civilian protections would be to undermine international security. Like Arnold-Forster, Brown hoped that the hunger blockade of the Great War would never have to be repeated. But he thought that the League should be able to use blockade legitimately, or otherwise its enforcement power had no use.[30]

Between 1928 and 1931, League advocates of collective security through economic blockade therefore confronted neutrals committed to an apolitical humanitarianism. Liberal internationalist efforts to turn Anglo-American navalism into the cornerstone of world order blocked a potential humanitarian turn in the treatment of wartime starvation. At the same time, the advent of the Great Depression produced a shift towards economic autarky and tariff protection that decreased international food trade and placed more emphasis on autonomous national and intra-imperial production. Material transformations in the world economy thereby reduced the vulnerability of many states to starvation. Looking back at the interwar years, it is clear that international law and its salience to the issue of food security and starvation was not only determined by power politics, but also by shifts in the structure of global food production and the trade in food commodities. Politics, in other words, was not the only contingent factor shaping international law—the development of the world economy played an important role.

IV. Blockade and starvation in the Second World War, 1939–1945

Every major power during the Second World War deprived enemy combatants and civilians of food supplies to weaken their fighting strength, to force them to surrender, or to kill them. At the most extreme, the Nazis devised a plan to deliberately starve millions of Jewish and Slav civilians across their newly conquered empire in Eastern Europe. The Hunger Plan was designed to feed Nazi occupation armies living off the land while starving out major Soviet cities and Soviet POWs. The expected result of this genocidal plan would be the death of up to 100 million 'useless mouths'. Although the Nazis were unique in their plans to systematically destroy entire civilian populations, they were far from the only imperial power which tried to deny their enemies access to calories.[31] Just as the British blockaded Nazi-occupied Europe during the war, so did the United States unleash a campaign of mass starvation on Japanese-occupied islands in the Pacific. The Japanese archipelago empire was turned into

[29] Brown to Draudt (7 July 1930) (PAAA R 53167).

[30] Sidney H Brown, 'Le Rôle de la Croix-Rouge en Cas d'Application de l'Article 16 du Pacte de la Société des Nations, et de Blocus en Temps de Guerre' (1930) 12 Revue Internationale de la Croix-Rouge 233.

[31] Lizzie Collingham, *The Taste of War. World War Two and the Battle for Food* (Allen Lane 2011) 5.

a patchwork of mass famine leading to the death of hundreds of thousands of Japanese soldiers, Allied POWs, and indigenous islanders.[32] In the spring of 1945, as part of 'Operation Starvation', US bombers laid vast minefields around the Japanese home islands to hasten their enemy's surrender, sinking over a million tonnes of shipping and raising the spectre of mass famine.

In their taxonomies of starvation, US and British officials and commentators used different legal arguments to justify blockade campaigns while rejecting outside aid to prevent mass famine. In the first place they arranged a one-way adverse relationship with enemy civilians in foreign territory.[33] By stressing the duty of the enemy belligerent to provide enough food for soldiers and civilians in its territories they effectively absolved themselves of any criminal conduct. If women and children were dying of starvation, then the occupier and not the blockader was held responsible.[34] Despite fierce criticism of the Allied blockade by neutrals, in the Second World War most Anglo-American commentators argued that it was practically impossible to distinguish military provisions from food destined for the civilian population.[35] Since some foodstuffs such as fats, oils, and fibres could be used to produce ammunition and weaponry, accepting the old principle that civilian food supplies were free goods came to be regarded as an unacceptable concession that would endanger the war effort.

The two major liberal powers effectively rejected the nineteenth-century principle of distinction between civilians and combatants.[36] In a 'totalitarian war', the influential British economist William Beveridge argued, virtually everyone and everything was involved in sustaining the enemy's war effort.[37] In his view, the tight control that dictatorships exercised over national food supplies abrogated the principle of distinction. With the virtual collapse of the nineteenth-century international legal order, Beveridge thought that a new system had to be imagined that would meet the demands of this novel type of inter-state war. In the fight for democratic freedoms against the dictatorships, Anglo-American commentators and officials felt that indiscriminate weapons like blockade and strategic bombing were not just permitted but necessary to hasten enemy surrender.[38]

The weapon of starvation was craftily integrated into international legal institutions created by the Allies after 1945. The drafters of the Genocide Convention and the Universal Declaration of Human Rights (1948) never specifically mentioned starvation as a method of mass murder. Nor did they accept a binding right to secure food supplies. In a similar way, the prosecutors in the Tokyo and Nuremberg Trials ignored the Allied starvation

[32] ibid 298.

[33] Carl Schmitt, *The Nomos of the Earth in the International Law of the Jus Publicum Europaeum* (GL Ulmen tr, Telos Press 2003) 317–18.

[34] William Beveridge, *Blockade and the Civilian Population* (The Clarendon Press 1939) 26–27.

[35] By the 1930s and 1940s such arguments were no longer new, but they could now be used in war against what were regarded as totalitarian societies in which the distinction between government and society had evaporated. WN Medlicott, *The Economic Blockade* (His Majesty's Stationery Office 1952) vol 1,12.

[36] For a critical history of the principle of distinction, see Helen Kinsella, *The Image Before the Weapon: A Critical History of the Distinction Between Combatant and Civilian* (Cornell University Press 2011).

[37] Hersch Lauterpacht, 'The Problem of the Revision of the Law of War' (1952) 29 British Yearbook of International Law 360, 373.

[38] Beveridge's essay was published at the time of the Molotov-Ribbentrop Pact. If there existed, he wrote, 'any similar obligation in respect of the feeding of the useless mouths', he wrote, 'the obligation rests upon the Government of the blockaded country... Nothing that Britain is able to do can either prevent German women and children from being secure that they are fed. That decision lies in the hands of the Nazi party and of their Soviet friends'. Beveridge (n 34) 31.

campaigns conducted during the war. Starvation was prosecuted as an Axis policy subsumed under meta-crimes such as extermination.[39] But even when specific starvation-related charges were brought against fascist officials, higher officers such as Karl Dönitz and Wilhelm von Leeb were not found guilty of criminal conduct as a result—most prominently when the Allies accepted its legality during the Nazi siege of Leningrad from 1941–1944, in which hundreds of thousands of civilians perished. The weapon of blockade was effectively legalised by Allied judges and treaty-drafters after the Second World War.[40] Ultimately, they did not so much reduce or limit its strength, but rather rendered it legal by creating ever more blockade-approving jurisprudence.

The Soviet Union supported restrictions on blockade in the interwar years—even floating a proposal for an international 'economic non-aggression pact' in 1931—and continued its humanitarian opposition to total economic war beyond the Second World War. Although they were ideologically opposed, both the Soviets and the ICRC challenged the legality of starvation in various ways. They endorsed the concept of distinction and demanded a right to humanitarian access for the victims of blockade.[41] The most promising wartime attempt to achieve those objectives was the ICRC plan to assist starving Greek civilians living under Axis rule, who since 1940 had been subjected to Allied blockade measures in the Mediterranean.[42] In mid-1941, the Geneva-based organisation started a major campaign to persuade British officials to temporarily lift the blockade of Greece.[43]

But the main agency organising the Allied blockade of occupied Europe, the British Ministry of Economic Warfare (MEW), initially rejected the ICRC relief plan.[44] The MEW argued that the Axis occupiers had the legal duty to ensure sufficient food supplies for the Greeks. Relief efforts, it argued, would only undermine Allied pressure on their enemy's war effort while a strict blockade could hasten the war's ending.[45] Privately, MEW officials expressed major concern about the ICRC's susceptibility to pressure from the Axis occupiers.

With the help of British humanitarians and US public pressure, the ICRC eventually succeeded in early 1942 in temporarily weakening the blockade of occupied Greece. Ships carrying wheat were allowed to dock in Greek ports, and from mid-1942 regular transports with food and medicine began arriving in famine-affected cities.[46] The aid operations were severely hampered, however, by Allied efforts to maximise the blockade's effects. For instance, relief shipments had to have special import and export certificates and lengthy negotiations followed between the British blockading authorities and the Joint Relief Commission (JRF), in which the ICRC acted as a key member.[47] The Anglo-American powers had virtually complete control over food markets and funds donated from Allied

[39] de Waal (n 5) 129.

[40] David Marcus, 'Famine Crimes in International Law' (2003) 97 The American Journal of International Law 245, 248.

[41] Reference is here made to the Soviet note of 25 October 1939, in which the Soviet government raised objections against the comprehensive British contraband lists.

[42] For official histories of the ICRC, see Catherine Rey-Schyrr, *De Yalta à Dien Bien Phu. Histoire du Comité international de la Croix-Rouge 1945–1955* (Georg-CICR 2007); and François Bugnion, *Le Comité International de la Croix-Rouge et la Protection des Victimes de la Guerre* (ICRC 2000).

[43] Collingham (n 31) 165–67.

[44] James Crossland, 'Expansion, Suspicion and the Development of the International Committee of the Red Cross: 1939–45' (2010) 56 Australian Journal of Politics & History 381, 384.

[45] *Report of the Joint Relief Commission of the International Red Cross, 1941–1946* (Geneva 1948) (ICRC Library, Geneva) 12–13.

[46] Collingham (n 31) 165–67.

[47] *Report of the Joint Relief Commission of the International Red Cross, 1941–1946* (n 45) 12.

countries could not be used for food purchases in Axis-occupied areas.[48] As a result of these systematic problems, the ICRC did not repeat the Greek campaign elsewhere during the war. Nor did it express much interest in those famines that were occurring outside Europe—in Bengal, China, and across the Pacific. This racial bias 'towards feeding a starving population when the starvation is in Europe', to quote a higher British imperial official,[49] weakened the Red Cross's official universalism and impartiality.

V. Questioning blockade at the drafting table, 1945–1949

As the war was drawing to a close in late 1944, the Legal Division of the ICRC started to revise the Geneva Conventions. Recognising that civilian starvation often failed to lead to surrender, the Red Cross lawyers argued that blockaders had legal obligations and that starving civilians were desperately in need of stronger protections.[50] Up to this point there was no international relief agreement or treaty which the ICRC could invoke to gain access to starving civilians; such concessions depended entirely on the will of the blockader.[51] In the following months the Legal Division drafted plans about the duties of occupiers, the role of humanitarian actors, the discretion of the blockading power, as well as the potential application of all these provisions to wars within states or empires.

In April 1947, after soliciting suggestions for the revision of the Conventions, the ICRC invited Allied government experts to Geneva. The ICRC's plans to restrict hunger blockades were motivated by two considerations. On the one hand, it wished to pivot international law from belligerent rights to civilian protections. On the other, it desired international recognition for its institutional role as a humanitarian actor fighting wartime starvation. The ICRC plan forced occupiers to ensure sufficient food supplies for gendered categories of victims (eg children, women) and obliged blockaders to allow the free passage of relief shipments.[52] This anti-starvation plan remained entirely silent, however, on the root causes of famine itself. By depoliticising relief, the ICRC regulated the effects of blockade without addressing the political and military causes of starvation. At a political level, this was a missed opportunity in post-war international legal history. In its efforts to keep the Anglo-American powers on board, the ICRC's focus on restricting starvation rather than outlawing it accepted the essential legality of enforcing deprivation against civilians.

Nonetheless, the Anglo-American representatives reacted to these proposals with alarm, questioning their broad scope while stressing the duties of occupiers under blockade. They resisted the suggested exemptions for children and disliked the mandatory nature of the ICRC suggestions. Britain and the United States provisionally accepted the right of free passage of relief, but only if it was obvious to all sides that the level of subsistence had fallen below a vaguely-defined 'minimum' necessary for human survival.[53] By trying to secure these discretionary sovereign powers, they hoped to neutralise the most dangerous

48 ibid 18–19.

49 Cited from: Collingham (n 31) 152.

50 René Provost, 'Starvation as a Weapon: Legal Implications of the United Nations Food Blockade against Iraq and Kuwait' (1992) 30 Columbia Journal of Transnational Law 577, 621.

51 See *Report of the Joint Relief Commission of the International Red Cross, 1941–1946* (n 45) 25–26.

52 ICRC Report on Civilian Convention (1947) (ICRC Library no CEG_1947_DOC_PROTCIV_ENG).

53 Minutes Meetings Commission III (1947) (ICRC Library no CEG_1947_COMM3_PV_03).

elements of the ICRC proposals. Moreover, British delegates accepted the text only as a 'basis' for future discussion, not as a potential draft of a future agreement.

The most important outcome of the Government Expert Conference in April 1947 was less the proposed regulation of blockade than the effective endorsement of the weapon itself. To the disappointment of the ICRC, European countries failed to challenge the discretionary powers of blockaders, placing the entire question of preventing starvation in belligerent territory outside the scope of the law.[54] Anglo-American drafters recognised that all these proposals, including those relating to colonial wars, were far from finalised, and could be revised at future drafting meetings. The ICRC began preparing drafts for a future Civilian Convention, to be presented at the Stockholm Conference held in August 1948. ICRC legal experts suggested regulating both the blockade of occupied territory (Article 49) and of belligerent territory (Article 20). This radical proposal, which struck at the root of the weapon of blockade, required the blockader to authorise food supplies for specific victim groups in belligerent territory.[55] In addition to these legal restrictions, a French Red Cross delegate also suggested a separate non-binding resolution that 'condemned blockade' as a response to the Greek disaster—unlike the French government representative, who rejected the proposal to keep his US allies on board.[56] However, the US delegation blocked this proposal before it was seriously discussed.[57] Calling the proposed restrictions 'politically inept',[58] US drafters also tried to undermine the mandatory nature of the ICRC's proposals.[59] They felt most strongly about losing the blockade-related permissions under international law 'from the point of view of [our] naked survival'.[60] Commonwealth delegates also expressed concern about losing a 'decisive' weapon that would protect Western (and British imperial) interests in future conflicts. The restrictions on blockade suggested by the ICRC undercut the security provided by Anglo-American naval power.[61]

The British government committed a strategic blunder by not sending a delegation to Stockholm. This allowed the ICRC to push through its 'blockade-bending' programme, one that was largely supported by Western European countries.[62] Despite Anglo-American opposition, the 1948 Stockholm Conference created a set of rules restricting the use of blockade for the first time in twentieth-century history. The ICRC was euphoric. Regardless of the controversy surrounding the blockade-breaking resolution, the organisation's drafters had gained widespread acceptance for their agenda to protect civilians against blockade-induced starvation. At the same time, there was no question of applying any criminal legal

[54] Report Dutch Delegation Government Experts' Conference, no 170 (1947) (Archief Rode Kruis Nederland [ARKN] The Hague).

[55] Draft Civilian Convention (1948) (ICRC Library no CI_1948_B3_01_ENG_03).

[56] It is interesting that Pictet, while considering the ICRC's important relations with its Anglo-American partners, proved unwilling to publicly condemn the resolution. See Minutes of Commission Juridique (1948) (ICRC Library no. CI_1948_COMJUR_02); and Memo Clattenburg on Plenary Sessions of Commission Juridique (26 November 1948) (National Archives and Records Administration [NARA] College Park, Maryland no Series 22, RG 43–5536).

[57] Minutes of Commission Juridique (1948) (ICRC Library no CI_1948_COMJUR_02).

[58] Report Clattenburg on Stockholm Conference (10 September 1948) (NARA no Series 22, RG 43–5536).

[59] Report of Canadian Sub-Committee on Civilian Convention (Library and Archives Canada [LAC] Ottawa, Ontario no 112–20 Vol I RG 19–Vol 480).

[60] Report Clattenburg on Stockholm Conference (10 September 1948) (NARA no Series 22, RG 43–5536).

[61] Report Canadian Delegation Stockholm Conference (1948) (LAC no Series 619–B–40, RG 25–Vol. 5020).

[62] The analytically useful distinction between blockade-bending as opposed to blockade-breaking is made by Geoffrey Best, *War and Law Since 1945* (Clarendon Press 2002) 122–23. For Best's apologetic views regarding blockade—'blockade is more humane than bombardment', see ibid 282–83.

framework to blockade. The debates in the 1940s merely succeeded in regulating what major powers portrayed as a necessary evil of modern total warfare, not in banishing the weapon of starvation itself.

VI. The mixed legacy of the Geneva Conventions, 1949

The Stockholm Conference's outcome led to major concern among British and American officials. Whitehall anticipated that, amidst growing tensions between the West and the socialist world, the Stockholm drafts would 'greatly weaken the weapon of blockade'.[63] It feared that in the case of a war with the Soviet bloc, communist countries would exploit the conventions by freely importing food supplies and stripping civilian hospitals to strengthen their own armed forces. The economic weapon was of critical importance to British warfighting strategy in particular, so the British delegation was instructed to 'firmly oppose' the right of free passage for foodstuffs, to undermine the law's mandatory elements, and to make only minimal compromises guaranteeing the blockader's discretionary powers.[64] By placing naval and air power outside of the scope of humanitarian law, Britain embraced a liberal exceptionalism. It launched an attack on the ICRC proposals, suggesting they were only superficially humanitarian but in fact undermined the defence of the free world.

Like its British counterpart, the US delegation was briefed to challenge the Stockholm draft's mandatory character and its proposed restrictions for blockade.[65] Originally Washington had supported guarantees for civilian food provision as a response to the wartime Greek disaster.[66] But in the wake of the war, the US Army began to express opposition to these safeguards.[67] The Pentagon wanted to minimise international restraints on US warfighting capabilities while the embarrassed delegation in Geneva feared critical press, the loss of support from Western European allies, and being outflanked by the Soviets.[68]

The Soviet Union surprised Western observers when it decided in April 1949 to end its boycott of the International Red Cross and sent a delegation to Geneva to participate in the drafting of the Conventions.[69] By adopting a pro-Stockholm approach, the two former antagonists became strategic partners at this gathering in Geneva, both intent on bending blockade.[70] Since they feared being targeted by future blockades, the Soviet-aligned delegations defended the Stockholm draft's starvation-related restrictions. Swiss representatives also largely supported the humanitarian ICRC agenda to protect individual victims of war. As their plans to remove all restrictions ran into broad opposition, the British were now forced to change their drafting strategy from *deleting* to *modifying* the blockade-related

[63] Briefing for UK delegation (February 1949) (The National Archives [TNA] Kew no 4145, FO369 (Foreign Office)).

[64] ibid.

[65] US Draft for the Civilian Convention (31 March 1949) Provost Marshal General, (NARA no 673).

[66] Cable from the State Department to the US delegation (22 April 1949) (NARA no Series 5, RG 43–40).

[67] See Best (n 62) 122–23; and Cable Harrison to State Department (25 April 1949) (NARA no Series 5, RG 43–40).

[68] Memo US Delegation for State Department (2 May 1949) (NARA no Series 5, RG 43–40).

[69] Boyd van Dijk, '"The Great Humanitarian": The Soviet Union, the International Committee of the Red Cross, and the Geneva Conventions of 1949' (2019) 37 Law and History Review 209.

[70] Report Soviet-Ukrainian Delegation (Tsentral'nyi derzhavnyi arhiv vyschykh organiv vlady ta upravlinnia Ukrainy [TSDAVO] Kiev, Ukraine no F. 2, Op. 12cc, Spr. 969, Ark. 60–76).

articles–and thereby subverting them. Their new approach was to reshape rather than reject the existing proposals, in line with Anglo-American strategic interests.[71]

To prevent an embarrassing defeat for their Anglo-American allies, a Norwegian drafter put forward a compromise proposal which appeased Britain and the United States by granting some blockade powers while assuaging continental European concerns about supplying occupied territory with sufficient food. The Norwegian proposal created a dilemma for Anglo-American drafters. While it presented a diplomatic way out of the drafting crisis, it broke with their original instructions requiring legal protection for 'one of [our] most effective weapons'.[72] In the end, the British Admiralty agreed to the Norwegian amendment since it largely secured its key interests by providing 'very widely drawn' discretionary powers to reject outside aid.[73] The emergent North Atlantic alliance recognised the need to protect a 'powerful instrument' with which it could fight Communism in a future war. Thus the majority of the drafting committee accepted the Norwegian amendment, despite continuing Swiss and Soviet opposition.[74]

In August 1949, the Diplomatic Conference of the delegates negotiating the Geneva Convention dealt a severe blow to the original blockade-bending proposals of the ICRC.[75] It passed a restrictive Article for belligerent territory (23) which endorsed blockade by 'recognizing that [it was] an essential feature of modern warfare'.[76] Under this new provision, the blockader's duty to accept food supplies was, in the words of one New Zealand delegate,

[71] See Memo Craigie on Blockade (15 June 1949) (TNA no 4153, FO369) and Correspondence Meeting Cabinet Office on Free Passage of Food and Medical Supplies (18-20 June 1949) (TNA no 21475, ADM1 [Admiralty]).

[72] See Correspondence Meeting Cabinet Office on Free Passage of Food and Medical Supplies (18–20 June 1949) (TNA no 21475, ADM1).

[73] Records Meeting Cabinet Office on Blockade (24 June 1949) (TNA no 21475, ADM1).

[74] Compte-rendu de la Séance Commission III (7 July 1949) (ICRC Library no CD_1949_Comm3_CR41).

[75] The reach of Article 55 applying to occupied territory is broader, applying to the population at large, not just expectant mothers and children—as Article 23 did. Moreover, it does not include a derogation clause like that in Article 23. Text of Article 55:

> To the fullest extent of the means available to it, the Occupying Power has the duty of ensuring the food and medical supplies of the population; it should, in particular, bring in the necessary foodstuffs, medical stores and other articles if the resources of the occupied territory are inadequate. The Occupying Power may not requisition foodstuffs, articles or medical supplies available in the occupied territory, except for use by the occupation forces and administration personnel, and then only if the requirements of the civilian population have been taken into account. Subject to the provisions of other international Conventions, the Occupying Power shall make arrangements to ensure that fair value is paid for any requisitioned goods. The Protecting Power shall, at any time, be at liberty to verify the state of the food and medical supplies in occupied territories, except where temporary restrictions are made necessary by imperative military requirements.

[76] Text of Article 23:

> Each High Contracting Party shall allow the free passage of all consignments of medical and hospital stores and objects necessary for religious worship intended only for civilians of another High Contracting Party, even if the latter is its adversary. It shall likewise permit the free passage of all consignments of essential foodstuffs, clothing and tonics intended for children under fifteen, expectant mothers and maternity cases. The obligation of a High Contracting Party to allow the free passage of the consignments indicated in the preceding paragraph is subject to the condition that this Party is satisfied that there are no serious reasons for fearing: (a) that the consignments may be diverted from their destination, (b) that the control may not be effective, or (c) that a definite advantage may accrue to the military efforts or economy of the enemy through the substitution of the above-mentioned consignments for goods which would otherwise be provided or produced by the enemy or through the release of such material, services or facilities as would otherwise be required for the production of such goods. The Power which allows the passage of the consignments indicated in the first paragraph of this Article may make permission conditional on the distribution to the persons benefited thereby being made under the local supervision of the Protecting Powers. Such consignments shall be forwarded as rapidly as possible, and the Power which permits their free passage shall have the right to prescribe the technical arrangements under which such passage is allowed.

'so circumscribed [that the] conditions [were] so stringent that the article [will] be of little practical value'.[77] In their reports, Anglo-American delegates noted with satisfaction that they had successfully undermined the ICRC proposals.[78]

By humanising blockade and rejecting the direct application of humanitarian law to internal wars, the Geneva Diplomatic Conference left a mixed legal legacy.[79] On the one hand, it rejected Nazi-style starvation policies such as killing civilians fleeing from a siege. This challenged the outcome of the High Command Trials in 1947–1948, which had acquitted German generals for such actions.[80] The restrictive measures adopted at Geneva represented a unique challenge to the weapon of blockade, laying the groundwork for future attempts that would restrict its use and strengthen the role of humanitarian actors. Yet at the same time the Diplomatic Conference accepted the legality of starvation as a weapon of war in principle. This strengthened blockaders' recourse to 'military necessity', and made Red Cross access to victims of man-made famine highly conditional. The Geneva Conventions ultimately produced a legally humanised form of blockade.

VII. The postcolonial afterlife of humanised blockade in Biafra, 1967–1970

The Biafrans were the most prominent victims of the legal regime for starvation as a war weapon created by Western delegates in Geneva. From 1967 onwards, the Nigerian government blockaded the breakaway province, massively contributing to famine and the death of thousands of civilians. The ICRC asked for access to these victims, invoking its right under Common Article 3 of the Geneva Conventions to regulate civil wars. Rather than applying this provision, the Nigerian government decided to put into operation the Civilian Convention's very permissive Article for blockade in belligerent territory. This decision gave it extensive discretionary powers to control and determine ICRC operations in Biafra.

The Nigerian government decided to apply humanitarian law to gain international recognition for its counter-insurgency campaign, which aimed to pressure the Biafran leadership into surrender. However, the Biafran leadership was unwilling to surrender, and frequently claimed it was the victim of genocide at the hands of the government. The Nigerians gradually lost the favour of Western publics, despite attracting continuing British and Soviet government support.[81] Nigerian generals expressed increasing resentment towards ICRC relief flights which in their eyes provided cover for arms transports.[82] This was

[77] Report of New Zealand Delegation to Diplomatic Conference of Geneva (1949) (Archives New Zealand [ANZ] Wellington AAYS 8638 W2054 ADW2054/1 220/3/3 (R18524114)).

[78] Report on the Work of the War Office Members of the UK delegation (1949) (TNA no 14038, WO32).

[79] Regulating armed conflicts within states or empires, Common Article 3 is a provision with a limited scope largely protecting the state's sovereign discretionary powers.

[80] For the history of the Nuremberg Military Tribunals, see Kevin Jon Heller, *The Nuremberg Military Tribunals and the Origins of International Criminal Law* (OUP 2012).

[81] On the genocidal dimensions of the Nigeria-Biafra War: Lasse Heerten and Dirk Moses, 'The Nigeria-Biafra War: Postcolonial Conflict and the Question of Genocide' (2014) 16 Journal of Genocide Research 169; Lasse Heerten, '"A" as in Auschwitz, "B" as in Biafra' in Heide Fehrenbach and Davide Rodogne (eds) *Humanitarian Photography: A History* (CUP 2015) 249; and GN Uzoigwe, *Visions of Nationhood: Prelude to the Nigerian Civil War, 1960–1967* (Africa World Press 2011).

[82] John Stremlau, *The International Politics of the Nigerian Civil War, 1967–1970* (Princeton University Press 1977) 281–82. It is correct that the Biafran rebels used those flights strategically as a cover for their arms transports. David Forsythe, *The Humanitarians: The International Committee of the Red Cross* (CUP 2005) 67; and Stremlau ibid 246–47.

not necessarily ungrounded, and Biafran rebels also used the horrific images of famine for political purposes to increase their legitimacy on the international stage.[83] By politicising relief in various ways, they pursued their secessionist struggle at the expense of starving Biafran civilians.[84] The politicisation of aid by both sides placed the ICRC in an extremely difficult position. Its delegation quickly learned that obtaining agreement between Lagos and the Biafrans on how relief flights should be conducted proved nearly impossible.[85]

The ICRC's delicate position was further weakened by its own charter, since Article 23 of the Geneva Conventions privileged the rights of the blockader, requiring the consent of the blockading to allow relief flights. This prompted severe criticism from humanitarian competitors and Western liberals.[86] In their eyes, the ICRC made a major mistake by not challenging the two sides' unwillingness to accept relief flights for Biafra. Bernard Kouchner argued that breaking humanitarian law and operating without the parties' consent served the higher moral purpose of saving starving Biafrans.[87]

Relief operations ended abruptly in June 1969 after the downing of an ICRC air plane. The organisation had to come to terms with its past track record as well as the legacy of the 1949 Geneva Conventions. It had to recognise after Biafra that its failed operations were at least partly caused by the Western-designed rules for blockade. The ICRC realised that as long as the Conventions failed to unambiguously outlaw starvation, humanitarian law would continue to endanger its own operations and the lives of suffering civilians in armed conflict.[88] The Biafran crisis served less as an example of the moral failure of humanitarian law than as a reminder that its foundational principles to protect civilians were in need of revision. Precisely for this reason, the Genevan legal experts tried to obtain stronger anti-blockade protections after 1970.

As the developing world asserted itself on the world stage in the 1970s under the aegis of the Group of 77 and the New International Economic Order, the drafters of the Additional Protocols to the Geneva Conventions finally succeeded in creating an historically unique prohibition against starvation as such.[89] Even though this cardinal principle came with various loopholes, the final text did include a unique (though conditional) prohibition against starvation, which represented a major conceptual shift in the history of blockade. Unsurprisingly, the Reagan administration opposed ratifying these Protocols. The US government was not interested in framing blockade as an indiscriminate weapon, or in accepting famine as an international crime. It thereby left a dangerous legal grey zone intact.[90] Since 1977, liberal

[83] Michael Barnett, *Empire of Humanity: A History of Humanitarianism* (Cornell University Press 2013) 134.
[84] Stremlau (n 82) 247.
[85] Forsythe (n 82) 67.
[86] What is striking about the legal arguments used by Western liberal commentators, such as Günter Grass and Western newspapers' commentaries, to criticise the ICRC's reluctance to operate without parties' consent is their neglect or ignorance of humanitarian law and its workings. Some referred to Common Article 3 without noticing its deliberate silence with regard to blockade; most others assumed that humanitarian law is always on the side of humanitarian solutions, rather than facilitating policies of starvation. For an example of this, see Marion Gräfin Dönhoff, Günter Grass, and Max Frisch, 'An die Adresse der Regierungen' *Die Zeit* (Hamburg, 23 August 1968) 3.
[87] Forsythe (n 82) 66–67. On Kouchner's reflections of the Nigerian-Biafra War: Bernard Kouchner, *Charité Business* (Le Pré aux Clercs 1986).
[88] Thierry Hentsch, *Face au Blocus. La Croix-Rouge Internationale dans le Nigéria en Guerre (1967–1970)* (Institut Universitaire de Hautes Études Internationales 1973) 227–28.
[89] Article 54, Protocol Additional to the Geneva Conventions of 12 August 1949, and Relating to the Protection of Victims of International Armed Conflicts, of 8 June 1977 ('Starvation of civilians as a method of warfare is prohibited'); Article 14, Protocol Additional to the Geneva Conventions of 12 August 1949, and Relating to the Protection of Victims of Non-international Armed Conflicts, of 8 June 1977 ('Starvation of civilians as a method of combat is prohibited'.).
[90] de Waal (n 5) 130–33.

states as well as illiberal states have continued to use the weapon of blockade, humanised to a greater or lesser degree according to the user, to fight wars. In doing so they have inflicted great suffering on civilians, from the US and UN sanctions regime against Iraq in the 1990s to the ongoing blockade-induced famines in Syria and Yemen.[91]

VIII. Conclusion

This article has reconstructed the long and winding road from the nineteenth-century law of blockade to the conditional abolition of starvation as a weapon of war in 1977. It is a story in which diplomats, colonial officials, politicians, and drafters changed the legal status of blockade-induced starvation across time. The proof of their agency lies in the fact that at several junctures, laws and principles preventing and restricting starvation were modified by treaty or in practice: the First World War, the interwar battles over belligerent rights in Geneva, the wartime humanitarian campaigns, and the diplomatic and legal wrangling before, during, and after the Conventions in the late 1940s represent key moments of historical contingency. A legal space for starvation was consistently preserved due to powerful hierarchies which structured international law and states' ability to make use of blockade. There were a number of different reasons that powerful states chose to preserve that space: as part of imperial projects to further colonial power; to promote liberal visions of an economic weapon in the service of world peace; as a fascist method to exterminate 'useless mouths'; or as a useful tool of anti-communist containment during the Cold War. Even postcolonial actors were able to exploit the Conventions to impose starvation on separatist rebels.

The late acceptance of the anti-starvation norm can be explained by several different factors. First, several anti-starvation campaigns emerged during the twentieth century from different ideological backgrounds, making it hard to find political agreement.[92] The Soviet anti-blockade platform in the interwar and Cold War period created tensions with the depoliticised and often conservative humanitarianism of the ICRC. International humanitarians in Geneva invoked the interests of humanity without addressing the political and strategic rationales behind famines that were the intentional result of state policy. Humanitarians were often very reluctant to outlaw starvation, let alone directly challenge the weapon of blockade, for fear of alienating powerful liberal allies, whether Britain in the interwar era or the United States since 1945.[93]

Second, we have drawn into question the equation of liberal democratic values with the rise of anti-starvation norms.[94] The conflicting character of liberal visions of humanity in war has never been entirely reconciled: if these visions sometimes pointed in the direction of banning starvation, by opposing and criminalising Nazi genocide, they could as easily point in the opposite direction, by giving Anglo-American powers the right to starve out

[91] Provost (n 50) 620.

[92] ibid 119.

[93] This helps to explain why international 'laws ... are reticent on naming starvation and famine as crimes and, specifically, framing the instruments for prosecuting famine perpetrators': de Waal (n 5) 134–35.

[94] Inspired by Amartya Sen's work, many scholars from various disciplines have convincingly shown how famine has never occurred in a functioning multiparty democracy. They have expressed much less interest, however, in exploring the role of liberal powers and ideas in undermining attempts to battle famine at the international stage. See Marcus (n 40) 251–52.

enemy resistance. The liberal form of total warfare was not focused on causing starvation as an end in itself. But it could readily accept that starvation occurred as a result of its policies, and was comfortable with using it as an instrument to achieve quick victory. To Anglo-American grand strategists, starvation was the unfortunate by-product of inflicting 'economic pressure' on enemy societies. Nonetheless, that by-product could be strategically useful, and so international law should not circumscribe it too tightly.

The third reason why an international legal order that allows starvation has persisted for so long—and continues to reappear in different disguises in our own time—is that it is extremely complicated to render the effects of blockade directly visible, and to prove culpability for the deaths that it causes. Whereas individual homicide has a certain immediateness that enables us to identify direct causality and hence legal consequences, an individual's death from starvation is often far-removed in space and time from the people shaping the policy that enables it. The distance between perpetrator and victim is mediated by several factors.[95] Mass famine can be triggered by malnutrition, disease, economic breakdown, market shocks, state intervention, persecution, state failure, natural disasters, or any combination of these factors.

As long as blockades are not publicly seen as part of the morally powerful category of 'indiscriminate weapons' (eg biological and chemical weapons), and as long as we do not recognise starvation as a multi-faceted and complex *social* rather than natural process, it is highly questionable whether international law can play a positive role in eradicating this slow but inhumane weapon. Law alone cannot fully address the challenge of blockade, but even political solutions will require significant mobilisation of opinion and expertise; the issue today lacks the political attention that it once enjoyed due to major public anti-blockade campaigns organised by progressive groups in Europe at the end of the First World War.[96]

The indiscriminate nature of blockade is not a bug but a feature of economic warfare. What united twentieth-century blockade planners was the view, which arose during the nineteenth century among Anglo-American as well as continental elites, that state warfighting power depended, most of all, on the people. Civil society was the backbone of military force. It applied the logic of the nation-in-arms in reverse: to weaken the forces in the field, one must strike the home front. What made the economic weapon of blockade so potent was that it severed targeted countries from the networks of exchange, circulation, and reproduction that sustained their social and economic fabric. It usually takes more than a single shock to the complex organisation of society for famine to occur. But under the influence of other pressures such as political and social upheaval, economic crisis, and the mobilisation of resources and people for war, the weight of a blockade can start to cause breakdowns in these networks that result in famine and subsequently the starvation of parts of a population.

The main reason why starvation did not become a war crime is not only because of the political power of the countries that used starvation blockades, but also because of the complex and nebulous nature of the process just described. The density of the social space

[95] de Waal (n 5) 127.

[96] Suda Lorena Bane and Ralph Haswell Lutz (eds), *The Blockade of Germany After the Armistice, 1918–1919* (Stanford 1942).; LJ Macfarlane, 'Hands Off Russia: British Labour and the Russo-Polish War, 1920' (1967) 38 Past & Present 126. See also the many contributions of the Women's International League for Peace and Freedom,whose feminist pacifism was aimed against blockade throughout the 1915–1919 period.

between the blockader and the starved is what renders the effort to deprive almost invisible. The paradigm of criminal law, whether international or domestic, is perhaps inherently unable to grasp phenomena that occur at this scale. It forces us to grapple with difficult questions about causation. These dilemmas often require identifying causal factors by specifying what would have happened in their absence. Understanding how people starve, and how and to what degree others might be held responsible for it, thus gets to the heart of questions of contingency and necessity.

E.

FOREIGN INVESTMENTS

23

The Law of State Responsibility and the Persistence of Investment Protection

Kathryn Greenman

I. Introduction

Over twelve days in March and April of 1930, the first international conference for the codification of international law (Codification Conference) was held in The Hague under the auspices of the League of Nations (League). One of the topics chosen for codification was state responsibility or, more specifically, 'whether, and in what cases, a State may be liable for injury caused on its territory to the person or property of foreigners'.[1] The Codification Conference was, however, unsuccessful in its efforts to conclude a treaty,[2] even though the Committee of Experts for the Progressive Codification of International Law had considered the topic's codification 'desirable and realisable at the present moment'.[3] A group of largely Latin American and former Austro-Hungarian states voted together to reject rules which favoured foreign commercial interests over their political and economic self-determination, and had been used to justify intervention. The rules that were defeated at The Hague sought to entrench an economic order that guaranteed continued metropolitan access to the markets and resources of newly decolonised states by protecting foreign trade and investment against political instability and economic nationalism therein. At the International Law Commission (ILC), the general rules of state responsibility, now embodied in the 2001 Articles on the Responsibility of States for Internationally Wrongful Acts (ARSIWA),[4] ended up being detached from any substantive obligations regarding the protection of foreign nationals. Nevertheless, important aspects of state responsibility for injuries to aliens, rejected in 1930, live on in international investment law.[5] International investment law has not only reasserted some of the particular rules of state responsibility for

[1] Committee of Experts for the Progressive Codification of International Law, 'List of Subjects for Study, Adopted by the Committee on April 6th and 8th 1925' (1926) 20 AJIL Special Supplement 13, 14.

[2] For recent accounts of this story, see Arnulf Becker Lorca, *Mestizo International Law: A Global Intellectual History 1842–1933* (CUP 2014) 317–26; Tzvika Alan Nissel, *A History of State Responsibility: The Struggle for International Standards (1870–1960)* (PhD thesis, University of Helsinki 2016) 311–18.

[3] Upon its establishment by the League in 1924, the first task of the Committee of Experts was to 'prepare a provisional list of the subjects of international law the regulation of which by international agreement would seem to be most desirable and realisable at the present moment': 'League of Nations Assembly Resolution of 22 September 1924' (1926) 20 AJIL Special Supplement 12.

[4] International Law Commission, 'Articles on Responsibility of States for Internationally Wrongful Acts' (2001) 2(2) Yearbook of the International Law Commission 26 (ARSIWA).

[5] See eg David Schneiderman, 'The Global Regime of Investor Rights: Return to the Standards of Civilised Justice?' (2014) 5 Transnational Legal Theory 60; Kate Miles, 'History and International Law: Method and Mechanism—Empire and "Usual" Rupture' in Stephan W Schill, Christian J Tams, and Rainer Hofmann (eds), *International Investment Law and History* (Elgar 2018) 136.

Kathryn Greenman, *The Law of State Responsibility and the Persistence of Investment Protection* In: *Contingency in International Law*. Edited by: Ingo Venzke and Kevin Jon Heller, Oxford University Press. © The Several Contributors 2021. DOI: 10.1093/oso/9780192898036.003.0023

injuries to aliens, but also reproduces its structure and effects in terms of the empowerment of international tribunals at the expense of national authority in matters of economic governance and the subordination of certain states as uncivilised, disordered, or illiberal.

In 1930, the law of state responsibility could have taken a different direction. However, the fact that this different path was not taken has not in the end, I argue, made a difference. Alternatively, I suggest here that the Codification Conference can be seen as a moment when the law of state responsibility *was* different. A block of newer and smaller states defeated the efforts of the colonial powers to codify rules that entrenched an economic order which favoured the latter's interests. However, the change did not stick; today international investment law embeds economic relations that continue to subordinate the Global South. In light of this, I want to explore the idea that there is something about international law which means its prioritisation of investment protection is a state of affairs that, despite contingency, is more likely to persist than not. In this chapter, my working assumption is that international law can be different but it cannot be anything and some things are more likely than others; in spite of contingency, the international legal order tends to favour certain outcomes. So, while I will begin by looking at how the law of state responsibility could have been different—and in a sense *was* different—I will finish by thinking about how things came to be as they are: that is, in important ways, continuous with what came before. If we want to understand how international law might have been or might be otherwise, it is essential to understand how certain potentialities have persistently won out, even in the face of resistance. In this respect, I will introduce two possible lines of thinking: fragmentation and structural bias.

II. State responsibility at the Codification Conference

The Codification Conference marked a point when the law of state responsibility could have taken a different direction. Under the Bases for Discussion prepared ahead of the Codification Conference,[6] and around which negotiations at The Hague were organised, state responsibility resulted from a breach of the standards, based on what 'could be expected from a civilised state',[7] regulating the treatment of foreign nationals or, as it was also referred to, the protection of aliens. State responsibility for injuries to aliens was controversial and its content had been contested, especially by Latin American international lawyers, since at least the mid-nineteenth century.[8] In his opening speech at the first meeting of the Third Committee, which had been assigned the topic of state responsibility, the chairman began by noting the importance of the subject, not just because 'the rules on responsibility are the key rules of any juridical system' but also 'because in the course of time and

[6] 'Bases of Discussion for the Conference Drawn up by the Preparatory Committee' in Conference for the Codification of International Law, *Acts of the Conference for the Codification of International Law* (League of Nations 1930) vol 4, 198–202.

[7] See 'Bases of Discussion' (n 6) nos 10, 17, 18.

[8] For an example of early Latin American resistance, see Carlos Calvo, 'De la Non-Responsabilité des États a Raison des Pertes et Dommages Éprouvés par des Étrangers en Temps de Troubles Intérieurs ou de Guerres Civiles' (1869) 1 (1st series) Revue de Droit International et de Législation Comparée 417. For the later debates among international lawyers, see eg James W Garner, 'Responsibility of States for Injuries Suffered by Foreigners Within Their Territories on Account of Mob Violence, Riots and Insurrection' (1927) 21 Proceedings of the American Society of International Law 49.

in various circumstances, political ambitions have only too often been concealed under a pretext of responsibility'.[9]

Upholding state responsibility for injuries to their nationals had often been used to justify intervention by the US and European powers, particularly in Latin America. For example, the US-Mexican War of 1848 in which Mexico lost half its territory, the French occupation of Mexico from 1862–1867, and the blockade of Venezuela by Britain, Germany, and Italy in 1902–1903 were all justified on the basis of enforcing claims for injuries to foreigners.[10] At the same time, the doctrine of state responsibility had emerged largely from arbitral practice, rationalised from the work of mixed claims commissions often imposed by force and on unequal terms, again mainly in Latin America.[11]

At stake in the debates about the rules of state responsibility was not only intervention, but also economic order. In the context of decolonisation and capitalist expansion in Latin America during the nineteenth century, the development of alien protection mediated the threat posed to US and European access to the natural resources and markets of the region by the formal sovereignty of Latin American states.[12] Capital-exporting countries wanted to protect their commercial interests in the decolonised world, first against political instability and later also against economic nationalism. State responsibility for alien protection—at least in the Anglo-American account that the Bases of Discussion prepared for the Codification Conference reflected—gave foreigners internationally enforceable rights to an international minimum standard of protection for their personal, property, and contractual interests.[13]

Ten Articles were adopted at first reading at the Codification Conference.[14] However, when it came to formally adopting a convention, which required a two-thirds majority, the forty-four delegations that participated in the Third Committee were deadlocked.[15] A block of seventeen largely Latin American and former Austro-Hungarian states voted together to reject rules which favoured the interests of capital-exporting states, and had been used to justify intervention.[16] The Articles adopted at first reading made the basis of responsibility

[9] *Acts of the Conference for the Codification of International Law* (n 6) 15.

[10] On Mexico, see John Bassett Moore, *History and Digest of the International Arbitrations to Which the United States Has Been a Party* (GPO 1898) vol 2, 1245–48, 1288–91. On Venezuela, see WL Penfield, 'The Anglo-German Intervention in Venezuela' (1903) 177 The North American Review 86; Amos S Hershey, 'The Venezuelan Affair in the Light of International Law' (1903) 51 American Law Register 249.

[11] See Kathryn Greenman, 'Aliens in Latin America: Intervention, Arbitration and State Responsibility for Rebels' (2018) 31 Leiden Journal of International Law 617; Frédéric Mégret, 'Mixed Claim Commissions and the Once Centrality of the Protection of Aliens' in Ignacio de la Rasilla and Jorge E Viñuales (eds), *Experiments in International Adjudication: Historical Accounts* (CUP 2019); cf Nissel (n 2), who also credits German theory.

[12] For an account from the time of the Codification Conference, see eg Frederick Sherwood Dunn, *The Protection of Nationals: A Study in the Application of International Law* (The Johns Hopkins Press 1932) 53–55. For more recent accounts, see Greenman (n 11); Mégret (n 11).

[13] Strictly the term 'international minimum standard' was not adopted until later.

[14] 'Texts Adopted by the Committee in First Reading as Revised by the Drafting Committee' in *Acts of the Conference for the Codification of International Law* (n 6) 236–37.

[15] For a list of the delegations, see *Acts of the Conference for the Codification of International Law* (n 6) 11–14. The delegation from the Soviet Union were observers.

[16] Regarding this block, see Edwin Borchard, '"Responsibility of States," at the Hague Codification Conference' (1930) 24 The American Journal of International Law 517, 518, 538–39; Green H Hackworth, 'Responsibility of States for Damages Caused in their Territory to the Person or Property of Foreigners: The Hague Conference for the Codification of International Law' (1930) 24 The American Journal of International Law 500, 514–15. Borchard and Hackworth did not specify explicitly which states were in the 'minority block', as they called it, but the implication is that it was the same states that voted against Article 10 of the Articles adopted at first reading. These were Brazil, Chile, China, Colombia, Czechoslovakia, Free City of Danzig, El Salvador, Hungary, Mexico, Nicaragua, Persia, Poland, Portugal, Romania, Turkey, Uruguay, and Yugoslavia.

'failure on the part of [a State's] organs to carry out the international obligations of the State which causes damage to the person or property of a foreigner on the territory of the State'.[17] When it came to the content of those obligations, there was a concern among states that had been subject to intervention to limit and define the sources of international law so as to prevent unclear or disputed standards being taken advantage of.[18] A provision was initially agreed upon, defining international obligations as those 'resulting from treaty, custom or the general principles of law designed to assure to foreigners in respect of their persons or property a treatment in conformity with the rules accepted by the community of nations'.[19] The block of seventeen, however, wanted this to be changed to 'indisputably accepted', to prevent rules that they had consistently contested being used as a basis for intervention.[20]

The most controversial provision provided for responsibility for damage caused by the acts of private persons where the state 'failed to take such measures as in the circumstances should normally have been taken to prevent, redress, or inflict punishment for the acts causing the damage'.[21] The Mexican delegate argued that the measures of protection due to foreigners were those afforded to nationals. He proposed a revised standard, namely, 'the precautions that [the state] usually adopts in regard to its own nationals', a position also proposed by China. The Salvadoran delegate rejected entirely the idea of responsibility for acts of private persons.[22] It was not just that more limited responsibility restricted the scope for intervention. The national treatment principle was a key tenet of the Latin American approach to alien protection—a means of empowering national authority to set standards. The block of seventeen also wanted a provision excluding responsibility for 'injury in insurrection, riot, [and] mob violence'.[23] This was important since many interventions and arbitrations had followed revolutions and civil wars.[24] At the same time, such a provision had the effect of allocating the (known) risk of political instability to foreign capital as the cost of entering profitable markets. Ultimately, the rules that the Conference sought to codify were rejected by the block of seventeen because they undermined their political and economic independence.

The law of state responsibility could thus, if the Anglo-American led block had got its way, have been different—a substantive doctrine tied to specific obligations regarding the protection of foreign nationals. One question is whether this was at all likely given the reality of numbers at the Conference. The Articles adopted at first reading simply never had sufficient support among the states of Latin America and Eastern Europe, which had the numbers to obstruct the adoption of any convention. With one vote per state, the balance of institutional power tipped away from traditional centres of economic and military

[17] 'Texts Adopted by the Committee in First Reading' (n 14) art 1.

[18] See *Acts of the Conference for the Codification of International Law* (n 6) 37–38, 144–45.

[19] 'Texts Adopted by the Committee in First Reading' (n 14) art 2.

[20] Borchard (n 16) 521.

[21] 'Texts Adopted by the Committee in First Reading' (n 14) art 10.

[22] *Acts of the Conference for the Codification of International Law* (n 6) 144 (El Salvador), 185 (China), 224 (Mexico).

[23] Hackworth (n 16) 514.

[24] See eg the mixed claims commissions set up between Britain and the United States in 1871 after the US Civil War and in 1923 after uprisings in Morocco; between Spain and the United States in 1871 after the insurrection in Cuba; with Chile in the 1890s following the Chilean Civil War of 1891; with Venezuela in 1903 following the revolutions and civil wars of 1892–1902; and with Mexico in the 1920s after the Mexican Revolution. AM Stuyt, *Survey of International Arbitrations, 1794–1938* (Martinus Nijhoff 1939). For examples of interventions, see n 10 and accompanying text.

dominance. This enabled new states and states traditionally excluded from significant influence over international law to block rules that did not reflect their interests. While the block of seventeen was willing to compromise within the framework of state responsibility for injuries to aliens instead of rejecting it outright, the positions of the capital-exporting and capital-importing states were nevertheless too far apart to find enough middle ground.

After the League's failed attempt to codify state responsibility, the ILC took up the task. The struggles of the ILC reveal just how difficult a job the League took on in 1930 in seeking to codify state responsibility in a multilateral organisation. It took fifty years for the ILC to adopt the ARSIWA.[25] The work of the first rapporteur, Francisco García-Amador, was marred by the same stalemate which paralysed negotiations at The Hague.[26] His reports retained alien protection, alienating those states that had objected to it at the Codification Conference, as well as the newly decolonised states, yet combined it with individual rights and state crimes, also alienating the rest.[27] While in 1930 capital-importing states had been willing to work within the framework of alien protection, after the Second World War, the so-called first generation of Third World international lawyers rejected injuries to aliens as the basis for state responsibility outright.[28] Consensus required separating the rules of responsibility from any substantive primary rules and gradually stripping them of content.[29]

Nevertheless, although a different outcome was not very likely, there were some concrete alternatives on the table, which were considered at the time as realistic. The doctrine of state responsibility debated at The Hague was very different to that which we have today under the ARSIWA: there was no concept of attribution or separation of primary and secondary rules, indeed responsibility was explicitly linked to a particular body of primary obligations regarding the protection of foreigners. 1930 was a fork in the road—a moment when the law of state responsibility began its turn away from alien protection and towards the abstract set of secondary rules that we know it as today.

III. The persistence of investment protection

However, although state responsibility could have been different, another question is whether the events at the Codification Conference have made any difference. That state responsibility was not codified on the basis of alien protection in 1930 has been presented as a 'great victory' or even as 'revenge' against economic imperialism for formerly-colonised states.[30] State responsibility, as a result, eventually became something neutral, at least in respect of the particular conflict over alien protection, although of course it has its other biases.[31] Such victory was, however, short-lived; alien protection has had its own revenge.

[25] ARSIWA (n 4).

[26] See eg 'International Responsibility: Report by Mr. F.V. Garcia-Amador, Special Rapporteur' UN Doc A/CN.4/96 (1956) Yearbook of the International Law Commission 2, 173.

[27] Nissel (n 2) 331–32, 336.

[28] See eg SN Guha-Roy, 'Is the Law of Responsibility of States for Injuries to Aliens a Part of Universal International Law' (1961) 55 American Journal of International Law 863.

[29] See eg Philip Allott, 'State Responsibility and the Unmaking of International Law' (1988) 29 Harvard International Law Journal 1.

[30] Becker Lorca (n 2) 305; Nissel (n 2) 290.

[31] See eg Christine Chinkin, 'A Critique of the Public/Private Dimension' (1999) 10 European Journal of International Law 387.

Important aspects of state responsibility for injuries to aliens that were rejected at The Hague live on in international investment law.[32]

For example, in the pivotal International Centre for Settlement of Investment Disputes (ICSID) award *AAPL v Sri Lanka*, which concerned the destruction of the claimant's prawn farm during the Sri Lankan Civil War, the tribunal relied on early twentieth-century arbitral awards based on alien protection to hold that during an insurrection failure to provide the requisite standard of protection—that of 'all possible measures that could be reasonably expected to prevent the eventual [losses]'—gives rise to the state's international responsibility for such losses.[33] Thus, the tribunal confirmed in the context of foreign investment one of the rules that had caused the most controversy at the Codification Conference. Even though neither side managed to adduce evidence as to how the farm was destroyed, the tribunal concluded that in any event, the government should have taken 'important precautionary measures' to get the suspected rebels out of the farm peacefully.[34] Sri Lanka's responsibility for breaching its obligations under the relevant bilateral investment treaty (BIT), particularly to provide 'full protection and security', was thus established. The claimant was awarded $460,000 plus interest.[35]

Today, international investment law has one of the strongest enforcement mechanisms in international law: over 900 cases are known to have been initiated in the last thirty years, and claimants regularly receive six-figure sums.[36] Despite state responsibility on the basis of alien protection being defeated, concerns similar to those that were raised in 1930—about the bias of international arbitration of disputes between states and foreign investors and the state's lack of authority over foreign capital—endure.[37] In the long term, the international judicialisation of economic governance has intensified—from mixed claims commissions to investor-state arbitration. Latin American efforts to resist the international enforcement of alien protection claims and assert national authority over foreign nationals in defence of their self-determination after decolonisation are now replaced by a more general pushback against international investment arbitration in the light of concerns about the capacity of public authorities to regulate in the interests of, for example, the environment. However, even if states like the United States and Canada are now regularly respondents, Latin America remains overrepresented in investor-state arbitration statistics.[38]

Thus, the change or the challenge to the status quo that the Codification Conference represented did not stick. In this section, I will explore how the prioritisation of investment

[32] See eg Schneiderman (n 5); Miles (n 5).

[33] *Asian Agricultural Products Ltd (AAPL) v Republic of Sri Lanka*, ICSID Case no ARB/87/3 (1991) 6(2) ICSID Rev 526 paras 72–75, 84(b).

[34] *AAPL v Sri Lanka* (n 33) para 85(d).

[35] *AAPL v Sri Lanka* (n 33) 572.

[36] Jonathan Bonnitcha, Lauge N Skovgaard Poulsen, and Michael Waibel, *The Political Economy of the Investment Treaty Regime* (OUP 2017) 25, 28. See also: UNCTAD, 'Investment Dispute Settlement Navigator' (*Investment Policy Hub*) <https://investmentpolicyhub.unctad.org/ISDS accessed 24 January 2021.

[37] See eg Amr A Shalakany, 'Arbitration and the Third World: A Plea for Reassessing Bias under the Specter of Neoliberalism' (2009) 41 Harvard International Law Journal 419; Gus Van Harten, 'Arbitrator Behaviour in Asymmetrical Adjudication: An Empirical Study of Investment Treaty Arbitration' (2012) 50 Osgoode Hall Law Journal 211; 'The Arbitration Game' *The Economist* (London, 11 October 2014); Martti Koskenniemi, 'It's Not the Cases, It's the System' (2017) 18 Journal of World Investment & Trade 343; Lora Verheecke, Pia Eberhardt, Cecilia Olivet, and Sam Cossar-Gilbert, *Red Carpet Courts* (Friends of the Earth Europe and International, Transnational Institute and Corporate Europe Observatory 2019).

[38] Cecilia Olivet, Bettina Müller, and Luciana Ghiotto, *ISDS in Numbers: Impacts of Investment Arbitration against Latin America and the Caribbean* (Transnational Institute 2017).

protection has persisted despite resistance from the Third World and beyond. This is a well-known story and one that has been more comprehensively told elsewhere.[39] My aim, however, is to look at certain aspects of it again with an eye to what they can tell us about contingency in the course of international law, through two lenses: fragmentation and structural bias. The goal is to start to understand the factors that contribute to certain potentialities persistently winning out so as to offer an insight into the possibilities and limitations of international law to change.

1. Fragmentation

In this section, I do not seek to intervene in the debates that have proliferated among international lawyers in recent years regarding whether fragmentation reflects a threat to the coherence of the international legal order or progress towards beneficial pluralism, or whether it is a good or bad thing for international law overall.[40] Rather I am interested in the story of the persistence of international law's prioritisation of investment protection as an example of how one effect of fragmentation can be, as Benvenisti and Downs have argued, to limit the influence of the states of the Global South in decisions that affect them and thus make it harder to change the status quo.[41]

The promise of the type of multilateral and multi-issue codification represented by the Codification Conference for challenging and changing international law has not been fulfilled. During the first decades of the twentieth century, Latin American international lawyers saw such codification as a means to assert regional interests and challenge the rules coming out of (arbitral) practice, which were seen as favouring powerful states and reinforcing the legal impact of intervention.[42] It offered an opportunity to improve upon practice and to 'perfect [rules] and bring them into harmony with new social conditions'; it was a chance for a new international law that reflected the interests of a broader community.[43] The idea that all the states of the world would come together and negotiate a comprehensive

[39] From a variety of different perspectives, see eg Antony Anghie, *Imperialism, Sovereignty and the Making of International Law* (CUP 2004) 196–244; Andrew Newcombe and Lluís Paradell, *Law and Practice of Investment Treaties: Standards of Treatment* (Kluwer 2009) sections 1.2–1.43; James T Gathii, 'War's Legacy in International Investment Law' (2009) 11 International Community Law Review 353; Sundhya Pahuja, *Decolonising International Law: Development, Economic Growth and the Politics of Universality* (CUP 2011) 95–171; Kate Miles, *The Origins of International Investment Law: Empire, Environment and the Safeguarding of Capital* (CUP 2013); Joost Pauwelyn, 'At the Edge of Chaos? Foreign Investment Law as a Complex Adaptive System, How It Emerged and How It Can Be Reformed' (2014) 29 ICSID Rev 372; M Sornarajah, *The International Law on Foreign Investment* (4th edn, CUP 2017) 23–36; Taylor St John, *The Rise of Investor-State Arbitration: Politics, Law, and Unintended Consequences* (OUP 2018); Stephan W Schill, Christian J Tams, and Rainer Hofmann (eds), *International Investment Law and History* (Edward Elgar 2018).

[40] See eg Martti Koskenniemi and Päivi Leino, 'Fragmentation of International Law? Postmodern Anxieties' (2002) 15 Leiden Journal of International Law 553; ILC, 'Fragmentation of International Law: Difficulties Arising from the Diversification and Expansion of International Law' (13 April 2006) UN Doc A/CN.4/L.682; Eyal Benvenisti and George Downs, 'The Empire's New Clothes: Political Economy and the Fragmentation of International Law' (2007) 60 Stanford Law Review 595.

[41] Benvenisti and Downs (n 40) 597.

[42] Becker Lorca (n 2) 305ff; Nissel (n 2) 292–94. The first binding international instrument to address alien protection was the Convention Relative to the Rights of Aliens adopted by the Second International Conference of American States in 1902. James Brown Scott (ed), *The International Conferences of American States 1889–1928* (OUP 1931) 91.

[43] Comments of the Portuguese delegate José Lobo d'Avila Lima at The Hague, *Acts of the Conference for the Codification of International Law* (n 6) 18. Regarding codification as improving practice, see the comments of TW Hu and Raymond Buell at the 1927 ASIL Annual Meeting in Garner (n 8) 69, 77–78.

code of international law represented a more democratic and egalitarian vision of international law.[44] Fragmentation makes such a project and the kind of resistance we saw at The Hague in 1930 more difficult and its impact less effective. It does so first, by allowing powerful states to 'switch venues' from more democratic and transparent institutions or mechanisms where weaker states can work together to those where they retain their (bargaining) advantages.[45] Second, through the proliferation of specialist regimes and institutions, fragmentation gives law-making power to non-representative bodies with particular biases in particular areas and enables preferences rejected in more democratic settings to continue to reassert themselves.[46]

This is not to say that fragmentation made the current situation inevitable. The bilateral development of international investment law into the form it takes today was also contingent upon complex political and economic factors. For example, there was the global recession of the late 1970s and the resulting Third World debt crisis, the widespread acceptance of neoliberal economics, and the collapse of the Soviet Union, all of which contributed to an explosion in the number of BITs during the 1980s and 1990s and in the membership of the ICSID.[47] There were also the actions of officials at the World Bank, such as Aron Broches, that led to adoption of the Convention on the Settlement of Investment Disputes between States and Nationals of Other States (ICSID Convention) in 1965 and its subsequent expansion.[48] Rather, my argument is that fragmentation made the persistence of international law's prioritisation of investment protection more likely, or more difficult to resist for those states opposed to it.

Following the Second World War, multilateral efforts to set international standards for investment protection—from the International Trade Organization (ITO) to the Multilateral Agreement on Investment (MAI)—repeatedly failed. However, the development of international standards of investment protection and rules of state responsibility for their breach has taken place outside of any formal codification process, largely through BITs, as well as 'minilateral' regional or sector-specific agreements, and the practice of arbitral tribunals. Certain processes of fragmentation thus enabled attempts by formerly-colonised states to change the status quo and assert national authority over foreign investment through multilateral codification to be sidestepped.

The establishment of investment protection standards multilaterally failed for all sorts of reasons, not just the objections of capital-importing states.[49] Such multilateral efforts also lacked the support of capital-exporting states out of concern that 'investment provisions negotiated at a multilateral conference might express the lowest common denominator of protection'.[50] The

[44] This is not to say that such 'constitutionalisation' cannot be used for other purposes or have other effects. See Ntina Tzouvala, 'The Academic Debate about Mega-Regionals and International Lawyers: Legalism as Critique?' (2018) 6 London Review of International Law 189, 201–202.

[45] Benvenisti and Downs (n 40).

[46] See eg Martti Koskenniemi, *From Apology to Utopia: The Structure of International Legal Argument* (rev edn, CUP 2005) 609; Anne Orford, 'Food Security, Free Trade, and the Battle for the State' (2015) 11(2) Journal of International Law and International Relations 1, 23.

[47] Sornarajah (n 39) 26–30.

[48] Convention on the Settlement of Investment Disputes between States and Nationals of Other States (adopted 18 March 1965, entered into force 14 October 1966) 575 UNTS 159. For analysis of the role of World Bank officials in the establishment and expansion of ICSID, see St John (n 39).

[49] Tension *between* capital exporters was just as important. St John (n 39) 117.

[50] Thomas L Brewer and Stephen Young, *The Multilateral Investment System and Multinational Enterprises* (OUP 1998) 66, quoting Clair Wilcox, *A Charter for World Trade* (MacMillan 1949).

Havana Charter for the ITO,[51] the first multilateral effort to develop an international regulatory framework for foreign investment in the 1940s, never entered into force after the US Congress refused to ratify it at least in part because of its weak investment provisions.[52] The OECD Draft Convention on the Protection of Foreign Property of 1962 (OECD Draft), another failure, also lost the support of key capital-exporting states.[53] Germany and Switzerland, for example, began to prefer bilateral treaties as 'easier, more strategic means of achieving the standards of investment protection they sought' and dropped their support for the 'compromises' of the OECD Draft.[54]

The OECD tried again in 1995. After only limited investment protections were adopted during the General Agreement on Tariffs and Trade Uruguay Round,[55] capital-exporting states decided to negotiate an agreement, the MAI, through the OECD.[56] The idea was that 'like-minded' states would agree high standards of protection. The resulting agreement could then be rolled out more widely as a fait accompli, making it hard for capital-importing states to object.[57] However, this attempt at venue switching was unsuccessful. Negotiations at the OECD failed due to lack of consensus—some states, for example, did not want to give up the competitive advantages they had in bilateral arrangements[58]—and the opposition of civil society.[59] After this failure, states switched back to bilateral or regional agreements to achieve investment protection.[60]

Nevertheless, despite these repeated failures, we have ended up in an analogous situation: a global network of over 2,000 bilateral and 'minilateral' agreements, connected by the growing jurisprudence of investor-state arbitral tribunals, have 'universalised' international investment law, creating an international regime that protects investments through the back door.[61] After the failure to establish the ITO, gradually '[b]ilateralism prevailed over multilateralism.'[62] Initiated by capital-exporting states, and generally establishing strong protections for investors, bilateral agreements became the principal means of establishing standards for the treatment of investments, particularly with the introduction of BITs in the late 1950s.[63] 165 BITs were signed between 1959 and 1979, mostly between European

[51] 'Havana Charter for an International Trade Organization' in United Nations Conference on Trade and Employment, *Final Act and Related Documents* (United Nations1948) 9. For the investment provisions see art 12.
[52] Brewer and Young (n 50) 66–68.
[53] See St John (n 39) 88–90.
[54] St John (n 39) 91, 93.
[55] For an overview, see Sornarajah (n 39) 310–14.
[56] Riyaz Dattu, 'A Journey from Havana to Paris: The Fifty-Year Quest for the Elusive Multilateral Agreement on Investment' (2000) 24 Fordham International Law Journal 275.
[57] ibid 276.
[58] Sergio Puig, 'Emergence and Dynamism in International Organizations: ICSID, Investor-State Arbitration and International Investment Law' (2013) 44 Georgetown Journal of International Law 531, 577.
[59] Dattu (n 56) 299.
[60] Tienhaara describes this as 'a classic example of forum shifting'. Kyla Tienhaara, 'Investor-State Dispute Settlement' in Peter Drahos (ed), *Regulatory Theory: Foundations and Applications* (Australian National University Press 2017) 679.
[61] See eg Jeswald Salacuse, 'The Emerging Global Regime for Investment' (2010) 51 Harvard International Law Journal 427. From a critical perspective David Schneiderman refers to this process as 'constitutionalisation'. David Schneiderman, *Constitutionalizing Economic Globalization: Investment Rules and Democracy's Promise* (CUP 2008). Stephan Schill, in contrast, calls it 'multilateralisation'. Stephan W Schill, *The Multilateralization of International Investment Law* (CUP 2009).
[62] Brewer and Young (n 50) 79. After the ITO, there were other multilateral, regional and private efforts to address investment issues internationally, of varying status and levels of success. See UNCTAD, *World Investment Report 1996: Investment, Trade and International Policy Arrangements* (United Nations 1996) 135–39 (Table V.2); Newcombe and Paradell (n 39) section 1.16.
[63] Brewer and Young (n 50) 74–75. Originally there were treaties of friendship, commerce, and navigation (FCNs) signed between the United States and European states in the context of the Marshall Plan during the 1940s

and developing states.[64] Such bilateral agreements form a 'formidable body of international law',[65] and the standards set therein for the treatment of foreign investment established core aspects of international investment law.[66] As is well known, during the 1980s and especially during the 1990s the numbers of BITs increased dramatically as, for reasons noted above, many states adopted economic liberalisation measures.[67] BITs functioned 'to lock in—through international agreements—the more liberalised national policies that had already been unilaterally adopted'.[68] In the early 1990s, two significant 'minilateral' agreements, the North American Free Trade Agreement (NAFTA) and the Energy Charter Treaty (ECT), with expansive investment protections, were also signed.

The 1990s also saw the beginnings of the rise in treaty-based investor-state arbitration that has been central to expansion of international investment protection. After the Second World War, use of mixed claims commissions, which had been central to the development and enforcement of state responsibility for injuries to aliens, declined. They could no longer be imposed by force and they were widely perceived as biased by the newly independent states, while the capital-exporting states also saw them as inadequate.[69] An alternative mechanism did not immediatelyb arise in their place. In 1966, however, at the instigation of World Bank officials, ICSID was founded.[70]

According to Sergio Puig, 'one of the reasons ICSID was established under the auspices of the [World Bank] was to insulate the discussion from the UN General Assembly'.[71] At the same time as the first BITs were being signed and ICSID was being negotiated, Third World states used those multilateral fora where they had the numbers, such as the UN General Assembly and UN Economic and Social Council (ECOSOC) to try and enact positive rules to protect their economic sovereignty and establish their authority over foreign investment in the context of the New International Economic Order (NIEO). They did not just reject state responsibility for injuries to aliens at the ILC. With a series of General Assembly resolutions, newly decolonised states asserted, among other things, their permanent sovereignty over their natural wealth and resources and their rights to nationalise foreign property and regulate foreign investment and transnational corporations.[72] These (one state, one vote) institutions were sidestepped via the World Bank.

and 1950s. The United States had been using FCNs since the nineteenth century to protect US nationals doing business overseas—a direct line with alien protection. For an overview of the types of protection afforded by BITs, see eg UNCTAD (n 62) 134.

[64] UNCTAD, *Bilateral Investment Treaties 1959–1999* (United Nations 2000) 1.

[65] Brewer and Young (n 50) 74.

[66] ibid 74; Rudolf Dolzer and Christoph Schreuer, *Principles of International Investment Law* (2nd edn, OUP 2012) 13.

[67] There were 165 BITs at the end of 1979, 365 at the end of 1989, and 1,857 at the end of 1999. UNCTAD (n 64) 1.

[68] Brewer and Young (n 50) 76. Investor-state arbitration functioned to the same effect, according to St John (n 39) 212.

[69] See Rudolf Dolzer, 'Mixed Claims Commissions' in *Max Planck Encyclopedia of Public International Law* (May 2011) <https://opil.ouplaw.com/view/10.1093/law:epil/9780199231690/law-9780199231690-e64> accessed 1 June 2020, para 8.

[70] ICSID does not provide the only institution or rules for investment disputes but it is the most important. ICSID had administered 63% of the 942 treaty-based investor-state arbitrations at the end of 2018 (based on available data). For detailed accounts of the establishment and development of ICSID, see Antonio R Parra, *The History of ICSID* (OUP 2012); Puig (n 58); St John (n 39).

[71] Puig (n 58) 542–43.

[72] See UNGA Res 1803 (XVII) (14 December 1962); UNGA Res 3281 (XXIX) (12 December 1974). For more on permanent sovereignty over natural resources and the NIEO, see Mohammed Bedjaoui, *Towards A New International Economic Order* (Holmes & Meier 1979); Nico Schrijver, *Sovereignty over Natural Resources: Balancing*

While the ICSID Convention was formally a multilateral treaty, its drafting process was, as Taylor St John has shown, deliberately designed 'in a way that made it difficult for potential opponents of investor-state arbitration to derail the proposal'.[73] The ICSID Convention was drafted within the World Bank, and then went through a series of regional 'roadshows' and a drafting committee. These were inclusive, with over 100 states represented in the drafting committee, but they were consultative, without formal power to amend the draft, and attended by experts not government representatives.[74] Issues that became controversial were excluded and resolved by working group or by World Bank officials.[75] The roadshows were arranged by region specifically to 'keep resistance to the Convention fragmented'.[76]

The fragmentation of international law into specialist regimes and the proliferation of specialist institutions here allowed the reassertion of investment protection and the circumvention of new preferences being expressed, for example, at the ILC or in the UN General Assembly. The World Bank took on the task of agreeing on a framework for the procedural protection of foreign investment since investment issues had been fragmented off from the questions of state responsibility being considered by the ILC. With the World Bank's less representative processes and mandate to promote investment, in contrast to the ILC, this made investment protection a more likely outcome.

ICSID did not originally have a lot of members. World Bank officials conducted a concerted campaign to increase ratifications, while Britain and France encouraged their former colonies to do so.[77] However, the states of Latin America, for example, all refused to ratify until the 1980s when in the context of the debt crisis and the widespread acceptance of neoliberal economics, the World Bank and International Monetary Fund made credit conditional upon joining ICSID. At the same time as the membership of ICSID was slowly growing with the encouragement and support of the ICSID Secretariat,[78] BITs started to provide for investor-state arbitration,[79] as later did NAFTA and the ECT.

Despite the vast potential scope of treaty-based arbitration without a contractual relationship, none of the states that ratified the ICSID Convention or agreed BITs giving access to investor-state arbitration intended or foresaw what followed.[80] There were only a handful of *contract-based* investment arbitrations between 1945 and 1990.[81] It was not until 2000, following some key high-profile cases during the 1990s, that there was an upsurge in the number of treaty-based claims, the vast majority under BITs, the ECT, or

Rights and Duties (CUP 1997); Antony Anghie, 'Legal Aspects of the New International Economic Order' (2015) 6 Humanity 145; Nils Gilman, 'The New International Economic Order: A Reintroduction' (2015) 6 Humanity 1.

[73] Taylor St John, 'Enriching Law with Political History: A Case Study on the Creation of the ICSID Convention' in Schill, Tams, and Hofmann (eds) (n 39) 288.

[74] ibid 310–11, 314.

[75] ibid 316–17.

[76] ibid 312.

[77] St John (n 39) 173–74.

[78] ibid 183–210.

[79] BITs provide for investor-state arbitration on quite varied terms. See Jan Paulsson, 'Arbitration Without Privity' (1995) 10 ICSID Rev 233, 236–38. Investor-state arbitration can also be provided for in investment contracts and domestic investment legislation.

[80] See Lauge N Skovgaard Poulsen and Emma Aisbett, 'When the Claim Hits: Bilateral Investment Treaties and Bounded Rational Learning' (2013) 65 World Politics 273; Lauge N Skovgaard Poulsen, 'Beyond Credible Commitments: (Investment) Treaties as Focal Points' (2020) 64 International Studies Quarterly 26. Nevertheless, some observers did have a sense of the possibilities back in the 1960s. St John (n 39) 131.

[81] These were important for the later treaty-based arbitration system, but they are distinct. See Sornarajah (n 39) 325, 349–51.

NAFTA.[82] This increase in investor-state arbitration has transformed international investment law, by both enforcing and developing protection standards. This not only makes the investment protection provisions in BITs and other agreements like NAFTA particularly effective, but also integrates them into a (relatively) coherent international regime.[83] This has given great power to investment tribunals—with their opaque processes and populated by a small elite of arbitrators—at the expense of national authorities and more representative international institutions and in a way that has favoured investment protection.

On one hand, the dominant professional sensibility of arbitrators has meant a tendency to preference investor interests and suspect state measures. Investment tribunals have tended to interpret protection standards (and their own jurisdiction) expansively,[84] as mixed claims commissions had done in respect of alien protection.[85] They have re-asserted and extended the standards of alien protection.[86] When it comes to state responsibility for breach of such standards, they have gone beyond the ARSIWA, citing alien protection claims and even the 1961 Harvard Draft Convention on the International Responsibility of States for Injuries to Aliens,[87] 'the high water mark of the failed codification of State responsibility as alien protection', which was rejected at the ILC.[88] At the same time, regardless of the outcomes of particular cases or the content of particular rules, as Martti Koskenniemi has argued, the very fact of the existence of investor-state arbitration delegitimises state intervention in the market and 'local self-determination in economic governance', and gives 'institutional backing' to investor interests in public decision making.[89] Where the international enforcement of state for responsibility for injuries to aliens once insulated foreign investment from political instability and economic nationalism, now investor-state arbitration insulates it against 'mass politics, organised labour and democratic imperatives'.[90]

Thus, in important respects, we are back where we started before the events at The Hague in 1930. Here I have tried to show the role of fragmentation in the difficulties in resisting this path. Where once there was state responsibility for injuries to aliens, there emerged three separate albeit overlapping regimes: international investment law, addressing the commercial aspects of alien protection; human rights law, into which the individual protection aspect of alien

[82] Only 44 of 942 (as of the end of 2018) investor-state claims were initiated before 2000. Over 900 of 942 were under BITs, the ECT, or NAFTA.

[83] The extent of the coherence of this jurisprudence is subject to much debate. Compare Schill (n 61) 278ff; Newcombe and Paradell (n 39) 59–60; Sornarajah (n 39) 1.

[84] See eg M Sornarajah, *Resistance and Change in the International Law on Foreign Investment* (CUP 2015) 147, 246ff; Gus Van Harten, *Sovereign Choices and Sovereign Constraints: Judicial Restraint in Investment Treaty Arbitration* (OUP 2014) 18.

[85] For example, early mixed claims commissions established their jurisdiction over claims based in contract, even if their founding instruments only provided for jurisdiction over claims for injuries to property and person. See the discussion in Moore (n 10) vol 4, 3425ff.

[86] Indeed, states have tried to use alien protection to try and *limit* expansive interpretations of the fair and equitable treatment standard. See eg Nathalie Bernasconi-Osterwalder, 'Giving Arbitrators *Carte Blanche*—Fair and Equitable Treatment in Investment Treaties' in CL Lim (ed), *Alternative Visions of the International Law on Foreign Investment: Essays in Honour of Muthucumaraswamy Sornarajah* (CUP 2016). See eg *AAPL v Sri Lanka* (n 33) for a reassertion of rules of alien protection.

[87] Louis B Sohn and Richard R Baxter, 'Convention on the International Responsibility of States for Injuries to Aliens: Draft no. 12 with Explanatory Notes' (1961) 55 American Journal of International Law 545. For references to investment tribunal decisions that have cited Sohn and Baxter, see Newcombe and Paradell (n 39) 22 n 126.

[88] Nissel (n 2) 336.

[89] Koskenniemi (n 37) 352–3. See also Shalakany (n 37).

[90] Ntina Tzouvala, 'Neoliberalism as Legalism: International Economic Law and the Rise of the Judiciary' in Ben Golder and Daniel McLoughlin (eds), *The Politics of Legality in a Neoliberal Age* (Routledge 2017) 116.

protection has been subsumed;[91] and state responsibility, which gradually became unhooked from alien protection and remains part of general international law. When it comes to state responsibility, the ILC has thus been left with formulating a residual regime. This has been part of a more general side-lining of the ILC for specialist institutions.[92] State responsibility under the ARSIWA is an abstract set of so-called secondary rules, which is always subject to special regimes combining primary and secondary rules.[93] Such a special regime—international investment law—has been developed, through less democratic and transparent mechanisms such as 'serial bilateralism' and arbitration, in a way that favours investment protection.[94] Fragmentation means that a change in one regime or institution can always be by-passed, making it difficult to change the overall course of the system once certain preferences have been entrenched: rather than changes in direction, what we end up with is temporary swerves.

2. Structural bias

So far, this is, on one hand, a rather instrumentalist account of international law. We could just say that the persistence of international law's prioritisation of investment protection is in part a reflection of the fact that powerful states are more likely to succeed in their efforts to instrumentalise law. A purely instrumentalist theory of international law is not, however, convincing or conducive to change. As Robert Gordon has argued:

> This method [of explaining anything that happens in the legal system by referring to someone's interest], subtly employed, yields narratives that are both subtle and exciting, but sooner or later, as every legal change is attributed in turn to a different set of bargains among interests, as a form of explanation it's going to seem discouragingly *ad hoc*.[95]

International law is not simply a neutral tool—even if there was such a thing—that can be used for varying ends depending on the circumstances in which it is being used and who is using it. Indeed, if this was true there would be little point in, or even possibility of, engaging with it as law; if international law did not have a certain autonomy from broader political, social and economic factors, it would be indistinguishable from them. At the same time, the rise of investor-state arbitration has also been a story of 'unintended consequences' and the actions of exceptional individuals at the World Bank.[96] This narrative does not offer much promise either when it comes to thinking about the role played by international law in how things came to be how they are and thus what needs to be undone for things to be different.

Instead, I suggest that the fact that certain 'uses' of international law and certain outcomes have prevailed historically, despite contingency, should make us stop and think

[91] See eg Richard Lillich, *The Human Rights of Aliens in Contemporary International Law* (Manchester University Press 1984).
[92] See Martti Koskenniemi, 'International Legislation Today: Limits and Possibilities' (2005) 23 Wisconsin International Law Journal 61; Martti Koskenniemi, 'The Fate of Public International Law: Between Technique and Politics' (2007) 70 Modern Law Review 1, 11.
[93] ARSIWA (n 4) art 55.
[94] See Benvenisti and Downs (n 40) 610–12.
[95] Robert Gordon, 'Critical Legal Histories' (1984) 36 Stanford Law Review 57, 87.
[96] This is Taylor St John's account (n 39) 131, although she refutes Pauwelyn's (n 39) chaos theory of the development of international investment law.

about its structural biases.[97] While different international institutions and regimes may have particular biases vis-à-vis each other—and in the previous section, I drew out something of the relative biases of the World Bank, ICSID tribunals and the ILC, and of the laws of state responsibility, international investment and human rights—in this section, I will consider the potential biases of two structural aspects of the discipline of international law that cross particular regimes and institutions, namely its sources and its commitment to the public-private divide.[98]

In the context of the efforts to establish the NIEO, arbitral awards ended up overriding democratic General Assembly resolutions. The World Bank was successful in getting a treaty agreed via unrepresentative processes, while ECOSOC, through the inter-governmental Commission on Transnational Corporations with its geographically equitable elected membership, was not.[99] The efforts to develop a binding code of conduct for multinational companies failed.[100] Instead, a series of international commercial arbitrations reasserted the international protection, rather than national regulation, of foreign investment.[101] General Assembly resolutions asserting permanent sovereignty over natural resources and national authority over foreign investment were not accepted as sources of binding international law.[102]

Just as sources were a key issue at The Hague in 1930 and in the contestation of state responsibility for injuries to aliens, they were too for the NIEO. Under orthodox sources doctrine, the General Assembly resolutions that asserted the NIEO, unlike binding treaty provisions under the UN Charter, could only be a source of international law as custom.[103] The fact that the formation of new customary international law requires generally uniform state practice—including that of specially-affected states, which concept has itself been used to favour Global North[104]—meant that, as Antony Anghie argues, a minority of Western states could block changes to custom, in whose formation new states had no opportunity to participate.[105] At the same time, the status of judicial decisions as formal, if subsidiary, sources of international law, empowered arbitrators—unaccountable and tending to be deferential to investor interests—to formulate law at the expense of more democratic mechanisms.[106] Thus international law's sources favoured both the status quo and—or as—investment protection.

[97] See eg Koskenniemi (n 46) 600–15; Rose Parfitt, *The Process of International Legal Reproduction: Inequality, Historiography, Resistance* (CUP 2019) 20–27.

[98] Antony Anghie has argued that the key factor behind the legal defeat of the NIEO was that these features made international law 'structurally immune from attempts to change': Anghie (n 72) 153.

[99] ECOSOC Res 1913 (LVII) (5 December 1974).

[100] See eg Jennifer Bair, 'Corporations at the United Nations: Echoes of the New International Economic Order?' (2015) 6 Humanity 159; Sundhya Pahuja and Anna Saunders, 'Rival Worlds and the Place of the Corporation in International Law' in Jochen von Bernstorff and Philipp Dann (eds), *The Battle for International Law in the Decolonization Era* (OUP 2019) 142.

[101] These culminated in *Texaco Overseas Petroleum Co v Libya* (1978) 17 ILM 1. For commentary see eg Anghie (n 39) 226–35.

[102] *Texaco* (n 101) paras 489–92.

[103] This was a matter of design of course. See Paul Kennedy, *The Parliament of Man: The Past, Present, and Future of the United Nations* (Random House 2006) 113–42.

[104] Kevin Jon Heller, 'Specially-Affected States and the Formation of Custom' (2018) 112 American Journal of International Law 191.

[105] Anghie (n 72) 149. On the bias of sources doctrine more generally, see Rose Parfitt, 'The Spectre of Sources' (2014) 25 European Journal of International Law 297; BS Chimni, 'Customary International Law: A Third World Perspective' (2018) 112 American Journal of International Law 1.

[106] Anghie (n 72) 152.

International law, as feminist scholars in particular have noted for a while, 'rests on a variety of distinctions between public and private worlds'.[107] This fundamental liberal tenet has favoured investment protection as an outcome, contributing to the failure of efforts to regulate multinational companies. As Anghie explains, 'the Third World initiative was unable to expand its reach to regulate power within the private sphere—in particular, the activities of corporations and the vision of property, contract, and economic relations that they furthered'.[108] Sundhya Pahuja and Anna Saunders have argued that the establishment of the Commission on Transnational Corporations, while a success in terms of creating a 'forum within in the [UN] for consideration of issues relating to transnational corporations',[109] had the effect of stabilising an understanding of corporations as private in a way that worked against the creation of a binding code to regulate multinational companies and establish national authority over foreign investment.[110] The public-private divide is also at the heart of the ARSIWA and its doctrine of attribution, meaning that states are not responsible as such for the actions of companies.[111] State responsibility for injuries to aliens may have been defeated, but the ARSIWA reinforced the idea of two distinct public and private spheres and that companies belong to the latter in a way which, delegitimising state intervention in the market, set back the task of asserting national authority over foreign investment.

IV. Conclusion

Anne Orford has argued that despite the fact that 'there is nothing inevitable about the particular forms that governance takes today ... it is still necessary to explore empirically how governance has come to take the forms it has taken, and the role that particular dominant modes of legal interpretation have played in that process.'[112] In this chapter, I have explored how international law's fragmentation, sources, and commitment to the public-private divide all contributed to the evolution of the current regime for the protection of foreign investment. They made investment protection a more likely outcome despite contingency and made it more difficult to resist for those with a different vision of international order. Today resistance against investor-state arbitration also comes from developed countries and mainstream international investment lawyers but to the extent that such resistance stays within international law's structural biases and fails to work against fragmentation, it is unlikely to effect change. Without understanding how we came to be where we are, it is hard to understand how things might have been different or could be different in the future. For agency to be effective, it must be accompanied by an understanding of the structures that it is working within and against.

[107] Hilary Charlesworth, 'Worlds Apart: Public/Private Distinctions in International Law' in Margaret Thornton (ed), *Public and Private: Feminist Legal Debates* (OUP 1995) 243. See also Chinkin (n 31).
[108] Anghie (n 72) 146.
[109] ECOSOC Res 1913 (LVII) (5 December 1974).
[110] Pahuja and Saunders (n 100).
[111] Unless special circumstances can be established, for example in accordance with ARSIWA art 5.
[112] Orford (n 46) 26.

24

Barcelona Traction Re-Imagined

The ICJ as a World Court for Foreign Investment Cases?

*Saïda El Boudouhi**

I. Introduction

The decline of diplomatic protection is usually related to the growth of other forms of investment protection, especially through investor-state dispute settlement (ISDS).[1] Conversely, a slight decline of the latter is quickly equated with a new rise of diplomatic protection.[2] It is thus not disputed that diplomatic protection and the origins of the protection of foreign investment are intimately related. Some even argue that in the nineteenth century 'foreign investment protection became part of ... the doctrine of diplomatic protection of aliens'.[3] The relationship between diplomatic protection and foreign investment protection is, however, complex: while the latter was born within the former, they then developed separately and even opposed to each other.

This ambiguous relationship between diplomatic and investment protection is puzzling and counterfactuals may prove to be a useful tool to disentangle it. Counterfactuals may also help to better understand the apparent 'mystery' of the sudden and inexorable expansion of international investment law. Indeed, while it has been one of the most dynamic chapters of international law, international investment protection has been subject over the last years to many challenges and criticisms, especially regarding its dispute settlement system. However, few sound alternatives have been provided, especially if we put aside the option of letting national tribunals be the sole judges for foreign investment disputes. Of course, if we look to the future, some real or alleged alternatives could well develop, such as bilateral investment courts or the seemingly utopian project of a multilateral investment court put forward by the European Union (EU). But what if we look to the past? What were the alternatives, if any? International investment law has changed the face of public international law over the last thirty years, but one can well wonder, in a historical perspective, whether it could have been otherwise. Is the current situation the only possible outcome of the history of international investment law?

Was there (and not only is there today) any other more (or less?) suitable solution? Was the large development of bilateral investment treaties (BITs), with each having its dispute

* The author is indebted to the editors for their valuable comments on previous versions of this work.

[1] *Ahmadou Sadio Diallo (Republic of Guinea v Democratic Republic of Congo)* (Preliminary Objections) [2007] ICJ Reports 88 (*Diallo*).

[2] See, for instance, Rodrigo Polanco, *The Return of the Home State to Investor-State Disputes: Bringing Back Diplomatic Protection?* (CUP 2019).

[3] Lauge N Skovgaard Poulsen, 'Sacrificing Sovereignty by Chance: Investment Treaties, Developing Countries, and Bounded Rationality' (PhD thesis, London School of Economics 2011) 31; see also Andrew Newcombe and Lluís Paradell, *Law and Practice of Investment Treaties* (Kluwer Law International 2009) 4–6.

Saïda El Boudouhi, Barcelona Traction *Re-Imagined* In: *Contingency in International Law*. Edited by: Ingo Venzke and Kevin Jon Heller, Oxford University Press. © The Several Contributors 2021. DOI: 10.1093/oso/9780192898036.003.0024

settlement system, a necessity from a historical perspective? Or is it contingent on the history of international law and an ever more globalised world? If so, what could be the legal (or extra-legal) facts that could have been turning points? To answer those questions, the chapter will refer to two legal theories which often appear as incompatible. While ultimately privileging an anti-formalist and a realist approach to law, the analysis will not deny all relevance to a formalist or normativist theory. The latter will be taken as a starting point from which the search for contingencies will have to depart and which can be mitigated in some cases. That is the result of an encounter between dominant French normativist doctrines derived from Kelsen's 'pure law' approach and realist theories as they have been developed in the United States or in Scandinavia. Such a hybrid approach finds inspiration in what has been called a 'normativist realism'.[4] Building on Michel Troper's 'realist theory of interpretation',[5] the method aims at overcoming the opposition between formalism/normativism, on the one hand, and realism/anti-formalism, on the other.

Section II will introduce the methodology and the concepts that are used. Section III will look at a few events in the history of foreign investment law in order to distinguish what was contingent and what was unavoidable while, at the same time, identifying what could be turning points. After having set the attention on the *Barcelona Traction* judgment as a contingent turning point among others, section IV will further assess the causal link between the judgment and foreign investment law through an exercise of imagination in which will be considered not only the possible but also the likely effects of a different outcome to the case. It is in this section that I will imagine what could have happened if the Court had responded positively to Belgium's request. By way of conclusion, section V will suggest that the *Barcelona Traction* judgment itself, rather than foreign investment law, was, however, so tightly constrained that it could hardly have been different even though the same cannot be said about the later *Diallo* case.

II. The possibility of contingency in (international) law

In order to set the theoretical foundations of the chapter, I will first examine the relationship between counterfactuals and contingency, on the one hand, and law on the other hand (1) before turning to the definition of contingent facts (2).

1. Counterfactuals and contingency in law

Contingency is a concept that is much appraised by philosophers and historians but it has drawn little attention in the legal scholarship overall.[6] But Susan Marks' 'False Contingency',

[4] Pierre Brunet. 'Le Réalisme n'est-il qu'une Théorie de l'Interprétation?' in Jean-Jacques Sueur and Pascal Richard (eds), *La Transgression* (Larcier 2013) 397.

[5] Michel Troper, 'Une Théorie Réaliste de l'Interprétation' in Michel Troper (ed), *La Théorie du Droit, le Froit, l'Etat* (PUF 2001) 74.

[6] While there is no mention of the word 'contingency' as an entry in any dictionary of legal theory or legal culture, Niklas Luhmann had already shown the necessity to reflect upon the relationship between 'Contingency and Law'. However, his perspective is an extra-legal one since he takes law as an object of a social sciences analysis: Niklas Luhmann, *Kontingenz und Recht* (Suhrkamp 2013) quoted by Klaus A Ziegert, 'Niklas Luhmann on Contingency and Law. The Theory Behind Systems Theory' (2017) 20 Soziale Systeme 421.

a reply to Roberto Unger's *False Necessity*,[7] or Ingo Venzke's more recent pieces,[8] have changed the landscape. Contingency is usually opposed to necessity and related to the counterfactual method. More exactly, the latter is based on the concept of contingency without which it would not exist. Although the counterfactual method seems to find its roots as far back in history as in Tite-Live's work, there seems to be a relative consensus that it has been reinvigorated in the 1990s, particularly in the English-speaking social sciences and especially in historical studies.[9] Contingency and counterfactuals are thus a common research field in social sciences and even in some hard sciences.

However, when related to legal studies, the concept of contingency may be puzzling, although counterfactuals have been incorporated as an explicit part of the legal reasoning in some areas. From the perspective of a formalist or normativist approach, contingency may well appear as unfit for legal reasoning which would arguably leave no room for imagination or creativity. And yet, as Jean Giraudoux has famously put it in his play *La Guerre de Troie n'Aura Pas Lieu*: 'le droit est la plus puissante des écoles de l'imagination'.[10] Although the playwright only referred to the way reality can be freely 'interpreted' by lawyers, imagination and law should be compatible. Still, lawyers, unless they are 'dreamers' or 'idealists', do not tend to look at 'what could have happened', except in the rare occasions where that is required by a legal norm itself. Therefore, one may wonder whether the counterfactual method is suited to the study of law at all. That depends on the legal theory that is privileged. A formalist approach to law does not pay much attention to alternatives to positive law, notwithstanding the obvious fact that examining 'what could have been' may sometimes prove useful for a better understanding of what actually is. On the contrary, an anti-formalist or a realist approach will tend to question what actually is and constantly look for how the legal system could have been otherwise.

More generally, for those who consider that law, and international law specifically, is a system and not simply a 'bric-à-brac',[11] it could be difficult to identify within it many contingent facts, at least not among the facts that have legal significance. The law is, because it has to be. Everything within the legal system is necessary. Formally, the establishment of a new norm or the adoption of a judicial decision is always part of a system as long as it is not arbitrary but based on some reasoning. It is arbitrary for instance, if it does not fit within one of the legal categories of the system. It is only within this limited context that a formalist approach to law would include contingency. Contingency could even be related to the will as the foundation of the international legal system. Any legal act is the result of will, therefore no legal act could ever be contingent. This of course begs the question of the customary norms which are the result of a process rather than an act. Are all customary norms contingent because they are not the result of a will? One cannot ignore that customary norms are nothing other than an addition of—often domestic—legal acts, tied together by an interpretive authority. Although it is not to be limited to, nor equated with randomness,[12]

[7] Roberto Unger, *False Necessity* (2nd edn, Verso 2004); Susan Marks, 'False Contingency' (2009) 62 Current Legal Problems 1.

[8] See for instance, Ingo Venzke, 'What if? Counterfactual (Hi)Stories of International Law' (2018) 8 Asian Journal of International Law 403.

[9] Quentin Deluermoz and Pierre Singaravélou, 'Explorer le Champ des Possibles. Approches Contrefactuelles et Futurs Non Advenus en Histoire' (2012/3) 59 Revue d'Histoire Moderne et Contemporaine 70, 86.

[10] 'Law is the most powerful school of imagination' (author's translation).

[11] Jean Combacau, 'Le Droit International: Bric-à-brac ou Système?' (1986) 31 Archives de Philosophie du Droit 85.

[12] See Samuel Moyn, in this volume, disagreeing with Susan Marks on the role of 'accident and randomness'.

contingency encompasses facts that appear by pure chance,[13] as opposed to facts that are the result of a will or of a system. Put this way, there would be no room for contingent legal facts and there would be no point in looking for them specifically in international law. From that formalist perspective, even when a decision is adopted by nine votes to eight,[14] it cannot strictly be said to be contingent even though it could obviously have been otherwise since the voting is 'on the edge'.[15] It is necessary and not contingent because it fits within a legal norm, that of the majority decision, no matter how tight the majority is. The legal fact could not be contingent because it is determined by the law. Of course, this is the perspective of an excessively formalist approach to law and sociologists of law such as Niklas Luhmann have long ago tried to show how even procedure and legal facts are contingent.[16]

If one departs from this reductionist approach to law, it may be easier to use the counterfactual method not only to understand what actually is, but also to be critical about it. Counterfactual reasoning can relate to many critical approaches to law. It shares some common features with the doctrine of legal indeterminacy as developed for instance by critical legal studies.[17] Indeed, contingency often lies in the interstices of indeterminacy. In that sense, assuming with critical legal studies scholars such as Martti Koskenniemi that the link between politics and law is particularly tight in international law,[18] the latter then becomes the ideal branch of law for testing the concept of contingency. Far from being purely epistemological, the counterfactual method yields a moral and political dimension which is often stressed by philosophers and historians.[19] In that sense, it also relates to comparative law methods that amount to assessing how similar institutions function in varying ways depending on different political choices and social constraints.

While the 'pure law' approach will not be discarded throughout this study, it is this more anti-formalist approach to law which will be privileged in order to provide for a more disruptive and critical perspective on the course of international law. It is thus postulated that contingency may lie not only within what is random or accidental but also within legal facts that are formally determined by the legal system.[20] Indeed, notwithstanding the wariness that counterfactual reasoning may arouse in legal scholars, law is more familiar with counterfactual reasoning than any other discipline in that it uses some techniques that are derived from it. The most obvious one is the but-for causation method which is widely used in

[13] Marks (n 7) 6: 'the emphasis is thrown on chance, accident and all that is random, indeterminate and up in the air'.

[14] As was the case, for example, in the controversial European Court of Human Rights (ECtHR) judgment in *Al-Adsani v United Kingdom* Application no 35763/97 (Judgment of 21 November 2001).

[15] The fact that in spite of such a tight vote the ECtHR has not changed the position it held in *Al-Adsani* in subsequent case law proves that that legal fact was not contingent.

[16] Luhmann (n 6).

[17] See for instance the presence of the concept of contingency in the work of Martti Koskenniemi, *From Apology to Utopia. The Structure of International Legal Argument* (Reissue with new Epilogue, CUP 2005).

[18] Among many other writings, see Martti Koskenniemi, 'The Fate of Public International Law: Between Technique and Politics' (2007) 70 Modern Law Review 1.

[19] Paul Ricoeur, *Temps et Récit* (Seuil 1983) 331–32: '[l]'estimation rétrospective des possibilités revêt ainsi une signification morale et politique, qui excède sa signification purement épistémologique: elle rappelle aux lecteurs d'histoire que le passé de l'historien a été le futur des personnages historiques'; for a historical perspective, see Deluermoz and Singaravélou (n 9).

[20] As for the concept of 'legal fact', I refer here to a general understanding in some legal systems such as the French one in which the legal fact is the one to which the law attaches some consequence. Jerzy Wróblewski provides a definition of 'legal facts' or of 'facts in law' when he asserts that 'each fact relevant in the application of law is either described or named in legal rule, or is related with such a fact' (Jerzy Wróblewski, *Meaning and Truth in Judicial Decision* (Juridica 1979) 116.

damages litigation,[21] especially in common law systems. Another example lies in the concept of legal fiction which consists of translating a 'what if' situation into an 'as if' one.

In order to set the boundaries of the object of study, the relationship between counterfactuals, contingency, and law must be examined. In other words, are we going to look at counterfactuals in law or at contingency in law? While the former points generally at the method that consists in rewriting history, history of law in our case, without necessarily hierarchising its different components, the latter is much narrower and focuses only on the events and facts that may be considered as contingent in the historical evolution of law. In an even more restrictive way, the analysis will be built on the idea of contingent facts taken individually, rather than on the concept of contingency *in abstracto*.

2. Defining contingent facts within the law

The gist of the argument will turn around whether a given fact, in this case the *Barcelona Traction* judgment, could be seen as a contingent fact within the course of foreign investment law.[22] This legal fact will be weighed against others that may also have contributed significantly to the current state of law. The research thus aims at distinguishing between the facts that are contingent and those that are not within the course of international investment law. Before proceeding any further, a preliminary definition of the contingent fact must be laid down.

To put it briefly, a contingent fact is usually a fact that could not have happened or that could have happened differently. Because the specificity of law as a science lies mainly in the existence of legal facts, ie facts the consequences of which are determined by the law, the analysis will focus on what legal facts within the examined field could be qualified as contingent. Indeed, the historian or the philosopher could look at any fact and see how it has affected the course of history or of philosophical thinking. The lawyer will pay the foremost attention to facts that exist within the legal world, ie legal facts or facts that have some legal significance. This does not exclude the possibility for a lawyer to act, concomitantly, as a social scientist and to also look at facts outside the law to understand how they have influenced a given legal norm or legal situation. That is what we do when we look, for instance, at the circumstances which have surrounded the judgment of the International Court of Justice (ICJ) in the *South Africa* case:[23] the death of one member of the bench and the illness of another are facts that may have weighed on the outcome of the case, and as such they are worthy of interest, but they are not accounted for by the law. They are therefore non-legal facts that this analysis will not ignore even though they are not at the centre of the study. While the analysis is embedded as much as possible within positive law, and as such will focus mainly on legal facts, it cannot ignore the role played by some non-legal facts in the course of international law.

Arguably, any fact could be looked at to determine its degree of contingency. However, for the purposes of the present research, both legal and non-legal facts must have a double

[21] We find an implementation of this method in the ELSI case before the International Court of Justice: *Elettronica Sicula SPA (ELSI) (United States of America v Republic of Italy)* (Judgment of 20 July 1989) [1989] ICJ Reports. The case was decided on the basis of the largely factual 'but-for' analysis.

[22] *Barcelona Traction, Light and Power Company, Limited* (Judgment) [1970] ICJ Reports 3 (*Barcelona Traction*).

[23] See Venzke (n 8).

characteristic to be worth being examined as a contingent fact: (i) they must be marginal in relation to a whole and (ii) they must have enough impact on that whole. Before dwelling on those two features, it is worth underlining that a fact that is not marginal enough will be considered as a necessary fact, while a fact which does not have enough impact will be deemed irrelevant and not necessary. Therefore, the facts that do not fulfil the two conditions will not all be necessary or non-contingent facts. Those that have no consequence on the course of the examined law will simply not deserve being examined for contingency purposes. This allows the contingency study to pinpoint those facts that are relevant, instead of indistinctly encompassing all the facts surrounding the emergence of a given norm, for instance.

Regarding the marginal character of the contingent fact, it is argued that a fact cannot be contingent in and of itself. It is contingent in relation to other facts. Therefore, to deserve the characterisation of a 'contingent fact', a given fact must be marginal enough for the studied structure to be able to stand without it. Otherwise, it would not be contingent but necessary in regards to the examined structure. The contingent fact would thus be the marginal, incidental, or peripheral fact in relation to an examined field. However, the contingent fact must not be confused with a fact that would be inconsequential. It has to make *some* difference as will be shown below.

Could, for instance, the Treaty of Westphalia be said to be a contingent fact? If the assessment of contingency were only about weighing probabilities, historians could probably point to different elements which restrained that fact, pre-determined it and made it more or less contingent. However, the question is interesting from a legal point of view only if the contingency is assessed in relation to another part of law, in this case the emergence of international law based on the concept of state sovereignty. In that regard, the Westphalia treaties are clearly not a marginal but a necessary fact in the emergence of international law since the latter could not exist without them. Indeed, while it may be stimulating to imagine what international law could have been without the Westphalia treaties, that would amount to imagining another system than international law as we know it. It would therefore not be a legal exercise anymore, but a purely fictional one. The Treaty of Westphalia is then an 'essential constraint' for the emergence of international law.[24] It is relatively easy, and therefore of little scientific interest from a legal point of view, to get rid of essential constraints and to imagine a whole different legal structure in a completely different world. It is more challenging to imagine 'small tweaks or adaptations' to the existent structure while keeping the essential constraints.[25]

Imagining an alternative to the Westphalia system is thrilling from a science fiction point of view or even from a literary point of view, but it would not help us understand the legal system we actually have. It may of course be objected that imagining another structure could also help understand the system in its core, such as in its emphasis on states and their will, as opposed to other kinds of 'foundations'. However, that would not be about international law as we know it and it may be of little use to improve the current system.

[24] Moyn, in this volume.

[25] Joost Pauwelyn, 'Infrastructure and Characteristics of the International Investment Regime' in Zachary Douglas, Joost Pauwelyn, and Jorge E Viñuales (eds), *The Foundations of International Investment Law: Bringing Theory into Practice* (OUP 2014) 11, 14.

As to the second characteristic, 'contingent facts' must be facts that are considered to have enough impact on the field at study. The assessment of the impact requirement must be a *prima facie* one: it may well be that a fact that is considered to have played an important role in the emergence of a given norm is eventually proved to be non-consequential at all. In other words, there has to be a real or supposed causal relationship between the contingent fact and the examined field. The importance of causality in counterfactuals has been stressed by Max Weber in his endeavour to provide historical studies with a methodology for identifying 'objective possibilities'.[26] Causality may be examined at two levels when one relates an allegedly contingent fact to a structure or a whole: one may look at the different possible 'causes' of the structure, among them the supposedly contingent fact, and hierarchise their influence; but one may also take a step back and search the causes of the contingent fact itself, thus assessing its probability. This latter option will be explored in Part V of the study.

One has to distinguish between absolute contingency (things would be exactly the same if the 'little', marginal, contingent fact had or had not happened; there is therefore no causal relationship between the examined field and the contingent fact) and relative contingency (although the overall structure would be more or less the same, things might have been different if the contingent fact had or had not happened because there is a causal relationship between the two elements). The idea of relative necessity, and thus of relative contingency, that is implied in Max Weber's work is indeed more appealing than that of 'false necessity' or 'false contingency' that has been respectively developed by Roberto Unger and Susan Marks.[27] While the argument made by Susan Marks in her famous essay is similar to Max Weber's, the formula 'false contingency' may suggest a binary thinking about what is contingent and what is not. On the contrary, thinking in terms of relative contingency amounts to assessing the constraints and assigning them relative importance.[28] Assessing the contingency of things amounts to weighing and balancing their influence on the course of events.

Within the context of a legal order, absolute contingency could apply to two categories of facts. The first ones would be those that were considered, *prima facie*, to have some impact and that eventually appear to have none. They are 'factually irrelevant' even though they may be legal facts: since they had no consequence on the examined structure or norm, they fall within absolute contingency. The second category of facts that could fall within the absolute contingency group are those that are legally irrelevant: what the judge has had for breakfast (despite the famous words attributed to Jerome Frank), and the nature of the relationship between the different judges sitting on the bench or even the accident that made for a given judge to be replaced, all seem to fall within absolute contingency because they are legally irrelevant. This does not mean, however, that these facts can never have a consequence on the decision. It simply means that such a consequence is not accounted for by law. These are non-legal facts which amount to 'external incentives to which the actors may be more or less sensitive' identified in another context.[29] In pure law, these should have no

[26] Max Weber, 'Troisième Essai, Essai sur Quelques Catégories de la Sociologie Compréhensive' in Max Weber, *Essais Sur la Théorie de la Science* (Julien Freund tr, Librairie Plon 1965) 325.

[27] ibid.

[28] Moyn, in this volume.

[29] Véronique Champeil-Desplats and Michel Troper, 'Proposition Pour une Théorie des Contraintes Juridiques' in Michel Troper, Véronique Champeil-Desplats and Christophe Grzegorczyk, *Théorie des Contraintes Juridiques* (LGDJ 2005) 13 (author's translation).

impact. But since they could, in some cases, have some social effect, they can move from absolute to relative contingency provided a non-formalist approach to law is privileged. If the objective of this collective project were 'simply' to proceed to an exercise of uchronia about different aspects of the international legal world, the analysis could focus on these absolutely contingent facts because they are what compares best to the famous example of Pascal on the length of Cleopatra's nose, often seen as the contingent fact par excellence. However, while it would probably be intellectually stimulating and enjoyable, delving into that kind of counterfactual reasoning would have little relevance from the point of view of a better understanding of positive law. This does not mean however that they may never be examined since they can move from absolute to relative contingency status; but only that their assessment should be secondary. The question may be raised at this point whether there is then any difference between this exercise of imagination embedded within the law – positive law – and pure legal commentary in which a good commentator is expected to raise and assess alternative paths. The main difference is probably historical hindsight. The difference is a matter of degree rather than of nature. Relative contingency is therefore what we are interested in for the purposes of better understanding how the law functions and how it could be improved: the contingent facts that deserve our attention are those that could have been different (they were only partially constrained) *and* that have had some influence on the course of the examined field, ie international investment law in this case. In other words, contingent facts must also be turning points within the law to deserve our attention. The identification of turning points that can be necessary or contingent facts is therefore an important methodological step.[30]

The gist of the juris-fiction exercise that is proposed in this chapter lies in the assessment of the relative importance of mainly legal, but also of some non-legal, facts that have paved the way for the emergence of foreign investment law; the same weighing and balancing exercise will further be used to determine whether the *Barcelona Traction* case, specifically, can be considered as a contingent fact or whether it was itself constrained by other legal—or non-legal—facts which made it a necessary and unavoidable legal fact.

III. Contingent facts and turning points in foreign investment law

The part of international law that is the object of the present analysis is foreign investment law, mainly in its procedural aspects as reflected in investor-state arbitration more specifically. The research therefore fits with the current and prolific debate surrounding the legitimacy of ISDS. The underlying question is whether investor-state arbitration could have taken another path, with perhaps a more balanced approach to private interests and protection of state sovereignty through an alternative dispute settlement system. Could investor-state arbitration have remained marginal instead of becoming one of the pillars of the protection granted to foreign investors? It is thus necessary to investigate the relatively brief history of foreign investment law in order to understand what could have been the turning points, the contingent turning points, that may have oriented the current evolution of this

[30] Andrew Abbott, 'À Propos du Concept de Turning Point' in Marc Bessin, Claire Bidart, and Michel Grossetti (eds), *Bifurcations. Les Sciences Sociales Face aux Ruptures et à l'Événement* (La Découverte 2010) 187, 191.

branch of international law in another direction than the one it has actually followed.[31] The aim is also to ask whether there is one contingent turning point which stands out or whether the current system is derived from a structure that made its course unavoidable with many factors pointing in the same direction. I will first consider foreign investment law generally and the different historical factors that have contributed to shaping it (1), before turning to the specific role that one of those factors, the *Barcelona Traction* judgment, may have played (2).

1. Possible turning points in the course of foreign investment law

For the evaluation of the *Barcelona Traction* case to be accurate, it is necessary to start with the identification of all other possible factors that may have shaped foreign investment law. These are possible turning points in the course of foreign investment law, but they are not necessarily contingent facts. They may well be facts that are necessary in regards to the current structure of foreign investment law. The approach adopted is similar to that relied on by Joost Pauwelyn who uses complexity theory to account for the evolution of foreign investment law.[32] Indeed, Pauwelyn considers that in accordance with complexity theory, foreign investment law must not be examined only through the lens of a 'reductionist' approach focusing on, for instance, the history of the International Centre for Settlement of Investment Disputes (ICSID) Convention or the history of the United States (US) BITs but must also be approached by looking at how different elements are interrelated.[33] In other words, instead of zooming in on one aspect, complexity theory invites us to look at the whole picture.

However, in order to gain an accurate knowledge of the whole picture, it is also necessary to zoom in on each aspect of the whole. Therefore, looking at foreign investment law through the lens of the *Barcelona Traction* judgment is tantamount to applying complexity theory and to widening even more the number of elements that may have led to the current state of law, while at the same time looking at them individually to assess their relative importance. Indeed, weighing the influence of the *Barcelona Traction* judgment does not exclude taking into account other elements which are more central in the field of foreign investment law. On the contrary, the decision's impact will be assessed in relation to other concomitant factors. Its contingency depends on its relationship with other elements. Therefore, looking at contingent legal facts that may have influenced the current state of foreign investment law postulates the relevance of complexity theory and extends Pauwelyn's analysis even to marginal elements. The approach is also indebted to Max Weber's causality theory mentioned above in that the objective is to assess the respective contribution of multiple factors in shaping not only past events, even legal ones, but also current legal situations.[34]

[31] It all depends on how investment is defined. See Patrick Juillard, 'Chronique du Droit International Économique' (1986) Annuaire Français de Droit International 399–400; H Neufeld, *The International Protection of Private Creditors from the Treaties of Westphalia to the Congress of Vienna (1648-1815)* (Sijthoff 1971). It may well be considered that foreign investment law goes as far back as the history of diplomatic protection in Latin America.

[32] Joost Pauwelyn, 'At the Edge of Chaos? Foreign Investment Law as a Complex Adaptive System, How It Emerged and How It Can Be Reformed' (2014) 29 ICSID Review 372.

[33] ibid 391–92.

[34] Weber (n 26).

The history of foreign investment law has already been described as being 'accidental', and thus supposedly made of contingent legal facts: Pauwelyn holds that foreign investment law 'was not rationally designed or entered into at one given point in time ... but gradually emerged from a series of small, historically contingent and at times accidental steps'.[35] Other scholars stress the role of 'chance' in the course of the investor-state arbitration system.[36] This makes foreign investment law particularly fit for research on contingency within international law,[37] even though the same could be said about other fields of international law such as human rights or international criminal law.[38] Foreign investment law directly challenges the heart and pillar of international law, ie state sovereignty, in a more profound way than any other branch of international law. Its development could even appear as counter-intuitive from a Westphalian perspective on international law. Would anyone have imagined at the beginning of the nineteenth century that private actors would curb state sovereignty so dramatically 100 years later? Of course the same could be said, *mutatis mutandis*, about human rights.[39] However, unlike human rights, foreign investment law seems to come with continuing puzzlement for external observers,[40] perhaps because it is still subject to existential tensions. These may be due to the fact that, somehow, investment law challenges sovereignty from 'outside' – through the protection of *foreigners'* rights – while human rights challenge it from 'within'. Be that as it may, and admitting that foreign investment law is at least partly counter-intuitive, it may be possible to assert that what is *counter*-intuitive is particularly fit for an exercise in *counter*factuals.

Among the several 'accidental steps', how does one identify those that are truly contingent or those that have had the greatest influence on the current state of foreign investment law? One of the 'accidental steps' that is often distinguished as being foundational is the *AAPL v Sri Lanka* arbitral award.[41] The award is even described by Pauwelyn as a 'silent revolution' or 'game changing' within foreign investment protection.[42] While this arbitral award has had an obvious and direct impact on the evolution of foreign investment law and the incremental course of investor-state arbitration, whether it is a foundational or a marginal fact regarding the course of foreign investment law is not as clear as one might think. While it may at first glance appear as a foundational element without which foreign investment law would not be what it is today, it may also be argued that its substance 'would have happened', sooner or later, since the US BITs already explicitly provided for direct access to arbitral tribunals by private investors on the sole basis of the treaty and for the purpose of judging not contract but treaty violations.[43] In that sense, the *AAPL* sentence may have been

[35] Pauwelyn (n 32) 374.

[36] Poulsen (n 3).

[37] While some critical legal theories perceive foreign investment law as a 'false contingency' and consider 'capitalism' as a determining force, they do so by looking at underlying political forces and ideologies (the 'superstructure'), rather than at the legal system within its social context.

[38] That is what Samuel Moyn does in his book *The Last Utopia* (Samuel Moyn, *The Last Utopia: Human Rights in History* (Harvard University Press 2010)).

[39] ibid.

[40] Pauwelyn (n 32) 372.

[41] *Asian Agricultural Products Ltd (AAPL) v Republic of Sri Lanka*, ICSID Case no ARB/87/3 (Final Award of 27 June 1990).

[42] Pauwelyn (n 32) 397.

[43] See for instance Samuel Asante, Dissenting Opinion, *AAPL v Sri Lanka*, ICSID Case no ARB/87/3 (1991) 6 ICSID Review—Foreign Investment Law Journal 574, 576–577. While the first BIT that provided for compulsory investor-state arbitration was the one concluded by the Netherlands with Indonesia in 1968, the US BITs were the ones that explicitly extended the tribunals' jurisdiction to treaty violations. See Pauwelyn (n 32) 417.

more constrained by other legal elements and less 'accidental' than is usually thought, notwithstanding the fact that there may have been room for another decision.[44]

Other legal and non-legal facts have greatly contributed to shaping foreign investment law as we know it. These elements and possible turning points may reduce the relative impact of the *Barcelona Traction* judgment on the course of foreign investment law. The legal fact which seems to have had the most direct influence on the current foreign investment law—by providing for the legal structure of the investor-state arbitration—is the ICSID Convention. Nine years before the *Barcelona Traction* judgment, in 1961, the World Bank developed the idea of drafting a multilateral instrument for the resolution of individual investment disputes. In 1965, twenty states, among which were both developed and developing states, immediately ratified it. This means that by 1970 the states had already manifested a preference for private arbitral dispute settlement, especially if we consider that Article 27 of the Convention explicitly prohibits the recourse to diplomatic protection in the case where consent for arbitral proceedings has been given. Therefore, it is argued that while it undoubtedly is a turning point, the ICSID Convention appears as a foundational, not a marginal, fact in regards to the development of foreign investment law. It cannot therefore be analysed as a contingent fact. Indeed, it is difficult to imagine that it could have been otherwise since it had been on corporations' and on some capital exporting states' minds since the 1950s, or even earlier, as is shown by Taylor St John in her book.[45] Without it, the whole of investment arbitration would not have emerged or would have emerged in such a scattered way that it would not be the phenomenon that we know today.[46] While the limited scope of this chapter does not allow for their thorough analysis, other legal or 'quasi-legal'[47] elements could equally be considered as turning points, but not necessarily as contingent facts in regards to foreign investment law: the Abs-Shawcross Draft Convention on Investments Abroad,[48] the very first BITs which provided for investor-state arbitration,[49] or even the first arbitral awards dealing with state contracts and opting for international law as the applicable law.[50]

As to the non-legal facts that could also qualify as turning points within the history of foreign investment law, economic globalisation certainly is the one that deserves most attention. It is tightly related to the 'prevailing political economy' that lies behind it, and has been

[44] On the room for another decision, see Pauwelyn (n 32) 415; Emmanuel Gaillard 'Observations on the AAPL Award' (1992) 119 Journal du Droit International 217, 227–29.

[45] Taylor St John, *The Rise of the Investor-State Arbitration: Politics, Law, and Unintended Consequences* (OUP 2018) 129.

[46] We can imagine that investment arbitration would have been limited to contract-based state consent. It is noteworthy that the Abs-Shawcross Draft Convention on Investments Abroad of 1959 did not include investor-state dispute settlement but only 'traditional' interstate arbitration. That was not the case of the version prepared by the Organisation for Economic Co-operation and Development (OECD) a few years later on the basis of the Abs-Shawcross Draft in which ISDS was included.

[47] The word refers here to draft conventions which have never become actual law. While they remain within the realm of fact, their similarity with legal elements is obvious. They would probably compare to the UN General Assembly resolutions which have a 'normative value' but not a binding effect (*Advisory Opinion on the Legality of the Threat or Use of Nuclear Weapons* [1996] ICJ Reports para 70).

[48] The Abs-Shawcross Draft Convention was prepared by the Association for the Promotion and Protection of Private Foreign Investment. It was later taken up by the OECD which transformed it into a Draft Convention on the Protection of Property that has greatly shaped the conclusion of bilateral investment treaties but which has never become a legal instrument in itself.

[49] Concluded on 25 November 1959 by Pakistan and Germany.

[50] For instance *Petroleum Development Ltd v The Sheikh of Abu Dhabi* (1951) 18 ILR 144; *Ruler of Qatar v International Marine Oil Co* (1953) 20 ILR 534.

characterised as a 'determining factor' in the course of foreign investment law.[51] Although the origins of foreign investment law can be dated back to the nineteenth century or even earlier,[52] its expansion and establishment in the second part of the twentieth century must be related to globalisation as a historical and economic fact to which international law could only adapt. Globalisation is certainly not a contingent fact in relation to foreign investment law. It is both an 'essential constraint' in the course of foreign investment law and a fact that it may be difficult to imagine not happening. The intensification of trade exchanges and investment flows has made it necessary to provide international protection for foreign investors. The correlation between globalisation and the recourse to arbitration has been shown beyond the field of investment protection.[53] In that sense, the international protection of foreign investors in itself appears to be a necessity in a world of globalised economy. It appears to be just as inexorable as was the failure of the New International Economic Order (NIEO) which was doomed to disappear given that none of the great industrialised powers supported it.[54] On the contrary, the emergence of the international protection of foreign investors is a result of the 'Great Compact' that has gathered both developed and developing states.[55]

2. The *Barcelona Traction* case as a contingent turning point?

The *Barcelona Traction* case dismissed by the ICJ in 1970 for Belgium's lack of legal standing could be one of those legal facts that is marginal enough to be considered as contingent, but the impact of which is sufficient for it to be considered as a turning point in the course of foreign investment law. In other words, even though *Barcelona Traction* is not necessary to the structure of foreign investment law, it could still be considered as a turning point if it can be shown that it has, indirectly, weighed sufficiently on its evolution.

Contingency has been defined in this chapter as intimately related to causality: the contingent fact that could have changed the course of foreign investment law must be a legal—or non-legal—fact with enough significance to have contributed to shaping the course of that part of law. This is where the distinction between absolute and relative contingency can be useful: is the *Barcelona Traction* judgment an absolutely contingent fact in relation to current foreign investment law? If it were so, it would be irrelevant to examine it for a better understanding of foreign investment law. It would be too marginal or too far away from the structure of foreign investment law to have had any impact. But it is undisputed that there is at least a historical relationship between diplomatic protection and the protection of foreigners' rights since the former has been established through customary rules for the

[51] Josef Ostřanský, in this volume.

[52] Charles Leben, 'Droit International des Investissements: un Survol Historique' in Charles Leben, *Droit International des Investissements et de l'Arbitrage Transnational* (Pedone 2015) 1, 6; see also Neufeld (n 31).

[53] Philippe Fouchard, 'L'Arbitrage et la Mondialisation de l'Économie' in *Philosophie du Droit et Droit Économique: Quel Dialogue? Mélanges en l'Honneur de Gérard Farjat* (Frison-Roche 1999) 381.

[54] For a different analysis of the 'possibilities of the past' through the NIEO, see Ingo Venzke, 'Possibilities of the Past: Histories of the NIEO and the Travails of Critique' (2018) 20 Journal of the History of International Law 263.

[55] W Michael Reisman, 'The Empire Strikes Back: The Struggle to Reshape ISDS' Presentation at the University of Miami (16 February 2017) <https://ssrn.com/abstract=2943514> accessed 1 June 2020.

exclusive purpose of guaranteeing the latter.[56] It is thus worth measuring the impact that *Barcelona Traction* may have had on the course of foreign investment law, the modern form of the protection of foreigners' rights.

Despite extensive literature on the link between the *Barcelona Traction* case and positive foreign investment law, it remains clear that the former is not a central part of the latter. At least, unlike the *AAPL* sentence or the ICSID Convention, the judgment does not appear at first sight as a foundational step within the field. It even seems to run counter to foreign investors' rights.[57] It is at the margins, if not outside, of that branch of international law as is shown by Article 27 of the ICSID Convention that renders the protection of foreign investment through arbitral proceedings incompatible with diplomatic protection. It has been regretted that the *Barcelona Traction* case is never discussed thoroughly in investment cases but treated with a 'dismissive attitude' for being irrelevant,[58] as is well illustrated in the *CMS v Argentina* award.[59] Even though investment tribunals could probably devote more attention to some of the ICJ's reasoning, as a matter of fact, it can hardly be claimed that the *Barcelona Traction* case is a central piece of foreign investment law. However, by indirectly setting diplomatic protection as an—exclusive—'alternative' to investor-state arbitration, the same ICSID Convention establishes an obvious relationship between the two which has been recently stressed in the context of the *Diallo* case before the ICJ.[60] Yet, *Barcelona Traction* has '*counter-intuitively*' boosted foreign investment law and investor-state arbitration through 'showing the States the inadequacy of customary law-making in the area; pushing the law-making resources into treaty-making; and clearly recognising and confirming the rights of States to provide more beneficial treatment to investors through treaty law unhindered by archaic and inappropriate customary law concepts'.[61] The counter-intuitiveness of the *Barcelona Traction* judgment thus seems to echo that of the exponential growth of investor-state arbitration.

[56] Pierre-Marie Dupuy, 'Unification Rather than Fragmentation of International Law? The Case of International Investment Law and Human Rights Law' in Pierre-Marie Dupuy, Ernst-Ulrich Petersmann, and Francesco Francioni (eds), *Human Rights in International Investment Law and Arbitration* (OUP 2009) 45, 47.

[57] See for instance Rosalyn Higgins, 'Aspects of the Case Concerning *Barcelona Traction, Light and Power Company, Ltd*' (1970–1971) 11 Virginia Journal of International Law 341; Richard B Lillich, 'The Rigidity of Barcelona' (1971) 65 American Journal of International Law 522, 552–57; Charles de Visscher, 'La Notion de Référence (Renvoi) au Droit Interne dans la Protection Diplomatique des Actionnaire de Sociétés Anonymes' [1971] Revue Belge de Droit International 1, 6.

[58] Zachary Douglas, 'Can a Doctrine of Precedent be Justified in Investment Treaty Arbitration?' (2010) 25 ICSID Review—Foreign Investment Law Journal 104,108–109; Alain Pellet, 'The Case Law of the ICJ in Investment Arbitration' (2013) 28 ICSID Review—Foreign Investment Law Journal 223, 232.

[59] *CMS Gas Transmission Company v Argentine Republic*, ICSID Case no ARB/01/8 (Decision on Jurisdiction of 17 July 2003) para 42.

[60] Christian J Tams and Antonios Tzanakopoulos, 'Barcelona Traction at 40: The ICJ as an Agent of Legal Development' (2010) 23 Leiden Journal of International Law 781, 790; Kate Parlett, 'Role of Diplomatic Protection in the Protection of Foreign Investments' (2007) 66 Cambridge Law Journal 533; Stephen J Knight and Angus J O'Brien, 'Ahmadou Sadio Diallo (Republic of Guinea v. Democratic Republic of the Congo): Clarifying the Scope of Diplomatic Protection of Corporate and Shareholder Rights' (2008) 9 Melbourne Journal of International Law 151, s IV D; Martins Paparinskis, 'Investment Arbitration and the Law of Countermeasures' (2008) 79 British Year Book of International Law 264, 281–97.

[61] Paparinskis (n 60) 342 (own emphasis); see also Stephen M Schwebel, 'Some Aspects of International Law in Arbitration between States and Aliens' (1986) reproduced in Stephen M Schwebel, *Justice in International Law: Selected Writings of Judge Stephen M. Schwebel* (CUP 1994) 196, 210–11; Frank Berman, 'The Relevance of the Law on Diplomatic Protection in Investment Arbitration' in Federico Ortino and others (eds) *Investment Treaty Law: Current Issues II* (BIICL 2007) 67, 69; *RomPetrol Group N V v Romania*, ICSID Case no ARB/06/3 (Decision on Respondent's Preliminary Objections on Jurisdiction and Admissibility of 18 April 2008) <www.italaw.com/sites/default/files/case-documents/ita0717.pdf> accessed 1 June 2020.

While it is certainly not the only factor that can account for the impressive development of BITs and investment arbitration, *Barcelona Traction* may be considered as a turning point in relation to foreign investment law. Almost fifty years later, the judgment still draws considerable scholarly attention regarding its legacy for shareholders' protection in international law.[62] By its unique position as the sole judgment delivered by the World Court establishing general international law in the field of diplomatic protection, the *Barcelona Traction* judgment may have contributed to dramatically shaping, if not changing, the course of international law at what could be considered a watershed moment, ie the first signs of globalisation through increasing internationalisation of shareholders.[63] Indeed, when the world generalist and permanent Court rejected the possibility for states to resort to diplomatic protection in favour of their nationals who were shareholders of foreign companies, international law had to turn to another solution that allowed for the protection of foreign investors as mere shareholders. It has been argued that the *Barcelona Traction* judgment 'contributed to kick-starting the present recognition of the central role of shareholders as investors under modern international investment law in instruments such as BITs'.[64] A study of over 850 BITs has correlated the *Barcelona Traction* case and treaty-making practice—the conclusion of BITs—and shown that the former directly shaped the scope of foreign investment law in some of its substantive aspects.[65] Thomas Wälde and Abba Kolo draw a more general conclusion when they consider? In considering? considering that the *Barcelona Traction* decision 'confirmed that the ICJ and inter-state litigation was not a suitable method for resolving investment disputes and thus helped to bring about direct, treaty-based investor-state arbitration as we know it now'.[66]

The assumption of the impact of *Barcelona Traction* on foreign investment law must, however, be tested negatively, ie imagining what would have happened if the outcome had been different than the one that we know.

IV. The possible and the likely effects of 'another' *Barcelona Traction*

To further assess the causal link between *Barcelona Traction* and the exponential growth of ISDS, it may be fruitful to proceed to an exercise of imagination in order to investigate what could have happened if the case brought by Belgium had not been dismissed by the ICJ; or, if 1970 were too early, to imagine what could have happened if the ICJ had changed its position in the *Diallo* case in 2007. On the one hand, the declining fate of the institution of

[62] Daniel Müller, *La Protection de l'Actionnaire en Droit International: l'Héritage de la Barcelona Traction* (Pedone 2015) preface; see also Tams and Tzanakopoulos (n 60) 781–800.

[63] It is to be stressed that the position later adopted by the International Law Commission on diplomatic protection in regards to shareholders relies extensively on what had been established by the ICJ. Indeed, the Special Rapporteur on diplomatic protection, John Dugard, declares in his fourth report that *Barcelona Traction* 'dominates all discussion of this topic': John Dugard, Fourth Report on Diplomatic Protection, UN Doc A/CN.4/530 (13 March and 6 June 2003) para 3.

[64] Ian A Laird, 'A Community of Destiny: The Barcelona Traction Case and the Development of Shareholder Rights to Bring Investment Claims' in Todd Weiler (ed), *International Investment Law and Arbitration: Leading Cases From NAFTA, ICSID, Bilateral Treaties and Customary International Law* (Cameron May 2005) 77, 77.

[65] Paul Peters, 'Some Serendipitous Findings in BITs: The Barcelona Traction Case and the Reach of Bilateral Investment Treaties' in Erik Denters and Nico Schrijver (eds), *Reflections on International Law from the Low Countries: In Honour of Paul de Waart* (Martinus Nijhoff 1998) 27.

[66] Thomas Wälde and Abba Kolo, 'Investor-State Disputes: The Interference Between Treaty-Based International Investment Protection and Fiscal Sovereignty' (2007) 35 Intertax 424, 426 n 8.

diplomatic protection as we know it today may not have been the same. It may have flourished. The concept of contingency allows here for a restrained freedom in trying to guess what could have happened. This is clearly an exercise of legal and institutional imagination rather than a legal argument. We could call it a 'juris-fiction'.

What could have happened if the Court had accepted the consideration that general international law allowed for states to exercise diplomatic protection on behalf of their nationals who were mere shareholders of a corporation injured by another state? It may have had more cases brought to it since a significant portion of foreign investors act in host states as shareholders of companies that do not have their nationality.[67] The ICJ has insisted in its 2007 *Diallo* judgment on the 'particular and relatively limited context [in which] the question of protection by substitution might be raised' thus suggesting that very few shareholders would be concerned since the great majority were already provided with standing before arbitral tribunals by BITs. However, this statement refers to the situation in 2007 and not in 1970. Somehow, the judgment of 1970 is partly responsible for this situation: since the path of diplomatic protection was closed to them as mere shareholders, foreign investors had to be provided with another mechanism, ie the investor-state arbitration mechanism inserted in the vast majority of BITs. It is no wonder that the *Barcelona Traction* judgment is seen as a 'friend of investment protection law'.[68]

Indeed, if the ICJ had decided otherwise in 1970, diplomatic protection would not be the dormant, if not dying, legal mechanism that it is today and investor-state arbitration would have been, perhaps not inexistent since it had already been introduced in some bilateral treaties, but probably much less developed. The activity of the ICJ could have grown in a significant manner that could have triggered the necessity for a chamber specialised in diplomatic protection in matters of foreign investment or simply in matters of diplomatic protection. Article 26 of the Statute of the Court mentions as examples, chambers on 'labour cases and cases relating to transit and communications' as technical fields requiring some specific expertise within international law. Foreign investment law would have been just one of those 'technical' fields. We would have had a world permanent judicial institution—comparable to the World Trade Organization dispute settlement system—which would provide a consistent case law where state and public interests would be sufficiently taken into account. Qualifications would certainly not have been an obstacle: the recommendation by the ICJ President that judges refrain from participation in investment arbitration is proof that the expertise of at least some of the judges qualifies them for investment disputes.[69] We would have had a midway before the ambitious Multilateral Investment Court pushed for by the EU and the current chaotic situation which has led to endless discussions on a possible reform of the system.[70] We could imagine that the procedural and political hurdles of diplomatic protection would have led some foreign investors to more easily reach

[67] Gabriel Bottini, 'The Admissibility of Shareholder Claims: Standing, Causes of Action, and Damages' (PhD thesis, University of Cambridge 2017).

[68] Martins Paparinskis, '*Barcelona Traction*: A Friend of Investment Protection Law' (2008) 8 Baltic Yearbook of International Law 105.

[69] Speech of the President of the ICJ Mr Abdulqawi A Yusuf before the UN General Assembly (25 October 2018) <https://www.icj-cij.org/public/files/press-releases/0/000-20181025-PRE-02-00-EN.pdf> accessed 1 June 2020. But see, despite that recommendation, the appointment of current judges in ICSID arbitrations: https://icsid.worldbank.org/cases/case-database/case-detail?CaseNo=ARB/20/22

[70] United Nations Commission on International Trade Law (UNCITRAL) Working Group III on the reform of the investor-state dispute settlement system.

an agreement with the host state. The case law before the specialised chamber of the ICJ would have been less massive than that submitted to ISDS in the last decades, but substantive enough to provide for some guarantee to foreign investors who would not be at the mercy of domestic tribunals. The home states may not have felt the need to systematically include in their BITs dispute settlement proceedings, given that they would have always had the possibility to espouse the claim of one of their nationals in case of gross violations, even for an indirect investment by a shareholder of a foreign company.

Their most important investors could always turn to their home state for diplomatic protection. Of course, the latter is discretionary and not all investments abroad would have qualified for diplomatic protection.[71] But, in turn, this would have lightened the litigating burden on host states. Foreign investors would have been dependent on the will of their home state as to the defence of their interests but this might have avoided some abusive proceedings. Investors may have been less tempted by the chaotic treaty shopping that is nowadays so harshly criticised and which is partly the result of the legal planning of investments in order to gain international legal protection.[72] Investors would have got a 'minimum' protection including diplomatic protection (in its judicial and non-judicial aspects), without the exponential growth of BITs.

Of course, the setting and functioning of a specialised chamber at the ICJ would have been costly, not only for the chancelleries, but also for the United Nations (UN) in case of increasing caseload for the ICJ. One must not forget however that one of the most hotly debated arguments against investor-state arbitration is its cost, particularly for host states faced with a multiplicity of proceedings.[73] Besides, one could imagine that states would have come up with an ingenious solution where the most active foreign investors would have contributed on a permanent basis to support the cost of possible litigation. Such imaginative solutions do exist within international law: in the field of maritime oil pollution, private companies entirely fund the functioning of an intergovernmental organisation, the International Oil Pollution Compensation (IOPC) Funds, whose task is to deal with the damages caused by an accident attributable to any company.[74]

But it must be recalled that if what has just been 'imagined' had lain among the 'possibilities' of international law right before the *Barcelona Traction* judgment, its likelihood is far from granted.

Indeed, however pleasant and thought-provoking it may be, the exercise of 'juris-fiction' must include an assessment of likelihood. Would the impact of the opposite solution have been so important? It is more likely that the admission of the Belgian request would not have changed much for current foreign investment law. The new costs of the proceedings for home states which would have to defend, even in court, the interests of their investors might have outweighed the current costs of arbitral proceedings for the host states.

[71] However, the discretionary character of diplomatic protection may have evolved too, either at the international level as is shown by the discussions that have taken place at the International Law Commission (John Dugard 'Articles on Diplomatic Protection' [2013] United Nations Audiovisual Library of International Law 4), or at the national level as is shown by the inclusion within the Lisbon Treaty of a—rather controversial—right to diplomatic protection (Treaty on the Functioning of the EU art 23).

[72] See the OECD Conference 'Conference on Treaty Shopping and Tools for Investment Treaty Reform' (Paris, March 2018); Jorun Baumgartner, *Treaty Shopping in International Investment Law* (OUP 2016).

[73] UNCITRAL Working Group III (Investor-State Dispute Settlement Reform), Possible Reform of Investor-State Dispute Settlement (ISDS)—Cost and Duration (31 August 2018) A/CN.9/WG.III/WP.153.

[74] Thomas Liebert, 'La Réparation du Préjudice Économique et Environnemental Causé par une Pollution: l'Exemple des FIPOL' in Saïda El Boudouhi (ed), *Les Transports au Prisme du Droit International Public* (Pedone 2019).

While discussions on more equitable cost sharing have emerged over the last years to provide a more 'sustainable' system,[75] the establishment of a mechanism by which foreign investors themselves would pay for the costs that the diplomatic protection would entail for their home states seems unlikely. A similar, yet informal, practice is observed only at the International Tribunal for the Law of the Sea where 'home' states' costs are entirely borne by private actors—shipowners—in prompt release proceedings.[76]

Besides, the IOPC Funds have been set up to cover not litigation fees, but the costs entailed by the reparation of damages caused to the marine environment, according to a pattern of objective responsibility by which damage caused to the marine environment automatically triggers an obligation for the Funds to provide for the remedies. But foreign investment law, with its utterly subjective interests, does not seem to leave any room for an objective responsibility system. Above all, even with such a mechanism, foreign investors would still expect their home states to provide for an alternative to diplomatic protection which would have continued to be seen as too discretionary and political, unless otherwise provided for. As to a special chamber for diplomatic protection or for foreign investment protection within the ICJ, the example of the Chamber for Environmental Matters that the Court created in 1993 is not promising. While states have agreed several times for the convening of a non-specialised chamber as is allowed by the Statute, including in a matter of foreign investments in the *ELSI* case,[77] no state has ever requested that a dispute be dealt with by the Chamber for Environmental Matters in its thirteen years of existence. The ICJ thus decided in 2006 not to hold elections for a bench within the said chamber. The interests at stake in cases of environmental protection and foreign investment law are, however, often not of the same type: one may imagine that when there are, in the shadow of the home state, powerful investors and huge economic interests, states could be expected to be more diligent in enforcing an adequate dispute settlement system.

V. Could the Court have decided otherwise? Probability between law and policy

Could the Court have really decided otherwise, as hindsight shows that more than thirty years later it reasserted its conservative position of 1970 in its 2007 *Diallo* judgment? In other words, is the legal fact '*Barcelona Traction* judgment' really contingent—ie it could have happened like it could have not happened? Or has it been conditioned by the nature and structure of international law and appears as necessary—unavoidable—in the course of international law?

It is time to examine the nature of the constraints that framed the contingent fact. Indeed, once it has been shown that the *Barcelona Traction* judgment was marginal enough and

[75] On the debate about the creation of an advisory centre on international investment law discussed within UNCITRAL Working Group III on the reform, see Karl Sauvant, 'An Advisory Center on International Investment Law: Key Features' (10 September 2019) Academic Forum on ISDS Concept Paper 2019/14 <www.jus.uio.no/pluricourts/english/projects/leginvest/academic-forum/papers/papers/sauvant-advisory-center-isds-af-14-2019.pdf> accessed 1 June 2020.

[76] *'Volga' case (Russian Federation v Australia)* (Prompt Release Proceedings, Judgment of 23 December 2002, Dissenting Op Judge ad hoc Shearer) ITLOS Reports 2002 para 19.

[77] *ELSI* (n 21); Sean D Murphy, 'The ELSI Case: An Investment Dispute at the International Court of Justice' (1991) 16 Yale Journal of International Law 391.

potentially influential in relation to foreign investment law and ISDS, it still remains to be seen whether there was any possibility of the *Barcelona Traction* judgment coming out a different way. Or, in Max Weber's words, the question must be asked whether it was an 'objective possibility'. To answer the question, it is necessary to examine not the aftermath of the judgment but the context within which it was delivered in 1970. That can be taken down to two elements: on the one hand, the law that the Court had to apply (after all the first and main constraint on the judge is the law, however indeterminate it may be); and on the other hand, beyond the applicable law, attention must also be paid to the social context of the judgment.

In the absence of an applicable treaty norm, the Court in the *Barcelona Traction* case had to look at the content of general international law, in that case at customary norms, to determine whether diplomatic protection could be used to defend shareholders' interests when the injury affected the company. In other words, the Court had to look for both a practice and an *opinio juris* that such a rule allowing for the diplomatic protection in favour of mere shareholders did exist. That is where contingency and indeterminacy meet. It may be held that international practice was at the time not 'ripe' enough to provide the substance of a customary rule for the lifting of the corporate veil in order to defend the rights of shareholders affected through their corporation, if only because most foreign investors signed state contracts with the host governments. The Court explains that 'the law on the subject has been formed in a period characterised by an intense conflict of systems and interests'.[78] However, after mentioning 'the important developments of the last half-century', it recognises that 'it may at first sight appear surprising that the evolution of law has not gone further and that no generally accepted rules in the matter have crystallised on the international plane'.[79] This 'surprise' effect is what contributes to making the *Barcelona Traction* case a good example of a 'turning point', just as the 'surprising' or 'accidental' exponential growth of foreign investment law is what makes it particularly suitable for a study on contingency.

The Court does of course not go as far as to say that the non-recognition of a general rule allowing for diplomatic protection in favour of shareholders is an 'accident' within the course of international law, but one may legitimately have that feeling in reading the judgment. What is most striking is that the Court, as it often does, introduces the absence of a general rule as if it were something that simply lay out before it, instead of being the result of a process in which the Court itself plays a decisive and creative role. Therefore, the Court could have decided otherwise on the basis of the applicable law: Article 38 of the ICJ Statute 'only' requires evidence of state practice and *opinio juris* for the recognition of a customary norm. This secondary norm is sufficiently indeterminate to leave enough leeway for a judge to decide either way in the presence of an undeniable emerging practice.

Even admitting with the Court that 1970 was too early for a general rule to emerge for the protection of shareholders through substitution, the same cannot be said in 2007. Indeed, the confirmation of the conservative position of the Court was harshly criticised and discussed.[80] The Court has in 2007 enough practice to decide otherwise. Instead, it opts for

[78] *Barcelona Traction* (n 22) 89–90.

[79] ibid 89.

[80] See the debate between Alain Pellet and Daniel Müller in Daniel Müller (ed), *La Protection de l'Actionnaire en Droit International: l'Héritage de la Barcelona Traction* (Pedone 2015). Pellet considers that the position of the ICJ, defended by Müller is excessively conservative. See also for a criticism of the *Barcelona Traction* solution, Francisco Orrego Vicuña, *International Dispute Settlement in an Evolving Global Society –Constitutionalization, Accessibility,*

considering that the extensive evidence provided by Guinea in favour of the shareholder protection 'is not sufficient to show that there has been a change in the customary rules of diplomatic protection'.[81] The Court immediately adds, quite ambiguously and perhaps inadvertently, that 'it could *equally* show the contrary'.[82] Match point. The practice required by the indeterminate applicable rule could be interpreted either way. The Court implicitly admits that the constraint is not legal but social. It comes from outside the law. Thus, the *Barcelona Traction* principle, as reasserted in the *Diallo* case, can be seen as a contingent legal fact in that it is the result of a political choice that was open to the Court. The constraint coming from the law is only relative.

As to the social context that could be more of an essential constraint, it can be summed up in the priority that both developing and developed states seemed to give to arbitral proceedings over diplomatic protection. In 1970, states had just adopted and ratified the ICSID Convention in which they had explicitly marginalised diplomatic protection. They were thus sending a clear message to the Court that they did not wish diplomatic protection to be strengthened through the relaxing of the conditions of its activation. Both groups, although for different reasons, wished to set aside diplomatic protection as regards foreign investors.[83] Developing states disliked it because they had too often been victims of political and even military pressure under the disguise of diplomatic protection on behalf of national investors. The Calvo Doctrine was elaborated by Latin American states with the purpose of setting aside diplomatic protection. Developed states were driven by another aim: their investors were demanding a more efficient and less political mechanism which would make them less dependent on their home states. It was in this political context that the Court decided the *Barcelona Traction* case. Was it an essential or a relative constraint? Given that the *Barcelona Traction* solution was voted by fourteen to one and the *Diallo* confirmation adopted by fifteen to one, and despite several separate opinions, particularly in *Barcelona Traction*,[84] it seems difficult to imagine that it could have really been otherwise and even that it could evolve in the near future, unless a sufficient number of states adopt a formal position in a treaty, for instance.

According to some recent research, diplomatic protection seems up in the air again as a remedy for the many flaws of ISDS.[85] This is backed up by all the recent draft treaties that scale back investment arbitration for foreign investors.[86] Through a revival of the remnants of diplomatic protection, the possibility of the past could well become a reality in the future provided some adaptations are made. Indeed, while it is unlikely that a resurgence of diplomatic protection as an alternative to ISDS would take place at the ICJ, given the huge hurdle

Privatization (CUP 2004) 42; Christoph Schreuer, 'Shareholder Protection in International Investment Law' (2005) 3 Transnational Dispute Management.

[81] *Diallo* (n 1) 90.

[82] ibid (my emphasis).

[83] Olivier de Frouville, 'Affaire *Ahmadou Sadio Diallo* (République de Guinée contre République Démocratique du Congo). Exceptions préliminaires: Le Roman Inachevé de la Protection Diplomatique' (2007) 53 Annuaire Français de Droit International 291, 315.

[84] On the absence of homogeneity in the voting of *Barcelona Traction*, see Peters (n 65).

[85] Rodrigo Polanco, *The Return of the Home State to Investor-State Disputes: Bringing Back Diplomatic Protection?* (CUP 2019).

[86] The recently renegotiated North American Free Trade Agreement (or United States-Mexico-Canada Agreement) is perhaps the most conspicuous example. The recent positions taken by several developing states at UNCITRAL Working Group III on the reform of the investment arbitration also point in the same direction.

of the amendment procedure of its Statute, it may be an easier task to create an entirely new multilateral institution, a 'world investment court' competent for interstate investment disputes. That would be a different path than the one currently pushed for at UNCITRAL by actors like the EU. The latter aims more at institutionalising, and thus saving, ISDS, than at putting forward a radical alternative recovered from the past.

25

From a Fortuitous Transplant to a Fundamental Principle of Law?

The Doctrine of Legitimate Expectations and the Possibilities of a Different Law

*Josef Ostřanský**

I. Introduction

The doctrine of legitimate expectations (LEs) is now considered a backbone of international investment law (IIL), particularly of the fair and equitable treatment standard (FET). Investors argue virtually all investment claims by reference to this notion, and many tribunals refer to it as the most important principle under FET.[1] The mainstream IIL literature has spilled a lot of ink on doctrinally justifying its pride of place in IIL.[2] We find works justifying the notion of legitimate expectations by reference to unilateral declarations of the state,[3] arguing that the notion is a general principle of law,[4] or simply deriving it through teleological interpretation of investment treaties by arbitral tribunals.[5] However, none of these approaches is entirely coherent even on its own terms.[6] Yet, currently it is hard to

* This chapter was finalised with the support of the Swiss National Science Foundation, Early Postdoc Mobility Grant (no. P2GEP1_188335).

[1] Eg *MTD Equity Sdn Bhd and MTD Chile SA v Republic of Chile*, ICSID Case no ARB/01/7 (Award of 25 May 2004) para 180 (*MTD v Chile); CMS Gas Transmission Company v The Republic of Argentina*, ICSID Case no ARB/01/8 (Award of 12 May 2005) para 279 (*CMS v Argentina*); *Azurix Corp v The Argentine Republic*, ICSID Case no ARB/01/12 (Award of 14 July 2006) para 372; *Electrabel SA v Republic of Hungary*, ICSID Case no ARB/07/19 (Decision on Jurisdiction, Applicable Law and Liability of 30 November 2012) part VII para 75 (*Electrabel v Hungary*); *William Ralph Clayton, William Richard Clayton, Douglas Clayton, Daniel Clayton and Bilcon of Delaware Inc v Government of Canada*, PCA Case no 2009-04 (Award on Jurisdiction and Liability of 17 March 2015) United Nations Commission on International Trade Law (UNCITRAL) (*Bilcon v Canada*).

[2] Eg Francisco Orrego Vicuña, 'Regulatory Authority and Legitimate Expectations: Balancing the Rights of the State and the Individual under International Law in a Global Society' (2003) 5 International Law FORUM du Droit International 188; Elizabeth Snodgrass, 'Protecting Investors' Legitimate Expectations—Recognizing and Delimiting a General Principle' (2006) 21 ICSID Review—Foreign Investment Law Journal 1; Rudolf Dolzer and Christoph Schreuer, *Principles of International Investment Law* (2nd edn, OUP 2012) 145–60; Michele Potestà, 'Legitimate Expectations in Investment Treaty Law: Understanding the Roots and the Limits of a Controversial Concept' (2013) 28 ICSID Review—Foreign Investment Law Journal 88; Martins Paparinskis, *The International Minimum Standard and Fair and Equitable Treatment* (OUP 2013) 251–59; Jonathan Bonnitcha, *Substantive Protection under Investment Treaties: A Legal and Economic Analysis* (CUP 2014) 167–94.

[3] Eg W Michael Reisman and Mahnoush H Arsanjani, 'The Question of Unilateral Governmental Statements as Applicable Law in Investment Disputes' in Pierre-Marie Dupuy and others (eds), *Common Values in International Law: Essays in Honour of Christian Tomuschat* (NP Engel Verlag 2006) 409.

[4] Eg Potestà (n 2).

[5] Stephen Fietta, 'Expropriation and the "Fair and Equitable" Standard: The Developing Role of Investors' "Expectations" in International Investment Arbitration' (2006) 23 Journal of International Arbitration 375; *MTD v Chile* (n 1) para 180; *CMS v Argentina* (n 1) para 279.

[6] For a critical overview of various doctrinal justifications see Josef Ostřanský, 'An Exercise in Equivocation: A Critique of Legitimate Expectations as a General Principle of Law under the Fair and Equitable Treatment Standard'

Josef Ostřanský, *From a Fortuitous Transplant to a Fundamental Principle of Law?* In: *Contingency in International Law*. Edited by: Ingo Venzke and Kevin Jon Heller, Oxford University Press. © The Several Contributors 2021. DOI: 10.1093/oso/9780192898036.003.0025

dispute that the doctrine of LEs is part of the modern canon of IIL. Open any recent textbook of IIL and you will find discussion on LEs as one of its core principles. Some authors view this development as a 'logical and practical necessity' which is 'useful and appropriate in the law governing investor-state relations'.[7] One tribunal went as far as stating that 'the most important function of the fair and equitable treatment standard is the protection of the investor's reasonable and legitimate expectations'.[8]

However, if one takes a step back, one may see that the notion of legitimate expectations simply appeared in early investment cases 'out of thin air'. After that, it was picked up and rationalised by later arbitral tribunals and scholarship. In this contribution, I adopt this perspective on the emergence of LEs not as logical and necessary, but rather as a contingent event.

At the same time, this contribution will argue that, while LEs' appearance in IIL practice may be viewed as contingent, its ascendance into the principal doctrine of substantive IIL with its specific parameters is neither entirely accidental nor random. The use and parameters of the doctrine have been allowed and facilitated by a specific historical context in which the notion became prominent. In this specific historical context it is: first, the indeterminate and semantically ambiguous legal form of IIL obligations which allows for a multiplicity of legal contents to be ascribed to those obligations; second, it is a particular political economy that the important actors project at a given historical period through IIL practice, which fosters a particular version of substantive IIL.

The consequence of this argument can be appreciated at two levels. First, it can be argued that even without the contingent ascendance of the notion of LEs, the field of IIL would likely have taken up a similar substantive trajectory. This is because the agents of IIL endowed with crucial capital could channel and accommodate the prevailing political economy through other international law concepts, doctrines, and techniques of similar malleability.[9] Second, this argument allows for the asking of questions about how a more substantial change in the regime might be effected, instead of merely reforming certain aspects of the regime without affecting its current premises, structure, substance, and teleology.

The chapter will proceed as follows. Section II will present the emergence of the doctrine of LEs in the practice and scholarship of IIL. By focusing on the political economy and form of the current IIL, section III will argue that it is unlikely that the practice of IIL would be much different without the emergence of LEs. Concluding section IV will examine the consequences of this argument on the possibilities of change and adaptation in the global regime of IIL.

By looking at the micro-level of a technical legal doctrine, this contribution seeks to explain the contingent emergence of the doctrine of LEs without siding with either the formalist accounts stressing the legal necessity and correctness of the turn to LEs or anti-formalist accounts reducing the law to the projection of extra-legal power relations. By doing so, the contribution underlines the difficulties in articulating plausibly what would

in Andrea Gattini and others (eds), *General Principles of Law and International Investment Arbitration* (Brill | Nijhoff 2018) 344.

[7] Snodgrass (n 2) 54, 57.
[8] *Electrabel v Hungary* (n 1) part VII(4) para 7.75.
[9] By agents with crucial capital, I mean chiefly arbitrators, counsel, but also commentators writing on IIL, and governmental and international organisation policy-makers.

have made a difference in a particular legal regime. These difficulties lead to questioning that some of the current reform initiatives will bear fruit in substantially changing the regime. The efforts must be equally directed at the change in the prevailing political economy and its ideational and material structures and practices. This is of course no small feat, but other reform attempts will most likely merely accommodate the critique and reproduce the existing underlying political economic arrangements.

II. The contingent emergence of the doctrine of legitimate expectations

Despite the numerous scholarly accounts justifying the emergence of the doctrine of LEs as a logical (and in this sense, necessary) application of investment treaties, one can also look at the emergence as a historically contingent event. Analysing IIL practice on LEs, one can see that the doctrine became part of the IIL toolkit through a rather fortuitous reference to expectations in early investment treaty arbitration cases. These early cases referred to investor's expectations in a non-technical sense. As will be discussed below, these cases did not expand on legal justifications for the reference to or relevance of the investor's expectations apart from a general reference to good faith.[10] Nevertheless, later cases and scholarship referred to the early case law as legal authority, and provided the necessary *ex post* juridical justification of the doctrine through legal reasoning.

1. Fair and equitable treatment and investors' expectations: recent beginnings

It should be stressed that cases referring to or applying the doctrine of LEs have done so in the context of interpretation and application of the obligation to provide FET—a notoriously open-textured and indeterminate standard. Over the last two decades, FET has developed from a seldom, if at all, negotiated provision[11] into a standard with breath-taking breadth.[12] This is despite the fact that the treaty formulations have hardly changed.[13] It has become a ubiquitous claim in investment arbitration. It can safely be said that claims under FET are the most successful investment claims.[14]

[10] For a detailed legal analysis of the early treaty arbitration jurisprudence on LEs, see Ostřanský (n 6) 370–76.

[11] Eg Scheuer's expert statement in *Wintershall Aktiengesellschaft v Argentine Republic*, ICSID Case no ARB/04/14 (Award of 8 December 2008) para 85.

[12] See the numerous monographs on FET, eg Paparinskis (n 2); Ioana Tudor, *The Fair and Equitable Treatment Standard in the International Law of Foreign Investment* (OUP 2008); Roland Kläger, *'Fair and Equitable Treatment' in International Investment Law* (CUP 2011).

[13] The new generation of treaties is clear in linking FET to the customary international law minimum standard: eg Trans-Pacific Partnership (text as of 26 Jan 2016) chapter 9, art 9.6. Some newer treaties seem to limit this standard denial of justice only, eg Morocco-Nigeria Bilateral Investment Treaty (signed on 3 December 2016) art 7(2)a; while others recognise that there is also a substantive element to it: eg EU-Vietnam Free Trade Agreement, chapter II, art 14(2), which in addition to denial of justice and due process protection includes manifest arbitrariness, targeted discrimination, abusive treatment, such as coercion, abuse of power, or similar bad faith conduct.

[14] For recent statistics see UNCTAD, 'Investment Dispute Settlement Navigator' (*Investment Policy Hub*) <https://investmentpolicy.unctad.org/investment-dispute-settlement> accessed 14 October 2019.

The first investment treaty arbitration case to refer to investor's expectations was *Metalclad v Mexico*; a well-known early NAFTA chapter 11 case where an investment into a landfill was defeated by non-granting of municipal permits, despite federal assurances. The Tribunal in that case stated:

> [A]ll relevant requirements should be capable of being readily known to all affected investors ... there should be no room for doubt or uncertainty ... Once central authorities become aware of any scope of uncertainty in this connection, it is their duty to ensure that the correct position is properly determined ... Metalclad was entitled to rely on the representations of federal officials and to believe that it was entitled to continue its construction of the landfill. ... Metalclad was merely acting prudently and in the full expectation that the permit would be granted.[15]

The case stands for a sweeping proposition that LEs exist whenever a state official advises an investor on the content of law and even requires officials to dispel possible uncertainties. One commentator mentioned that outside of the context when the body consulted is tasked with the official authoritative interpretation, one can hardly think of a commercial or administrative relationship in which one party has to act as legal counsel for the other, or in which one party had to rely wholly on legal advice from the other.[16] The Tribunal seemed to assume that the entitlement to have the expectations protected stems from the subjective expectation itself. The Tribunal explained that this entitlement is required by the obligation of transparency which is part of FET.[17]

The tribunal in *Metalclad* was of high calibre. The Tribunal's president was Sir Elihu Lauterpacht, a towering figure in international law, whereas the wing arbitrators too were of important stature and reputation. Benjamin Civiletti was a former US Attorney General who appeared before the ICJ in the *Tehran Hostage* case.[18] José Luis Siqueiros, a professor at Universidad Iberoamericana in Mexico, was a former President of the Inter-American Juridical Committee of the Organization of American States.[19] Sir Elihu, in particular, left an important legacy in the field of IIL, as he was a crucial figure in the drafting of important twentieth-century documents aiming at the codification of IIL, such as the Abs-Shawcross Draft on Protection of Foreign Investment and the OECD Draft Convention on Investment Abroad.[20] His ideas, informed by the experience of the nationalisation of the Anglo-Iranian Oil Company in the 1950s, contributed in important ways to, for instance, the creation of

[15] *Metalclad Corporation v The United Mexican States*, ICSID Case no ARB(AF)/97/1 (Award of 30 August 2000) paras 76, 89 (*Metalclad v Mexico*).

[16] Christopher Campbell, 'House of Cards: The Relevance of Legitimate Expectations under Fair and Equitable Treatment Provisions in Investment Treaty Law' (2013) 30 Journal of International Arbitration 361, 366.

[17] Interestingly, the decision was partly annulled on the grounds that the NAFTA chapter 11 does not include a stand-alone obligation of transparency, which the tribunal read into Article 1105 via reference to Article 102(1). *The United Mexican States v Metalclad Corp*, Supreme Court of British Columbia [2001] BCSC 664 (2 May 2001).

[18] 'Legends in the Law: Benjamin R. Civiletti' (*DC Bar Report*, December/January 2019); United States Diplomatic and Consular Staff in Tehran (*United States of America v Iran*), Verbatim Record (1979) Oral Arguments on the Request for the Indication of Provisional Measures, Minutes of the Public Sittings, 15.

[19] International Council for Commercial Arbitration, Advisory Members <www.arbitration-icca.org/about/governing-board/ADVISORY-MEMBERS/Jose_Luis_Siqueiros.html> accessed 14 October 2019.

[20] Yuliya Chernykh, 'The Gust of Wind: The Unknown Role of Sir Elihu Lauterpacht in the Drafting of the Abs-Shawcross Draft Convention' in Stephan Schill and others (eds), *International Investment Law and History* (Edward Elgar 2018) 241; Squire Law Library, 'Eminent Scholars Archive, Sir Elihu Lauterpacht', <www.squire.law.cam.ac.uk/eminent-scholars-archive/professor-sir-elihu-lauterpacht> accessed 14 October 2019.

the modern mechanism of investor-state treaty-based arbitration and the emergence of umbrella clauses.[21] Additionally, serving as a president of the World Bank Administrative Tribunal from 1996 to 1998, he decided cases which operated with the notion of legitimate expectations, although in an entirely different legal context.[22] Importantly, however, apart from a passing reference to investors' expectations, the Tribunal did not apply anything resembling a doctrine, principle or a rule of LEs.

The second case alluding to expectations also dealt with revocation of a permit to operate a landfill in Mexico. The *Tecmed v Mexico*[23] tribunal divined a standard that has been criticised as an ideal governance programme and which, similarly as in *Metalclad*, was not even applied in the case (because the Tribunal found a violation of procedural propriety).[24] A far-reaching conception of LEs, unsupported by any authority apart from good faith is showed in the oft-cited quote:

> [G]ood faith principle established by international law, requires the Contracting Parties to provide to international investments treatment that does not affect the basic expectations that were taken into account by the foreign investor to make the investment. The foreign investor expects the host State to act in a consistent manner, free from ambiguity and totally transparently in its relations with the foreign investor, so that it may know beforehand any and all rules and regulations that will govern its investments, as well as the goals of the relevant policies and administrative practices or directives, to be able to plan its investment and comply with such regulations.[25]

Metalclad and *Tecmed*'s sweeping dicta were later picked up by other cases, and referred to as authority supporting the principle of LEs, although the two cases in fact had not applied the protection of LEs to the cases at hand.[26]

It was not until the case of *Thunderbird v Mexico* that the doctrine of LEs was actually applied in investment treaty arbitration.[27] *Thunderbird*, in particular Wälde´s separate

[21] Chernykh (n 20); Anthony Sinclair, 'The Origins of the Umbrella Clause in the International Law of Investment Protection' (2004) 20 Arbitration International 411.

[22] Eg *Joseph Lopez v IBRD*, World Bank Administrative Tribunal Decision no 147 (14 May 1996). The case dealt with the question of whether Lopez's service was properly terminated by the Bank for unsatisfactory performance. Lauterpacht found that the delay of the Bank's review of Lopez's objection 'infringed upon his procedural rights and his legitimate expectation to have a speedy disposition of his complaints (para 54)'. As a side note, one of the vice presidents of the Tribunal deciding on the Lopez case was the late Francisco Orrego Vicuña, who later became an important arbitrator in many investor-state treaty disputes and one of the early scholars justifying reference to legitimate expectations in arbitral practice. Orrego Vicuña (n 2).

[23] *Técnicas Medioambientales Tecmed, SA v The United Mexican States*, ICSID Case no ARB (AF)/00/2 (Award of 29 May 2003) (*Tecmed v Mexico*). The composition of the *Tecmed* tribunal was also interesting. The Tribunal was presided over by the former Secretary General of the International Chamber of Commerce Court of Arbitration, an expert in private international law and commercial arbitration, Argentine professor Horacio Grigera Naón. The other two arbitrators were, José Carlos Fernandez Rosa, professor of private international law at Universidad Complutense in Madrid and later a member of l'Institut de Droit International, and Carlos Bernal Verea, a private practitioner in Mexico, who later became a professor at Instituto Tecnológico Autónomo de México in Mexico City.

[24] Zachary Douglas, 'Nothing if Not Critical for Investment Treaty Arbitration: Occidental, Eureko and Methanex' (2006) 22 Arbitration International 27, 28.

[25] *Tecmed v Mexico* (n 23) para 154.

[26] Eg *Bayindir Insaat Turizm Ticaret Ve Sanayi AS v Islamic Republic of Pakistan*, ICSID Case no ARB/03/29 (Award of 27 August 2009) paras 179–80; *MTD v Chile* (n 1) paras 114–15; *LG&E Energy Corp, LG&E Capital Corp, and LG&E International, Inc v Argentine Republic*, ICSID Case no ARB/02/1 (Decision on Liability of 3 October 2006) para 127 (*LG&E v Argentina*); *Saluka Investments BV v The Czech Republic*, UNCITRAL (Partial Award of 17 March 2006) para 302 (*Saluka v Czech Republic*).

[27] *International Thunderbird Gaming Corporation v The United Mexican States*, UNCITRAL (Award of 26 January 2006) (*Thunderbird v Mexico*).

opinion, nodded to *Tecmed* and *Metalclad*, but also expended substantial efforts to argue that LEs are a general principle of law. Albert Jan van den Berg, a renowned expert on the New York Convention with extensive practice in commercial and investment arbitration, presided over the Tribunal, with Agustín Portal Ariosa, a Mexican private practitioner who had worked for the Mexican government, and the already mentioned late Thomas Wälde serving as co-arbitrators. Thomas Wälde, who penned the influential separate opinion, was a prominent person in the field of investment treaty arbitration since its emergence as a booming field of practice. Former UN Inter-Regional Advisor on Petroleum and Mineral Legislation, a seasoned UN official, international law practitioner and academic, who worked with Detlev Vagts, Richard Baxter, and Rosalyn Higgins, Wälde came to prominence in the IIL community as someone who created important platforms for exchange of opinions among the constituencies interested in IIL. He set up the Centre for Energy, Petroleum and Mineral Law and Policy at the University of Dundee, but more importantly, he established OGEMID,[28] an influential listserv connecting actors in the emerging IIL community of practitioners and academics. In addition, he was an active commentator on new developments in IIL, arbitration and oil and gas in the Transnational Dispute Settlement (TDM), an online journal on the just mentioned matters.[29] Through these activities Wälde created highly influential venues for the exchange of information among like-minded actors with an interest in the field of IIL.

In his separate opinion, Wälde argued that LEs are a 'self-standing subcategory and independent basis for a claim'.[30] Wälde's comparative review of European Union law, national administrative law systems, as well as World Trade Organization jurisprudence, lead him to argue the existence and validity of the doctrine of LEs in IIL, while he admitted that its exact contours are not yet clear. He also claimed that international law has long applied the doctrine of LEs of the kind applied by modern investment tribunals.[31] Upon closer look, however, none of Wälde's references really have much in common with the conception of LEs as we know it in IIL today. For instance, *Schufeldt*, to start, was not about an illegal contract later reneged on; this was merely a defence put forward by Guatemala. The arbitrator held the contract valid and the repudiation decree was held as an internationally unlawful sovereign interference into a contract.[32] Similarly, *Aminoil* and *Amoco* referred to LEs only as a consideration applied to the calculation of damages, in order to help establish what could be a reasonably foreseeable profit.

Be that as it may, already in the early 2000s, IIL scholars (many of whom also practitioners in the field) started publishing articles explaining and justifying the application of LEs as a doctrine of IIL,[33] sometimes speaking of its emergence as a 'logical and practical

[28] 'About OGEMID', (*Transnational Dispute Management*) <www.transnational-dispute-management.com/ogemid/> accessed 14 October 2019.

[29] An impressive list of his commentaries and short articles spanning wide range of topics related to IIL and arbitration published in TDM can be found at 'Professor Thomas Wälde' (*Transnational Dispute Management*) <www.transnational-dispute-management.com/journal-author-articles.asp?key=6> accessed 14 October 2019.

[30] *Thunderbird v Mexico* (n 27) Separate Opinion of Thomas Wälde para 37.

[31] He referred to *Shufeldt Claim (Guatemala, USA)* (24 July 1930) [1949] United Nations Reports of International Arbitral Awards 2, 1079 (*Schufeldt Claim*); *Kuwait v The American Independent Oil Company (AMINOIL)* (1982) 21 ILM 976 para 149; *Amoco International Finance Corp v Iran* (1987) 15 Iran-US Claims Tribunal 189.

[32] *Schufeldt Claim* (n 32) 1088. Alternatively, the circumstances of the *Schufeldt* case may be viewed as an example of estoppel precluding Guatemala's defence of illegality. Derek Bowett, 'Estoppel Before International Tribunals and its Relation to Acquiescence' (1957) 33 British Yearbook of International Law 176, 186.

[33] Eg Orrego Vicuña (n 2); Snodgrass (n 2); Potestà (n 2).

necessity'.[34] By the 2010s, LEs were established as the most important aspect of FET, and thus arguably of substantive IIL.[35] This is despite the fact that most of the legal justifications suffer from important flaws and leave many questions unanswered.[36] Few commentators have pointed to the problematic juridical nature of the application of the doctrine of LEs in the investment context;[37] some of them, while clearly recognising the doctrinal inconsistency of applying LEs within the context of FET, admitted that their usage in arbitral practice is now well established.[38]

The bottom line of this section is that despite its contingent emergence in the early cases, LEs are now considered an established part of the legal toolkit of IIL—what is essentially contingent looks natural, automatic, and necessary. However, despite this contingency, would IIL be really different without LEs? I argue in the negative, and the next section develops this argument.

III. The law would not be that different without legitimate expectations

Histories of IIL show that actors in influential positions and institutions made choices that were partly the result of their own agency, but were also framed by discursive frameworks, normative and structural features of international law, personal experiences, prevailing underlying political economy, institutional, and resource constraints, etc.[39] As Susan Marks put it, 'things can be, and quite frequently are, contingent without being random, accidental, or arbitrary'.[40] What we now consider an established canon of IIL could have been different if these actors had decided differently. But their decisions were situated against the background of the underlying political, economic, and social circumstances that these actors did not choose, as well as against international law's constraining yet pliable normative and institutional structures.

This chapter emphasises two elements of this background framework, which I view as the most relevant for the appreciation of the role of LEs in the current version of IIL. One factor points in the direction of allowing greater agency, the other points in the direction of constraining the exercise of this agency. Those factors are (i) the semantic ambiguity and structural indeterminacy of investment treaty law, and (ii) the political economy prevailing at the time of the emergence of LEs. Whereas the indeterminacy of IIL would suggest many possible contents of legal obligations, the prevailing politico-economic dynamics make intelligible why a particular version of LEs has arisen and help explain why other doctrines and techniques from the international law toolbox could have achieved similar results.

[34] Snodgrass (n 2) 54–56.

[35] Eg *Electrabel v Hungary* (n 1) part VII para 75: 'It is widely accepted that the most important function of the fair and equitable treatment standard is the protection of the investor's reasonable and legitimate expectations'.

[36] See Ostřanský (n 6).

[37] Eg Campbell (n 16).

[38] Paparinskis (n 2) 259.

[39] Eg Taylor St John, *The Rise of Investor-State Arbitration* (OUP 2018); Quinn Slobodian, *Globalists: The End of Empire and The Birth of Neoliberalism* (Harvard University Press 2018); Ntina Tzouvala, 'The Ordo-Liberal Origins of Modern International Investment Law: Constructing Competition on a Global Scale' in John D Haskell and Akbar Rasulov (eds), *New Voices and New Perspectives in International Economic Law* (Springer 2020) 37.

[40] Susan Marks, 'False Contingency' (2009) 62 Current Legal Problems 1, 2.

1. The semantic ambiguity and structural indeterminacy of IIL sources

The generally open-ended and indeterminate nature of international law sources is a well-established proposition in international legal scholarship.[41] The language of investment treaty standards is particularly known for suffering from substantial indeterminacy. This is evidenced by various conclusions as to the content of investment treaty obligations that have occurred in the jurisprudence and scholarship of IIL and that are considered legally plausible. The interpretation of the open-textured obligations of international investment agreements thus allows tribunals to project the dominant political economy through semantically ambiguous language.[42]

The obligation to provide FET in particular is inherently open-ended.[43] On the one hand, this indeterminacy may be used as an argument that any of the conclusions on the spectrum of plausibility can be adopted by an arbitral tribunal. In this sense, the fact that the early cases applied rather expansive conceptions of legitimate expectations can be viewed as an accidental event. Some authors have argued that the current IIL regime is indeed a result of a panoply of random and accidental events and individual free-floating decisions.[44] However, it would be an indefensible position to contend that anything goes in arguing what is the correct interpretation and application of FET. I will return to this point when discussing why only certain conceptions of LEs have been adopted, and not others, and why the fact that it was only those conceptions still matters little for the global trajectory of IIL over the last three decades.

On the other hand, the toolkit of international law techniques has been deployed to show that there is specific technical content to the obligation of FET by linking it to some general abstract principle, policy or purpose.[45] This is what legal doctrinal scholarship has by and large been providing to the activity of law-applying organs—reasoned elaboration of law which is purposive, generalising, and idealising.[46] However, most of these doctrinal accounts fail in explaining the whole of IIL practice without siding with one or only some of the actually existing interpretations: there are always some 'wrong' international law interpretations. This means there is little possibility to reconcile all the existing interpretations by a unifying principle, as they all start from different assumptions or emphasise different principles or purposes.[47]

[41] This is no place to discuss the varieties of the indeterminacy thesis in legal scholarship, such as American legal realism, structural indeterminacy, linguistic indeterminacy, critical legal studies, Marxism, TWAIL, etc; see eg Cameron Miles, 'Indeterminacy' in Jean d'Aspremont and Sahib Singh (eds), *Concepts for International Law* (Edward Elgar 2019) 447. Most typically Martti Koskenniemi, *From Apology to Utopia: The Structure of International Legal Argument* (CUP 2005); David Kennedy, 'When Renewal Repeats: Thinking Against the Box' (2000) 32 New York Journal of International Law and Politics 335, 404–408; Robert Knox, 'Marxism, International Law, and Political Strategy' (2009) 22 Leiden Journal of International Law 413.

[42] See III.2.

[43] FET seems to comport both to semantic indeterminacy as 'penumbra' in the Hartian sense; HLA Hart, 'Positivism and the Separation of Law and Morals' (1957-1958) 71 Harvard Law Review 593, 606–15; as well as to structural indeterminacy as understood by Kennedy and Koskenniemi.

[44] Joost Pauwelyn, 'At the Edge of Chaos? Foreign Investment Law as a Complex Adaptive System, How It Emerged and How It Can Be Reformed' (2014) 29 ICSID Review—Foreign Investment Law Journal 372. Pauwelyn's conclusions have been challenged on historical grounds by various authors such as St John (n 39).

[45] Paparinskis (n 2); Todd Weiler, *The Interpretation of International Investment Law: Equality, Discrimination and Minimum Standards of Treatment in Historical Context* (Martinus Nijhoff 2013).

[46] Roberto Mangabeira Unger, *The Critical Legal Studies Movement: Another Time, A Greater Task* (Verso 2015) 16.

[47] Koskenniemi (n 41) 59–67; similarly, Pierre Schlag, *The Enchantment of Reason* (Duke University Press 1998).

In other words, traditional doctrinal accounts present their specific solutions behind the veil of more general and abstract legal notions, which are indeed incontestable in the abstract. But there is always another competing principle, value, or goal which may lead to another resolution. Who would say that it is bad to protect investors' legitimate expectations?[48] At the same time, legitimate expectations must have limits. They must be balanced against the state's legitimate interest in regulating for the public purpose.[49] Protecting investor's legitimate expectations allows investors to use their economic resources efficiently and thus allows economic development.[50] Stability of the legal framework is paramount to FET,[51] and equally, it is an important element in the rule of law, hence legitimate expectations must be protected.[52] Yet, the investors must take cognisance of the fact that the regulatory environment is bound to change.[53] These various and somewhat stylized legal propositions about FET and LEs are but a sample of existing justifications and as such are simplifying. The general point is that virtually all cases eventually justify their specific conclusions by reference to a general legal principle, rule, or purpose, or by limiting the rule through an exception stemming from other equally abstract and important principles, and by doing so these accounts dismiss the competing interpretations that start from different principles, assumptions, or starting points.[54] The doctrine of LEs thus offers a terrain for a useful application of the basic tenets of classical critical legal studies.[55] We can also see that there is Koskenniemi's oscillation between ascending (apologetic)[56] and descending (utopian)[57] international law arguments at play here.

What is common to both of these approaches (ie the approach stressing the entirely accidental nature of IIL, and the traditional doctrinal approaches struggling over the correct and necessary interpretation) is that they indirectly justify the status quo and allow for limited possibility of change. In the case of the former, presenting existing IIL as entirely accidental delegitimises and discourages the efforts to change it from the outset, because we cannot ever know what our interventions will lead to.[58] In the case of the latter, they present the existing regime as a rational design stemming from a higher-level principle or deployed for an abstract cognisable purpose; the regime's outcomes are perceived necessary, logical, and desirable and as such serve an important ideological function, consciously or not.[59] The

[48] *Tecmed v Mexico* (n 23), *Metalclad v Mexico* (n 15).

[49] *Total SA v The Argentine Republic*, ICSID Case no ARB/04/01 (Decision on Liability of 27 December 2010) para 128 (*Total v Argentina*).

[50] *Suez and others v Argentina*, ICSID Case no ARB/03/17 (Decision on Liability of 30 July 2010) para 203 (*Suez v Argentina*).

[51] *CMS v Argentina* (n 1) para 279; *Occidental Exploration and Production Company v The Republic of Ecuador* (Final Award of 1 July 2004) London Court of International Arbitration Case no UN3467 paras 183–86; *LG&E v Argentina* (n 26) para 137.

[52] The notions of the rule of law, economic development, and depoliticisation permeate the doctrinal accounts of IIL.

[53] *El Paso Energy International Company v Argentina*, ICSID Case no ARB/03/15 (Award of 31 October 2011) para 352.

[54] Schlag (n 47); compare the arguments on LEs in Orrego Vicuña (n 2); Snodgrass (n 2) with those in Campbell (n 16), and James Crawford, 'Treaty and Contract in Investment Arbitration' (2008) 24 Arbitration International 351.

[55] Eg Unger (n 46) chapter 1, in which Unger describes this method of explanation and justification of legal conclusions as 'reasoned elaboration'.

[56] Eg Campbell (n 16), *Total v Argentina* (n 49); or *Glamis Gold, Ltd v The United States of America* UNCITRAL (Award of 8 June 2009) para 766.

[57] See Orrego Vicuña (n 2); and *Metalclad v Mexico* (n 15).

[58] Pauwelyn (n 44).

[59] EP Thompson, *Whigs and Hunters* (Peregrine Books 1977) 263.

a-historicism of these two approaches to IIL has been recently questioned by accounts of IIL that use various historical methods.[60] Drawing on this body of work and my own research, I ask what the emergence of one specific legal doctrine such as LEs can tell us about the possibility of change in the IIL regime.

2. The prevailing political economy of IIL as a determining factor

If the adopted legal solutions are neither random nor necessary, ie are contingent, it is possible to view some conclusions as more plausible than others if one takes into account other factors. Among these factors is especially the prevailing political economy. By this I mean the prevailing economic arrangements including their discursive justifications, in other words, material and ideological reasons. The prevailing political economy not only creates incentives for the actors who decide,[61] but it also frames what is perceived as a preferable and acceptable decision to take.[62]

Based on my previous research on legal concepts expressing the regulatory powers of the state in IIL,[63] I argue that many IIL concepts apart from LEs became part of the IIL toolkit due to contingent events, but their actual uses reflect a rather specific political economy. If we look at the actual application of the legal concepts expressing the state's regulatory powers, we see that notions ostensibly used to promote public interest and public welfare (eg police powers doctrine) are in practice either disregarded, stripped to the bones, or relegated to an exception.[64] On the other hand, LEs, as a doctrine devised to protect investors' interests, are in practice expansive, almost all-encompassing and indiscriminate,[65] or at best, lead to idiosyncratic balancing against the public interest.[66] Likewise, other techniques such as proportionality and reasonableness are used in conceptions that are rather expansive, blunt, and prone to unhindered balancing.[67]

[60] Slobodian (n 39); Tzouvala (n 39), exploring intellectual history; St John (n 39), using historical institutionalism; Andrea Leiter, 'The Silent Impact of the 1917 Revolutions on International Investment Law' (2017) 6 ESIL Reflections 10, using material and intellectual history; Nicolás Perrone, 'UNCTAD's World Investment Reports 1991–015: 25 Years of Narrative Justifying and Balancing Foreign Investor Rights' (2018) 19 Journal of World Investment & Trade 7; Kate Miles, 'History and International Law: Method and Mechanism—Empire and "Usual" Rupture' in Schill and others (eds) (n 20) 136; Kate Miles, *The Origins of International Investment Law: Empire, Environment and the Safeguarding of Capital* (CUP 2013).

[61] One can think of reputational and economic incentives of international adjudicators to interpret their jurisdictional mandates broadly.

[62] That is, adjudicators' world views about the role of private property and foreign investment in national, regional, and global economy and about the role and functions of the state vis-à-vis the economy and other policies.

[63] Josef Ostřanský, 'The State´s Regulatory Powers in International Investment Law' (PhD thesis, Graduate Institute of International and Development Studies 2017).

[64] This framework holds even for cases that applied the doctrine: eg *Saluka v Czech Republic* (n 26) speaks of 'exception to an exception' at paras 254–62; *Methanex Corp v US*, UNCITRAL (Final Award on Jurisdiction and Merits of 3 August 2005) Part IV, chapter D, para 7; *Burlington Resources Inc v Ecuador*, ICSID Case no ARB/08/5 (Decision on Liability of 14 December 2012) para 506; *Suez v Argentina* (n 50) para 148.

[65] *Tecmed v Mexico* (n 23); *Bilcon v Canada* (n 1); *Masdar Solar & Wind Cooperatief UA v Kingdom of Spain* ICSID Case no ARB/14/1 (25 September 2018) (*Masdar v Spain*).

[66] *Total v Argentina* (n 49); *Continental Casualty Company v The Argentine Republic*, ICSID Case no ARB/03/9 (Award of 5 September 2008) paras 255–61.

[67] ibid; also see eg *Tecmed v Mexico* (n 23) paras 122, 133; *Azurix Corp v The Argentine Republic* ICSID Case no ARB/01/12 (Award of 14 July 2006) para 311; *LG&E v Argentina* (n 26) para 194; *Philip Morris Brands Sárl, Philip Morris Products SA and Abal Hermanos SA v Uruguay*, ICSID Case no ARB/10/07 (Award of 8 July 2016) paras 305–306.

Analysis of the arbitral decision-making and other legal materials point in the direction of a political economy that gives primacy to the individual and corporate economic actors in the questions of national economic ordering—most of IIL is based on the classic liberal state-individual/enterprise dichotomy.[68] This political economy also presumes that private capital and individual enterprise is pre-existing and is creative of public wealth and economic development, the latter being abstract and semantically vague concepts. The role of the state is not passive, as it requires active measures on its part in order to put in place legal infrastructure to facilitate market exchange and competition, and to liberalise the market.[69] Nevertheless, the state's role is obscured by the emphasis on private enterprise.

We can see that the semantic ambiguity allows for reproducing the particular economic arrangements or projecting certain visions of global order. As Andrea Leiter argues, the switching of the *raison d'être* of the global property protection regime from property simpliciter to investment and economic development has allowed for the projection of the vague normative goal of economic development. This has contributed to the multilateralisation of global property protection.[70] The normative goal of the regime is essentially an empirical proposition that private investment contributes to development, without necessarily defining what is meant by the latter, and without empirically testing the proposition.[71]

The political economy which underlies most of the current IIL practice thus appears to project a knee-jerk suspicion towards state intervention that would go beyond market-inducement and correction of market failures.[72] It gives preference and protection to property as a means of wealth maximisation over other societal purposes of property.[73] It supports the state's maintenance of generalised competition.[74] Finally, it projects an idea of one-directional regulatory stability, ie it condones regulatory changes that create possibilities for investors' wealth maximisation, while it rejects regulatory changes that limit wealth maximisation for the protection of other societal goals.[75] This apparent suspicion towards state interference, however, obscures that private market interaction is in fact premised on state involvement at every turn, since the state and market power are always already deeply intertwined and co-constitutive.[76] It is against this political economy of investment treaties and arbitral practice, that the claim of accidental emergence of a particular calibration of the notion of LEs becomes less persuasive.

[68] Slobodian speaks of the 'doubled world' of *imperium* and *dominium*, typical of the intellectual forefathers of current global economic governance, such as Hayek and Röpke; see Slobodian, *Globalists* (n 39) chapter 1.

[69] See specifically on IIL, Perrone (n 60), documenting the discursive framework through which the role of the state *vis-à-vis* foreign investment has been constructed in UNCTAD World Investment Reports; for the intellectual history of ideas behind the political economy of the investment regime see Slobodian (n 39); Tzouvala (n 39).

[70] Leiter (n 60).

[71] St John documents through her archival work that international officials promoting investor-state arbitration were conscious of the lack of empirical grounding for their proposition, but through various strategies avoided it as defining the success of their mission: St John (n 39).

[72] Perrone documents how UNCTAD's narrative post-2007 World Investment Reports is more sensitive to public regulation of investment for certain goals, but they still do not abandon the commodity conception of investment, let alone move towards a conception of investment which would reflect local preferences, Perrone (n 60) 12.

[73] Nicolás Perrone, 'The Emerging Global Right to Investment: Understanding the Reasoning Behind Foreign Investor Rights' (2017) 8 Journal of International Dispute Settlement 673.

[74] Tzouvala (n 39).

[75] Ostřanský (n 63).

[76] I thank Umut Özsu for highlighting this for me. More generally, see Werner Bonefeld, *The Strong State and the Free Market* (Rowman & Littlefield 2017), and specifically with respect to IIL see Tzouvala (n 39).

Just as other conceptions of the notion of LEs could possibly have been adopted but were not, other established legal doctrines of similar semantic ambiguity (eg good faith, vested rights, regulatory stability, consistency, estoppel, and proportionality)[77] may have easily replaced the doctrine of LEs to allow for the equivalent level of protection of foreign investment and corresponding substantive outcomes.

In this sense, although the resort to the aforementioned legal doctrines would be contingent, as IIL obligations allow other plausible justifications to be furnished within the vague and open-textured investment standards, the dominant political economy of the IIL regime shared by the relevant actors projects historically specific prevailing economic arrangements and allows only certain interpretations to emerge as more likely than others.[78] If some of the micro-level events of the IIL world, such as the emergence and use of the doctrine of LEs, can be viewed as contingent though not arbitrary or random, and their occurrence might not have had important consequences, we are left with the question as to what would have made a difference?

IV. In lieu of conclusion: responses, adaptation, and change in IIL?

The analysis presented in this chapter prompts the question of how to effect change that brings fundamental and emancipatory consequences. Can this be done without change in the prevailing political economy underlying the IIL regime and its practice? This concluding section merely aims to canvas, with broad brush strokes, (im)possibilities of change that have been put forward in the debates about the reform of IIL and that could be pursued in light of the analysis presented above. Let me start with a few caveats.

First, change in IIL is happening constantly: bilateral investment treaties (BITs) with investor state dispute settlement (ISDS) were not prevalent until the late 1980s; treaty arbitration cases did not exist on a mass scale until the late 1990s; the cases from the early 2000s are not decided in the same way despite deployment of the same techniques and reasoning as those in the 2010s; BITs of the late 2000s and onwards are different from those of the 1990s; and the scholarly discussion and public perception has changed (or rather emerged). But despite these constant permutations, can we say that something remains constant and prevalent?

It should be noted that the application of the doctrine of LEs in IIL practice from 2007 onwards has been marked by a more circumscribed interpretations as compared to the early expansive conceptions.[79] But we still find decisions that adhere to the far-reaching

[77] Some of the doctrinal accounts argue that cases applying the doctrine of LEs could be better explained by applying some of these cognate legal concepts. Ostřanský (n 6); Paparinskis (n 2) 259.

[78] It is worth noting that more recent cases applying a more restrictive understanding of legitimate expectations arose mostly after the 2007–08 financial crisis. The decisions that first openly opposed the sweeping statements of early awards (*MTD v Chile* (n 1) (Decision of the Ad Hoc Committee of 31 March 2007); *CMS v Argentina* (n 1) (Decision of the Ad Hoc Committee of 25 September 2007)) have a commonality: Judge Crawford sitting on both ad hoc committees. Interestingly, earlier investment awards with Crawford nn the panel do not mention LEs as a standalone part of FET (see eg *Waste Management (No 2) v Mexico*, ICSID Case no ARB(AF)/00/3 (30 April 2004) para 93).

[79] *Total v Argentina* (n 49); *Toto Costruzioni Generali SpA. v The Republic of Lebanon*, ICSID Case no ARB/07/12 (Award of 7 June 2012); *Gold Reserve Inc v Bolivarian Republic of Venezuela*, ICSID Case no ARB(AF)/09/1 (Award of 22 September 2014). A similar account with respect to trade law can be found in Robert Howse, 'The World Trade Organization 20 Years On: Global Governance by Judiciary' (2016) 27 European Journal of International Law 9.

interpretations of LEs of much younger vintage.[80] This change may, first, be taken as evidence of the malleability of juridical concepts of an open-ended and semantically indeterminate nature (and as such should not be surprising). Second, this practice can be explained as an accommodation of external and internal critiques in order to reproduce the dominant political economy or, less radically, as a reaction to external circumstances shaping the reference points of the prevailing political economy.[81]

Nevertheless, the broad discursive frameworks, political economic underpinnings, intellectual frames and representations have been quite stable and resistant over the last thirty years. The core presumptions manifested in the structure and telos of the IIL regime can be identified in virtually all cases: the individual/state dichotomy; the presumption of the beneficial role of foreign investment; the ambiguity as to the meaning of economic development; the kepticism towards the state intervention of other than market-facilitating and market-protecting nature; the importance of protecting foreign property; the insistence on the particular type of stability of legal regimes. So, what can the various explored and unexplored avenues of change offer?

Under the circumstances, would an individual decision or aggregate approach by arbitrators have made a difference? It seems quite unlikely. This makes propositions about the potential of a 'reform from within', ie reform and change carried out by arbitrators/adjudicators themselves,[82] a questionable contender for bringing about important changes to the prevailing political economy.[83]

When it comes to the modification of investment treaties, the prospects are mixed. On the one hand, the treaties have hardly changed.[84] For one thing, the changes have not diverged from the prevailing rationales, and there is currently little global discussion about the reform of substantive investment law.[85] A multilateral treaty regulating substantive investment norms has been repeatedly abandoned due to its highly contested nature. The historical decisions to move 'from substance to procedure' (eg conclusion of the ICSID Convention) and from multilateral to bilateral arrangements attest to the resilience of the international regime of property protection and its underlying logic through internalisation of critique.[86] On the other hand, several states are forging paths that break from the existing global regime of investment protection to some extent.[87]

[80] *Bilcon v Canada* (n 1) para 447; *Masdar v Spain* (n 65); *Antaris Solar GmbH and Dr Michael Göde v Czech Republic*, PCA Case no 2014-01 (2 May 2018) (Dissenting Opinion of Gary Born).

[81] See most clearly in Perrone (n 60).

[82] For an assessment of these proposals see Joshua Paine, 'Project of System-Internal Reform in International Investment Arbitration: An Appraisal' (2015) 6 Journal of International Dispute Settlement 332.

[83] If further reforms bring about bases for establishing investors' responsibility in ISDS, one can, nevertheless, imagine some progressive minor victories. See eg essays in the Symposium 'Investor Responsibility: The Next Frontier in International Investment Law' (2019) 113 AJIL Unbound.

[84] Tomer Broude, Yoram Z Haftel, and Alexander Thompson, 'Legitimation Through Renegotiation: Do States Seek More Regulatory Space in Their BITs?' in Ole Fauchald and Daniel Behn (eds), *Empirical Perspectives on the Legitimacy of International Investment Tribunals* (forthcoming, CUP).

[85] Although more and more states are challenging the limited dispute-settlement focus of the UNCITRAL reform process, such as South Africa and Indonesia. See eg Anthea Roberts and Taylor St John, 'UNCITRAL and ISDS Reforms: Agenda-Widening and Paradigm-Shifting' (*EJIL:Talk!*, 20 September 2019) <www.ejiltalk.org/uncitral-and-isds-reforms-agenda-widening-and-paradigm-shifting/> accessed 14 October 2019.

[86] Eg Miles, 'History and International Law' (n 60); Miles, *The Origins of International Investment Law* (n 60); Slobodian (n 39); Alessandra Asteriti, 'Gramsci in Washington: "Molecular Initiative" and International Investment Law' (*Legal Form*, 27 October 2017) <https://legalform.blog/2017/10/27/gramsci-in-washington-molecular-initiative-and-international-investment-law-alessandra-asteriti/≥ accessed 19 October 2019.

[87] Brazil and South Africa are moving away from the protective rationale of IIL, as does the Indian Model BIT, which, however, offers a rather confusing mix of reactionary statism in its content with the classical investment protection treaty in its form.

So, what about a different dispute settlement mechanism? Here, the debate is under way.[88] Apart from the few states mentioned above which propose a more radical departure from the existing regime, this reform debate, however, focuses on either technical improvements in the existing ISDS mechanisms or on establishing a permanent investment tribunal or an appellate body.[89] But this will likely achieve little in terms of changing the underlying politico-economic rationales of the current IIL. Dispute settlement reforms, especially when legitimated through the vernacular of the rule of law, may instead further entrench the contested material norms of investment protection and foreclose future avenues of change. Between the lines, these efforts seem to echo Tancredi in the Leopard: 'If we want things to stay as they are, things will have to change'.[90]

Miles and others have made an argument about continuity of the current ISDS system with previous forms of international law protection of commerce and property, thus linking international law generally and IIL specifically to imperialism.[91] Should this mean that we need to reject international law wholesale if we are to hope in substantially different outcomes? That is perhaps too pessimistic, as there are still avenues for resistance and change, though limited, within the current form of international law.[92] Yet, we should not forget about (imagining) other routes that may not necessarily feature any gadgets from the international law toolbox. The current era of challenges to the global economic order does not necessarily mean either more technical international law solutions or a withdrawal to nostalgia of the twentieth-century statism.[93] Technical adjustments, no matter how important they may be, are a far cry from serious and honest reconsideration of the political economy underlying not only IIL but the structures of the current international economic law. This chapter cannot be a place for providing more concrete answers to those large questions. Instead, its modest contribution was to emphasise that individual legal doctrines, such LEs, are not and should not be the main battleground. But their short history in IIL can give us hints as to from where we can, or rather cannot, expect a more radical change. This may help in redirecting our search.

[88] UNCITRAL 'Working Group III: Investor-State Dispute Settlement Reform' (*United Nations Commission on International Trade Law*) <https://uncitral.un.org/en/working_groups/3/investor-state> accessed 1 June 2020; CIDS, 'Academic Forum on ISDS', 'Matching Concerns and Reform Options' (*CIDS*) <www.cids.ch/academic-forum-concept-papers> accessed 19 October 2020.

[89] Anthea Roberts, 'Incremental, Systemic, and Paradigmatic Reform of Investor-State Arbitration' (2018) 112 American Journal of International Law 410; this is by no means to belittle the importance of the multiple ailments that have been identified as suffered by the current ISDS and which the UNCITRAL reform process aims to cure.

[90] Giuseppe Di Lampedusa, *The Leopard* (Random House 2007) 22.

[91] Miles, *The Origins of International Investment Law* (n 60); Slobodian (n 39); Antony Anghie, *Imperialism, Sovereignty and the Making of International Law* (CUP 2004).

[92] Knox (n 41); Isabel Feichtner, 'Critical Scholarship and Responsible Practice of International Law: How Can the Two be Reconciled?' (2016) 29 Leiden Journal of International Law 979.

[93] Ntina Tzouvala, 'The Academic Debate about Mega-Regionals and International Lawyers: Legalism as Critique?' (2018) 6 London Review of International Law 189. Also see David Kennedy, 'Law and the Political Economy of the World' (2013) 26 Leiden Journal of International Law 7.

F.

THE NEW INTERNATIONAL ECONOMIC ORDER

26

Bandung's Fate

*Kevin Crow**

There were limitations on what actors believed in the past and there are argumentative constraints in the present on what to make of that past.[1]

I. Introduction

The 1955 Bandung Conference, also known as the Asia-Africa Conference, had limited possibilities of affecting the emerging international legal order when it occurred, but it has created new possibilities for the present because it occurred. The Conference produced documents and declarations that have consistently challenged how international lawyers understand the structure and purpose of international law, first through a series of Declarations that culminated in the New International Economic Order (NIEO) and as a reference point (even if mythical) for the founding of Third World Approaches to International Law (TWAIL) at a period in history during which much of the present world order was taking form. The Conference also faced serious obstacles: the United States (US) Government tried to prevent it and the Soviet Union tried to co-opt it. In spite of this, it articulated a clear vision for international engagement distinct from the First or Second World visions. But after all was said and done, the Conference's immediate influence on the international legal order was negligible.

Without diminishing Bandung's importance to present day understandings of international law, this chapter argues that its anticlimactic impact was almost inevitable. This is what I refer to as Bandung's 'fate': a narrow understanding of Bandung's legal utility in its immediate present that was in many ways preordained. I draw this understanding primarily from reports that detail perceptions of Bandung from the 'First World' and contrast them with reports that detail perceptions from the 'Third World'. To the nations that controlled international law, Bandung served preordained purposes that undermined its immediate impact. But recent scholarship revisiting and revising the story of Bandung,[2] along with

* Many thanks to Nicoll Soedarko for her research and translation assistance and to the editors of this volume for their very insightful comments on earlier drafts of this chapter.

[1] Ingo Venzke, 'Possibilities of the Past: Histories of the NIEO and the Travails of Critique' (2018) 20 Journal of the History of International Law 263, 271; see also Lena Salaymeh, *The Beginnings of Islamic Law: Late Antique Islamicate Legal Traditions* (CUP 2016) 15–16.

[2] See generally Luis Eslava, Michael Fakhri, and Vasuki Nesiah (eds), *Bandung, Global History, and International Law: Critical Pasts and Pending Futures* (CUP 2017); see also eg Seng Tan and Amitav Acharya, *Bandung Revisited: The Legacy of the 1955 Asian-African Conference for International Order* (National University of Singapore Press 2008).

Kevin Crow, *Bandung's Fate* In: *Contingency in International Law*. Edited by: Ingo Venzke and Kevin Jon Heller, Oxford University Press. © The Several Contributors 2021. DOI: 10.1093/oso/9780192898036.003.0026

renewed interest in what the failure of the NIEO can teach us in the present,[3] indicates that the Conference created a 'normative surplus'[4]—an unveiling of acceptable norms at a particular point uncodified in law. In this light, Bandung is not a story of possibilities lost but a catalyst to imagine new possibilities for the present. After all, the act of judging an event's 'success' or 'failure' is itself contingent upon the temporal vantage point of the judge; potentiality is greater than possibility.

Among other things, the Bandung Principles unambiguously declare a preference for a consensus-based rather than adversarial approach to dispute settlement (as it now prevails in the World Trade Organization (WTO) Appellate Body and the European Court of Human Rights (ECtHR), for example). The Principles also prohibit sovereign interference in the absence of consent from the sovereign (in contrast to understandings of the responsibility to protect).[5] While explicitly affirming many of the values set out in the Universal Declaration of Human Rights (UDHR), the Bandung Communiqué repeatedly condemns colonialism and cautions against covert interference from previous colonial powers through the guises of international 'rule of law'.[6] Postcolonial scholars view these documents as founding incarnations of TWAIL,[7] a springboard for the Non-Aligned Movement,[8] and an inspiration for the NIEO.[9] More critical voices highlight missed opportunities in the construction of the Committees,[10] participants' slavish emphasis on remaining uncontroversial,[11] or a misguided belief that 'Capitalism as Development' could be an anecdote to illnesses caused by 'Capitalism as Colonialism'.[12] Either way, existing scholarship tends to focus on the event itself as 'success' because of the political movements it hatched, or as 'failure' because Bandungian values never meaningfully transformed the practice or structure of international law (adversarialism won out over consensus in dispute settlement, responsibility to protect (R2P) won out over non-intervention, the separation of political and economic rights still debatably undermines both conceptions of rights, and the NIEO succumbed to an age of neoliberal globalism).

But these characterisations of the event itself can distract from its living potential. Hence, this chapter suggests that, regardless of whether the lauders or the critics veer closer to the 'truth' of the Conference, Bandung most likely could not have yielded a greater normative influence on the mid-twentieth-century incarnation of international law because the narrative of its significance in the West was in many ways constructed before the Conference even began. From there, international lawyers can consider what it means to the present. At

[3] See eg Nils Gilman, 'The New International Economic Order: A Reintroduction' (2015) 6 Humanity Journal 7; see also Venzke, 'Possibilities of the Past' (n 1).

[4] See Venzke (n 1).

[5] Ministry of Foreign Affairs Republic of Indonesia, *Asia-Africa Speaks from Bandung* (1955); see also Anne Orford, *International Authority and the Responsibility to Protect* (CUP 2011).

[6] See the Final Communiqué in Indonesia, *Bandung*; see also Gilbert Rist, *The History of Development: From Western Origins to Global Faith* (Zed Books 2002).

[7] See eg Antony Anghie, *Imperialism, Sovereignty, and the Making of International Law* (CUP 2005).

[8] Though it is often credited as the first, the Bandung Conference was actually the second non-aligned movement gathering. See Albania, Ministry of Foreign Affairs, Report on the First and Second Conference of Non-Aligned Countries (1961). An English translation is available at Wilson Center Digital Archive <https://digitalarchive.wilsoncenter.org/document/110537> accessed 1 May 2019.

[9] See generally Eslava, Fakhri, and Nesiah (n 2).

[10] Antony Anghie 'Bandung and the Origins of Third World Sovereignty' in Eslava, Fakhri, and Nesiah (n 2) 535.

[11] Priya S Gupta 'From Statesmen to Technocrats to Financiers' in Eslava, Fakhri, and Nesiah (n 2) 481.

[12] Rist (n 6).

present, international law is (re)entering an era in which past possibilities are again future realities. I believe this era can find inspiration from the foreclosed possibilities of the past. If this is true, Bandung's life (long thought to be over) may have barely begun.

After providing a brief background on Bandung and its aftermath (section II), I suggest that contemporary perceptions of Bandung in the West limited its impact at the outset for at least two reasons. First, the novelist and independent observer Richard Wright claimed disproportionate influence upon the Western imagination of Bandung in an account that sought to claim it primarily as a rebuke of colonialism. And second, the coverage of Bandung in papers like the *New York Times*, *Der Spiegel*, and *Le Monde* created narratives that served the political predispositions of American and European audiences, foreclosing a serious public discussion in the West on the issues raised at the Conference. Indeed, the Indonesian Government's English-language Asian-African Conference Bulletin along with several Indonesian-language reports support the notion that public perceptions in the West were a strong determinant in the development of international law, and that Bandung's coverage fell in line with pre-existing perceptions. I suggest that a fatalistic understanding of these perceptions and their impact in the past might enable international lawyers to resist parallel perceptions in the present (section III). With these points aired, I suggest that Bandung's 'normative surplus' raises at least two questions worth sustaining: first, what can Bandung's legacies teach us about how the use of dominant discursive structures and vocabularies foreclose the possibility of radical critique? And second, how can Bandung's normative surplus inform the concept of 'development as cooperation'? Emphasising 'appropriateness' rather than 'justice' is one possibility (section IV). I then conclude by suggesting that, contrary to one conventional narrative, ideology is not something that should be purged from the production of international law. It is rather something continually imbedded in law. Accepting and acknowledging ideology as ever-present permits international lawyers to air it openly, freeing the legal imagination from rigid conceptions of 'justice', 'best practices', and other false necessities (section V).

II. Bandung's legacies: documents, disciples, discontents

The Bandung Conference was the first large-scale conference of newly decolonised or otherwise newly independent states. Its participants comprised representatives from twenty-nine countries representing more than half of the Earth's human population (roughly 54%).[13] The aim of the Conference was to set out an agenda for intercultural global economic and political cooperation that opposed or resisted colonialism or neo-colonialism, albeit limited to the forms visible at the time.[14] In order to execute this aim, the Conference produced Committee records and the Communiqué (documents) (1). These documents inspired a range of views and discussions in the years following the conference (disciples) (2). While many important initiatives grew out of these discussions, the present international economic order manifests many of Bandung's fears (discontents) (3).

[13] Wisma Warnapala, 'Bandung Conference of 1955 and the Resurgence of Asia and Africa', *Sri Lanka Daily News* (21 April 2005).

[14] For a discussion of other forms, see eg Anghie (n 7).

1. The Bandung Communiqué

The Communiqué makes 'development' a major theme. It welcomes 'development' initiatives from the West and assumes in many aspects that economic activity will take place within the context of a West-dominated world economy, not in a regional one.[15] The language of the text, however, incorporates several limiting clauses indicating a deliberate effort to retain regional power on this global economic frontier. Such clauses include, 'as far as practicable and desirable', 'wherever economically feasible', 'on the basis of mutual interest', 'as far as possible', and so on.[16] This language in the context of the Communiqué suggests that participants wanted the option to push back against external forces that moved too boldly against the long term economic goals of Bandungian states.

The "Economic Cooperation' section of the Communiqué understands cooperation amongst Third World states as a stalwart shelter against potential economic imperialism resulting from foreign aid.[17] Some scholars have characterised this principle as 'timidly asserted' because it is accompanied by references to the 'valuable contribution' made from 'outside the region' to the development of participating countries.[18] Nevertheless, this was the first allusion to what the NIEO would later sanctify as 'collective self-reliance',[19] or even later, 'South–South cooperation'.[20]

It is tempting to view the composition and varying influence of Bandung's Committees as evincing 'missed legacies' when considering what Bandung's influence on international law could have been. Bandung was divided into five Committees,[21] three of which issued widely publicised statements. These were the Political Committee composed of political officials of varying backgrounds, the Economic Committee composed of 'experts', and the Cultural Committee.[22] The Political Committee proceedings dominated the Conference. Despite the large number of socialist leaders—many of whom saw politics, culture, and economics as part of a single whole—the Political Committee was separated from other committees in an effort to mirror what the participants viewed as 'international expectations'.[23] The participants wished to cater to these expectations because many were most concerned with representation at the United Nations (UN) General Assembly—which required cohesion with UN understandings of international economics—along with a desire for non-alignment with and especially non-interference from the 'Great Power' politics of the Cold War.[24]

While the Political Committee focused largely on how to engage capital from the West without subjugation to the West, the Economic Committee's less publicised statement

[15] Indonesia (n 5).
[16] ibid.
[17] Rist (n 6).
[18] Indonesia (n 5).
[19] UN Resolution S6/3201 (SVI), 'Declaration on the New International Economic Order'.
[20] UN Resolution 29/3281 (XXIX), 'Charter of Economic Rights and Duties of States'; UN Resolution 41/128, 'Declaration on the Right to Development'.
[21] Ministry of Foreign Affairs, Republic of Indonesia, 'Asian-African Bulletin No 2' [1955] 3.
[22] See generally ibid.
[23] Gupta (n 11).
[24] ibid.

seemed to assume that national independence and sovereignty were preconditions to social and economic progress.[25] The Committee's work provided the impetus for a range of new initiatives that sought to reconfigure the economic structure of international legal relations.[26] These initiatives—which included the right to development, the economic rights and duties of states, and most famously the NIEO—are amongst the most significant efforts made to date to de-normalise the inherited post-Second World War economic order. Some recent scholarship has mourned their non-manifestation.[27]

In contrast to the prevailing model of international 'development' promoted by Truman and Keynes,[28] the 'development' envisaged at Bandung resisted hierarchical categorisations of states in economic terms on the international stage. Discussions that began at Bandung later generated visionary alternative proposals for how to form and codify the concept of 'development' in international law. (See notable examples in 1962,[29] 1974,[30] 1975,[31] and 1986.[32]) Unfortunately, these proposals also served as catalysts for old colonial economic structures to re-express themselves in new terms.[33] Newly independent states quickly became characterised in international law as 'developing states' and therefore in need of developmental interventions. Presently, the circumstances under which these interventions can take place are characterised as 'exceptions' in WTO instruments,[34] even though economically speaking, highly developed states are the global 'exceptions'.

2. Understandings of Bandung

Bandung is broadly seen as an effort by Asian and African nations, many of which were left out from the United Nations Conference in San Francisco, to engage with international law on their own terms—to set out boundaries and parameters to international economic and political relations at a time when many of the participants had just emerged from the humiliations of colonialism. Beyond those general terms, interpretations of this effort are as diverse as the Conference itself. For example, whereas Antony Anghie sees the Bandungian theory of sovereignty as a great intervention to supplant the nineteenth-century European ideal that only 'civilised' states were fully sovereign,[35] Obiora Okafor reads Bandungian sovereignty as essentially defensive—an effort to escape manipulation

[25] Indonesia (n 5).
[26] ibid.
[27] See eg John Linarelli, Margot E Salomon, and M Sornarajah, *The Misery of International Law: Confrontations with Injustice in the Global Economy* (OUP 2018).
[28] I refer here to Harry Truman's famous 'Point Four' speech, which for the first time declared that Western powers had a responsibility to assist 'developing countries', and to John Maynard Keynes' prominent influence at the Bretton Woods Conference, which established the first incarnation of the present global economic order.
[29] UN Resolution 1803 (XVII).
[30] UN Resolution S6/3201 (n 19).
[31] UN Resolution 29/3281 (XXIX), 'Charter of Economic Rights and Duties of States'.
[32] UN Resolution 41/128, 'Declaration on the Right to Development'.
[33] See generally Eslava, Fakhri, and Nesiah (n 2).
[34] See eg World Trade Organization, Ministerial Declaration of 14 November 2001, WT/MIN(01)/DEC/1, 41 ILM 746 (2002) (Doha Declaration).
[35] Anghie (n 10).

rather than to reform.[36] Whereas Eslava and his collaborators argue that Bandung was the moment at which international law truly became international because it supplanted deficiencies in perspective amongst the fifty states present at the San Francisco Conference,[37] Umut Özsu views the same Conference—and particularly the notion of solidarity—as masking an empty politics concerned primarily with symbolic valorisation of the Third World rather than substantive initiatives.[38]

Whatever the mythical or symbolic triumphs or deficiencies of Bandung,[39] what seems substantively clear from the Communiqué is that participants desired an international law with codified prohibitions on 'coercion' and 'intervention'. They saw in the UDHR provisions that could internationally fortify self-determination for their communities over the political rights of individuals.[40] The lingering question is, if the language of the Communiqué found this possibility readily apparent in the UDHR, and if the Communiqué in fact demanded that international law take this possibility seriously, why were international lawyers so inclined to do otherwise?

3. Missed Legacies?

Some forty years after the conclusion of Bandung, the Marrakesh Agreement set out a basic narrative eerily similar to the economic situations against which the Conference participants hoped to rally.[41] At least three immediate Bandungian fears are manifest through Marrakesh. First, as noted earlier, the Marrakeshian narrative is one that presupposes the authorship of 'developed' countries because it carves out exceptions for 'developing' nations rather than making rules based on the needs of developing nations and carving out exceptions for the most 'developed' nations.[42]

Second, the adversarial approach to dispute settlement at the Panel and Appellate Body (AB) codified in the Dispute Settlement Understanding (DSU) runs against the grain of the preference for consensus-based settlement expressed at Bandung and individually amongst a vast number of Asian states.[43] And while not explicitly provided in the DSU, the adversarial function of the WTO's AB has allowed for the 'judicial' importation of legal tools from European and American jurisprudence that facilitate hierarchical understandings of

[36] Obiora Chinedu Okafor 'The Bandung Ethic and International Human Rights Praxis' in Eslava, Fakhri, and Nesiah (n 2) 515.

[37] Luis Eslava, Michael Fakhri, and Vasuki Nesiah 'Introduction' in Eslava, Fakhri, and Nesiah (n 2) 1.

[38] Umut Özsu 'Let Us First of All Have Unity Among Us' in Eslava, Fakhri, and Nesiah (n 2) 293.

[39] On mythical elements of Bandung, see Robert Vitalis, 'The Midnight Ride of Kwame Nkrumah and Other Fables of Bandung' (2013) 4 Humanity Journal 261.

[40] See Indonesia (n 5).

[41] Agreement Establishing the World Trade Organization 1867 UNTS 154 (1994) (Marrakesh Agreement).

[42] General Agreement on Tariffs & Trade 1994, 1867 UNTS 190 (1994) (GATT 1994). The Marrakesh Agreement itself does not reference developing countries; when I use the term 'Marrakeshian', I am here referring to the group of instruments Annexed to the Marrakesh Agreement that established the WTO, including the GATT 1994, which carves out exceptions for 'less-developed' and 'least-developed' countries.

[43] Understanding on the Rules and Procedures Governing the Settlement of Disputes 1869 UNTS 401 (1994) (Dispute Settlement Understanding). Bandung's approach to non-intervention can also be seen as inconsistent with adversarial procedure at the earlier-established ICJ. See United Nations Charter, Statute of the International Court of Justice, USTS 933, ch III (1946) (ICJ statute).

cultural values, for example in the use of 'balancing' in General Agreement on Tariffs and Trade (GATT) XX 'public morals' cases.[44]

Finally, the WTO treaties assume a 'development' of intervention, which was a fear expressly debated in the build-up to Bandung during meetings at which future participants decided upon how to organise and compartmentalise the agenda.[45] At least through implication, the Bandung Conference facilitated a non-rights-based approach to economic matters through its separation of the political and economic committees and through its primary emphasis on the findings of the Political Committee.[46] This separation—envisaged at Bandung and perhaps necessitated by the Cold War, codified by the International Covenant on Civil and Political Rights (ICCPR) and International Covenant on Economic, Social and Cultural Rights (ICESCR), challenged by the NIEO and then reinforced by the WTO—is articulated on the defensive wherever it encounters 'development'.[47] One fine example is the 2001 Doha Ministerial Conference Declaration, which begins with a justification for the continuation of the status quo in an apologetic tone ('We are determined [...] to maintain the process of reform and liberalisation of trade policies, thus ensuring that the system plays its full part in promoting recovery, growth and development') at the same time as it proclaims that the 'international trading system' is responsible for all economic growth, employment, and development in the last fifty years.[48] (A fair point from a correlative standpoint, but highly debatable and empirically dodgy.[49])

In telling the post-Second World War (hi)story of international law, the gap between Bandungian and Marrakeshian aspirations for the global economic order has often required that Bandung be cast in a somewhat mournful role or ignored entirely.[50] I would like to offer an alternative role for Bandung that understands its lack of immediate impact as inevitable. By adopting this fatalistic view, international lawyers can free it from the past and embrace its enduring utility. As I will argue based on the reporting below, Bandung's aspirations never had a realistic chance of becoming codified in international law at the Bandung moment. Nevertheless, its enduring utility has always been its ability to sustain discussion. It sustains discussion because of its potentiality: the Committee records and the Communiqué it produced provide present international

[44] See WTO, *Korea: Measures Affecting Imports of Fresh, Chilled and Frozen Beef—Report of the Appellate Body* (11 December 2000) WT/DS161/AB/R, WT/DS169/AB/R 164; WTO, *Brazil: Measures Affecting Imports of Retreaded Tyres—Report of the Appellate Body* (17 December 2007) WT/DS332/AB/R 156; see also WTO, *United States: Measures Affecting the Cross-Border Supply of Gambling and Betting Services—Report of the Appellate Body* (7 April 2005) WT/DS285/AB/R; WTO, *Dominican Republic: Measures Affecting the Importation and Internal Sale of Cigarettes—Report of the Appellate Body* (25 April 2005) WT/DS302/AB/R.

[45] Gupta (n 11); Indonesia, 'Bulletin No 2' (n 21).

[46] Final Communiqué in Indonesia (n 5).

[47] See UN General Assembly, *International Covenant on Civil and Political Rights*, 1999 UNTS 171 (1966) (ICCPR); UN General Assembly, *International Covenant on Economic, Social and Cultural Rights*, 993 UNTS 3 (1966) (ICESCR); Resolution S6/3201 (n 19).

[48] Doha Declaration (n 34) [1].

[49] See eg, Esteban Ortiz-Ospina, Diana Beltekian, and Max Roser, 'Trade and Globalization' (*Our World in Data*, October 2018) <https://ourworldindata.org/trade-and-globalization> accessed 1 May 2019.

[50] Many histories of international law overlook Bandung, eg Alexander Orakhelashvili, *Research Handbook on the Theory and History of International Law* (Edward Elgar 2011); Otto Kimminich, 'History of the Law of Nations: Since WWII' in Rudolf Bernhardt (ed), *Max Planck Encyclopedia of International Law* (vol 7, Elsevier 1984) 262 (ignores Bandung but mentions NIEO); Martti Koskenniemi, 'History of International Law, since World War II' in Rüdiger Wolfrum (ed), *Max Planck Encyclopedia of International Law* (vol 4, OUP 2011) 902 (ignores Bandung but mentions NIEO). For many scholars that cast Bandung in a mournful light, see Eslava, Fakhri, and Nesiah(n 2).

lawyers with a springboard from which to articulate alternate possibilities for international legal and governance institutions. In a fatalistic reading, these possibilities did not exist at the Bandung moment. Yet without Bandung, they would not exist today.

III. Western understandings of 'The Possible' at Bandung around 1955

In his 'What Should Legal Analysis Become?', Roberto Unger describes an institutional 'fetishism' in international law.[51] He was grappling with the idea that public institutions are organised in a manner which gains 'a pseudoscientific respectability through a largely implicit but nevertheless influential idea: the notion of a convergence towards a single set of best available practices throughout the world'.[52] He noted that fetishising this notion restricted the 'legal imagination' in that it required of international lawyers a universal understanding of what was 'best' and a procedural apparatus through which to achieve this on the international stage.[53] Unger calls this a 'regressive thesis' because it necessitates functional requirements that undermine institutional responses;[54] in other words, institutions lose the freedom to reflect and react flexibly to the will of the societies which produced them, and this eventually reduces freedom for most individuals in those societies. On the international stage, Unger suggests, institutional fetishism has caused international lawyers to choose one economic shape of civilisation over another.[55] On this view, one might understand Bretton Woods in 1944 and San Francisco in 1945 as articulating choices about which concept of 'best' the world should converge towards. Indeed, by the 1955 Bandung moment, the West had in many ways already fetishised the institutions engaged in the production of international law. And as the subsections below demonstrate, the Western imagination of whether a Bandungian vision of international law could converge with its existing institutions was determined largely by reporters who did not have the benefit of, say, Edward Said's *Orientalism*,[56] James Baldwin's *Nobody Knows My Name*,[57] or even the civil rights movement to foster and sustain introspective examinations of 'othering'.[58] Even at the Bandung moment, Bandung was already a fantasy in the West.

One author in particular—the African American novelist and independent observer Richard Wright—claimed disproportionate influence upon the Western imagination of Bandung, due to his pre-existing fame, the readability and comprehensiveness of his narrative, and due to lack of other thorough English language accounts. In the following subsections I turn first to an analysis and critique of his work (1). I then broaden the scope to Bandung's coverage in the *New York Times*, *Der Speigel*, and *Le Monde*, and to an analysis of Indonesian publications reporting on coverage throughout the Global North (2).

[51] Roberto Unger, *What Should Legal Analysis Become?* (Verso 1996) 8.
[52] ibid 9.
[53] ibid.
[54] ibid 20.
[55] ibid 9.
[56] Edward Said, *Orientalism* (Pantheon 1978).
[57] James Baldwin, *Nobody Knows My Name* (Dial 1961).
[58] Said's seminal work coined the term 'othering' and had an immense impact in many disciplines, including critical legal studies (CLS) and TWAIL. Edward Said, *Orientalism* (n 56).

1. Richard Wright's understanding of 'The Possible': *The Color Curtain* and other writings

While the Conference made room for roughly '400 pressmen',[59] the academic narrative was initially dominated by writer Richard Wright. Wright's novels *Native Son* and *The Outsider* depicting pre-civil rights era African American life had earned him international acclaim.[60] His status as a self-exiled African American in Paris bolstered his work's cosmopolitan pull, and his initial 'independent' reports and later book *The Color Curtain* were early authorities on prevailing attitudes at Bandung.[61] His work is referenced in many of the periodicals detailed further below.

Although recent scholarship has revealed grievous inaccuracies in Wright's account (largely due to his cultural misunderstandings),[62] I argue that even if Richard Wright had been a different American or European observer, it is unlikely that such inaccuracies would not have been presented to the Western audience. This is because, even though Wright considered himself an outsider, he was in many ways representative: he was a Westerner who predominantly saw in Bandung a rebuke of capitalism, colonialism, consumerism, and more generally, the proverbial 'White Man'.[63] Many subsequent authors have observed that Wright's focus on these themes did not so much express the zeitgeist at Bandung as it expressed Wright's desire to see Bandung as a rebuke of these themes.[64]

To gather a sense of whether these criticisms are contingent on Wright, the question must not be whether Wright was right or wrong in his assessment of Bandung, but rather whether another observer in Wright's position would have been less wrong or right. Wright's own account—especially taken together with Western media narratives and the meticulous verification work of Bandung historians Brian Roberts and Keith Foulcher[65]—suggests that this is unlikely. In *The Color Curtain*, Wright describes the atmosphere at Bandung with assumptions that reaffirm what he would have read in American and French papers before the conference took place: America was a champion of the Indonesian struggle for independence and therefore the Conference,[66] but the Conference was disappointing because 'representatives of Negro-Africa have neither brought up a single question nor produced a single constructive idea',[67] a simultaneous animosity towards and fear of China,[68] and a pre-Conference chapter setting out presumptions later to be confirmed by Wright's assessment: that the Conference was overshadowed by tensions regarding 'race and religion, two of the most powerful and irrational forces in human nature'.[69] Indeed, by Wright's own account, he travelled to Bandung because he read an account in *Le Monde* that primed him to view Bandung as an expression of racial animosity.[70] *Le Monde* and Wright shared the

[59] Ministry of Foreign Affairs, Republic of Indonesia, 'Asian-African Bulletin No 1' (1955) 11.
[60] Richard Wright, *Native Son* (Harper 1940); Richard Wright, *The Outsider* (Harper 1953).
[61] Rist (n 6); see also Brian Russell Roberts and Keith Foulcher, *Indonesian Notebook: A Sourcebook on Richard Wright and the Bandung Conference* (Duke University Press 2016).
[62] Roberts and Foulcher (n 61).
[63] Richard Wright, *The Color Curtain* (World 1956); Rist (n 6).
[64] See eg Eslava, Fakhri, and Nesiah (n 2).
[65] Roberts and Foulcher (n 61).
[66] 'Indonesian Impresario Foundation' *Java Bode* (Jakarta, 15 April 1955).
[67] 'Famous U.S. Negro Author Disappointed' *Indonesian Observer* (Jakarta, 23 April 1955).
[68] See warnings regarding Chou En-Lai in Wright (n 63) ch 5.
[69] ibid ch 1.
[70] Roberts and Foulcher (n 61).

notion of 'Bandung as irrational' in their pre-Conference writings—a notion that would spread to the English-language reports Wright influenced during the Conference and spread in public perceptions due to the report he wrote afterwards.

If one takes a transcendental approach to Wright's account—ie ask not whether Wright's premise was reasonable, ask rather what Wright would need to believe was reasonable in order to reach the conclusions he reached—it is difficult to imagine anyone in Wright's position reporting in any significantly different way. Critical voices on Wright scrutinise his racial radicalisation of the Bandung narrative,[71] but overlook the fact that Wright wanted Bandung to be radical in a distinctly Western way. Specifically, Wright wanted to see direct confrontation at Bandung, and this misunderstood especially Asian approaches to politics.[72] Even as Wright focuses on racial tension, his assessment is shot through with assumptions about the superiority of Western approaches to governance, diplomacy, and problem solving. He favours adversary over consensus, pragmatism over face-saving, free markets over planned economies.[73] In sum, Wright's ideas are temporally standard: the way in which he focuses on race would likely have emerged from any American intellectual at the time; the parallels between the plight of decolonised peoples and the plight of African Americans in the United States were difficult to miss, even if superficial. Despite any solidarity Wright may have felt as an African American amongst peoples he viewed as oppressed, he nevertheless writes steadfastly as a Westerner and deploys a full arsenal of 'othering' language, especially when speaking about people from African countries and Indonesians.[74] Finally, and most subtly, the notion that Bandung's participants were irrational—whether driven by religious belief or racial animosity—runs throughout Wright's narrative. In my reading, Wright's narrative delicately undermines the seriousness of the issues raised at the Conference; it was in many ways culturally determined and politically belittling. But perhaps Wright's temporal vantage point rendered this perspective almost inevitable.

2. Understandings of 'The Possible' through the lens of news reports

While Wright's most thorough account is retroactive,[75] he corresponded regularly with and informed many of the journalists writing during the Bandung moment.[76] His contemporaneous influence upon the coverage is apparent both in articles about him and in the correspondents that echo his impressions.[77] Nevertheless, the following subsections seek to tighten the discussion's proximity to the Bandung moment by investigating public understandings of Bandung as they occurred simultaneously in multiple locales. This coverage both shaped and was shaped by the perceptions put forward in Wright's later, more cohesive narrative. The following subsections seek to understand this narrative through newspaper

[71] ibid.

[72] See eg Deepak Nair, 'Saving Face in Diplomacy: A Political Sociology of Face-to-Face Interactions in the Association of Southeast Asian Nations' (2019) 25 European Journal of International Relations 672; Mely Caballero-Anthony, 'Mechanisms of Dispute Settlement: The ASEAN Experience' (1998) 20 Contemporary Southeast Asia 38.

[73] Wright (n 63); Roberts and Foulcher (n 61).

[74] Roberts and Foulcher (n 61).

[75] Wright (n 63).

[76] Roberts and Foulcher (n 61).

[77] See ibid; see also eg 'Famous U.S. Negro Author Disappointed' *Indonesian Observer* (Jakarta, 23 April 1955).

coverage of the event in the Western states which overwhelmingly controlled the construction of international law (i), and through an analysis of Indonesia's reporting on the newspaper coverage in other states (ii). These sources reveal that even as the Conference occurred there was no single truth to the story of Bandung.

i. Indonesia's reporting on the pre-conference news of other countries

Leading up to and immediately following the Bandung Conference, the Indonesian Government published the Asian-African Conference Bulletin—an English-language report on the proceedings, the volumes of which are held at the National Library of the Republic of Indonesia (*Perpustakaan Nasional Republik Indonesia*) in Jakarta, along with Indonesian-language reports.[78] The Bulletin summarised coverage of the Conference from Indonesian newspapers as well as select international newspapers. Much of this coverage from Asia focused on questions of solidarity. For example, before the Conference, the *Times of India* is quoted as speculating on the question of China's solidarity: 'Much [of Bandung's fate] will depend on whether Peking considers itself more Asian than Communist or vice versa'.[79] At the same time, the *Pakistani Standard* emphasised religious solidarity, highlighting the ability of Islam to transcend borders, language, and culture, and quoting then-Prime Minister Mohammed Ali's appeal to the Indonesian people: 'When you fought for your independence, the hearts of our people and prayers were with you ... When you suffered, we suffered too in our hearts'.[80] Even the government-critical Indonesian paper *Jana* projected that the Conference could only produce desired results if the governments of the Conference were to collectively 'assert themselves'.[81] However, in the pre-Conference coverage, assumed hierarchies appear amidst the professed solidarity. Even typically critical *Jana* viewed the task of Asian-African 'cooperation' as one in which 'Asian nations which have developed their own administrative skills' can assist 'the African regions [in which either] a deliberate policy of the rulers or ... the cultural backwardness of some of its peoples [produced a situation where] skilled indigenous administrators are scarce'.[82]

By contrast, pre-Conference coverage in the West focused on the politics of exclusion. For example, the *Sydney Telegraph* bemoaned the fact that, although Australia was geographically close to Indonesia and had championed Indonesia during its 'UN fight for nationhood', it was not invited to the Conference. The *Tasmania Examiner* feared that the conference 'could be the beginning of an upsurge of racial hatreds',[83] notwithstanding the fact that combating racialism was among the four primary purposes of the Conference from the beginning.[84] The London *Times* and Italy's *Avanti* focused on the question of whether China should be excluded on the basis of its alignment with great Cold War power Russia,[85] and on the decision to include some Middle Eastern states but not newly established Israel.[86] Moreover, as early as January 1955, the Moscow *Literary Gazette* reported that the United States was attempting to undermine Bandung's agenda by 'get[ting] the [C]onference to

[78] Many thanks to Nicoll Soedarko for translation assistance.
[79] Indonesia, 'Bulletin No 1' (n 59).
[80] ibid.
[81] ibid.
[82] Indonesia, 'Bulletin No 2' (n 21).
[83] Indonesia, 'Bulletin No 3'.
[84] ibid.
[85] ibid.
[86] Indonesia, 'Bulletin No 2' (n 21).

limit itself to discussion on cultural and economic relations and not touch on political problems'.[87] Whether or not it was the Dulles Department's plan, as the *Gazette* alleged, the concern that the focus on economic issues would detract from the ability of the 'awakened peoples of the East' to use 'power and resolution to decide their fate' did not land far from the Conference's immediate result.[88]

In the United States, the *New York Herald Tribune* noted 'two main criteria of non-admission. One is to be now a satellite or colony of the West. Formosa and Korea are not to be treated as "independent government". The second criterion is not to be of Asian stock'.[89] Likewise, the *Montreal Star* reported that amongst the invitees, it was 'possible to think of only two common qualities. One is that all the nations involved are non-white. The other is that all of them have emerged, or are emerging, from some form of subject or inferior status'.[90] And indeed, 'that status was imposed in all cases by the white peoples of the western world'.[91] The cautionary tone in the West avoids discussion on what the fresh colonial pasts of Bandung's states—fuelled by international capitalism—meant for the economic future of those states.

Hence, while the pre-Conference coverage from invited countries focused on the politics and dynamics of solidarity, the pre-Conference coverage from excluded countries focused on the politics of exclusion. With the exception of Russia, excluded countries feared that the conference represented a solidarity and independence from the West that could insight hatred towards the West. In my reading, an underlying concern in reports from Western countries was that solidarity could result in coordinated efforts for international economic reforms that might hurt the West—the United States feared economic injury to capitalism and Europe feared economic backlash against colonialism. But as the next subsection shows, after the opening speeches condemned colonialism and after the Communiqué embraced development, European papers (many of whose reporters corresponded with Wright) began to characterise Bandung as incompetent, while non-colonialist America's tone changed to one of subtle approval.

ii. Themes from Western newspapers during and after the conference

The prevailing American public perception of Bandung can be at least partially understood through the lens of the *New York Times* and the Associated Press, which treated Bandung as a positive affirmation of Capitalism's superiority: China was clumsy and floundering, eg its diplomats were ideologically defensive and materially indulgent,[92] and its airplanes were falling from the sky due to its own incompetence even as it blamed the West.[93] Meanwhile, European news outlets—such as *Der Spiegel* and *Le Monde*—characterised Bandung as a political façade, unfocused, while *Jana* produced a widely reprinted report regarding 'comfort girls' for delegates.[94] These narratives likely both reflected and informed public

[87] Indonesia, 'Bulletin No 4'.
[88] ibid.
[89] Indonesia, 'Bulletin No 3' (n 83).
[90] ibid.
[91] ibid.
[92] Tillman Durden, 'Asia-Africa Unity Hailed as Parley Opens in Bandung' *New York Times* (New York, 18 April 1955).
[93] Tillman Durden, 'Premier Says Peiping Does Not Want War with This Country' *New York Times* (New York, 19 April 1955).
[94] Roberts and Foulcher (n 61).

understandings of Bandung in the West at a time when international law was overwhelmingly shaped by the West.

To provide a few examples: while *Der Spiegel* characterised Bandung's participants as drawn together by 'negative principles (*negativen Grundsätzen*)' and insisted that capital vulnerability and 'weakness of social order (*schwache Gesellschaftsordnung*)' would derail meaningful decisions,[95] *Le Monde* ridiculed Bandung's anti-colonialist themes as 'emotional in nature, and therefore irrational (*de nature essentiellement émotive, et, par là même irrationnelle*)'.[96] The *New York Times* emphasised a Bandungian desire for economic development, highlighting the opening speeches that called for an 'international development corporation, which should include in its activities the undertaking of equity investment'.[97] It also noted an emphasis on 'promoting joint ventures among Asian-African countries in so far as this will promote their common interest'.[98] However, it did not report on the explicit Bandungian desire that the Asian-African bloc be consulted by Western powers on decisions that affected its members.[99] And although *The Times* noted that the right to self-determination was a dominant theme at the Conference,[100] it did so only in relation to an overarching embrace of the Universal Declaration of Human Rights—the UN document in which a reference to the rights of 'all peoples' had its debut appearance.[101] These themes, in combination with an unsurprising belittling of the 'Reds' in China and Vietnam,[102] gave the impression that Bandung embraced the economic and civil institutions on offer via the UN and Bretton Woods.

Where Wright's voice emerges, it paints a picture of peoples differentiating the wrongs of past colonialism (which Wright uses to catalyse claims of reverse racism) from the unquestionable 'right' of international finance and access to liberal markets (which Wright largely assumes).[103] Colonial resentment belonged to the political past, and as such, the economic future bears no innate responsibility to remedy those wrongs. In this way, these narratives are consistent with the logic through which economic 'advantages' are seen as 'entitlements' which rich states 'grant' to the poor in the form of 'exceptions' as well as 'capacity building' and 'enabling' clauses.

These narratives also beg the question: who tells the story? Who owns the law? Who grants exceptions, builds capacity, and enables? International law in the years since Bandung began to institutionally reflect the 1955 perception that developing states were abnormalities orbiting the developed nucleus of the West, and that the law should move those abnormalities towards normality (the West), especially since the late 1980s.[104] However, as the

[95] Internationales, 'Die Konferenz von Bandung' *Der Spiegel* (Hamburg, 20 April 1955) (author's translations).

[96] F Van Langenhove, 'L'anticolonialisme des nations émancipées est parfois à sens unique' *Le Monde* (Paris, May 1955).

[97] Tillman Durden, 'Excerpts from Opening Speeches at the Asian-African Conference in Bandung' *New York Times* (New York, 19 April 1955).

[98] ibid.

[99] Indonesia (n 5).

[100] Durden (n 97).

[101] UN General Assembly, *Universal Declaration of Human Rights* (10 December 1948), 217 A(III), Preamble (UDHR).

[102] Durden (n 92).

[103] This is apparent in Wright (n 63); but Wright's reports during the conference were influential upon American and European journalists writing on Bandung from their home countries. See Roberts and Foulcher (n 61).

[104] For a visual to conceptualise the novelty of the term 'capacity building' since the late 1980s, see <https://books.google.com/ngrams/graph?content=capacity+building&year_start=1800&year_end=2000&corpus=15&smoothing=3&share=&direct_url=t1%3B%2Ccapacity%20building%3B%2Cc0≥ accessed 12 October 2019.

newspaper articles and reports above indicate, these attitudes did not emerge after the Cold War or even after Bandung. These perceptions existed prior to and contemporaneously with Bandung. Thus, rather than bemoan the inaccuracies that Wright and Western news outlets propagated, overshadowing the participants' clear desire to be consulted on decisions affecting Asia,[105] and rather than bemoan the participants' debatable error in separating the Political and Economic Committees,[106] it might be more constructive to accept the narratives those outlets put forward as pre-determined, dominant because they were already accepted, and in this way, inevitable before the Conference ever took place.

The course for international law had already been set elsewhere—in San Francisco[107] and at Bretton Woods[108]—and had already been absorbed by the most economically powerful actors on these terms.[109] The reports above suggest that, at the Bandung moment, some immediate possibilities for the Communiqué had already been foreclosed by other political and social interests. On the one hand, Bandung was claimed by those *New York Times*-ers who sought to use it as a 'shield' against Communism or condemnations of colonialism. On the other hand, it was claimed by those Richard Wright-ers who sought to use it as a 'sword' whose hilt was gripped by the resurgence of 'colored peoples' and the Third World against those states and peoples which would rather oppress them, and whose blade was the UDHR. Against this backdrop, it would have been unlikely that, for example, UN regulators would perceive that the Communiqué's demands for 'consultation' were distinct from systems already in place: These states had representation in the UN General Assembly, so an argument could always be made that they were already consulted on international decisions affecting them made by Western powers. The pre-existing availability of institutional and normative claims to equitable international representation rendered public perception in the West a determinant in the development of international law. In other words, Great Power states had a 'first mover' advantage set in motion long before Bandung. By 1955, the concept of human rights had already taken on an individualist, liberal, Christian-naturalist tone (eg an understanding of the UDHR that emphasised the intrinsicality of individual rights[110]) and the concept of international development had already been infused with Trumanism and hijacked as a tool for capitalist intervention by the wake of the Cold War.[111] Likely by 1955 and certainly by the failure of the NIEO, these perceptions had been fetishised as 'best'. Bandung's fate, in the time that it occurred, was to be used rather than embraced by the dominant narratives that were already shaping international law.

[105] Indonesia (n 5).

[106] Gupta (n 11).

[107] United Nations Conference on International Organization, 25 April–26 June 1945, where the United Nations Charter took form.

[108] United Nations Monetary and Financial Conference, 1–22 July 1944, where the IMF, GATT 1948, and World Bank were first fertilised.

[109] In many instances, because newly decolonised states viewed the Charter and UDHR as safeguards to prevent encroachments on hard-won sovereignty.

[110] See eg, Samuel Moyn, *Christian Human Rights* (Harvard University Press 2015); on Adam Smith, see also Amos Funkenstein, *Theology and the Scientific Imagination* (Princeton University Press 1986).

[111] At the Bretton Woods Conference itself, officials and analysts of poorer countries were well represented and discussions on how to reconcile the liberal economic order with the aspirations of emerging powers played a larger role than is often acknowledged. But the 'development' that took structural form in the years following the Conference more closely resembled Truman's vision. On the former point, see Eric Helleiner, *Forgotten Foundations of Bretton Woods: International Development and the Making of the Postwar Order* (Cornell University Press 2016); on the latter point see Rist (n 6).

In sum, the public perceptions of the Conference prior to its beginning were focused on how to define solidarity, on whom to exclude, and on whether the Third World would lean closer to the East or the West. And during the Conference, Western perceptions referenced dominant domestic political predispositions. Indeed, these predispositions were almost inevitable: while records of the Conference indicate the participants believed a co-operative economic future could be best obtained by consigning discussions of racism and colonialism to the political past, the Communiqué provides ample evidence that Bandung embraced a Western economic future through its welcoming of 'development'. As difficult as systemic legacies of imperialism and racism are to identify and eliminate in today's institutions, they were likely more difficult to identify and eliminate in 1955 before so many lights were shined to expose them. In part because of this, much of Bandung's contingency does not rest on the event itself, but on how the event was used by external actors, and how that use was, for the immediate follow-up, shaped or reaffirmed by reporting.

San Francisco, Bretton Woods, and Bandung were all just 'events'—none of them speak for themselves as defining the trajectory of international law—yet San Francisco and Bretton Woods were *absorbed* as definitive, authoritative, and legitimate whereas Bandung was absorbed in different places as a different (less significant) thing or not absorbed at all. Why was this so? At least part of the answer is that the strength of public perception in the West was a determinant in the development of international law. As the reporting above has shown, perceptions of Bandung as irrational, incompetent, or subservient placed discursive limits on the effect it could have on the form international law was assuming in 1955. Leading up to the Conference, reporting from papers such as *The Times of India*, *The Pakastani Standard*, and *Jana* emphasised the solidarity of participants at the same time as they referenced hierarchies amongst them. During and after the Conference, reporting from *Der Spiegel* and *Le Monde* portrayed Bandung as irrational or doomed, whereas the United States emphasised China's unpopular role amongst a prevalence of participants eager to partake in the spoils of American capitalism and to welcome foreign investment to their shores. All of these news outlets focused on participant speeches and publications from the Political Committee, so in the Bandung moment and the immediate aftermath, the achievements of the Economic Committee went unsung. It would be almost two decades before the economic work that took place at Bandung came close to fruition through the NIEO, but a number of circumstantial elements also cut the NIEO's life short. The issues raised by both efforts, and especially the distributive economic concerns that run through them, remain very much alive today.[112]

It is clear that the present version of international economic law has in fact exacerbated global inequality, both amongst and within states.[113] And it is clear that international human rights law has done nothing and perhaps can do nothing to curtail this.[114] It would seem, therefore, that many of the concerns raised by the economic committee and the NIEO were correct, and that many of the undesirable futures envisaged in the past have in fact become our present. By studying the perceptions of the Bandung moment at the time it occurred, perhaps international lawyers can more readily recognise falsehoods in our perceptions of

[112] See eg Thomas Piketty, *Capital in the Twenty-First Century* (Harvard University Press 2013).

[113] See ibid; see also Quinn Slobodian, *Globalists: The End of Empire and the Birth of Neoliberalism* (Harvard University Press 2018).

[114] Ingo Venzke, 'International Law and the Spectre of Inequality' [2019] Inaugural Lecture No 607, University of Amsterdam <http://cf.bc.uva.nl/download/oraties/oraties_2019/Venzke_Ingo.pdf≥ accessed 12 October 2019.

present radical proposals for global economic reform. Perhaps now, international lawyers can more readily heed Duncan Kennedy's pleas to reclaim human agency against all efforts to present the 'actual' as the 'natural, necessary, and just'.[115]

IV. Bandung's normative surplus

In an article considering the unrealised possibilities of the NIEO, which grew out of Bandung's Economic Committee, Ingo Venzke recently wrote that the NIEO's 'normative surplus ... sustains and permeates present debates about international economic justice. A project long believed dead breathes new life as it shows its unrealised potential. [When a dominant rationality is exposed as ideology], it then belongs to the past and the present is freed from it'.[116] If past perceptions of Bandung had sealed the fate of its immediate impact before the Conference even took place, what then can be gained from regaining a sense of the possibilities opened at Bandung? What dominant rationalities are today exposed as ideologies?

Bandung's normative surplus is vast, and many have already made important contributions to debates on equality, sovereignty, and ideology that Bandung sustains. Moreover, Bandung's mythos has served to promote a variety of political missions over time—anticolonialism at the outset, nonalignment shortly thereafter, centralised planning for international economic activity still later, and today, in my reading at least, an invaluable articulation of an unrealised normative vision that can help international lawyers move beyond universalising impulses. Along these lines, here I would like to briefly raise two questions inspired by two particles of 'normative surplus' from Bandung that I believe are worth sustaining in our present.

First, is it desirable or even possible to separate the political from the economic in international law? Bandung's participants appear to have adopted this separation because they believed it would match the compartmentalisation deployed in San Francisco and would therefore increase Bandung's communicability.[117] But this merely reinforced the groundwork for a remaking of international trade and investment systems in a (neo)liberal image: internal regulation of state economies should be organised around what is best for international markets;[118] international markets are 'natural' and must therefore be insulated by the international system from the whims of democracy;[119] and human rights are 'intrinsic' and therefore must be protected by the international system from the whims of state authority.[120] Yet at the same time, the 'natural' forces of the economy must be imbedded by the state; international law governs the course of economic activity between states but domestic law is responsible for systems of distribution. Thus, the prevailing logic of today's

[115] Duncan Kennedy, 'Introduction to Legal History', undated post on author's webpage, but a mantra in much of Kennedy's works and public statements <www.duncankennedy.net/legal_history/index.html> accessed 8 November 2019.

[116] Venzke (n 1).

[117] See Gupta (n 11).

[118] This is the international implication of Ricardo's theory of comparative advantage, on which the WTO is explicitly (if naively) based. See World Trade Organization, 'Understanding the WTO: Basics: The Case for Open Trade' <www.wto.org/english/thewto_e/whatis_e/tif_e/fact3_e.htm≥ accessed 1 May 2019.

[119] An assumption exposed in Slobodian (n 113).

[120] The UDHR makes explicit references to the intrinsicality of some rights with which humans are 'endowed', but these include no economic rights; see also Venzke (n 114).

system holds that political rights are internationally 'intrinsic' and equality is domestically relative. The market and moral focus of this logic disregards the notion that both international and domestic systems are expressivist phenomena, shot through with structural imprints and logics reflective of the powers and ideologies that create them. Keeping this in mind, the first particle of Bandung's normative surplus is cautionary: buying into dominant (discursive) structures undermines radicality. Movements of resistance and change should always be sensitive to this: before (or after) the lawmaking process, the role of activism should be to push public discourse as far as possible beyond the status quo. One present-day example might be found in the United States, where politicians generally cannot publicly advocate for the abolition of municipal police if they hope to be reelected. However, Black Lives Matter activists certainly can, and these activists have pushed the public discourse on municipal police reform by rejecting the very idea that police can be reformed. Compromise is a place that law will eventually reach; public discourse can change the terms of that compromise. Perhaps for this very reason, the NIEO set out to revive Bandungian notions by collapsing the political/economic distinction, proposing an extension of the notion of sovereignty from the political to the economic.[121] It also sought to empower the majority of states and peoples to manifest such reforms by proposing that the UN General Assembly be vested with legislative authority to make binding international law.[122] These proposals sought in international law a more accurate reflection of the political nature of market-making. Discussions along these lines are worth sustaining.

Second, what does 'development as cooperation' truly mean for international law? As Lixinski and Ingulstad note in a previous chapter in this book,[123] the promise of development prior to the form it took in the mid-1950s was frustrated by the international investment regime because it displaced other legal initiatives intended to empower developing states in the foreign investor-state relationship, eg Permanent Sovereignty over Natural Resources.[124] The same can be said of the Calvo Doctrine.[125] Bandungian development emphasised non-intervention and cooperation as opposed to 'development as trade' or 'development as investment', much less the 'development as hierarchy' implicit in the provisions of many trade agreements,[126] and implicit in the 'graduation' language deployed by the World Bank.[127] I want to suggest that the NIEO's understandings of investment arbitration—which more closely mirrored the Calvo Doctrine than the present investor-state dispute settlement (ISDS) status quo—can provide some insight into what was meant by this. The Calvo Doctrine that dominated Latin American foreign investment until the second generation of international investment disputes generally prohibited international intervention, diplomatic or otherwise.[128] After the success of the Organization of the

[121] See Resolution S6/3201 (n 19).
[122] ibid.
[123] Luxinski and Ingulstad, in this volume.
[124] For an overview on the topic, see eg Nico Schrijver, *Sovereignty over Natural Resources: Balancing Rights and Duties* (CUP 1997).
[125] For understandings of the Calvo Doctrine in the decade prior to the Bandung moment in 1955, see Alwyn V Freeman, 'Recent Aspects of the Calvo Doctrine and the Challenge to the International Law' (1946) 40 American Journal of International Law 121.
[126] For a detailed discussion of this concept, see Kevin Crow, 'The Concept of Development in International Economic Law: Three Definitions and an Inquiry into Origin' (2017) 14 Manchester Journal of International Economic Law 168.
[127] ibid.
[128] For an overview of the changing dynamics in the three generations of BITs, see Diane Desierto, *Public Policy in International Economic Law: The ICESCR in Trade, Finance, and Investment* (OUP 2015).

Petroleum Exporting Countries (OPEC) buoyed the NIEO in 1974, the General Assembly adopted the Charter on the Economic Rights and Duties of States, which resembled Calvo in its procedural requirements but granted a right to nationalise or expropriate to the 'host' state at the same time as it accorded the host state the right to determine the parameters of compensation.[129] One specific particle of normative surplus that could facilitate a non-coercive form of 'development as cooperation' as described in the Communiqué was expressed in Article 2(2)c of the Charter:

> [Each State has the right to] nationalise, expropriate or transfer ownership of foreign property, in which case appropriate compensation should be paid by the State adopting such measures, taking into account its relevant laws and regulations and all circumstances that the State considers pertinent. In any case where the question of compensation gives rise to a controversy, it shall be settled under the domestic law of the nationalising State and by its tribunals, unless it is freely and mutually agreed by all States concerned that other peaceful means be sought on the basis of the sovereign equality of States and in accordance with the principle of free choice of means.[130]

Foreign investment in raw materials production and extractive industries have characterised North-South economic relations for centuries, even before the colonial era. But in the post-Second World War era, the technology of production in extractive industries was becoming standardised to the extent that it was no longer necessary to welcome foreign investment in order to maintain or increase levels of production.[131] The foreign extractive investments made in the decades leading up to the NIEO created a form of corporate sovereignty over the natural resources multinationals invested to extract.[132] This form of corporate sovereignty, along with the hierarchical notion that developing states 'graduate' to the level of developed ones, comprises an uncomfortable parallel with the nineteenth-century European notion that 'non-civilised' states are not really sovereign at all; that colonial corporations are 'natural, necessary, and just'. It also directly clashes with understandings of sovereignty set out in the Communiqué (non-intervention, non-coercion).[133] The international investment system nevertheless moved further towards alienation and away from cooperation, and today, the fact that it quite blatantly favours intervention not only from developed economies, but also from multinational corporations, has bolstered serious efforts for reform.[134] Again, Bandung's life, and its progeny in Article 2(2)c above, may have barely begun. While Article 2(2)c might be read as a universalisation of the Calvo doctrine,

[129] UNGA Resolution S6/3281 (XXIX), 'Charter of the Economic Rights and Duties of States', 12 December 1974; see also M Sornarajah, 'The New International Economic Order, Investment Treaties, and Foreign Investment Laws in ASEAN' (1985) 27 Malaya Law Review 443.

[130] UNGA Resolution S6/3281 (XXIX) (n 129) art 2(2)c.

[131] Jeffrey A Hart, *The New International Economic Order: Conflict and Cooperation in North-South Economic Relations* (Palgrave Macmillan 1983).

[132] A thorough discussion on the concept of corporate sovereignty is beyond the scope of this chapter, but for an introduction (rooted in the police power and the 'ban'), see Joshua Barkan, *Corporate Sovereignty: Law and Government Under Capitalism* (Minnesota Press 2013).

[133] Indonesia (n 5).

[134] For a recent example, see United Nations, *UNCTAD's Reform Package for the International Investment Regime: 2018 Edition* (2018). For an overview of several the most contentious clauses typical to IIAs, see Christian Tietje and Kevin Crow, 'The Reform of Investment Protection Rules in CETA, TTIP, and Other Recent EU-FTAs: Convincing?' in Stefan Griller, Walter Obwexer, and Erich Vranes (eds), *Mega-Regional Agreements: TTIP, CETA, TiSA. New Orientations for EU External Economic Relations* (OUP 2017) 87.

the language above differs in one significant, cooperation-building regard: it places the onus regarding compensation for expropriation, appropriation, or nationalisation not on what is 'just' but on what is 'appropriate', and it grants the host state the ability to choose what 'appropriate' means.

V. Conclusion: on ideology and the possibilities of the present

Even if Bandung was inevitably uninfluential at the time that it occurred, the fact that it occurred has shaped and will likely continue to shape the future of international law. With this chapter, I hope to add to Bandung's potentiality by more directly acknowledging the fact that Western perceptions were a determinant in the development of international law in 1955. The perceptions revealed through contemporaneous records indicate that in many cases Bandung was pre-ordained to be 'irrational' (because it acknowledged suffering caused by racism and religion), 'incompetent' (because of organisational or diplomatic faux pas), or 'unable' (because of the diversity of interests represented). These narratives foreclosed possibilities for Bandung, and may have precluded it from being taken seriously as articulating a vision for what international law should become. Today, we are again free to take Bandung's vision seriously as we seek to remake the present and thereby the future.

Citing Richard W Cox's work on the NIEO from the early 1970s, Ingo Venzke correctly noted '[s]ignificant change is possible when a previously dominant rationality is widely exposed as ideology'.[135] We can observe this process in the recent past: in the decade or so since the financial crisis of 2008, rich bodies of work in a variety of fields have made new efforts to expose market fundamentalism as ideology;[136] as humanitarian intervention and claims to just war have exacerbated violence and inflamed new intercultural tension, new scholarly efforts have been made to expose dominant rationalities of intrinsic human rights as ideology;[137] the COVID-19 pandemic has, *inter alia*, thrust a swath of systemic global and domestic legal inequities to the fore, exposed false assumptions in cherished economic wisdoms, and pushed private sector champions of free expression to suppress certain types of speech. In the words of Kurt Vonnegut, 'So it goes.'[138] Or rather, in the words of Richard W Cox, '[i]deological analysis is, of course, a critic's weapon and one most effectively used against the prevailing orthodoxies which, when stripped of their putative universality, become seen as special pleading for historically transient but presently entrenched interests. Social science is never neutral'.[139]

Just as Cox revealed in his assessment of contemporary understandings of the NIEO, the Bandung Conference too has potential to expose ideology in international law—to inform discussion on how ideas on the 'nature' of markets justified separating the economic from the

[135] Venzke (n 1).

[136] A full list of this work would fill libraries, but for some excellent recent work see eg, Slobodian (n 113); Samuel Moyn, *Not Enough: Human Rights in an Unequal World* (Harvard University Press 2018); Wolfgang Streeck, *How Will Capitalism End?: Essays on a Failing System* (Verso 2016); M Sornarajah, *Resistance and Change in International Investment Law* (CUP 2015).

[137] See eg Stephen L B Jensen, *The Making of International Human Rights: The 1960s, Decolonization, and the Reconstruction of Global Values* (CUP 2016); Moyn (n 110); Orford (n 5).

[138] A recurring motif in Kurt Vonnegut, *Slaughterhouse-Five, or The Children's Crusade: A Duty-Dance with Death* (Dell 1972).

[139] Robert W Cox, 'Ideologies and the New International Economic Order: Reflections on Some Recent Literature' (1979) 33 International Organization 257.

political, but how in fact, the market is an institutional expression of ideologies. The 'market' as a natural force and articulations of individual and community rights in international law are expressions of ideology that have often laid claim to rationality, to universality. But there is no 'God's-eye-view' achievable through international law.[140] We cannot now claim that, finally absolved of ideology, law can discover some purely rational state. In fact, Bandung's fate perhaps most clearly reveals that the opposite is true. It exposes international law's proponents of 'global constitutionalism' as advocates of an ideology of Kantian (or Christian) individualism,[141] and it exposes 'global administrative law' as an ideology favouring managerialism, or law's managerial potential.[142] It shows that rationalities of accession should not be mistaken for rationalities of consent, that rationalities of accession favour ideologies that view acceptance as agreement, which is worlds apart from those that view consensus as agreement, as in present-day Association of Southeast Asian Nations (ASEAN) and much of South Asia.[143] Bandung is living proof that the international legal imagination can do better than this; it can do better than claiming pure rationality by admitting that law is an expressivist phenomenon; and from there, international lawyers might imagine how a single legal institution can express multiple ideologies at the same time.

[140] Borrowing a favourite phrase from Thomas McCarthy.

[141] Proponents of global constitutionalism claim, among other things, that a global constitution would create a desirable hermeneutic device to provide a vocabulary to condemn extreme violations of human equality and autonomy. This is an ideological claim: it assumes that the highest purpose of law is to protect a Kantian concept of individual dignity that elevates individual suffering to the realm of the 'non permissible'. On this view, treating a person as a means to an end is globally repugnant in all instances, even if, in the judgment of a given society, individual suffering is necessary in the short term for the long-term benefit of that society. This Kantian (and ultimately Christian) concept of dignity, and thereby fundamental (in)justice, is a concept that is not universally held. A society might just as well take a utilitarian approach to justice, allowing for individuals to be means to the end of creating a society that provides more good for more people; there is nothing inherent to utilitarian thought or Kantian thought that justifies the elevation of either approach as superior to the other. Those are just two broad categories amongst the many available and legitimate root concepts upon which law could possibly be grounded. Thus, while global constitutionalists seek to create a vocabulary that elevates humanity (a noble goal), they inadvertently assume the superiority of a concept of that elevation that favours individual dignity, which is a reflection of Western values. On global constitutionalism, see eg, Anne Peters, 'The Merits of Global Constitutionalism' (2009) 16 Indiana Journal of Global Legal Studies 397; see also Martti Koskenniemi, 'Constitutionalism as a Mindset: Reflections on Kantian Themes About International Law and Globalization' (2007) 8 Theoretical Inquiries in Law 9. On the Christian roots of human dignity in international law, see Moyn (n 110).

[142] For a positive overview of global administrative law, see Sabino Cassese, 'Global Administrative Law: The State of the Art' (2015) 13 ICON 465.

[143] For a detailed discussion of how this process works in ASEAN's legal systems, see Robert Beckman and others, *Promoting Compliance: The Role of Dispute Settlement and Monitoring Mechanisms in ASEAN Instruments* (CUP 2016).

27

'Poisonous Flowers on the Dust-heap of a Dying Capitalism'

The United Nations Code of Conduct on Transnational Corporations, Contingency and Failure in International Law

Michelle Staggs Kelsall

I. Introduction: Transnational corporations, economic self-determination, and the United Nations Code of Conduct

In this chapter, I wish to revisit a recent moment in the institutional life of international law:[1] namely, the attempt by the United Nations Commission on Transnational Corporations (UNCTNC) to draft a Code of Conduct for (later: on) Transnational Corporations.[2] The UNCTNC was established by the Economic and Social Council (ECOSOC) in 1974.[3] It was inaugurated in response to calls for institutional reform outlined in two resolutions adopted by the United Nations General Assembly (UNGA) during its sixth Special Session in support of a New International Economic Order (NIEO).[4] The Code negotiations, which were the UNCTNC's *raison d'être*, marked a final attempt to secure economic self-determination for newly emerging states in the postcolonial period.[5] The attempt failed: after over a decade of negotiations, the Code was relegated to the archives of the ECOSOC.

Like no initiative before it, the NIEO marked a sustained attempt by the Group of 77 nations (G-77) 'to craft a new international law that would facilitate resource redistribution in a world economy whose regulatory architecture had revealed itself to be fragile, if not obsolete'.[6] However, calls to regulate Transnational Corporations (TNCs) are often underplayed when scholars consider the G-77's demands for permanent sovereignty over natural resources (PSNR), greater aid, debt relief, and more favourable terms of trade in the

[1] Sundhya Pahuja, *Decolonising International Law: Development, Economic Growth and the Politics of Universality* (CUP 2011) 2. On institutional internationalism, see Glenda Sluga, *Internationalism in the Age of Nationalism* (University of Pennsylvania Press 2013) 57.

[2] Annex VI: Draft United Nations Code of Conduct on Transnational Corporations (as of mid-1989) in Sidney Dell, *The United Nations and International Business* (United Nations Institute for Training and Research 1990). See also, 'Code of Conduct on Transnational Corporations' (1983) 22 International Legal Materials 192.

[3] Jennifer Bair, 'Corporations and the United Nations: Echoes of a New International Economic Order?' (2015) 6 Humanity: An International Journal of Human Rights, Humanitarianism and Development 159, 160.

[4] UNGA Res 3201 (S-VI) (1 May 1974) UN Doc A/Res/S-6/3201 at para 4(g); UNGA Res 3202 (1 May 1974) UN Doc A/Res/S-6/3202 at para V.

[5] Bair (n 3).

[6] Umut Özsu, 'Neoliberalism and the New International Economic Order: A History of "Contemporary Legal Thought"' in Justin Desautels-Stein and Christopher Tomlins (eds), *Searching for Contemporary Legal Thought* (CUP 2017) 330, 332. See also: Umut Özsu, 'Rendering Sovereignty Permanent? The Multiple Legacies of the New International Economic Order' (2016) European Yearbook of International Economic Law 1.

Michelle Staggs Kelsall, *'Poisonous Flowers on the Dust-heap of a Dying Capitalism'* In: *Contingency in International Law*. Edited by: Ingo Venzke and Kevin Jon Heller, Oxford University Press. © The Several Contributors 2021. DOI: 10.1093/oso/9780192898036.003.0027

international system. In the most common telling of the NIEO story, even before Code negotiations began, the '*real* new international economic order'—that of neoliberalism—had already come to dominate a variety of different legal responses to economic inequality.[7]

Yet the question of how to regulate the TNC formed a key part of the NIEO's programmatic platform. Arguably, its failure has had wider and deeper ramifications in the international system than this state-centric narrative admits. As Quinn Slobodian asserts, for the chief representative of corporations at the United Nations—namely, the International Chamber of Commerce (ICC)—the point in jettisoning Third World attempts at gaining power on the international stage was not to advocate for United States' hegemonic stability. Rather, it was to reduce the need for states altogether.[8]

The question the chapter therefore poses is: what were the necessary determinants precipitating the failure of the Code negotiations? By 'necessary determinants' I am referring to factors which 'orient change without actually predetermining it'.[9] The three 'necessary determinants' discussed in this chapter are structure, form, and actor participation: namely, (1) the structure of the negotiating entity (what this structure meant for what it could achieve); (2) the form international law took in these negotiations (both how the TNC was formally construed and what form regulating that object took); and (3) those actors who were present at (and who remained absent from) the proceedings. Conversely, I then ask: what contingencies arose from these necessary determinants that could have brought about the Code's success? And what does 'success' mean, in this context?

At first glance, the project of this chapter appears very modest. For the contemporary international lawyer, in the best-case scenario, the chapter crafts a revisionist history in which a soft law instrument is agreed that provides no more than a modicum of regulation for the TNC. Yet in a second register, what this chapter argues is that the Code negotiations reveal a deeper, normative contingency present within international law itself:[10] namely, that 'consent' in international law is more accurately construed as co-existing dissent. Hence, in this register, I argue that rather than focusing on the decay of consent, international lawyers may do well to consider the possibilities created through mutual dissensus.[11] This focuses our attention on international law as a site of ongoing struggle, rather than letting us assume that law remains beyond this critical instability.

When viewed from within the struggle to create international law, mutually-agreed dissensus is international law's greatest strength and signals its 'success'. This is because dissensus provides the freedom for state representatives to agree tacitly to a diverse set of teleological interpretations of what aims international law will serve. The uncertain certainty provided by international law is *both* necessary and contingent: it allows the greatest space for state representatives to determine how international law will operate (contingency) yet it is precisely what enables international law to come into being *as law* (necessity). Pondering this uncertainty gives international lawyers pause for greater reflection on

[7] Ibid. Oszu 2017 (emphasis added).

[8] Quinn Slobodian, *Globalists: The End of Empire and the Birth of Neoliberalism* (Harvard University Press 2018) 133.

[9] Susan Marks, 'False Contingency' (2009) 62 Current Legal Problems 1, 9.

[10] With sincere thanks to Mats Ingulstad for pointing this out.

[11] Nico Krisch, 'The Decay of Consent: International Law in an Age of Global Public Goods' (2014) 108 American Journal of International Law 1.

the possibilities contained within international law (and by extension, international lawyering) at any given moment in time.

The 'normative surplus' of the NIEO embodied in these proceedings, therefore, remains ripe for re-examination.[12] By re-considering the necessary determinants and embedded contingencies associated with institutional structure, legal form, and actor-participation, twenty-first-century international lawyers are provided with a prudent opportunity. The path from NIEO to now is one in which the TNC is often relegated to the role of handmaiden to the United States and its allies, a mere bit-player in the background of a pervasive and trenchant realpolitik embodied in Cold War international law.[13] Focusing instead, on how international civil servants attempted to navigate the relationship between TNCs and states illuminates a more complex story, in which our telling of the ascendance of the global North needs to further accommodate the rise of the First World in the Third and the Third World in the First—a rise which the TNC undoubtedly helped facilitate.[14]

II. A question of structure—development and the struggle to regulate the transnational corporation at the UNCTNC

By the 1970s, international jurists were deeply concerned with the perceived threat of the TNC in the post-Second World War period. In the seminal corporations case inaugurating that decade, *Barcelona Traction, Light and Power Company*, Justice Padilla Nervo polemically noted:

> It is not the shareholders in those huge corporations who are in need of diplomatic protection; it is rather the poorer or weaker States, where the investments take place, who need to be protected against encroachment by powerful financial groups, or against unwarranted diplomatic pressure ... Perhaps modern international business practice has a tendency to be soft and partial towards the powerful and rich, but no rule of law could be built on such flimsy bases.[15]

For many Third World statesmen and jurists, Justice Nervo articulated a belief they shared: the TNC should be seen as nothing other than an entity from whom they—and, to some extent, *all* states—were in need of protection.[16] The idea of investigating the TNC

[12] Ingo Venzke, 'Possibilities of the Past: Histories of the NIEO and the Travails of Critique' (2018) 20 Journal of the History of International Law 263.

[13] Margot E Salomon, 'From N.I.E.O. to Now and the Unfinishable Story of Economic Justice' (2013) 62 International & Comparative Law Quarterly 31. Note however, forthcoming: Matthew Craven, Sundhya Pahuja, and Gerry Simpson, *Cold War International Law* (CUP, in press).

[14] On this point, see in particular fellow travellers in what has been identified as the TWAIL II scholarship: BS Chimni, *International Law and World Order: A Critique of Contemporary Approaches* (CUP 2018) 16. Muthucumaraswamy Sornarajah, 'The Myth of International Contract Law' (1981) 15 Journal of World Trade 187; Muthucumaraswamy Sornarajah, 'The Climate of International Arbitration' (1991) 8 Journal of International Arbitration 47; Muthucumaraswamy Sornarajah, *The International Law on Foreign Investment* (CUP 2004).

[15] *Barcelona Traction, Light and Power Company, Limited (Belgium v Spain)*, Second Phase [1970] ICJ Rep 3 Judge Padilla Nervo, Separate Opinion at 250. See also Markos Karavias, 'Shared Responsibility and Multinational Enterprises' (2015) 62 Netherlands International Law Review 91 (citing Judge Nervo at 91).

[16] Sundhya Pahuja and Anna Saunders, 'Rival Worlds and the Place of the Corporation in International Law' in Jochen von Bernstorff and Philip Dann (eds), *The Battle for International Law: South-North Perspectives on the Decolonization Era* (OUP 2019) 141. See also Anthony Anghie, 'Legal Aspects of the New International Economic

gained momentum, fuelled by state representatives supporting the NIEO. In keeping with the NIEO's central ethos, the Charter of Economic Rights and Duties of States (CERDS) included provisions calling for TNCs' regulation.[17]

The gap between incomes of Third World and developed world countries had become enormous. According to Franck and Munansungu, developed market-economies enjoyed about two-thirds of the world's income.[18] In contrast, Third World economies housing almost 50% of the world's population (excluding the People's Republic of China) received only one-eighth of its income.[19] Between 1953 and 1972, this had corresponded with an increase in the share of world trade for developed countries from 64.9% to 71.5%, while developing countries had a share of only 13% (excluding petroleum-exporting countries). Although these figures were disputed, the fact that economic growth was disproportionately benefiting the developed world was not.[20]

In one register, establishing the UNCTNC can be read as states agreeing an institutional antidote to this growing inequality. Although since largely ignored or considered weak by those who paid it attention, the UNCTNC provided Third World states with the political machinery and technical expertise to continue to assert their claims to regulate foreign investment in an international fora.

The resolution calling for the UNCTNC's establishment placed a primacy on institutionalising a system enabling the Third World to monitor and document the inner workings of the TNC.[21] Hence, like the League of Nations before it, the UNCTNC sought to discover the interiority of the transnational firm—conceived by several prominent theorists at the time as an entity that was able to construct its own universe, through the marshalling of extensive resources and capital across state lines.[22]

As Anthony Anghie has noted, international jurists in the era of the League sensed that access to the interior of the state would 'revolutionise their discipline in much the same way that Joyce had revolutionised the novel and Freud had revolutionised our understanding of human nature'.[23] It was precisely through the Mandate system that international law and

Order' (2015) 16 Humanity: An International Journal of Human Rights, Humanitarianism and Development 145, 150–54.

[17] Charter of Economic Rights and Duties of States, UNGA Res 3281 (XXIX) (12 December 1974) UN Doc A/Res/3281(XXIX) (CERDS). Article 2(1) states that: 'Every State has and shall freely exercise full and permanent sovereignty, including possession, use and disposal over its wealth, natural resources and economic activities.' Article 2(2)(b) states that:

> Each State has the right: (b) To regulate and supervise activities of transnational corporations within its jurisdiction and take measures to ensure that such activities comply with its law, rules and regulations and conform to its economic and social policies. Transnational corporations shall not intervene in the internal affairs of a host State. Every State should, with full regard to its sovereign rights, cooperate with other states in the exercise of the right set forth in this paragraph.

[18] Thomas Franck and Mark M Munansangu, 'The New International Economic Order: International Law in the Making?' Policy and Efficacy Studies No 6 (United Nations Institute for Training and Research 1982) 3, 20.

[19] Franck and Munansangu (n 18) 20.

[20] ibid.

[21] Öszu, 'Neoliberalism and the New International Economic Order' (n 6) 341 and Salomon (n 13). See also ECOSOC 'The Impact of Transnational Corporations on the Development Process and International Relations' Res 1913 (LVII), E/5782, United Nations Economic and Social Council official records, Supp (No.5) 3.

[22] Tagi Sagafi-nejad with John H Dunning, *The UN and Transnational Corporations: From Code of Conduct to Global Compact* (Indiana University Press 2008) 96. See also Raymond Vernon, *Sovereignty at Bay: The Multinational Spread of U.S. Enterprises* (Basic Books 1971). Both Dunning and Vernon were advisors to the Centre for Transnational Corporations.

[23] Antony Anghie, *Imperialism, Sovereignty and the Making of International Law* (CUP 2007) 135.

institutions had complete access to the interior of society—and with which the violence of that law could be further sustained.[24]

Many member states' representatives conceived of the TNC with similar aversion, but subverted violence with passive resistance. The UN Centre on Transnational Corporations (the Centre) supporting the UNCTNC was able to provide Third World economies with the chance to test propositions regarding the benefits they were presumably accruing from TNC presence on their soil, and decide for themselves whether or not these entities were working to the benefit of their societies. Issues such as the veracity of claims regarding technology transfer to the Third World (and whether technology remained an enclave within the TNC or was diffused through the country through linkages) were given fine-grained analysis enabling states to determine their truth and the desirability of TNCs more generally.[25]

Hence, the UNCTNC's 'civilising therapy' was not aimed at the interior of the sovereign state but instead, the interior of the TNC. The TNC's role as an agent of foreign direct investment became the subject of studies,[26] reports, and panel discussions with relevant groups;[27] technical cooperation and the rendering of advisory services (for states, regarding industry);[28] and ongoing exchanges of views amongst governmental, business, trade union, non-governmental, and consumer organisations.[29] It provided an opportunity for Third World representatives to challenge claims of 'barbarism' from the West, by utilising the United Nations' machinery to investigate one of the West's most loved associational forms.[30]

By its second meeting, the UNCTNC had assembled the machinery to service its highest priority: the creation of a Code of Conduct.[31] Work to this end would proceed along two interrelated paths. On the one hand, it assembled an information-gathering system through the Centre. On the other, the Commission appointed an Intergovernmental Working Group (IGWG) to undertake the task of producing drafts of the Code of Conduct.[32]

The Centre was tasked with gathering, analysing, and disseminating information on TNCs through the creation and maintenance of a comprehensive database.[33] In addition, it conducted research on the political, legal, economic, and social aspects of TNCs (including in support of the Code of Conduct negotiations).[34] Finally, it provided 'technical cooperation' programmes, upon request by Member States, in order to 'increase their negotiating capacity vis-à-vis transnational corporations'.[35] Technical cooperation was primarily financed by the UN Development Programme from 1979 onwards.[36]

24 ibid.

25 Sagafi-nejad (n 22) 96–97.

26 ECOSOC Res 1913 (LVII) (n 21) at para 3(d).

27 ibid.

28 ibid at para 3(c)

29 ibid at para 3(b).

30 Pahuja and Saunders (n 16).

31 For a comprehensive overview of the Code, see Karl Sauvant, 'The Negotiations of the United Nations Code of Conduct on Transnational Corporations: Experiences and Lessons Learned' (2015) 16 Journal of World Investment and Trade 11.

32 Sauvant (n 31).

33 Sagafi-nejad (n 22) 96.

34 Economic and Social Council, United Nations Commission on Transnational Corporations (UNCTNC) E/C.10/16 (1–12 March 1976) para 39.

35 UNCTNC, Third Session (Summary Record of 25th Meeting), Comments of Mr Aissa (Algeria), E/C.10/SR.25 (2 May 1977) 2 para 7; as noted in Office of the Secretary-General, Organization Manual: Section T—A Description of the functions and organization of the United Nations Centre on Transnational Organizations, ST/SGB/Organization Section T/Rev.1 (28 June 1979) 2 (United Nations Archives and Records Management Services [UN-ARMS] New York, File No. S-1051/10/1/92/155 (on file with the author).

36 ibid 2.

The IGWG would meet during seventeen sessions, between 1976 and 1983, to compile the draft. The IGWG worked in tandem with the Centre to produce what the UNCTNC still hoped would culminate in a multilateral framework supported by all United Nations member states. Yet from the moment negotiations began, states' perspectives on the TNC were divergent. After the first meeting of the IGWG (charged with drafting the Code), Klaus Sahlgren would send an internal memo to Secretary-General Kurt Waldheim, stating that:

> Even though, as was expected, the 48-member Intergovernmental Working Group was not able to endorse in a committing manner the annotations of the Chairman, it is remarkable that it did agree to incorporate the Chairman's annotated outline in its report on the understanding that it would serve as the basis for future work. The fact that . . . the Working Group's report does not contain any brackets is, in my view, a significant achievement . . . [37]

Proceedings were stymied by an inability to determine what the TNC actually *was*, and how it should be treated. The IGWG fielded distinct views about the form of the corporation. The German Democratic Republic (GDR) reiterated the principles contained in the CERDS and argued for 'controlling the activities of TNCs and subordinating their activities to the national jurisdiction of states'.[38] 'An effective curtailment of the neo-colonialist practices of transnational corporations', was conceived by the GDR as 'a pre-requisite for establishing truly equitable international economic relations based on the principle of mutual advantage'.[39]

Jamaica went even further in asserting states' sovereignty against the TNC. States should ensure TNCs and their direct affiliates 'operate as good corporate citizens and not act against the state objectives of host countries'.[40] Somewhat paradoxically, Jamaica further asserted that this would include conforming 'in the case of apartheid' to the laws of *that* state, rather than the home state.[41]

Ecuador asserted the Code should be addressed to TNCs to ensure they 'effectively participate in the process of development'.[42] Japan argued Code negotiations should proceed without a definition of the TNC. Delegates could learn through the process and experience of the Code's formulation how to define its object.[43]

Although the Soviet Union did not initially express a view, ongoing work on the Code would reveal it considered any definition to preclude publicly-owned and mixed enterprises. According to this view 'enterprises of the socialist countries had nothing in common with transnational corporations'.[44]

The United Kingdom maintained the Code's purpose was to secure effective international arrangements to promote TNC's contribution to 'national developmental goals and world

[37] Inter-Office Memorandum, Klaus Sahlgren to UN Secretary-General (13 May 1977) at 2 (UN-ARMS File No 0897/7/4—Secretary-General Kurt Waldheim's Administrative Files (New York, New York)) viewed from 13–26 May 2017 (copy on file with the author).

[38] ECOSOC, 'Transnational Corporations: Views and Proposals of States on a Code of Conduct: Report of the Secretariat' (30 December 1976) E/C.10/19 7 at para 23 ('Views of States') (considered at the Intergovernmental Working Group of the Whole of the Code of Conduct, First Session, 10–14 January 1977).

[39] ibid 7 at para 23.

[40] ibid 9 at para 40.

[41] ibid.

[42] ibid 5 at para 15.

[43] ibid 11 at para 51.

[44] UNCTNC 'Report of the Eighth Session' E/C.10/1982/18 (30 August–10 September 1982) 40 at para 142.

economic growth'.[45] Additionally, however, states should conform to extant international law, even as states required TNCs to conform to their national laws.[46] The United States went even further, noting domestic enterprises as well as TNCs should be included, wherever possible.

The response of Sten Niklasson, the appointed Chairman of the IGWG and his successors, to the question of corporate form was largely to defer determining what the TNC *was* and focus instead on its 'activities' and 'effects'. As states' representatives continued to debate the extent to which the TNC could be embedded within the social institutions of the nation, international civil servants continued to maintain that they should proceed with 'pragmatism and imagination', focusing all the while on the art of the possible.[47]

Throughout the 1980s, the UNCTNC and the Centre produced a body of work documenting the 'effects' of TNCs in intimate detail. The Centre's output was vast: between 1975 to 1992 it produced a total of 265 publications—one for every month of its lifetime.[48] The UNCTNC and the Centre proved to be a genuine source of information-gathering and Third World resistance, in that it engaged in critical research about TNCs and refused to bow to pressure from states that saw its work as detrimental to *their* corporations.[49] This was pragmatism, late twentieth-century style: unlike the League of Nations, the UNCTNC was not concerned with challenging positivist ideas about international law or furthering particular social ends. Instead, reports evidence an ongoing attempt to mobilise instrumental management and bureaucratic process in order to achieve specific, measurable outcomes. The technology of technocracy was prioritised by the Centre—as civil servants worked towards the goal of harnessing the TNC to do the sovereigns' bidding.

The structural constraints of the UNCTNC's process, however, meant that the leviathan representatives sought to tame was never fully within their grasp. Pahuja and Saunders argue that these constraints were intentional: the task set for the UNCTNC, from the very outset, had been one in which the possibility of determining a legally binding agreement had become remote. With only the possibility of a non-binding Code of Conduct on the table, the work of the Centre and the IGWG could only ever become a footnote in the history of international law.[50]

I argue the situation was more nuanced. As will be discussed in the section which follows, between the need for more law and the inability to agree to it lay an opportunity to reconfigure the material sources of custom as more aligned with the practice of Third World states. Justice Padillo's warning at the start of the 1970s could have resulted in the 'flimsy bases' of international law being strengthened by the Code. Yet the deferral of the question of definition meant that the TNC *was* reduced to being a 'business enterprise', largely eschewing any question of states grappling with the politics to which its form gave rise.[51]

[45] ECOSOC E/C.10/19 7 (n 38) 14 at para 72.
[46] ibid.
[47] UNCTNC 'Report on the Fifth Session' (14–25 May and 16–17 July 1979) E/C.10/59 9 at para 14.
[48] Khalil Hamdani and Lorraine Ruffing, *United Nations Centre on Transnational Corporations Corporate Conduct and the Public Interest* (Routledge 2015) 49.
[49] ibid 50.
[50] Pahuja and Saunders (n 16) 169.
[51] See: UNCTNC 'Work related to a Definition of Transnational Corporations' (14–25 May 1979) E/1979/38/Rev.1 para 130; Interoffice Memorandum From Sidney Dell, Executive Director of the Centre for TNCs, to the Secretary-General (Javier de Pérez Cuéllar) EO/433 (5 July 1984) (UN-ARMS Folder S-1048-21-2-95-3) 1 (copy on file with the author).

Although the Soviet Union's representatives largely saw TNCs as 'poisonous flowers on the dust-heap of a dying capitalism', international law proved to be a paltry antidote for this particular toxicodendron.[52] The forty-eight member panel comprising the UNCTNC's proceedings was *too* democratic: the inability to reach decisions was tempered only by generating reports, the assumption being that this would lead to Third World empowerment against TNCs, over time. What this shows, however, is that in addition to providing us with a normative surplus, the NIEO reveals a descriptive deficit in our understanding of international law. The descriptive deficit arises from the need for greater inquiry and historical analysis of the making of international law, in all its forms. This is so, even (or perhaps, especially) when those forms lie in the messy formative space between law and non-law and the line between a private history of international law and a history of private international law is at its most blurred.[53]

III. A question of form—custom, conduct, contract, and the battle for [re]new[ed] international law

A second necessary determinant analysed in my assessment of the Code negotiations, is the form which international law would take through this process. I use the term 'necessary determinant' drawing from the work of Susan Marks with regard to false contingency. Marks argues that, in international jurists' efforts to evade determinism in their readings of history, they fail to consider certain determin*ing* factors which may contribute towards necessary constraints on the possibilities of the past. As I have noted, determining factors set limits or exert certain pressures (necessity) that can be contrasted with 'accidental' or 'voluntary' factors (contingency).

In this next section, I argue that the question of form—whether the Code should be mandatory or voluntary; whether it should be declaratory of custom, crystallise as custom over time, or support a 'new' international contract law—was *both* a determinant and a normative contingency within the Code negotiations. The determinant (or determining constraint) lay in the power differential between states representatives, and the capacity of some Western states to exert pressure, as champions of both extant European international law and novel international contract law, as to how that law should come into being. The contingency lay in the timing at which this form was taking shape, which gave both states' representatives and international civil servants the chance to work towards shaping a Code that was responsive to the desires of the Third World, even if not symbolic of a new international economic order.

Although it has often been stated that the Third World sought to obtain a 'legally binding' instrument and developed states did not, the position of several states' representatives was more nuanced than this would suggest. The fault lines lay between those states who wanted the Code to form part of custom and those who saw TNC regulation as distinct from it. The former—largely comprising G-77 nations—wanted to maintain, within the instrument

[52] Cited in Klaus A Sahlgren, 'Scenes from my UN Journey' in Martti Ahtisaari (ed) *Finns in the United Nations* (Finnish UN Association 1996) 205.

[53] For a wonderful discussion of the former as it relates to permanent sovereignty over natural resources, see Lucas Lixinski and Mats Ingulstad, 'Contingent Economic Legal Ordering: Permanent Sovereignty Over Natural Resources and International Commodity Agreements' in this volume.

drafted, the contingent possibility that its status as customary international law would be determined over time. In keeping with the Charter on the Economic Rights and Duties of States, states would maintain their individual right to 'regulate and supervise the activities of transnational corporations' while securing a collective duty of cooperation in the exercise of that right as states would individually determine.[54] This would allow for the terms of foreign direct investment to remain largely at the behest of individual states (rather than a pre-conceived agreement in international law).

The latter—for whom the United Kingdom and United States were the chief proponents—wanted instead to champion further what Muthucumaraswamy Sornarajah has termed the 'myth' of international contract law.[55] As AA Fatouros would reiterate, the idea of international contract law reflected a significant doctrinal trend of the 1950s and 1960s perpetuated primarily (though not exclusively) by Western lawyers. The trend encompassed formulating international legal norms that would ensure the freedom of contract of investors in host states. Yet ironically, attempts to uphold this position had been in the minority prior to the negotiations. The myth of international contract law would further sustain the fallacy that TNCs and other business enterprises were at once not obliged to be regulated by international law in terms of their conduct, but must be guaranteed a right through international contract to full return on their investments.[56]

Third World states championed the primacy of the NIEO informing the proceedings and being the Code's *modus operandi*.[57] Yet states' representatives of the G-77 recognised that as an international code, its legality would need to be evidenced through customary international law and any 'bindingness' as such would be centred in state practice once the instrument itself had been drafted. The problem became how customary international law was determined, which, as Samuel Asante recalls, remained 'highly controversial' throughout the proceedings.[58]

It is perhaps more accurate to state that Third World countries wanted TNCs to be bound by the terms of an international instrument which states themselves could implement in keeping with their own development policies. As such, they wanted corporate conduct to be highly regulated, but foreign investment terms to remain highly flexible. This caused tensions after 1980, when it became clear that developed states wanted the Code to be *both* on and *for* TNCs, including provisions pertaining to the treatment of TNCs in the Code that would safeguard the demands of foreign investors.[59]

Latin American countries argued that attempts to utilise international law to regulate TNCs had to be balanced against states' interest to utilise them as '*real* mechanisms for progress'.[60] Specifically, the government of Ecuador recommended that the Code should 'be addressed to transnational corporations *only* and not the States themselves' to enable states

[54] CERDS (n 17) art 2(2).

[55] Sornarajah, 'The Myth of International Contract Law' (n 14). See also Robert Brown, 'Choice of Law Provisions in Concession and Related Contracts' (1976) 39 Modern Law Review 625, 632.

[56] AA Fatouros, 'International Law and the Internationalized Contract' (1980) 74 American Journal of International Law 134, 135. See also Theodore Kill, 'Don't Cross the Streams: Past and Present Overstatement of Customary International Law in Connection with Conventional Fair and Equitable Treatment' (2008) 106 Michigan Law Review 853.

[57] See in particular, UNCTNC (Fifth, Sixth and Seventh Sessions, 11 April 1979) E/C.10/46, 6 at para 24–26.

[58] Samuel KB Asante, 'Doctrinal Differences on the Code' in Hamdani and Ruffing (n 48) 91–92.

[59] See submissions of Chile, Ecuador, and Jamaica in UNCTNC E/C.10/19 (30 December 1976). Sauvant (n 31) and Asante (n 58) 91.

[60] UNCTNC E/C.10/19 (n 59) 5, 13 paras 13–16.

to maintain 'the sovereign right to enact national laws to determine how the Code would be implemented'.[61]

Switzerland and Japan stressed the importance of the scope of application over form, although both countries ultimately favoured guidelines which were *not* legally binding.[62] Japan took the view that the Code should basically cover TNC's activities but should also contain provisions covering government policies (eg nationalisation, taxation, anticorruption) to enable uniformity in the treatment of TNCs.[63] This may in part have reflected the states' own desire to protect the interests of the *keiretsu* (Japanese TNCs), which are characterised by small, intra-group cross-shareholdings coupled with strong coordinated management.[64] Switzerland favoured a Code that would enable governments to refrain, as much as possible, from intervening in the economic decisions of the private sector, preferring instead to use 'other methods to influence such decisions'.[65]

For their part, submissions from the United States and the United Kingdom made it clear from the outset of negotiations that the Code should be a 'voluntary' instrument, which would influence, rather than regulate, corporate behaviour. Any national laws and policies that states sought to use to regulate the TNC 'should in turn be clearly stated and conform to [extant] international law'.[66] The United Kingdom insisted that expropriation should be 'in accordance with the rules of international law' and compensation should amount to 'the market value of the investment appropriated'.[67]

Neither state seemed to acknowledge the precariousness upon which their claims regarding 'international law' were made. As Theodore Kill has documented, the principle of fair and equitable treatment of investors (which the United States agitated for) did not arise from multilateral agreements negotiated under the auspices of the UN but rather, from the Organisation for Economic Cooperation and Development (OECD) (on the one hand) and the ICC on the other. The OECD Draft Conventions on the Protection of Foreign Property ((1962) and (1967)) purported to ground the fair and equitable treatment provision in customary international law. Yet at the time, 'the idea that customary international law imposed an obligation to treat foreign commerce fairly and equitably emerged only in the 1950s and only among rich countries'.[68]

Similarly, the United Kingdom's claim that the terms of expropriation should be 'in accordance with [extant] international law' and investors should be compensated 'at market value' assumed that the original investments had been undertaken in accordance with, and adherence to, fair and equitable principles for which there would be no need to renegotiate or from which Third World states may wish to claim equitable estoppel.[69] Yet as Samuel

[61] ibid 5, 15 paras 13–16.

[62] ibid 3 paras 51–53 (Japan), 18 paras 97–106 (Switzerland).

[63] ibid 3 paras 51–52.

[64] Law on Prohibition of Private Monopoly and Ensuring of Fair Trade (Anti-Monopoly Law) Law No.54 (1947) (Japan) art 9. See also Peter Muchlinski, *Multinational Enterprises and the Law* (OUP 2007) 63–64.

[65] UNCTNC E/C.10/19 (n 59) 18–19, at paras 97–106 at 101.

[66] ibid 18–19.

[67] ibid 14 para 72.

[68] Kill (n 56) 880.

[69] Here I am adopting the broad view of estoppel in international law, although it is arguable that even on the stricter view, estoppel in international law is so broad as to accommodate these claims. See Ian MacGibbon, 'Estoppel in International Law' (1958) 7 International & Comparative Law Quarterly 468. Note *contra* Derek Bowett, 'Estoppel Before International Tribunals and its Relation to Acquiescence' (1957) British Yearbook of International Law 176. For a good analysis see Andreas Kulick, 'About the Order of Cart and Horse, Among Other Things: Estoppel in the Jurisprudence of Investment Tribunals' (2016) 27 European Journal of International Law 107.

Asante notes, the legacy of colonialism meant that many corporations continued to utilise the concession agreement as a form through which they could exercise 'a virtual assumption of sovereignty over a nation's natural resources'.[70] According to Asante:

> The consideration for these exclusive economic benefits was patently ludicrous. In many cases the companies paid a nominal rent of say, GBP150 for a whole concession, plus one or two bottles of rum ... The title to the natural resource passed to the transnational corporation at the point of extraction.[71]

That the United Kingdom was now insisting upon 'market value' for the investments appropriated seemed to forget this legacy of abuse or at the very least, to assume it had no effect on how the terms of the contracts in existence between TNCs and states should be governed. Conveniently, the determinant imposed by the United Kingdom was that extant international law should be maintained only insofar as it ensured customary practice regarding a state's right to secure a diplomatic remedy for its citizens extraterritorially, as in earlier cases pertaining to state responsibility. This much became clear in the United Kingdom's claim that while host countries were free to regulate the operations of transnational corporations within their jurisdiction, international law *and international agreements to which governments have subscribed* should be respected.[72] Hence the contingency for the United Kingdom was the possibility that any *novel* reading of international law through the Code would be restricted by terms which favoured investors obtaining market value for their investments, regardless of whether that compensation was 'fair and equitable' from the perspective of the host state.

Similarly, the United States' position throughout the Code negotiations continued to evoke the 'myth' of international contract law.[73] This view had been upheld in a series of arbitral decisions during the late 1970s and early 1980s.[74] As Fatouros noted, international contract law eviscerated the sovereignty of newly emerging states by wresting from their authority the capacity to determine investment disputes nationally. The paradoxical result of the creation of international contract law was to prevent a diversity of state practice and *opinio juris* in the international system to crystallise into customary international law norms. According to Fatouros:

> Once international law is thus opened up, its vaunted diversity somehow disappears ... But if the international law of contracts is identical in content with the international law of treaties, why is it necessary to stress the distinction? If the multiplicity of subjects and kinds of international law is to have any meaning, there has to be *at least a possibility* of variation in outcomes.[75]

[70] Samuel KB Asante, 'Restructuring Transnational Mineral Agreements' (1979) 73 American Journal of International Law 335.

[71] ibid 339.

[72] Views of States (n 38) 16 para 88.

[73] Brown (n 55) 632.

[74] *Texaco Overseas Petroleum Co & California Asiatic Oil Co v Libyan Arab Republic* (1978) 17 ILM 1, 29 (Dupuy arb); *Kuwait and American Independent Oil Co* (1982) 66 ILR 519, 21 ILM 976 (Reuter, Sultan, and Fitzmaurice arbs).

[75] Fatouros (n 56) 135 (my emphasis).

At the same time, other jurists had argued for an emerging 'international law of development' which attempted to delegitimate certain legal principles and practice regarded by several Third World countries as being inimical to their needs for development.[76] This view found support in the International Law Commission, where it had been noted that the body of international law was growing to incorporate a 'duty to cooperate in the promotion of national and human *welfare*'.[77]

These two contrasting positions—one that viewed the form of international law as based upon safeguarding contractual primacy and the other, viewing law's form as ensuring endogenous development supported by existing customary international law and an emerging duty to cooperate in the promotion of welfare—framed many of the debates about the form that the Code should take.

Based on the reports produced from the meetings for the UNCTNC, the question as to the legality of the Code appeared at its most heightened during the first,[78] sixth,[79] seventh,[80] and fifteenth[81] sessions of the IGWG—the last of which included reviewing a draft Code which was tabled by Venezuela on behalf of the G-77 nations.[82] Despite 'exhaustive' discussions on the topic, any final determination as to the legality of the Code was 'by consensus, deferred to the concluding phase of the negotiations' and was still outstanding at the time the IGWG delivered its draft to the UNCTNC in 1983.[83]

In reality, international law came out of these proceedings as only able to chart a midway path between consent and consensus.[84] Writing to the Secretary-General in 1984, following a special session in which the UNCTC had attempted to obtain broad member state support for the Code, the then Executive Director of the Centre, Sidney Dell, noted:

> On international law, it was recognized that there existed a fundamental difference of opinion between the OECD countries and the developing countries on the relationship between international law, including customary international law, and the Code. It was also agreed by *all sides* that the only way of dealing with this matter was to employ language that was *sufficiently ambiguous to be interpreted differently by the various groups*. Although the need for ambiguity was *generally recognized*, the search for a formula was unsuccessful.

[76] Oscar Schachter, 'The Evolving International Law of Development' (1976) 15 Columbia Journal of Transnational Law 7.

[77] Yearbook of the International Law Commission (United Nations 1971) vol 2, part 2, 34–5 (my emphasis). See also FV Garcia Armador 'The Proposed New International Economic Order: A New Approach to the Law Governing Nationalization and Compensation' (1980) 12 Lawyer of the Americas 1, 16.

[78] UNCTNC Report of the Intergovernmental Working Group on a Code of Conduct (Third Session, 4 May 1977) E/C.10/31.

[79] UNCTNC Report of the Intergovernmental Working Group on a Code of Conduct (Fifth Session, 11 April 1979) E/C.10/46, 4 para 16 (noting 'At its sixth session, the Working Group concentrated its deliberations on the legal nature of a Code of Conduct').

[80] UNCTNC Report of the Intergovernmental Working Group on a Code of Conduct (Fifth, Sixth and Seventh Sessions, 11 April 1979) E/C.10/46, 4–5.

[81] UNCTNC Report of the Intergovernmental Working Group on a Code of Conduct (Fifteenth, Sixteenth and Seventeeth Sessions, 5 June 1982) E/C.10/1982/6, 3 para 11.

[82] UNCTNC E/C.10/1983/S/4 'Draft Code of Conduct for Transnational Corporations—Proposed by Venezuela on behalf of the Group of 77' (21 January 1983).

[83] 'United Nations Commission on Transnational Corporations: Information Paper on the Negotiations to Complete a Code of Conduct on Transnational Corporations' (1983) 22 International Legal Materials 177, 185.

[84] On the distinction between consent and the formation of custom as international jurists during this period considered it, see in particular, Anthony D'Amato, 'The Concept of Human Rights in International Law' (1982) 82 Columbia Law Review 1110, 1117–18. Compare: Franck and Munansangu (n 18).

> Numerous drafts were considered, but all were viewed by one group or another as compromising its *fundamental position of principle* ...[85]

The question to which this gives rise, then, is not (or not solely) how or why international law safeguarded the interests of the powerful, but rather, what the inability to reach agreement evidenced about the creation of international law. As I have argued throughout this chapter, that the intent and purpose of international law should be to provide enough flexibility for all parties to interpret the Code's provisions *differently*, rather than to settle on an *agreed* interpretation of provisions, reveals international law's normative contingency. By 'normative contingency', I am referring to the ongoing possibility contained within international law to wage a struggle to create meaning from vocabulary: it is the possibility of that struggle that is international law's greatest strength.

In this respect, the role assigned to international law was not to secure agreement or consensus, but to enable dissent to co-exist. The failure of the Code negotiations was as much due to states' incapacity to facilitate multiple interpretations of the Code as it was due to a lack of agreement between the parties about what provisions should be included in it. Viewed from this perspective, international law is not governing by consensus, but rather, mutually agreed dissensus.

International law's contingency, in this moment, therefore, was limited to maintaining stasis. That states' representatives refrained from compromising on 'fundamental positions of principle' can be read not as the failure of these negotiations, but instead, their resounding success. That international law failed to be agreed in form reveals the intransigence of states' determinations in substance. Yet it also evidences the significance placed on agreeing any law at all. In my critical re-reading of these negotiations, that states refused to compromise on principle shows the genuine power of international law, and the contingent opportunity within that law for states, once agreed. The question then becomes why states could not agree, and whether the presence of the TNC could have changed the parameters of this mutual dissensus.

IV. Merchants of peace—business' participation in the code proceedings as a precursor to their 'success'

A final determinant worthy of consideration in the Code negotiations is the question of actor participation in the UNCTNC's proceedings. The failure to include TNCs more readily in the Code negotiations has been attributed to its failure by several commentators, the most famous of which is perhaps Jonathan Charney. Writing in the aftermath of the first near-final draft of the Code in 1983, Charney argued:

> Failing to bring the major international actors into this process does little to advance relevant interests and imposes unnecessary risks on the inherently frail international legal system ... Expanding the role that TNCs and other major interest groups play in the

[85] Interoffice Memorandum from Sidney Dell, Executive Director of the Centre for TNCs, to the Secretary-General (Javier de Pérez Cuéllar) (5 July 1984) EO/433, 1 (UN-ARMS Folder S-1048-21-2-95-3) (copy on file with the author) 2 (my emphasis).

process of developing and implementing these rules might be one way to avoid these negative results.[86]

In coming to this conclusion, Charney understated the role of business interest groups in the process, who remained present throughout the UNCTNC's proceedings and provided their views to the IGWG drafting the Code. For Charney, the presence of these groups did little to guarantee business' interests, because they could not directly participate in the norm development process.

Yet Charney proceeds from the assumption that the strength TNC participation would provide would have proved favourable to states, if not individually, at least collectively. This fails to understand the intimate connection between sovereignty and property already operative within the proceedings and the desire to keep these spheres distinct from one another precisely to diminish the role of the former in permitting the facilitation of the latter. In other words, far from *strengthening* the international legal system, increased presence of TNCs could very well have resulted in ensuring that the frailty of that system was not appreciated for what it was and in fact diminished it further. The struggle amongst states to maintain mutual dissensus, to ensure the greatest amount of freedom between them to determine the parameters of the law accorded with that of the political communities they represented, may have become jettisoned for the demands of the facilitation of capital that key players at the UN—notably, the ICC—were already seeking to safeguard.

As such, Charney's views have since been discredited by scholars who document the instrumental role that business-interest groups, and in particular the ICC, have played in actively sponsoring and heavily contributing towards the development of international trade law. Originally a network of nationally and locally-based chambers of commerce in the nineteenth century, the ICC had assumed the form of a federation of national-based chambers with a Paris-based secretariat in the aftermath of the First World War.[87] During the 1920s, it employed eminent economists Friedrich Hayek, Ludwig von Mises, Gottfried Haberler, and Fritz Machlup—all of whom historian Quinn Slobodian has recently credited with being neoliberal luminaries of the Geneva school.[88]

During the Second World War, the ICC established a close working relationship with the UN. It attempted to safeguard the neoliberal ethos of its formative protagonists by institutionalising the globalist ethos that would maintain the 'human right of capital flight'.[89] In this respect, Hayek and his contemporaries believed that the global economy was not, nor should it be, self-regulating.

As Slobodian argues, for Hayek, and the neoliberals thereafter, law should *encase* the global economy in institutional relationships for the benefit of capitalist elites.[90] Democracy became a problem that needed to be managed. The idea that 'successive waves of clamoring demanding masses' would be able to determine the course of their own history was palpably anxiety-inducing.[91] That they would be able to claim the *right* to do so, was further

[86] Jonathan Charney, 'Transnational Corporations and Developing Public International Law' (1983) Duke Law Journal 748, 754 .

[87] Slobodian (n 8) 5.

[88] ibid 8.

[89] ibid 134.

[90] ibid 2.

[91] ibid 17.

emblematic of the 'rabies democratica' that was spreading in the aftermath of the Second World War.[92]

The UNCTNC's Centre solicited the views of non-state actors for the IGWG's consideration. In this respect, business organisations favoured a voluntary instrument and trade unions supported a legally binding Code. Similar to many Third World countries and the G-77's combined proposal, however, any legally binding instrument should provide a maximum amount of flexibility to government to regulate TNCs.[93]

Perhaps not surprisingly, business organisations, including the ICC, the International Organisation of Employers, the Business Interest Advisory Council (of the OECD), and the Chamber of Commerce of the United States of America, largely favoured standardised international guidelines that would be voluntary and serve the purpose of increased foreign investment by corporations 'in the overall development context'.[94] In particular, the ICC noted in 1977, that because only 25% of total investment was in developing countries, a United Nations code would be primarily applicable within developed market economies.[95]

On definition and scope, the ICC stressed that all TNCs—private, mixed, and state-owned—should be included under the term used. The main reason given for adopting such a definition was to 'avoid discrimination and distortion between national corporations and transnational enterprises as well as between private and public sectors'.[96] The Code should be 'voluntary in nature, non-binding in character and flexible enough to allow for different situations not only arising out of varying national legislation and practices but also out of different kinds of TNCs'.[97] This plea for flexibility was in keeping with the neoliberal ethos the organisation sought to defend: the movement of capital remained the primary *modus operandi* which representatives of the ICC believed the Code should embody.

In 1984, with a full draft of the Code to hand, all states expressed the view that the utmost effort should be made to conclude negotiations and to adopt the Code 'without delay'.[98] Yet the UNCTNC's proceedings continued for another eight years without agreement being reached. For an additional two years, the UNCTNC maintained that delegates should prioritise 'not its legal form but the political commitment of all parties to it' and see it as 'an important step towards international economic cooperation'.[99] Yet by 1987, the tone had changed remarkably:

> [T]he Executive Director of the United Nations Centre on Transnational Corporations recalled that the international debate on *foreign direct investment* and transnational corporations began with the creation of the Commission on Transnational Corporations *which was given the mandate, as its main priority, to establish an international framework in that area* ... he stressed the importance of concluding the code so that, among other things, countries desiring larger flows of foreign direct investment could obtain them.[100]

[92] ibid 124 quoting Röpke.

[93] ECOSOC, UNCTNC 'Transnational Corporations: Views and Proposals of Non-Governmental Interests on a Code of Conduct' (30 December 1976) E/C.10/20, 15.

[94] ibid 6 para 15.

[95] ibid 7 para 23.

[96] ibid.

[97] ibid 8 para 32.

[98] UNCTNC 'Report on the Tenth Session' (17–27 April 1984), E/C.10/1984/20 18 para 40.

[99] UNCTNC 'Report on the Eleventh Session' (10–19 April 1985) E/C.10/1985/19 20 para 38; 'Report on the Twelfth Session' (9–18 April 1986) E/C.10/1986/19 20 paras 41–42.

[100] UNCTNC 'Report on the Thirteenth Session' (7–16 April 1987) E/C.10/1987/16 23, para 62 [My emphasis].

V. Conclusion: A moment of failure, in fact a success?

Exploring both the necessary determinants and contingencies associated with form, structure, and actor-participation in the Code negotiations helps to reveal the precariousness with which international law was advanced in support of state interests (either for or against the interests of TNCs) in the final quarter of the twentieth century at the UNCTNC. The implications of this chapter are not, however, that a better institution, more (or better) law, and greater participation from TNCs would have led to the more robust regulation of TNCs by international law in our contemporary moment. Such an insipid conclusion is too facile. Nor is it to assert, as others in this volume have, that the sovereignty of the corporation should be reconsidered in response to the contingency of the nation state and its sovereign form.

Rather, I would argue that it is our conception of international law itself that needs to be reconfigured. When considering the contours of institutionalisation, form, and actor-participation, international law emerges from these proceedings as the product of experts through the rise of managerialism; a means through which permitting dissent to co-exist is sought; and a tool through which business ensured the human right of capital flight.

Viewed from another perspective, however, what emerges is that international law has a normative contingency founded in its critical instability. The question that the contingency of failed proceedings provokes is therefore, not (or not solely) how international law could have been but instead, how international lawyers can maintain the latent potential of international law and enable that potential to exist at all times. The frailty of the international system in fact enables international law to always have a 'could have been' moment: in this respect, further reflections on the failure of international law to emerge or exist, reminds us that the 'could have been' is always, in fact, within our midst. It also further assists us in filling the descriptive deficit to which the normative surplus associated with contingency gives rise. As international lawyers, therefore, contingency provides a moment of possibility through which law can always be interpreted differently. In the pendulum swing between apology and utopia, there may yet be a moment through which we can effect transformative change.

G.

ERUPTIONS

28

Contravention and Creation of Law during the French Revolution

Edward Kolla

I. Introduction

Moments of great infraction of international law often help change the system and create law.[1] They are examples of contingency in the history of international law because they represent a departure from what was, to contemporary observers, correct and lawful and seems, to historians, deterministically preordained in retrospect. Instead of corresponding to extant ideologies and idioms, these events open new horizons and can render what was previously unthinkable not only possible but also, in some cases, an entirely new norm. The French Revolution was one such instance.

The central feature of that momentous occurrence was 'the transfer of ultimate authority from the public person of the sovereign to the sovereign person of the public', as Keith Baker describes it.[2] Unintended by revolutionaries, the notion of popular sovereignty quickly bled from domestic politics, into international law, and became a new justification for claims to territory—as opposed to older dynastic and hereditary entitlements. By the twentieth century, the idea that peoples ought to have a say in their international status came to be called national self-determination. Aside from its novelty in 1789, this principle's contingency during the Revolution is most important in terms of the unintentional motive of its actors in heralding what became a critical innovation. What is more, these events were not only unplanned; they have remained unrecognised, for the most part, with few scholars having noted their true significance.

Historians of international law have traditionally followed one of two paths. Either they have ignored the French Revolution, like Arthur Nussbaum, who marvelled: 'To what extent the general transformation of political ideas wrought by the Revolution has ... influenced international law, is not easy to say.'[3] Or, they have ascribed to revolutionaries a proactive agenda of transformation of the law, derived from Enlightenment critiques of

[1] Jean-Louis Halpérin has argued that 'legal systems have evolved without great ruptures' although he admits that '*in some situations* [Halpérin's emphasis] legal revolutions have occurred' in *Five Legal Revolutions since the 17th Century: An Analysis of a Global Legal History* (Springer 2014) x–xi. He also identifies a problem: 'Lawyers have always been reluctant to analyse revolutions', vii.

[2] Keith Michael Baker, 'Public Opinion as Political Invention' in Keith Michael Baker, *Inventing the French Revolution: Essays of French Political Culture in the Eighteenth Century* (CUP 1990) 172. Elsewhere he has written: 'That the principle of national sovereignty lay at the very heart of the French Revolution need hardly be insisted upon. That this principle was created—and implemented—by transferring absolute sovereignty from the king to the nation is a truism worth repeating.' See his 'Sovereignty' in François Furet and Mona Ozouf (eds), *A Critical Dictionary of the French Revolution* (Arthur Goldhammer tr, Belknap Press 1989) 844.

[3] Arthur Nussbaum, *A Concise History of the Law of Nations* (Macmillan 1947) 133.

Edward Kolla, *Contravention and Creation of Law during the French Revolution* In: *Contingency in International Law*. Edited by: Ingo Venzke and Kevin Jon Heller, Oxford University Press. © The Several Contributors 2021. DOI: 10.1093/oso/9780192898036.003.0028

ancien régime diplomacy.[4] The latter camp are helped along by a few incendiary, but misleading, pronouncements by prominent revolutionaries. The Jacobin journalist and politician, Camille Desmoulins, once averred that: 'The public law of Europe ought to be treated as Luther treated the canon law: all of the books about it should be thrown into the fire'.[5] The reality is quite a bit more nuanced.

Popular sovereignty entered the discourse of international law unexpectedly and idiosyncratically, as revolutionaries broke older dynastic and positive obligations *not* out of a grand rejection of all extant commitments or based on a preconceived programme. Rather, a series of diplomatic imbroglios, starting in 1789, forced them to navigate between the Scylla of commitment to their lodestar, the will of the people, and Charybdis of respect for the contemporary international system—at least initially.[6] The best example comes from Avignon, a city where the people declared independence from their erstwhile sovereign, the pope, and proclaimed a desire to join France in June 1790. For fear of alienating His Holiness (who, among other more important things, was at the time contemplating the revolutionary reorganisation of the church in France) and most European courts (this was long before the outbreak of the Revolutionary Wars) deputies in Paris dithered for almost a year and half before accepting the request of the sovereign people of Avignon, and annexing the city. One of the few to advocate a pure application of revolutionary ideology at the time, consequences be damned, was the 'incorruptible' himself, Maximilien Robespierre, who declared that the 'cause of Avignon is that of the universe, it is that of liberty'.[7]

Fortuitous and haphazardly applied, revolutionaries' new ideas about international law went on to have great purchase during the nineteenth century, in spite of attempts made at the Congress of Vienna and afterwards to put the proverbial genie, of popular sovereignty, back in the bottle. Then, these ideas acquired even wider application, and the neologism 'national self-determination', in the early twentieth century.[8] Today the principle is averred in the first Article of the 1945 Charter of the United Nations.[9]

That a transformation of international law occurred, between the French Revolution and today, from a territorial order based on dynastic claims to one founded on the will and desires of peoples, is apparent.[10] Understanding *how* this transformation took place is, however, a much trickier proposition. Not only was this change contingent insofar as it broke with a longstanding and deeply entrenched legal culture, but also, the very agents of the change did not mean proactively for it to happen. It is necessary to go beyond an exposition

[4] See the works of Marc Belissa, *Fraternité Universelle et Intérêt National (1713–1795): Les Cosmopolitiques du Droit des Gens* (Kimé 1998) and *Repenser l'Ordre Européen (1795–1802): De la Société des Rois aux Droits des Nations* (Kimé 2006).

[5] From Desmoulins' *Révolutions de France et de Brabant*, cited in Pierre Gaxotte, *The French Revolution* (Walter Alison Phillips tr, Charles Scribner's Sons 1932) 188.

[6] Edward James Kolla, *Sovereignty, International Law, and the French Revolution* (CUP 2017).

[7] *Archives Parlementaires de 1787 à 1860: Recueil Complet des Débats Législatifs et Politiques des Chambres Françaises* (Dumont 1885) vol XX, 525 (my translation). This quotation comes from a debate on 18 November 1790.

[8] Credit often goes to American President Woodrow Wilson, and his 'Fourteen Points', first articulated in a speech on 'War Aims and Peace Terms', in January 1918, for coining the idea and the term. Putting aside the French revolutionary origin of the principle, more contemporaneously, Wilson was responding to Vladimir Lenin's 'Decree of Peace', of November 1917, promoting independence from (Western) European empire. As Lenin foresaw, self-determination would ideologically underpin the decolonisation of Asia and Africa in the mid- and later-century.

[9] 'The Purposes of the United Nations are ... [t]o develop friendly relations among nations based on respect for the principle of equal rights and self-determination of peoples'.

[10] Again, this is a point I have argued in previous scholarship. See Kolla (n 6).

of the content in legal debates at the time, which show the revolutionary transition from a dynastic to popular idiom occurring even though (or, especially because) no one set out to create it. Instead, one must explain how these new ideas implanted themselves and acquired a legal force, contingently, relative to the will of French revolutionaries. My initial supposition consists of a three-pronged hypothesis set out in this chapter. After a brief, narrative overview of the role played by the principle of popular sovereignty in international law in the long nineteenth century, and its evolution into national self-determination, I will focus in turn on each of three elements. I propose that the principle of popular sovereignty entered international law through a mix of increasingly favourable international 'public opinion', jurisprudential *and* moral legitimacy, and military force.

The last point may seem incongruous. However, military force was key for the will of the people to achieve widespread legal acceptance in the late eighteenth century, just as it was nearly a hundred years later when national self-determination was imposed in central and eastern Europe after the First World War. Military action or its aftermath is a necessary but not sufficient factor for such widespread change in international law; other intangible factors are also essential, as Victor Hugo's famous dictum affirms: 'No army can stop an idea whose time has come'.[11]

II. Self-determination and international law, circa 1789–1918

In Ernest Renan's lecture, 'What is a Nation?' he asserted that: 'It is the glory of France to have announced, by the French Revolution, that nations exist by themselves'.[12] He went on to claim that a 'nation's existence' is 'a daily plebiscite'.[13] Today, people often associate national self-determination and plebiscites with the process by which some states have achieved independence, or regions clamour for freedom from existing states. Late twentieth and early twenty-first century examples include referenda in places as diverse as Quebec, Timor-Leste, Scotland, Iraqi Kurdistan, and Catalonia.

However, when the principle of popular sovereignty emerged during the French Revolution, its first application to international territory actually helped areas to join with and integrate into France. Corsica was the first place where the principle was invoked in international law.[14] France had occupied the Mediterranean island according to a 1768 agreement with its formal sovereign, the city-state of Genoa. However, in 1789, people on Corsica demanded formal incorporation with France and the National Assembly duly decreed it—in blatant contravention of the existing treaty law and the overall ethos of the times.[15]

[11] Victor Hugo, *Histoire d'un Crime* (written 1852, Calmann Lévy 1878) vol II, 331.

[12] Ernest Renan, *Qu'est-ce qu'une nation?* (Conférence en Sorbonne, le 11 mars 1882, Ethan Rundell tr) available at <http://ucparis.fr/files/9313/6549/9943/What_is_a_Nation.pdf> accessed 15 July 2020.

[13] ibid.

[14] One of the few historians to recognise the importance of Corsica, if not the specifics of this episode, was Franco Venturi in his magisterial *Settecento Riformatore*: Franco Venturi, *The End of the Old Regime in Europe, 1768–1776: Part I: The Great States of the West* (R Burr Litchfield tr, Princeton University Press 1991) vii.

[15] This important point has been overlooked because the facts of the situation have often been misconstrued. Both William Doyle and Paul Schroeder, for example, write that France 'took over' or acquired Corsica in 1768 without highlighting its complex legal status. See, respectively, William Doyle, *The Oxford History of the French Revolution* (2nd edn, OUP 2002) 2 and Paul W Schroeder, *The Transformation of European Politics, 1763–1848* (OUP 1994) 35–36.

Next came the plebiscites that Renan mentions so casually and that have become a fixture of international law—albeit still controversial at times and in places. Public consultations were first used by the French in 1791 to canvas opinion in Avignon, the papal enclave in southern France, to confirm the desire to join France.[16] After war broke out, in April, 1792, and although the French became more chauvinist and expansionist, they still based all their territorial annexations on the will of the people—although these justifications mutated creatively and repeatedly to suit local realities in the various places French armies conquered. The process continued through to the time of Napoleon Bonaparte's empire: although hypocritical, new acquisitions, even as far-flung as the Dalmatian coast, continued to be announced as according to the wishes of local peoples.

These new ideas were so powerful, especially as popular sovereignty began to fuse with national allegiance, that they started to be used by Napoleon's enemies, between 1807 and 1815. They are perceptible starting with the 'guerilla' or little war in Spain, and then the defence of Russia after the ill-fated 1812 invasion, so well described as a national struggle by Tolstoy in his 1867 masterpiece, *War and Peace*.[17] In Germany, incipient nationalism was forcefully articulated in Johann Fichte's 1808 *Addresses to the German Nation* and helped swell numbers at 'The Battle of the Nations', fought near Leipzig in October 1813, between 191,000 Frenchmen and more than 300,000 coalition allies.[18]

But then, after Napoleon's defeat, the settlement negotiated at the Congress of Vienna, in 1814–1815, tried to expunge the idea of national peoples having a stake and say in international law. In contradistinction to revolutionaries' original lack of intentionality, the hereditary rulers of Europe tried to return to a dynastic idiom in international law. This is the classic thesis of the 'Restoration' era.[19] However, in spite of the Vienna architects' best efforts, revolutionary ideas subsisted; or, to paraphrase Hugo, Restoration armies could not stop them.

Just as revolutionaries' actions were unpremeditated in creating this wellspring, so has its repercussions often gone unrecognised. Simply canvassing the highlights of nineteenth-century European diplomatic history shows, however, the continued role of popular and increasingly national sovereignty in relation to territorial change. The Greek revolt of the 1820s against Ottoman overlordship culminated in independence, in 1832, based in part on a distinct identity and recognised as such by pan-Hellenists in both the Orthodox-sympathetic East and in the West, among elites with a classical education.[20] Not only did Belgium also became independent, based on its people's perceived difference from the Dutch in 1830, but also, the new state and its neutrality were guaranteed in positive law in the 1839 Treaty of London—which German Chancellor Bethmann-Hollweg called a 'scrap of paper' at the outbreak of the First World War.[21]

The 1848 Revolutions, though generally remembered as failures, have often been called the 'Springtime of the Peoples' and indeed the legal mechanisms by which those people

[16] A classic work is René Moulinas, *Histoire de la Révolution d'Avignon* (Aubanel 1986).

[17] Dominic Lieven, *Russia Against Napoleon: The True Story of the Campaigns of War and Peace* (Penguin 2011).

[18] Gregory Moore (ed), *Fichte: Addresses to the German Nation* (CUP 2008).

[19] Though nuanced in recent years, the broad strokes of the classic thesis still obtain for the purposes here. For a recent re-evaluation, see Brian Vick, *The Congress of Vienna: Power and Politics after Napoleon* (Harvard 2014).

[20] See Gerry Simpson, *Great Powers and Outlaw States: Unequal Sovereigns in the International Legal Order* (CUP 2004) ch 8.

[21] This line forms part of the title of Isabel V Hull, *A Scrap of Paper: Breaking and Making International Law during the Great War* (Cornell University Press 2019).

could enact territorial change was fraught. Lord John Russell, British Prime Minister at the time, opposed recognising the people's desires in Schleswig-Holstein, arguing that self-determination was 'too new in Europe' and that 'the Great Powers had not the habit of consulting populations when questions affecting the Balance of Power had to be settled'.[22] Thus, the London Protocol of 1852 forbade annexation of the duchy by either Prussia or Denmark. This different 'scrap' would not prevent Bismarck, riding a wave of national enthusiasm that would climax in German unification, from seizing them fifteen years later.

The legacy of the 1790s is even clearer by the time of Italian unification. By then, Russell had changed his mind. Acting then as British Foreign Secretary, he sanctioned unification because it was based, as he put it in October 1860, on the will of the people.[23] At the same time, John Stuart Mill wrote, 'it is in general a necessary condition of free institutions that the boundaries of governments should coincide in the main with those of nationalities'.[24] Plebiscites also reappeared. Romans voted to join the new Kingdom of Italy by a margin of 40,000 for and only forty-six against! Just as during the French Revolution, and more recently with Schleswig-Holstein, territorial change transpired in contravention of historical possession and existing treaty law—not least the Final Act of the Congress of Vienna. This is not to say that unadulterated nationalist sentiment drove Italian or German unification, nor that these unifications were an expression of or even an exercise in national sovereignty. Rather, they illustrate, in both rhetoric and actions like the sham plebiscites in the Roman case, that the will of the people persisted as an underlying rationale, and was therefore a legal legacy from the Revolution.

National self-determination had, therefore, had a lively and significant history before Woodrow Wilson enunciated his 'Fourteen Points' and applied the principle, after the calamity of the First World War, in establishing new states in eastern Europe at the Paris Peace Conference.[25] The reality of this trajectory, between the French Revolution and the twentieth century, has been widely overlooked in the historical literature, just like its contingent genesis after 1789. In his survey of the history of international law, Wilhelm Grewe argues that the idea of self-determination 'lay dormant' from the time of the Revolution, 'until 1919, when [it] experienced an astonishing rebirth'.[26] The principle was not dormant, so much as inadvertent and then unheralded.

III. Legal conscience as popular opinion?

If the application of the principle of popular sovereignty in international law was contingent relative to the aims of French revolutionaries how, precisely, did it acquire force as a norm? Moreover, how did self-determination then subsist and affect international relations so demonstrably over the course of the long nineteenth century—especially in opposition to the explicit aims set out in the Vienna settlement and other positivist treaty instruments?

22 Cited in AJP Taylor, *The Struggle for Mastery in Europe, 1848–1918* (OUP 1954) 151.

23 ibid 124.

24 John Stuart Mill, 'Of Nationality, as Connected with Representative Government' ch XVI of *Considerations of Representative Government* (first published 1861, Henry Holt 1873) 313.

25 The triumphalist Wilsonian narrative has been nuanced recently, for example with Erez Manelas, *The Wilsonian Moment: Self-determination and the International Origins of Anticolonial Nationalism* (OUP 2007).

26 Wilhelm G Grewe, *The Epochs of International Law* (Michael Byers tr, De Gruyter 2000) 414.

One first factor relates to a conjecture articulated by the Dutch jurist Hugo Krabbe in the 1920s. He believed that, prior to the French Revolution, the true source of law was 'authority' as vested in established power structures; however, during the Revolution, this traditional authority was toppled and replaced by what Krabbe dubbed 'legal conscience'.[27] This new force derived its potency from the principle of popular sovereignty and the institutions of popular government. In a paradox worthy of the Christopher Nolan thriller *Inception*, it is impossible to explain the genesis by which the will of the people legitimised itself, the people's own conscience, and henceforth went on to underpin new claims in law. However, according to Krabbe, the fact remains.

If Krabbe is correct that the principle of popular sovereignty came, via what he terms legal conscience, to act as a fountainhead for future changes in the law, an important distinction might need to be drawn between domestic and international law. To return to Renan's 'daily plebiscite', in the domestic sphere, the people's will is made manifest most obviously, and increasingly over time, when the public is actually consulted—in elections to representative assemblies, or at times through direct interrogation in the form of referenda, and the like. But how is legal conscience engendered in international life? Absent active consultation, could international law be underpinned, nonetheless, through something like a daily plebiscite? One way is perhaps through international public opinion.

The rise of modern international law, in the late seventeenth century, and the heyday of the Westphalian system for the hundred and fifty years afterwards coincide with when Jürgen Habermas famously identified as the emergence of the bourgeois public sphere.[28] To cite an even more precise congruence of dates and events, one scholar has argued that 1618 marked a decisive shift with respect to the public sphere due to what she calls 'the news fever sparked by the start of the Thirty Years' War'.[29] And, of course, every student of international relations knows the Thirty Years' War to have catalysed the creation of a new international system and its law—even if this idea is now widely criticised by scholars for its oversimplifications.[30]

Public opinion was even more crucial during the French Revolution. Specialists of the linguistic and cultural turns in the history of the French Revolution—such as Roger Chartier, Robert Darnton, Mona Ozouf, and Keith Baker—have critically interrogated the public sphere, drawing particular attention to how transforming and transformed semantic meaning among an ever-more politically cognisant population was crucial to gaining, maintaining, and consolidating power.[31] A notorious example of the perils of having public opinion turn against you at the time is provided by Marie-Antoinette, the French queen.

[27] Hugo Krabbe, 'L'idée Moderne de l'État' (1926) 13 Recueil des Cours de l'Académie de Droit International 509, 559.

[28] Jürgen Habermas, *The Structural Transformation of the Public Sphere: An Inquiry into a Category of Bourgeois Society* (first published 1962, Thomas Burger and Frederick Lawrence trs, MIT 1989).

[29] Cited in Edward Keene, 'International Intellectual History and International Relations: Contexts, Canons and Mediocrities' (2017) 31 International Relations 341, 349; from Carmen Espejo, 'European Communication Networks in the Early Modern Age' (2011) 17 Media History 189, 192.

[30] See for example Pärtel Piirimäe, 'The Westphalian Myth and the Idea of External Sovereignty' in Hent Kalmo and Quentin Skinner (eds), *Sovereignty in Fragments: The Past, Present and Future of a Contested Concept* (CUP 2010) 64. See also Andreas Osiander, 'Sovereignty, International Relations, and the Westphalian Myth' (2001) 55 International Organization 251.

[31] See for example Roger Chartier, *The Cultural Origins of the French Revolution* (Lydia G Cochrane tr, Duke University Press 1991); Daniel Gordon, 'The Great Enlightenment Massacre' in Haydn T Mason (ed), *The Darnton Debate: Books and the Revolution in the Eighteenth Century* (Voltaire Foundation 1998) 129, 153–54; and the works of Ozouf (n 2) and Baker (n 2) previously referenced.

She was discredited by everything from sexual libels, which sapped her and the monarchy's ethical credibility, to the 'Diamond Necklace Affair', in which her pecuniary extravagance scandalised an impoverished nation, to her Austrian origins in an increasingly jingoistic country.[32]

From 1789 on, Baker has argued that public opinion is indispensable to understanding the shift from absolutist to revolutionary political culture; moreover, with respect to inter-state relations, he characterises the public as 'an abstract authority invoked at a point when older principles of hierarchy and order in the international domain had lost their power to constrain political actors', in an echo of Krabbe's emphasis on the transition from old to new sources of law.[33] Mlada Bukovansky goes so far as to argue that public opinion became a source of authority in its own right.[34] The stress Krabbe placed on the institutions of popular government is, again, resonant where Habermas himself argued that, through the French Revolution, the creation of representative assemblies inspired and empowered people to become acutely aware of the political functions of the public sphere.[35] No less a recent authority than Martti Koskenniemi has also linked the ideas of popular institutions and international society to Habermas, among others: 'Habermas, and most European international lawyers have insisted that the acceptability of the postnational constellation will require functional equivalents to the administrative state to interact with individual rights on the one hand, and a cosmopolitan social realm on the other'.[36]

On a practical level, popular institutions were important, but certainly not alone, in instantiating public opinion as a political force at the time of the Revolution. Participation in actual elections—from the selection of deputies for the Estates-General in early 1789; through choosing members for the Legislative Assembly envisaged in the 1791 Constitution, via an expanded electorate; to the election in 1792 of the Convention, for the first time, under universal manhood suffrage—was important both insofar as public opinion was canvassed and also seen to have effects.[37] These effects were not thought to be limited to domestic politics. The affair of the *princes possessionnés* was an important diplomatic and legal quarrel in which the French were embroiled before the outbreak of the Revolutionary Wars. German titleholders with longstanding claims in France, guaranteed in no less a treaty than the 1648 Peace of Westphalia, saw their rights and dues disappear when France ceremoniously abolished feudalism in the fall of 1789. At the time, one deputy, for example, spoke about the 'tribunal of public opinion' and the need for international diplomatic activity to be 'in a state to be universally judged'.[38] This universal opinion was promoted also by the explosion of popular pamphlet literature that circulated during the Revolution, in part because of

[32] For the first, see Lynn Hunt, *The Family Romance of the French Revolution* (University of California Press 1992); with respect to foreign policy, see Thomas Kaiser, 'From the Austrian Committee to the Foreign Plot: Marie-Antoinette, Austrophobia, and the Terror' (2003) 26 French Historical Studies 579.

[33] Keith Michael Baker, 'Politics and Public Opinion Under the Old Regime: Some Reflections' in Jack R Censer and Jeremy D Popkin (eds), *Press and Politics in Pre-Revolutionary France* (University of California Press 1987) 204, 214.

[34] Mlada Bukovansky, *Legitimacy and Power Politics: The American and French Revolutions in International Political Culture* (Princeton University Press 2002) 101, 181.

[35] Habermas (n 28) 70.

[36] Martti Koskenniemi, 'Global Governance and Public International Law' (2004) 37 Kritische Justiz 241, 244.

[37] Malcolm Crook, *Elections in the French Revolution: An Apprenticeship in Democracy, 1789–1799* (CUP 1996).

[38] Opinion de M de Noailles, 'Sur les Mesures Définitives Prises Contre les Ennemis Extérieurs, & sur les Dispositions des Puissances Étrangères, Relatives à la France' Procès-verbal de l'Assemblée Nationale, séance de 5 septembre 1791 (Archives départementales du Bas-Rhin: I L 333 757) (my translation).

the breakdown of the royal censorship system. One such brochure (self-referentially, since it was referring to the very types of intellectual activity increasingly possible because of publications such as itself) argued, again on the subject of international law, that through public understanding people could now 'learn to interpret treaties that, hitherto, were granted no interpretation'.[39]

These French revolutionaries were not alone in linking public opinion to international law at the time. In the same year as the outbreak of the Revolution, Jeremy Bentham coined the term 'international law'. Bentham also envisaged a 'Public Opinion Tribunal' in his *Constitutional Code*, which one scholar has described 'as an alternative system of law to that emanating from legislators'.[40] Given that the international system lacks a legislature enacting formal law, it would seem that public opinion is especially well suited to the elucidation of international law. Even more explicitly, Bentham claimed: 'Public Opinion may be considered as a system of law, emanating from the body of the people'.[41]

Eighteenth- and early nineteenth-century counterparts of Bentham also highlighted the importance of public opinion for international law. American legal theorist, and one of the six original justices of the United States Supreme Court, James Wilson asserted that: 'As the practice of the law of nations, therefore, must, in a free government, depend very considerably on the acts of citizens, it is of high import, among those citizens, its knowledge be generally diffuse'.[42] Fellow American law scholar James Kent believed international law:

> has a real and propitious influence on the fortunes of the human race ... The law of nations is placed, in the first place, under the protection of public opinion. It is enforced by the censures of the press, and by the moral influence of those great masters of public law, who are consulted by all nations as oracles of wisdom ... No nation can violate public law, without being subjected to the penal consequences of reproach and disgrace.[43]

On the subject of such reproach, the twentieth-century jurist and historian Nussbaum contended that, due to the Napoleonic Wars, emergent public opinion was inclined to gauge a government's action based on international law.[44] Bentham also believed in the 'censorial' potential of public opinion and its ability to 'maximize [the] responsibility' of officials.[45]

To summarise—the rise of public opinion and the public sphere in the seventeenth and eighteenth centuries, which commentators have both highlighted and linked to international law, could, therefore, have served as an international 'legal conscience', as posited by Krabbe. This conscience, in turn, could have helped establish the people's will as a force in international territorial claims, even though revolutionaries originally had no such

[39] *Lettre d'un Citoyen François, à un Député de l'Assemblée Nationale, Sur le Discours de M. Maihle, Membre du Comité Diplomatique, dans l'Affaire des Princes Possessionnés en Alsace, Prononcé à la Séance du Samedi 25 Février 1792* (La Feuille du Jour 1792) (Bibliothèque nationale de France: 8-LB39-5808) (my translation).

[40] Frederick Rosen, 'Introduction' in Xiaobo Zhai and Michael Quinn (eds), *Bentham's Theory of Law and Public Opinion* (CUP 2014) 2–3.

[41] Jeremy Bentham, *The Collected Works of Jeremy Bentham, Constitutional Code: Volume I* (first published 1843, F Rosen and J H Burns eds, Clarendon Press 1983) 36.

[42] James Wilson, *The Works of James Wilson* (Robert Green McCloskey ed, Belknap Press 1967) vol I, 148.

[43] James Kent, *Commentaries on American Law* (O Halsted 1826) vol I, 169.

[44] Nussbaum (n 3) 178.

[45] Jeremy Bentham, *The Collected Works of Jeremy Bentham, First Principles Preparatory to Constitutional Code* (first published 1822, Philip Schofield ed, Clarendon Press 1989) 28.

intention, and despite the opposition of those powers which hewed to traditional authority even into the late nineteenth century.

IV. Moral and legal legitimacy

If legal conscience, at the international level, opens the way for public opinion to provide a potential source of law, other factors are necessary to understand precisely why certain beliefs or standards acquire legal force. Not every idea becomes law. Certain ones—specifically, in this case, the principle of popular sovereignty—acquire legitimacy, both legal and moral.

One framework for determining or evaluating a norm's legal legitimacy has been elaborated by Thomas Franck.[46] He identifies four indicators of legitimacy—determinacy, symbolic validation, coherence, and adherence.[47] Examining these markers for the principle of popular sovereignty, domestically as well as for its application to territorial claims in international law, is elucidating. Starting with determinacy, from the earliest moments of the French Revolution, this principle was proclaimed and defended—at times heroically. On 14 June 1789, exactly a month before the fall of the Bastille, a perhaps more momentous event occurred. Deputies of the Third Estate, which represented all the people of France who were not of the First and Second—the clergy and nobility, respectively—declared themselves a National Assembly.[48] Days later, on 20 June 1789, members gathered in the royal tennis court in Versailles, when they found their regular meeting room locked and under guard. Fearing a royal counter-offensive, they took what is now called the 'Tennis Court Oath' and vowed memorably 'not to separate, and to reassemble wherever circumstances require, until the constitution of the kingdom is established'. Soon thereafter, these assertions of the primacy of the people, in representing the nation and dictating its new political structure, were codified in the 'Declaration of the Rights of Man and Citizen' and especially Article 3 that asserts that 'all sovereignty resides essentially in the nation'.[49] The 'Declaration' was soon appended to France's first written constitution, in 1791. As Francis Harry Hinsley put it in an authoritative work, this determinacy has continued to spread over time: since the French Revolution, popular sovereignty 'has sooner or later come to be the prevalent doctrine' in almost all 'political societies'.[50] Hinsley did not explicitly include international society, though it clearly has had an effect there, too.

Symbolic validation of the will of the people was acquired, in part, through some of the high drama of the Revolution, not least the two events already described from June 1789.

[46] Thomas M Franck, *The Power of Legitimacy among Nations* (OUP 1990). Now, Franck explicitly looks at international law in a positivist framework but absent a coercive mechanism, in which legitimacy or legitimation could aid compliance, 15–16. Nonetheless, his schema is enlightening for other contexts.

[47] Franck (n 46) 49. Determinacy is based on '1. the transparency of the standard established in the rule text; and 2. the extent to which the rule is accessible to legitimate clarifying procedures', 67; just as determinacy represents the literary-structural component of legitimation, symbolic validation, ritual, and pedigree provide legitimation's cultural and anthropological dimension, 91; coherence is the ability of the legal cue to communicate the reality of a given situation, 135; adherence is fairly self-explanatory. Franck's work on international law's legitimacy is one of the many offspring of the classic Louis Henkin, *How Nations Behave: Law and Foreign Policy* (2nd edn, Columbia University Press 1979).

[48] One of their most important points of inspiration was a pamphlet: Emmanuel Joseph Sieyès, 'Qu'est-ce que le Tiers État' published in January 1789.

[49] The Declaration was approved by the National Assembly on 26 August 1789.

[50] FH Hinsley, *Sovereignty* (2nd edn, CUP 1986) 154.

However, historians have moved away from 'recounting the narrative of the revolutionary events' and, according to Lynn Hunt, tried instead to 'uncover the rules of political behavior'.[51] This means examining: 'The values, expectations, and implicit rules that expressed and shaped collective intentions and actions'.[52] This examination, in turn, requires analysis of symbolic forms, because 'during the Revolution, even the most ordinary objects and customs became political emblems'.[53] Hunt goes on to list (not even exhaustively) liberty trees, liberty caps, female figures of liberty, ritual observances like festivals, school contests, club meetings, statues of liberty, and festivals of reason—and, at the same time, an end to emblematic connections to the king's body and monarchy in general.[54] This all gave symbolic validation to a new political culture predicated on the sovereignty of the people, whether domestic or international. No wonder Louis XVI lamented, after having accepted the new constitution on 14 September 1791: 'What remains to the king, other than the empty simulacrum of royalty?'[55] Of course, the French would soon abolish the monarchy altogether, and Louis would not even keep his life. It is hardly a surprise, given this weight of symbolism, that revolutionaries' validation of popular sovereignty would seep from its initial, explicit context in France, to a new vision of international relations and law.

As for coherence and adherence, revolutionaries were fairly consistent, intellectually and pragmatically, in both these matters—at least in the early Revolution. In a bridge between these two criteria, and to return to determinacy, in 1791, the French Ministry of Foreign Affairs sent a letter from the king to all the courts of Europe. The purpose was to communicate, clearly, the changes that had occurred in France.

> The Estates General were assembled and took the title of National Assembly: soon a Constitution appropriate to the happiness of France and the Monarch replaced the old order of things... The National Assembly adopted the form of representative government, joined to hereditary monarchy. The Legislative Corps was declared permanent ... What some are calling the Revolution was nothing but the annihilation of a mass of abuses accumulated over the centuries... They no longer exist: the sovereign Nation now only has citizens equal in rights, no despot other than the law, no organs other than public functionaries, and the King is the first of these functionaries. Thus is the French Revolution.[56]

These precepts, and what was developing inadvertently into a new, popular paradigm in international law in general, did not coexist peacefully with the old dynastic paradigm for long. Moreover, the French became less coherent as time went on, even if they did adhere to the principle of popular sovereignty only as a legal fig leaf to justify later territorial acquisitions.

[51] Lynn Hunt, *Politics, Culture, and Class in the French Revolution* (University of California Press 1984) 10.
[52] ibid.
[53] ibid 53.
[54] ibid 67.
[55] *Archives Parlementaires* (Dupont 1887) vol XXVII, 379. The citation is from the 'Déclaration du Roi Adressée à tous les Français à sa Sortie de Paris', and was read on 21 June 1791 (my translation).
[56] 'Copie d'une Lettre du Ministre des Affaires Etrangères, Adressée, par Ordre du Roi, à tous les Ambassadeurs & Ministres de Sa Majesté dans les Cours Etrangères' (Paris 1791) (Archives national de France: AD-XV-38-105-7) (my translation).

Although Franck intentionally leaves 'justice' out of his interpretation of legal legitimacy, French revolutionaries did not—with historical consequences.[57] They passionately believed in the moral rectitude of what they were doing. And yet, in the classic Westphalian system, prior to the French Revolution, theorists did not recognise other normative systems in addition or as superior to international law. That system was underpinned, theoretically, by the freedom and autonomy of sovereigns, uninhibited by moral constraints.[58] Hugo Grotius may deserve his epitaph as the father of modern international law for two philosophical innovations: he highlighted the singular virtue of self-preservation in a theoretical state of nature, and then made the moral analogy of people in that state of nature and sovereign states in the international system, and thereby reimagined international law.[59] As Hersch Lauterpacht observed:

> In stressing the practical analogy of states and individuals Grotius derived substantial assistance from the fact that in the century in which he wrote the emerging territorial state was a creature of personal rule. Marriage settlements and testamentary dispositions continued to be an important medium of territorial changes.[60]

This makes the use, by revolutionaries, of the principle of popular sovereignty to supersede *ancien régime* territorial claims all the more provocative. Nonetheless, the French increasingly invoked the will of the people in this way. Unpremeditated, revolutionaries started to claim with vehemence that 'people cannot be sold or trafficked like simple... property'.[61] In the National Assembly, a deputy ventured: 'one does not cede men; one does not cede nations. There must be no doubt on this principle'.[62] By 1795, in the second article of his 'Perpetual Peace: A Philosophical Sketch', Immanuel Kant forbade states from acquiring others 'through inheritance, exchange, purchase or gift'.[63]

Claims based on moral legitimacy, in this case territorial claims by the people concerned, thereby re-entered the discourse of international law. And, as described above, these claims went on to have huge repercussions through the nineteenth century—again, without any basis in (and often in explicit contravention of) traditional title or treaty law. This process occurred, it seems, through the progressive entrenchment in international public opinion of the tenet as valid. Like Russell who shifted his opinion about 'consulting populations' between 1848 and the time of Italian unification, people came to assume the norm's legitimacy.

[57] Franck (n 46) 208.

[58] See for example Leo Gross, 'The Peace of Westphalia, 1648–1948' (1948) 42 American Journal of International Law 20, 26–28.

[59] Richard Tuck, *The Rights of War and Peace: Political Thought and the International Order from Grotius to Kant* (OUP 1999) 82.

[60] Hersch Lauterpacht, 'The Grotian Tradition in International Law' (1946) 23 British Yearbook of International Law 1, 28–29.

[61] 'Déclaration et Protestation de l'Assemblée des Etats du Comté Venaissin, Réunis aux Membres du Comité des Mêmes Etats, Contre la Motion Faite, au Sujet de cette Province, à l'Assemblée Nationale de France' (25 November 1789) (Archives départementales de Vaucluse: 9/J/7/1) (my translation).

[62] *Archives Parlementaires* (Dupont 1880) vol XI, 269–70 (my translation). This citation comes from a debate that took place on 21 January 1790, and was by Dominique Garat, a Third Estate deputy from Bordeaux.

[63] Immanuel Kant, *Political Writings* (Hans Reiss ed, HB Nisbet tr, 2nd edn, CUP 1991) 94.

V. The use(fullness) of force?

Which brings us back to armies. Adam Watson, channelling Max Weber, has asserted that: 'Legitimacy is the acceptance of authority ... as distinguished from the power to coerce. It is determined by the attitudes of those who obey an authority'.[64] While the point stands, legitimacy and coercion had a synergistic relationship in the case of the principle of popular sovereignty and its emergence in international law.

The French armies of the Revolution spread the idea of popular sovereignty throughout continental Europe. This was based, at first, on what historians have dubbed the 'decree of fraternity', in which France pledged in November 1792, to 'accord fraternity and assistance to all peoples who wish to recover their liberty'.[65] In some places, that liberty was sought and willingly embraced by locals in a reflection of its expanding acceptance in continental public opinion. In others, however, so certain were the French of the principle's legitimacy, they invoked it to impose the institutions of popular government precisely *against* the wishes of most inhabitants. There, revolutionary officials claimed that they were empowered to 'abolish all the social institutions' of 'tyranny' against the desire of locals if the latter lacked the foresight or 'courage to want to be free'.[66] This is but one of the contingencies of the story. Having started out *not* planning to export popular sovereignty, revolutionaries slowly began to support militarily those foreigners who shared their views. Then, they began to impose it by force, paradoxically, against people's will and based on the righteous certainty of its moral superiority. Thus, the will of the people became the self-justifying mechanism for its own propagation. This story reached its hypocritical apex when Napoleon used 'liberty' and the people's choice as a pretext to conquer much of Europe. However, two important facts show that this hubris and hypocrisy were not without lasting impact.

First, the French could have reverted to the older legal logic of conquest and dynasty, especially after the creation of the Napoleonic empire.[67] But they continued using the language of popular consent. An amusing example comes from Elba, because Napoleon would—of course—later be exiled there briefly before his 'Hundred Day' return and ultimate banishment to St Helena. When he annexed the island in August, 1802, the law proclaimed it to be 'in the name of the French people'.[68] It is a thought-provoking counterfactual to imagine how the history of Europe and of nationalism would be different—especially the history of nineteenth-century diplomatic activity, described above, justified by the will of national peoples—had the French during the later Revolution and under Napoleon *not* disingenuously but consistently legitimised what they were doing by claiming to respect and represent the people's choice. The seeds of the principle of popular sovereignty might not have been sown so far and wide.[69]

64 Adam Watson, *The Evolution of International Society: A Comparative Historical Analysis* (Routledge 2009) 17.

65 *Archives Parlementaires* (Dupont 1898) vol LIII, 474 (my translation).

66 'Observations sur le Décret du 15 Xbre 1792' (Archives national de France: D/§2/4-5 (Armée du Nord en Belgique), dossier 5) (my translation).

67 For example, see James Q Whitman, *The Verdict of Battle: The Law of Victory and the Making of Modern War* (Harvard University Press 2012).

68 'Sénatus-Consulte Organique Portant Réunion de l'Ile d'Elbe au Territoire de la République' (8 Fructidor X/ August 26, 1802) (Archives national de France: AD/XV/41) (my translation).

69 I had the honour to debate this point with Lionel Jospin, the former Prime Minister of France, at a roundtable about his book *Le Mal Napoléonien* (Seuil 2014) in Melbourne at the 22nd annual conference of the Australian Society for French Studies.

Secondly, it shows the power of what later came to be called national self-determination that so many European dynastic powers embraced the language of the people rising up, to defeat Napoleon. Ultimately, their rhetoric proved just as self-serving, dishonest, and hypocritical as had Napoleon's—especially given the way that they backtracked on promises after the Corsican's defeat. But it was precisely in response to these dashed hopes that many of the various revolts and revolutions of the nineteenth century occurred—not to mention later territorial change done in the name of the people.

The principle of popular sovereignty was not only spread by France's revolutionary armies. According to Bukovansky, it also 'could vastly enhance state power and mobilisation capacity, and this development enhanced the potential destructiveness of warfare'.[70] Other countries, therefore, mimicked many of the institutional innovations of revolutionary and Napoleonic France, so as to buttress state power. At the same time, they ultimately and inadvertently furthered a popular agenda.

VI. Conclusion

If what came, by the twentieth century, to be called self-determination was actually born in the late eighteenth century, but in a way that was unintended by French revolutionaries; and if it went on to be invoked through the nineteenth century, but in a way that actors then and historians since have failed to fully recognised, how does one account for the innovation and subsequent perpetuation of this norm? The proposition I have elaborated in this chapter is that, in the case of the principle of popular sovereignty, a 'legal conscience' analogous to international public opinion and increasing legal and moral legitimacy, along with its spread through Europe by revolutionary and Napoleonic armies, resulted in the will of the people acquiring an international legal force, in spite of the inadvertency of this story.

To go beyond to this singular case study, there are other, possible, and modern analogues that reflect a similar trajectory—in which principles acquire international legal force quickly, during times of tumult. These instances of collective and public moral transformation, often accompanied by military activity, indicate that this process was not, perhaps, limited to the episode here described during the French Revolution.

One example in the twentieth century probably comes after the Second World War, at the Nuremberg Trials of Nazi officials. Humanity's collective moral revulsion at the Holocaust led to the elaboration of new international sanctions for newly-defined crimes against humanity.[71] To cite Ingo Venzke from the introduction to this volume, but relating to a different instance of contingency, this innovation in the 1940s would certainly have 'come as a surprise' to late nineteenth- and early twentieth-century jurists and diplomats.[72] One of the era's great international lawyers, Hersch Lauterpacht, was instrumental in both the elaboration of the idea of crimes against humanity *and* getting 'general principles of the

[70] Bukovansky (n 34) 165.

[71] Coincidentally, it was a trial during the French Revolution that some historians have argued was, in fact, the first to raise the issue of 'crimes against humanity'. See Jacques Dupâquier, 'Le Procès de Carrier' in Michel Vovelle (ed), *Le Tournant de l'An III: Réaction et Terreur Blanche dans la France Révolutionnaire* (CTHS 1997) 27–35.

[72] Venzke, in this volume.

law' recognised as a source of international law in the statute of the International Court of Justice.[73] Philippe Sands argues that Lauterpacht 'believed in the possibility of reining in the power of the state ... to this end, he wanted an international law ... more open to outside influence'.[74] This 'more open' international law, based in part on norms without formal codification and possibly derived from 'general principles', reflects a contingent interpretation of the history of international law in which both self-determination and crimes against humanity arose surprisingly, but went on to have significant effect.

A more recent, and controversial, illustration of potential change in international law based on evolving public attitudes about what is legally or morally appropriate occurred in 1999. Members of the North Atlantic Treaty Organization (NATO) bombed Serbia in support of ethnically Albanian Kosovars, even though legal scholars and practitioners were almost unanimous in believing that this action contravened the legal prohibition against the use of force, without Security Council authorisation, in the United Nations' charter.[75] Human rights advocates argued, however, that a moral obligation to protect an oppressed minority supplanted existing law—and many people in the Western world agreed.[76] Some lawyers cited an emerging principle known as 'the Responsibility to Protect' though it was and remains by no means universally accepted as an international legal obligation. Koskenniemi holds up the example of Kosovo to argue that 'in the 1990's a fundamental discrepancy was revealed between the international *governance ethos* and public international law'; he goes on: 'And let me be clear: it was the internationalists who thought this. It was *they* who felt that, well, if the law does not permit us to do what is right, then all the worse for law'.[77]

Meanwhile, Henry Kissinger (someone who flouted international law when in officialdom) contended that the bombing of Kosovo represented a departure from the Westphalian status quo, and Grotian moral minimalism:

> Those who sneer at history obviously do not recall that the legal doctrine of national sovereignty and the principle of noninterference—enshrined, by the way, in the U.N. Charter—emerged at the end of the devastating Thirty Years' War, to inhibit a repetition of the depredations of the seventeenth century, during which perhaps 40 percent of the population of Central Europe perished in the name of competing versions of universal truth.[78]

[73] Lawyers habitually cite the sources of international law in keeping with Article 38 of the 1946 Statute of the International Court of Justice (ICJ), which include conventions or treaties, international custom, and 'the general principles of the law recognized by civilized nations'. The Statute is an annex to the Charter of the United Nations.

[74] Philippe Sands, *East West Street: On the Origins of 'Genocide' and 'Crimes Against Humanity'* (Vintage 2017) 86.

[75] Article 2, 4 of the Charter states that '[a]ll members shall refrain in their international relations from the threat or use of force against the territorial integrity or political independence of any state' and Chapter VII specifically empowers the Security Council only to authorise the use of force that is not conducted in self-defence. NATO lacked Security Council authorisation for military action in Kosovo because Russia, allied with Serbia, vowed to veto any resolution authorising force.

[76] In response to atrocities in Bosnia and Rwanda, the Canadian government convened an International Commission on Intervention and State Sovereignty in September 2000. In 2001, it issued a report titled 'The Responsibility to Protect'.

[77] Koskenniemi (n 36) 248–49.

[78] Henry A Kissinger, 'The End of NATO as We Know It?' *Washington Post* (Washington, 15 August 1999), cited in Gary J Bass, *Freedom's Battle: The Origins of Humanitarian Intervention* (Knopf 2008) 13.

Did the destruction wrought by the Thirty Years' War ultimately provide stability in the international system, for centuries to follow, by emphasising sovereign independence and delegitimising conflict based on shifting perceptions of what is legal or moral 'truth', as Kissinger believes? Or, did the rise of the public sphere at that same time ultimately provide a new forum in which competing ideas about legality and morality, sometimes disseminated with military force, provide a process of legal transformation? In other words, perhaps the contravention and subsequent creation of international law, which Kissinger warns against, is in fact intimately intertwined with the birth of a new norm when that idea's 'time has come'.

29

Contingencies in the Rise of European and Latin American Private International Law, 1850 to 1950

Ana Delic

I. Introduction

Nestled in the archive of the founder of the Hague Conference for Private International Law (HCCH), Tobias Asser, is a curious 1907 article by the Argentinian professor Estanislao Zeballos on the codification of private international law (PrIL).[1] This was a copy presumably sent by Zeballos to Asser of his inaugural address delivered on 7 April 1907 at the University of Buenos Aires. The Argentinian professor went against mainstream historiography of the rise of multilateralism in PrIL, which views a multilateral PrIL as part of the legacy of the Italian Pasquale Stanislao Mancini, who had submitted to the Italian Chamber of Deputies in 1861 and 1863 motions expressing the desire to negotiate PrIL conventions. Zeballos offered a different version of events.[2] In 1855, Dalmacio Vélez Sarsfield was entrusted by the Argentinian President with editing the civil code. Sarsfield's preliminary sketch had gone unnoticed by jurists at the University of Buenos Aires until Zeballos discovered it as the most advanced synthesis of PrIL to date. Zeballos wrote:

> Had not Velez Sarsfield been the codifier of a modest and unknown country, his glory would be universal and the name of his country would occupy a lofty space in the annals of jurisprudence and its progress. Nevertheless, Europe attributes the commencement of codification to a celebrated Italian jurist, only because he had the glorious pedestal which was wanting to us.[3]

Zeballos argued that the Argentinian could claim the honours for the first steps towards codification. Already before the publication of the Italian Civil Code (1865) in 1861, Sarsfield had printed a copy of the draft code for consideration by Argentinian jurists.[4] Despite the fact that this article was certainly known to Europeans at the time—it sits in a box of Asser's

[1] Inventaris van het archief van het geslacht Asser (1610) 1797–1940, inventory number 2.21.014.274 (The Hague: National Archives (NA)).
[2] Estanislao S Zeballos, *Codification of Private International Law* (Albion 1907) 6.
[3] ibid.
[4] ibid 7.

Ana Delic, *Contingencies in the Rise of European and Latin American Private International Law, 1850 to 1950* In: *Contingency in International Law*. Edited by: Ingo Venzke and Kevin Jon Heller, Oxford University Press.
DOI: 10.1093/oso/9780192898036.003.0029

papers after all—this episode is not mentioned in global historiographies of multilateral private international law.

The 'glorious pedestal' upon which Mancini sits is but one example of Western-centric tendencies in the conventional historiography of PrIL: specifically its focus on Europe and the United States[5] at the expense of Latin America.[6] However, the inclusion of Latin American contributions to the rise of multilateralism is not so unexpected if we consider works from the 1880s onwards on what was termed Latin American, Hispano-American, or American private international law.[7] Western and Latin American PrIL historiographic traditions differed in that the latter claimed to be a universal system while the former was transparent vis-à-vis its regional nature. The comparison of Western and Latin American PrIL in this chapter thus strives to pierce the veil of Western universality by delineating how both these legal traditions were highly regional during this period.

The chapter will explore organisational and doctrinal contingencies in PrIL's multilateral codification movements involving European and Latin American states (with interference from the United States). Firstly, in terms of the initial wave of PrIL congresses, it will look at the manner in which multilateralism was, in Hegel's language, 'infected' by contingencies related to the will of sovereign states[8] and then parse out which other factors were at play in the formation of PrIL. Secondly, concerning doctrinal contingencies, it will show how the choice of whether to include nationality or domicile in the governance of personal law was the most controversial issue of the century. The outcome of that debate was crucial—and far from certain.

II. Organisational contingencies

This section will discuss attempts, four European and four Latin American, to convene PrIL congresses. Of these eight attempts, the majority were failures, but there was one successful European conference (the Hague Conference on Private International Law and two successful Latin American congresses, the Montevideo Congress and the Pan-American Conference). The successes as well as the failures will be summarised in order to understand which contingencies, including and beyond state voluntarism, were at play.

[5] Friedrich K Juenger, 'A Page of History' (1984) 35 Mercer Law Review 419; Kurt Lipstein, *Principles of the Conflict of Laws National and International* (Martinus Nijhoff Publishers 1981) vol I; Alex Mills, 'The Private History of International Law' (2006) 55 International and Comparative Law Quarterly 1.

[6] With emphasis on Latin America: Kurt H Nadelmann, 'Multilateral Conventions in the Conflicts Field: An Historical Sketch' (1972) 19 Netherlands International Law Review 107.

[7] Alexandre Àlvarez and Charles Hitchcock Sherrill, *Le Droit International Américain, Son Fondement—Sa Nature, d'après L'Histoire Diplomatique des Etats du Nouveau Monde et leur vie Politique et Économique* (Pédone Paris 1910); Cecilio Bàez, *Curso de Derecho Internacional Privado Americano* (Imprenta Nacional 1926); Rafael Fernando Seijas, *El Derecho Internacional Hispano-Americano: Público y Privado* (El Monitor 1884); Jesús María Yepes, 'La Contribution de l'Amérique Latine au Développement du Droit International Public et Privé' (1930) 32 Recueil des Cours 691.

[8] Georg Wilhelm Friedrich Hegel, *The Philosophy of Right* (Samuel Walters Dyde tr, 6th edn, G Bell 1896) section 333; Immanuel Kant, *Perpetual Peace: A Philosophical Essay* (M Campbell Smith tr, Allen & Unwin 1915) section II.

1. Four European attempts to achieve multilateral private international law

There were four attempts to achieve multilateral PrIL in the century under investigation: (1) Mancini's failed Italian congress (1861); (2) Asser's failed Dutch congress on recognition and enforcement (1874); (3) Mancini's cancelled congress of Rome (1885); and (4) Asser's HCCH (1893) as well as the early Hague Conventions (1900s).

Firstly, Mancini submitted to his government proposals to create PrIL regulation in 1861.[9] In 1867, Urbano Rattazzi, the president of the Italian council of ministers, charged Mancini, then the Minister of Public Instruction, with official and confidential negotiations with various governments to extend the rights of foreigners.[10] Mancini was granted the Italian government's permission to circulate the unofficial proposition to the governments of France, the North German Bund, and Belgium.[11] There were favourable responses from Brussels and Berlin. In Paris, while the initial response was likewise positive, political incidents between Italy and France discontinued negotiations.[12] The end of Rattazzi's political career because of domestic politics meant that Mancini lost his great political supporter and the project was sidelined.[13]

On 24 November 1873, Mancini also presented a speech to the parliament in which he insisted on arbitration and the codification of the private law of states, which was received positively by the government spokesman.[14] Mancini's first failed attempt to inaugurate a congress demonstrates a trend we witness throughout the race for multilateral PrIL: the way in which the initial call for action was contingent upon the convening state's domestic political climate. The convenor had to have the majority's government's ear either by virtue of being a government official, as in Mancini's case, or by at least having political ties. This first attempt reveals the way in which voluntarism was coloured with the international relations of the convening state and the invited states, specifically the interruption of negotiations between Italy and France for political reasons.

Secondly, in 1874, Asser persuaded the Dutch ministers to initiate an international conference devoted to investigating the recognition and enforcement of foreign judgments.[15] In January 1874, the Dutch representatives to Austria-Hungary, Belgium, France, Italy, and Great Britain received instructions to propose an intergovernmental meeting of experts to unify rules in the area of PrIL.[16] Russia and the United States were among the governments briefed on the project and invited to send experts to the meetings. The memorandum

[9] Francesco Contuzzi, *II Codice Civile nei Rapporti del Diritto Internazionale Privato* (Stabilimento Tipografico N Jovene 1902) vol 6.

[10] Pasquale Stanislao Mancini, 'De l'Utilité de Rendre Obligatoire pour tous Les Etats, sous la Forme d'un on de Plusieurs Traités Internationaux, un Certain Nombre de Règles Générales du Droit International Privé pour Assurer la Décision Uniforme des Conflits entre les Différentes Législations Civiles et Commerciales' (1874) 1 Journal Du Droit International Privé 220, 285.

[11] Pasquale Stanislao Mancini, 'Négotiations Diplomatiques du Gouvernment Italian'(1886) 8 Journal de Droit International Privé 36, 39.

[12] Enrico Catellani, *Il Diritto Internazionale Privato e I Suoi Recenti Progressi* (Unione Tipografica-Editrice 1888) 966.

[13] Pasquale Stanislao Mancini, *La Vita de' Popoli nell' Umanita-Prelezioni al Corso di Diritto Internazionale Pubblico, Privato e Marittimo* (Stabilimento Tipografico 1872).

[14] Catellani (n 12) 967.

[15] Inventaris van het archief van het geslacht Asser (1610) 1797–1940, inventory number 2.21.014.114 (The Hague: NA).

[16] Nadelmann (n 6) 113.

written by the Dutch foreign minister, Louis Gericke van Herwijnen, indicated the need for an international legislative commission tasked with drawing up a set of rules that could be incorporated into national legal systems via domestic legislation or international treaties. The call to codification had a very mild reception: the Italians alone were in full support; the Belgians and Austrians were generally in favour; the Russians expressed interest and the Scandinavian countries were hesitant.[17] Opposition came from the French, who stressed that bilateral treaties were the only acceptable approach.[18] The newly founded German Empire was engaged in the preparation of a code of civil procedure with rules covering recognition and did not want to involve themselves in international projects.[19] Hamilton Fish, the American Secretary of State, acknowledged the importance of the project but declined the invitation because of the US's federal constitution.[20]

The project would lie dormant until December 1878, when the Dutch parliament pressed for further development in PrIL. A government spokesperson deemed the recognition of judgments project doomed because of France's opposition.[21] Asser's first call for multilateralism took on the limited PrIL field of recognition and enforcement but with little success despite the modest ambit of the proposal. One of the reasons behind the failure was certainly the tradition of bilateral treaty-making dealing with matters of recognition and enforcement, as France's opposition clarified. The importance of French support for the Dutch government initiative was apparent by the statement of the governmental official who deemed the project doomed without it.

Thirdly, in September 1881, after Mancini became the Italian Minister of Foreign Affairs, he sent out instructions to diplomatic representatives in both Europe and Latin America to determine whether governments were interested in signing bilateral PrIL treaties with Italy.[22] It appeared that he was testing the waters to see if the response was more favourable to the traditional bilateral approach to PrIL-making than it was to the multilateral approach. The Netherlands said it preferred a multilateral approach.[23] Among other negative responses were France; Great Britain, which feared clashes with domestic legislation; Russia; Belgium; and Denmark.[24] Favourable responses came from Switzerland, Spain, Portugal, Greece, Brazil, Argentina, and Chile.[25] Austria-Hungary was undecided and Germany expressed interest.[26]

On 19 September, an official note on the status of the project was sent to the foreign ministers of Greece, Germany, Switzerland, Denmark, Peru, Portugal, Britain, Spain, Uruguay, France, Russia, Brazil, Chile, Sweden, and Austria-Hungary.[27] In early 1884, Mancini addressed the Italian government personally with the request for a diplomatic conference to

[17] ibid 113–14.

[18] Louis Renault, 'Le Droit International Privé et la Conférence de la Haye' (1894) 9 Annales de l'Ecole Libre des Sciences Politiques 310, 319–20.

[19] Tobias Michael Carel Asser, 'Droit International Privé et Droit Uniforme' (1880) 12 Revue de Droit International et de Legislation Comparée 1, 2.

[20] *Papers Relating to the Foreign Relations of the United States* (United States Government Printing Office 1874) documents 506–507, 509.

[21] Michael Hendrik Godefroi, 'Le Droit International Privé au Parlement Hollondais' (1879) 6 Revue du Droit International Privé et de la Jurisprudence Comparée 369.

[22] Mancini (n 11) 36.

[23] ibid 49.

[24] ibid 45–51

[25] ibid 49–51.

[26] ibid 47.

[27] ibid 52.

be established by the Association for the Reform and Codification of the Law of Nations (founded 1873).[28] Although the call for action only included matters of recognition and enforcement, Mancini hoped to introduce his project on choice of law.[29] The report highlighted how enforcement of foreign judgments should occur automatically without consideration of the merits of the case as long as doing so was not against the public policy of the recognising state. The combination of Mancini's memorandum and the report received mostly positive responses from foreign governments, with two exceptions. Germany had recently introduced legislation which made reciprocity a requirement for recognition and enforcement and this was not included in Mancini's drafts.[30] The US State Department replied that the approach taken to recognition in the proposal was already nationally incorporated.[31]

In March 1884, Mancini sent out instructions to the Italian diplomatic representatives in Europe, Latin America, and the United States to disseminate the conference report as well as a letter signed by Mancini himself urging for participation in a diplomatic conference to be held in Rome.[32] On 28 June 1885, Mancini sent a letter regretfully cancelling the first multilateral congress on PrIL to Argentina, Austro-Hungary, Belgium, Colombia, Costa Rica, Denmark, France, Great Britain, Greece, Guatemala, Honduras, the Netherlands, Peru, Portugal, Romania, Serbia, Spain, Sweden and Norway, Switzerland, and Venezuela.[33] This correspondence indicated the plan to recommence the work in November. The reason for the cancellation was the fifth and last major international outbreak of cholera of the nineteenth century, which led the Italian government to convene the sixth Sanitary Conference to standardise quarantine regulation. Shortly after the note announcing the cancellation of the congress, Mancini resigned as Minister of Foreign Affairs. A green book which Mancini submitted to the parliament in June 1885 made all the preparatory materials available,[34] and he also published the memoranda in the Journal de Droit International Privé.[35] Mancini died soon afterwards in 1888.

One of the most important aspects of Mancini's second call to action was that both Western and Latin American states were invited to participate. Learning from the opposition to Asser's multilateral recognition and enforcement project, Mancini first surveyed the invitees to assess whether multilateralism was off the table, forging ahead when he received positive responses and even hoping to bridge choice of law matters as well. Comparing Asser and Mancini's similar calls to action one can note the more favourable response to the former, indicating how the formation of international law was contingent on who did the

[28] In 1895 this became the International Law Association. Dr Ruth Frendo, 'Archives of the International Law Association' (*International Law Association*) <http://www.ila-hq.org/images/ILA/docs/international_law_association_article_-_dr_ruth_frendo.pdf> accessed 28 August 2020.

[29] Ministero degli Affari Esteri, *Documenti Diplomatici Presentati alla Camera dal Ministro degli Affari Esteri (Mancini) con Lettera alla Presidenza in Data 28 Giugno 1885: Negoziati e Convocazione di Conferenza Diplomatica in Roma per Norme Convenzionali di Diritto Internazionale Privato e per la Esecuzione dei Giudicati Stranieri (1881-85)* (Tipografia della Camera dei Deputati 1885) document 167.

[30] Ludwig von Bar, *Theory and Practice of Private International Law* (George Robertson Gillespie tr, Green & Sons 1892) 977.

[31] Ministero degli Affari Esteri (n 29) documents 164–65.

[32] Mancini (n 11) 55.

[33] ibid.

[34] Ministero degli Affari Esteri (n 29) document 40.

[35] Mancini (n 11) 35.

convening. Specifically, Mancini was a distinguished statesman acting as foreign minister at the time of his second attempt, which compelled positive responses. Mancini's approach to this topic was a radical expression of mutual trust: allowing for immediate automatic recognition and enforcement if not against the recognising nation's public policy. The demise of the project was contingent not on voluntarism but on a twist of fate in the shape of a cholera outbreak.

Fourthly, in 1891, Asser convinced the newly instated Prime Minister, Gijsbert van Tienhoven, to hold a conference on PrIL in the Netherlands. In August 1892, Asser embarked on legislation regarding general principles of choice of law.[36] An invitation to convene a congress was sent out by the Dutch government to only Western states: Belgium, Great Britain, France, Germany, Italy, the Netherlands, the United States, Austro-Hungary, Denmark, Spain, Luxemburg, Portugal, Romania, Russia, and Switzerland. All civil law jurisdictions participated in the proceeding conferences and Great Britain opted out.

The first HCCH session lasted two weeks, from 12 to 27 September 1893, with delegates from Austria, Belgium, Denmark, France, Germany, Italy, Luxemburg, the Netherlands, Portugal, Romania, Russia, Spain, and Switzerland. During the afternoon of the second day, 13 September 1893, Asser conceded the critiques of the other delegates from that morning who argued that the scope of the conference as delineated in his questionnaire tackling general PrIL principles was too expansive, abstract, and unpractical.[37] By that afternoon, the delegates decided that the fields treated by the conference would be choice of law in matters of marriage, the form of legal acts, succession, and judicial competence.[38] Eventually, the law applicable to form of legal acts was abandoned.[39]

Throughout the subsequent conferences, new participants were added. During the Second Hague Conference (25 June–13 July 1894), Sweden-Norway joined the conference. While no new participants were added during the Third Hague Conference (29 May–18 June 1900), during the Fourth Hague Conference (16 May–7 June 1904) Japan became the first non-Western nation to join.[40] The inclusion of Japan as the only non-European nation in the HCCH hinged on the Japanese Civil Code (1896) and the Law No 10 of 1898 Concerning the Application of Laws in General (*Hôrei*), which incorporated Westernised private law and PrIL into Japanese law. In order to be accepted as a member, the Japanese submitted a memorandum outlining their legal system.[41] However, the inclusion of Japan was not simply a matter of legal and judicial Westernisation, because if that was the requirement Latin American states would have been invited by the HCCH organisers from the beginning. Inclusion was a politically motivated gesture indicating that Japan belonged to the PrIL 'family of [Western] states', while Latin America remained at the periphery.[42]

[36] Tobias Michael Carl Asser, 'Note Mémoire: Projet d'une Programme' in *Actes de la Conférence la Haye Chargée de Réglementer Diverses Matières de Droit International Privé (12–27 Septembre)* (Imprimerie Nationale 1893).
[37] ibid.
[38] ibid 33.
[39] ibid 85–86.
[40] *Actes de la Quatrième Conférence de la Haye Chargée de Réglementer Diverses Matières de Droit International Privé 16 Mai–7 Juin 1904* (Imprimerie Nationale 1904).
[41] ibid 139.
[42] This was different for public international law. While only Mexico participated in the First Hague Peace Conference (1899), eighteen Latin American states participated in the Second Hague Peace Conference (1907).

The first four HCCH sessions achieved conventions in the areas of marriage (1902), divorce (1902), guardianship (1902), the effects of marriage (1905), and civil procedure and the deprivation of civil rights (1905). The fifth and sixth sessions (1925, 1928) were devoted to protocols concerning the earlier Hague Conventions, introduced a model bilateral treaty on recognition and enforcement, and prepared a draft convention on the law applicable to the international sale of goods. No other sessions were held until 1950 because of the Second World War.

Overall, Asser's successful formation of the HCCH included only Western participants (with the exception of Japan)—a stark contrast to Mancini's doomed project. Certainly, Mancini's inclusion of Latin American invitees spoke to the strong ties between Italy and these states to which large numbers of Italian had emigrated. The Dutch government did not have such links, which could be one reason for the exclusion. On the other hand, Latin American regional multilateral PrIL had been forming since the late 1880s, before the first HCCH session in 1893, which could have compelled the Europeans to likewise create their own regional PrIL conference. The path to voluntarism in multilateral European PrIL was arduous as countless pages of minutes of discussions between delegates testify. It was also limited to areas of continental European PrIL which were largely harmonised (ie family law) or necessary for the proper functioning of regional legal relations (ie civil procedure and civil rights).

To summarise, the history of the rise of European multilateral PrIL was contingent upon factors other than simply the will of states. These factors included the political influence of the individuals convening the congresses, by the international relations between the hosting and participating states, by the drafting procedure, and by whether there was national PrIL harmonisation, which eased the road towards multilateral codification. Lastly, history was also contingent on externalities beyond law-making. With regard to personalities, Mancini is hailed as the first government official to attempt to convene a congress, thereby inaugurating a race to achieve multilateral conventions that Asser won due to the unfortunate cancellation of the congress of Rome. PrIL historiography has lingered on the victor of this race, Asser and the foundation of the HCCH, which would be formally institutionalised by its statute of 1955. Mancini's failures have been excluded from serious attention, missing the fact that had the Italian's Rome congress succeeded, it would have been the first *international* congress, as both European and Latin American states were invited and willing to participate. With regard to the influence of international relations, the failure of Mancini's and Asser's first attempts to convene a congress were strongly influenced by tense relations with France in the latter instance and French disinterest in the former case. Italy's strong ties with Latin American states because of emigration certainly compelled Mancini to include them as invitees for the 1885 congress. In terms of drafting procedure, European participants of the HCCH wilfully ratified conventions because of a collaborative methodology: comparative national legal studies and arduously negotiated drafts were undertaken before consensus was reached and final versions were adopted. The early Hague Conventions were a testament to how PrIL harmonisation of international family law at the national level eased the road for multilateral codification. Lastly, the doomed congress of Rome had all the makings of a successful congress delineated above, but its demise was contingent upon an unfortunate outbreak of cholera due to which law-making was set aside to focus on public health.

2. Four Latin American attempts (with some US-American interference) to achieve multilateral private international law

As in Europe, there were four Latin American attempts to achieve multilateral PrIL codification: (1) the Failed Congress of Lima, the first PrIL congress ever held; (2) the Montevideo Congress, which resulted in the Montevideo Treaties (1888–1889, amended 1939–1940), the first PrIL multilateral conventions ever concluded; (3) Zeballos' failed Argentinian Congress (1909); and (4) the Pan-American Union Conferences and the Pan-American Code of Private International Law (1928).

Firstly, the editor of Peru's official gazette, *Gaceta Oficial*, Manuel Atanasio Fuentes, published a memorandum in November 1875[43] concerning the unification of private law, PrIL rules, civil rights protections for foreigners, recognition of foreign judgements, and a postal convention.[44] The Peruvian government accepted the idea and an invitation was sent to all American states in December 1875. The United States declined the invitation, citing federalism as well the uniqueness of its common law system.

The Congress of Lima (1877–1878) organised by Peru was the first PrIL congress. Delegates from Bolivia, Chile, Cuba, Ecuador, and Peru were present at the opening of the congress in December 1877, while delegates from Costa Rica, Honduras, Uruguay, and Venezuela arrived later. The Peruvian Supreme Court member, Antonio Arenas, was president of the conference. On 9 November 1878, the treaty to establish rules in the matter of PrIL was signed by the delegates of Peru, Argentina, Chile, Ecuador, Bolivia, Venezuela, and Costa Rica.[45] This treaty of Lima of 1 January 1879 was ratified only by Peru and never came into effect, although the provisions were later replicated in a bilateral treaty between Colombia and Ecuador.[46] The main reasons for the Treaty of Lima's eventual fate as dead law were the Pacific War (1879) between Bolivia, Chile, and Peru and the movements against the principle of nationality, as the treaty deemed national law as applicable to personal law, family law, and succession. The failure of the Congress of Lima was contingent on the breakdown of international relations due to war involving the convening state and some of the participatory states and the lack of doctrinal congruity at the national PrIL level.

Secondly, Gonzalo Ramírez, chair of private international law at the University of Montevideo and afterwards Uruguayan ambassador to Argentina, took note of Mancini's green book and the project of multilateral private international conventions. In a memorandum of 21 June 1887 to the Foreign Minister of Uruguay, Ramírez suggested that Uruguay and Argentina should try to convene a Latin American conference to establish a PrIL treaty and submitted a draft of the proposed codification, which the Argentinian government approved. On 14 February 1888, the Argentine Foreign Affairs Minister, Norberto Quirno Costa, and Ramírez met to organise the congress. In 12 March 1888, a joint invitation by the Argentinian and Uruguayan governments was sent to Latin American states.[47] The note included mention of the Lima Congress, the Institut de Droit International's (IDI) resolutions, and American David Dudley Field's draft code of international law.[48]

43 Alberto Ulloa y Sotomayor, *Congresos Americanos de Lima* (Torres Aquirre 1938) 406, 408.
44 ibid 109–10.
45 Haroldo Valladão, 'Le Droit International Privé des Etats Américains' (1952) 81 Recueil des Cours 93–98.
46 Treaty of Quito (signed 18 June 1903) 2346 UNTS 11–1284.
47 *Actas y Tratados Celebrados por el Congreso Internacional Sud-Americano de Montevideo* (Tipo-Litografía 'Oriental' 1889) IX–XIV, XV–XXIII.
48 David Dudley Field, *Outlines of an International Code* (Diossy & Company 1872) Division Two.

The Congress of Montevideo (25 August 1888 and 18 February 1889) included delegates from Argentina, Bolivia, Brazil, Paraguay, Peru, and Uruguay. The minutes refer to the theories of global PrIL experts: Europeans like Mancini and Friedrich von Savigny; Americans like Joseph Story and Field's draft code; and the Argentinians Carlos Calvo and Amancio Alcorta, who had recently published comprehensive PrIL manuals.[49] The first successful multilateral instruments of PrIL worldwide, the eight Montevideo Treaties—ratified by Argentina, Bolivia, Paraguay, Peru, and Uruguay and acceded to by Columbia and Ecuador –covered civil law, commercial law, penal law, procedural law, exercise of liberal professions, protection of literary and artistic property, commercial and industrial trademarks, and letters patent.

The Second Montevideo Congress was organised by the governments of Argentina and Uruguay on the fiftieth anniversary of the first congress. Two sessions (18 July–3 August 1939, 6 March–19 March 1940) were attended by delegates from Argentina, Bolivia, Chile, Paraguay, Peru, and Uruguay. The purpose of the sessions was to re-examine the Montevideo Treaties in order to adopt necessary solutions for current problems and to reaffirm the Americas' PrIL doctrine. Advancements to technology, science, and banking were reflected in new treaties on international commercial law and international commercial navigation law. The eight amended treaties were not as well received as the original legal instruments and only Paraguay and Uruguay (and in some cases Argentina) ratified them.

The success of the original Montevideo Treaties hinged on the productive partnership of Ramírez and Costa and the governments of Uruguay and Argentina, as well as on the wish of participatory states to strengthen mutual political, economic, and legal bonds. The wide scope of the Montevideo Treaties speaks to the degree of national PrIL harmonisation among the ratifying states. The second Montevideo Congress was less successful because of the rise of a competing PrIL order established by the Pan-American Union discussed subsequently.

Thirdly, the year Zeballos wrote about the historiographic negation of Sarsfield—1907—was the same year he began work on a congress that would inevitably fail and be mostly forgotten.[50] As newly instated Foreign Minister (1907), he began to assess whether there was interest for a diplomatic conference in Buenos Aires, inviting states which adhered to domicile as opposed to the nationality principle.[51] The president of Argentina sent out a letter on 15 June 1908 to the British Empire, Switzerland, Austria-Hungary, Denmark, the United States, Uruguay, and Paraguay. The instructions of the US ambassador in Buenos Aires concerning the project articulated that Washington was 'sympathetic'.[52] The congress was scheduled to take place in July 1909. Zeballos' international congress sought to unify legislation on domicile and the rules on the acquisition and loss of nationality. However, Zeballos resigned as Foreign Minister in June 1908 and his conference was cancelled because of impeding presidential elections. Zeballos' congress thus did not go beyond the preliminary stages because of his fall from domestic politics.

[49] Carlos Calvo, *Manuel de Droit International Public et Privé Conforme au Programme des Facultés de Droit* (Rousseau 1881); Amancio Alcorta, *Curso de Derecho Internacional Privado* (Lajouane 1892) vols 1–3.

[50] Except in the work of Nadelmann (n 6).

[51] ibid 128.

[52] ibid.

Fourthly, the United States Secretary of State James G Blaine established the International Union of American Republics (later called the Pan-American Union) in 1890 with its headquarters in Washington. An agreement of 23 August 1906 to appoint a commission of five jurists to elaborate public and private international law codes,[53] which had been initiated by the Brazilian José Hygino Duarte Pereira, was presented and accepted during the twentieth session of the third congress (20 December 1906). During the twenty-third session of 30 December 1906, the Haitian delegate, Jacques Nicolas Léger, proposed amendments to the first three Articles of the project because they limited the scope of the international codification to the Western hemisphere only. In his view, the project should have included Europe.[54] The Mexican Francisco de la Barra disagreed, stating that too much time would be lost in trying to come to a legal consensus if Europe was included in the project. In the end, only Léger voted in favour of European inclusion.

The first session of this commission took place in Rio de Janeiro on 26 June 1912 with the participation of most American states, apart from Haiti, Honduras, and Nicaragua. The commission appointed six sub-commissions. The fifth sub-commission met in Montevideo in that year and was entrusted with issues surrounding capacity, persons, condition of foreigners, family, and succession.[55] The next session scheduled for 1914 never took place because of the Second World War. On 2 March 1925, American Secretary of State Charles Evans Hughes, in his role as chairman of the governing board of the Pan-American Union, requested that the American Institute of International Law (AIIL) prepare a code of PrIL. The AIIL was initially the idea of Chilean Alejandro Àlvarez, and in 1912 he founded the organisation together with the American James Brown Scott) in order to examine American problems in the light of international law, form societies in capitals of the Americas to popularise it, and become an organ of juridical conscience of the continent. A committee of four individuals was asked to prepare the code on conflict of laws, comprised of Antonio Sánchez de Bustamante y Sirvén (Cuba), who was chairman; José Matos (Guatemala); Rodrigo Octávio (Brazil); and Eduardo Sarmiento Laspiur (Argentina).[56] AIIL president Brown Scott instructed Bustamante—explicitly excluding the other Latin American jurists[57]—to prepare the code to be considered and revised in the meeting at Havana during December 1925 by the same small group.

The Sixth Inter-American Conference, held in Havana in 1928, approved the Convention on Private International Law in the Annex.[58] The Pan-American Code of Private International Law (also called the Bustamante Code) of 20 February 1928 was ratified by fifteen (of the then-twenty) Latin American states. Like the Montevideo Treaties, the breadth of this instrument was expansive, covering civil, mercantile, penal, and procedural international law. The Pan-American initiatives were shaped by the powerful position of the

[53] Ernest G Lorenzen, 'The Pan-American Code of Private International Law' (1930) 4 Tulane Law Review 499, 499–501.

[54] John Vavasour Noel, *History of the Second Pan-American Congress* (Guggenheimer Weil & Co 1902) 207–13.

[55] Charles Noble Gregory, 'Congress of Jurists at Rio de Janeiro' (1912) 6 American Journal of International Law 931.

[56] International Commission of Jurists, 'Private International Law: Project to be Submitted for the Consideration of the Sixth International Conference of American States' (Sessions Held at Rio de Janeiro, 18 April–20 May 1927) (Pan American Union 1927).

[57] Juan Pablo Scarfi, *The Hidden History of International Law in the Americas* (OUP 2017) 110–13.

[58] Joseph Fuller (ed), *Papers Relating to the Foreign Relations of the United States, 1928* (US Government Printing Press 1942) vol 1, 356–69.

United States as convening nation and the (unrealised) possibility of multilateral PrIL for the entire Western hemisphere. The success of the Pan-American Code was contingent on the involvement of AIIL president Brown Scott, who entrusted the whole drafting project to Bustamante. The one-man drafting process was certainly speedier and the ambit of the code more expansive than would have been the case if negotiation sessions had taken place in the manner of the HCCH. The fact that most Latin American states ratified the Pan-American Code speaks to the degree to which it reflected a PrIL doctrinal consensus and doctrinal compromises where consensus could not be reached.

To summarise, as in Europe, the history of the rise of Latin American multilateral private international law was contingent upon factors other than the will of states: the political influence of the convenor(s); the international relations between the convening, invited, or participatory states; the drafting procedure; national PrIL confluence paving the way for multilateralism; and Latin American states' shared experience of decolonialisation and novel nationhood. In terms of the political influence of the convenors, diplomats Ramírez and Costa successfully garnered the support of their governments while Zeballos' congress was quickly set aside as he lost his position as Foreign Minister. International relations were key to voluntarism: the failure of the Congress of Lima was influenced by the outbreak of war, while the success of the Pan-American congresses was shaped by the looming power of the United States as the puppet master of codification—recalling Scott Brown's exclusive choice of Bustamante to draft a code—even though it ultimately refused ratification. The only inclusive PrIL congress initiated by Zeballos that invited European and Latin American states as well as the United States was a failure, and regional multilateralism reigned in Latin America with the Montevideo and Pan-American regimes despite Léger's failed attempt to include European invitees to the latter.

In terms of drafting procedure, Montevideo and Pan-American PrIL were achieved through a less collaborative process than the HCCH conventions: Ramírez prepared all the items on the Montevideo Congress programme,[59] and the Pan-American Code was drafted by Bustamante. Certainly, the expansive scope of both these multilateral projects speaks to the acceptability of singular drafting endeavours, an approach which had been immediately rejected at the first HCCH session as even Asser's preliminary questionnaire was deemed impractical and abstract. PrIL confluence at the national levels paved the way for multilateralism, specifically assuming singular or compromised doctrinal solutions so that ratification could be achieved.

Finally, the success of Latin American PrIL during this period must be attributed to colonial trauma and post-independence solidarity, as pointed out by Àlvarez.[60] Although the idea of a Latin American confederation was abandoned as the fear of European re-conquest diminished, this family of states '[s]trove to strengthen the bonds of friendship and commerce while regulating uniformly the juristic relations in many of the matters which are included in Private International Law'.[61]

[59] International American Congress, *Reports of Committees and Discussions Thereon* (Government Printing Press 1890) vol II, 76.

[60] Alejandro Àlvarez, 'Latin America and International Law' (1909) 3 American Journal of International Law 269, 300–301.

[61] ibid.

III. Doctrinal contingencies

The most pronounced PrIL controversy of this period was which doctrine to apply to personal law: nationality (*lex patriae*), domicile (*lex domicilii*), or habitual residence. Nationality could be conferred by the *jus sanguinis* (ie, endowed as a result of the parents' status) or *jus soli* (ie, given by the fact that the child was born on national territory). Domicile entailed an intention to make a jurisdiction a permanent home, while habitual residence was connected to where the individual was consistently living. The Western PrIL tradition was epitomised by the dividing line between the common law's preference for domicile and the civil law's adherence to nationality *jus sanguinis*, with domicile or habitual residence as the exceptions to the rule. The separating line between Western and Latin American PrIL was the adherence to domicile or nationality *jus soli*. This section will explore how regional doctrinal preferences with regards to personal law were impacted by such aspects as movements of immigration or emigration, colonialism or decolonialisation, and the Second World War.

1. Domicile or nationality *jus sanguinis* in Western private international law

The common law states, but also German states before the civil code (1896) and some Scandinavian states, adhered to domicile. Savigny promoted this principle because it was connected to territory as opposed to the person, discussing how nationality was historically tied to the nomadic tribes although the Turks and the Jews still adhered to it.[62] Both the German and common law traditions considered that domicile meant the person intended to choose a permanent abode and centre of his relations and undertook acts to realise this intention[63]—or at least the 'absence of intention to live elsewhere.'[64] German Ludwig von Bar pointed out that English and American approaches to domicile were more inclined to refuse change in domicile than continental European states, although the English Albert Dicey allowed for the possibility of modification if a new domicile was acquired or an old domicile was resumed.[65] The US preference for domicile was influenced by it being both an immigrant and federal nation.

The continental European preference for nationality began with the Napoleonic Code (1804), which ordained that the laws of France on status and capacity governed Frenchmen even when residing abroad.[66] During his inaugural lecture as professor of private international law in Turin (1851), Mancini promoted nationality by way of *jus sanguinis*, because for him each nation was characterized by its national race, language, religion, history, tradition, social institutions, and moral conscience.[67] In discussions over the drafting of

[62] Friedrich Carl von Savigny, *A Treatise on the Conflict of Laws and the Limits of Their Operation in Respect of Place and Time* (William Guthrie tr, Clark 1880) 15–16.

[63] Bar (n 30) 113; Albert Venn Dicey, *A Digest of the Law of England with Reference to the Conflict of Laws* (Stevens and Sons 1908) vol XXV; Joseph Story, *Commentaries on the Conflict of Laws Foreign and Domestic* (Little and Brown 1846) section 43; Francis Wharton, *A Treatise on the Conflict of Laws: or Private International Law* (Kay and Brother 1881) 351; John Westlake, *A Treatise on Private International Law or the Conflicts of Law* (W Maxwell 1858) 304; The First Restatement of Conflict of Laws (1934) sections 9–41.

[64] *Williamson v Osenton* (1914) 232 US, 619, 624.

[65] Bar (n 30) 113; Dicey (n 63) vol XXXVI, 463.

[66] Napoleonic Code, article 3(3); Austrian Civil Code, articles 4, 34.

[67] Pasquale Stanislao Mancini, *Della Nazionalità come Fondamento del Dritto delle Genti* (Tipografia Eredi Botta 1851).

the Italian nationality provisions, Mancini emphasised nationality *jus soli* as a servitude or a vestige of feudalism, making man 'an accessory of soil'.[68] Domicile had no value since man was born of a family and the nation was an aggregate of families. This approach was appropriated in French scholarship (1890s): the *jus soli* was in contradiction to human liberty, since it negated the attachment for one's nation of origin.[69] When Mancini became draftsman of the Italian Committee on Legislation, he successfully incorporated provisions in the Italian Civil Code (1865) which stipulated that the national law of a person would govern status and capacity, family relations, and even succession. Shortly thereafter, almost all continental European states prescribed nationality for personal law international disputes,[70] although domicile continued to apply for intra-state disputes in Germany, Japan, and Switzerland.[71]

Nationality reigned in the pre-First World War approaches of the IDI and the HCCH. Mancini, the first IDI president, made a report (1874) which prescribed nationality for personal and family law matters but domicile for intra-state conflicts.[72] During the IDI's 1879 session, the Belgian Egide-Rodolphe-Nicolas Arntz and the Englishman John Westlake presented a model law inspired by this report. Article VI determined nationality governed status and capacity or domicile of origin for intra-state conflicts or if the person had no nationality.[73] Before the first session of the HCCH, Asser compiled a questionnaire and the first question concerned whether nationality or domicile applied to the status and capacity of individuals.[74]

Although status and capacity were quickly set aside during the initial sessions, personal law matters figured prominently in the drafting of the choice of family law provisions. The Marriage Convention offered a compromise solution between nationality and domicile by specifying in Article 1 that the national law of the future spouses applied unless it referred to another law. This approach was influenced by both the French and Belgian delegates, who specified that domicile or the place of the marriage's conclusion could only apply if the national law so determined.[75] Danish, French, Swedish, and Norwegian comments all argued that the applicability of domicile or the place of the marriage's conclusion (if the national law of the spouses permitted) should be made explicit in Article 1.[76] Both Denmark and Norway applied domicile while Sweden followed nationality.[77] The predominance of nationality was passed without comment in the first Article of the other family law conventions: divorce

[68] Sabina Donati, *A Political History of National Citizenship and Identity in Italy 1861–1950* (Stanford University Press 2013) 27; Pasquale Fiore, *Droit International Privé, ou Principes pour Résoudre les Conflits entre les Législations Diverses en Matière de Droit Civil et Commercial* (A Durand et Pedone-Lauriel 1875) 635.

[69] George Cogordan, *La Nationalité au Point de Vue des Rapports Internationaux: Droit des Gens* (Larose & Forcel 1890) 9; Albert Geouffre de Lapradelle, *De la Nationalité d'Origine* (A Giard & E Brière 1893) 11.

[70] Germany (Bürgerliches Gesetzbuch, article 7); Belgium (Civil Code, article 3(3)); Spain (Civil Code, article 9); Japan (*Hôrei*, article 3).

[71] Kurt H Nadelmann, 'Mancini's Nationality Rule and Non-Unified Systems: Nationality versus Domicile' (1968) 17 American Journal of Comparative Law 418, 440–41.

[72] Mancini (n 67); Institut de Droit International, 'Travaux Préliminaires La Session de la Haye 1874–1875 1ere Commission-Droit International Privé' (1875) 6 Revue de Droit International et de Législation Comparée 329.

[73] *Annuaire de L'Institut de Droit International III & IV 1879–1880* (Libraire C Muquardt 1882) vol 1, 190–91, 197.

[74] *Actes de la Conférence la Haye Chargée de Réglementer Diverses Matières de Droit International Privé (12–27 Septembre)* (Imprimerie Nationale 1893) 7.

[75] ibid 40–41, 49, 52.

[76] *Documents Relatifs à Troisième Conférence de la Haye pour le Droit International Privé* (Imprimerie Nationale 1906) 5–6.

[77] Nadelmann (n 71) 441.

was legal if the spouses' national law and the place of the request allowed it, and nationality regulated guardianship of a minor and the spouses' rights and obligations.

After the First World War, both European scholarship and the multilateral codification movement witnessed the beginnings of nationality's fall from grace. German and French scholars became disillusioned with nationality. Walter Simons, president of the Reichsgericht, determined that Mancini had misleadingly swayed Germany's abandonment of domicile.[78] Paul Lerebours-Pigeonnière favoured domicile's possibilities of assimilation.[79] René Cassin argued that nationality was an approach too simplistic for the complex needs of international life while domicile offered both a link to the personal and territorial.[80] Jean-Paulin Niboyet propagated the inclusion of domicile in the reform of the French Civil Code.[81]

At the sixth HCCH session (1928), the nationality principle adhered to in the family law conventions needed amendments due to the surge of double nationality and statelessness. The First World War's mass migrations of individuals from ancestral homes left many stateless. The rise of double nationality occurred as a result of enhanced ease of travel; the rise of women's rights, which meant that marriage to a foreigner no longer extinguished the wife's original nationality but she still became a national of her husband's nation; and mass migrations of workers from Europe to states in the Western hemisphere. In the questionnaire concerning amendments to the family law conventions sent out to the delegates previous to the HCCH 1928 session, domicile was the favoured approach for stateless and dual nationals in familial relations.[82]

However, there were exceptions: Germany (and at times Italy and Hungary) preferred habitual residence; and Italy promoted nationality *jus sanguinis* for dual nationals.[83] During the 1928 HCCH session discussions, German Karl Neumeyer proposed that matrimonial capacity of the stateless person be the law of habitual residence, arguing that this approach better ensured continuity of the individual's legal situation than domicile, which had different meanings in the common law versus civil law countries.[84] While the German proposal met with little support from the other delegates, the drafting committee agreed with it, extending habitual residence to instances of dual nationality as well. The proposals of the drafting committee were unanimously adopted.

At the IDI's sessions in Cambridge (1931) and Oslo (1932), domicile prevailed over nationality with regard to the capacity to conclude legal acts and guardianship, because it provided more efficient protection of the individual unless the domicile was unknown, in which case 'actual residence' applied.[85] The members voted strongly in favour of domicile as

[78] Walter Simons, 'Conception du Droit International Privé d'Après la Doctrine et la Pratique en Allemagne' (1926) 15 Recueil des Cours 433, 480–83.

[79] Paul Lerebours-Pigeonnière, *Précis de Droit International Privé* (6th edn, Dalloz 1954) 245.

[80] René Cassin, 'La Nouvelle Conception du Domicile dans le Règlement des Conflits de Lois' (1930) 34 Recueil des Cours 655, 771–72.

[81] M Niboyet, 'Le Domicile dans le Projet de la Commission de Réforme du Code Civil' (1953) 9 Travaux du Comité Français de Droit International Privé 65.

[82] *Documents Rélatifs à la Sixième Conférence de la Haye pour le Droit International Privé* (Imprimerie Nationale 1928) 403–33.

[83] ibid.

[84] Hague Conference on Private International Law (HCCH), *Actes de la Sixième Conférence de la Haye pour le Droit International Privé* (Imprimerie Nationale 1928) 110, 113, 416–20.

[85] *Annuaire de l'Institut de Droit International 1932* (Goemaere 1932) 185–230.

opposed to habitual residence because it was already defined at the domestic levels and the two principles yielded the same results in practice.[86]

In sum, the main approaches to personal law were domicile among common law states and Mancini-inspired nationality among civil law states. That latter approach also prevailed in the multilateral family conventions of the HCCH. Exceptions to these general tendencies include the reference that the IDI resolution of 1879 made to domicile with regard to intra-state conflict of laws rules; the 1828 HCCH proposal for amendments to the family law conventions, which highlighted the applicability of habitual residence for dual nationals and stateless individuals; and the IDI resolution of 1932, which preferred domicile when it came to guardianship and the capacity to conclude legal acts. The IDI's resolution favouring domicile over nationality cemented a wider trend of nationality's demise in the European context, but the persistence on the old doctrine of domicile can be read as a failed moment to foreshadow its eventual substitution with the doctrine of habitual residence. The shift from domicile to habitual residence was sparked with amendments to the HCCH family law conventions in cases of dual nationality or statelessness and fully realised in European PrIL from the late twentieth century onwards.

2. Domicile or nationality *jus soli* in Latin American private international law

Among Latin American states, doctrinal divisions were apparent between domestic PrIL legislation that preferred domicile[87] as opposed to nationality.[88] At the level of scholarship, Argentinians promoted domicile, while Colombians, Chileans, and Brazilians were on the side of nationality *jus soli*. Both approaches shared concerns over Western infringements on Latin American sovereignty. Argentinians Alcorta and President Domingo Sarmiento believed that the principle of nationality allowed the immigrant to be controlled by their national state, which was against the political project of populating Argentina with Europeans to create a civilised and capitalist society.[89] Carlos Saavedra Lamas argued that nationality would allow foreign creditors to adjudicate claims outside of national courts, opening the floodgates of foreign intervention.[90] Lamas thus positioned nationality as contrary to the Calvo Doctrine (1868), which determined that aliens could not be accorded more rights or privileges than nationals and that aliens could only redress grievances locally without special diplomatic protection.[91]

[86] ibid 169–70.

[87] Argentina (Civil Code, arts 6, 7, 138); Uruguay (Civil Code, art 2393); Paraguay (Civil Code replicated the Argentinian PrIL provisions).

[88] Brazil (Civil Code, art 9); Chile (Civil Code, art 15); Colombia (Civil Code, art 19); Ecuador, (Civil Code, art 14); Nicaragua (Civil Code, art 15); San Salvador (Civil Code, art 15); Uruguay (Civil Code, art 4).

[89] Pilar González Bernaldo de Quirós, 'Primeras Iniciativas de Regulación Global de las Migraciones: Estanislao Zeballos y la Doctrina Argentina del "Derecho Privado Humano" (1873–1923)' (2018) 22 História Unisinos 170; Ernesto Quesada and Adolfo Mitre, *Derecho Internacional Privado: Curso de 1878 Dictado por el Doctor A. Alcorta. Apuntes por Ernesto Quesada y Adolfo Mitre* (Imprenta de La Nación 1878) 492; Domingo Faustino Sarmiento, *Condición del Extranjero en América* (La Facultad de Juan Roldán, 1928) 549.

[90] Carlos Saavedra Lamas, *La Crise de la Codification et la Doctrine Argentine du Droit International* (Editions Internationales 1931) 757–54.

[91] Carlos Calvo, *Derecho Internacional Teórico y Pràctico* (D'Amyot 1868) section 256.

Contrariwise, the Chilean Àlvarez defended nationality as requiring a uniquely American approach because the creoles in their plight for independence had become the nationals of the states they emancipated.[92] Both Àlvarez and the Columbian Jesús María Yepes discussed how the bonds of attachment and memories of the nationality of origin lessen each generation incited by budding nationalism felt towards the Latin American state.[93] Brazilian Raul Pederneiras argued that if Mancini's nationality *jus sanguinis* applied instead of *jus soli*, many states would cease to exist and become absorbed by old colonial metropoles, remaining dependent as colonies.[94]

Certainly, emigration as a tool of colonial expansion was on Mancini's political agenda in talks surrounding Italy's participation in the scramble for African colonies. In an 1885 speech to the Chamber of Deputies as Foreign Minister, Mancini disagreed with mainstream Italian politics that tried to curb mass emigration because of its detriment to agriculture.[95] As opposed to Italians emigrating to a foreign place where they needed to seek protection from the foreign government, Mancini considered emigration to an Italian colony more advantageous to aid in the colonial process. Mancini postulated that the economic achievement of Italians in South America indicated that similar feats were possible in Africa. At first, South America was like Africa, sparsely populated; but now Italian emigrants 'return[ed] home with conspicuous wealth legitimately earned to enjoy a happy age'.[96] Mancini's insistence on nationality *jus sanguinis* must be understood in line with the view of emigration as a tool of colonialism and eventually as a source of wealth as emigrants returned to the motherland with heavy pockets.

The division between Latin American states which preferred nationality as supposed to domicile was clearly evidenced by the negotiations and output of the four Latin American congresses. Firstly, during the debates at the Congress of Lima, Peruvian delegates preferred nationality. One of the reasons for the Lima Treaty's fate as dead law were movements against the principle of nationality. Secondly, reflecting Ramírez's initial memorandum (1887), the Montevideo treaties adopted domicile, going as far as conceptualising 'commercial domicile'.[97] During negotiations, Brazilian Domingos de Andrade Figuera solely voiced resistance against domicile citing its feudal origins as opposed to nationality as a modern PrIL principle.[98] The Montevideo Civil Law Treaty amended Article 1, providing that domicile applied to personal law matters such that 'no incapacity of a penal character nor for reasons of religion, race, nationality or opinion will be recognized'.[99] This amendment further strengthen the applicability of domicile by preventing a public policy exception from denying its application based on prejudicial grounds. Thirdly, Zeballos' memorandum accompanying the invitation for a congress introduced Argentinian doctrine centred around

[92] Alexandre Àlvarez, *La Nationalité Dans le Droit International Américain* (Pedone 1907) vol VII, 8.

[93] ibid vol XIII; Yepes (n 7) 749–50.

[94] Raul Pederneiras, *Direito Internacional Compendiado* (Freitas Bastos 1931) 26; Arno Dal Ri, 'Mancini in the Platine Basin: The Reception of the Principle of Nationalities in Argentina, Uruguay and Brazil' (2018) 1 Forum Historie Iuris—Internetzeitschrift für Rechtsgeschichte in Europa 1, 2.

[95] *Atti Parlamentari Camera dei Deputati Legislatura XV 1a Sessione 27 January 1885*, document number 371, 11067.

[96] ibid (my translation).

[97] Montevideo Treaty on International Civil Law, arts 1–4, 7; Montevideo Treaty on International Commercial Law, art 2.

[98] *Actas y Tratados* (n 47) 185, 617–25, 881–85.

[99] Ernst Rabel, 'The Revision of the Treaties of Montevideo on the Law of Conflicts' (1941) 39 Michigan Law Review 517, 519.

the free choice of domicile.[100] Argentinian doctrine or 'human private law'[101] protected modern man and his rights as he traversed the globe, emphasising the individual rather than territory or community of origin, as Europeans did. Fourthly, the approach of Bustamante's draft to personal law was similar to the early HCCH Marriage Convention: capacity was governed by nationality with the exceptions delineated by the code or local law.[102]

The comprise approach stemmed from Bustamante's and Brown Scott's view that American states were divided on this question, making compromise the only way to achieve ratification.[103] Argentina, Guatemala, the Dominican Republic, and Paraguay all made reservations, stipulating that principles modifying the law of domicile would not be accepted.[104] Argentina and Paraguay never ratified the code. Bolivia and Peru ratified both the Montevideo Treaties and the Bustamante Code. In the case of Bolivia, the Montevideo Treaties took precedence. The Dominican Republic offered a reservation that national law was supreme in all questions relating to status and capacity. Columbia and Costa Rica's identical declaration emphasised that future juridical unity should revolve around domicile as 'one of the most characteristic aspects of juridical Pan Americanism' and not European-favoured nationality, which created 'in America a State within a State' akin to the 'capitulation regime which Europe imposed during centuries on the states of Asia, which she considered as inferior in their international relations'.[105]

All in all, the prevention of European re-colonialisation through the extraterritorial application of national *jus sanguinis* law was a prevalent theme throughout Latin American PrIL at the level of scholarship as well as multilateral law-making. The prevalence of domicile and nationality *jus soli* demonstrates Latin American PrIL doctrines of resistance against interferences to national sovereignty, which simultaneously created the possibility of immigrating to populate newly independent states. Mancini's speeches reveal that his approach preferring nationality *jus sanguinis* certainly had to do with colonialism as well as the preservation of economic bonds between Italian emigrants in Latin America and the Italian motherland.

IV. Conclusion

The rise of multilateralism in PrIL is laden with contingencies. In relation to the organisation of congresses, including but beyond Hegel's notion of voluntarism infecting international law with contingency, other factors at play were the political influence exerted by the convenor; the international relations between the convening, invited, or participatory states; drafting procedure; and national PrIL harmonisation easing the road for multilateral codification. Lastly, there were more regionally specific contingencies: the European

[100] Estanislao S Zeballos, 'Motion sur le Système Argentin de Droit International Privé' in Association de Droit International, *Report of the Thirty-First Conference held at the Palace of Justice, Buenos Aires 24 August–30 August 1922* (Sweet & Maxwell 1923) 405, 413–14.

[101] ibid 408–10.

[102] Antonio Sánchez de Bustamante, 'La Nationalité et le Domicile' (1927) 22 Journal du Droit International Privé et de la Jurisprudence Comparée 375, 381.

[103] ibid; James Brown Scott, 'The Gradual and Progressive Codification of International Law' (1927) 21 American Journal of International Law 417, 448–49.

[104] 'Convention on Private International Law (Bustamante Code)' (*Organization of American States*) <www.oas.org/en/sla/dil/inter_american_treaties_A-31_Bustamente_Code_signatories.asp> accessed 15 November 2019.

[105] ibid.

cholera outbreak, which resulted in the Rome Congress being cancelled, and colonial trauma and post-independence solidarity, which buttressed Latin American PrIL.

Furthermore, organisational contingencies demonstrate tendencies of exclusion, leading to regional, as opposed to international, multilateralism. There were moments of failed internationalism: Mancini's and Zeballos' cancelled congresses, Léger's failed attempt to include European invitees in the Pan-American PrIL project, and Japan's participation in the HCCH but without ratification of the early conventions. While European PrIL remained regionally insular, Latin American PrIL took inspiration from European multilateral movements. Asser's initial memorandum included delineation of all previous codification attempts in Europe and Latin America.[106] During the session of 19 September 1893, Asser informed the delegates that the Uruguayan consul in London had sent a referential copy of the Montevideo Treaties, but subsequent sessions did not reveal any inspection of Latin American multilateral approaches by the delegates convened in The Hague.[107]

On the other hand, Mancini's failed congress lived on in Latin America. First, the Montevideo Congress took the place of Mancini's failed congress and became the first successful international congress worldwide, three years before Asser would hold the first session of the HCCH. Secondly, Ramírez was inspired by Mancini's green book in the foundational stages of the Montevideo Congress. Unlike in Europe, where bilateral agreements and the emphasis on reciprocity prevailed, both the Montevideo Treaty on International Procedural Law (1889/1940) and the Bustamante Code provided mandatory enforcement of the judgments of other signatory states. In this way, both examples of Latin American PrIL replicated Mancini's initial proposal.

As concerns doctrinal contingencies, European and Latin American PrIL demonstrate distinct tendencies with regards to personal law impacted by regional realities of immigration or emigration, colonisation or decolonialisation, and the First World War. Immigrant societies, such as Latin American states and the United States, adopted domicile or nationality *jus soli* in domestic legislation as well as multilateral instruments like the Montevideo Treaties and the Pan-American Code in order to populate their lands with newly arrived citizens. Italy, as a nation of emigrants, promoted nationality to keep the bond between those that moved abroad to their nation of origin; an approach which was readily accepted in other national continental European codifications and the HCCH family law conventions.

Mancini and Latin American scholars and statesmen were aware that nationality *jus sanguinis* had colonial connotations, creating extraterritorial jurisdictions of European nationals in Latin America or enabling the return of emigrants and the flow of their New World wealth to the motherland. Latin American international lawyers persistently responded to these colonial and economic threats with a preference for nationality *jus soli* and domicile in scholarship and multilateral conventions. After statelessness swept Europe as a result of the First World War and dual nationality increased due to the enhanced ease of travel, the rise of women's rights, and mass migrations of European workers to the Western hemisphere, the doctrine of nationality began to show its flaws. HCCH delegates proposed amendments to nationality in the family law conventions applying habitual residence in cases of the stateless or dual nationals and the IDI resolution indicated that domicile should

[106] HCCH (n 84) 6.
[107] ibid 34.

govern guardianship and capacity to conclude legal acts. At the close of the mid-twentieth century, Zeballos' 'human private law', with its emphasis on the individual as opposed to the community of origin, domicile of choice (or increasingly habitual residence) and the protection of the modern person traversing the world, was becoming the global doctrine governing personal law.

IV
OUTLOOK

30

From Situated Freedom to Plausible Worlds

Samuel Moyn

I. Introduction

Most of the metaphysical systems and social visions we know about have been necessitarian. Anyone interested in contingency is someone in the minority in world history, boldly making a bet that there were past and are future alternatives in a world that looks to be so profoundly under the rule of various laws—natural, divine, human. The appeal of contingency, philosophical and practical, is recent, and its power has always been the belief in freedom that underpins it. Routinely, not enough room is made for the freedom that not only accounts theoretically for contingent possibility, but practically gives rise to the incentive for recovering it in the past and seeking it in the present.

Sometimes an understandable emphasis on determination threatens this incentive and substitutes for it an ancient hankering for contemplative serenity, in the face of a world and society that seems depressingly closed to change, as if understanding our unfreedom might make up for its endurance. 'The wise man', the grim determinist Benedict Spinoza said in concluding the *Ethics*, 'is scarcely at all disturbed in spirit, for, being conscious of himself, and of God, and of things, and their certain eternal necessity, always possesses true acquiescence of his spirit.'[1] Contemplative serenity, on this account, is a consolation prize once one realises one cannot, actually, resist determination. Comply with necessity: it is the oldest injunction of religion and philosophy. Yet it is also a massive concession to the reality of human freedom that it denies.

Only recently, in the long view, has there emerged insight into contingent alternatives, in nature itself, and in our own individual and collective lives. And yet today, some of the defenders of freedom themselves complain about those who want to eke out more freedom. They insist that natural and social structures are unfailingly determinative (which of course they are), and that even what production of contingency there is in our malleable worlds, when it emerges at all, mostly ratifies and certainly does not automatically undermine illicit power. Ironically, some of the chief defenders of the goal of human freedom themselves willingly court the risk of extinguishing or marginalising the very possibility they in fact want to coax into actuality, coming near undermining the plausibility of their own stated goals.

But we all know that freedom is not merely a ruse. Alongside false necessity, it is valuable to emphasise false contingency—but not if doing so is a monument to our depression about the possibility of change, and not if it overcomes the far more pertinent truth that defenders of the contingent have barely made a dent so far in the millennial traditions—religious or

[1] Benedict de Spinoza, *The Chief Works of Benedict de Spinoza* (RHM Elwes tr, George Bell and Sons 1891) vol 2, 270.

Samuel Moyn, *From Situated Freedom to Plausible Worlds* In: *Contingency in International Law*. Edited by: Ingo Venzke and Kevin Jon Heller, Oxford University Press. DOI: 10.1093/oso/9780192898036.003.0030

secular, conservative or radical, Western or Eastern—that agree, like neoliberalism today, that there is no alternative to their prescriptions.

This volume has provided a potent reminder of the need for a cautious and intelligent embrace of contingency in explaining the past and framing hopes for the future of international law. The contingent, properly understood, is neither the utterly random nor the wholly determined. At its best, interest in contingency expresses a commitment to a theory of situated freedom, as I will try to sketch, and a desire to reach a proper sense of what options are available to us, neither conceding to the claims of unbending necessity nor pretending to an unbound and utopian sense of anarchic possibility that generally collapses into its opposite when it crashes into a recalcitrant world. The point of revealing contingency in the past, for its best analysts, is to explore social institutions and legal rules that can expand practical freedom in the midst of the powerful forces that undoubtedly shape so much of natural processes and social life—for we already know that societies mainly differ from one another in the extent to which their institutional designs structurally produce individual and collective freedom rather than determination.

After making these points in a bit more detail, I want to argue that a stress on possibility in the past and hope for the future has been deployed in our scholarship in many different ways for many different reasons, before closing with some thoughts about the scholarly uses of counterfactuality and need to organise our thinking around plausible worlds within the multiverse of alternative scenarios.

II. Origins

In Western intellectual history, God not man was the first truly free actor, and reflecting on the mythology of the divine proved the laboratory for later hopes for human possibility.

For those who exaggerated the implications of divine omnipotence (or took it to its ultimate conclusions), God faced no structural necessity, and suffered—at least according to the most radical theoreticians of his omnipotent will—no false contingency. God was free from his prior choices; in voluntarist theory, his will could never be bound, not even by necessity he imposed on himself. Occasionalists (so-called) even drew the conclusion that God's unbound freedom meant that he could only create, never endure, and if the world appeared to be the same from one moment to the next it was because of an active choice of a contingent possibility rather than because God suffered any necessity. There were no 'voluntarist mystifications', in Susan Marks's phrase, in this theory.[2] Possibility going forward and perhaps even backwards—there was no reason God couldn't change the past—was his most essential feature. Voluntarist mystification was the theory.

According to many historians, such theologies paradoxically led to intellectual secularisation—both due to their own internal dynamics and because students of human agency increasingly noticed that humanity enjoyed aspects of the possibility that had originally been projected on the divine.

The internal theological story has been studied brilliantly by Amos Funkenstein and others, but the main idea is that an anarchic God is no longer worth tracking, and indeed

[2] Susan Marks, 'False Contingency' (2009) 62 Current Legal Problems 1, 2.

may lead people to want to exit his world and create their own order and regularities, as in different ways occurred in early modern natural science and political theory.[3]

'How can a necessary being exist totally polluted with the contingent?' the monk Adso asks his teacher in Umberto Eco's *The Name of the Rose*. 'What difference is there, then, between God and primigenial chaos? Isn't affirming God's absolute omnipotence and His absolute freedom with regard to His own choices tantamount to demonstrating that God does not exist?'[4] And, as I said, thinkers also began reflecting on the contingency of human choice, missed in prior metaphysics. It is not just that choice subjectively always seems like it can go either way, no matter how many forces—natural or structural necessity—may bear down on us. It was also that thinkers about nature and society like Francis Bacon and Niccolò Machiavelli came to see human society as artifactual and manmade. Not that society lacked powers over those it shaped in social reproduction, but it was also at an eternal crossroads, with different possibilities of development. (The same was true of nature, as a scientific revolution increasingly discovered that knowing what something is depends on knowing what it can become and therefore exploring what humans make of it.)

Even then, in this early stage in the discovery of contingency, the chief problem was how to square local human possibility with the overall necessity of a divine plan, as in Leibniz, whose theory of the best of all possible worlds was premised on the idea that God would select among the possibilities introduced by the contingent events of nature and humanity—in order to make the providentially best available outcome come to pass from the options. As Fleur Johns might have anticipated, GW Leibniz didn't 'cover up' contingency in celebrating God's rule in and through history; at this transitional moment, divine power was exercised *on the basis* of human contingency.[5] It is thus not a new thing that contingency can serve power; according to Leibniz's apologia, it was the most conclusive witness to God's majesty that he could wisely transform contingency into optimality—not far from the neoliberal thinking of Friedrich Hayek about spontaneous order.

But, in spite of the fact that insight into contingency emerged within frameworks of necessity, it ultimately slipped the grasp of providentialist systems. Possibilities once reserved to God were increasingly arrogated by and assigned to human beings, for whom there seemed much more play in allegedly constraining systems of natural and social necessity than previously thought. Politically, Thomas Hobbes remains the greatest antinaturalist who founded modern political theory on the proposition in *Leviathan* that it is up to us how we live together and even to interpret a world that is meaningless until we accord it meaning first.[6] Of course, no one could posit for people the kind of unbridled freedom that God had enjoyed in theist mythology, and it was difficult to know for sure that people had any freedom at all. But a long campaign was launched to explore how the constraints humanity experiences are real but mostly self-imposed, and the task of social theory became to understand those constraints and their flexibility without reverting to the gloomy sense that there is no alternative—a sense that had been characteristic not only of most of the history of metaphysics and politics, but also remains the stock in trade of today's dominant ideologies.

[3] Amos Funkenstein, *Theology and the Scientific Imagination from the Middle Ages to the Seventeenth Century* (Princeton University Press 1986).
[4] Umberto Eco, *The Name of the Rose* (William Weaver tr, Harcourt Brace Jovanovich 1983) 528.
[5] See Fleur Johns' contribution in this volume.
[6] Thomas Hobbes, *Leviathan* (first published 1651, Penguin 1985).

III. Determinism

The unprecedented embrace in modernity of the contingency of our societies has, of course, been haunted by new forms of determinism, which have paradoxically found a welcoming home in progressive thought. In the vein of Plato and Spinoza, necessity was recuperated in social analysis as real developments were finally giving it the lie more and more. Many modern social thinkers, such as Immanuel Kant and GWF Hegel, and certainly Karl Marx in their train, sometimes look to have done little more than update Leibniz's old providentialist view that there is a hidden plan of nature, a cunning of reason, or a history working behind the backs of men, even if God did not author it. All these views concerning an immanent teleology are implausible, but their staying power is remarkable, no less than the nakedly and sentimentally teleological bromide of my country's last president that the moral arc of history bends towards justice on its own. No wonder, then, that in her classic essay Susan Marks identified contingency that disrupts necessity and teleology—the discovery that history is made and can be remade—as 'a cardinal principle of all progressive thought', adding that 'the work of drawing out its multifarious implications is as urgent as it is endless.'[7] Let's never forget to savour that line, even as we also insist on the need to keep contingency in its place.

I find nothing to quarrel with in Marks's careful argument that false necessity and false contingency are corresponding sins. There is one flaw in her approach, however, since she sometimes implies, and it has been repeated since, that a devotion to contingency consists in allegiance to the powerful role of mere accident or randomness. Not really. There is no reason to mortgage our interest in contingency to a claim about the role of accident or chance, and indeed in my understanding it has been rare to do so. Let me explain.

Contingency is not normally allowance for the accidental and stochastic—like the inexplicable swerve of the atoms in Epicurean physics. Rather, it is the acknowledgment that structures, however dominating they are on the agents that build and inhabit them, never admit of only one outcome. And no one ever fully knows in advance how much give they have until their prospective mutability is made the pressing question, analytically or politically. Reciprocally, no structuralist approach, including a Marxist one, could afford to scant the play in the system of causation and domination, a play that allows possibilities to mushroom, including sometimes to escalate beyond anyone's initial expectations, for good or ill. Even to the extent these are structured possibilities, rather than random mutations, they allow for affirming contingency without pretending that possibility is simply inexplicable and unbidden.

It is therefore a bad result if tensions about exactly how to characterise the reciprocal dependence of a plausible theory of determination on a plausible theory of contingency devolve into mutual sniping about who has gotten the balance wrong; both sides presuppose a common commitment to situated freedom, which forbids some simple choice between causation and freedom, whether the goal is to explain past actors, or bring about change ourselves. It follows that, just as a stress on contingency is not normally a thesis about the randomness of events, it is even more rarely a theory of indeterminacy—since an awareness

[7] Marks (n 2).

of the underdeterminacy of history, like that of texts, hardly implies it can mean anything at all.

Why not, then, agree on a common premise of situated freedom as in fact the only credible basis of social thought—as Maurice Merleau-Ponty argued in first trying to salvage Marxism from its nineteenth century-scientism before deciding he had to replace it altogether?[8] Contingency and determination are from this perspective not mutually exclusive but both required for any sensible approach to social explanation and programmatic thinking. Without contingent freedom, explanation devolves into the vindication of fate, as Roberto Unger memorably called it; without contingent freedom, action risks paralysis through the belief that the forces of history are all controlling, a self-fulfilling prophecy that feeds much demobilisation and withdrawal past and present.[9]

This has implications for what theorists we read and tasks we consider pressing. Unger (Susan Marks's target only after she volunteered to offer a modest corrective to his thought) is the chief theoretician of structure and contingency not only in law—but also, and at least to the best of my limited knowledge, in the whole history of social theory. His goal was to install neither arbitrariness nor indeterminacy in how law and society are conceived but (in his words) to 'place explanatory ambition on the side of an acceptance of contingency and an openness to novelty.'[10] Let me now classify some possible approaches to contingency to explain why I still think this goal is the best one.

IV. A typology of approaches to contingency

After all, the emphasis on contingency past or present is never a standalone programme. In fact, it figures in radically alternative intellectual enterprises, and anyone interested in contingency has to choose among them. Consider three briefly. Call the first genealogical delegitimation, the second narrative liberation, and the third radical strategy.

The contingent is often associated with genealogical inquiry, in the tradition of Friedrich Nietzsche. In fact, it was not a major theme in it originally. The point of classic genealogies was not to liberate practically, or at least not precisely. The dominant emphasis, rather, was the base origins of things we consider noble, with no particular insistence that it might have been or even still could be otherwise. At no moment in the *Genealogy of Morals* did Nietzsche pause to contemplate precisely what would have happened had Jesus never lived, or Paul slipped on a banana peel on the road to Damascus instead. Even augmented by a stress on the accidental, at their best, genealogical thinkers tend to avoid the search for alternatives, except ones that lurk mysteriously on the margins or beyond the frame, like Michel Foucault's tradition of mad poets confined and marginalised by reason, or David Kennedy's appeal to a somewhat mystical unknowing as an alternative to expertise.[11]

Fleur Johns, following Susan Marks, persuasively suggested that there is a love affair with contingency in current international legal scholarship. But there is room for the opposite

[8] Maurice Merleau-Ponty, *Phénoménologie de la Perception* (Librairie Gallimard 1945).
[9] Roberto Mangabeira Unger, *False Necessity* (CUP 1987).
[10] Roberto Mangabeira Unger, *What Should Legal Analysis Become?* (Verso 1996) 124.
[11] David Kennedy, *A World of Struggle: How Power, Law and Expertise Shape Global Political Economy* (Princeton University Press 2016); Samuel Moyn, 'Knowledge and Politics in International Law' (2016) 129 Harvard Law Review 2164–89.

worry that in fact we frequently run across genealogical accounts that do not make enough of contingency. As an example, let me take my own old account of the rise of human rights *The Last Utopia*, which is notorious in some quarters for its stress on contingency—yet in fact it lacks much emphasis at all on whether there were real alternatives for and to human rights in the accumulation of small events over the short term that I claimed cast the die for our time a few decades ago.[12] Like the *Genealogy of Morals*, it is a genealogy of an allegedly disastrous mistake, rather than a vivid portrait of what options were live, or what else, counterfactually might have come to pass instead.

Of course, we can imagine genealogical accounts that might make much not just of contingent mistakes but also illustrate past alternatives in our road to the present. The point is that their distinctive features limit their aims, insofar as the stress still falls on a disaster that contingently occurred and might have been avoided, as mourned by its disappointed heirs. There is an important contribution of delegitimation of resulting triumphalism that genealogical accounts add, but their strategy goes no further. Without more, genealogical delegitimation might even redouble the sense of disappointment, since it might imply that the heirs of the mistake lost a chance they will never get back. TW Adorno argued that philosophy lives on because the chance to make good on its promises was missed, and nearly everybody has their story of the one that (contingently) got away.[13] A genealogy that deploys contingency for the sake of mourning its loss is hardly a good use of it.

A more productive use of contingency, narrative liberation, is to dwell on it as a kind of spiritual tonic for those who hope to contemplate the past, not to reaffirm its necessity, but to remind themselves that no one is ever a mere pawn of massive forces, and can always still act.

As an example of this strategy, consider the rather brilliant and neglected and highly pertinent theory of narrative offered by literary critics Michael André Bernstein in his *Foregone Conclusions* and Gary Saul Morson in his *Narrative and Freedom: The Shadows of Time*.[14]

For this school of critics, the trouble with our familiar narrative techniques in fiction and history is that they have a bias for *post hoc ergo propter hoc*. In response, Bernstein and Morson insisted that the famous narrative technique of foreshadowing, however effective for readers, is a moral error. According to Bernstein and Morson, foreshadowing was typically reinforced by a narrative technique they called 'backshadowing', which went beyond merely anticipating future events for the reader but implied that characters in the fiction *should have known* what was necessarily to come. Through such devices, contingency was banned narratively, as if characters convinced of the openness of history and the reality of their own freedom were blind and obtuse. The truth, of course, is that the epistemological advantage of hindsight often leads narrators to overstate what their characters—historical or unreal—could and must have known, closing history narratively after time has already shut the door.

Bernstein gave the example of Aharon Appelfeld's chilling novella *Badenheim 1939*, which portrays Austrian Jews on a final summer holiday who do not realise their extinction is nigh. 'What fools!' Appelfeld's implicitly Zionist account leads the reader to think. They

[12] Samuel Moyn, *The Last Utopia: Human Rights in History* (Harvard University Press 2010).
[13] TW Adorno, *Negative Dialectics* (EB Ashton tr, Seabury Press 1973) 1.
[14] Michael André Bernstein, *Foregone Conclusions: Against Apocalyptic History* (University of California Press 1994); Gary Saul Morson, *Narrative and Freedom: The Shadows of Time* (Yale University Press 1994).

do not know that Central Europe is not for them and bury their hands in the sand. This message is nowhere stated; rather, it is narratively implied by the constant foreshadowing of apocalyptic doom in the text, and backshadowed judgement on those who lived their lives and treated their futures as if they would have time to flee or lives to continue—when in fact, the die had supposedly been cast for their later fate.

What were the alternatives to foreshadowing offered by these theorists? They advised the narrative strategies of 'sideshadowing'. Robert Musil was the great exponent of this narrative practice. 'The course of history was therefore not that of a billiard-ball', Musil wrote in *The Man without Qualities*, 'which, once it had been hit, ran along a definite course; on the contrary, it was like the passage of the clouds, like the way of a man sauntering through the streets—diverted here by a shadow, there by a little crowd of people, or by an unusual way one building jutted out and the next stood back from the street—finally arriving at a place that he had neither known of nor meant to reach.'[15] When we write fiction or history, we can narrate the sense of possibility in every present, even when the future has since supervened to select among them in one way rather than another. It might well be an equal moral error to overstate, currently or retroactively, the range of options that people experience. But sideshadowing is a crucial mode of narrative that reanimates the freedom people actually have had and do have, to whatever limited extent it obtains.

Now this narrative mode is just one example of the way that, in narrative liberation, emphasis on contingency, past or present, is part of a family of tonics—its ultimate point is to remind ourselves that we can always regard ourselves as free to some extent, even if in the past we forsook or misused that freedom, or continue to do so. It thus goes beyond genealogical delegitimation in its focus on a kind of present liberation. As Bernstein and Morson emphasised, a narrative commitment to freedom is as much a spiritual stance as a literary technique.

But there are limits, too, to this second approach precisely to this extent, especially because its invocation of contingency is really about reaffirming a kind of personal freedom in the face of structural necessity that, while valuable, ignores that structures liberate as well as constrain and that different structures bring about different amounts or experiences of freedom. As we know, freedom is not the absence of structure but the presence of the kinds of structures that create and liberate individual and group agents, a truth that an emphasis on the always oppressive character of structures is apt to obscure. More interesting, therefore, is a comparative science of structures for the diverse freedoms allowed—as a comparison of the premodern world with our own age self-evidently proves.

Equally important, Bernstein and Morson's strategy of dwelling on contingency, however productive, ignores the big task. It is not enough to emphasise that no one knew what was coming, and to preserve the contingency of their present in our narrative. For we have to know what options each moment plausibly generates. Some outcomes were ruled out and others were indeed inevitable, for sure. After a certain point in my life, I could not become a professional athlete, assuming I could have to begin with. And some space of alternatives generally remains in human experience, it is less and less fulsome the closer a given event approaches and as the conditions for its occurrence accumulate. Reconciling the contingency of action with the determinative pressures of structures depends on a

15 Robert Musil, *The Man Without Qualities* (Eithne Wilkins and Ernst Kaiser trs, Secker and Warburg 1966) vol 2, 74–75.

precise account of situational possibility, and the claim that whatever the situation people retain some freedom and some contingency is too vague. Sideshadowing contingency fails to explore what the actual alternatives for action were, and fails to develop tools to assess the boundaries and range of options. The plurality of future worlds from any point in time means there is always more than one choice, but there is not an infinite number, and some are easier to reach than others. And freedom itself is at stake in which one results. A man in a straitjacket can be sideshadowed as easily as one with agonising choices—and it matters not just that he has them, but what they are.

Lastly, then, there is a stress on contingency as explanation of the interaction of freedom and structure and the exploration of real alternatives. Unger, the great neglected thinker of contingency in the historical process and political present, called for 'sever[ing] the link between our ability to explain past or present situations and the premise that these situations were or are necessary.'[16] The point was to *preserve* the goals of explanatory social theory, never to exult in contingency, and certainly not to enshrine the accidental and the random as the way of the world. Instead, as Susan Marks acknowledged (perhaps a bit too grudgingly), the aim was to develop a theory of structure more compatible than prevailing versions with our freedom.

Of course, it would be utterly unpersuasive to ditch determination in our explorations of the contingency of the past. But that was not Unger's goal, and it should not be ours. Rather, the point was to avoid a marionette understanding of history as something that merely guides us as puppets driven by unseen forces, in order to understand how determination and freedom go together. This is not to say it's easy to reconcile the forces of powerful structures and the contingent alternatives they always nonetheless allow, in general or in any specific situation past or present. But doing so is always our crucial intellectual task.

This approach should not be confused with mere consciousness raising about contingency. For sure, a different practice of explanation that refuses to kowtow to determination certainly is a potential incitement to present action, much as determinism risks shutting action down. But there is no doubt that outcomes typically depend on a huge number of other factors, and nobody ever achieves the aims of their free acts exactly. In any case, only a few who have emphasised contingency, for example Richard Rorty in his *Contingency, Irony, and Solidarity*, have ever thought that mere redescription by liberated intellectuals could enact social change.[17] Yet it could throw an accelerant into a fire. Conversely, it will be a dark day should intellectuals (including professors and students) ever abandon belief in the potential moral importance of their own work in enacting or quickening possibility, however unlikely they are in this task and however much they rightly emphasise the need for others to shoulder the burden of change.

Today it seems as if some feel contingency in history or international legal history is becoming a bit boring and hackneyed. Contingency is yesterday's fashion, the rule of structural necessity that an emphasis on contingency supposedly forgot or the participation of contingency in the rule of power themselves alternatives to consider. In contrast, I am not sure how much the world needs the depressing but obvious message that structures are resilient; for the recollection of contingency never implied that transformation was going to

[16] Roberto Mangabeira Unger, *Social Theory: Its Situation and Its Task* (CUP 1986) 1.
[17] Richard Rorty, *Contingency, Irony, and Solidarity* (CUP 1989).

be easy or quick. In the end, it remains the case that the incipient transformability even of seemingly resilient structures is what we should care most about.

In this volume, there is a great deal of creative thinking about how to characterise this transformability in the past. Clearly, it is inadequate to pretend, not only that constraint and freedom are alternatives, but that all constraint is created equal. To grasp some moment or other, it is critical to assign relative importance to constraints. We do not know how to do that well yet, in social theory let alone in international legal history. And it is possible that counterfactual reasoning is not an essential tool but an easily abused one.

V. On counterfactuality

So let me turn to that last point. For all the importance of a recovery of contingency, I think we should be very wary of moving too quickly from some sort of acknowledgment of the uses of emphasising contingency to the role of counterfactual scenarios (what if?) to explore them. But counterfactual narratives—what another literary critic, Catherine Gallagher, recently called 'telling it like it wasn't'—are certainly not the exclusive mode of exploring contingency, and come with their own risks.[18]

Asking 'what if?' raises fascinating questions to which one can imagine equally wonderful responses. Yet there remains the chief risk of counterfactuals, which is that they devolve into a mere parlour game. As Geoffrey Hawthorn developed long ago in his great book *Plausible Worlds*, we need to deploy counterfactuals responsibly, if at all, to recover the precise extent and kind of transformability of past situations—without pretending that actors, lacking the right exits, might simply walk through the walls that confine them.[19] As Hawthorn taught, the essential task is to augment our sense of *possibility* with one of *plausibility* so we know what the adjacent alternatives were and are—not unavailable ones.

The New International Economic Order of the 1970s, for example, may have had next to no chance to be realised in practice, after its proclamation.[20] Yet it was frightening to many observers, including Henry Kissinger, who proceeded accordingly in their diplomatic manoeuvres. The challenge is to reconstitute the world in which the event was surprising, and seemed to portent possibility, even if it is obvious in retrospect why it went down to defeat in the end. And while it would make sense as an enjoyable exercise to determine what obstructions, once cleared, might have changed the result, simply removing the constraint of plausibility could function as an analytical indulgence rather than an action-guiding inquiry.

Other events may call for historians to recover contingency when a sense of fate has deadened our imaginations. For example, consider the novelist Nicholson Baker's extraordinary reconstruction of the years leading to American intervention in the Second World War, the better to advance a pacifist ideology.[21] It is, among other things, a classic example

[18] Catherine Gallagher, *Telling It Like It Wasn't: The Counterfactual Imagination in History and Fiction* (University of Chicago Press 2018).

[19] Geoffrey Hawthorn, *Plausible Worlds: Possibility and Understanding in History and the Social Sciences* (CUP 1991).

[20] Ingo Venzke, 'Possibilities of the Past: Histories of the NIEO and the Possibilities of Critique' (2018) 20 Journal of the History of International Law 263.

[21] Nicholson Baker, *Human Smoke: The Beginnings of World War II, the End of Civilization* (Simon & Schuster 2008).

of narrative backshadowing to make an event that hitherto seemed necessary—American entry in the Second World War—seem not merely a genuine choice, but also a disastrous mistake. Baker's book counteracts the sense that American intervention was delayed but foreordained by an emphasis on how many plausible alternatives there were, almost up to the very day that Pearl Harbor seemed to force Franklin Roosevelt's hand. The inevitability of war—not merely its justice—has been drummed into generations, but there were a number of plausible alternatives to it. Once again, those alternatives have to be available to be useful. It is one thing to recover the fragility of the American consensus around military intervention even in the two years after Pearl Harbor, and thus the profusion of choices before. It is another to imagine what might have been had Adolf Hitler simply dropped dead the night before he declared war on the United States on 11 December 1941.

We can defend fanciful or utopian thinking—whether Hitler's death or the reign of justice—on other grounds. But it is not going to help in understanding specific moments of the past or our own present, precisely because utopianism absconds from the difficult situational analysis of the real constraints and potentialities from time to time and place to place. Counterfactuality thus has to be allied to a case for plausibility, for both explanatory and moral purposes. We can then defend utopian thinking for our own present insofar as it encourages us to look for different exits than we can find. Much like insight into both contingency and constraint in the first place, situational and radical counterfactuality are, in the history of international law and in our own present, crucial allies, not enemies.

Index

For the benefit of digital users, indexed terms that span two pages (e.g., 52–53) may, on occasion, appear on only one of those pages.